Finding·God

Our Response to God's Gifts

Parish Catechist Guide

Barbara F. Campbell, M.Div., D.Min.
James P. Campbell, M.A., D.Min.

LOYOLA PRESS.
A JESUIT MINISTRY
Chicago

D1261580

Imprimatur	In Conformity
In accordance with c. 827, permission to publish is granted on March 10, 2011 by Rev. Msgr. John F. Canary, Vicar General of the Archdiocese of Chicago. Permission to publish is an official declaration of ecclesiastical authority that the material is free from doctrinal and moral error. No legal responsibility is assumed by the grant of this permission.	The Subcommittee on the Catechism, United States Conference of Catholic Bishops, has found the doctrinal content of this manual, copyright 2013, to be in conformity with the *Catechism of the Catholic Church*.

Finding God: Our Response to God's Gifts is an expression of the work of Loyola Press, a ministry of the Chicago-Detroit Province of the Society of Jesus.

Senior Consultants
Jane Regan, Ph.D.
Richard Hauser, S.J., Ph.D., S.T.L.
Robert Fabing, S.J., D.Min.

Advisors
Most Reverend Gordon D. Bennett, S.J., D.D.
George A. Aschenbrenner, S.J., S.T.L.
Paul H. Colloton, O.P., D.Min.
Eugene LaVerdiere, S.S.S., Ph.D., S.T.L.
Gerald Darring, M.A.
Thomas J. McGrath, M.A.

Catechetical Staff
Jeanette L. Graham, M.A.
Jean Hopman, O.S.U., M.A.
Joseph Paprocki, D.Min.

Grateful acknowledgment is given to authors, publishers, photographers, museums, and agents for permission to reprint the following copyrighted material; music credits where appropriate can be found at the bottom of each individual song. Every effort has been made to determine copyright owners. In the case of any omissions, the publisher will be pleased to make suitable acknowledgments in future editions. Acknowledgments continue on page T-346. Children's Book acknowledgments begin on page 275.

Cover design: Loyola Press
Cover Illustration: Rafael López
Interior design: Loyola Press and Think Bookworks

ISBN-13: 978-0-8294-3177-3
ISBN-10: 0-8294-3177-2

Copyright © 2013 Loyola Press, Chicago, Illinois.

Manufactured in China.

LOYOLAPRESS.
A JESUIT MINISTRY

3441 N. Ashland Avenue
Chicago, Illinois 60657
(800) 621-1008

www.loyolapress.com
www.ignatianspirituality.com
www.other6.com

13 14 15 16 17 18 RRD 10 9 8 7 6 5 4 3

Contents

CONTENTS

Finding·God
Our Response to God's Gifts

"The desire for God is written in the human heart."

Catechism of the Catholic Church (CCC 27)

We desire to know God in a personal way in order to find meaning and purpose in our lives. This is the aim of catechesis as expressed in the *General Directory for Catechesis:* "to put people, not only in touch, but also in communion with Jesus Christ" (*GDC* 80). Loyola Press has designed *Finding God: Our Response to God's Gifts* as a successful way to invite children and the adults who care for them to enter into a deeper relationship with God and the Catholic Church in service to the world.

Inspired by the life and work of Saint Ignatius of Loyola, the Ignatian approach of *Finding God: Our Response to God's Gifts* invites all who experience the program to recognize the presence of God in the sacraments and in their communities of faith, and realize the presence of God in their experiences of God's creation and in their lives as people for others.

Finding God: Our Response to God's Gifts is an authentic expression of the Catholic faith, found to be in conformity with the *Catechism of the Catholic Church* by the Subcommittee on the Catechism. The program reflects a vision of our Catholic faith grounded in Scripture and Tradition. The expression of the vision is based on our Catholic belief that effective catechesis

▶ reflects the love of the Father, the Son, and the Holy Spirit.

▶ centers on the Person of Jesus Christ.

▶ proclaims the liberating good news of Salvation through Jesus Christ.

▶ leads the Christian into the world in mission and action.

▶ addresses the needs of the culture in which it is presented.

▶ invites believers to reflect on personal experience as they grow in relationship with God.

▶ leads to a full, conscious, active participation in the liturgical life of the Church.

▶ fosters a climate of prayer and nurtures a faith that is expressed in prayer.

So enjoy *Finding God: Our Response to God's Gifts,* knowing that you will be successful in helping children and families experience the full and authentic teaching of the Church while entering more deeply into a meaningful, lifelong relationship with God.

Catholicism is more than just an interesting theological proposition— it's the way you live your life.

Our faith is meant to be lived out in our homes, at school, on our jobs, and in the community. *Finding God: Our Response to God's Gifts* provides an invitation into a way of living in relationship to God, family, parish, and neighbor. This compelling and comprehensive program provides sound and substantial lessons in the faith and delivers those lessons through experiential activities that make these essential lessons part of a lifelong practice. *Finding God* involves the whole child: mind and heart, body and soul.

With *Finding God,* faith comes alive through

▶ **Dramatized Scripture stories** that place the child in the scene

▶ **Recorded guided meditations** that lead to prayerful encounters with Jesus

▶ **Diverse opportunities for prayer** that mentor children into a lifelong habit of praying

▶ **Connections** to the feasts, seasons, and liturgical life of the Church

▶ **Exploring Faith Through Art**—beautiful and inspiring Art Prints that creatively engage children with essential concepts of our faith

And *Finding God* engages parents and other family members through

▶ **Faith Moves,** a spiral-bound deck that helps parents nurture family faith in the course of their busy lives

▶ **Family E-newsletters** delivered online for easy distribution

▶ **Online resources** for living faith in the home, on the job, and in the community

▶ **Intergenerational events** that engage the whole parish community in exploring and celebrating our faith

You want to lead the children in your care to the blessings of a lifelong faith. *Finding God* offers you an impressive array of tools and resources to help you do just that.

Program Components

Soundly grounded in Scripture, Church Tradition, and prayer, *Finding God: Our Response to God's Gifts* offers catechists everything they need to inspire and guide children's faith formation. Engaging, developmentally appropriate content and faith experiences for children have been paired with easy-to-use, supportive catechist tools and materials to develop a comprehensive, integrated, relevant program.

Exploring Faith Through Art

25 prints per easel, each Art Print accompanies Children's Book pages, has catechist instructions, and is brimming with fine art, experiential activities, and prayer. (24 x 18 in.)

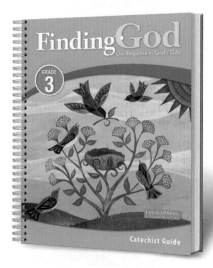

Catechist Guide

Each guide includes complete catechetical background, clear plans, step-by-step support, and additional activities—with custom guides for parish and school.

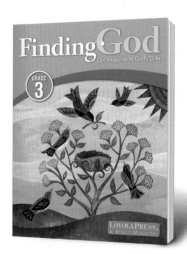

Children's Book

The truth and beauty of the Catholic faith is shared through prayer, Scripture, story, article, song, illustration, and experience.

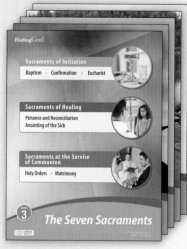

Poster Set

Posters at every grade level include relevant topics and beautiful visuals. (17 x 22 in.)

Scripture Stories and Guided Reflections Spoken Word CD

Dramatized recordings of Scripture stories bring the Bible to life; meditations mentor children to live a life of prayer.

Vocal, Instrumental, and Reflective Music CD

Recorded by the internationally known L.A. Children's Chorus, these songs reflect the diversity and unity of the Catholic Church.

Director Quick-Start Guide

It's easy to begin with clear, concise plans for step-by-step program implementation.

Finding God Together: An Intergenerational Events Kit

As optional unit openers, these parish-wide plans offer five intergenerational events that include skits, crafts, grade-level saint stations, and family faith formation experiences and projects.

Faith Moves

These family faith formation activities are for children of all ages. This deck is pocket-sized for use anytime, anywhere, and aligns with the five overarching themes in the program.

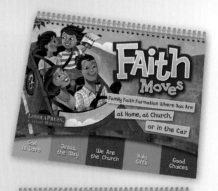

Leader Guide

Saint Station Posters

Five posters per grade feature unit-opener saints. (17 x 22 in.)

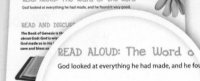

Technology—*Helpful Resources for Everyone*

DRE/Principal
- Director Guide Supplements
- *Finding God Together* Skit Scripts and Support Pieces
- Family E-Newsletters

Catechist/Teacher
- Activity Finder
- Prayer Services
- Blackline Masters
- Lesson Planner
- Links to Other Resources
- Assessments

Families
- At-Home Learning Guide
- Spanish Support

Children
- Spanish and English Glossaries
- Session Reviews
- Study Guides
- Games

 www.findinggod.com

To take full advantage of the secured items on the site, directors of religious education, principals, catechists, and teachers should register online with this **access code: FG-2013**

Spiral Curriculum

An integrated curriculum that spirals through the grades, *Finding God: Our Response to God's Gifts* provides support when and how it is needed. As children are introduced to and revisit concepts and vocabulary from one year to the next, their knowledge and experience both broaden and deepen.

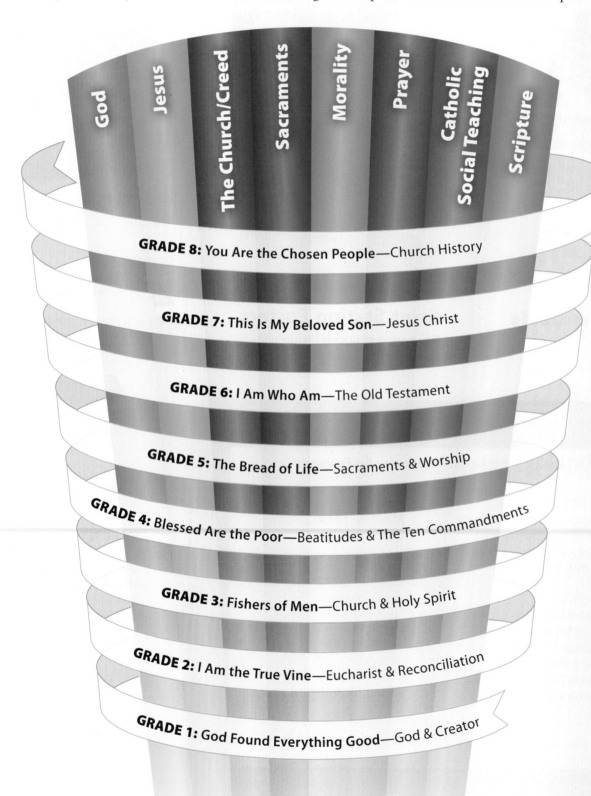

God   Jesus   The Church/Creed   Sacraments   Morality   Prayer   Catholic Social Teaching   Scripture

GRADE 8: You Are the Chosen People—Church History

GRADE 7: This Is My Beloved Son—Jesus Christ

GRADE 6: I Am Who Am—The Old Testament

GRADE 5: The Bread of Life—Sacraments & Worship

GRADE 4: Blessed Are the Poor—Beatitudes & The Ten Commandments

GRADE 3: Fishers of Men—Church & Holy Spirit

GRADE 2: I Am the True Vine—Eucharist & Reconciliation

GRADE 1: God Found Everything Good—God & Creator

Varied Catechetical Approaches

Finding God: Our Response to God's Gifts offers catechists and teachers a variety of catechetical approaches so that all children's needs are met and so that children, families, parishes, and schools are nurtured to grow in faith and become living examples of God's love.

Core Content as Catechesis

This program presents the Church's doctrine and Tradition accurately, comprehensively, and with approval by the United States Conference of Catholic Bishops. Direct references to the *CCC* and *GDC* are included in the Catechist Preparation section of each session.

Prayer as Catechesis

Finding God: Our Response to God's Gifts nourishes a relationship with God through traditional prayer, meditation, liturgical prayer, and praying with Scripture. At least five opportunities to pray are woven into each of the 25 sessions. Prayer services are provided for each Seasonal Session and online for each unit.

Liturgical Experiences as Catechesis

This series echoes our belief that the Eucharist is the "source and summit of the Christian life" (*CCC* 1324). For example, each Celebrating Session (Sessions 5, 10, 15, 20, and 25) helps children connect to their faith through the celebration of the Mass and to join in more meaningful participation in the Church's sacramental and liturgical life.

Scripture as Catechesis

Scripture sets the foundation for the truths reflected on in each session. The authentic teaching of the Church is revealed through Scripture and presented with ample opportunities for reflection and discussion.

Service/Catholic Social Teaching as Catechesis

Every session in this program provides children and adults with opportunities to explore and act on their commitment to the principles of Catholic Social Teaching.

A Blend of Traditional and Intergenerational Catechesis

The whole faith community is invited to experience *Finding God: Our Response to God's Gifts* through the supplemental intergenerational events kit titled *Finding God Together.* Through these creative, optional unit openers, catechesis can be extended to parishioners of all ages.

The Children's Book

Catholic content shared in a rich context, beautiful images, thoughtful prayer, and engaging activities and experiences draw children in to fully learn, experience, and express their faith.

Unit Opener

Each unit opens with a saint whose holy life and response to God's love reflect the unit theme.

Fact-filled biographies bring to life our Catholic faith, history, and Tradition.

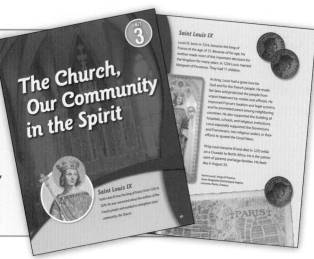

Explore Further

Learning comes alive as children explore and discuss traditional and modern art-works from around the world and connect the themes to Catholic Scripture, Tradition, and beliefs.

Integral to each session, children further explore catechetical content as it relates to the Art Print faith focus and the session themes.

Engage

Each session begins at a natural starting point—the child's own life.

Thought-provoking questions and an opening prayer lead children into the session.

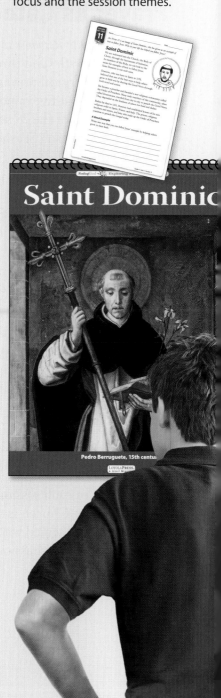

Explore

Children deepen their understanding of the Catholic faith as they read, discuss, experience, and pray.

Activities abound so that children can record their reflections and learning.

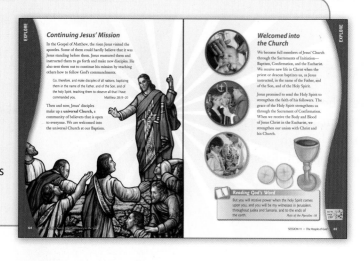

Reflect

Various forms of prayer draw children into a personal relationship with God.

Children are invited to express thoughts and ideas as another way to process and reflect.

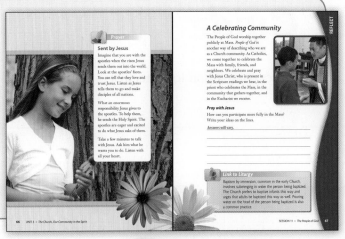

Support

Prayers and Practices
Children can reinforce and extend their learning with an age-appropriate reference to Catholic prayers, Tradition, beliefs, and music.

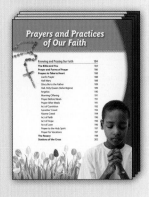

Respond

Children review what they've learned and pray in gratitude for God's gifts.

Families are invited to live their faith through simple, life-enriching experiences, discussions, and prayers.

Glossary An extensive Glossary provides further support so that reading is comprehensible.

Seasonal Sessions

The Year in Our Church seasonal sessions provide options for learning more about the liturgical year and its feasts.

Celebrating the Liturgical Year

Celebrating Sessions highlight the Mass and how and why we celebrate throughout the liturgical year.

The Catechist Guide

So easy to use, the Catechist Guide is the perfect companion for catechists and teachers of every experience level.

Catechist Preparation

 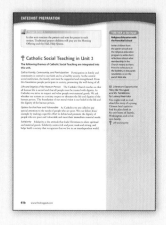  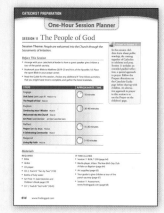

Overview
To begin each unit, catechists are introduced to the unit theme, session descriptions, and the unit-opener saint.

Catholic Social Teaching
For each unit, catechists are provided with an overview of prayer experiences and Catholic Social Teaching themes.

Literature Opportunity
Catechists can incorporate popular and classic literature as another way to explore the unit theme.

Together as One Parish
This idea provides an opportunity for the parish to come together when both the religious education program and the Catholic school are using the *Finding God* curriculum.

Retreat/Background
To begin each session, catechists are invited to pray in preparation. Then they read to gain background knowledge in Scripture, Tradition, and catechesis that children will experience.

One-Hour Planner
This easy-to-follow, one-hour lesson plan guides catechists to implement the session. (A five-day session plan is provided in the school edition Catechist Guide.)

A Choice for How to Open Each Unit

Stay in the Book
Catechists employ this approach to use the Children's Book as a more traditional way to introduce children to the unit theme and unit saint.

Intergenerational Event
If your parish adopts this supplement, children can be introduced to the unit theme and saint by attending an exciting intergenerational event.

Start at the Heart of a Child's Life

Every session opens by inviting children to talk about themselves, their friends, and their family—to tell their own stories as an entry point for discovering the session theme.

Engage

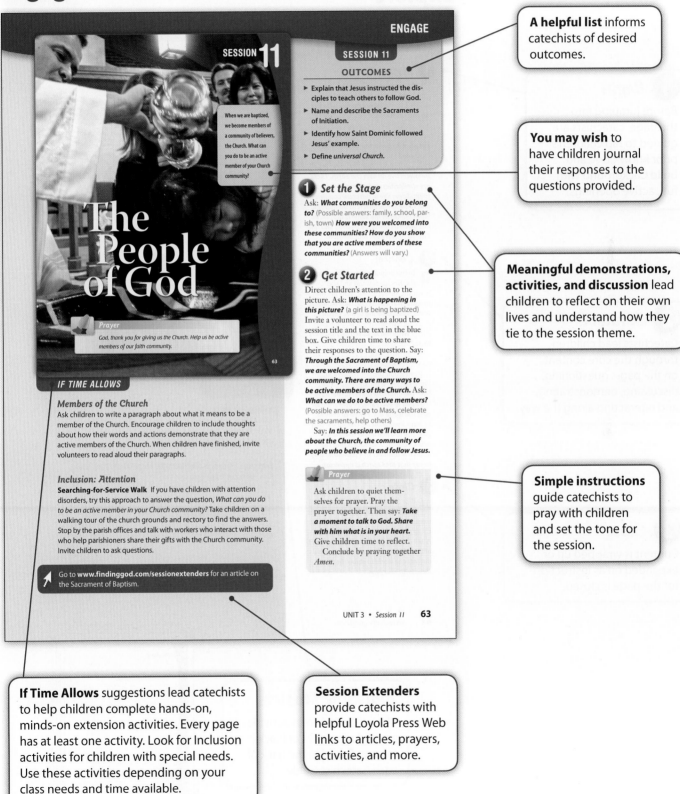

A helpful list informs catechists of desired outcomes.

You may wish to have children journal their responses to the questions provided.

Meaningful demonstrations, activities, and discussion lead children to reflect on their own lives and understand how they tie to the session theme.

Simple instructions guide catechists to pray with children and set the tone for the session.

If Time Allows suggestions lead catechists to help children complete hands-on, minds-on extension activities. Every page has at least one activity. Look for Inclusion activities for children with special needs. Use these activities depending on your class needs and time available.

Session Extenders provide catechists with helpful Loyola Press Web links to articles, prayers, activities, and more.

Rich Instruction in Three Simple Steps

Finding God teaches concepts in context—through Scripture, story, articles, engaging photographs, and interactive writing and drawing opportunities. In addition to definitions and facts, this program makes content connections that translate into a life of faith.

Explore

 Begin

Before jumping into the page, catechists are guided to tap children's prior knowledge and build background with fun, active openings.

 Connect

Catechists lead children through the core content on the page, questioning, discussing, demonstrating, and interacting along the way.

 Close

Content is wrapped up or expanded on as instruction for the page is closed.

EXPLORE

 Begin
Display a globe. Ask: *What is this?* (a globe) *What does it represent?* (the planet Earth) *How are people who live on earth different?* (Possible answers: They speak different languages. They live in different countries.) *How are people who live on earth the same?* (Possible answers: They are all human. They are all God's children.) Say: *Jesus' followers live all over the earth. There are similarities and differences among them. Some live in different countries, and some speak different languages. What makes us the same is that Jesus has given us the same mission and one Church to carry out that mission.*

 Connect
Invite volunteers to read aloud the first paragraph and the Scripture passage. Ask: *Why did the apostles have a difficult time believing Jesus was appearing before them?* (Possible answer: They thought he was dead.) *What did Jesus tell his followers to do?* (go forth and make new disciples, continue his mission by teaching others how to follow God's commandments)
Read aloud the last paragraph. Point out the term *universal Church.* Say: *The Church is universal because it is open to everyone. People from all over the world are invited to believe in Jesus and follow his teachings. Last year you learned about the Marks of the Church. One Mark is that the Church is catholic. This is another way to say that the Church is universal.*

Close
Play "Two by Two" [CD 2, Track 9]. As children listen to the song, ask them to follow along, using the lyrics in the back of their books. After children listen, say: *As members of the universal Church, Jesus sends us out into the world to share the Good News with everyone.*

64 www.findinggod.com

EXPLORE

Continuing Jesus' Mission

In the Gospel of Matthew, the risen Jesus visited the apostles. Some of them could hardly believe that it was Jesus standing before them. Jesus reassured them and instructed them to go forth and make new disciples. He also sent them out to continue his mission by teaching others how to follow God's commandments.

> Go, therefore, and make disciples of all nations, baptizing them in the name of the Father, and of the Son, and of the holy Spirit, teaching them to observe all that I have commanded you. *Matthew 28:19–20*

Then and now, Jesus' disciples make up a **universal Church**, a community of believers that is open to everyone. We are welcomed into the universal Church at our Baptism.

64 UNIT 3 • *The Church, Our Community in the Spirit*

IF TIME ALLOWS

Session 11 BLM
Carrying On Jesus' Mission Have children complete the Session 11 Blackline Master [T-309] to have them reflect on ways they can carry out Jesus' mission in the world today.

Message Through Media: **The New Birth Day Club: A Video on Baptism**
Have children watch this 12-minute video that makes a connection between a young boy's desire to belong to a community and the Sacrament of Baptism. After watching the video, ask children to list and explain the symbols and gestures that are part of the Sacrament of Baptism.

✝ *Family and Community*

Blackline Masters

Many If Time Allows activities are tied to a series of Blackline Masters found in the back of each Catechist Guide.

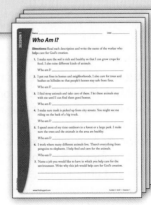

Catechists and teachers are supported every step of the way. The guides are so easy to navigate that even first-year catechists and teachers can use them with confidence.

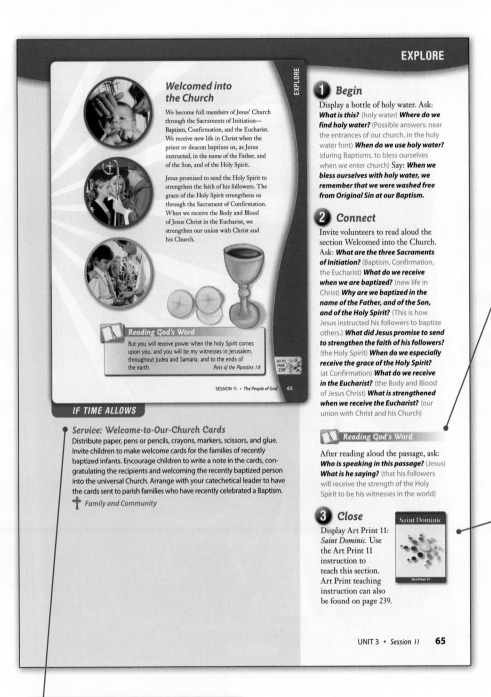

Special Features

With these special features, Catholic faith is highlighted through Scripture, liturgical references, interesting facts, and information about saints and sacred sites.

 Reading God's Word

 Link to Liturgy

 Did You Know?

 Meet a Saint or Holy Person

 Sacred Site

Go to the Art Print

Children explore concepts further with this exciting new session element that takes them out of the books and into discussion, reflection, prayer, experience, and expression. See pages OV-16 and OV-17 for a full explanation of how to implement the Exploring Faith Through Art portion of the session.

 Service Suggestion

Every session includes an idea for serving others, a real-life application of Catholic Social Teaching themes. For a full explanation of Catholic Social Teaching, visit the USCCB Web site.

The Session Continues

Integrated into every session and woven into the Children's Book, the Exploring Faith Through Art easel and catechist instructions make *Finding God* the most experiential program of its kind. Appealing to a variety of learning styles, only *Finding God* offers this rare opportunity to enliven and enrich your program—without any need for technology. The sturdy easel stands 18 x 24 inches.

Explore Faith Through Art

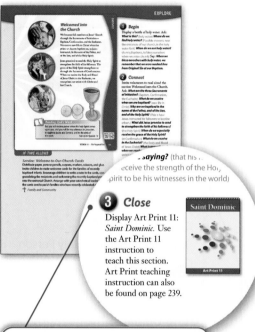

Finding God · Exploring Faith Through Art

Saint Dominic

Pedro Berruguete, 15th century.

LOYOLA PRESS.
A JESUIT MINISTRY

ART PRINT 11

③ Close
Display Art Print 11: *Saint Dominic.* Use the Art Print 11 instruction to teach this section. Art Print teaching instruction can also be found on page 239.

Display the Art Print

This step in the Catechist Guide directs catechists to display and use the session Art Print.

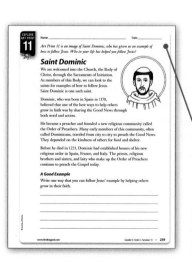

Children's Page

After discussing the artwork, catechists lead children through related content that furthers their learning.

Art Print Easel

Each session Art Print coincides with the session theme. Paintings, sculpture, stained glass, and other forms of visual art from every era spark the imagination as they reflect Catholic themes and ideas.

Guided Instruction on the Back of Each Art Print

About the Artist
Provided for catechist background and group sharing, biographical information is presented for each artist.

Art·i·facts
This feature provides information about the artwork's medium or main theme.

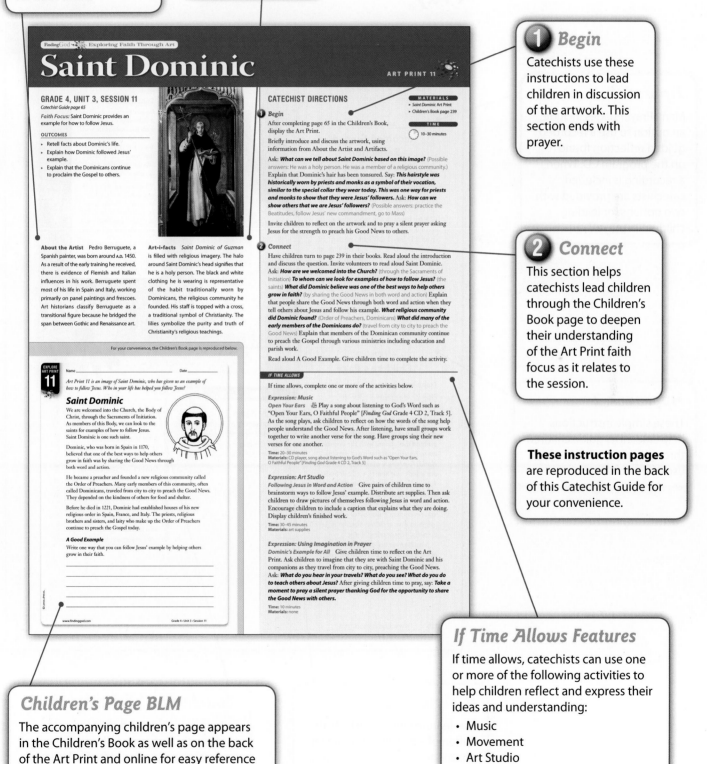

1 Begin
Catechists use these instructions to lead children in discussion of the artwork. This section ends with prayer.

2 Connect
This section helps catechists lead children through the Children's Book page to deepen their understanding of the Art Print faith focus as it relates to the session.

These instruction pages are reproduced in the back of this Catechist Guide for your convenience.

Children's Page BLM
The accompanying children's page appears in the Children's Book as well as on the back of the Art Print and online for easy reference and reproduction.

If Time Allows Features
If time allows, catechists can use one or more of the following activities to help children reflect and express their ideas and understanding:
• Music
• Movement
• Art Studio
• Using Imagination in Prayer

Helping Children Enter into a Deeper Relationship with God

Finding God **consistently provides opportunities** for catechists and children to experience and cherish prayer as a deeply important, always present opportunity to grow in relationship with God.

Pray

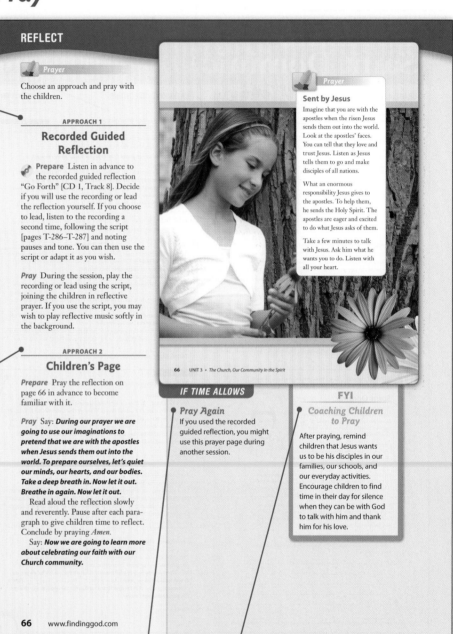

Approach 1

Many Prayer pages include an option to use a recorded guided reflection found on the program CD. When a recording is included, catechists are provided with two options for leading children in prayer.

Approach 2

These simple instructions help catechists guide children through prayer without the use of a recording.

If Time Allows

This feature gives catechists the option of expanding the prayer experience in meaningful ways.

Coaching Children to Pray

To help catechists and children enter confidently and more fully into prayer, a coaching tip is offered for each prayer.

Reflection Through Personal Expression

After prayer, and through personal expression, children are encouraged to take time to reflect—to recognize God's presence in their lives and in the world.

Reflect

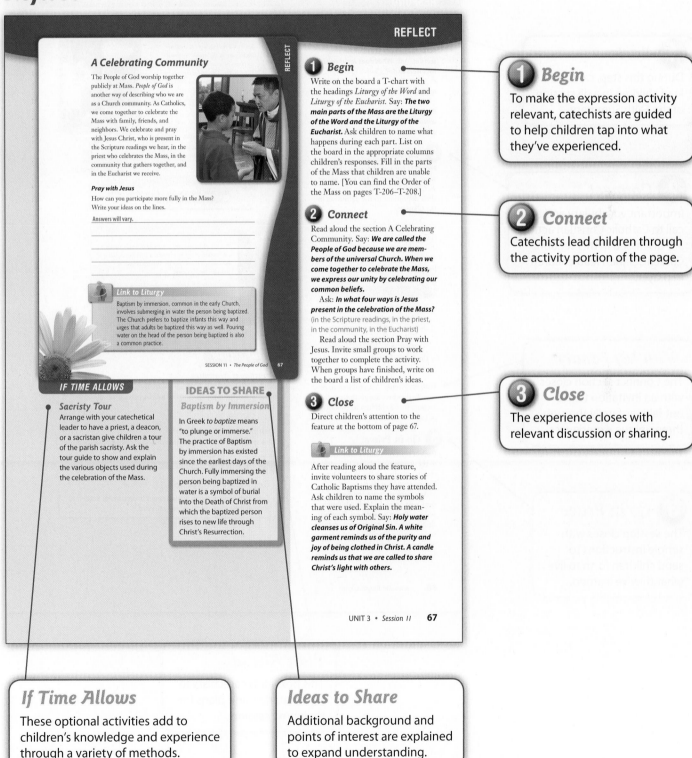

REFLECT

A Celebrating Community

The People of God worship together publicly at Mass. *People of God* is another way of describing who we are as a Church community. As Catholics, we come together to celebrate the Mass with family, friends, and neighbors. We celebrate and pray with Jesus Christ, who is present in the Scripture readings we hear, in the priest who celebrates the Mass, in the community that gathers together, and in the Eucharist we receive.

Pray with Jesus

How can you participate more fully in the Mass? Write your ideas on the lines.

Answers will vary.

Link to Liturgy

Baptism by immersion, common in the early Church, involves submerging in water the person being baptized. The Church prefers to baptize infants this way and urges that adults be baptized this way as well. Pouring water on the head of the person being baptized is also a common practice.

SESSION 11 • *The People of God* 67

IF TIME ALLOWS

Sacristy Tour
Arrange with your catechetical leader to have a priest, a deacon, or a sacristan give children a tour of the parish sacristy. Ask the tour guide to show and explain the various objects used during the celebration of the Mass.

IDEAS TO SHARE

Baptism by Immersion
In Greek *to baptize* means "to plunge or immerse." The practice of Baptism by immersion has existed since the earliest days of the Church. Fully immersing the person being baptized in water is a symbol of burial into the Death of Christ from which the baptized person rises to new life through Christ's Resurrection.

① Begin

Write on the board a T-chart with the headings *Liturgy of the Word* and *Liturgy of the Eucharist.* Say: **The two main parts of the Mass are the Liturgy of the Word and the Liturgy of the Eucharist.** Ask children to name what happens during each part. List on the board in the appropriate columns children's responses. Fill in the parts of the Mass that children are unable to name. [You can find the Order of the Mass on pages T-206–T-208.]

② Connect

Read aloud the section A Celebrating Community. Say: **We are called the People of God because we are members of the universal Church. When we come together to celebrate the Mass, we express our unity by celebrating our common beliefs.**

Ask: **In what four ways is Jesus present in the celebration of the Mass?** (in the Scripture readings, in the priest, in the community, in the Eucharist)

Read aloud the section Pray with Jesus. Invite small groups to work together to complete the activity. When groups have finished, write on the board a list of children's ideas.

③ Close

Direct children's attention to the feature at the bottom of page 67.

Link to Liturgy

After reading aloud the feature, invite volunteers to share stories of Catholic Baptisms they have attended. Ask children to name the symbols that were used. Explain the meaning of each symbol. Say: **Holy water cleanses us of Original Sin. A white garment reminds us of the purity and joy of being clothed in Christ. A candle reminds us that we are called to share Christ's light with others.**

UNIT 3 • *Session 11* **67**

---

① Begin

To make the expression activity relevant, catechists are guided to help children tap into what they've experienced.

② Connect

Catechists lead children through the activity portion of the page.

③ Close

The experience closes with relevant discussion or sharing.

If Time Allows

These optional activities add to children's knowledge and experience through a variety of methods.

Ideas to Share

Additional background and points of interest are explained to expand understanding.

Look Back and Send Forth

Through a review of key concepts and vocabulary, children identify how they can respond to God's invitation as they live each day. Families are invited to "bring the learning home" with three varied experiences that include activities, discussion, and prayer.

Living My Faith

1 Begin

During this step, catechists lead children in a discussion of the Faith Summary.

2 Connect

Important vocabulary and a call to Catholic Christian action are discussed in this section. Catechists then lead children in prayer.

With My Family

The Connect section closes with an invitation to live out faith as family through three unique experiences.

3 Go in Peace

The session closes with simple instructions to send children forth to live what they've learned.

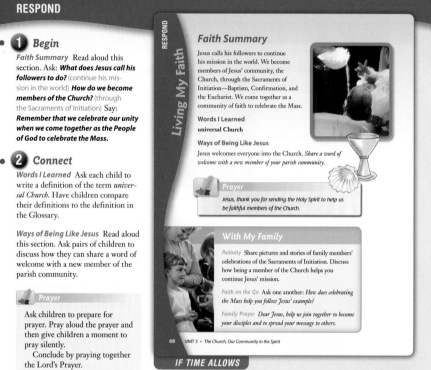

RESPOND

1 Begin

Faith Summary Read aloud this section. Ask: **What does Jesus call his followers to do?** (continue his mission in the world) **How do we become members of the Church?** (through the Sacraments of Initiation) Say: **Remember that we celebrate our unity when we come together as the People of God to celebrate the Mass.**

2 Connect

Words I Learned Ask each child to write a definition of the term *universal Church*. Have children compare their definitions to the definition in the Glossary.

Ways of Being Like Jesus Read aloud this section. Ask pairs of children to discuss how they can share a word of welcome with a new member of the parish community.

Prayer

Ask children to prepare for prayer. Pray aloud the prayer and then give children a moment to pray silently.
Conclude by praying together the Lord's Prayer.

With My Family Ask children to read silently the three suggestions in this section. Invite children to choose one or more to complete at home.

3 Go in Peace

Collect materials and return them to the appropriate places. Encourage children to discuss the With My Family section at home.
As a farewell, trace the Sign of the Cross on each child's forehead and say: **Peace be with you.** Remind children that the priest performs this action during Baptisms to welcome new members into the Church.

68   www.findinggod.com

RESPOND / Living My Faith

Faith Summary

Jesus calls his followers to continue his mission in the world. We become members of Jesus' community, the Church, through the Sacraments of Initiation—Baptism, Confirmation, and the Eucharist. We come together as a community of faith to celebrate the Mass.

Words I Learned

universal Church

Ways of Being Like Jesus

Jesus welcomes everyone into the Church. *Share a word of welcome with a new member of your parish community.*

Prayer

Jesus, thank you for sending the Holy Spirit to help us be faithful members of the Church.

With My Family

Activity Share pictures and stories of family members' celebrations of the Sacraments of Initiation. Discuss how being a member of the Church helps you continue Jesus' mission.

Faith on the Go Ask one another: *How does celebrating the Mass help you follow Jesus' example?*

Family Prayer Dear Jesus, help us join together to become your disciples and to spread your message to others.

68   UNIT 3 • The Church, Our Community in the Spirit

IF TIME ALLOWS

Newspaper Headlines
Write on the board the vocabulary term. Then have children write a headline and the topic sentence for a newspaper article about the universal Church.

Session Assessment Option
An assessment for this session can be found at **www.findinggod.com**.

PLAN AHEAD

Get Ready for Session 12
Consult the catechist preparation pages to prepare for Session 12 and determine any materials you will need.

Plan Ahead

This box leads catechists to find materials and plans for their next session.

A Complete Program

The continuation of faith formation at home and the ability to monitor progress are key elements of a comprehensive curriculum. *Finding God* offers unique ways to engage families and utilizes quality assessments and study tools to be sure children are supported in every way.

For the Family

Faith Moves

Family Faith Formation Wherever You Are—at Home, at Church, or in the Car!

Geared for families with children of all ages, this action-packed deck makes family faith formation accessible and fun for everyone. It's the take-anywhere answer to "How do I get families involved?" Card themes are aligned with the *Finding God* Program.

Sold separately.

Available in English and Spanish.

Assessment

Session Assessments

Available as PDFs on the Web, these assessments track children's progress for all 25 sessions.

Unit Assessments

Five unit assessments are bound in the Catechist Guide as Blackline Masters in addition to being provided as PDFs online.

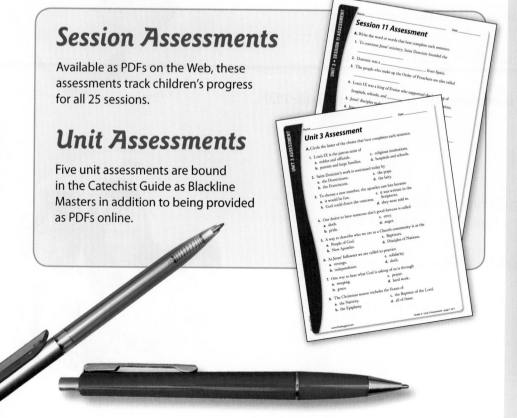

Online Resources

For Families

Finding God E-Newsletters

Provided seven times a year, these e-newsletters give parents inspiring suggestions for raising faith-filled kids. Articles and special features on topics such as saints, what it means to be Catholic, and media reviews make these newsletters relevant and inviting. Available in English and Spanish.

For Catechists and Children

Games, Reviews, and Study Guides

Online games, interactive reviews, and study guides help children prepare for assessment.

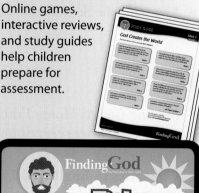

Online Support

A Web site that offers a wealth of resources to support and enhance the program, **www.findinggod.com** has the entire faith community in mind. To access secured materials such as assessments, directors of religious education, principals, catechists, and teachers should register online with this **access code: FG-2013**

Directors of Religious Education and Principals

▶ **Director Guide:** Practical plans for introducing and implementing the program. Includes PDFs of sample presentation slides.

▶ *Finding God Together* **Kit:** Skit scripts and support pieces for parishes and/or schools that wish to use the alternative unit openers by holding intergenerational events.

▶ **Family E-Newsletters:** Offered seven times a year. Available in English and Spanish.

Catechists and Teachers

▶ **Activity Finder:** Hundreds of activities for every grade level, grouping, and learner.

▶ **Prayer Services:** Printable prayer service PDFs for every unit and season.

▶ **Blackline Masters:** For easy access all Blackline Masters are available as PDFs online.

▶ **Lesson Planner:** Fast and easy to use. Takes the guesswork out of lesson planning.

▶ **Session Extenders:** Helpful Loyola Press Web links to articles, prayers, activities, and more.

▶ **Assessments:** Session and unit assessments are available as printable PDFs.

Families

▶ *Finding God* **At-Home Edition:** For homeschoolers or for long absences. Provides everything for families to complete the program independently at home.

▶ **Glossaries in English and Spanish:** A definition for every vocabulary word in the program.

▶ **Spanish Support:** Support and resources for parents whose primary language is Spanish.

Children

▶ **Interactive Session Reviews:** To reinforce comprehension and prepare for upcoming assessments.

▶ **Online Games:** An entertaining and educational way to reinforce content.

▶ **English Glossary:** A definition for every Word I Learned in the program.

▶ **Spanish Glossary:** For children and parents whose primary language is Spanish.

Everyone

LoyolaPress.com

▶ **3-Minute Retreats online:** Available in English and Spanish for your computer, iPhone®, or iPad®. Great for personal use or to open sessions or meetings.

▶ **Sunday Connection:** Useful background and activities to explain the upcoming Sunday's Scripture readings.

▶ **Family, Faith, and Fun:** Fun activities to help parents see family life as an opportunity to recognize the grace of God.

▶ **Saint Resources:** Activities, biographies, reflections, and stories.

▶ **Our Catholic Faith Resources:** Articles, activities, and facts about Catholic life.

Note: Be sure children are closely supervised by adults when on the Internet.

IgnatianSpirituality.com

▶ **What Is Ignatian Spirituality?:** Relevant articles and information about Saint Ignatius of Loyola and his teachings.

▶ **Ignatian Prayer:** A variety of prayers developed or inspired by Saint Ignatius.

▶ **Making Good Decisions:** Information on discernment, spiritual direction, and life vocations.

▶ **Ignatian Voices:** Articles and biographies about those inspired by Ignatian spirituality.

▶ **Ignatian Community:** Connections to Jesuit and Ignatian organizations and communities.

Other6.com

▶ **Online Community:** An inspirational place to connect with other Catholics to answer two profound questions: *Where have you found God today? Where do you need to find God today?*

Unit	Session	Session Theme	Scripture	CCC References
1 God, Our Creator and Father	**1** God Creates Us	God created the world to show us how much he loves us.	1 Timothy 4:4; Genesis 1:1–31	290–292, 307
	2 God Gives Us Jesus	Jesus is the Son of God who comes to save us.	Matthew 1:18–24, 28:20	422–424, 430–432
	3 God Is Our Father	We call Jesus the Son of God because he reveals to us his loving Father.	Matthew 6:25–34; 1 Peter 5:6–7	65, 2786–2793
	4 God's Life for Us	All good things we do and the good decisions we make come from the Holy Spirit.	Luke 2:25–32; Matthew 5:14–16; Isaiah 49:6	733–736, 739
	5 Celebrating Ordinary Time	Ordinary Time is a time to be fed by Jesus, the Bread of Life.	John 6:48	533
2 Jesus, Our Lord and Savior	**6** Jesus Is Faithful	With God's help, we can follow the Commandments and live in peace with one another.	Exodus 20:1–17; Luke 2: 41–52	534, 2052, 2197–2246
	7 Jesus Saves Us	Jesus is the model for the love and goodness in our lives.	Isaiah 35:5; Luke 7:18–22	427, 459, 520, 532, 581, 2607
	8 Jesus Calls Us to Love	Jesus calls us to the Kingdom of God.	Matthew 4:23; Luke 14:16–23	541–556, 2632, 2816–2821
	9 Jesus Cares for Us	The parable of the lost sheep shows God's loving concern for us.	Matthew 18:10–14; John 10:11; Psalm 23	553, 861–862, 881, 896, 1465
	10 Celebrating Advent	Advent is a time to prepare for Jesus and make room for him in our lives.	Ephesians 5:8	524
3 The Church, Our Community in the Spirit	**11** We Worship God	The sacraments help us to worship God in a special way.	John 15:1–6; Galatians 5:22	Part 2
	12 Celebrating Reconciliation	When we celebrate the Sacrament of Reconciliation, we are reconciled with God and with others.	Luke 12:33, 19:2–9	1422–1484
	13 The Sacrament of Reconciliation	In the Sacrament of Reconciliation, our sins are forgiven.	Luke 1:77; Mark 2:1–12	1468–1470, 1849–1869
	14 Mary Shows Us the Way	Mary is the great example of what it means to obey God.	Luke 1:39–55, 2:19	717, 2617–2619, 2676–2679
	15 Celebrating Christmas	Christmas is a time to celebrate the birth of Jesus with our families.	Matthew 1:23	525–526
4 Sacraments, Our Way of Life	**16** New Life in Jesus	When we receive the Sacraments of Initiation, we receive new life in Jesus.	Revelation 22:17; Acts of the Apostles 2:38	1212–1274, 1285–1314, 1322–1405
	17 Jesus Loves the Church	One way we can see God's love in the world is the way we celebrate the Eucharist.	Luke 24:13–31; Acts of the Apostles 2:42	329, 1347
	18 Gathering for Mass	When we gather for Mass, we hear the Word of God.	2 Timothy 3:14–17	1348–1349
	19 Celebrating the Eucharist	Celebrating the Eucharist is central to Christian life.	Luke 22:14–20; Hebrews 10:12	1350–1355
	20 Celebrating Lent and Holy Week	Lent and Holy Week are times to ask for God's help in becoming the person he calls me to be.	Ephesians 4:22–24	1438
5 Morality, Our Lived Faith	**21** Being Like Jesus	Jesus shows us how to love through his words and deeds.	Luke 10:25–37; Matthew 5:7	512–560
	22 We Share God's Life	God helps us follow our conscience so that we can be truly free and happy.	Deuteronomy 30:16–18; John 14:6	1749–1756, 1776–1794
	23 Following Jesus	We can be like Jesus by treating others fairly and with justice.	Matthew 22:37–38, 5:1–10; 1 John 3:17–18	1716–1719, 1725–1728
	24 Making Choices	God wants us to respect one another's good name and property.	1 Peter 3:10–12; Psalm 34:12–15	120–127, 2779–2783
	25 Celebrating Easter	Easter is a time to reflect on eternal life.	John 10:28	639–644

A sixth unit includes separate sessions for these liturgical seasons: Advent, Christmas, Lent, Holy Week, Easter, Pentecost, and All Saints Day. A Scope and Sequence is on page 151a.

Words Learned	Saints and Holy People	Prayers / Parts of the Mass	Catholic Social Teaching Themes	Service Suggestion
Eucharist, holy, Sacrament of Penance and Reconciliation	St. Isidore the Farmer St. Maria de la Cabeza Holy Family Joseph Simeon of Jerusalem	Glory Be to the Father, Sacrament of the Eucharist	Family and Community, God's Creation, Work and Workers	Grounds Cleanup
Blessed Sacrament, consecration, Emmanuel, genuflect, Savior, tabernacle			Family and Community	The Gift of Time
petition, praise		Lord's Prayer, Prayer of Petition, Prayer of Praise	Family and Community, Solidarity	Garden for God
faith, Messiah, Temple		Prayer to the Holy Spirit	Solidarity	Pen Pals
Bread of Life, chasuble			Solidarity	Welcome a New Family
Ten Commandments	St. Anne St. Joachim John the Baptist St. Martin de Porres St. Peter		Family and Community	Honoring Our Elders
miracle			Poor and Vulnerable, Solidarity	Our Prayer Tree
bishop, crosier, parable, pope			Poor and Vulnerable, Solidarity	A Great Leader
deacon		Psalm 23	Family and Community, Solidarity	Show Thanks
			Poor and Vulnerable	A Servant's Heart
Fruits of the Holy Spirit, Original Sin, rite	St. Ignatius of Loyola Mary Elizabeth Zacchaeus		Family and Community, Poor and Vulnerable	Spirituality in Action
confession, contrition, examination of conscience, mortal sin, venial sin		Act of Contrition	Family and Community, Solidarity	Serve Others
absolution, seal of confession			Life and Dignity, Solidarity	Signs of Peace
Magnificat		*Magnificat*	Family and Community, Solidarity	Make a Visit
Nativity scene			Solidarity	Adopt a "Grandfriend"
Body and Blood of Christ, Confirmation, Holy Communion, Sacraments of Initiation	Pope Saint Pius X St. Peter John Luke Mark Matthew	Holy Communion	Family and Community, Solidarity	Prayer Cards
disciple, ministry, Sacrifice of the Mass		Celebration of the Eucharist, Prayer Before Meals	Family and Community, Solidarity	Our Daily Bread
ambo, Evangelists, homily, *Lectionary for Mass*, Liturgy of the Word		Creed, Entrance Chant, *Gloria*, Homily, Introductory Rites, Liturgy of the Word	Family and Community	Volunteer at Mass
altar, Holy Days of Obligation, Liturgy of the Eucharist, transubstantiation		Concluding Rites, Eucharistic Prayer, Lamb of God, Liturgy of the Eucharist	Family and Community, Poor and Vulnerable	Book Drive
		Penitential Act	Family and Community	Easter Egg Hunt
Beatitudes	St. Martin of Tours Moses St. Elizabeth Ann Seton Peter	the Eucharist	Life and Dignity, Poor and Vulnerable, Rights and Responsibilities, Solidarity	Seasonal Service
conscience, moral choice			Poor and Vulnerable, Family and Community	Sock Hop for Those Who Are Homeless
Great Commandment, New Testament, Old Testament			Solidarity, Poor and Vulnerable	Act Justly
peacemaker, sign of peace		Sign of Peace	Solidarity, Family and Community, Life and Dignity	Respect Posters
eternal life			Family and Community	Reading Hour

Art Print titles and themes are found at the end of this section.

Unit	Session	Session Theme	Scripture	CCC References
1 God, Our Creator and Father	1 Created to Be Happy	God wants us to know him.	Psalm 148:7–14; Genesis 1:31	41, 222–227
	2 Created to Be Together	The love of the Father, Son, and Holy Spirit is the source of the love we have for one another.	I John 4:16, 4:7–11	2196
	3 God Is Our Father	Jesus reveals to us that God is our loving Father, who calls us to live in peace with one another.	Matthew 6:9–14; 2 Corinthians 1:3–4	2786–2796
	4 Jesus Is with Us	The Father sends Jesus to save us.	Matthew 1:18–23; Deuteronomy 31:8	430–433, 441–444
	5 Celebrating Ordinary Time	Ordinary Time is a time to grow and be grateful we belong to our church community.	Colossians 3:16; Psalms 118:24	775
2 Jesus, Our Lord and Savior	6 Jesus' Good News	Jesus teaches us how to love the Father, others, and ourselves.	Matthew 13:31–32, 13:33	541–556
	7 Following Jesus	Jesus call us to love God and others.	Mark 10:17–23; Matthew 6:21	2052–2055
	8 Jesus Gathers Disciples	Jesus invites his followers to enter the Kingdom of God.	Luke 5:1–5, 5:6–11, 10:2	2044–2046
	9 Jesus Dies and Rises	Through Jesus' Death and Resurrection, we receive Salvation.	John 11:25–26; I Corinthians 15:1–5	599–618, 638–655, 659–664, 731–732
	10 Celebrating Advent	Advent is a time to prepare ourselves and our homes for the celebration of Jesus' birth.	Luke 2:12	524
3 The Church, Our Community in the Spirit	11 Jesus Sends the Holy Spirit	Jesus sends the Holy Spirit to bring life into the Church.	Galatians 5:22–23; Acts of the Apostles 2:1–12	731–741
	12 The Catholic Church	Jesus gives us leaders in the Church.	John 21:17; Matthew 16:18–19	858–862, 880–886
	13 The Church Prays	Jesus Christ is especially present in the celebration of the sacraments.	Luke 7:1–10, 17:21	798, 947, 1088, 1097, 1118, 1123
	14 Mary Is Holy	Mary is the Church's model of faith and love.	Luke 1:45–54	717, 946–959, 971, 2617–2619, 2676–2679
	15 Celebrating Christmas	Christmas is a time to prepare to celebrate as a Church the birth of Jesus.	Micah 5:1	525–526
4 Sacraments, Our Way of Life	16 Sacraments of Initiation	Through the Sacraments of Initiation, we receive fullness of the Spirit and become members of the Church.	Ephesians 4:4; Acts of the Apostles 8:26–34, 8:35–40	1212–1274, 1285–1314, 1322–1405
	17 Celebrating Reconciliation	When we fail to love God and others because of sin, Jesus calls us to forgiveness though the Sacrament of Reconciliation.	John 20:19–23; Psalm 85:9	1422–1470
	18 Celebrating the Eucharist	The celebration of the Eucharist is at the center of parish life.	I Corinthians 11:23–26; John 6:48	1396
	19 Christian Living	We are called by God to do special work as either a sister, brother, priest, married, or single person.	1 Corinthians 12:4–11; I Peter 4:10	1350–1355
	20 Celebrating Lent and Holy Week	Lent and Holy Week are times to think of how we treat others.	Tobit 4:7; Matthew 4:10, 25:40; Luke 21:1–4	1438
5 Morality, Our Lived Faith	21 Faith, Hope, and Charity	We live like Jesus when we practice the virtues of faith, hope, and charity.	I Thessalonians 1:2–4; I Corinthians 13:13	1812–1829
	22 Making Good Choices	Jesus gives us the help we need to make good moral choices.	Colossians 3:17; Matthew 4:1–11	2052–2074
	23 Living as God's Children	Jesus helps us to love and respect one another.	Galatians 6:2; Philippians 1:3–11	1878–1885, 2196
	24 All Life Is Sacred	Jesus calls us to share with one another in any way we can.	I John 4:7; Psalm 8:6–10	2258–2262, 2415–2418
	25 Celebrating Easter	Easter is a time to reflect on God's merciful love.	John 20:27	639–644

A sixth unit includes separate sessions for these liturgical seasons: Advent, Christmas, Lent, Holy Week, Easter, Pentecost, and All Saints Day. A Scope and Sequence is on page 151a.

Words Learned	Saints and Holy People	Prayers / Parts of the Mass	Catholic Social Teaching Themes	Service Suggestion
apostle, Apostles' Creed, creed	St. Ignatius of Loyola Trinity Joseph Mary St. Elizabeth of Hungary St. Joseph	Apostle's Creed	God's Creation	Poster Campaign
Sign of the Cross		Sign of the Cross, Glory Be to The Father	Family and Community, Life and Dignity, Solidarity	Nursing Home Letters
Abba		The Lord's Prayer	Poor and Vulnerable, Solidarity	Food Collection
Scriptures		Apostles' Creed	Family and Community, Poor and Vulnerable,	Read to Children
community			Poor and Vulnerable, Solidarity	Make Snack Bags
monastery	St. Scholastica St. Benedict St. Peter St. Paul		Poor and Vulnerable, Solidarity	Book Collection
conversion			Poor and Vulnerable, Solidarity	Collect Money
Gospel, mission			God's Creation, Family and Community,	Performance
Paschal Mystery		Apostles' Creed	Family and Community	Design a Poster
			Family and Community	Make a Prayer Tree
witness	St. Katharine Drexel St. Peter Mary Elizabeth	Prayer to the Holy Spirit	Solidarity	Bookmarks
apostolic, Marks of the Church, Mystical Body of Christ, one, pastor, Vicar of Christ		Apostles' Creed	Family and Community, Solidarity	Letters to Pastor
blessing, sacramental			Life and Dignity	Sacramental Collection
Annunciation, Communion of Saints, Rosary, Visitation		*Magnificat*, Rosary	Poor and Vulnerable	Clothing Collection
			Family and Community	Pen Pal
People of God	St. Paul the Apostle St. Philip St. Andrew Kim Taegon	Renewing the Baptismal Promises at Mass; Sacraments of Baptism, Confirmation, and Eucharist	Family and Community, Life and Dignity	Baby Items Collection
personal sin		Act of Contrition, Sacrament of Penance and Reconciliation	Family and Community	Peace Garden
epistle, worship		Liturgy of the Eucharist, Eucharistic Prayer	Family and Community, Solidarity	Spread the Word
Holy Orders, Matrimony, vocation		Sacrament of Holy Orders, Sacrament of Matrimony	Work and Workers, Family and Community	Thank-You Cards
almsgiving		Prayer of the Faithful	Family and Community	Record a Book
charity, hope, virtues	St. Monica St. Jeanne Jugan St. Augustine St. Paul St. Louise de Marillac Blessed Frederic Ozanam		Poor and Vulnerable, Life and Dignity, Solidarity	Toiletries Collection
moral law		The Ten Commandments, Morning Offering	Solidarity	Mini-Posters
justice			Life and Dignity, Poor and Vulnerable	Clothing Collection
Dismissal			God's Creation, Life and Dignity, Poor and Vulnerable, Rights and Responsibilities	Pet Supplies Collection
Lamb of God, mercy		Lamb of God	Family and Community	Spread Easter Joy

Art Print titles and themes are found at the end of this section.

Unit	Session	Session Theme	Scripture	CCC References
1 God, Our Creator and Father	1 God Creates the World	God's love for us is revealed through his creation.	Psalm 65:10,14; Sirach 39:33	296–298
	2 Our Father in Heaven	Jesus teaches us that God is our loving Father.	Matthew 7:9–11; John 14:7	120–127, 2779–2783
	3 God's Plan for Salvation	God responds to the sin of Adam and Eve with the promise of a Savior.	Genesis 3:1–24	410–412
	4 God Calls Us to Obey	God speaks to us through our conscience.	1 Corinthians 13:2; Galatians 5:22–23, 6:9–10; Matthew 6:10	1783–1794
	5 Celebrating Ordinary Time	Ordinary Time is a time to grow as Jesus' disciples.	Ephesians 5:8–10; Luke 4:17–19	533
2 Jesus, Our Lord and Savior	6 Jesus' Law of Love	Jesus' law of love allows us to live peacefully with one another.	John 13:34	1822–1826, 1889, 2011, 2083, 2196
	7 The Beatitudes	The Beatitudes show us how we can be truly happy and share happiness with others.	Matthew 5:2–10; Psalm 73:1	1716–1719
	8 Jesus Our Redeemer	Jesus redeemed us from our sins through his life, Death, and Resurrection.	Luke 23:39–43; Acts of the Apostles 4:12	571, 601, 669
	9 Jesus Sends the Spirit	Jesus shares his new life with us through the power of the Holy Spirit.	Acts of the Apostles 2:1–4, 9:32–43	731–732, 737–741
	10 Celebrating Advent	We can prepare to welcome Jesus into our lives by making good moral choices.	Luke 3:4	524
3 The Church, Our Community in the Spirit	11 The People of God	People are welcomed into the Church through the Sacraments of Initiation.	Matthew 28:19–20; Acts of the Apostles 1:8	751–752, 1140–1141
	12 The Church Teaches Us	Jesus calls the Church to continue his mission.	Romans 12:4–5; Acts of the Apostles 1:21–26	888–892, 2041–2043
	13 God Is Our Friend	Jesus calls us to forgiveness and offers us the grace of reconciliation when we sin.	Isaiah 49:15; Matthew 18:21–22; Luke 15:8–24	1440–1442, 1854–1863
	14 Serving God and Others	Mary, the Mother of God and the Mother of the Church, is the perfect model of Christian discipleship.	Luke 1:26–38,45–46	484–507
	15 Celebrating Christmas	During Christmas we celebrate Jesus' birth.	John 6:35	525–526
4 Sacraments, Our Way of Life	16 Celebrating Reconciliation	Through the Sacrament of Reconciliation, we renew our relationship with God and others.	Isaiah 40:11; Luke 15:4–7	1422–1470
	17 The Sacrament of the Eucharist	Jesus is really present to us in the Sacrament of the Eucharist.	Matthew 26:26–30; Mark 6:34–44, 14:22–26; Luke 22:14–20; 1 Corinthians 10:16	1322–1405, 1548–1553, 2174–2188
	18 Anointing of the Sick	We celebrate the healing presence of Jesus in the Sacrament of the Anointing of the Sick.	Luke 5:17–20; James 5:14–16; Matthew 11:4–5	1499–1525
	19 Sacraments of Service	Matrimony and Holy Orders are Sacraments at the Service of Communion.	John 15:9–10,12–13	1536–1589, 1601–1658
	20 Celebrating Lent and Holy Week	Lent and Holy Week are times to be more like Jesus.	John 3:16	1423, 1427, 1431
5 Morality, Our Lived Faith	21 The Ten Commandments	By using the Ten Commandments as guide for our actions, we are able to make good moral choices.	Exodus 3:4–17, 7:14—11:10, 14:5–30, 19:1—20:17; Matthew 5:17	2052–2074
	22 Loving God Above All	The first three commandments teach us to love God above all.	Mark 12:29–33; Exodus 20:2–3,7–8; Luke 4:8	2084–2195
	23 Loving Our Family	The Fourth through Sixth Commandments teach us to live in good relationship with others.	Exodus 20:12–14; 1 Kings 8:57–58; Matthew 5:43–44	2201–2233
	24 Jesus Calls Us to Love Others	To choose to follow God's Ten Commandments is to choose life.	Exodus 20:15–17	2410–2557
	25 Celebrating Easter	Easter is a time to reflect on Jesus' gift of peace.	John 14:47	639–644

A sixth unit includes separate sessions for these liturgical seasons: Advent, Christmas, Lent, Holy Week, Easter, Pentecost, and All Saints Day. A Scope and Sequence is on page 151a.

Words Learned	Saints and Holy People	Prayers / Parts of the Mass	Catholic Social Teaching Themes	Service Suggestion
free will, psalm, soul	St. Teresa of Ávila St. Peter Canisius	Responsorial Psalm	God's Creation, Rights and Responsibilities, Work and Workers	Recycling
Theological Virtues		Lord's Prayer, Communion Rite, Act of Faith	Family and Community, God's Creation, Rights and Responsibilities, Solidarity,	Care-for-Creation Signs
Salvation		Act of Hope, Penitential Act	Family and Community, Life and Dignity	A Picture-Book Library
prudence		Examination of Conscience	Family and Community, Life and Dignity, Rights and Responsibilities	Cards for Others
discipleship			Family and Community	Liturgical Ministry
fortitude, Torah	St. John Baptiste Vianney St. Francis of Assisi St. Augustine Blessed Teresa of Calcutta St. Vincent de Paul St. Jerome	Prayer of the Faithful, Act of Love	Family and Community, Rights and Responsibilities, Solidarity	Praying for Others
Sermon on the Mount		Sign of Peace, Peace Prayer of St. Francis	Family and Community, Solidarity	Random Acts of Kindness
Ascension, Redeemer, redemption		Mystery of Faith, Apostles' Creed	Poor and Vulnerable	Birthday Boxes
Corporal Works of Mercy, Spiritual Works of Mercy		Holy Spirit Prayer of St. Augustine	Family and Community, Poor and Vulnerable, Solidarity	Food Drive
Angelus		Angelus	Poor and Vulnerable	"I Care" Kits
universal Church	St. Louis IX Blessed Miguel Pro St. Dominic Matthias Mary		Family and Community, Life and Dignity	Welcome-to-Our-Church Cards
cast lots, diocese, Precepts of the Church		Morning Offering	Family and Community, Solidarity	Collection for Catholic Relief Services
capital sins, envy, pride, sloth			Family and Community	Book Collection
solidarity		Salve Regina	Family and Community, Solidarity	Clothing Drive
			Poor and Vulnerable	Gift Basket
repentance	St. Ignatius of Loyola Venerable Pierre Toussaint Hildegard of Bingen	Act of Contrition	Family and Community, Life and Dignity	Sacrament of Reconciliation Advertisements
compassion			Family and Community, Poor and Vulnerable	A Parish Celebration
Anointing of the Sick, oil of the sick		Prayers of Intercession	Family and Community	Toy Drive
ordained			Family and Community	Congratulations Cards
Holy Thursday		Stations of the Cross	Family and Community	Prayer Partners
covenant, plague	St. Francis Xavier St. Thomas More	Prayer to the Holy Spirit	Family and Community	Cards for RCIA Candidates
Divine Praises, idolatry		Divine Praises	Family and Community, Rights and Responsibilities	Write Articles About Loving God
obedience			Family and Community, Life and Dignity	Respect Life
covet, Temperance		Concluding Rites	Rights and Responsibilities, Work and Workers	Thank-You Cards
gift of peace			Poor and Vulnerable	Share Peace with Others

Art Print titles and themes are found at the end of this section.

Grade 3 Art Prints at a Glance

During every *Finding God* session, children experience catechesis through the use of an Art Print, an accompanying Children's Page, and direct instruction. Use this handy guide to see the faith focus of each Art Print portion of a session.

GRADE 3

Unit	Session Number	Art Print Title	Art Print Faith Focus
1	1	Paradise Garden	We give glory to God for the wonders of creation.
	2	Elizabeth of Hungary	We share God's love with others.
	3	The Peace Offering	God calls us to care for others by forgiving one another.
	4	Names of Angels	The names we use for Jesus reveal him to us.
	5	Eucharist	Ordinary Time reminds us to be thankful for God's presence each day.
2	6	Saint Benedict	Saints Benedict and Scholastica spread God's love to others.
	7	Young Christian Girl	Jesus calls us to be closer to God and show our love for others.
	8	Acts of the Apostles	Jesus invites us to proclaim the Kingdom of God.
	9	Saint Paul the Apostle	Like Saint Paul, we can spread God's message to help others believe and be saved.
	10	Prepare for Christmas	Advent is a time to prepare for the celebration of Jesus' birth.
3	11	The Doves III	Jesus sends the Holy Spirit to be with us and guide us.
	12	Saint Peter	Jesus chose Peter to be the rock on which to build the Church.
	13	The Centurion Kneeling	Jesus Christ reaches out to all people.
	14	Annunciation	Mary is blessed by God.
	15	Nativity	We celebrate Christmas as a Church community.
4	16	The Ethiopian Baptized	The disciple Philip continues Jesus' mission.
	17	Greetings	When we fail to love God and others because of sin, Jesus calls us to forgiveness through the Sacrament of Reconciliation.
	18	First Communion	The celebration of the Eucharist is at the center of parish life around the world.
	19	A Sunny Corner	The Holy Spirit gives us spiritual gifts so that we can serve God and others.
	20	Christ on the Cross	Lent is a time to think about how we can make our hearts ready for Easter.
5	21	The Sacred Heart	We live like Jesus when we practice the virtues of faith, hope, and charity.
	22	In the Wilderness	Jesus gives us the help we need to make good moral choices.
	23	Saint Paul	Paul was happy when he saw how his Church family grew in their faith.
	24	Light Work	Jesus calls us to share with one another in any way we can.
	25	The Lamb of God	Easter is a time to celebrate God's merciful love.

THE EFFECTIVE CATECHIST

A Catechist's Role

As a catechist you are responding to a call to share the gift of faith with others, even as you deepen your own faith. This call may have reached you through your pastor, the director of your parish's religious education program, or through your role as a Catholic school teacher. But know that this calling ultimately comes from God whose Holy Spirit inspires and guides you. Know that this *Finding God* **Catechist Guide** was designed to accompany you every step of the way with abundant resources, practical tips, and support.

Fundamental Characteristics of Your Role

As catechists we yearn for the knowledge and skills that help us gently nurture children to experience their faith. We ground our efforts in these fundamentals:

▶ a basic understanding of Catholic teaching, Scripture, and Catholic Tradition

▶ honest and respectful relationships with children

▶ effective teaching methods and techniques

Qualities of an Effective Catechist

As catechists we share our personal faith and humanity. The ability to share authentically requires certain qualities that include

▶ a desire to grow in our faith

▶ an awareness of God's grace and the desire to respond to that grace

▶ a commitment to the Church's liturgical and sacramental life and moral teachings

▶ a strength of character built on patience, responsibility, confidence, and creativity

▶ required or voluntary training to protect God's children, such as Virtus® training

▶ an understanding of the developmental level of the children with whom you work (go to www.findinggod.com for more information)

▶ a generosity of spirit, respect for diversity, and a habit of hospitality and inclusion

As you reflect on your role as a catechist, know that support abounds in *Finding God: Our Response to God's Gifts.* Through the catechist preparation pages in this guide, at www.loyolapress.com, and professional development opportunities such as webinars and workshops, Loyola Press is your partner on the journey.

This catechist guide accompanies you every step of the way with resources, practical tips, and support.

Sacred Space

Preparing the Learning Environment

When Jesus planned a special meal with his apostles during Passover, he sent Peter and John ahead of him, saying, "Go and make preparations for us[.]" (Luke 22:8) In the same way, preparing the physical space for faith formation is important.

Prayer Center and Table

Arrange a focal point with symbols that express the presence of the Word of God and communicate a sense of the sacred. Set up your own prayer center and table with these supplies:

▶ small table, prominently placed

▶ cloth table cover, changed to reflect each liturgical season

▶ Bible

▶ small plant or flowers

▶ candle (if allowed)

▶ one or more of the following: bowl of holy water, crucifix, religious image, or statue

Seating Arrangement

Choose a seating arrangement that fosters community and is appropriate for the activity being experienced. Consider these ideas:

▶ seats in a large circle or semicircle for whole-group discussions

▶ several chairs around tables for small-group work

▶ relaxed "open seating" of choice for silent reading or guided reflections

Visuals/Audio

To give children a sense of belonging and sacred space no matter your environment, consider displaying one or more of the following:

▶ *Finding God* session Art Print, on its stand-up easel

▶ *Finding God* poster, chosen from set

▶ photographs or objects relevant to session topic

▶ music that sets desired mood as appropriate

▶ cross or crucifix

> "Go and make preparations for us..."
>
> Luke 22:8

Presentation Tips

Jesus possessed the quality of positive presence, the ability to communicate with enthusiasm, confidence, authority, hospitality, and sensitivity. Here are some ways that you can present your sessions in a similar way.

Use Technology and Media

Look for opportunities to use media to enrich your presentations. Here are some ideas.

▶ During prayer or reflective experiences, play instrumental versions of the songs featured in the *Finding God* program, found on the **music CD.**

▶ Look for the **Message Through Media** film suggestions in the **If Time Allows** features in each session. Consider showing these clips or films to solidify concepts.

▶ Project a daily **3-Minute Retreat** found at **www.loyolapress.com** and lead children through it.

▶ Invite children to experience the online activities at **www.findinggod.com.**

Note: The USCCB provides a list of recommended films. For movies with a rating of A-II, obtain parental permission for viewing and show only preselected scenes. Always preview films to be sure they are appropriate for the children with whom you work.

Communicate with Care

As you work through the Children's Books and Art Prints, be sure to

▶ refer to each child by name.

▶ move around the room and use gestures and body movements.

▶ make eye contact with each child.

▶ use facial expressions to show your enthusiasm, compassion, and kindness.

▶ speak as the gentle, confident voice of authority.

▶ speak clearly and appropriately and vary your tone of voice and volume.

Lead Lively Discussions

Try these tips to lead lively discussions.

▶ Read your session in advance, and highlight the questions you will ask. Think about the best way to ask the questions. For example, will you use a prop or a gesture to help illustrate the concept?

▶ Ask questions with curiosity and enthusiasm.

▶ Rephrase questions if only a few children raise their hands.

▶ Give children "think time" (10–15 seconds) before calling on a child to answer.

▶ Affirm acceptable responses, and gently redirect incorrect responses.

. . . communicate with enthusiasm, confidence, authority, hospitality, and sensitivity.

Diversity

As a catechist you can help all children recognize themselves in the story of Salvation History and celebrate the Church's diversity. This richness in diversity is reflected and celebrated throughout *Finding God: Our Response to God's Gifts*. Here are some examples.

Art

▶ Photographs in the Children's Book portray people of various cultures and backgrounds.

▶ **Exploring Faith Through Art** easel features artworks from different heritages and time periods throughout the Church's history.

▶ Featured artists reflect the ethnic diversity of the Church.

Saints and Holy People

▶ Featured saints and holy people show diversity in culture, personality, and gifts from God.

▶ Brief biographies and informational sections honestly examine what it means to be part of a diverse Church and society.

Music

▶ Melodies and instrumental arrangements represent music styles from across the globe.

▶ Lyrics reflect a variety of cultures.

▶ Musical activities invite children from all backgrounds to participate.

Ritual and Tradition

▶ A rich variety of traditions are integrated throughout the program.

▶ Draw on the popular devotions and prayer expressions in your community that respond to the needs of various ethnic and cultural groups.

▶ Catechist preparation pages include the **Together as One Parish** features to help religious education programs and Catholic schools come together as one while celebrating the uniqueness of each situation.

> *As a catechist you can help all children recognize themselves in the story of Salvation History and celebrate the Church's diversity.*

Inclusion: Special Needs

Among the children you serve, some may have special needs. *Finding God: Our Response to God's Gifts* includes If Time Allows activities in each Catechist Guide that adapt teaching approaches so that all children are included and can successfully enter into the faith experience. In addition, the following Catholic resources offer suggestions for helping children with special needs.

Among the children you serve, some may have special needs.

Inclusion in this Guide

Inclusion: Look for the title *Inclusion* in the Catechist Guide to find lesson adaptations for children with special needs in the following categories: attention disorders, autism spectrum disorders, chronic illness, cognitive differences, communication disorders, emotional needs, gifted, hearing impairments, physical challenges, vision challenges, and specific learning disorders.

Autism Spectrum

Autism resources from the **National Catholic Partnership on Disability:**
http://www.ncpd.org/ministries-programs/specific/autism

Chronic Illness

An Apostolate for People with Chronic Illness or with Disabilities:
www.cusan.org

Cognitive Differences

Resources from **The National Apostolate for Inclusion Ministry:**
www.nafim.org

Hearing Challenges

National Catholic Office for the Deaf:
http://www.ncod.org/BreakingNews.asp

Physical Challenges

Resources from the University of Dayton Institute for Pastoral Initiatives,
The Network of Inclusive Catholic Educators:
http://ipi.udayton.edu/nice.htm

Vision Challenges

Xavier Society for the Blind:
http://www.xaviersocietyfortheblind.org

Long-Range Planning

The following is a sample long-range plan for faith formation sessions that take place from the end of August to early June. You can modify this plan to fit your needs, using page EC-7 or by accessing the customizable online lesson planner at www.findinggod.com.

AUGUST

Unit 1
- Session 1 plus related Blackline Masters
- The Year in Our Church Introduction
- Optional Session Assessment (www.findinggod.com)

SEPTEMBER

Unit 1
- Sessions 2 to 5 plus related Blackline Masters
- Optional Session Assessments (www.findinggod.com)
- Unit 1 Assessment

OCTOBER

Unit 2
- Sessions 6 to 8 plus related Blackline Masters
- All Saints Day and All Souls Day Seasonal Session
- Optional Session Assessments (www.findinggod.com)

NOVEMBER

Unit 2
- Sessions 9 and 10 plus related Blackline Masters
- Advent Seasonal Session
- Optional Session Assessments (www.findinggod.com)
- Unit 2 Assessment

DECEMBER

Unit 3
- Session 15 plus related Blackline Masters
- Christmas Seasonal Session
- Optional Session Assessment (www.findinggod.com)

JANUARY

Unit 3
- Sessions 11 and 12 plus related Blackline Masters
- Optional Session Assessments (www.findinggod.com)

FEBRUARY

Unit 3
- Sessions 13 and 14 plus related Blackline Masters
- Optional Session Assessments (www.findinggod.com)
- Unit 3 Assessment

MARCH

Unit 4
- Sessions 16 to 18 plus related Blackline Masters
- Optional Session Assessments (www.findinggod.com)
- Lent Seasonal Session

APRIL

Unit 4
- Sessions 19 and 20 plus related Blackline Masters
- Holy Week Seasonal Session
- Easter Seasonal Session
- Optional Session Assessments (www.findinggod.com)
- Unit 4 Assessment

MAY

Unit 5
- Sessions 21 to 24 plus related Blackline Masters
- Pentecost Seasonal Session
- Optional Session Assessments (www.findinggod.com)

JUNE

Unit 5
- Session 25 plus related Blackline Masters
- Optional Session Assessment (www.findinggod.com)
- Unit 5 Assessment

Your Long-Range Plan

Use the example on page EC-6 and modify the plan to fit your calendar year.
Or you may wish to use the online lesson planner at www.findinggod.com.

AUGUST

Week 1
Week 2
Week 3
Week 4

SEPTEMBER

Week 1
Week 2
Week 3
Week 4

OCTOBER

Week 1
Week 2
Week 3
Week 4

NOVEMBER

Week 1
Week 2
Week 3
Week 4

DECEMBER

Week 1
Week 2
Week 3
Week 4

JANUARY

Week 1
Week 2
Week 3
Week 4

FEBRUARY

Week 1
Week 2
Week 3
Week 4

MARCH

Week 1
Week 2
Week 3
Week 4

APRIL

Week 1
Week 2
Week 3
Week 4

MAY

Week 1
Week 2
Week 3
Week 4

JUNE

Week 1
Week 2
Week 3
Week 4

JULY

Week 1
Week 2
Week 3
Week 4

The First Day

Beginnings are always important. Here are some tips to help you make your first day a good experience.

Prepare in Advance

Advance preparation is important to a successful session. You can get ready by doing the following:

▶ Read the Catechist Preparation pages for Unit 1, Session 1.

▶ Gather materials for the lesson and the If Time Allows activities that you choose to do.

▶ Survey the room in which the session will take place. Plan for the best seating arrangement. Adorn the space with suggestions from page EC-2.

▶ If needed, prepare name tags or name tents for children.

Set the Stage

To begin the session, consider incorporating the following suggestions:

▶ Greet the children warmly and explain the purpose of your time together.

▶ Arrange children according to your preplanned seating arrangement and play a "get to know your name" game if children are unfamiliar to you or one another.

▶ Invite each child to tell you one thing he or she wants to learn or experience about Catholic faith formation. Say: **As we spend time together this year, let's remember these ideas and explore them further as they come up during our sessions.**

Present the Books

Follow this plan to help children appreciate the value of this special, sacred time together:

▶ Call each child by name and invite him or her to come forward to receive a book. Say: **May your life be changed by recognizing God in all things.**

▶ When all books are distributed, read aloud the book title, *Finding God: Our Response to God's Gifts*, and explain what it means.

▶ Have children open their books and fill in the name plate on the inside front cover.

▶ Slowly and prayerfully pray aloud the Scripture verse below the name plate. Then pray together the prayer on the title page: **As I open this book . . .**

▶ Invite pairs of children to look through the book and discuss what they see. Invite children to share their ideas with the group.

▶ Begin Unit 1, Session 1.

Beginnings are always important.

UNIT 1

Catechist Preparation pages open each unit and session.

God, Our Creator and Father   1

UNIT 1
God, Our Creator and Father

UNIT SAINT
Saint Ignatius of Loyola

Ignatius of Loyola had a deep appreciation for the role of nature in helping people to find God in all things.

Unit 1 focuses on God as our Creator and Father with an emphasis on how we can love and care for his creation, the world he gave us. In this unit children will learn the following concepts.

SESSION 1 Created to Be Happy

God's beauty is reflected in all of creation. God created the world for reasons of love, and everything has come from and returns to God. We learn about the true nature of God by reading the Bible. God showed his love by creating us and revealing himself to us. We are called to make him the first priority in our lives.

SESSION 2 Created to Be Together

The Trinity is a community of God's love. God created all things out of love, Jesus came to tell us of God's love, and the Holy Spirit helps us show God's love to others. Those who make and keep a commitment to love God and their neighbor can look forward to living happily with God at the end of their lives.

SESSION 3 God Is Our Father

Jesus, the Son of God, teaches us to pray the Lord's Prayer so that we can become more like our heavenly Father and learn to trust him more completely. God's care and concern for us is most clearly seen in Jesus. Through Jesus we learn to love God and one another. Jesus teaches us that God is our loving Father. All prayer is primarily addressed to God as our Father.

SESSION 4 Jesus Is with Us

The Salvation promised in the Old Testament is fulfilled in Jesus. *Jesus* means "God saves." *Christ* means "the anointed one," or the one especially chosen by God to be our Savior. Joseph responded to God's call to be the foster father of Jesus and cared for Jesus and Mary for the rest of his life. Mary became the mother of Jesus through the action of the Holy Spirit.

SESSION 5 Celebrating Ordinary Time

Children learn the meaning of Ordinary Time, why we celebrate it, and explore how Ordinary Time is celebrated in our Church.

In each session of Unit 1, establish the pattern and tone for prayer. During an introduction to the first part of the Apostles' Creed, children learn to pray their belief in the Trinity. Children also review and pray the Sign of the Cross and the Glory Be to the Father. In a guided reflection, they meditate on the meaning of the Lord's Prayer.

✝ Catholic Social Teaching in Unit 1

In the story of the Good Samaritan (Luke 10:29–37), Jesus makes clear our responsibility to care for those in need. The Church articulates this responsibility in Catholic Social Teaching. Following are the themes of Catholic Social Teaching integrated into this unit.

Call to Family, Community, and Participation Participation in family and community is central to our faith and to a healthy society. As the central social institution, family must be supported and strengthened. From this foundation people participate in society, fostering a community spirit and promoting the well-being of all.

Care for God's Creation God is the Creator of all people and all things, and he wants us to enjoy his creation. The responsibility to care for all God has made is a requirement of our faith. We are called to make moral and ethical choices that protect the ecological balance of creation both locally and worldwide.

Life and Dignity of the Human Person The Catholic Church teaches us that all human life is sacred and that all people must be treated with dignity. We are called to ask whether our actions as a society respect or threaten the life and dignity of the human person.

Option for the Poor and Vulnerable In our world many people are wealthy, while at the same time, many are poor. As Catholics we are called to pay special attention to the needs of those who are poor. We can follow Jesus' example by making a specific effort to defend and promote the dignity of those who are poor and vulnerable and meet their immediate needs.

Solidarity Because God is our Father, we are all brothers and sisters with the responsibility to care for one another. Solidarity unites rich and poor, weak and strong, and helps build a society that recognizes that we live in an interdependent world.

TOGETHER *as One Parish*

Religious Education with the Parochial School

To nurture parish unity, celebrate the beginning of a new year of faith formation. Add an insert to your parish bulletin that introduces the religious education team in one combined list with catechists' names from both your religious education program and parochial school. Introduce the list by sharing common goals for children to participate in the programs.

Literature Opportunity
***Pinduli* by Janell Cannon**
You might wish to read aloud this story of a young hyena that discovers how both good and bad words can affect one creature and an entire community.
✝ *Life and Dignity*

Created to Be Happy

3-Minute Retreat

Before you prepare the session, pause and be still. Take three deep breaths and be aware of the loving presence of God, who is with you on this journey of growth and discovery.

Psalm 148:12–13

Young men and women too,

> *old and young alike.*

Let them all praise the LORD's name,

> *for his name alone is exalted,*

> *majestic above earth and heaven.*

Reflection

All of creation reveals the wonder of God and teaches us about God's great love for us. In this Psalm nature itself gives praise to God the Creator. Revealed in creation and in the Bible, God wants to be known intimately by each of us. God's gift of love calls forth a response of love.

Question

With the glory of God's creation all around me, for what am I most grateful?

Prayer

Speak to God, using the words of this prayer or your own.

> *Praise God from whom all blessings flow.*

> *Praise him all creatures here below,*

> *Praise him above, ye heavenly host:*

> *Praise Father, Son, and Holy Ghost.*

Knowing and Sharing Your Faith in Session 1

Consider how Scripture and Tradition can deepen your understanding of the session content.

Scripture

Psalm 148:7–14 summons all creation to praise the Lord.

Genesis 1:31 tells us that God looks at creation and finds it very good.

Tradition

The Scripture verses from Psalm 148 call us to praise God for the wonders of the earth and the heavens. These wonders are awesome and humbling. In praise we profess our faith, acknowledge our dependence on God, and recognize that creation is a continual sign of God's blessing. The created world is the result of God's decision to share his life and love with us. God created the world for reasons of love. Everything has come from and returns to God. God's love and beauty are reflected in all of creation. We can know God by reflecting on the beauty of the world. The Bible—the Word of God—teaches us to praise God for the wonder and beauty of creation.

Catholic Social Teaching

In this session the integrated Catholic Social Teaching theme is **Care for God's Creation.** See page 1b for an explanation of this theme.

Window on the Catechism

The importance of loving God above all is presented in *CCC* 222–227. The value of understanding God as reflected in nature is found in *CCC* 41.

General Directory for Catechesis

The understanding of God as the Father of all creation is discussed in *GDC* 100.

One-Hour Session Planner

SESSION 1 Created to Be Happy

Session Theme: *God wants us to know him.*

Before This Session

▶ Prepare a prayer center. See page EC-2 for ideas.

▶ Establish group rules and procedures. See page EC-2–EC-3 for ideas.

▶ Bookmark your Bible to Psalms 148:7–14 and Genesis 1:31. Place the Bible open to either of these passages in your prayer center.

▶ Listen to the songs to become familiar with the content and pacing.

▶ Display the *Finding God* poster Apostles' Creed.

▶ Read the Guide for this session, choose any additional If Time Allows activities that you might have time to complete, and gather the listed materials.

STEPS	APPROXIMATE TIME
Engage *Unit Saint:* Saint Ignatius of Loyola PAGES 1–2 *Created to Be Happy* PAGE 3	10 minutes
Explore *We Believe in God* PAGE 4 *All Creation Praises God* PAGE 5 *Art Print:* Paradise Garden ART PRINT AND PRINT BACK	30–40 minutes
Reflect *Prayer:* A Special Faith Prayer PAGE 6 *Knowing God* PAGE 7	15–20 minutes
Respond *Living My Faith* PAGE 8	5–10 minutes

Prayer in Session 1

In this first session, be sure to promote a quiet and meditative environment for prayer. The opening prayer is a prayer of petition, and the closing prayer is a prayer of thanks. These prayers will focus on caring for God's world as well as provide an opportunity for children to add their personal intentions. Children will also learn the first line of the Apostles' Creed. Children will learn the remainder of the Creed in future sessions.

Materials

REQUIRED

▶ Bible

▶ Art Print 1: *Paradise Garden* and Children's Book page 227

▶ Writing supplies

▶ Art supplies

▶ CD player

▶ CD 2, Track 3: "All You Works of God" (3:59)

▶ CD 2, Track 4: "All You Works of God" (Instrumental)

▶ *Finding God* poster: Apostles' Creed

IF TIME ALLOWS

▶ Magazines, newspapers (page 3)

▶ Construction paper (page 3, 7)

▶ Art supplies (page 3, 7)

▶ Session 1 BLM, T-293 (page 4)

▶ *Godspell* on VHS or DVD, media player (page 4)

▶ Poster board (page 5)

▶ Red construction paper (page 7)

▶ Session 1 Assessment, www.findinggod.com (page 8)

UNIT 1

God, Our Creator and Father

Saint Ignatius of Loyola

Saint Ignatius of Loyola recognized God in every living creature in the heavens and on earth. He saw God in plants, in animals, and especially in people.

1

Saint Ignatius of Loyola

Saint Ignatius of Loyola was born in Spain in 1491. He grew up in a noble family in the castle of Loyola. He was a soldier until he was wounded in a battle. He went home to get well. There he read about the lives of Jesus and the saints. He wanted to become a saint too.

Ignatius traveled to a monastery in Spain at Montserrat. There he saw the mountain and many of God's wonderful creatures. He prayed at the shrine of Our Lady of Montserrat. He laid down his sword and pledged his life to God. He gave away his fine clothes and dressed as a poor man.

From *The Spiritual Journey of St. Ignatius*

Later Ignatius wrote what he learned about God and Jesus. His book is called *Spiritual Exercises*. He wrote it to help people grow closer to God. He tells us that God cares for all the things he created. If we want to know God, we can begin by caring for the world God gives us. Ignatius's feast day is July 31.

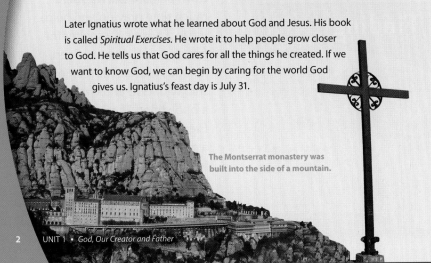

The Montserrat monastery was built into the side of a mountain.

5-MINUTE APPROACH
Children's Pages

1 Begin

Smile and greet children. Introduce yourself and explain why you became a catechist. Say: *I am excited to get to know each of you.* Invite children to say their names and something about themselves. Distribute the Children's Books. Say: *Please receive this book with the blessing of Jesus.*

Have children open their books to page 1. Read aloud the unit title. Say: *Our first unit helps us understand that God is our Creator and Father. God's creation shows us his love for us.*

2 Introduce the Saint

Focus children's attention on the picture. Ask: *Why do you think the artist showed a light around Ignatius's head?* (because he is holy and special) Say: *Artists use a halo to show that someone is holy.*

Have a volunteer read aloud the text on page 1. Ask: *Why do you think Ignatius recognized God in every living creature?* (They are all part of God's creation.)

Have children turn to page 2. Read aloud the first paragraph. Explain that Ignatius's family was wealthy. Then read aloud the second paragraph. Explain that a monastery is a place where some men live apart from the everyday world to give their lives to God. Read aloud the last paragraph. Ask: *What did Ignatius say we should do if we want to know God?* (We can start by taking care of the world around us.)

✝ **God's Creation**

This page describes a program-wide intergenerational event that is offered in a supplemental component.

OPTIONAL UNIT OPENER

Intergenerational Event

1 Prepare

Work with your catechetical leader to use the *Finding God Together* kit to plan an intergenerational event for Unit 1.

2 Open the Event

Gather families in one space. Use *Finding God Together* to open the event, introduce *Finding God*, and discuss the main theme for Unit 1. Together, enjoy an entertaining skit.

3 Implement the Saint Stations

Use *Finding God Together* to help families learn more about the saints at their grade-level saint stations. Be sure all families feel welcome and are engaged in the process.

4 Close

Gather families in one space for a guided reflection. Use *Finding God Together* to close the event.

5 Transition to Children's Book

When children arrive for the faith formation session, discuss the event, distribute the Children's Books, and review information about the unit saint. Have children open their books to page 3.

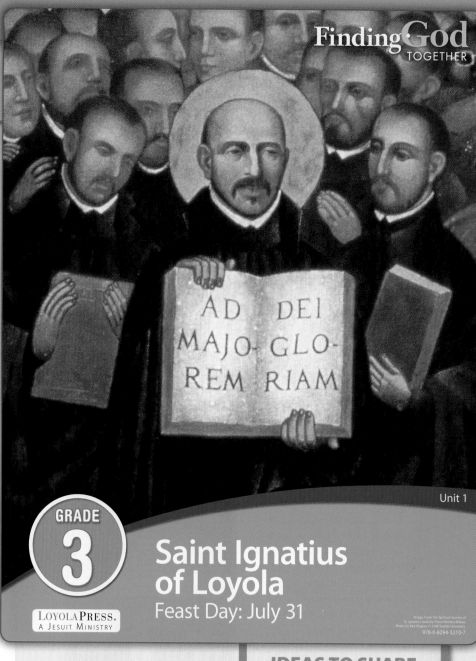

Finding God TOGETHER

Unit 1

GRADE **3**

LOYOLA PRESS.
A JESUIT MINISTRY

Saint Ignatius of Loyola
Feed Day: July 31

Image: From The Spiritual Journey of St. Ignatius Loyola by Drea Klachkova Ethaca. Photo by Ken Wagner © 1998 Seattle University.

978-0-8294-3210-7

Events Guide

Finding God Together: An Intergenerational Events Guide
by Mary Lynn Hendrickson and Tom McGrath

Finding God TOGETHER

AN INTERGENERATIONAL
EVENTS GUIDE

IDEAS TO SHARE

Saint Ignatius of Loyola

When Ignatius left Montserrat, he went to the town of Manresa. He spent much time praying and helping in a hospice, a shelter for travelers and those in need. Ignatius grew in his relationship with God and wrote a book titled *The Spiritual Exercises*. He was ordained a priest, and in 1540 he founded the religious order known as the Society of Jesus, the Jesuits.

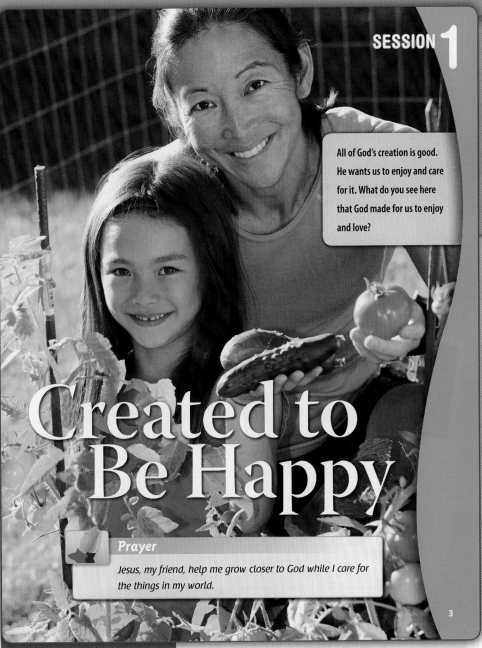

All of God's creation is good. He wants us to enjoy and care for it. What do you see here that God made for us to enjoy and love?

Created to Be Happy

 Prayer

Jesus, my friend, help me grow closer to God while I care for the things in my world.

3

IF TIME ALLOWS

Our Beautiful World

Distribute magazines and newspapers that contain pictures of beautiful things from nature. Lead a discussion on how to care for these gifts from God. Have children mount collages of the pictures on construction paper. Display the collages.

† *God's Creation*

Go to **www.findinggod.com/sessionextenders** for a three-minute retreat on how we are called to care for God's garden.

OUTCOMES

▶ Explain that all nature is part of God's creation, and it reflects his love.

▶ Discuss God's presence, his invitation, and our response.

▶ Define *apostle, Apostles' Creed,* and *creed.*

① *Set the Stage*

Have children close their eyes. Say: ***Imagine you are outside. What do you see? What do you hear? What do you smell?*** Pause to allow children to share ideas. Say: ***All things in nature are part of God's creation.***

Direct children's attention to the picture on page 3. Ask: ***What can this child do to care for God's creation?*** (Possible answer: She can water the vegetables.)

② *Get Started*

Read aloud the session title and the text in the blue box. Invite children to name things in the picture that God made for us. (vegetables, each other, sunshine)

Say: ***In this session we will learn about the wonders of God's creation and how we are called to take care of it.***

 Prayer

Tell children it is time to pray to Jesus and to ask for his guidance. Say: ***Please fold your hands and pray silently as I pray aloud.*** Pray the prayer in a loving tone. Give children time to talk to Jesus and to offer prayers of petition. Close by praying *Amen.* Say: ***We pray Amen after a prayer because we are saying yes to God. Let our hearts be open to God's guidance and love during this session.***

1 Begin

Have children turn to page 4. Say: **These are pictures of how we can hold our hands when we pray.** Fold your hands in prayer and have children do the same. Say: **We are going to learn about a special prayer called the Apostles' Creed.**

2 Connect

Read aloud the heading and first paragraph. Have a volunteer read aloud the second paragraph. Point to the words in bold type and explain their meanings. Say: **The apostles were close friends of Jesus'. They followed him and taught others about him.**

Say: **The Apostles' Creed is a prayer that states what members of the Catholic Church believe. Today we are going to learn part of this Creed.** Write *Apostles' Creed* on the board and ask a volunteer to define it, using information on this page.

Read aloud the first part of the prayer. Have children repeat it after you. As a group read the sentence one more time. Say: **This Creed is a very long prayer, so we will learn it in small parts.** Tell children they will learn the rest of the prayer later.

You can find the complete prayer in the Prayers and Practices of Our Faith section.

3 Close

Direct children's attention to the feature at the bottom of page 4.

Reading God's Word

From your Bible read aloud the passage from Genesis. Tell children that Genesis is the first book in the Bible. Say: **The word Genesis comes from a word that means "beginning." In Genesis we read about the beginning of the universe and all of God's creation, including people.**

We Believe in God

We see the world around us and know that God blesses us and cares for us. We depend on him. We praise God to show that we believe in him.

We pray a special prayer called the **Apostles' Creed** to show our faith. An **apostle** was a special follower of Jesus'. A **creed** tells us what people believe. The Apostles' Creed tells us what the apostles believed. It states the beliefs of our Catholic faith. This is how the Apostles' Creed begins. Learn this part and pray it often.

I believe in God,
the Father almighty,
Creator of heaven and earth,

Reading God's Word

God looked at everything he had made, and he found it very good.
Genesis 1:31

4   UNIT 1 • *God, Our Creator and Father*

IF TIME ALLOWS

Session 1 BLM

The Apostles' Creed Have children complete the Session 1 Blackline Master [T-293], a puzzle, to find words from the Apostles' Creed.

Message Through Media: Godspell

Have children view a 5- to 10-minute excerpt from *Godspell,* a movie based on the Gospel according to Matthew. In particular show children the scenes in which the actors sing and perform "Day by Day," a song about daily prayer. Write the lyrics on the board and have children sing along as they watch the movie.

All Creation Praises God

We have a feeling of wonder when we see the things God made for us. We tell God that we believe in him and love him. We sing praise to God.

> Let all God's creation praise him, from the animals in the sea to the clouds in the sky. Mountains and trees, birds and animals praise God their creator. People young and old sing praise to God. His name alone is greater than heaven and earth.
>
> *adapted from Psalm 148:7–13*

Your Own Song of Praise

On the lines below, write a message to praise God for something beautiful you saw this week.

_____

_____

_____

_____

_____

_____

_____

_____

GO TO PAGE 227

SESSION 1 • *Created to Be Happy*   5

IF TIME ALLOWS

Service: Poster Campaign

Discuss how walking and biking are good for the environment. Provide poster board and markers for children to create posters encouraging people to walk or to ride bikes. Suggest including pictures and words reminding people of the beauty of God's world. Ask your catechetical leader where children can post these in the church or school.

✝ **God's Creation**

---

1 Begin

Open the Bible to the Book of Psalms and show children where the psalms are located. Say: **A psalm is a prayer in the form of a poem or song that uses colorful language to praise God.**

2 Connect

Invite a volunteer to read aloud the heading and the first paragraph.

✝ Have children follow along as you read the adaptation of Psalm 148:7–13. Invite volunteers to read it again, one sentence at a time. Pause after each child reads to point out the diversity in creation.

🎵 Play "All You Works of God" [CD 2, Track 3]. Ask: **What is this song asking all the works of God's creation to do?** (praise God) Have children look at the words in the back of their books. Say: **This song reminds us of the psalms because the lyrics speak beautifully of the world God gives us.** Encourage the children to sing along as you play the song a second time.

Read aloud the directions for Your Own Song of Praise. Say: **Close your eyes and imagine a special place filled with beautiful things. Think of colorful words to describe what you see. Use those words to praise God for the things you see.**

 Have children write their messages on the page. Play the instrumental "All You Works of God" [CD 2, Track 4] in the background. Invite volunteers to share their messages.

3 Close

Paradise Garden

Art Print 1

Display Art Print 1: *Paradise Garden.* Use the Art Print 1 instruction to teach this section. Art Print teaching instruction can also be found on page 227.

REFLECT

Prayer

Follow the steps to guide children through the prayer on page 6.

Children's Page

Prepare Display the *Finding God* Apostles' Creed poster. Pray the prayer in advance to become familiar with it.

Pray Say: ***Prayer is our special time with God. We quiet ourselves to be more aware of his presence.*** Focus children's attention on the picture on the page. Ask: ***What is the child doing?*** (enjoying the fresh air and warm sun) ***Why should we take care of the world?*** (because God made it for us)

Say: ***Let's remember how much God loves us and pray the part of the Apostles' Creed that we learned today. Focus your mind and heart on God. Let all other thoughts drift away as we pray.***

Play the instrumental "All You Works of God" [CD 2, Track 4] to help children relax and concentrate while they pray silently. Play the music quietly in the background.

Read aloud the first paragraph. Then pray the first line of the Apostles' Creed. Have children pray aloud after you. Read aloud the next two lines. Tell children that when they want to talk to God, they may use these words or any words they wish.

Ask children to bow their heads and fold their hands. Read aloud the last paragraph. Say: ***Let's take a moment of silence so that you can speak to God, using your own words.*** Take four deep breaths. Say: ***Let's close by praying the Sign of the Cross. Now we will discover ways to live what we have learned today.***

Prayer

A Special Faith Prayer

These are the first words of the Apostles' Creed, our very special faith prayer. Pray these words often.

I believe in God,
the Father almighty,
Creator of heaven and earth,

Knowing that God is in your heart, think about him as the Father of Jesus and your Father too. Then think about God making everything in the universe. Tell God how awesome he is. Thank him for his gift of creation. Tell God how you will keep our world beautiful.

IF TIME ALLOWS

My Creed

Have children write the first three lines of the Apostles' Creed. Collect the papers and return them each time children learn more of the Creed.

FYI

Coaching Children to Pray

Set the tone for prayer by using a relaxed, confident, reverent tone of voice. Say: ***Remember that you are in the holy presence of God.***

Knowing God

The beauty of the world helps us to know God. We see that God created all things because of his love. Because he created us and loves us, we make God important in our lives. We can know about God and creation by reading the Bible, which is the Word of God.

Loving God's Creation

We can love all of God's creation. Think of three people, animals, or parts of nature that you love, and write them on the lines. Draw pictures of them in the hearts.

I love . . .

SESSION 1 • *Created to Be Happy*　**7**

 Begin

Hold up your Bible. Ask children to think about where they have seen a Bible. Ask: **Where have you seen Bibles used or displayed?** (Possible answers: church, home, someone else's home) Ask children if they have ever looked through the pages of a Bible. Explain that we can learn about God and how much he loves us by reading the Bible. Show children the Book of Genesis and the Book of Psalms.

 Connect

Read aloud the heading and the first paragraph on page 7. Ask: **Why did God create all things?** (because of his love) **Why must we make God an important part of our lives?** (because he created us and loves us)

Distribute crayons, colored pencils, or markers. Ask a volunteer to read aloud the second paragraph. Brainstorm ideas for people, animals, and parts of nature. Draw a chart on the board and record children's ideas. Say: **Now choose three parts of God's creation and write them on the lines.** Have children draw pictures inside the hearts. Walk around the room while children work. Ask them to raise their hands if they need help spelling a word.

✝ God's Creation

 Close

When children are finished, encourage them to share their drawings. Ask volunteers to talk about why they chose the people, animals, or parts of nature they did. Say: **After seeing everyone's drawings, we are reminded of all the beauty around us. Let us take a moment to thank God.** Give children quiet time to be with God and pray together *Amen.*

IF TIME ALLOWS

God Loves Us

Distribute red construction paper. Show children how to cut a heart from the paper and have them do so. Have each child write his or her name on the heart. On a large sheet of paper or poster board, write *God Loves Us.* Ask each child to come forward with his or her paper heart. Say: **God loves [name].** Glue the hearts on the poster. Then display the poster.

Begin

Faith Summary Read aloud this section. Ask: **What does the beauty in our world help us to do?** (to know God and to love God) Say: **Think of the psalm we read today that praises God for his creation. What are ways we can care for and respect God's creation?** (Possible answers: do not litter; be kind to animals; recycle)

✝ *God's Creation*

 Connect

Words I Learned Call on volunteers to pronounce and define each term. If needed, refer children to the Glossary definition.

Ways of Being Like Jesus Read aloud this paragraph. Invite children to give examples of how they can respect people and animals. Say: **When you show respect for God's creations, you are being like Jesus.**

 Prayer

Have children close their eyes and fold their hands. Ask them to take a few moments thanking Jesus as they pray the prayer silently. Allow some time for children to pray silently. Then pray together *Amen.* Say: **Jesus is always with you and ready to hear your prayers of thanks.**

With My Family Ask children to read silently the three suggestions in this section. Invite children to choose one or more to complete at home.

 Go in Peace

Collect materials and return them to the appropriate places. Encourage children to discuss the With My Family section at home. Say: **When you come back, you can tell me about what you did with your family to care for God's creation.**

8 www.findinggod.com

Faith Summary

We believe in God our Father, who created the world out of love for us. God wants us to know him and love him through the beauty of our world that leads us to him.

Words I Learned	Ways of Being Like Jesus
apostle	Jesus loves and cares for all God's people.
Apostles' Creed	*Be kind to people and animals around you.*
creed	

 Prayer

Jesus, thank you for helping me to know and love God. Help me to care for God's world as he cares for me.

With My Family

Activity Work together as a family to keep your neighborhood neat. Take a walk around the block and pick up litter you find lying on the ground.

Faith on the Go Ask one another: *Think about our wonderful earth. What do you think is the most beautiful part of God's creation? Why?*

Family Prayer Dear God, bless our family as part of your creation. Help us to show love for your creation by taking care of the world around us. Amen.

8 UNIT 1 • *God, Our Creator and Father*

IF TIME ALLOWS

Session Assessment Option

An assessment for this session can be found at **www.findinggod.com.**

PLAN AHEAD

Get Ready for Session 2

Consult the catechist preparation pages to prepare for Session 2 and determine any materials you will need.

Created to Be Together

3-Minute Retreat

Before you prepare the session, sit quietly for a few moments and clear your mind of distractions. Take three deep breaths and call to mind the love of the Trinity. Reflect on the love and the inspiration you receive from the Holy Trinity.

> *1 John 4:9,11*
>
> *In this way the love of God was revealed to us: God sent his only Son into the world so that we might have life through him. . . . Beloved, if God so loved us, we also must love one another.*

Reflection

Love is a life-giving force. It pushes aside isolation and fear. In this Scripture passage, the Father, Son, and Holy Spirit are made known to us as a community of love. The unity of the Trinity is a beautiful model of a loving union. When we experience the love of God, our life is changed both internally and externally. In Jesus we experience a new life. Filled with the love of God, we respond to loving others.

Question

How is the new life I have received in Jesus reflected in the way I relate to others?

Prayer

Give thanks for the love of the Trinity, using the words of this prayer or your own.

> *Blessed Trinity, Father, Son, and Holy Spirit, help me to reflect your love and to care generously for the needs of others, especially those of the children.*

Knowing and Sharing Your Faith in Session 2

Consider how Scripture and Tradition can deepen your understanding of the session content.

Scripture

1 John 4:7–11 speaks of God's great love for us in sending his Son and calls us to love one another.

1 John 4:16 says that, through love, God lives in us and we in him.

Tradition

God is the source of all love. God shows his love in creation by sending his only Son to save us. John explores the truth that we are capable of love because God loved us first. When we love others and ourselves, we are bringing to life the love God has for all. When we reflect on the love God has for us in Jesus Christ, we are reflecting on the essential mystery of the Trinity. The Trinity is the revelation of God as Father, Son, and Holy Spirit. We are called to love God and our neighbor.

Catholic Social Teaching

In this session the integrated Catholic Social Teaching themes are **Call to Family, Community and Participation; Life and Dignity of the Human Person;** and **Solidarity.** See page 1b for an explanation of these themes.

Window on the Catechism

The relationship between love of God and love of our neighbor is presented throughout the *Catechism.* See especially *CCC* 2196.

General Directory for Catechesis

Jesus said that love of God and neighbor is the basis of the Law and the prophets. This is reviewed in *GDC* 115.

One-Hour Session Planner

SESSION 2 Created to Be Together

Session Theme: *The love of the Father, Son, and Holy Spirit is the source of the love we have for one another.*

Before This Session

▶ Bookmark your Bible to 1 John 4:7–11 and 1 John 4:16. Place the Bible open to either of these passages in your prayer center.

▶ Read the Guide for this session, choose any additional If Time Allows activities that you might have time to complete, and gather the listed materials.

STEPS	APPROXIMATE TIME
Engage ***Created to Be Together*** PAGE 9	10 minutes
Explore ***Sign of the Cross*** PAGE 10 ***Another Prayer to the Trinity*** PAGE 11 **Art Print:** *Elizabeth of Hungary* ART PRINT AND PRINT BACK	30–40 minutes
Reflect **Prayer:** A Reminder of the Trinity PAGE 12 ***Gentle Jesus*** PAGE 13	15–20 minutes
Respond ***Living My Faith*** PAGE 14	5–10 minutes

Prayer in Session 2

In this session continue to establish the pattern and tone for prayer. The short opening and closing prayers invite children to engage in prayers of petition and thanks related to the Trinity. Each prayer provides an opportunity for children to add their personal intentions. Children review the Sign of the Cross and Glory Be to the Father as ways of giving honor and praise to the Trinity.

Materials

REQUIRED

▶ Bible

▶ Art Print 2: *Elizabeth of Hungary* and Children's Book page 228

▶ Art supplies

▶ CD player

▶ CD 2, Tracks 17 and 18: "Reflective Music"

IF TIME ALLOWS

▶ Magazines (page 9)

▶ Poster board (page 9)

▶ Session 2 BLM, page T-294 (page 10)

▶ Art supplies (pages 9, 12)

▶ Drawing paper (page 12)

▶ Session 2 Assessment, www.findinggod.com (page 14)

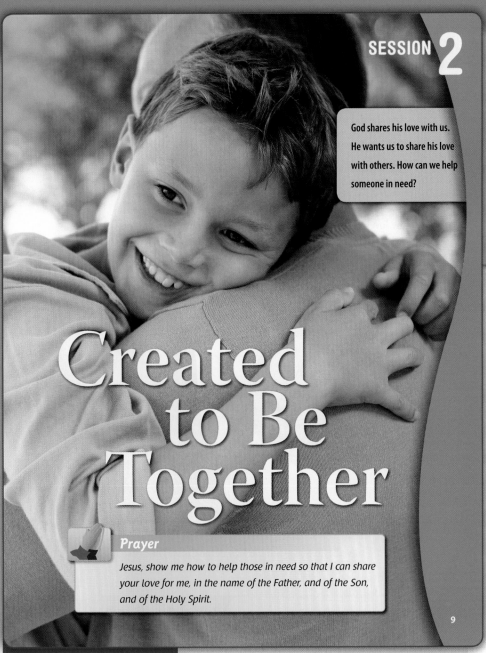

Created to Be Together

SESSION 2

God shares his love with us. He wants us to share his love with others. How can we help someone in need?

 Prayer

Jesus, show me how to help those in need so that I can share your love for me, in the name of the Father, and of the Son, and of the Holy Spirit.

9

IF TIME ALLOWS

Inclusion: Autism Spectrum

Community Pantomime If you have children with autism spectrum disorders, you can present the page content in a more visual way. For example, to illustrate community, ask children to stand in a group. Gesture with wide arms to show inclusion while saying aloud the word *community*. Have children act out scenarios of helping one another.

Future Helpers

Discuss what roles as Church community helpers children might be interested in doing in the future. For example, ask if they have a specific interest, such as music. Suggest that they can use their interest in music to be in the church choir. Then have children make a group collage using pictures of these helpers from old magazines.

Go to **www.findinggod.com/session extenders** to read an article about how to incorporate a tradition of giving to people in need.

SESSION 2

OUTCOMES

▶ Explain that we worship the Trinity when we pray the Sign of the Cross.

▶ Explain that we bring God's love to life in our world by loving others.

▶ Identify practical ways to act on God's invitation in everyday living.

▶ Define *Sign of the Cross*.

① Set the Stage

Discuss the meaning of a community. Say: *Some communities are made up of people who have the same beliefs, interests, or jobs. Can you name a community you are part of based on similar beliefs?* (Church community)

Discuss community helpers. Ask: *Can you name helpers in your Church community?* (Possible answers: altar servers, catechists, lectors) Say: *How can you serve your Church community?* (Possible answer: help with a service activity)

✝ *Family and Community*

② Get Started

Ask a volunteer to read aloud the session title and the text in the blue box. Encourage children to suggest various answers to the question. Say: *In this session we will learn how to give praise to God and how to share God's love with others and help people in need.*

✝ *Solidarity*

 Prayer

Have children fold their hands and pray the Sign of the Cross. Then lead them in praying together the prayer. Conclude by praying *Amen*. Say: *We pray the Sign of the Cross as a way of remembering the Trinity. Let us be aware of God's presence during our session.*

1 Begin

Point to the picture of the girl. Ask: ***What is the girl doing?*** (praying) Encourage children to talk about their own experiences praying. Ask: ***When do you like to pray? Is it quiet? Do you tell God about your day?*** (Answers will vary.)

2 Connect

Read aloud the heading and first paragraph. Call on a child to read aloud Julia's question. Ask children to predict Katie's answer. Have volunteers read aloud the last two paragraphs. Ask: ***Who are the three Persons of the Holy Trinity?*** (God the Father, the Son, and the Holy Spirit) Ask: ***What have we learned about our Father?*** (He created all things because he loves us.) ***Why did Jesus come?*** (Jesus, the Son of God who became man, came to tell us of the Father's love and to save us.) ***What does the Holy Spirit do?*** (helps us understand how much God loves us, helps us love others) Say: ***Look at the symbol that represents the Trinity. The hand represents God, the cross represents Jesus, and the dove represents the Holy Spirit. Let us think of the Trinity as we pray the Sign of the Cross together.*** Lead children in praying the Sign of the Cross.

Link to Liturgy

Ask a volunteer to read aloud the feature. Say: ***At the beginning of the Mass, the priest walks to the altar, bows, and leads the people in praying the Sign of the Cross. Praying together the Sign of the Cross unites our Church community.***

Sign of the Cross

Each night before bed, Katie prayed the **Sign of the Cross** as she began her evening prayers. Julia copied her older sister, but she did not understand what her sister was doing.

"Why do we make that sign when we pray?" Julia asked.

Katie explained that the Sign of the Cross reminds us of the Trinity. We pray to the Father, the Son, and the Holy Spirit.

We pray to God our Father. He created all things because he loves us. We pray to the Son, Jesus. Jesus, the Son of God who became man, came to tell us of the Father's love and to save us. We pray to the Holy Spirit. The Holy Spirit helps us to understand how much God loves us. The Spirit helps us show God's love to others.

Link to Liturgy

We begin Mass with the Sign of the Cross. The priest also blesses us with the Sign of the Cross at the end of Mass.

10   UNIT 1 • *God, Our Creator and Father*

IF TIME ALLOWS

Session 2 BLM

Love Bug Have children complete the Session 2 Blackline Master [T-294] to list ways they can show their love for others in their community.

Teaching the Prayer

Group children in pairs. Ask one child in each pair to imagine he or she has never prayed the Sign of the Cross. Have the other child in the pair teach this prayer to his or her partner. The child who teaches can choose to explain the prayer verbally or guide the partner's hands through the prayer. Have children switch roles. When they are finished, discuss the ways children taught the prayer.

Another Prayer to the Trinity

Katie told Julia of another prayer that praises God as the Trinity. She said, "When we pray the Glory Be to the Father, we are praising God, who created us. He is with us now, and he always will be." Katie helped her sister pray this prayer.

Glory be to the Father, and to the Son, and to the Holy Spirit. As it was in the beginning, is now, and ever shall be, world without end. Amen.

As they closed their prayer with the Sign of the Cross, Julia smiled. From now on, when she prays these prayers, she will think of the Trinity: the Father, the Son, and the Holy Spirit.

Reading God's Word

We have come to know and to believe in the love God has for us. God is love, and whoever remains in love remains in God and God in him.

1 John 4:16

GO TO PAGE 228

Read aloud the heading on page 11. Ask a child to read aloud the paragraph. Ask: **What is another prayer that praises God as the Trinity?** (Glory Be to the Father) Ask: **What does the Glory Be to the Father help us remember about God?** (He created us; he is with us now and always will be.)

Pray aloud the prayer as children pray silently. Have them close their books as you pray aloud the prayer again.

Read aloud the last paragraph. Ask: **What do the Sign of the Cross and the Glory Be to the Father have in common?** (They praise God as the Trinity.)

Reading God's Word

Read aloud the passage from the First Letter of John while children follow along. Hold up your Bible and show where the passage is in the book. Say: **John wrote several letters to his friends about the importance of spreading God's love. We can read his letters in the Bible.**

Ask children to tell how others have shown God's love to them by helping them with something. (Possible answers: a parent who is always there for them; a teacher who helped them understand something)

3 Close

Display Art Print 2: *Elizabeth of Hungary.* Use the Art Print 2 instruction to teach this section. Art Print teaching instruction can also be found on page 228.

Elizabeth of Hungary

Art Print 2

IF TIME ALLOWS

Service: Love Is in the Mail

In advance obtain permission from your catechetical leader to proceed. Then tell children: **Saint John wrote to friends as a way of sharing love of the Trinity.** Discuss with a nursing home's representative to see if residents are interested in receiving letters from children. Obtain residents' names and have children write letters. Discuss writing ideas, such as what children are learning about God and the Church. Have children write short, neat letters. Send the letters to the nursing home.

✝ *Life and Dignity*

Prayer

Follow the steps to guide children through the prayer on page 12.

Children's Page

Prepare Pray the prayer in advance to become familiar with it.

Pray Say: **It is now time to reflect on today's session and pray our special prayer of praise to the Trinity.** Quiet children and dim the lights, but be sure children can still see their books. Tell children that you will read parts of the prayer and then you will pause so they can imagine what you describe. Tell them you will ask questions and they should think about the answers. Say: **Our special prayer today is the Sign of the Cross. Let us bow our heads.**

Invite children to pray the Sign of the Cross with you. Then read aloud the first paragraph.

Play reflective music [CD 2, Tracks 17 and 18] in the background as you read the rest of the reflection. Read slowly and prayerfully, pausing for several seconds after each sentence to give children time to reflect. Read the last paragraph, giving children a few minutes to be with Jesus. Take five deep breaths and end with *Amen*.

Say: **The love and peace of the Trinity is with us at all times. Let us move on to finish our session and find ways we can share this love with others.**

Prayer

A Reminder of the Trinity

Let the Sign of the Cross be our prayer today. Think about the meaning of the words as we pray them.

Sign of the Cross

In the name of the Father,

Bring to mind some of the wonderful things God the Father has created.

and of the Son,

Imagine that you are walking with Jesus. What is Jesus telling you about God?

and of the Holy Spirit.

Think about the kind and caring things you do for others. The Holy Spirit helps you do these things.

Amen.

Spend a few more minutes with Jesus. Tell him how you will follow the guidance of the Holy Spirit. Tell him something you will do for another person. Thank him for his love.

12   UNIT 1 • *God, Our Creator and Father*

IF TIME ALLOWS

Prayer Pictures
Have children draw a picture of themselves praying the Sign of the Cross.

FYI

Coaching Children to Pray

Establish a pattern for beginning prayer time by inviting children to quiet themselves as they prepare to pray.

Gentle Jesus

Jesus showed us how to love others. He used gentle words when he talked to people.

What Would Jesus Say?

Read the sentences below. Make a smiling face in the circle next to each sentence that Jesus would like to hear you say. Make a frowning face in the circle next to the unkind sentences.

☹ You cannot have any of my candy.

☺ You can go first.

☺ Do you want to come to my house?

☹ I do not like you.

☺ Let's ask Michaela to play.

☹ You cannot join my team.

Kindness Counts

Draw a scene where two people are being kind to each other. Add balloons that show words they are saying to each other.

SESSION 2 • *Created to Be Together*   13

IF TIME ALLOWS

Kind Conversations

Have children practice gentle conversation with one another. Group children in pairs. Explain that the first partner starts with a sentence of his or her choice and the second partner responds with an appropriate gentle sentence. Have partners switch roles so that all children have a chance to start a kind conversation.

---

1 Begin

Ask children to think about how they feel when they fight with a friend. Ask: **How do you feel when you are angry with your friends or family?** (Possible answers: mad, hurtful)

Say: **Think about the pictures and sculptures of Jesus you've seen in our church and in books.** Ask: **How have we heard stories about him?** (Bible stories, stories catechists have told) Ask: **How does Jesus act in these pictures and stories?** (Possible answers: kind, loving, understanding) Say: **To be like Jesus, we must treat people gently.**

2 Connect

Ask children to look at the picture on page 13. Ask: **What do you notice about these children?** (Possible answers: They look happy. They look like they are friends and like one another.) Tell children that they will now learn how important it is to treat people lovingly as Jesus did.

Read aloud the two paragraphs at the top of the page. Make sure children understand what they are to do. Have them complete the activity independently. Walk around the room while they work and answer any questions.

Go over the sentences together. Encourage children to change the unkind sentences to gentle ones that Jesus would have used.

3 Close

Read aloud Kindness Counts. Distribute crayons or colored pencils for children to do the drawing activity. Invite children to show their drawings and explain the scenes.

✝ *Life and Dignity*

Begin

Faith Summary Read aloud the paragraph. Ask: **Who is the source of the love we have for one another?** (the Trinity) **What prayers give praise and honor to the Trinity?** (Sign of the Cross, Glory Be to the Father) Ask: **What are ways that you can share your love and serve the community?** (Possible answers: donate food to a food bank; be a crossing guard) Discuss how the children in the pictures are following Jesus' example.

 Solidarity

Connect

Words I Learned Read aloud the term. Review the term in the Glossary if necessary.

Ways of Being Like Jesus Read aloud the paragraph. Ask children how they could respond to people who are sick or who are poor as Jesus did. (Possible answers: visit a person who is sick; make a healthful snack for someone)

 Life and Dignity

 Prayer

Ask children to bow their heads and fold their hands. Say: **Let's pray and thank Jesus for what we've learned today.** Lead children in praying the Sign of the Cross, ending with *Amen*.

With My Family Ask children to read silently the three suggestions in this section. Invite children to choose one or more to complete at home.

Go in Peace

Collect materials and return them to the appropriate places. Encourage children to discuss the With My Family section at home. Say: **Remember to share God's love by speaking gently, as Jesus would, when you talk to other people.**

14 www.findinggod.com

Faith Summary

The love of the Trinity—Father, Son, and Holy Spirit—is the source of our love. God wants us to share his love with others.

Words I Learned

Sign of the Cross

Ways of Being Like Jesus

Jesus helped people when they were sick or in need. *Treat people kindly. Offer to help others, even when you are busy.*

 Prayer

Jesus, thank you for showing me how to help others. Let me care for others like you did so I can grow closer to you.

With My Family

Activity Decide with your family what you can do together to help others. Some choices are making a food basket for a family in need, shopping for a wish-tree gift at Christmas, or helping a sick or elderly neighbor with chores around the house.

Faith on the Go Ask one another: *If you could help one person, whom would it be? Why?*

Family Prayer Pray the Sign of the Cross and the Glory Be to the Father with your family. Then spend a few minutes talking about the Trinity.

14   UNIT 1 • *God, Our Creator and Father*

IF TIME ALLOWS

Session Assessment Option

An assessment for this session can be found at **www.findinggod.com**.

PLAN AHEAD

Get Ready for Session 3

Consult the catechist preparation pages to prepare for Session 3 and determine any materials you will need.

God Is Our Father

3-Minute Retreat

Before you prepare the session, pause to quiet your mind. Take three deep breaths and remember that God the Father is with us at all times. Bring the love of his presence to your session.

Matthew 6:9

This is how you are to pray:

Our Father in heaven,

hallowed be your name[.]

Reflection

Jesus shares the intimate relationship he has with God when he teaches us to pray to God as Father. Raising our hearts and minds in prayer, we address God in a personal way as our Father. The intimacy of a loving family mirrors the relationship we have with God as the Father who sustains us, forgives us, leads us, and protects us from evil.

Questions

Do the words I use in prayer reflect a more intimate or distant relationship with God? How does the way I address God help me grow in appreciation in the value of all human life, including my own?

Prayer

Jesus invites you to speak to the Father, using the words of this prayer or your own.

Abba, Father, embrace me with your love.

Knowing and Sharing Your Faith in Session 3

Consider how Scripture and Tradition can deepen your understanding of the session content.

Scripture

Matthew 6:9–14 teaches the Lord's Prayer through Jesus' words.

2 Corinthians 1:3–4 tells of God's compassion and encourages all people to be compassionate toward others.

Tradition

When we say "Our Father," the Lord's Prayer calls us to express the qualities of childlike trust, intimacy, and ready access to God. Jesus prayed to God simply as *Abba. Abba*, an affectionate term, speaks to the intimate relation of Jesus with God. Jesus shares the meaning of his relationship with God with his disciples and with the entire human family. In the first part of the Lord's Prayer, we praise and honor God. In the second part of the Lord's Prayer, we pray for our welfare. Accepting God's forgiveness, we take the first step toward forgiving one another. We ask God to help us receive what God wants for us, especially in times of temptation.

Catholic Social Teaching

In this session the integrated Catholic Social Teaching themes are **Solidarity** and **Option for the Poor and Vulnerable.** See page 1b for an explanation of these themes.

Window on the Catechism

God as Father is discussed in *CCC* 2786–2793. Heaven as God's dwelling place, as near to us as the heart of Jesus, is discussed in *CCC* 2794–2796.

General Directory for Catechesis

The role of prayer in catechesis, specifically the Lord's Prayer, is explored in *GDC* 85.

One-Hour Session Planner

SESSION 3 God Is Our Father

Session Theme: *Jesus reveals to us that God is our loving Father, who calls us to live in peace with one another.*

Before This Session

▶ Bookmark your Bible to Matthew 6:9–14 and 2 Corinthians 1:3–4. Place the open Bible in your prayer center.

▶ Play the song and the guided reflection to become familiar with both.

▶ Read the Guide for this session, choose any additional If Time Allows activities that you might have time to complete, and gather the listed materials.

STEPS	APPROXIMATE TIME
Engage *God Is Our Father* PAGE 15	10 minutes
Explore *Jesus Reveals God as Our Father* PAGE 16 *Jesus Teaches Us to Pray* PAGE 17 *Art Print: The Peace Offering* ART PRINT AND PRINT BACK	30–40 minutes
Reflect *Prayer:* Grow Closer to God PAGE 18 *Show Forgiveness* PAGE 19	15–20 minutes
Respond *Living My Faith* PAGE 20	5–10 minutes

Prayer in Session 3

In this session children review the words and meaning of the Lord's Prayer. Session 3 includes an extended guided reflection titled "The Lord's Prayer." As you prepare to share this prayer experience with children, listen to the recorded guided reflection "The Lord's Prayer" [CD 1, Track 6] as a prayerful experience for yourself. When you play the recording during the session, join children in reflective prayer. If you choose to lead the guided reflection yourself, listen to the recording a second time, following the script [pages T-282–T-283]. You can use the script or adapt it. An alternative approach is to use the Prayer on the children's page.

Materials

REQUIRED

▶ Bible

▶ Art Print 3: *The Peace Offering* and Children's Book page 229

▶ CD player

▶ CD 2, Track 2: "Song of Love" (Instrumental)

▶ CD 1, Track 6: "The Lord's Prayer" (12:00)

IF TIME ALLOWS

▶ Drawing paper (pages 15, 16)

▶ Art supplies (pages 16, 17)

▶ Session 3 BLM, page T-295 (page 16)

▶ Large cardboard boxes (page 17)

▶ Session 3 Assessment, www.findinggod.com (page 20)

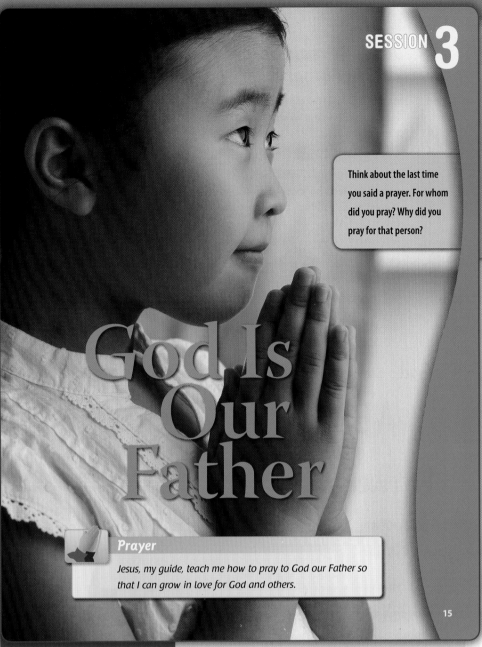

SESSION **3**

Think about the last time you said a prayer. For whom did you pray? Why did you pray for that person?

God Is Our Father

Prayer

Jesus, my guide, teach me how to pray to God our Father so that I can grow in love for God and others.

15

IF TIME ALLOWS

Questioning the Mark

Tell children to draw a large question mark that covers an entire sheet of paper. Have them think of questions that they would ask Jesus. Then tell them to write their questions around the outline of their question mark. Say: **Think of these questions as we move through this session and see how many answers we find.**

Ways to Pray

Remind children of the four ways to pray: Please/Thanks/Ow!/Wow! Review the definition of each. Ask volunteers to give examples of each type of prayer. Say: **God listens to all our prayers.**

 Go to **www.findinggod.com/sessionextenders** to learn more about the *Pray Me a Story* series that teaches you how to use popular storybooks as a springboard for prayer.

OUTCOMES

▶ Describe the Lord's Prayer as the way Jesus wants us to pray to God.

▶ Practice forgiving others as Jesus forgives us.

▶ Recognize that God is our Father, revealed by Jesus.

▶ Define *Abba*.

① Set the Stage

 Play the instrumental "Song of Love" [CD 2, Track 2] as children enter.

Have children turn to page 15 and look at the picture. Ask: **What is this child doing?** (praying) Say: **People have many questions about God. God sent Jesus to answer these questions, and Jesus taught us how to pray to God.**

② Get Started

Read aloud the session title and the text in the blue box. Talk about why we pray. Share this easy recall for ways of prayer:

Please: prayers of petition, which is asking for self, and intercession, which is asking on behalf of another

Thanks: prayers of gratitude and thanksgiving

Ow!: prayers for forgiveness and of sorrow

Wow!: prayers of adoration and praise

Say: **In this session we are going to learn about a very special way in which Jesus taught us to pray.**

✝ Solidarity

 Prayer

Say: **We can pray to Jesus at any time. Let us pray for his guidance.**
Ask children to fold their hands and bow their heads.

Give children quiet time with Jesus. After a brief time, pray *Amen*.

Begin

Point to the picture of the children. Say: ***The children might be of different ages and backgrounds, but they play together. This is what living in peace means.***

Connect

Read aloud the heading and the first paragraph. Ask: ***What does*** **reveal** ***mean?*** (making known what was not known before) Write the word on the board. Ask children for examples. (Possible answers: telling the ending of a movie; telling about a place they have never been to before) Explain that Jesus reveals God to us. Say: ***Jesus revealed to us what God is really like. He told us that God is our Father who loves and cares for us. Jesus said that God forgives us when we do something wrong and asks us to forgive others.***

Read aloud the second paragraph. Write *Abba* on the board and pronounce it [AH bah]. Say: ***This is how Jesus referred to God, just as some children refer to their fathers as Dad or Papa.***

Ask a child to read aloud the last paragraph. Encourage children to respond to the last question. Ask children to think about people who care for them. Say: ***God our Father loves and cares for us just as our families and friends love and care for us.***

Close

Direct children's attention to the feature at the bottom of page 16.

 Did You Know?

Ask a child to read aloud the paragraph. Have children pray together the Lord's Prayer. Encourage them to lift their minds and hearts to God when praying. Say: ***In the Lord's Prayer, we praise God. We ask him to give us what we need, and we ask for his forgiveness.***

16   www.findinggod.com

Jesus Reveals God as Our Father

As God's Son, Jesus shows us what God is really like. He reveals that God is our Father, who cares for us as his children.

As God's children, we call God our Father, as Jesus did. *Father*, for Jesus, means the one who loves, forgives, and is good to his children. Sometimes Jesus called God **Abba.** That is a special name like Dad or Papa.

Children all over the world use Father in their own language when they call God. The word for father in Spanish is *padre*; in German it is *Vater*. Do you know the word for father in another language?

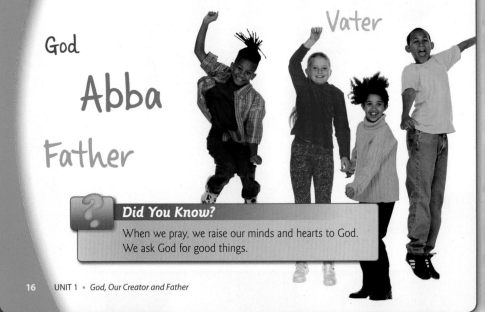

Did You Know?

When we pray, we raise our minds and hearts to God. We ask God for good things.

16   UNIT 1 • *God, Our Creator and Father*

IF TIME ALLOWS

Session 3 BLM

Praying to God Our Father Have children complete the Session 3 Blackline Master [T-295] to learn about praying to God our Father.

Write to Our Father

Distribute paper and crayons so that children can write a short prayer to God our Father. Tell them that it can be a prayer of forgiveness, thanks, praise, or petition.

Jesus Teaches Us to Pray

Jesus went up the side of the mountain and sat down. His disciples gathered around him. Jesus began to teach them.

This is how you are to pray:

Our Father in heaven, hallowed be your name, your kingdom come, your will be done on earth as in heaven. Give us today our daily bread; and forgive us our trespasses as we forgive those who trespass against us; and lead us not into temptation, but deliver us from evil.

If you forgive others for the wrongs they do, your heavenly Father will forgive you.

adapted from Matthew 6:9–14

Forgive Each Other

Write about a time when you forgave someone or someone forgave you.

_____

_____

_____

_____

_____

Link to Liturgy

We pray the Lord's Prayer as we prepare to receive Holy Communion.

SESSION 3 • *God Is Our Father* 17

---

1 Begin

Read aloud the heading. Say: **Jesus is with us today in many ways. He is with us when we pray.**

2 Connect

Read aloud the first paragraph. Say: **This is a review of the Lord's Prayer. Hallowed** *is another word for* **holy. Trespasses** *are things we do that hurt someone, things that are wrong to do.*

 Read aloud the adaptation from Matthew. Say: **When we pray the Lord's Prayer, we are telling God we love him. We are asking God for things that we think will be good for us and asking him to give us the strength to forgive others. Forgiveness is impor-tant to live together in peace.**

Pray the Lord's Prayer together slowly. Say: **These are Jesus' words to us. He taught us how God wants us to be forgiving.**

Read the activity Forgive Each Other and invite children to share their experiences from the activity.

 Link to Liturgy

Read aloud the feature. When we pray the Lord's Prayer at Mass, we hold our hands in the *orans* position. The priest uses this position when praying the Lord's Prayer and when giving the final blessing at Mass. He holds out his arms, elbows bent a little, hands open, and palms up.

3 Close

Display Art Print 3: *The Peace Offering.* Use the Art Print 3 instruction to teach this section. Art Print teach-ing instruction can also be found on page 229.

IF TIME ALLOWS

Service: Caring Friends' Food Drive

Arrange with your catechetical leader to place collection boxes in front of the main office and outside your classroom. Bring in card-board boxes and art supplies. Have children label the boxes for a food drive. Periodically tell children how much food has been collected and take it to a local food pantry.

✝ *The Poor and Vulnerable*

Prayer

Choose an approach and pray with children.

APPROACH 1

Recorded Guided Reflection

Prepare Listen in advance to the recorded guided reflection "The Lord's Prayer" [CD 1, Track 6]. Decide if you will use the recording or lead the reflection yourself. If you choose to lead, listen to the recording a second time, following the script [pages T-282–T-283] and noting pauses and tone. You can then use the script or adapt it as you wish.

Pray During the session, play the recording or lead using the script, joining the children in reflective prayer. If you use the script, play reflective music [CD 2, Tracks 17 and 18] softly in the background.

APPROACH 2

Children's Page

Prepare Pray the prayer on page 18 in advance to become familiar with it.

Pray Ask children to quiet themselves for prayer. Say: **Now we are ready to begin our prayer.** Then say: **This prayer is a reflection on the Lord's Prayer, the prayer that Jesus gave us so we could speak to God our Father.** Read aloud the first paragraph. Pray the first part of the Lord's Prayer.
   Read aloud the second paragraph and the second part of the prayer.
   Read aloud the third and fourth paragraphs. Then give children time to talk to Jesus in their own words. Pray aloud *Amen.* Then lead children in praying the Sign of the Cross. Say: **With the same spirit of quiet and prayerfulness, let's talk about ways we can put Jesus' teachings into practice.**

Prayer

Grow Closer to God

Jesus taught us the Lord's Prayer. He wanted to bring us closer to God the Father, to himself, and to one another. God is our loving Father, and we pray the Lord's Prayer to him.

Lord's Prayer

Our Father, who art in heaven,
hallowed be thy name;
thy kingdom come,
thy will be done
on earth as it is in heaven.

We give glory to God, whose name is holy. We pray that what he wants for us and for the world will happen.

Give us this day our daily bread,
and forgive us our trespasses,
as we forgive those who trespass against us;
and lead us not into temptation,
but deliver us from evil.
Amen.

We ask God for what we need to live. We tell him we will forgive others as he forgives us. We ask him to keep us from evil.

Imagine that you are with Jesus and his disciples on the mountain. You have a chance to talk to Jesus alone. Tell Jesus what the most important part of the prayer is for you. Listen in your heart for what he wants you to know.

18   UNIT 1 • *God, Our Creator and Father*

IF TIME ALLOWS

Pray Again

If you used the recorded guided reflection, you might use this prayer page during another session.

FYI

Coaching Children to Pray

Before starting the prayer, ask children to picture themselves having a conversation with Jesus. Say: **This is your opportunity to open your heart to Jesus about whatever is happening in your life.**

Show Forgiveness

In the Lord's Prayer, Jesus tells us that God wants us to forgive others.

What Would You Do?

How would you show forgiveness in these situations? Write your answers on the lines. Then draw a picture of one of your answers.

1. You found your new souvenir from the museum in your sister's room. Earlier you told her that it was fragile and that she couldn't play with it.

   Possible answer: I would ask her how it got in her room. Then I would say she

   can hold it when she is with you, but not alone because it's fragile.

2. Your good friend forgot to invite you to his laser tag birthday party. Later he said he was sorry he did not invite you.

   Possible answer: I would tell him that I was happy

   he talked to me about it and wish him a happy birthday.

Reading God's Word

Blessed be the God and Father of our Lord Jesus Christ. God the Father always shows us mercy. He encourages us. He supports us when we are troubled. He wants us to do the same for others who are suffering.

adapted from 2 Corinthians 1:3–4

SESSION 3 • *God Is Our Father* 19

IF TIME ALLOWS

Letter to Saint Paul

Tell children that when we write a letter or an e-mail, we like to receive one in return. Suggest that they write a short letter to Saint Paul, responding to the part of his letter on this page. Encourage children to thank Saint Paul for reminding them of all that God does for us and to say how they will help others as Saint Paul did.

1 Begin

Read aloud the heading. Say: *In the Lord's Prayer, we ask God to forgive us as we forgive others.* Ask: *What does forgive mean?* (Possible answer: not holding it against someone for doing something that hurts you or your feelings) Say: *It takes love and strength to forgive someone. That is why we are like Jesus when we forgive people.*

2 Connect

Have a child read aloud the introduction and the activity What Would You Do? Ask a volunteer to read aloud the first situation. Give children a few moments to write a response they think is appropriate. Move on to the second situation. Give children time to write their responses.

Ask volunteers for their responses to the first situation. Look for responses that demonstrate forgiveness. Say: *It is always better to forgive than to stay angry and hold a grudge.* If a child's response does not reflect forgiveness, point out ways in which he or she might respond differently. Move to the second situation and ask for children's responses, pointing out those that show forgiveness. Have children draw one of their answers.

3 Close

Direct children's attention to the feature at the bottom of page 19.

Reading God's Word

Read the adapted passage from 2 Corinthians 1:3–4 as children follow along. Ask: *What does this reading have to do with the activity we just did?* (God helps us and shows us mercy. He wants us to help others and forgive them and show mercy. We just talked about ways to do this.) Say: *This passage is from a letter in the Bible that Saint Paul wrote to his friends so that they would understand how important it is to help others.*

1 Begin

Faith Summary Read aloud the paragraph. Ask: **What prayer did Jesus give us so that we could speak to God?** (the Lord's Prayer) Ask: **Jesus tells us we may address God using what words?** (Our Father) **Why does God want us to call him Father?** (God wants us to know that he loves us, cares for us, answers our prayers, and forgives us.)

2 Connect

Word I Learned Ask a volunteer to define the word. See if anyone can remember the word *father* in another language.

Ways of Being Like Jesus Read aloud the section. Say: **Think of someone you should forgive but haven't. Think about reaching out to that person. We can always pray to God and Jesus to help us be forgiving.**

 Prayer

Invite children to quiet their thoughts. Say: **Let us pray a prayer of thanks to Jesus for giving us the Lord's Prayer.** Ask children to close their eyes. Have them pray silently as you pray the prayer aloud reverently.

Invite children to open their eyes. Give them time to offer personal prayers of thanks. Then pray *Amen.*

With My Family Ask children to read silently the three suggestions in this section. Invite children to choose one or more to complete at home.

3 Go in Peace

Collect materials and return them to the appropriate places. Encourage children to discuss the With My Family section at home. Say: **Remember that God forgives your wrongs so forgive others for wrongs they do.**

RESPOND

Living My Faith

Faith Summary

By teaching us the Lord's Prayer, Jesus reveals God as our Father. He tells us God wants us to forgive one another.

Word I Learned

Abba

Ways of Being Like Jesus

Jesus forgave others. *Ask God to help you learn forgiveness from him.*

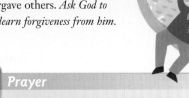

 Prayer

Jesus, thank you for showing us how to pray to God our Father. Help me forgive others so I can be more like you.

With My Family

Activity Take a walk with your family in a peaceful environment, such as a forest or a park. Enjoy each other's company.

Faith on the Go Think back to a time when you might not have been forgiving. Ask one another: *What happened? What would you do differently now?*

Family Prayer Dear God, help us to ask for forgiveness when we hurt others. Help us to keep our hearts open to love others and forgive them when they hurt us. Amen.

20   UNIT 1 • God, Our Creator and Father

IF TIME ALLOWS

Session Assessment Option

An assessment for this session can be found at **www.findinggod.com.**

PLAN AHEAD

Get Ready for Session 4

Consult the catechist preparation pages to prepare for Session 4 and determine any materials you will need.

Jesus Is with Us

3-Minute Retreat

Before preparing the session, take a few moments to rest in the presence of God. Breathe deeply three times and reflect on the great gift God has given us in his Son, Jesus.

Matthew 1:20–21

Such was his intention when, behold, the angel of the Lord appeared to him in a dream and said, "Joseph, son of David, do not be afraid to take Mary your wife into your home. For it is through the holy Spirit that this child has been conceived in her. She will bear a son and you are to name him Jesus, because he will save his people from their sins."

Reflection

God sent Jesus to be our Salvation. Through the action of the Holy Spirit, Mary became the mother of Jesus. Joseph, a good man, knowing that he was not the father of Mary's child, trusted God and accepted Mary, and thereby Jesus, into his home. Accepting Jesus into our lives also requires trust in God. *Jesus* means "God saves," foreshadowing the outcome of our lives when we trust God and accept Jesus into our lives.

Question

How can I encourage children to trust God and accept Jesus into their lives?

Prayer

Speak to the Holy Family, using the words of this prayer or your own.

Jesus, Mary, and Joseph, pray for me that my heart might trust God. Help me to encourage others and learn from children's trust in you.

Knowing and Sharing Your Faith in Session 4

Consider how Scripture and Tradition can deepen your understanding of the session content.

Scripture

Matthew 1:18–23 tells of Mary conceiving Jesus through the Holy Spirit in fulfillment of the prophecy of Isaiah.

Deuteronomy 31:8 proclaims God's devotion to his people.

Tradition

Jesus ministered on earth, especially to those who were poor and suffering. He lived in perfect obedience to the Father to counteract the effect of the disobedience of Adam and Eve. The angel that appeared to Joseph told him not to be afraid to take Mary as his wife. Joseph was open to the grace of God and listened to the angel. He cared for Mary and Jesus for the rest of his life. God the Father and Jesus the Son send the Holy Spirit to give us the grace to understand who Jesus is and what he has done for us. We too are called to trust God and accept Jesus into our lives.

Catholic Social Teaching

In this session the integrated Catholic Social Teaching themes are **Call to Family, Community, and Participation** and **Option for the Poor and Vulnerable.** See page 1b for an explanation of these themes.

Window on the Catechism

The mission of Jesus in fulfilling the promises of the Old Testament and saving us is found in *CCC* 430–433, 441–444.

General Directory for Catechesis

The role of Jesus in revealing God's plan of Salvation is explained in *GDC* 40.

One-Hour Session Planner

SESSION 4 Jesus Is with Us

Session Theme: *The Father sends Jesus to save us.*

Before This Session

▶ Bring children's Creed papers to the session so that children can add to them.

▶ Bookmark your Bible to Matthew 1:18–23 and Deuteronomy 31:8. Place the open Bible in your prayer center.

▶ Play the reflective music with any activity or prayer time to make a quiet and meditative atmosphere.

▶ Display the *Finding God* poster Apostles' Creed.

▶ Read the Guide for this session, choose any additional If Time Allows activities that you might have time to complete, and gather the listed materials.

> **Prayer in Session 4**
>
> In this session children learn the next lines of the Apostles' Creed, "[I believe] in Jesus Christ, his only Son, our Lord, who was conceived by the Holy Spirit, born of the Virgin Mary."

STEPS	APPROXIMATE TIME
Engage ***Jesus Is with Us*** PAGE 21	10 minutes
Explore ***Trust in God*** PAGE 22 ***Listening and Trusting*** PAGE 23 **Art Print:** *Names of Angels* ART PRINT AND PRINT BACK	30–40 minutes
Reflect **Prayer:** We Believe in Jesus PAGE 24 ***Examples for Living*** PAGE 25	15–20 minutes
Respond ***Living My Faith*** PAGE 26	5–10 minutes

Materials

REQUIRED

▶ Bible

▶ Art Print 4: *Names of Angels* and Children's Book page 230

▶ Art supplies

▶ CD player

▶ CD 2, Tracks 17 and 18: "Reflective Music"

▶ *Finding God* poster: Apostles' Creed

IF TIME ALLOWS

▶ Drawing paper (pages 21, 22)

▶ Art supplies (pages 21, 22, 25)

▶ Session 4 BLM, T-296 (page 22)

▶ My Creed papers from Session 1 (page 24)

▶ Magazines (page 25)

▶ Session 4 Assessment, www.findinggod.com (page 26)

SESSION **4**

Mary and Joseph prepared for Jesus to be born. How do you think they got ready for Jesus? If you had been there, how would you have helped Mary and Joseph?

Jesus Is with Us

Prayer
Jesus, Savior, help me to learn from your life so that I can live as God wants me to live.

21

OUTCOMES

▶ **Give examples of how we can trust in God.**

▶ **Pray the next part of the Apostles' Creed.**

▶ **Explain the meanings of Jesus' different names.**

▶ **Define** *Scriptures***.**

1 *Set the Stage*

Begin a discussion about your family and ask children to talk about theirs. Explain that each child's family is special. Tell children that they will be reading about a special family in this session. Ask: **Can you guess what family that is?** (Holy Family)

Point to the picture on page 21. Ask: **How do you think the big sister feels about the new baby in her family? How can she help care for the baby?** (Possible answers: She may be excited about having a new baby in the house. She can bring toys to the baby.)

2 *Get Started*

Read aloud the session title and the text in the blue box, pausing for children to answer the questions. (Possible answers: prepared their home for a new baby; comfort Mary; be kind to Mary and Joseph because they are new, loving parents) Say: **In this session we will learn how God sent his Son, Jesus, to save us and to teach us how to live.**

Prayer

Say: **Let us pray and ask Jesus for his guidance. Quiet your minds, hearts, and bodies. Pray silently as I pray the prayer. You can then tell Jesus whatever you would like.** Pray aloud, and then allow time for children to finish their silent prayer. Lead children in praying the Sign of the Cross.

IF TIME ALLOWS

Inclusion: Emotional
Welcome Jesus Give children with emotional disorders a chance to show what they feel about the page content through art. Ask them to illustrate what they feel about Jesus by drawing pictures of themselves welcoming Jesus to their homes. Say: **Think about how you can welcome Jesus into your lives and into your hearts.** Encourage children to display their pictures in their homes, where they can see them every day.

A Special Prayer Book
Invite children to write short prayers for special little ones in their lives or write prayers for all new babies. Then have children draw small illustrations next to their prayers. Collect their papers and make a book or binder showcasing their work.

 Go to **www.findinggod.com/sessionextenders** to review a Sunday Connection where Jesus tells his disciples he is the Way, the Truth, and the Life.

1 Begin

Read aloud the heading. Discuss what it means to trust. Ask: **Do you trust your parents when they say they will pick you up at a friend's house? Why?** (Possible answers: Children have faith that their parents tell them the truth. They know their parents love them and want what is best for them.) Say: **That is how Joseph trusted in God.**

Tell children they will hear a story adapted from the Gospel of Matthew about how Mary and Joseph trusted in God. Say: **In the Bible, Matthew tells us of God's promise to send his Son to his people. Matthew also tells us that when Jesus came, that promise came true.** Point to the picture of the angel. Say: **You are going to learn about an angel's visit to Joseph.**

2 Connect

Read aloud the adaptation from Matthew. When you have finished reading, ask: **What did the angel tell Joseph?** (that Mary would have a baby through the Holy Spirit) **What does the name Jesus mean?** ("God saves us.")

Write the words *Son of God* on the board. Say: **There are many names for Jesus. No matter what name we use, we can always think of him as the Son of God.** Read aloud the paragraph below the Scripture passage. Say: **Joseph believed the angel's message. He trusted God and knew that God wanted what was best for Joseph and his family.**

3 Close

Direct children's attention to the feature at the bottom of page 22.

❓ Did You Know?

Call on a volunteer to read aloud this section. Say: **Can anyone tell us three of the names for Jesus that are on this page?** (Emmanuel, Savior, Son of God)

Trust in God

A young woman named Mary was engaged to a good man named Joseph. An angel visited Joseph in a dream and told him that Mary would have a baby through the Holy Spirit. The angel said the baby's name would be Jesus, which means "God saves us." Jesus was to be our Savior. Jesus would also have the name Emmanuel, which means "God is with us."

adapted from Matthew 1:18–23

Joseph listened to the angel and trusted in God. He and Mary got married. Jesus, the Son of God, was born. Joseph cared for Mary and Jesus.

❓ Did You Know?

The name Christ means "the anointed one." That means the one chosen by God to be our Savior.

trust in God

22

IF TIME ALLOWS

Session 4 BLM

An Angel's Visit Have children complete the Session 4 Blackline Master [T-296], a crossword puzzle, about the angel's visit.

Show the Story

Distribute crayons and drawing paper. Have children illustrate the angel visiting Joseph. Encourage them to give Joseph and the angel facial expressions that communicate how they must have felt. Have children give their pictures titles that reflect the meaning of the story. Examples of titles are Trust in God or Faith Comes from Trust.

Listening and Trusting

In the **Scriptures** we learn that the angel visited Joseph in a dream. Joseph listened to the angel. He trusted in God and cared for Jesus and Mary.

We trust in God. Jesus, God's Son who became man, is with us always. Even when we are alone or afraid, Jesus is with us.

Sometimes we must listen to others. We trust our parents and teachers when we do not know what to do.

Can you think of a time when you listened and trusted what someone told you? On the lines below, share what happened.

_____

_____

_____

listen and trust

 Reading God's Word

The Lord leads you. He will always be with you. He will never disappoint you or abandon you. Do not be afraid or discouraged. *adapted from Deuteronomy 31:8*

 GO TO PAGE 230

SESSION 4 • *Jesus Is with Us* 23

IF TIME ALLOWS

Service: Building Trust Through Teaching

Consult your catechetical leader before arranging with a catechist of younger children to combine classes for a few minutes. Tell your children that they will read to the younger children. Have them practice reading the adapted Scripture passage from Matthew on page 22. In the combined class, have the older children read to the younger children and teach them the names for Jesus.

 The Poor and Vulnerable

---

1 Begin

Point to the photo near the bottom of the page. Ask: *What do you see in this picture?* (a child holding hands with a grown-up) Say: *These people love and trust each other. Why do we love and trust our parents and friends?* (Possible answers: They teach, help, and love us.)

Write *Scriptures* on the board. Say: *Scriptures are the holy writings in the Old and New Testaments of the Bible.*

2 Connect

Read aloud the heading and the first paragraph. Say: *The story on page 22 is in the New Testament, the second part of the Bible.*

Call on a volunteer to read aloud the second paragraph. Ask: *How do you feel knowing that God sent his Son to be with you always?* (Possible answers: secure, confident)

Read aloud the last two paragraphs. Invite volunteers to share their experiences.

 Reading God's Word

Tell children that you will read an adaptation of a Scripture passage from the Old Testament, the first part of the Bible. Read aloud the passage. Say: *Trust that the Lord is always with you.* For more information on Scripture, refer children to page 184 in the Knowing and Praying Our Faith section of the Children's Book.

3 Close

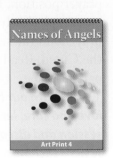

Display Art Print 4: *Names of Angels.* Use the Art Print 4 instructions to teach this section. Art Print teaching instruction can also be found on page 230.

Prayer

Follow the steps to guide children through the prayer on page 24.

Children's Page

Prepare Pray the prayer on page 24 in advance to become familiar with it. Display the *Finding God* Apostles' Creed poster where children can see it.

Pray Invite children to relax and quiet themselves. Say: ***Let's get ready for our special prayer time—when we take time to talk to God and listen to him in our hearts.*** Have children look at the picture on the page. Say: ***This child is opening her arms because she feels God's love all around her.***

Ask: ***What prayer are we beginning to learn in which we profess our belief in God?*** (the Apostles' Creed) Say: ***The first part of the Creed reminds us of creation and Jesus' birth.***

Point to the poster. Invite children to read the first phrase with you. Remind them that they learned this phrase—*I believe in God, the Father almighty, Creator of heaven and earth*—in the first session. Run your finger under the rest of the words as you read them aloud from the poster.

If you wish, play the reflective music [CD 2, Tracks 17 and 18] while you pray the reflection. Ask children to fold their hands in a prayer position. Read aloud the first paragraph slowly. Then have children pray aloud the second sentence of the Creed. Read aloud the second paragraph.

Say: ***With our hearts open to Jesus' love and care, let us continue our session and discover ways to practice Jesus' teachings.***

Prayer

We Believe in Jesus

Joseph believed and trusted the angel who appeared to him. We tell God we believe in Jesus when we pray this part of the Apostles' Creed.

[I believe] in Jesus Christ,
his only Son, our Lord,
who was conceived by the Holy Spirit,
born of the Virgin Mary,

Pray this part of the Apostles' Creed in the presence of Jesus. Spend some time talking with him. Invite him to be at home in your heart just as he was at home with Joseph and Mary. Think about how you will make Jesus at home in your heart. Talk it over with him. Remember to say "Thank you!"

24 UNIT 1 • *God, Our Creator and Father*

IF TIME ALLOWS

My Creed

If you began this activity in Session 1, continue it. Distribute children's Creed papers. Have them copy the new words of the Creed from the poster. Collect the papers. If you did not begin this activity in Session 1, have children copy the prayer from the beginning and stop after this new part.

FYI

Coaching Children to Pray

Make suggestions to children that connect the final phrases or words of the prayer. For example, say: ***You can spend special time with Jesus any time.***

Examples for Living

Jesus showed us how to live the way God wants us to live. Jesus spent his life teaching and healing others. Joseph also showed us ways of living a good life. He trusted in God and took care of Mary and Jesus.

Good Examples

People in our lives can show us good ways to live. Circle the pictures of the people below who set good examples for us.

Write a short prayer thanking God for people who show you how to live a good life. Use at least two of the following words in your prayer: *thanks, trust, lead, teach, God.*

Dear God,
_____
_____
_____
_____
_____

IF TIME ALLOWS

Picture This

Distribute magazines, scissors, glue, and paper. Have children find pictures of people acting like good role models. Some examples include a nurse caring for someone, a teacher with students, a police officer, or a firefighter serving the community. Have children make a collage with a phrase under each picture, explaining how the person sets a good example.

---

1 Begin

Ask: **Do your parents or teachers ever tell you that you should be a good example for others? What does that mean?** (Possible answer: act appropriately so that others follow and do the right thing) Ask: **For whom can you be a good example?** (Possible answers: younger sisters and brothers, cousins, neighbors) Tell children that they will read about people who are good examples.

2 Connect

Read aloud the heading and ask a volunteer to read aloud the following paragraph. Ask: **What are some ways that Jesus lived a good life and cared for others?** (Possible answers: He taught others about God; helped Mary and Joseph; healed sick people.) **How did Joseph live a good life?** (Possible answer: He took care of Mary and Jesus and trusted in God.) **How did Mary live a good life?** (Possible answers: She gave us Jesus, loved and cared for him, trusted in God.)

Read aloud the activity Good Examples and the first paragraph. Give children time to complete the activity. Then ask volunteers to explain their reasons for choosing the pictures they circled.

✝ *Family and Community*

3 Close

Read aloud the following paragraph, and give children time to complete their prayers. Ask volunteers to share the prayers they wrote. Allow time for everyone to share if they like. Then say: **Remember that one way to pray is to say a prayer of thanksgiving. That is the type of prayer you wrote today. You thank God for people who show you how to live a good life.**

1 Begin

Faith Summary Read aloud the paragraph. Ask: **Why did God our Father send his Son to us?** (to save us, teach us, be with us) Ask: **How is Jesus a good example for us to follow?** (Possible answers: He was generous and loving toward all people. He helped others find God. He trusted in God the Father.) Ask: **How did Joseph trust in God when the angel visited him?** (Possible answers: He believed what the angel said; he promised to care for Mary and Jesus.)

2 Connect

Word I Learned Write the word *Scriptures* on the board. Ask: **What does this word mean?** (holy writings about God and Jesus found in the Old and New Testaments in the Bible)

Ways of Being Like Jesus Have a volunteer read aloud this section. Ask: **Why should we be kind to others?** (We follow Jesus' good example.) Ask: **How can you be like Jesus and be good in your everyday lives?** (Possible answers: Smile and greet people cheerfully. Help clean the kitchen. Speak in a gentle way.)

 Prayer

Invite children to pray the prayer silently as you pray aloud. Allow for a few seconds of silent reflection. Then pray together *Amen.*

With My Family Ask children to read silently the three suggestions in this section. Invite children to choose one or more to complete at home.

3 Go in Peace

Collect materials and return them to the appropriate places. Encourage children to discuss the With My Section at home. Say: **Remember to trust in God this week whenever you need his guidance or support.**

Faith Summary

We believe that God sent his Son to save us and to be with us at all times. Through his own life, Jesus reveals God's love for us and teaches us what it means to live as God wants us to live.

Word I Learned

Scriptures

Ways of Being Like Jesus

Jesus always helped others and was good to everyone. *Follow Jesus' example by looking for ways to help others.*

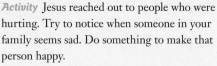

 Prayer

Jesus, thank you for always being with me. Help me to reach out to others and treat them kindly, as you did.

With My Family

Activity Jesus reached out to people who were hurting. Try to notice when someone in your family seems sad. Do something to make that person happy.

Faith on the Go Ask one another: *Name a person that treats other people with love. What does that person do for others?*

Family Prayer Dear God, help us to know when other people need us. Teach us how to care for them. Amen.

26   UNIT 1 • *God, Our Creator and Father*

IF TIME ALLOWS

Session Assessment Option
An assessment for this session can be found at **www.findinggod.com**.

PLAN AHEAD

Get Ready for Session 5
Consult the catechist preparation pages to prepare for Session 5 and determine any materials you will need.

Celebrating Ordinary Time

3-Minute Retreat

As you prepare the session, pause, be still, and be aware of the loving presence of God.

Colossians 3:16

Let the word of Christ dwell in you richly, as in all wisdom you teach and admonish one another, singing psalms, hymns, and spiritual songs with gratitude in your hearts to God.

Reflection

For the early Church, Christian life was never a private affair. To be Christian identified you with the Church, where Christ dwells. The letter to Colossians calls us to treat one another with "heartfelt compassion, kindness, humility, gentleness, and patience" (Colossians 3:12). When we are able to relate to one another by practicing these virtues, we can praise God, singing together psalms, hymns, and spiritual songs. This is the life Jesus calls us to as we celebrate the Mass during Ordinary Time. We respond to Jesus' gift in thanksgiving.

Question

What can I do to participate even more fully at Mass?

Prayer

Speak to your heavenly Father, using this prayer or one of your own.

God, you call us together to be your people. Help me take the steps to celebrate more fully with others.

Knowing and Sharing Your Faith in Session 5

Consider how Scripture and Tradition can deepen your understanding of the session content.

Scripture

Colossians 3:16 reminds us to always be grateful to God by singing hymns and psalms of praise.

Tradition

Ordinary time is celebrated on Sundays in two distinct periods. The first period is after the Christmas season until Ash Wednesday. The second period is after the Easter season until the First Sunday of Advent. There may be 33 or 34 Sundays in Ordinary Time. The term *Ordinary Time* is based on the word *ordinal*, meaning "numbered days." These are the Sundays in which the Church reflects on the mystery of Christ in his day-to-day life. It is during this time we ask for Christ's saving help, especially by receiving him in the Eucharist. We live out our commitment to Christ in our daily lives through the community of the Church. Together with the Church we are a sign of Christ's presence in the world.

Catholic Social Teaching

In this session the integrated Catholic Social Teaching themes are **Solidarity** and **Option for the Poor and Vulnerable**. See page 1b for an explanation of these themes.

Window on the Catechism

The Church as a sign and instrument of God's presence is found in *CCC* 775.

General Directory for Catechesis

The Church as the seed of the Kingdom of God is found in *GDC* 102.

One-Hour Session Planner

SESSION 5 Celebrating Ordinary Time

Session Theme: *Ordinary time is a time to grow and be grateful we belong to our Church community.*

Before This Session

▶ Determine whether you will use the Unit Assessment option listed on page 30.

▶ Determine whether you will also discuss the All Saints Day and All Souls Day seasonal pages in the back of the Children's Book.

▶ Bookmark your Bible to Colossians 3:16. Place the open Bible in your prayer center.

▶ Read the Guide for this session, choose any addition If Time Allows activities that you might have time to complete, and gather the listed materials.

STEPS	APPROXIMATE TIME
Engage *Celebrating Ordinary Time* PAGE 27	🕐 10 minutes
Explore *We Grow in Community During Ordinary Time* PAGE 28	🕐 25–35 minutes
Reflect *Mass During Ordinary Time* PAGE 29 *Art Print: Eucharist* ART PRINT AND PRINT BACK	🕐 20–25 minutes
Respond *Living My Faith* PAGE 30	🕐 5–10 minutes

Prayer in Session 5

The opening and closing prayers relate to the focus of this session, asking Jesus to help children be a part of their Church community. Prayer time includes the opportunity for children to pray to God, using their own words. During this time children may wish to share with God anything that is on their minds or in their hearts.

Materials

REQUIRED

▶ Bible

▶ Parish bulletin

▶ Art Print 5: *Eucharist* and Children's Book page 231

IF TIME ALLOWS

▶ Long strips of paper (page 27)

▶ Glitter, art supplies (page 27)

▶ Cardstock (page 27)

▶ Session 5 BLM, T-297 (page 28)

▶ Brown paper bag (page 29)

▶ Session 5 Assessment, www.findinggod.com (page 30)

▶ Unit 1 Assessment, pages T-298–T-300 (page 30)

Celebrating Ordinary Time

Each year the Church celebrates special feasts and seasons that help us remember the great things God has done to save us and how much he loves us.

The liturgical year is the Church's calendar. Ordinary Time is celebrated two times during each liturgical year—between Christmas and Ash Wednesday, and between Easter and Advent.

Prayer

Dear Jesus, I know you are with me during each day of Ordinary Time. As you walk with me, help me to serve others the best I can.

27

IF TIME ALLOWS

Inclusion: Autism Spectrum

Feasts and Seasons Cards If you have children with autism spectrum disorders, you can make a cue card for the main feasts or seasons of the liturgical year. On the card write the name of the feast or season and draw a symbol for it. Use these cards as visual aids when you are discussing various seasons and feasts.

You might say: ***Ordinary Time*** [display card] ***is a time to be grateful.***

Make Your Own Time Line

Distribute a long strip of paper, perhaps cut from a roll, to each child. Provide markers, glitter, and other tools so that children can make colorful time lines of their own. Have children show each month of the year. Encourage them to make Ordinary Time stand out however they wish. Save their time lines so they can add special feasts and seasons they learn about during Celebrating sessions.

SESSION 5
OUTCOMES

▶ Explain that in Ordinary Time, we are grateful to belong to our Church community.

▶ Discuss how we grow in community by being Christ to the world.

▶ Define *community.*

① Set the Stage

Ask children how many months are in a year. (12) Then ask: **How many seasons are there?** (4) Have children name some important holidays we celebrate during these seasons. Say: **Our Church celebrates special feasts in seasons too. Let's learn about our Church's celebrations!**

② Get Started

Read aloud the session title and the first paragraph. Have children turn to page 151 in their books to look at the liturgical calendar. Ask: **What are some of the Church seasons and feasts that we celebrate?** (Advent, Christmas, Lent, Easter, Ordinary Time) Have a volunteer read aloud the second paragraph on page 27. Ask: **When do we celebrate Ordinary Time?** (between Christmas and Ash Wednesday, and between Easter and the first Sunday of Advent)

Draw a time line on the board, showing these dates.

Say: **In this session we'll read about Ordinary Time—the time of year when we learn to be grateful for our Church community.**

Prayer

Lead children in praying together the prayer. Say: **Let's take a moment to talk to Jesus in our hearts.** Allow time for children to finish their silent prayers. Pray together the Sign of the Cross.

1 **Begin**

Ask children if anyone knows what the word *community* means. Say: **We are going to learn what the word community means and how our Church is involved.**

2 **Connect**

Have a volunteer read aloud the heading and the first paragraph. Tell children about the importance of community and working together to serve others.

Read aloud the question below the first paragraph. Invite volunteers to share their responses, discussing ways that Church communities can be Christ to the world, such as working in soup kitchens or outreach programs and participating in mission trips.

 Solidarity

Have a volunteer read aloud the section Be Like Christ. Offer an example for the activity: **One way I can be more like Christ in my home and school is by being patient with others.** Invite children to complete the activity independently or with partners.

3 **Close**

Direct children's attention to the feature at the bottom of page 28.

 Reading God's Word

Read aloud the verse adaptation as children follow along in their books. Ask: **How do you feel when someone tells you thank you. Do you smile? When you thank friends for something they did for you, how do they react? How do you think God feels when we remember to say thank you to him?**

We Grow in Community During Ordinary Time

Ordinary Time is a time to be grateful that we belong to our church **community**. Together we work to serve others as Jesus did. We grow in community by being Christ to the world.

What is one way that your church community is Christ to the world?

Be Like Christ

During Ordinary Time how can you be more like Christ at home and in your school? Write your idea on the lines.

_____

_____

_____

grow
in your
community

Reading God's Word

Be thankful in your hearts to God.

adapted from Colossians 3:16

28   UNIT 1 • *God, Our Creator and Father*

IF TIME ALLOWS

Session 5 BLM

My Parish Have children complete the Session 5 Blackline Master [T-297] to draw their families and explain the importance of community at Mass.

Seasonal Session: All Saints Day and All Souls Day

Work with children through pages 177–180 of the Children's Book and this guide. This special session can take up to one hour to complete.

Mass During Ordinary Time

When you go to Mass during Ordinary Time, you often receive a parish bulletin that tells about the life of the church.

As you read the bulletin, you will learn about opportunities to love and serve others in your community and around the world.

What We Experience

When you look around your church, you will see parish members praying and singing together as a community. Watch closely as they share in a sign of peace.

My Parish

Write a word on each line in the cross that tells something about your parish.

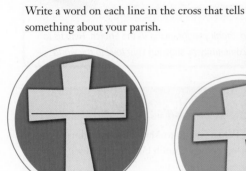

Did You Know?

Each Sunday you can find out which liturgical season or feast we are celebrating by looking in your parish missal or in your parish bulletin.

GO TO PAGE 231

IF TIME ALLOWS

Service: Snack Bags for People Who Are Homeless

Have each child decorate a brown paper bag with pictures and words of encouragement. Encourage children to take their bags home and fill them with nonperishable snack items. Collect the bags and drop them off at a local homeless shelter.

✝ *The Poor and Vulnerable*

1 Begin

Hold up a parish bulletin. Ask: **Does anyone look at their parish bulletins? What kind of information do you read in them?** (Accept reasonable answers.)

2 Connect

Read aloud the heading and the first two paragraphs. Explain that a parish bulletin tells about the events and activities in a church. Hold up the bulletin again and read aloud a few examples. Ask: **What do these examples say about the Church community?** (Possible answer: that parish members look to serve others in the community and around the world)

Ask a volunteer to read aloud the section What We Experience. Discuss the importance of going to church with others. Ask: **How would Sunday Mass feel different if you attended alone?** Then invite children to complete the activity My Parish.

Did You Know?

Read aloud this section. Explain that a parish missal contains the information needed to participate in Mass and states the season or feast being celebrated that week. Invite children to search a parish bulletin to see if they can find the same information.

3 Close

Display Art Print 5: *Eucharist.* Use the Art Print 5 instructions to teach this section. Art Print teaching instruction can also be found on page 231.

1 Begin

Faith Summary Ask a volunteer to read aloud this section. Ask: **Why should we be thankful for community during Ordinary Time?** (Possible answers: Share in Mass together. Pray as a group. Participate in service together.)

2 Connect

Word I Learned Read aloud the word. Ask children to name examples of groups of people in their Church community. Review the word in the Glossary if necessary.

Ways of Being Like Jesus Have a volunteer read aloud this section. Say: **Tell a partner about a time when you were like Jesus.**

Prayer

Ask children to close their eyes, fold their hands, and pray silently as you pray aloud. Allow a few seconds for silent reflection. Pray *Amen* and then pray the Sign of the Cross together.

With My Family Ask children to read silently the three suggestions in this section. Invite children to choose one or more to complete at home.

3 Go in Peace

Collect materials and return them to the appropriate places. Encourage children to discuss the With My Section at home. Say: **During Ordinary Time this year, tell me some of the ways you've found to act more like Jesus. I can't wait to hear!**

Faith Summary

Ordinary Time is celebrated twice during each liturgical year. It is a time to grow in community by being Christ to the world. We are grateful that we belong to our church community.

Word I Learned

community

Ways of Being Like Jesus

Jesus served those in need.
Spend time visiting with an elderly neighbor.

Prayer

Dear God, thank you for giving us the Church. Help us to grow in community by showing your love to the world.

With My Family

Activity When you go to Mass during Ordinary Time, bring home a church bulletin and discuss the information you read.

Faith on the Go Ask one another: *How can I become more involved in my church community?*

Family Prayer Use Ordinary Time to invite family members to grow in faith together by making a prayer box for special prayer intentions or requests.

30   UNIT 1 • *God, Our Creator and Father*

IF TIME ALLOWS

Session Assessment Option

An assessment for this session can be found at **www.findinggod.com.**

Unit Assessment Option

If you wish, photocopy the Unit Assessment on pages T-298–T-300. Administer the assessment during the session or send it home.

PLAN AHEAD

Get Ready for Session 6

Consult the catechist preparation pages to prepare for Session 6 and determine any materials you will need.

UNIT 2

Catechist Preparation pages open each unit and session.

Jesus, Our Lord and Savior   31

UNIT 2

Jesus, Our Lord and Savior

Unit 2 focuses on the call to serve the Kingdom of God. Jesus invites us to be helpers in the Kingdom of God, serving and caring for others. In this unit children will learn the following concepts.

SESSION 6 *Jesus' Good News*

Jesus teaches us about the Kingdom of God by using parables. The parables of the mustard seed and of the yeast reveal the kingdom and teach us how to serve the kingdom through our love of God, our neighbors, and ourselves. As disciples of Jesus, we are called to serve the Kingdom of God through acts of kindness.

SESSION 7 *Following Jesus*

Jesus calls us to love God and others by following the Ten Commandments. Through the grace of the Holy Spirit, we are called to conversion, prompting us to be generous toward those who are less fortunate. As followers of Jesus, we must take extra steps to help those around us.

SESSION 8 *Jesus Gathers Disciples*

Jesus invites his followers to work together to spread God's love. Jesus chose apostles and disciples to help him spread the Good News of the kingdom. The apostles and disciples accepted Jesus' mission to proclaim God's kingdom. We are called to work together as disciples of Jesus, proclaiming the Kingdom of God in Jesus' name.

SESSION 9 *Jesus Dies and Rises*

God loves us so much that he sent his only Son, Jesus, to save us through his life, Death, and Resurrection. Saint Paul wrote letters proclaiming the Paschal Mystery of Jesus' Death and Resurrection. We proclaim our belief in the Paschal Mystery when we pray the Apostles' Creed. Through the grace of the Holy Spirit, we are called to be faithful to Jesus and to serve others.

SESSION 10 *Celebrating Advent*

Children learn the meaning of Advent, why we celebrate it, and explore how Advent is celebrated in our Church.

UNIT SAINTS

Saint Scholastica and Saint Benedict

Scholastica and Benedict were a brother and sister who lived during the sixth century in Italy. Scholastica and Benedict shared great faith in God and dedicated their lives to living as Jesus' disciples and serving the Kingdom of God.

Prayer in Unit 2

Unit 2 continues the pattern and tone for prayer in each session. The opening and closing prayers invite children to reflect on the focus of each session. Each prayer session provides an opportunity for children to add their personal intentions. In the first three sessions, children pray while reflecting on Scripture passages. Then children relate the story to their own relationship with God. In the fourth session, children continue learning the Apostles' Creed.

Catholic Social Teaching in Unit 2

Following are the themes of Catholic Social Teaching integrated into this unit.

Call to Family, Community, and Participation Participation in family and community is central to our faith and to a healthy society. As the central social institution, family must be supported and strengthened. From this foundation people participate in society, fostering a community spirit and promoting the well-being of all.

Care for God's Creation God is the Creator of all people and all things, and he wants us to enjoy his creation. The responsibility to care for all God has made is a requirement of our faith. We are called to make moral and ethical choices that protect the ecological balance of creation both locally and worldwide.

Option for the Poor and Vulnerable In our world many people are wealthy, while at the same time, many are poor. As Catholics we are called to pay special attention to the needs of those who are poor. We can follow Jesus' example by making a specific effort to defend and promote the dignity of those who are poor and vulnerable and meet their immediate needs.

Solidarity Because God is our Father, we are all brothers and sisters with the responsibility to care for one another. Solidarity unites rich and poor, weak and strong, and helps build a society that recognizes that we live in an interdependent world.

TOGETHER *as One Parish*

Religious Education with the Parochial School

To nurture parish unity, choose a program-long theme, such as the military, poverty, or immigration, so that the school and religious education share a common goal. Organize and advertise school and religious education service projects—one to open the year, one during the Christmas season, and one to close the year.

Literature Opportunity

***A Bus of Our Own* by Freddi Williams Evans**

You might wish to read aloud this story a young African American girl facing challenges during a difficult time in American history. The story explains how a community worked together so that the children could go to school.

✝ *The Poor and Vulnerable*

Jesus' Good News

3-Minute Retreat

As you prepare the session, pause for a few moments. Take three deep breaths and be aware of the loving presence of God, who guides and comforts you.

Matthew 13:31–32

He proposed another parable to them. "The kingdom of heaven is like a mustard seed that a person took and sowed in a field. It is the smallest of all the seeds, yet when full-grown it is the largest of plants. It becomes a large bush, and the 'birds of the sky come and dwell in its branches.'"

Reflection

Jesus presents an image that equates the Kingdom of Heaven with a seed of insignificant size. Our life, if given over to the direction of God, can bloom and grow in the same miraculous way as the mustard seed grows. All the great accomplishments of the saints and the holy men and women begin with a small seed of faith. God continues to plant such seeds of faith today.

Questions

How can I best serve the Kingdom of God in my life? How can I nurture the seeds that have been planted today?

Prayer

Speak to Jesus, using this prayer or your own.

Jesus, sower of the kingdom, help me to nurture the seed of the Kingdom of God that you have planted in my heart.

Knowing and Sharing Your Faith in Session 6

Consider how Scripture and Tradition can deepen your understanding of the session content.

Scripture

Matthew 13:31–32 compares the Kingdom of God to the tiny mustard seed that grows to be the largest of plants.

Matthew 13:33 compares the Kingdom of God to the leavening property of yeast.

Tradition

Over the centuries the Church as taken different perspectives when defining the Kingdom of God. The contemporary perspective is based on the teachings of the Second Vatican Council. The Council describes the kingdom as eternal and universal, a kingdom of truth and life, of holiness and grace, of justice, love, and peace. The Church is not the kingdom but rather the seed and the beginning of the kingdom. For this reason we can describe the Church as the Kingdom of Christ already present in mystery. It is the mission of the Church to proclaim and establish among all peoples the Kingdom of God on earth. The kingdom breaks through at times, as it did in the life of Jesus, but it will not reach its perfection until the end of time.

Catholic Social Teaching

In this session the integrated Catholic Social Teaching themes are **Option for the Poor and Vulnerable** and **Solidarity**. See page 31b for an explanation of these themes.

Window on the Catechism

The rich imagery of the Kingdom of God is explored in *CCC* 541–556.

General Directory for Catechesis

The proclamation of the Good News of the Kingdom of God is highlighted in *GDC* 97.

One-Hour Session Planner

SESSION 6 Jesus' Good News

Session Theme: *Jesus teaches us how to love the Father, others, and ourselves.*

Before This Session

▶ Visit www.catholicrelief.org to learn more about Catholic Relief Services and be prepared to share information with children.

▶ Bookmark your Bible to Matthew 13:31–32 and 33. Place the open Bible in your prayer center.

▶ Play the guided reflection to become familiar with it.

▶ Read the Guide for this session, choose any additional If Time Allows activities that you might have time to complete, and gather the listed materials.

STEPS	APPROXIMATE TIME
Engage ***Unit Saints:*** Saint Scholastica and Saint Benedict PAGES 31–32 ***Jesus' Good News*** PAGE 33	10 minutes
Explore ***The Kingdom of God*** PAGE 34 ***We Serve God's Kingdom*** PAGE 35 ***Art Print:*** *Saint Benedict* ART PRINT AND PRINT BACK	30–40 minutes
Reflect ***Prayer:*** Thanking Jesus for His Parables PAGE 36 ***Yeast Is Like the Mustard Seed*** PAGE 37	15–20 minutes
Respond ***Living My Faith*** PAGE 38	5–10 minutes

Prayer in Session 6

Children learn to practice praying while reflecting on Scripture readings, such as the parables of Jesus. A special approach to prayer in Session 6 is an extended guided reflection entitled "Kingdom of God." To prepare this prayer experience, listen to the recorded guided reflection "Kingdom of God" [CD 1, Track 7]. When you play the recording during the session, join children in reflective prayer. If you choose to lead the guided reflection yourself, listen to the recording a second time, following the script [pages T-284–T-285] or you may choose to adapt it. An alternative approach is to use the Prayer on the children's page.

Materials

REQUIRED

▶ Bible

▶ Art Print 6: *Saint Benedict* and Children's Book page 232

▶ Loaf of bread

▶ Writing supplies

▶ CD player

▶ CD 1, Track 7: "Kingdom of God" (10:32)

IF TIME ALLOWS

▶ Collection of Aesop's fables (page 33)

▶ Session 6 BLM, T-301 (page 34)

▶ Large cardboard box (page 35)

▶ Art supplies, computer with Internet access (page 37)

▶ Session 6 Assessment, www.findinggod.com (page 38)

Jesus, Our Lord and Savior

UNIT 2

Saint Scholastica and Saint Benedict

Saint Scholastica and her twin brother Saint Benedict lived in the hills of northern Italy. As adults, they each started a religious community.

31

Saint Scholastica and Saint Benedict

Saint Scholastica and her brother Saint Benedict grew up together in the hills of northern Italy. They were best friends. When they moved apart, they missed each other very much.

Benedict went to study in Rome. Scholastica stayed close to home. She loved to study and to take care of people who were poor or sick.

Later, Scholastica started a community of nuns. It was about five miles from the monastery where Benedict had started a community of monks. Scholastica and Benedict met once a year in a little house nearby. They prayed and talked about their love of God.

Saint Scholastica and her brother Saint Benedict.

At the end of one visit, Scholastica asked her brother to stay longer. When he refused, she prayed that he would stay. A powerful storm started, and Benedict could not leave. Scholastica explained that since he would not listen to her, she had asked God. She said God had heard her prayer. They talked and prayed all night. Scholastica's feast day is February 10. Benedict's feast day is July 11.

32   UNIT 2 • Jesus, Our Lord and Savior

Choose one approach to open the unit.
5-Minute Approach . . . . below
Optional Unit Opener . . . . next page

5-MINUTE APPROACH
Student Pages

1 Begin

Smile and greet children warmly. Say: **Today we will begin a new unit in which we will learn more about Jesus' life.** Discuss relationships with best friends. Share a story about a friend of yours who moved away but with whom you kept in touch. Ask: **Have you ever had a best friend move away? How did you feel?** Discuss how friends and family are special to us.

Say: **In this unit we will learn about Jesus' friendships with the apostles and disciples. We will learn how we can be good friends and followers of Jesus' as well as good friends to one another.**

2 Introduce the Saint

Have children turn to page 31 and look at the picture. Say: **Saints Scholastica and Benedict were brother and sister as well as best friends.** Read aloud the unit title and caption. Ask: **What is a religious community?** (a group of men or women who live, work, and pray together to serve God and others)

Have children turn to page 32 and look at the picture. Say: **This is what an artist thought they looked like as children. Scholastica holds a dove, a symbol of her spirit. Benedict holds a raven that once saved his life.** Read aloud the first paragraph. Say: **Remember our discussion about how important friends are to us.** Have children read the next paragraph silently. Then have volunteers read aloud the remaining paragraphs. Ask: **What was so important about this storm?** (It showed that God had heard Scholastica's prayer.)

This page describes a program-wide intergenerational event that is offered in a supplemental component.

OPTIONAL UNIT OPENER
Intergenerational Event

1 Prepare

Work with your catechetical leader to use the *Finding God Together* kit to plan an intergenerational event for Unit 2.

2 Open the Event

Gather families in one space. Use *Finding God Together* to open the event and discuss the main theme for Unit 2. Together, enjoy an entertaining skit.

3 Implement the Saint Stations

Use *Finding God Together* to help families learn more about the saints at their grade-level saint stations. Be sure all families feel welcome and are engaged in the process.

4 Close

Gather families in one space for a guided reflection. Use *Finding God Together* to close the event.

5 Transition to Children's Book

When children arrive for the faith formation session, discuss the event and review information about the unit saint. Have children open their books to page 33.

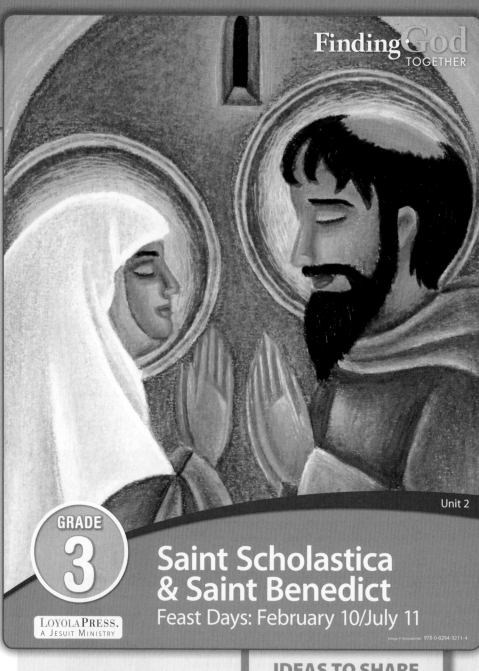

Finding God TOGETHER

GRADE 3

LOYOLA PRESS.
A JESUIT MINISTRY

Unit 2

Saint Scholastica & Saint Benedict
Feast Days: February 10/July 11

978-0-8294-3211-4

Events Guide
Finding God Together: An Intergenerational Events Guide
by Mary Lynn Hendrickson and Tom McGrath

IDEAS TO SHARE
The Holy Twins

Pictured on page 32, the dove Scholastica is holding is a symbol of her spirit. Accounts of her death have described her spirit ascending to heaven in the likeness of a dove. The raven is from a story of a raven that saved Benedict's life. A priest in Italy was jealous of Benedict's fame as a holy man. The priest sent Benedict a poisoned loaf of bread. The raven jumped on the bread to warn him. Once Benedict realized that the bread was poisoned, he had the raven get rid of it.

SESSION **6**

Many stories teach lessons about how we should live. Name a fable or another story that teaches a lesson.

Jesus' Good News

Prayer

Jesus, my teacher, help me to understand your stories so that they can help me to know and love God and others.

33

IF TIME ALLOWS

Inclusion: Specific Learning

Story Time If you have children with specific learning disabilities, you can present the page content in a very direct way. For example, before reading the fable to children, position yourself in front of those children if possible. Maintain eye contact with them as you read the story and allow extra time for them to discuss the story's moral.

Recall Familiar Morals

Invite children to think of some morals they are familiar with and ask them to share with the class. Write them on the board. See if children can connect stories or movies they have seen to the morals on the board. Conclude by reading a fable and having children guess what the moral is. Then read a few more morals from a collection of Aesop's fables and see if children can identify their morals.

 Go to **www.findinggod.com/sessionextenders** to learn more about books on parables, such as *A Child's Book of Parables* by Sister Kathleen Glavich.

OUTCOMES

▶ Explain why Jesus told parables.

▶ Describe ways that we can serve God's kingdom.

▶ Discuss how Saints Benedict and Scholastica served the Kingdom of God.

▶ Define *monastery*.

① Set the Stage

Point to the picture on page 33. Ask: **What are these people doing?** (reading a bedtime story) **Do you read at bedtime? What kinds of stories do you like to read in the evening or before bed?**

② Get Started

Read aloud the title of the session and the text in the blue box. Have children name a story that teaches a lesson. Remind them about fables, such as those found in a collection of Aesop's fables. Say: **Jesus knew people enjoyed stories, so he told a lot of them. He wanted us to learn from them. Jesus told us parables to teach us about God and his creation. In this session we will learn why Jesus told parables and what these stories taught.**

 Prayer

Invite children to pray the prayer. Say: **Sit comfortably and quietly as I pray aloud. Then you will have time to talk quietly with Jesus.** Pray aloud the prayer again. Give children enough time to talk quietly with Jesus and pray together *Amen.*

1 Begin

Say: ***Sometimes we can explain something by comparing it to something else. For example, if I say that Jenna walked home from a day at the beach like an old horse, how would you describe how she walked?*** (Possible answers: slowly, wobbly, tired) ***Jenna was very tired, so I compared her walk to that of an old horse's walk. Comparing can help us understand something. Jesus did this in a special kind of story called a parable. Jesus told a parable to help us understand what the Kingdom of God is.***

2 Connect

 Read aloud the first paragraph. Then ask a volunteer to read aloud the parable. Say: ***This parable helps us understand the Kingdom of God.*** Ask children what they think Jesus meant when he taught about the growth of the tiny mustard seed. Discuss that small things are important and that something little can spread far and serve many.

Ask a volunteer to read aloud the last paragraph. Ask: ***What are small acts that we might do to serve the kingdom?*** (Possible answers: respect elders, greet neighbors, help with chores)

Have children turn to page 35 and have a volunteer read aloud the title and the first paragraph. Ask: ***How can you live according to God's direction?*** (obey the Ten Commandments; follow Jesus' example of helping others; share God's love) ***What did Jesus do to show us how to serve the Kingdom of God?*** (He worked hard, practiced his faith, and loved all people.) Say: ***We have learned that Jesus showed us how working hard, having faith in God, and showing kindness toward others are ways of serving God's kingdom on earth.*** Ask: ***Who else have we learned about that helped serve God's kingdom?*** (Saints Benedict and Scholastica)

The Kingdom of God

Many people gathered around to hear Jesus speak. Jesus wanted them to understand what the Kingdom of God is like. He told them this parable, or story.

> The Kingdom of God is like a mustard seed that is planted in a field. It is the smallest of all seeds, but it grows to be the largest of plants. It becomes a bush so large that birds come and nest in its branches.
> *adapted from Matthew 13:31–32*

Jesus used this parable to show how, with God's help, a great, welcoming kingdom can grow from small beginnings. Small acts of kindness can help many people feel welcomed by God.

34 UNIT 2 • *Jesus, Our Lord and Savior*

IF TIME ALLOWS

Session 6 BLM

My Own Parables Have children complete the Session 6 Blackline Master [T-301] to write their own parables.

Message Through Media: **Parables for Kids, Vol. 1**
Have children view "The Good Samaritan," one of five parables in this animated collection. After the story is over, ask children what they think Jesus teaches with this story. Guide them to recognize the kindness the Samaritan shows to a man he did not even know.

We Serve God's Kingdom

When we love one another and live according to God's rule and direction, we serve the Kingdom of God just like Jesus did. During his life in Nazareth, Jesus worked hard and observed the rules of the Jewish faith. He loved all people. Jesus showed that we can serve God's kingdom in our daily lives.

A Small Act of Kindness

Here is an example of what Jesus meant. Anna, a third grader, goes to Mass on Sunday mornings with her family. One Sunday the priest said there were children in the parish who needed hats and gloves for winter. Anna went home and returned with a pair of warm mittens. Her friend Tara saw her and did the same thing. Soon many others did too. Anna's actions grew into something that served many people. Her small beginning served God's kingdom.

Random Acts of Kindness

Think about acts of kindness that you can do for others in your family or community. Pick someone you know, such as your little sister, your grandfather, or a neighbor, and write something you can do to make that person feel welcome in God's kingdom.

Possible answers: I could play a game with my little sister on a rainy day. I could make my grandfather a nice card or picture to brighten his day. With my parents' permission, I could offer to help clean up my neighbor's yard or take out the trash.

GO TO PAGE 232

SESSION 6 • *Jesus' Good News* 35

IF TIME ALLOWS

Service: Little Things Mean a Lot

Plan with children to donate used books to a neighborhood resource center. Say: **Just as the tiny mustard seed grew to be a great bush, small acts make a big difference to those in need**. Place a cardboard box in a prominent place and tell children to put books inside. Emphasize making others happy by sharing.

✝ **Solidarity**

Read aloud A Small Act of Kindness. Encourage children to talk about what Anna did. Ask: **Have you ever given away something to help someone in need? What are some other ways we can help those in need?** (Possible answers: donate toys at Christmas; give money or items to charity) Say: **When others see our good deeds, it encourages them to do good deeds as well.**

✝ **The Poor and Vulnerable**

Return to the words *Kingdom of God*. Say: **Describe the kingdom in your own words.** (Possible answers: God's love is for all people. All are welcome in the kingdom. Everyone can serve the kingdom if he or she follow Jesus' teachings.)

Read aloud the activity Random Acts of Kindness. Make sure children understand what to do. Walk around the room while children work. When they are finished, ask children to share their ideas for acts of kindness.

③ Close

Display Art Print 6: *Saint Benedict*. Use the Art Print 6 instruction to teach this section. Art Print teaching instruction can also be found on page 232.

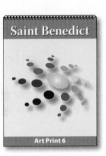

Saint Benedict

Art Print 6

Prayer

Choose an approach and pray with the children.

APPROACH 1

Recorded Guided Reflection

Prepare Listen in advance to the recorded guided reflection "Kingdom of God" [CD 1, Track 7]. Decide if you will use the recording or lead the reflection yourself. If you choose to lead, listen to the recording a second time, following the script [pages T-284–T-285], noting pauses and tone. You can then use the script or adapt it as you wish.

Pray During the session, play the recording or lead using the script, joining children in reflective prayer. If you use the script, play reflective music softly in the background.

APPROACH 2

Children's Page

Prepare Pray the prayer on page 36 in advance to become familiar with it.

Pray Say: ***Taking quiet moments to pray can make a big difference in our lives. Through prayer God's love takes root inside us. Before we begin, find a comfortable position. Relax. Close your eyes and take three deep breaths.*** Pause while children do this.

Read aloud the first three paragraphs slowly in a soft, prayerful voice. After each sentence and question, give children time to reflect.

Read aloud the last paragraph. Give children a few moments to thank Jesus and to think of what they can do to serve God's kingdom. Then pray *Amen.* Say: ***Open your eyes. Now let us learn more about how we can serve the Kingdom of God in our lives.***

Prayer

Thanking Jesus for His Parables

Jesus' parables are like puzzles. When Jesus told the parables, people sometimes asked for help to understand them. Think about the parable of the mustard seed.

Imagine that you are there when Jesus is telling this parable. Who is with you? Do people look puzzled as Jesus tells the story?

Do you understand what Jesus is saying about the Kingdom of God? How does the parable help you understand what he means?

Now spend some time with Jesus. Thank him for telling parables to help you understand God's direction in your life. Tell him one thing you will do to serve God's kingdom.

IF TIME ALLOWS

Pray Again

If you have used the recorded guided reflection, you may wish to use this prayer page during another session.

FYI

Coaching Children to Pray

Remind children to be aware of the presence of God in their lives. Say: ***Remember that you are in the holy presence of God, who loves you.***

Yeast Is Like the Mustard Seed

Jesus told the people a parable about yeast.

He said the Kingdom of God is like yeast that a woman mixes with wheat flour to make dough rise. Even though the amount of yeast is small, it can make the dough rise.   *adapted from Matthew 13:33*

When we make a loaf of bread, we add just a little yeast to make the dough rise. Yeast is like the mustard seed—a little bit makes a big difference.

Can You Be Like Yeast?

Small things we do can be like yeast. By doing small things, we can serve God's kingdom. On the lines below, write one small thing you can do to serve the kingdom. Explain how this act helps the kingdom grow.

_____

_____

_____

_____

_____

SESSION 6 • *Jesus' Good News* 37

IF TIME ALLOWS

Service: Catholic Relief Services

Before your session, visit the Catholic Relief Services Web site at www.CRS.org. The site gives information about the organization's international relief efforts. Read aloud the list of countries where CRS is established. Invite small groups to write thank-you note to CRS. Encourage children to include what they have learned about serving God's kingdom. Remind them that you will mail the letters.

✝ Solidarity

REFLECT

1 Begin

Show children a loaf of bread. Ask them to name some common ingredients used to make bread. Ask: *What ingredient makes the dough rise so that bread is light and fluffy?* (yeast)

2 Connect

 Read aloud the heading and the first sentence. Say: *Now sit quietly and listen as Jesus tells us a parable about yeast and the Kingdom of God.* Ask a volunteer to read aloud the passage. Say: *When dough is baked without yeast, the bread will be flat. But if we add a little yeast to the dough, it will rise and bake into a bread loaf that is much larger than before it was baked.* Ask: *How does this story help us understand how to serve the Kingdom of God?* (Each little thing that we do for others helps us serve the Kingdom of God.) *What other story that we heard has the same lesson?* (the story about the mustard seed) *What is the lesson they both teach?* (Small things can make a big difference.)

Have a volunteer read aloud the second paragraph.

3 Close

Read aloud the activity Can You Be Like Yeast? Say: *Think about the parables we have learned and what they taught us about serving God's kingdom.* Remind children that little things can have far-reaching effects.

Give children time to write their ideas in the space provided. Walk among children as they work to make sure they know what to do. Invite volunteers to share what they wrote.

Say: *Think about how much the Kingdom of God will grow when we do all these little things.*

Begin

Faith Summary Read the paragraph to children. Call on volunteers to retell the parables of the mustard seed and of the yeast. Ask: **What did we learn from the parables?** (that small deeds can serve God's kingdom in small ways)

 Connect

Word I Learned Have a volunteer read aloud the word and use it in a sentence. Ask: **What do we call men who live in a monastery?** (monks) Review the word in the Glossary if necessary.

Ways of Being Like Jesus After a volunteer reads aloud the paragraph, ask: **How does God want you to live at home and in school?** (study hard, be kind to classmates and family, help others without being asked) Tell children that by doing these things, they are serving the Kingdom of God.

Prayer

Say: **Today we have learned about Jesus, the stories he told, and what we can learn from them. Let us be quiet now and spend some time thanking Jesus.** Ask children to think of how they will try to make a difference. Have them pray the prayer silently.

With My Family Ask children to read silently the three suggestions in this section. Invite children to choose one or more to complete at home.

 Go in Peace

Collect materials and return them to the appropriate places. Encourage children to discuss the With My Family section at home. Say: **Remember Jesus' parables and try to share their messages with others this week.**

RESPOND

Living My Faith

Faith Summary

Jesus' parables teach us that we can serve the Kingdom of God in our own lives. Jesus teaches us that small acts of kindness can make a big difference.

Word I Learned

monastery*

Ways of Being Like Jesus

Jesus served the Kingdom of God by doing small things to help others. *Say something nice to a classmate and offer your help at home when it is needed.*

 Prayer

Thank you, Jesus, for teaching me the importance of all the things that I do. Help me as I try to make a difference.

With My Family

Activity Bake some bread with your family. As you bake, talk about the yeast parable.

Faith on the Go Ask one another: *What is your favorite parable? What does it teach?*

Family Prayer *Dear God, help us to see ways that we can show kindness to other people. Lead us in finding ways to serve your kingdom. Amen.*

38 UNIT 2 • *Jesus, Our Lord and Savior*   * This word is taught with the Art Print. See page 232.

IF TIME ALLOWS

Word Research

To review the new word in the session—*monastery*—have children use computers and search for the word online. Allow time for children to share the names of the different monasteries and any pictures they found.

Session Assessment Option

An assessment for this session can be found at **www.findinggod.com**.

PLAN AHEAD

Get Ready for Session 7

Consult the catechist preparation pages to prepare for Session 7 and determine any materials you will need.

Following Jesus

3-Minute Retreat

Before preparing the session, pause for a moment to turn your focus inward. Be still and pay attention to your breathing and your heartbeat as you recognize that God is with you.

Mark 10:21

Jesus, looking at him, loved him and said to him, "You are lacking in one thing. Go, sell what you have, and give to [the] poor and you will have treasure in heaven; then come, follow me."

Reflection

Initially the rich young man affirms his devotion to following the Ten Commandments. Jesus shows his love for the rich young man by challenging him to not only follow the Commandments but also to become a disciple, allowing his love of God to be more important than anything in the world. We too are meant to keep the Ten Commandments. We are also called to conversion, turning our lives over to God by following the teachings of Jesus Christ and by serving others.

Questions

What do I find hard to let go of in my journey to follow Jesus? How can I help others to trust completely in God?

Prayer

Speak to the Lord, using these words or your own.

Lord Jesus, you know me, and you love me.
Help me to give my whole self to your direction
and care.

Knowing and Sharing Your Faith in Session 7

Consider how Scripture and Tradition can deepen your understanding of the session content.

Scripture

Mark 10:17–23 encourages seeking heavenly rather than earthly treasures.

Matthew 6:21 teaches that one's heart is where one's treasure is.

Tradition

Christians have always considered that following the Ten Commandments is the basis for a life of fidelity to God. However, Jesus made it clear that the call to conversion means more than just following the commandments. Jesus conveyed this same message in his Sermon on the Mount. The Ten Commandments are binding. Therefore, we are called to view them as the obligatory first steps on the road to full discipleship of Jesus. We are called to view them as leading us in the direction of full participation in the divine life.

Catholic Social Teaching

In this session the integrated Catholic Social Teaching themes are **Option for the Poor and Vulnerable** and **Solidarity**. See page 31b for an explanation of these themes.

Window on the Catechism

Jesus takes a unique approach to the Ten Commandments. This is explored in *CCC* 2052–2055.

General Directory for Catechesis

The love of God and neighbor, lived in the spirit of the Beatitudes, as proclaimed by Jesus in the Sermon on the Mount, is examined in *GDC* 115.

One-Hour Session Planner

SESSION 7 Following Jesus

Session Theme: *Jesus calls us to love God and others.*

Before This Session

▶ Research local social service facilities to learn which ones accept donations for people who are poor. Bring the contact information with you to your session to share with children.

▶ Bookmark your Bible to Mark 10:17–23 and Matthew 6:21. Place the open Bible in your prayer center.

▶ Plan enough time for children to view a listing of the Ten Commandments in the back of their books. They will learn more about the commandments in Unit 5. Display the *Finding God* poster The Ten Commandments.

▶ Read the Guide for this session, choose any additional If Time Allows activities that you might have time to complete, and gather the listed materials.

> **Prayer in Session 7**
>
> In this session children reflect on the story of Jesus and the rich young man by placing themselves in the story. In a guided reflection, children imagine how they would answer Jesus' call. Continue to provide time for personal reflection after the short opening and closing prayers.

STEPS	APPROXIMATE TIME
Engage *Following Jesus*　PAGE 39	10 minutes
Explore *The Rich Young Man*　PAGE 40 *Choosing God*　PAGE 41 *Art Print:* Young Christian Girl　ART PRINT AND PRINT BACK	30–40 minutes
Reflect *Prayer:* A Quiet Walk with Jesus　PAGE 42 *Obey the Ten Commandments*　PAGE 43	15–20 minutes
Respond *Living My Faith*　PAGE 44	5–10 minutes

Materials

REQUIRED

▶ Bible

▶ Art Print 7: *Young Christian Girl* and Children's Book page 233

▶ CD player

▶ CD 1, Track 1: "The Rich Young Man" (2:43)

▶ CD 2, Track 2: "Song of Love" (Instrumental)

▶ CD 2, Tracks 17 and 18: " Reflective Music"

▶ *Finding God* poster: The Ten Commandments

IF TIME ALLOWS

▶ Drawing paper (pages 39, 40)

▶ Art supplies (pages 39, 40, 43)

▶ Session 7 BLM, T-302 (page 41)

▶ CD player, CD 2, Track 1: "Song of Love" (page 41)

▶ Poster board (page 43)

▶ Session 7 Assessment, www.findinggod.com (page 44)

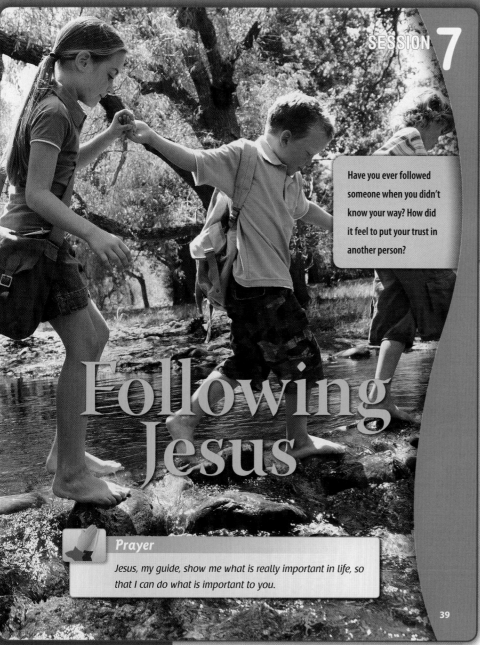

SESSION 7

Following Jesus

Have you ever followed someone when you didn't know your way? How did it feel to put your trust in another person?

Prayer

Jesus, my guide, show me what is really important in life, so that I can do what is important to you.

39

IF TIME ALLOWS

Trustworthy Acrostics

Distribute drawing paper and crayons or markers. Have each child write his or her VIP's name in large letters on the paper. Say: **Think of words that tell why you trust this person. These words should start with the letters that make up the person's name. For example, if your VIP's name is Tom, the first letter, T, stands for Truthful.** Have children make acrostics by writing each "trust" word so that it starts at a letter in the name and runs down the paper. Make time for children to share their "trustworthy" word pictures.

Go to **www.findinggod.com/sessionextenders** to do a daily examen that can help guide us in following in Jesus' footsteps.

SESSION 7

OUTCOMES

▶ Discuss how God calls us to follow the Ten Commandments.

▶ Discuss how being generous with ourselves helps us follow Jesus.

▶ Identify ways to show our love for God and our neighbor.

▶ Define *conversion.*

1 Set the Stage

 Play the instrumental "Song of Love" [CD 2, Track 2] as children enter. Say: **Jesus is someone we look up to because he lived a holy life.**

When children are seated, say: **Name a person who is very important to you. Why did you choose this person?** (Possible answers: I learn from him; she cares about me.) Say: **When have you trusted this person?** (Possible answers: when he or she took me someplace new or asked me to try something new)

2 Get Started

Read aloud the title of the session and the questions in the blue box. Discuss children's answers. Ask: **Whom can you trust and follow all the time?** (Jesus) Ask: **Why do you trust Jesus?** (Possible answers: He loved others and always did what was right.) **How do you feel when you follow Jesus?** (Possible answers: happy, loved, at peace)

Say: **In this session we will find out how we can become Jesus' faithful followers.**

 Prayer

Invite children to get ready for prayer. Say: **Pray the prayer silently as I pray it aloud. Then you will have time to add your own prayers.** Pray the prayer slowly. Give children time to finish their prayers. Pray *Amen* together.

1 Begin

Invite the children to name some of their favorite things, such as an MP3 player or a bike. Then ask them to consider silently how it would feel if they have to give that item away forever. Read aloud the heading on page 40. Point to the picture and ask: **Who is with Jesus?** (a young man) **How can you tell that the man is rich?** (He is dressed well.)

2 Connect

Invite volunteers to read the story. Then tell children you will now play a recorded version of the story. Say: **Imagine how Jesus and the rich young man acted toward each other.**

Ask children to sit quietly. Then play "The Rich Young Man" [CD 1, Track 1]. Afterward, ask: **Do you think Jesus' request of the rich young man to keep the Ten Commandments is easy?** (Answers will vary.) Say: **The Ten Commandments are rules that God gave us to live by. God wants us to obey the Commandments, but we can do more to show our love for him and others.**

Ask: **What else did Jesus ask the young man to do?** (sell his belongings, give money to the poor, follow Jesus) Encourage children to explain what the young man decided to do and why. Ask: **Which was more important to the young man, keeping his money or following Jesus?** (keeping his money) Ask the question at the bottom of the page. (Possible answers: He will not follow Jesus' example; he will have a change of heart and give up his riches.)

3 Close

Ask: **Why might it be difficult for those who are rich to follow Jesus?** (They have more money and possessions.)
Say: **Jesus wants us to share our riches with others in any way we can. We all have gifts we can share.**

✝ **The Poor and Vulnerable**

The Rich Young Man

In the story below, Jesus meets a rich young man and talks about choosing God's kingdom.

One day a young man stopped Jesus. "Good teacher," he asked, "what must I do to gain eternal life?"

You must keep the Ten Commandments," Jesus replied.

The young man smiled. "That is easy. I have kept the Commandments since I was a child," he said.

Jesus looked at the young man with love. "There is one more thing you should do, " he said. "Sell everything you own and give the money to the poor. Then come, follow me."

The young man frowned. He went away, for he was very rich.

Jesus said to his disciples, "It is not easy for people with wealth to choose God's kingdom!"

adapted from Mark 10:17–23

What do you think the rich young man will do next?

Christ and the Rich Young Ruler, Heinrich Hofmann.

40 UNIT 2 • *Jesus, Our Lord and Savior*

IF TIME ALLOWS

Giving for Others

Ask children to think about the difficult position the rich young man was in. Ask them if they would be able to give up some of their possessions in order to serve others. Give each child a sheet of paper. On one side of their papers, have children draw pictures of themselves with something they could give to someone else. On the other side, have them draw pictures of individuals to whom they could give the item or a place to which they could donate it.

Choosing God

God does not expect us to give up everything we have, but he does call us to change. He wants us to love him above all else. He wants us to love one another as much as we love ourselves.

God gave us the Ten Commandments to show us how to love him and one another. When we make wrong choices, we turn away from God and others. These choices lead us into sin. God calls us to be sorry for our sins. The Holy Spirit gives us the grace to turn back to God. We then mend our relationships with God and others. This is called **conversion.**

Every day we make choices about how to act toward God and others. The Ten Commandments help us to follow God and to care for others. On the lines below, share a recent choice that you made that brought you closer to God.

_____

_____

_____

 Link to Liturgy

When we follow the Ten Commandments, we live peacefully with one another. During the Sign of Peace at Mass, we share the peace of Christ with one another.

GO TO PAGE 233

SESSION 7 • *Following Jesus* 41

IF TIME ALLOWS

Service: Change for Change

Talk about what spare change can buy for people in need. Ask children to bring in change to donate to Catholic Relief Services or a local charity.

✝ *Solidarity*

Session 7 BLM

Singing of Love Have children complete the Session 7 Blackline Master [T-302] to learn the actions for "Song of Love" [CD 2, Track 1].

 Begin

Read aloud the heading. Ask: **How does the heading relate to the story we just read?** (Possible answer: The man did not choose God's kingdom.) Say: **Now we will learn how to follow God.**

2 Connect

Have a volunteer read aloud the first paragraph. Ask: **What are the two things God calls us to do?** (love him above all else, love one another as much as we love ourselves)

Read aloud the second paragraph. Ask: **What do we do when we make wrong choices?** (turn away from God, commit sin) **What does it mean to sin?** (to make a choice that hurts our friendship with God and other people) **Who gives us the grace to turn back to God?** (the Holy Spirit)

Say: **Conversion means "change." It is a change of heart that directs us away from sin and toward God.** Ask if children have ever had a change of heart. Say: **The change from selfishness to caring is a conversion.**

Read aloud the third paragraph. Say: **When we make a good choice, we strengthen our friendship with God.** Have children write on the lines a choice that brought them closer to God. Invite volunteers to share their answers.

 Link to Liturgy

Have a volunteer read aloud this section. Say: **When we offer a sign of peace, we recognize those around us as brothers and sisters of Jesus'.**

3 Close

Display Art Print 7: *Young Christian Girl.* Use the Art Print 7 instruction to teach this section. Art Print teaching instruction can also be found on page 233.

Prayer

Follow the steps to guide children through the prayer on page 42.

Children's Page

Prepare Pray the prayer on page 42 in advance to become familiar with it.

Pray Put all materials aside and quiet children. Say: ***Today we have learned about the rich young man. He talked to Jesus and asked him for advice. Now we will spend some time with Jesus and ask for his help.*** Tell children to spend a few quiet moments looking at the girl walking down a path in the picture. Say: ***Jesus loved to spend time outside with nature.*** Tell children to close their eyes, fold their hands, and imagine they are in this peaceful setting as you read aloud.

Say: ***Now I will read the reflection and ask questions that will help you imagine the scene.*** If you wish, play reflective music. Read aloud the first paragraph softly and slowly, pausing for five seconds after each sentence for children to imagine themselves in the scene.

Read aloud the next paragraph, pausing at the end to allow children to answer the questions silently. Close the reflection time by praying *Amen.* Then have children open their eyes.

Say: ***We have reflected on Jesus' challenge to the rich young man. We have also thought of how Jesus challenges us. We answer his challenge by our actions every day.*** Tell children that they will learn other ways they can answer Jesus' challenge in their daily lives.

Prayer

A Quiet Walk with Jesus

Imagine you are there when Jesus is talking to the rich young man. You see and hear everything. You see how sad Jesus is as he watches the young man walk away. If you could talk with the young man, what would you say?

After Jesus watches the young man leave, you and Jesus take a walk. When he looks at you, what do you tell him? What do you ask him? Walk quietly with Jesus, glad to be together.

42   UNIT 2 • *Jesus, Our Lord and Savior*

IF TIME ALLOWS

Prayerful Preparation

Talk about the importance of silence and stillness during prayerful reflection. Invite children to share how they prepare to speak to God during prayer.

FYI

Coaching Children to Pray

Prayer gives children an opportunity to speak to God about what they learned in a session. Remind children that we need silence during prayer so that God can speak to us in our hearts. Help everyone understand the importance of not disturbing someone else's prayer.

Obey the Ten Commandments

By obeying the Ten Commandments, we show respect to God and others and live our lives without harming anyone. Jesus teaches us that this is a good thing. But Jesus asked the rich young man to do more. He asked him to give up all that he owned and follow him. The rich young man was not willing to do this.

What I Want and What I Need

Sometimes we are called to give up things we want but do not need. Draw an X through the things you may want but do not need.

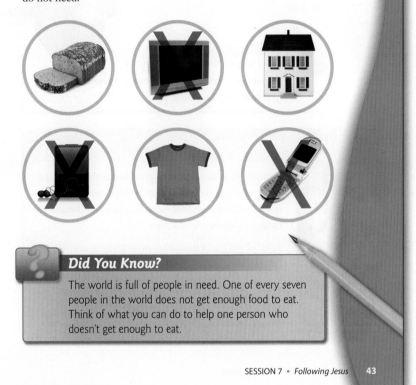

Did You Know?

The world is full of people in need. One of every seven people in the world does not get enough food to eat. Think of what you can do to help one person who doesn't get enough to eat.

SESSION 7 • *Following Jesus* 43

IF TIME ALLOWS

It Is Better to Give

Ask children to think of a time they have shared or given something to another person. Ask them to draw a picture of what they shared. Write these words on poster board: *It is more blessed to give than to receive.* When children have finished their drawings, have them cut out and glue the pictures on the poster board.

 Begin

Display the Finding God poster *The Ten Commandments*. Ask a volunteer to read aloud the First Commandment, then choose someone else for the second, and so on.

 Connect

Read aloud Obey the Ten Commandments. Say: ***It is very important to obey the Ten Commandments that God gave us. However, Jesus asked the rich young man to do even more. Being generous helps us follow Jesus. We often give only to those we love. Jesus loves all people very much, and the Gospels are filled with stories of him helping all people in need. By following his example, you are taking the next step in being a good Christian.***

Read aloud the directions for the activity. Circulate among children to answer any questions they might have as they work. Ask volunteers to share answers and the reasons they circled the items they did. Say: ***This activity helps us see what possessions we really need and which ones we just want.***

Discuss what it means to give up something to help others. Say: ***Think of belongings you have. Now think of someone who might need them more than you do.*** Encourage children to discuss their thoughts about sharing what they have.

 Close

Direct children's attention to the feature at the bottom of page 43.

Did You Know?

Ask a volunteer to read aloud the section. Ask for suggestions of what they can do to feed people who are hungry. Write children's ideas on the board, such as donating non-perishables to a food bank or baking food with their family to give to a homeless shelter. Say: ***See all we can do to help.***

 The Poor and Vulnerable

1 Begin

Faith Summary Read aloud the paragraph. Ask: **What rules did God give us to live by?** (the Ten Commandments) Ask: **What does the story of the rich young man teach us?** (Jesus calls us to obey the Commandments, follow him, and share with others.) **What are ways God wants us to show our love for him and others?** (sharing and helping others, living in peace) **What does the Holy Spirit give us to help us do what God wants?** (grace)

2 Connect

Word I Learned Say the word *conversion* aloud. Say: **Remember, conversion is the change of heart that directs each person away from sin and toward God.**

Ways of Being Like Jesus Read aloud the paragraph. Invite children to share times they could do things cheerfully for one another, such as stop watching a favorite TV show to wash dishes or give allowance money to a collection for those who are poor.

✝ *The Poor and Vulnerable*

Prayer

Say: **Let's thank Jesus for his help.** Pray aloud the prayer slowly. Tell children to add what they would like to say. Give children a brief time to pray. Pray together *Amen.*

With My Family Ask children to read silently the three suggestions in this section. Invite children to choose one or more to complete at home.

3 Go in Peace

Collect materials and return them to the appropriate places. Encourage children to discuss the With My Family section at home. Say: **Every day try to think of something to give up for the benefit of others, just as Jesus did for us.**

Living My Faith

Faith Summary

The Ten Commandments tell us how to love God and others. God gives us the grace to change and to cooperate with him.

Word I Learned

conversion

Ways of Being Like Jesus

Jesus helped those in need. *Do things for others cheerfully, even if it's not easy, to be like Jesus.*

Prayer

Thank you, Jesus, my friend, for showing me how to love you so much. I will follow you.

With My Family

Activity Find items around your home that someone else could use, such as clothes or toys that are in good condition. Gather them in a box and donate them to a shelter or charity.

Faith on the Go Ask one another: *If you were rich, who would you help with your money? Why?*

Family Prayer Dear God, help us to use our free will to obey the Ten Commandments and follow you in all things. Amen.

IF TIME ALLOWS

Word Act

To review the new word in this session—*conversion*—have children act out situations in which they would have a change of heart and turn toward God.

Session Assessment Option

An assessment for this session can be found at **www.findinggod.com**.

PLAN AHEAD

Get Ready for Session 8

Consult the catechist preparation pages to prepare for Session 8 and determine any materials you will need.

Jesus Gathers Disciples

3-Minute Retreat

As you prepare the session, pause and pay attention to your breathing. Take three deep breaths and reflect on the love you receive from the Father, the Son, and the Holy Spirit.

Luke 5:10

Jesus said to Simon, "Do not be afraid; from now on you will be catching men."

Reflection

Following an unsuccessful night of fishing, Peter meets Jesus and Peter's life is changed forever. We too can find our lives transformed as we listen to and act on the words of Jesus. We, like Peter, may prefer the familiar and be fearful when life is not what we expect. Jesus assures us that when we respond to his call, we will in time bear fruit as God intends. Joining in Jesus' mission, we follow the well-traveled path of the apostles and earliest disciples.

Question

What do I find challenging about the mission and call to follow Jesus?

Prayer

Pray, using these words or your own.

Jesus, transform my life with your acceptance and love that I may, without fear, do your work in the world.

Knowing and Sharing Your Faith in Session 8

Consider how Scripture and Tradition can deepen your understanding of the session content.

Scripture

Luke 5:1–11 tells us that Simon Peter is to be a fisher of men.

Luke 10:2 tells us that Jesus needs more people to help spread his message.

Tradition

Christians have long reflected on the mission of the Church. Our contemporary understanding of this mission is reflected in the documents of the Second Vatican Council. The Council tells us that we have been sent by Christ to reveal and to communicate the love of God to all people and all nations. The goal is to bring all people to share in Christ's saving redemption. The Council summarizes this by saying that it is the mission of the Church to proclaim the Kingdom of God. The Church proclaims the coming of the kingdom through its preaching but also through its very being, for the Church is the initial budding forth of the kingdom. The Council completes the picture when it says that it is the mission of the Church to serve the Kingdom of God everywhere for the glory of God the Father.

Catholic Social Teaching

In this session the integrated Catholic Social Teaching themes are **Care for God's Creation** and **Call to Family, Community, and Participation.** See page 31b for an explanation of these themes.

Window on the Catechism

The mission of the Church in the world is summarized in *CCC* 2044–2046.

General Directory for Catechesis

The role of the Paschal Mystery in catechesis is examined in *GDC* 85.

One-Hour Session Planner

SESSION 8 Jesus Gathers Disciples

Session Theme: *Jesus invites his followers to enter the Kingdom of God.*

Before This Session

▶ You may wish to obtain a copy of *Scripture Comes Alive 2: New Testament* published by Loyola Press. It contains models for dialogues and can be used for some activities in this session.

▶ Bookmark your Bible to Luke 5:1–11 and Luke 10:2. Place the open Bible in your prayer center.

▶ Read the Guide for this session, choose any additional If Time Allows activities that you might have time to complete, and gather the listed materials.

STEPS	APPROXIMATE TIME
Engage ***Jesus Gathers Disciples*** PAGE 45	10 minutes
Explore ***Jesus Calls Peter*** PAGES 46–47 ***Art Print:*** *Acts of the Apostles* ART PRINT AND PRINT BACK	30–40 minutes
Reflect ***Prayer:*** Following Jesus PAGE 48 ***Working Together to Follow Jesus*** PAGE 49	15–20 minutes
Respond ***Living My Faith*** PAGE 50	5–10 minutes

Prayer in Session 8

The opening and closing prayers relate to the focus of this session— following Jesus. The Reflect step is a short guided reflection on the story of Jesus calling Peter to follow him. The guided reflection provides the opportunity to help children pray in silence, relating the main focus to their personal prayers.

Materials

REQUIRED

▶ Bible

▶ Art Print 8: *Acts of the Apostles* and Children's Book page 234

▶ Fishing pole or fishing lure

▶ CD player

▶ CD 1, Track 2: "Jesus Calls Peter" (2:57)

▶ CD 2, Track 5: "Here I Am, God" (1:45)

▶ CD 2, Tracks 17 and 18: "Reflective Music"

IF TIME ALLOWS

▶ Construction paper (page 45)

▶ Art supplies (pages 45, 48, 49)

▶ Session 8 BLM (page T-303) (page 46)

▶ Netting (pages 46, 47)

▶ Drawing paper (pages 48, 49)

▶ Session 8 Assessment, www.findinggod.com (page 50)

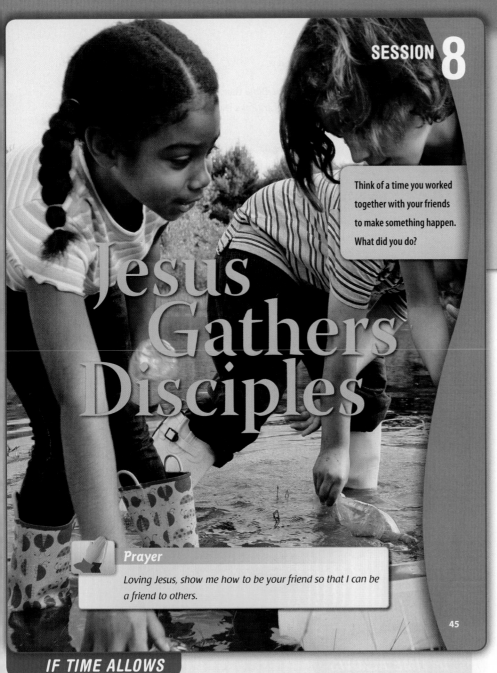

SESSION 8

Jesus Gathers Disciples

Think of a time you worked together with your friends to make something happen. What did you do?

 Prayer

Loving Jesus, show me how to be your friend so that I can be a friend to others.

45

IF TIME ALLOWS

Inclusion: Chronic Health Conditions

Friendship Stories Children with chronic health conditions may find it helpful if they can express how they feel in writing. Ask children to write about how important friends have been to them. Allow children to share their stories. Be sensitive about the need to talk about the role of friends in children's own health journey.

Say Thanks

Distribute construction paper and markers to the children. Ask them to choose a friend for whom they are thankful. Tell them they may choose a sibling or a cousin if they wish. Have children make a thank-you card to give to that person. Explain that they can thank the person for one thing in particular or give a general thanks.

↗ Go to **www.findinggod.com/sessionextenders** to read various articles on how you can participate in missionary work and about others who have led lives of missionary services.

ENGAGE

 SESSION 8

OUTCOMES

▶ Tell the story of how Jesus chose Peter to follow him.

▶ Explore why Jesus needed apostles and disciples to help him.

▶ Discuss reasons why we need to work together to serve the kingdom.

▶ Define *Gospel* and *mission*.

 Set the Stage

Ask: *How do friends show they care for each other?* (Possible answers: do nice things for each other, support each other) *How do you make friends with someone?* (Possible answers: be honest with them, share things with them) Say: *Jesus liked to have friends too. The way Jesus cared for and loved others shows us how we should treat friends.*

Point out the picture on page 45. Say: *The people here are helping do something important.* Ask: *What are they doing?* (picking up garbage) *How do you think they feel?* (Possible answers: proud, helpful) Say: *Working together peacefully to help God's creation is one way of being like Jesus.*

✝ God's Creation

 Get Started

Read aloud the session title and the paragraph in the blue box. Encourage children to share their responses to the question. Say: *In this session we will learn that Jesus wants us to know that we can accomplish much when we work together.*

 Prayer

Say: *Focus your mind and heart on Jesus and ask him to help us be good friends to others.* Pray aloud the prayer. Invite children to pray silently and spend a few moments with Jesus. Lead children in praying *Amen.*

UNIT 2 • *Session 8* **45**

① Begin

Show children a fishing lure or a pole. Ask if anyone has ever used one of these and invite a volunteer to tell about a fishing experience. Say: **Sometimes when you fish, you catch a few fish, and sometimes you won't catch anything. Now we're going to read a fishing story from the Bible.**

② Connect

Read aloud the heading. Say: **Peter was one of Jesus' apostles. Now we will learn how Jesus called Peter to follow him.** Ask a volunteer to explain *apostle.* (a special friend of Jesus, a man who traveled with Jesus in his ministry and witnessed his Resurrection)

Read aloud the first paragraph. Write *Gospel* on the board. Help children pronounce it. Ask: **Where have you heard that word?** (at Mass, when the priest reads about Jesus' life)

 Say: **The word Gospel means "good news." The Gospel tells us the Good News about God's mercy and love, as well as stories of Jesus' life and teachings. These stories are in four books in the New Testament. The books are the Gospels of Matthew, Mark, Luke, and John. Today's story is from the Gospel of Luke.** Show children the Gospels in your Bible.

Tell children that Peter was a fisherman before he followed Jesus. Say: **Fishing boats were like those we use today. The large nets were made of thick rope. Fishermen threw nets into the water to catch fish. This is how they earned a living.**

Invite volunteers to read aloud the story on page 46. Then ask the question below it before reading the story's conclusion on page 47.

Ask: **Why did Peter lower the nets if he didn't think he could catch anything?** (He trusted Jesus.) **Why might it be hard for Peter to trust Jesus?** (He did not know Jesus.) **Why did Peter tell Jesus to leave him?** (He felt he was not good enough to be a follower of Jesus.)

Jesus Calls Peter

The **Gospels** are parts of the Bible that tell the good news of Jesus' life. In the Gospel of Luke, we learn how Jesus called Peter to follow him.

Jesus was near a lake, sharing the word of God with many people. He saw two boats with fishermen washing their nets. Jesus got into Peter's boat and asked him to move the boat away from the shore. Jesus taught the crowd from the boat.

Later, he asked Peter to move the boat into deeper water and to lower the fishing nets. Peter answered, "We have worked all night long without catching anything. But if you tell me to, I will lower the nets.
adapted from Luke 5:1–5

Would you trust Jesus as Peter did?

46

IF TIME ALLOWS

Session 8 BLM

Fishing for Good Deeds Have children complete the Session 8 Blackline Master [T-303] to "fish" for good deeds they can do for others. Provide a basket for children to place their fish.

Role-play the Story

Invite volunteers to role-play the story of Jesus and Peter. Give children time to reread silently the story, thinking about how each character would act and look. Choose volunteers to play Jesus, Peter, other fishermen, and narrators. Have the narrators read aloud slowly and with expression while actors pantomime the actions.

Peter Answers the Call

Peter knew he could do more with Jesus' help than by himself.

He trusted Jesus and lowered the nets into the water. The fishermen caught so many fish that their nets were tearing. They called to their partners on the other boat to come and help them.

Soon both boats were so full of fish that they almost sank. The fishermen were amazed. Peter knelt in front of Jesus and said, "Leave me, Lord, for I am a sinful man."

"Do not be afraid," Jesus said to him. "From now on you will be catching people instead of fish." When they reached the shore, Peter and the others left everything behind and followed Jesus.

adapted from Luke 5:6–11

Jesus accepted Peter as he was. He called Peter to help him bring others to God.

GO TO PAGE 234

SESSION 8   *Jesus Gathers Disciples*   47

IF TIME ALLOWS

Service: Spread the Good News with Friends

First, consult your catechetical leader. Then talk to another catechist to arrange a time when your children can visit their class to act out the story of Jesus choosing Peter. Have children practice their skit before the visit. They can carry netting to emphasize Jesus' apostles becoming "fishers" of people.

✝ *Family and Community*

Ask: **What did Jesus mean when he said they would be catching people?** (They would bring more people to follow Jesus, just as they caught more fish when they lowered their nets again.) **What does it mean that Jesus accepted Peter as he was?** (Jesus knew Peter was trying his best to be a good person.) Say: **Jesus knows we aren't perfect, but he accepts us the way we are. He wants us to hear his call to follow him.**

After reading aloud the story, invite children to imagine the scene as they listen to a recording of it [CD 1, Track 2]. Note that the stories on CD are dramatized versions of the stories in their books.

Say: **In the early years of the Church, Christians used the shape of a fish as a symbol of their faith.** Then prepare the children to do a fish craft. Have children make fish out of a 12-inch-long craft stem. Bend the stem in half and twist it together near the end to make a tail. Pull the middle apart to resemble a fish.

Say: **I am going to play a song that we can sing to tell God that we will answer his call. The words of this song remind us of how the apostles felt when they met Jesus and decided to serve him.** Have children turn to the back of their books to find the words to "Here I Am, God" [CD 2, Track 5]. Play the song. Ask: **How does this song encourage us to follow Jesus?** (Accept a variety of responses.)

③ Close

Display Art Print 8: *Acts of the Apostles.* Use the Art Print 8 instruction to teach this section. Art Print teaching instruction can also be found on page 234.

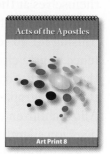

Prayer

Follow the steps to guide children through the prayer on page 48.

Children's Page

Prepare Pray the prayer on page 48 in advance to become familiar with it.

Pray Invite children to be still. Point to the picture. Tell them you will play the song "Here I Am, God" [CD 2, Track 5] to help them relax and concentrate on what they've learned today. Say: **Think about Jesus and Peter and the importance of working with friends as you listen to the song.**

After listening, suggest that the words of the refrain, "I am coming. I will do your will. Here I am, God. I am coming. My delight is to do your will," might be similar to what Peter said to Jesus at the lake. Turn off the music.

Say: **Peter listened when Jesus called him. Jesus is calling us too. When we quiet ourselves for prayer, we can listen for Jesus' call and respond to him in our hearts. Let's spend time with Jesus and listen for his call.**

Tell children that you will read the reflection while they imagine the scenes. Ask them to quiet their bodies, minds, and hearts, and close their eyes. Tell children to picture themselves at the lake with Jesus. Read the aloud first paragraph slowly, pausing for 10 seconds after each sentence to give children time to imagine the scene. Read aloud the second and third paragraphs, pausing after each. Allow children time to answer the question silently.

Read aloud the last paragraph. Tell children you will give them a few moments to be alone with Jesus. Pause for a few moments and then pray *Amen.* Say: **Now that we have told Jesus that we will follow him, let's review some ways of following Jesus in our daily lives.**

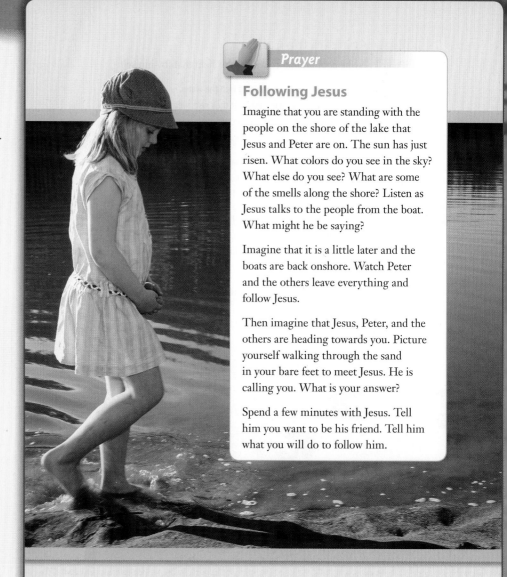

Prayer

Following Jesus

Imagine that you are standing with the people on the shore of the lake that Jesus and Peter are on. The sun has just risen. What colors do you see in the sky? What else do you see? What are some of the smells along the shore? Listen as Jesus talks to the people from the boat. What might he be saying?

Imagine that it is a little later and the boats are back onshore. Watch Peter and the others leave everything and follow Jesus.

Then imagine that Jesus, Peter, and the others are heading towards you. Picture yourself walking through the sand in your bare feet to meet Jesus. He is calling you. What is your answer?

Spend a few minutes with Jesus. Tell him you want to be his friend. Tell him what you will do to follow him.

48   UNIT 2 • *Jesus, Our Lord and Savior*

IF TIME ALLOWS

Standing with Jesus

To extend the reflection, give children paper and crayons. Have them draw the scene they imagined. Encourage children to show themselves in the picture, perhaps talking to Jesus.

FYI

Coaching Children to Pray

Tell children that this is an opportunity to use their imagination in prayer. Explain that they can use their senses—sight, smell, hearing, and touch—as they imagine the scene and speak to Jesus heart to heart.

Working Together to Follow Jesus

Sometimes it takes many people working together to do a job. Jesus' apostles learned to work together when they went out to proclaim God's Word. Write how you could work with others to follow Jesus' path.

Possible answer:

I could work with my class to read Bible stories to younger children.

Reading God's Word

Jesus told his disciples to gather followers. He said they would be like workers during a harvest. He said, "There is a large crop but few workers. More workers are needed to bring in the crop." *adapted from Luke 10:2*

SESSION 8 • *Jesus Gathers Disciples* 49

IF TIME ALLOWS

Friends Are Special People

Discuss the qualities of a good friend. Ask children to think of some describing words. Distribute drawing paper and crayons. Invite children to draw pictures of themselves with their best friends. Say: *Just as we are friends with others, we are also friends with Jesus.*

① Begin

Read aloud the heading and talk about the idea of working together. Ask children how they work together as a group, such as cooperating on projects or by cleaning up at the end of a session. Say: *Jesus knew that he could accomplish more with the help of his friends, the apostles.*

② Connect

Ask a volunteer to read aloud the paragraph. Before children write their responses, suggest ideas to make sure they understand the activity. Provide examples, such as working with friends at a parish function and helping to organize a neighborhood cleanup crew.

Give children time to write their responses. When children are finished with the activity, encourage volunteers to share their responses.

✝ *Family and Community*

③ Close

Direct children's attention to the feature at the bottom of page 49.

Reading God's Word

Ask a volunteer to read aloud this passage. Ask: *What did Jesus tell his disciples to do?* (gather followers) *What did he compare his disciples to?* (workers during a harvest) *How does this passage relate to the activity that we just did?* (It shows how people need to work together to accomplish something.) *Why did Jesus need more workers?* (It takes many people to accomplish a big job.)

1 Begin

Faith Summary Read aloud the paragraph. Review ways we can proclaim the Kingdom of God. Ask: **What did we learn from Jesus about working together?** (He worked with the apostles and disciples to proclaim the Kingdom of God. He wants us to follow his example.)

2 Connect

Words I Learned Review the meaning of each word. For *Gospel*, point out Luke's Gospel in the Bible. Then ask: **What is your mission as a follower of Jesus'?** (to serve God's kingdom by following Jesus and serving others)

Ways of Being Like Jesus Discuss how being respectful to our peers serves the Kingdom of God. Say: **Let's make it our mission to work well with others when working to serve the kingdom.**

✝ Family and Community

 Prayer

Invite children to be quiet for the closing prayer. Say: **It's time to thank Jesus for his guidance.** Ask children to sit quietly with their hands folded and pray together the prayer. Pause for a moment and then lead children in praying the Sign of the Cross.

With My Family Ask children to read silently the three suggestions in this section. Invite children to choose one or more to complete at home.

3 Go in Peace

Collect materials and return them to the appropriate places. Encourage children to discuss the With My Family section at home. Say: **Let us always remember to be good friends to one another just as Jesus was to the apostles.**

Living My Faith

Faith Summary

Jesus chose apostles and sent them on a mission to preach the Word of God. He also chose disciples to help him. Jesus wants us to proclaim the Kingdom of God.

Words I Learned

Gospel
mission*

Ways of Being Like Jesus

Jesus chose special people to help him. *When you work in a group, listen to others and respect their ideas.*

 **Prayer**

Dear Jesus, like Peter, I trust you to guide my life. Thank you for calling me to follow you.

 ## With My Family

Activity Jesus called Peter personally. As a family, choose a relative or a friend who lives alone. Phone or visit that person.

Faith on the Go Ask one another: *What do you think life was like for Peter when he decided to follow Jesus? Why?*

Family Prayer *Dear God, help us to answer Jesus' call to follow him every day. Amen.*

50   UNIT 2 • *Jesus, Our Lord and Savior*   * This word is taught with the Art Print. See page 234.

IF TIME ALLOWS

Session Assessment Option
An assessment for this session can be found at **www.findinggod.com.**

PLAN AHEAD

Get Ready for Session 9
Consult the catechist preparation pages to prepare for Session 9 and determine any materials you will need.

Jesus Dies and Rises

3-Minute Retreat

As you prepare the session, pause for a few quiet moments. Take three deep breaths and know that God lives in you and that his love works through you.

1 Corinthians 15:3–4

For I handed on to you as of first importance what I also received: that Christ died for our sins in accordance with the scriptures; that he was buried; that he was raised on the third day in accordance with the scriptures . . .

Reflection

Finding life through death is a difficult paradox to understand. The apostle Paul identifies the Death and Resurrection of Jesus as an important truth. The Apostles' Creed, which we profess, echoes this truth. The path that Jesus took to lead us to Salvation is through death. After his death he was raised by the work of the Father. Jesus shares his divine life with us through the Holy Spirit. We receive grace from Jesus through the Holy Spirit that helps us to live faithful lives.

Question

What do I need to do so that others may see Christ in me?

Prayer

Pause to pray, using this prayer or your own.

Jesus, you show me the path to eternal life. Give me the grace to share my faith and serve others.

Knowing and Sharing Your Faith in Session 9

Consider how Scripture and Tradition can deepen your understanding of the session content.

Scripture

1 Corinthians 15:1–5 tells us the message to proclaim is Christ's Death, burial, and Resurrection.

John 11:25–26 tells us that Jesus says that those who believe in him will never die.

Tradition

The word *paschal* comes from the Greek word *pascha*, which means to pass over. The Paschal Mystery is the single event of our Salvation accomplished through Jesus Christ's Passion, Death, Resurrection, Ascension, and gift of the Holy Spirit. It is called paschal because it reflects the Passover event of the Old Testament, the deliverance of the people of Israel from slavery in Egypt. Christ passed over to the Father in Heaven and draws all people and all human history with him.

Catholic Social Teaching

In this session the integrated Catholic Social Teaching theme is **Call to Family, Community, and Participation.** See page 31b for an explanation of this theme.

Window on the Catechism

The Passion and Death of Jesus are presented in *CCC* 599–618. Jesus' Resurrection is discussed in *CCC* 638–655. Jesus' Ascension is explored in *CCC* 659–664, and Pentecost is discussed in *CCC* 731–732.

General Directory for Catechesis

The role of the Paschal Mystery in catechesis is examined in *GDC* 85.

One-Hour Session Planner

SESSION 9 Jesus Dies and Rises

Session Theme: *Through Jesus' Death and Resurrection, we receive Salvation.*

Before This Session

▶ Bookmark your Bible to 1 Corinthians 15:1–5 and John 11:25–26. Place the open Bible in your prayer center.

▶ Display the *Finding God* poster Apostles' Creed.

▶ Read the Guide for this session, choose any additional If Time Allows activities that you might have time to complete, and gather the listed materials.

STEPS	APPROXIMATE TIME
Engage ***Jesus Dies and Rises*** PAGE 51	10 minutes
Explore ***We Proclaim Jesus' Death and Resurrection*** PAGE 52 ***We Believe in the Paschal Mystery*** PAGE 53 ***Art Print:*** *Saint Paul the Apostle* ART PRINT AND PRINT BACK	30–40 minutes
Reflect ***Prayer:*** A Special Faith Prayer PAGE 54 ***Celebrating New Life*** PAGE 55	15–20 minutes
Respond ***Living My Faith*** PAGE 56	5–10 minutes

Prayer in Session 9

Continue praying with children slowly and reverently, allowing time for silent reflection. In this session children learn the section of the Apostles' Creed that states our belief in the Paschal Mystery. In the Link to Liturgy, children learn about the memorial acclamation at Mass when we proclaim our faith in the Paschal Mystery.

Materials

REQUIRED

▶ Bible

▶ Art Print 9: *Saint Paul the Apostle* and Children's Book page 235

▶ Art supplies

▶ *Finding God* poster: Apostles' Creed

▶ CD player

▶ CD 2, Tracks 17 and 18: "Reflective Music"

IF TIME ALLOWS

▶ Session 9 BLM (page T-304) (page 52)

▶ Drawing paper (pages 52, 54)

▶ Art supplies (pages 52, 53, 54)

▶ Construction paper or poster board (page 53)

▶ My Creed papers (page 54)

▶ Book about butterflies (page 55)

▶ Session 9 Assessment, www.findinggod.com, (page 56)

SESSION **9**

Have you ever handled a new baby? Have you taken care of a puppy, a kitten, or another young animal? What did you do?

Jesus Dies and Rises

 Prayer

Jesus, our risen Lord, help me to be a faithful disciple so that I can share in your new life.

51

IF TIME ALLOWS

A Circle of Hands

Distribute construction paper, scissors, glue, and pencils. Tell children that we think of a circle as having no beginning and no end, just as God's love for us is boundless. Cut a large circle out of poster board or construction paper. Have each child trace his or her hand on construction paper and cut it out. Ask children to write their names on the paper hands and glue the cutouts around the outer part of the circle to symbolize helping hands working together without end.

 Go to **www.findinggod.com/sessionextenders** to read a selection of Sunday Connections about the Paschal Mystery.

OUTCOMES

▶ Discuss Jesus' passage from Death to Resurrection.

▶ Describe what Saint Paul wrote about the Paschal Mystery in his letters.

▶ Explain that we show our love for others through our actions.

▶ Define *Paschal Mystery*.

❶ Set the Stage

Share a time when someone close to you showed love for you. Ask children to share their own stories. Make a list of ways to show love, such as hugging, giving, sharing, and comforting. Say: *We can tell people we love them, but our actions also show our love. Now we will read about someone who loves us very much and who did something very special to show his love.* Ask: *Who was this special person?* (Jesus)

❷ Get Started

Have children turn to page 51. Point to the picture. Ask: *How does the girl show she cares?* (by being gentle and caring to the lamb)

Call on a volunteer to read aloud the session title and the questions in the blue box. Discuss children's answers. Ask: *How can we show our love?* (Answers will vary.)

Say: *In this session we will learn that Jesus proclaimed his love for us in a very special way.*

 Prayer

Ask children to quiet themselves. Say: *Let's pray to Jesus to help us live as he did, and then share our own thoughts with Jesus.* Invite children to bow their heads, fold their hands, and close their eyes. Ask children to pray silently as you pray aloud. Pray slowly. After a few quiet moments, pray together *Amen.*

1 Begin

Share stories of when the children have spread good news, such as the birth of a new sibling. Then read aloud the heading. Ask: **What does proclaim mean?** (to announce publicly)

2 Connect

Read aloud the first paragraph. Ask: **Why would we proclaim this news?** (It is exciting that Jesus died and rose from the dead. He did it for love of us.) Write *Paschal* [PAS kuhl] *Mystery* on the board. Say: **The term Paschal Mystery describes how Jesus saved us through his life, Death, and Resurrection.**

Point to the picture. Say that it is a painting of the Resurrection. Point to the cross. Say: **The cross is a symbol, or an image that reminds us of something important. What does the cross represent?** (Jesus' Death) Tell children that the cross also represents how Jesus, by his Death, was able to open the gates of Heaven for all his friends who had died. Say: **They had been waiting to be saved by Jesus so that they could enjoy Heaven.**

Read aloud the second paragraph and ask: **How does Jesus share his life with us?** (He sends us the Holy Spirit.) **What do we receive from the Holy Spirit?** (the grace to be faithful to God and serve others)

3 Close

Direct children's attention to the feature at the bottom of page 52.

Reading God's Word

Tell children that this is a reading from the Gospel of John. Read aloud the passage. Ask: **What does Jesus mean when he says that if we believe in him, we will never die?** (If we are faithful to God and serve others, we will live with Jesus in Heaven forever.) Say: **Every time we pray the Apostles' Creed, we proclaim our belief in Jesus' Resurrection and our hope for Heaven.**

We Proclaim Jesus' Death and Resurrection

After he died, Jesus opened the gates of Heaven for the just people who had died before him. Then he rose from the dead and appeared to Peter and the apostles. We call Jesus' passage from Death to Resurrection the **Paschal Mystery.**

Because Jesus Christ is God, we call him Lord. He was raised by the Father through the power of the Holy Spirit. Jesus Christ shares his life with us by sending the Holy Spirit to us. From the Holy Spirit, we receive the grace to be faithful to God and serve others. Jesus is with us today and awaits us at the end of life.

The Holy Resurrection, Nana Quparadze.

Reading God's Word

Jesus said, "I am the resurrection and the life. Everyone who lives and believes in me will never die."

adapted from John 11:25–26

52

IF TIME ALLOWS

Session 9 BLM

Paschal Mystery Have children complete the Session 9 Blackline Master [T-304] to unscramble words about the Paschal Mystery.

Community Helpers

The Holy Spirit gives us the grace to serve others. Tell children that many people in the community serve others. Ask: **Who are some of these people?** (Possible answers: nurses, firefighters) Provide other examples, such as hospice workers who comfort people who are dying and their families, and volunteers who help at homeless shelters. Discuss how the work of each is an example of following Jesus. Distribute paper and crayons or markers. Have children draw a picture of one of these people. Then have children share their pictures.

We Believe in the Paschal Mystery

In this part of the Apostles' Creed, we proclaim our belief in the Paschal Mystery. Pray this part of the Creed.

[He] suffered under Pontius Pilate,
was crucified, died and was buried;
he descended into hell;
on the third day he rose again from the dead;
he ascended into heaven,
and is seated at the right hand of God the Father almighty;
from there he will come to judge the living and the dead.

EXPLORE

Jesus is with us.

Link to Liturgy

At Mass we pray: "We proclaim your Death, O Lord, and profess your Resurrection until you come again."

SESSION 9 • *Jesus Dies and Rises*   53

IF TIME ALLOWS

Service: Proclaim Jesus' Death and Resurrection

Give small groups poster board and markers. Have each group design a poster that shows symbols of Jesus' Death and Resurrection. Ask children to write the headline *We Believe* at the top. Obtain permission to tape the posters around the building to be shared with your parish community.

✝ **Family and Community**

IDEAS TO SHARE

Paschal Mystery

Paschal comes from a word that means "to pass over." We call this the Mystery of Faith because we are acclaiming Jesus' passing over from Death to Resurrection and his promise to come again. The Mystery of Faith is sung or said during the Eucharistic Prayer at Mass.

① Begin

Point to the picture on page 53. Say: **This is another picture of Jesus' Death and Resurrection, or the Paschal Mystery. How do you know this is Jesus?** (There is a golden halo behind his head.) **Jesus is holding an Easter lily. What is it a symbol of?** (new life, Easter, the Resurrection)

② Connect

Ask a volunteer to read aloud the heading and the first paragraph. Display the *Finding God* poster Apostles' Creed. Say: **Now we will learn more of the Apostles' Creed.** Before reading the new part, explain that Pontius Pilate was the Roman governor of Judea who ordered that Jesus be crucified.

Read together the next part of the prayer. Say: **This states our belief in God the Creator; his Son, Jesus Christ; and the power of the Holy Spirit. Each sentence describes part of the Paschal Mystery. We proclaim our belief in the Paschal Mystery when we pray the Apostles' Creed.**

Suggest that children practice this part of the Apostles' Creed at home so that they can learn the whole prayer by the end of the year.

 Link to Liturgy

Read aloud the feature. Say: **This summarizes the basic meaning of the Paschal Mystery.**

③ Close

Display Art Print 9: *Saint Paul the Apostle.* Use the Art Print 9 instruction to teach this section. Art Print teaching instruction can also be found on page 235.

Prayer

Follow the steps to guide children through the prayer on page 54.

Children's Page

Prepare Pray the prayer on page 54 in advance to become familiar with it. Display the *Finding God* Apostles' Creed poster.

Pray Say: *Today we have learned more of the Apostles' Creed. Can anyone remember the first part of the Creed?* Ask volunteers to recite the first part of the Creed. If they cannot remember it, point to the poster and read it together. Say: *Now we are going to spend time with Jesus and pray the new section of the Apostles' Creed.*

Invite children to be quiet for prayer. Point to the cross on the page. Say: *The cross serves as a symbol of the Paschal Mystery, which we remember when we pray the Creed. We pray to Jesus, who died and rose from the dead for us.*

Move to the prayer center with children. Have them bring their books. Play the reflective music at the end of CD 2 as you read the reflection. Read aloud the first paragraph. Then have children look at their books and pray the new part of the Creed with you. Remind them to pause after each sentence.

Ask children to prepare themselves for prayer and to close their eyes. Read the last paragraph slowly. Give children time to be with Jesus. Then pray together *Amen.*

Have children open their eyes. Say: *We told Jesus that we believe. Let us now learn about a symbol of the Resurrection.*

Prayer

A Special Faith Prayer

You have learned more of our special faith prayer, the Apostles' Creed. Pray these words now. Pause after each line to tell Jesus what the words mean to you.

*[He] suffered under Pontius Pilate,
was crucified, died and was buried;
he descended into hell;
on the third day he rose again
    from the dead;
he ascended into heaven,
and is seated at the right hand
    of God the Father almighty;
from there he will come to judge
    the living and the dead.*

Spend a few quiet moments with Jesus. He loves being with you. You are content in each other's company. If there is something you want to ask Jesus or tell him, do it now. Listen to him.

54   UNIT 2 • *Jesus, Our Lord and Savior*

IF TIME ALLOWS

My Creed
If children have been writing the Creed as they learn it, return their papers and ask them to add the sentences about the Paschal Mystery. Collect the papers when children are finished.

Drawing the Creed
Have children illustrate one of the lines they just learned in the Apostles' Creed. Then display their drawings in the order of how the lines appear in the prayer. Encourage children to use the drawings as visual aids in memorizing the Creed.

FYI

Coaching Children to Pray

Remind children that when we pray the Apostles' Creed, we are affirming the basic truths of our faith. It is important to pray with meaning and to reflect on the specific beliefs as we pray.

Celebrating New Life

Liliana and Rosa peeked excitedly into their butterfly box. They had seen the eggs hatch into caterpillars. The caterpillars ate so many leaves that they outgrew their skins several times. Then each caterpillar spun a silky chrysalis around itself and rested.

Two weeks later, the girls wondered if this would be the day the former caterpillars would fly off and start their new lives as butterflies.

Liliana told Rosa that she learned in church that the butterfly is a symbol of Jesus' Resurrection. When the butterfly comes out of the chrysalis and begins a new life, we are reminded of Jesus' Resurrection.

Color the Butterfly

Color this butterfly that is ready to fly off to a new life.

SESSION 9 • *Jesus Dies and Rises* 55

IF TIME ALLOWS

Butterfly Books

Bring in a book on the life cycle of a butterfly. Choose a book that shows a caterpillar, a chrysalis, and a butterfly. Read aloud the section that describes how a caterpillar becomes a butterfly. Ask volunteers to explain how the caterpillar's metamorphosis is similar to the Resurrection. Point out that the caterpillar changes form and goes on to lead a more beautiful life.

1 Begin

Ask: **What are butterfly boxes?** (cardboard boxes with plastic windows and leaves inside for caterpillars) Children may have seen one in science class. If not, describe it or show one. Say: **This is a place for the caterpillar to live as it waits to become a beautiful butterfly.**

2 Connect

Ask a volunteer to read aloud the heading and the first paragraph. Ask: **What happens to a caterpillar in the chrysalis?** (It turns into a butterfly.)

Ask a volunteer to read aloud the second paragraph. Say: **The caterpillar and the butterfly are the same being—it has simply changed form.** Guide the discussion so that children understand the nature of the transformation.

Read aloud the last paragraph. Remind children that the cross is a symbol of Jesus' Death and Resurrection. Say: **After waiting in its chrysalis, the butterfly rises up to an even more beautiful life, just as Jesus did on Easter. When we see a butterfly, it reminds us of Jesus and his new life after he rose from the dead. The butterfly is a symbol of Jesus' Resurrection.**

Distribute crayons for the Color the Butterfly activity. Give children time to color their butterflies.

3 Close

When children finish coloring, ask them to share their pictures. Say: **New life is a happy thing. Jesus rising from the tomb was a wonderful event. The caterpillar rising out of the box as a butterfly reminds us of the joy of the Resurrection.**

1 Begin

Faith Summary Have a volunteer read aloud the paragraph. Ask: **How are we saved?** (through Jesus' Death and Resurrection)

2 Connect

Words I Learned Call on a volunteer to tell you what *Paschal Mystery* means. Have children look up the definition in the Glossary. Say: **Jesus died and rose from the dead and because of this saved us from our sins.**

Ways of Being Like Jesus Ask a volunteer to read aloud the paragraph. Give children a few moments to think about someone they could forgive. Say: **Jesus finds it easy to forgive us because he loves us so much. If he can do this great thing for us, we too can forgive others.**

Prayer

Invite children to be still and quiet. Say: **It is time to pray and thank Jesus for all the wonderful things he does for us.** Read the prayer aloud. Invite children to take a few quiet moments to thank Jesus for something he has done for us. Pause for a moment, then pray *Amen.*

With My Family Ask children to read silently the three suggestions in this section. Invite children to choose one or more to complete at home.

3 Go in Peace

Collect materials and return them to the appropriate places. Encourage children to discuss the With My Family section at home. Say: **As we move through our week, let us all try to put the needs of others before our own, just as Jesus did.**

Living My Faith

Faith Summary

Jesus suffered and died for us. By the power of the Holy Spirit, he rose from the dead. Through his Death and Resurrection, we are saved.

Words I Learned

Paschal Mystery

Ways of Being Like Jesus

Before Jesus died, he asked the Father to forgive his enemies. *Forgive those who hurt you.*

Prayer

Jesus, Lord, thank you for giving your life to save me. Help me to live my life to help others.

With My Family

Activity As a family, decide to help one another with chores that family members usually do alone.

Faith on the Go Ask one another: *Do we help out each member of the family as much as we can? If not, what prevents us?*

Family Prayer Dear God, thank you for the gift of your Son, Jesus Christ. Help us to remember that Jesus suffered and died for us. Amen.

56   UNIT 2 • *Jesus, Our Lord and Savior*

IF TIME ALLOWS

Session Assessment Option

An assessment for this session can be found at **www.findinggod.com.**

PLAN AHEAD

Get Ready for Session 10

Consult the catechist preparation pages to prepare for Session 10 and determine any materials you will need.

Celebrating Advent

3-Minute Retreat

As you prepare the session, pause, be still, and aware of the loving presence of God.

Luke 2:12

And this will be a sign for you: you will find an infant wrapped in swaddling clothes and lying in a manger.

Reflection

As we begin the Church's liturgical year in Advent, the decorations in the Church are more solemn and the color is purple (except for Gaudete Sunday). In the commercial world, Christmas decorations and sales promotions start earlier every year. In both worlds we anticipate the celebration of the birth of a babe wrapped in swaddling clothes, lying in a manger. The commercial world tries to fulfill the promise of this child with glitz and glitter. As Christians we know in faith that by making room in our hearts, we will be prepared to celebrate more fully he who is our true Lord.

Question

What am I doing to make room for a new birth of Jesus in my heart?

Prayer

Speak to your heavenly Father, using this prayer or one of your own.

Jesus, help me to live in anticipation of a rebirth of your presence in my heart. I pray that it will manifest itself in care for others.

Knowing and Sharing Your Faith in Session 10

Consider how Scripture and Tradition can deepen your understanding of the session content.

Scripture

Luke 2:12 reminds us that we are preparing to receive Jesus in our hearts.

Tradition

The word *advent* is from the Latin *adventus*, meaning "coming" or "arrival." The season of Advent prepares us to celebrate the "coming" of Jesus as Messiah, Christ, or King. The Scripture readings during Advent include passages from the Old Testament telling of the promise of a Messiah. Many New Testament passages concern Jesus Christ's Second Coming as judge of all people. Since Advent prepares us to celebrate Christmas and is not part of the Christmas season itself, Christmas hymns or readings are not used. The liturgical color of Advent is purple, except for the third Sunday of Advent. This is often called Gaudete Sunday on which rose-colored vestments may be used. During Advent we prepare to receive Jesus in our hearts to share with others.

Catholic Social Teaching

In this session the integrated Catholic Social Teaching theme is **Family and Community.** See page 31b for an explanation of this theme.

Window on the Catechism

A deeper understanding of the season of Advent is described in *CCC* 524.

General Directory for Catechesis

The importance of understanding the centrality of Jesus for our Salvation is found in *GDC* 98.

One-Hour Session Planner

SESSION 10 Celebrating Advent

Session Theme: *Advent is a time to prepare ourselves and our homes for the celebration of Jesus' birth.*

Before This Session

- ▶ Determine whether you will use the Unit Assessment option listed on page 60.

- ▶ Determine whether you will also discuss the Advent seasonal pages in the back of the Children's Book.

- ▶ Bookmark your Bible to Luke 2:12. Place the open Bible in your prayer center.

- ▶ Collect tree branches, a small Christmas tree, or cardboard to make a prayer tree.

- ▶ Read the Guide for this session, choose any additional If Time Allows activities that you might have time to complete, and gather the listed materials.

Prayer in Session 10

The prayers in this session encourage children to prepare room for Jesus in their lives. The prayer times include time for children to talk with God in the silence of their hearts and to share with him any of their thoughts and concerns.

STEPS	APPROXIMATE TIME
Engage ***Celebrating Advent*** PAGE 57	10 minutes
Explore ***We Prepare During Advent*** PAGE 58	25–35 minutes
Reflect ***Mass During Advent*** PAGE 59 **Art Print:** *Prepare for Christmas* ART PRINT AND PRINT BACK	20–25 minutes
Respond ***Living My Faith*** PAGE 60	5–10 minutes

Materials

REQUIRED

- ▶ Bible
- ▶ Advent calendar
- ▶ Lyrics to "O Come, O Come Emmanuel"
- ▶ Art Print 10: *Prepare for Christmas* and Children's Book page 236

IF TIME ALLOWS

- ▶ Red and white construction paper, stapler, art supplies (page 57)
- ▶ Session 10 BLM, T-305 (page 58)
- ▶ Tree branches, a small Christmas tree, or cardboard (page 59)

- ▶ Session 10 Assessment, www.findinggod.com, (page 60)
- ▶ Unit 2 Assessment, T-306–T-308 (page 60)

Celebrating Advent

The Church's liturgical year begins with Advent. Advent is the season before Christmas. It begins four Sundays before December 25 and ends at Christmas Mass.

Advent is a time to prepare our hearts and our homes to celebrate the birth of Jesus. We use this season to pray and to prepare ourselves to welcome him into our lives.

Love

Hope

Joy

Peace

Prayer

Dear Jesus, on each day of Advent, I am preparing to celebrate your birth. Fill my heart with love and joy.

57

IF TIME ALLOWS

Inclusion: Attention

Favorite Memories Use this activity if you have children with attention differences. Invite children to act out their favorite events or memories from past Advent seasons. Ask: **What do you remember about Advent?** Allow children an opportunity to share their answers.

Pockets of Love

Have each child fold a large sheet of red construction paper in half so that the short sides meet, and cut two hearts from the folded paper at the same time. Staple the hearts around the outside edges, leaving the tops open to form a pocket. Let children decorate the hearts, perhaps labeling it *My Advent Pocket of Love*. Give children small strips of white paper on which to write messages to family members that express how they feel. Have children fold the papers and put them in the pocket. Children can also add a paper carry strap or use a hole punch and string. Tell children to offer a love message every day during Advent.

✝ *Family and Community*

▶ Explain that Advent is a time to prepare our hearts and our homes to celebrate the birth of Jesus.

▶ Discuss that Advent is a time for preparing, praying, and remembering.

① Set the Stage

Point to the Advent wreath on the page. Say: **This is an Advent wreath. When do we light the candles?** (We light one candle each Sunday during Advent.) Say: **In this session called Celebrating Advent, we'll learn more about this wreath and about this time of year when we prepare to celebrate the birth of Jesus.**

Have children turn to page 151 in their books. Remind them of the liturgical calendar. Ask: **What are some seasons on the calendar?** (Advent, Christmas, Lent, Easter, Ordinary Time) Then point to the season of Advent.

② Get Started

Invite volunteers to read the paragraphs on page 57. Ask: **When do we celebrate Advent?** (after Ordinary Time and before Christmas) **When does Advent begin and end?** (begins four Sundays before Christmas Day and ends at Christmas Mass) **What do we use this season to do?** (pray and prepare ourselves to welcome Jesus)

Prayer

Say: **Now close your eyes, and take a moment to imagine a peaceful night sky.** Pray aloud the prayer. Then say: **Let's take a minute to talk to Jesus in the quiet of our hearts.** Allow time for children to finish their prayers. Pray *Amen* and conclude with the Sign of the Cross. Ask children to open their eyes.

Begin

Display an Advent calendar. Say: **Some families hang an Advent calendar. They use this calendar to prepare for the birth of Jesus.** Ask: **What does your home look like during Advent?**

 Connect

Have a volunteer read aloud We Prepare During Advent. Say: **Advent is a time of preparation.** Ask: **How can we open our hearts to make room for Jesus?** (by helping others) Say: **Preparing our homes is another way that we get ready for Christmas.** Remind children of the symbolism of the Advent wreath: round shape for God's unending love, evergreens for new life, candles for Jesus, and the Light of the World. Ask: **How were Mary and Joseph faithful to God?** (Mary agreed to become the mother of Jesus. Joseph agreed to marry Mary and become the foster father of Jesus.)

Have a volunteer read aloud the activity directions. Offer an example for the activity. Say: **During Advent I prepare for Christmas by arranging my Nativity scene.** Invite children to complete the activity independently or with partners.

 Close

Direct children's attention to the feature at the bottom of page 58.

 Reading God's Word

Read aloud the passage from the Bible as children follow along in their books. Explain the passage in simple terms. Say: **Jesus' birth was a sign to the world that God loves us. Can you imagine seeing baby Jesus wrapped in swaddling clothes, lying in a manger? The story of his birth is always told each year at Christmas Mass.**

EXPLORE

We Prepare During Advent

Advent is a time to seek Jesus and to make room for him in our lives. We open our hearts by helping others. We also remember how faithful Mary and Joseph were to God's plan. Decorating our homes is another way we prepare for celebrating Jesus' birth. One way you can prepare your home for Advent is by setting up an Advent wreath or hanging up an Advent calendar.

We Prepare, We Remember

Think about what you will do this Advent to prepare to celebrate the birth of Jesus. Then finish each sentence on the lines below.

1. During Advent I prepare for Christmas by _____
_____.

2. During Advent I remember that _____
_____.

3. During Advent my family and I _____
_____.

Reading God's Word

"And this will be a sign for you: you will find an infant wrapped in swaddling clothes and lying in a manger."

Luke 2:12

58

IF TIME ALLOWS

Session 10 BLM

We Prepare for Jesus Have children complete the Session 10 Blackline Master [T-305] to make an Advent candle.

Seasonal Session: Advent

Work with children through pages 153–156 of the Children's Book and this guide. This special section can take up to one hour to complete.

Mass During Advent

During Advent we long for Jesus, and we look forward to the celebration of his birth on Christmas Day. When you go to Mass during Advent, you might hear hymns such as, "O Come, O Come Emmanuel." Songs like this help us recognize how much we long for Jesus.

What We Experience

When you look around your church during Advent, you might see an Advent wreath with candles, which reminds us that we are preparing the way for Jesus, the Light of the World. You will also see the color purple on the altar cloth or priest's vestments. The color purple reminds us that Advent is a time of preparation.

My Advent Hymn

Imagine you are writing an Advent hymn. Write some of the words or phrases that you might include below.

_____

_____

_____

_____

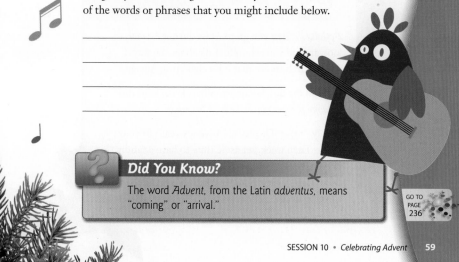

Did You Know?

The word *Advent*, from the Latin *adventus*, means "coming" or "arrival."

GO TO PAGE 236

SESSION 10 • *Celebrating Advent* **59**

IF TIME ALLOWS

Service: Prayer Tree

Use tree branches, a small Christmas tree, or cardboard to make a class prayer tree. Contact your parish office and ask for a list of members in need of prayers.

Copy each name onto a small piece of paper and hang it on the class prayer tree. Then have children choose a tag from the prayer tree. Tell children to pray for that person each day. Near the end of Advent, have them make a Christmas card for that person, telling him or her that they prayed for that person during Advent.

✝ *Family and Community*

1 Begin

Provide children with a copy of the lyrics to "O Come, O Come, Emmanuel" and sing aloud together. Then discuss how the song reminds us of what God has done for us. Point out that God sent his Son, Jesus, to show us how to live and to save us from our sins.

2 Connect

Read aloud the first two paragraphs. Ask: **What are some items that you see in church during Advent?** (Possible answers: evergreen trees, poinsettias, tree with tags of children's names so that parishioners can purchase gifts) Ask: **What is the color of the priest's vestments or altar cloth during Advent?** (purple)

Have children complete the My Advent Hymn activity. Invite the children to pair up to brainstorm ideas before coqaampleting the activity independently. When children are done, ask them to share some words or phrases that they used and write them on the board.

Did You Know?

Read aloud the feature. Remind children that during Advent we are waiting for the "coming" or "arrival" of Jesus. Ask: **Why is this arrival so important?** (It shows God's love for us.)

3 Close

Display Art Print 10: *Prepare for Christmas.* Use the Art Print 10 instruction to teach this section. Art Print teaching instruction can also be found on page 236.

Begin

Faith Summary Invite a volunteer to read aloud the paragraph. Ask: **Why do we celebrate Advent?** (to prepare our hearts and homes for the birth of Jesus)

 Connect

Ways of Being Like Jesus Have a volunteer read aloud this section. Say: **Tell a partner about a time you were like Jesus in this way.**

 Prayer

Ask children to close their eyes, fold their hands, and pray silently as you pray aloud. Allow a few seconds for silent reflection. Pray *Amen* and pray the Sign of the Cross together.

With My Family Ask children to read silently the three suggestions in this section. Invite children to choose one or more to complete at home.

 Go in Peace

Collect materials and return them to the appropriate places. Encourage children to discuss the With My Family section at home. Say: **During Advent this year, tell me some ways you've found to act more like Jesus. I can't wait to hear!**

RESPOND

Living My Faith

Faith Summary

Advent is a season of preparing and remembering. We prepare our hearts and our homes to celebrate the birth of Jesus.

Ways of Being Like Jesus

Jesus was always thinking of others before himself. *This Advent I will put someone else's needs before my own.*

 Prayer

Dear Jesus, as I prepare for the celebration of your birth, I know you are with me. Help me to remember to spread the joy of the Advent season to those I meet.

With My Family

Activity When you go to Mass during Advent, look around your church. Talk about the ways your church shows that it is celebrating Advent.

Faith on the Go Ask one another: *What more can we do to prepare our home for Christmas?*

Family Prayer Display an Advent wreath in your home. Each week, set aside time to have a family prayer service, using the wreath. Read from the Bible, light the Advent candles, and pray for those in need.

60 UNIT 2 • *Jesus, Our Lord and Savior*

IF TIME ALLOWS

Session Assessment Option

An assessment for this session can be found at **www.findinggod.com.**

Unit Assessment Option

If you wish, photocopy the Unit Assessment on pages T-306–T-308. Administer the assessment during the session or send it home.

PLAN AHEAD

Get Ready for Session 11

Consult the catechist preparation pages to prepare for Session 11 and determine any materials you will need.

UNIT 3

Catechist Preparation pages open each unit and session.

The Church, Our Community in the Spirit   61

UNIT 3

The Church, Our Community in the Spirit

This unit focuses on continuing Jesus' mission by being active members of the Catholic Church. In this unit children will learn the following concepts.

UNIT SAINT
Saint Katharine Drexel

SESSION 11 *Jesus Sends the Holy Spirit*

In this session children learn that Jesus sent the Holy Spirit to help the disciples carry out his mission. The Holy Spirit helps us today by teaching us to be witnesses to Jesus.

SESSION 12 *The Catholic Church*

In this session children see how Jesus calls us to be part of the Church community. Peter and the apostles were the first leaders of the Church. Today the pope, bishops, and pastors are our leaders. Jesus calls us to be part of the Catholic Church, which is one, holy, catholic, and apostolic.

SESSION 13 *The Church Prays*

Jesus gives us the sacraments to help us worship God. In this session children learn how Jesus is present to us through the celebration of the sacraments and the grace of the Holy Spirit. Jesus reached out to heal the Roman officer's servant. In the same way, he reaches out to us through the sacraments.

SESSION 14 *Mary Is Holy*

The Church is united before God in the Communion of Saints. Children learn that Mary, the Mother of Jesus and of the Church, is our model. Through her life she shows us how to believe and how to love. When praying the Rosary, we remember the principal events in the lives of Jesus and Mary.

SESSION 15 *Celebrating Christmas*

Children learn the meaning of Christmas, why we celebrate it, and explore how Christmas is celebrated in our Church.

Katharine Drexel dedicated her life to continuing Jesus' mission. Katharine was born to a wealthy family in Pennsylvania in 1858. As she traveled the United States, she witnessed how Native Americans and African Americans suffered because of social injustice. She decided to use her wealth to ease their suffering. Katharine founded a religious order called the Sisters of the Blessed Sacrament. She founded several schools and missions throughout the United States, spending $20 million of her own money. Pope John Paul II named her a saint in 2000.

Prayer in Unit 3

In this unit continue to establish a prayerful environment that is consistent with the theme and tone of each prayer, and be sure to always provide ample opportunity for individual prayer following the prayers of petition and gratitude. Throughout this unit children will reflect on the following: the Prayer to the Holy Spirit, the last part of the Apostles' Creed, and the important events in the lives of Jesus and Mary.

✝ Catholic Social Teaching in Unit 3

The following themes of Catholic Social Teaching are integrated into this unit.

Call to Family, Community, and Participation   Participation in family and community is central to our faith and to a healthy society. As the central social institution, family must be supported and strengthened. From this foundation people participate in society, fostering a community spirit and promoting the well-being of all.

Life and Dignity of the Human Person   The Catholic Church teaches us that all human life is sacred and that all people must be treated with dignity. We are called to ask whether our actions as a society respect or threaten the life and dignity of the human person.

Option for the Poor and Vulnerable   In our world many people are wealthy, while at the same time, many are poor. As Catholics we are called to pay special attention to the needs of those who are poor. We can follow Jesus' example by making a specific effort to defend and promote the dignity of those who are poor and vulnerable and meet their immediate needs.

Solidarity   Because God is our Father, we are all brothers and sisters with the responsibility to care for one another. Solidarity unites rich and poor, weak and strong, and helps build a society that recognizes that we live in an interdependent world.

TOGETHER *as One Parish*

Religious Education with the Parochial School

To nurture parish unity, celebrate Catholic Kids Week in addition to celebrating Catholic Schools Week. Invite both school and religious education to celebrate together with special events. End the week with a special children's liturgy.

📖 *Literature Opportunity*
Say Something
by Peggy Moss
You might wish to read aloud this story of how a young girl witnesses the bullying of children at school. She doesn't get involved, but then realizes that not participating in the bullying is not enough to help others.

✝ **Life and Dignity**

Jesus Sends the Holy Spirit

3-Minute Retreat

Pause for a few moments before preparing for the session. Take three deep breaths. Know that Jesus' love and his great gift of the Holy Spirit are alive and active in you.

Acts of the Apostles 2:2–3

And suddenly there came from the sky a noise like a strong driving wind, and it filled the entire house in which they were. Then there appeared to them tongues as of fire, which parted and came to rest on each one of them.

Reflection

On Pentecost the disciples' fear was blown away as the Holy Spirit entered their lives, filling them with the fire to proclaim Jesus' message. From fearfully hiding together behind locked doors, they proceeded to go out with fervor to speak to the crowds gathered in Jerusalem from every nation. Under the influence of the Holy Spirit, the disciples spoke boldly, and the people heard and understood their message. We share in the same Spirit and the dramatic potential to serve God.

Questions

Am I excited, discouraged, doubtful, or fearful that the Holy Spirit could work through me like the Spirit worked through the disciples? What am I capable of with the help of the Spirit?

Prayer

Pray to the Holy Spirit, using this prayer or one of your own.

Come Holy Spirit, dwell in me. Embolden me by your presence to speak about Jesus and continue his mission with my life.

Knowing and Sharing Your Faith in Session 11

Consider how Scripture and Tradition can deepen your understanding of the session content.

Scripture

Acts of the Apostles 2:1–12 recounts the coming of the Holy Spirit.

Galatians 5:22–23 lists the Fruits of the Holy Spirit.

Tradition

The story of Pentecost in the Acts of the Apostles is only the beginning of the account of the Holy Spirit's presence in the early Church. Peter was filled with the Holy Spirit when he spoke. We encounter Stephen, a man filled with faith and the Holy Spirit as he prepared for his martyrdom. We meet Paul, who was filled with the Holy Spirit after his conversion. We are told that all the disciples were filled with the joy of the Holy Spirit. In the Acts of the Apostles, we learn that the disciples were filled with the Holy Spirit and continued to speak the Word of God with boldness and that with the consolation of the Holy Spirit, the Church grew in numbers. The message is clear: the Holy Spirit is actively involved in the life of the Church and its members.

Catholic Social Teaching

In this session the integrated Catholic Social Teaching theme is **Solidarity.** See page 61b for an explanation of this theme.

Window on the Catechism

The action of the Holy Spirit in the Church is explored in *CCC* 731–741.

General Directory for Catechesis

The Holy Spirit as the "animator" of catechesis is discussed in *GDC* 34 and 288.

One-Hour Session Planner

SESSION 11 Jesus Sends the Holy Spirit

Session Theme: *Jesus sends the Holy Spirit to bring life into the Church.*

Before This Session

▶ Bookmark your Bible to Acts of the Apostles 2:1–12 and Galatians 5:22–23. Place the Bible open to either passage in your prayer center.

▶ Read the Guide for this session, choose any additional If Time Allows activities that you might have time to complete, and gather the listed materials.

Prayer in Session 11

Through a short guided reflection, children invite the Holy Spirit into their hearts by praying the Prayer to the Holy Spirit.

STEPS	APPROXIMATE TIME
Engage *Unit Saint:* Saint Katharine Drexel PAGES 61–62 *Jesus Sends the Holy Spirit* PAGE 63	10 minutes
Explore *A Wind from Heaven* PAGES 64–65 *Art Print: The Doves III* ART PRINT AND PRINT BACK	30–40 minutes
Reflect *Prayer:* Thankful for the Holy Spirit PAGE 66 *The Fruits of the Holy Spirit* PAGE 67	15–20 minutes
Respond *Living My Faith* PAGE 68	5–10 minutes

Materials

REQUIRED

▶ Bible

▶ Art Print 11: *The Doves III* and Children's Book page 237

▶ Fan

▶ CD player

▶ CD 2, Track 7: "Come, O Holy Spirit/ Wa Wa Wa Emimimo" (1:11)

IF TIME ALLOWS

▶ Poster board or heavy paper, magazines, art supplies (page 63)

▶ *The Acts of the Apostles* on VHS or DVD (page 64)

▶ Premade blank bookmarks or card-stock (page 65)

▶ CD 2, Track 7: "Come, O Holy Spirit/Wa Wa Wa Emimimo" (1:11) (page 66)

▶ Session 11 BLM, T-309 (page 67)

▶ Session 11 Assessment, www.findinggod.com (page 68)

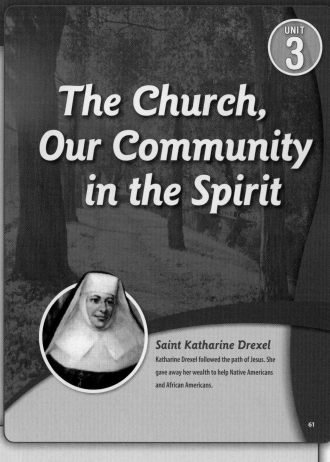

The Church, Our Community in the Spirit

Saint Katharine Drexel

Katharine Drexel followed the path of Jesus. She gave away her wealth to help Native Americans and African Americans.

61

Choose one approach to open the unit.
5-Minute Approach . . . . below
Optional Unit Opener . . . . next page

5-MINUTE APPROACH
Children's Pages

1 Begin

Greet children warmly. Say: **In this unit we will learn more about the Catholic Church and its gifts, as well as about important leaders of the Church.** Write *mission* on the board. Ask: **What is a mission?** (Possible answer: a job or goal to achieve) Say: **In Unit 2 we learned that Jesus sent his apostles and disciples on a mission. What was the mission?** (to proclaim God's Word and continue the work of Jesus Christ) Read aloud the unit title. Say: **Since then, many members of the Church have accepted a mission to continue the work of Jesus Christ through the Holy Spirit.**

2 Introduce the Saint

Point to the picture on page 61. Tell children that Katharine Drexel accepted a mission from the pope to serve the Kingdom of God. Read aloud the text. Say: **People who go to places to help people and tell about God are missionaries.**

Have children turn to page 62. Ask volunteers to read aloud the text. Say: **Katharine continued the work of Jesus Christ through her generosity to Native American and African American people.** Ask: **What group did she organize to help others?** (Sisters of the Blessed Sacrament)

✝ *The Poor and Vulnerable*

Ask: **What is Jesus' mission for you?** (be generous and kind, help and respect others, obey parents, share God's love)

Saint Katharine Drexel

Katharine Drexel was born to a wealthy family in Pennsylvania in 1858. Her parents taught her to use her wealth to help others.

After Katharine's parents died, she traveled around the country. She saw the suffering of the Native Americans and African Americans. She decided to use her fortune to help them.

Katharine asked Pope Leo XIII to send missionaries to help people in need. The pope replied, "Why don't you become a missionary?" She knew the pope was challenging her to do more. She started the Sisters of the Blessed Sacrament.

Mother Katharine Drexel began about 60 schools and missions in the United States. She spent many millions of her own money to help others. Katharine Drexel accepted Jesus' mission by giving up her wealth and following him. Her feast day is March 3.

St. Katharine Drexel,
Robert Lentz, 2012.

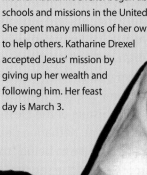

This page describes a program-wide intergenerational event that is offered in a supplemental component.

OPTIONAL UNIT OPENER

Intergenerational Event

1 Prepare

Work with your catechetical leader to use the *Finding God Together* kit to plan an intergenerational event for Unit 3.

2 Open the Event

Gather families in one space. Use *Finding God Together* to open the event and discuss the main theme for Unit 3. Together, enjoy an entertaining skit.

3 Implement the Saint Stations

Use *Finding God Together* to help families learn more about the saints at their grade-level saint stations. Be sure all families feel welcome and are engaged in the process.

4 Close

Gather families in one space for a guided reflection. Use *Finding God Together* to close the event.

5 Transition to Children's Book

When children arrive for the faith formation session, discuss the event and review information about the unit saint. Have children open their books to page 63.

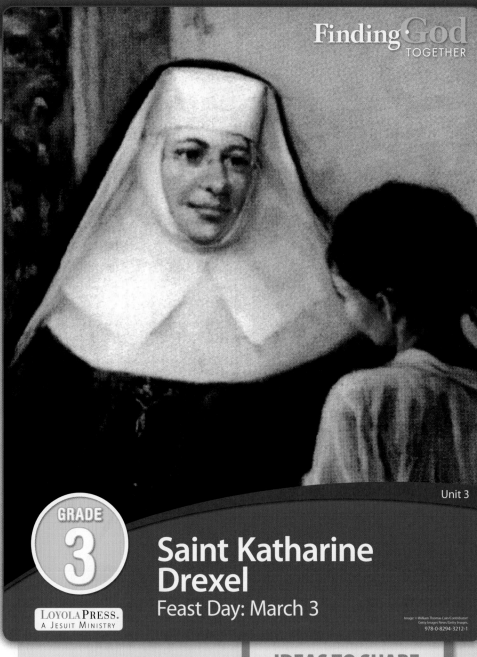

Finding God TOGETHER

Unit 3

GRADE 3

LOYOLAPRESS.
A JESUIT MINISTRY

Saint Katharine Drexel
Feast Day: March 3

Image © William Thomas Cain/Contributor/
Getty Images News/Getty Images
978-0-8294-3212-1

Events Guide

Finding God Together: An Intergenerational Events Guide
by Mary Lynn Hendrickson and Tom McGrath

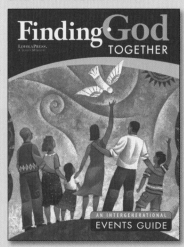

IDEAS TO SHARE

Saint Katharine's Call

In 1885 Pope Leo XIII asked Katharine to become a missionary. In the United States, Katharine started schools for Native American children and helped those who were poor. In 1891 Katharine became the first member of the Sisters of the Blessed Sacrament. Katharine dedicated her life to being "the mother and the servant" of the Native American and African American peoples. She died March 3, 1955. Pope John Paul II canonized her on October 1, 2000.

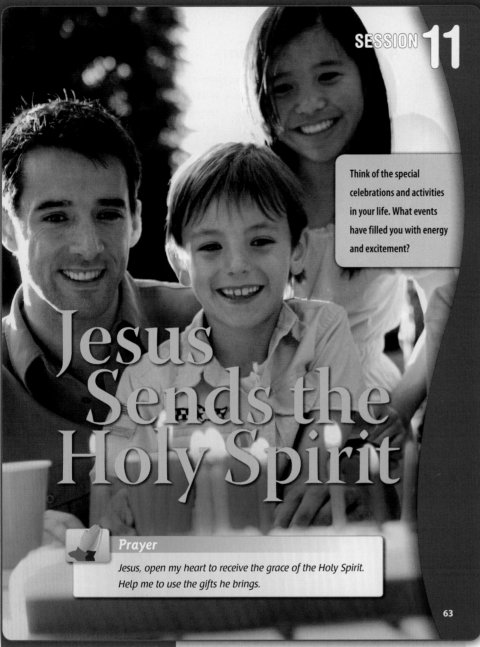

SESSION **11**

Think of the special celebrations and activities in your life. What events have filled you with energy and excitement?

Jesus Sends the Holy Spirit

 Prayer

Jesus, open my heart to receive the grace of the Holy Spirit. Help me to use the gifts he brings.

63

IF TIME ALLOWS

Celebrations

Provide poster board, magazines, scissors, and glue. Have children look for pictures of celebrations. Ask them to look for pictures in which people look happy and excited. Have children arrange the pictures in collages on the poster board. Title their collages *Celebrating with Family and Friends*.

Go to **www.findinggod.com/sessionextenders** to read articles and learn more about Saint Katharine Drexel.

▶ Tell the story of the Holy Spirit coming to the disciples at Pentecost.

▶ Describe how the Holy Spirit helps us live prayerful lives.

▶ Discuss the Fruits of the Holy Spirit.

▶ Define *witness*.

1 Set the Stage

Invite children to use their imaginations. Say: ***Imagine that it is your birthday and that your parents are hosting your birthday party. How do you feel?*** (Possible answers: excited, enthusiastic, loved) Say: ***Think of these words when we read the story today about the disciples and the Holy Spirit.*** Ask: ***What is a disciple?*** (a person who is a follower of Jesus')

2 Get Started

Have children turn to page 63 and read aloud the session title. Point to the picture and emphasize the expressions on the people's faces. Ask: ***How do they feel about this party?*** (Possible answer: excited) Read aloud the text in the blue box, giving children a chance to talk about other events that gave them the same feeling. Say: ***In this session we learn how the disciples were excited when the Holy Spirit visited them.***

Prayer

Ask children to be mindful of Jesus' presence. Say: ***The Holy Spirit came to the disciples to help them. The Spirit helps us too. Pray aloud with me.***

Read aloud the prayer. Then say: ***Open your heart to the Holy Spirit. Pray quietly to Jesus.*** Pause for a few moments while children reflect. Then pray the Sign of the Cross together.

1 Begin

Set up a large fan in front of the group or on a desk and, without preparing the children, turn it on to the highest setting. Leave it on for a few seconds, letting the children feel the strong wind. Then read aloud the heading. Say: **There was a strong wind when the Holy Spirit first visited the disciples.**

✝ Tell children that they will read an adapted version of a story from the Bible. Point out the source line, Acts of the Apostles 2:1–12. Show them the passage in the Bible.

2 Connect

✝ Read aloud the first paragraph. Ask: **How does a strong wind sound?** (Children may imitate a wind sound.) Explain that "tongues of fire" are small flames that represent the enthusiasm with which the disciples were filled. Ask: **Who had come to the disciples?** (the Holy Spirit)

Read aloud the second paragraph. Ask: **Why were people confused?** (They heard a loud noise.) **What amazed the crowd?** (They spoke different languages, but each person could understand everything the disciples said.) Say: **The Holy Spirit was making it possible for the disciples to reach all people with God's message.**

Point to the painting on page 64. Say: **This was painted by a Greek painter, El Greco, around 1600.** Ask: **Who is in this painting?** (Mary, apostles, disciples) **What is above their heads?** (tongues of fire) **What is at the top of the painting?** (a dove) **What do the flames and the dove symbolize?** (the coming of the Holy Spirit)

Ask: **What does the expression "fired up" mean?** (to become excited) Say: **The Holy Spirit got the disciples "fired up" to tell the world about Jesus.**

A Wind from Heaven

After Jesus' life on earth ended, his disciples gathered in Jerusalem during the celebration of Pentecost. Suddenly the sound of a strong wind filled the house. Tongues of fire appeared over each person's head. Jesus' disciples were filled with the Holy Spirit and began to speak in different languages.

Hearing the noise, a crowd gathered and began talking and shouting. They were confused. People from all over the world were there. They spoke many different languages. Yet each heard the disciples' message in his or her own language. They asked one another, "What does this mean?"

adapted from Acts of the Apostles 2:1–12

Pentecost, El Greco.

64   UNIT 3 • *The Church, Our Community in the Spirit*

IF TIME ALLOWS

Message Through Media: The Acts of the Apostles
Have children view *The Acts of the Apostles,* an animated film that tells the story of Pentecost. After the movie, either view the tutorial that is included or review the story.

Accepting Jesus' Mission

The disciples realized that the Holy Spirit had come to them, just as Jesus had promised. They were excited. The Holy Spirit gave them strength to continue Jesus' mission. The disciples were ready to tell people all over the world about Jesus. Each disciple would be a **witness** to Jesus.

The Holy Spirit Builds the Church

At Pentecost the Holy Spirit gave the disciples the strength to continue Jesus' mission. The Holy Spirit began building the Church. Today the Spirit builds the Church through us, filling the Church with life. The power of the Holy Spirit is like the wind—though we cannot see it, we can feel its strength. The Holy Spirit gives us strength to continue Jesus' mission in our lives by being witnesses to him.

Jesus' Mission in Our Lives

Share your ideas about how you can continue Jesus' mission in your life.

_____

_____

_____

_____

Link to Liturgy

The Feast of Pentecost is celebrated seven weeks after Easter Sunday.

GO TO PAGE 237

SESSION 11 • *Jesus Sends the Holy Spirit* 65

IF TIME ALLOWS

Service: Good-News Bookmarks

Have children make bookmarks that spread the Good News. Use pre-made blank bookmarks or cut out strips of cardstock. Have children write messages such as "Jesus Loves You" and include images, such as the tongues of fire, on their bookmarks. Have children bring home their bookmarks to share with a family member or distribute the bookmarks to children in other grades.

 Solidarity

Read aloud the first heading on page 65. Write *witness* on the board and read aloud the paragraph. Ask: **What do witnesses do?** (tell what they see or experience) **What does a witness to Jesus do?** (believes in and tells other people about Jesus; continues Jesus' mission) Say: **Every Christian has a duty to give witness to the Good News about Jesus, which is that he loves us and wants us to love God and one another.**

Point to the photos on the page. Ask: **How are these children being witnesses to Jesus and carrying out his mission?** (Possible answers: helping others, enjoying each other, caring)

Read aloud the second heading and the paragraph. Ask: **How did the Holy Spirit begin building the Church?** (by giving disciples the strength to continue Jesus' mission) **How does the Holy Spirit continue to build the Church today?** (by giving us the strength to be witnesses to Jesus and to spread God's Word)

Read aloud Jesus' Mission in Our Lives and discuss children's answers.

Ask: **How do you see the wind at work?** (Possible answer: It moves our hair and the leaves on trees.) Ask: **How was the Holy Spirit working like the wind?** (The Spirit stirred up the disciples.) Say: **The Holy Spirit is at work in us when we are excited about spreading God's love to others.**

 Link to Liturgy

Read aloud the feature. Say: **On Pentecost Sunday, priests wear red vestments in memory of the tongues of fire at the first Pentecost.**

3 Close

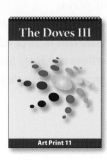
The Doves III
Art Print 11

Display Art Print 11: *The Doves III.* Use the Art Print 11 instruction to teach this section. Art Print teaching instruction can also be found on page 237.

Prayer

Follow the steps to guide children through the prayer on page 66.

Children's Page

Prepare Pray the prayer in advance to become familiar with it.

Pray Ask children to sit quietly and prepare to pray. Say: **We have learned that the Holy Spirit helps us live prayerful lives. We invite the Holy Spirit to stay in our hearts, so our actions reflect the Fruits of the Holy Spirit**.

Remind children that Jesus' disciples were "fired up" by the Holy Spirit. Tell children that *consolation* near the end of the prayer means "comforting." Say: **Let us pray, asking the Spirit to be with us as he was with the disciples. He will help us lead prayerful lives.**

Ask children to fold their hands and sit quietly. Read aloud the heading and the first paragraph. Invite children to pray aloud the prayer with you. When you have finished, read aloud the last sentence. Pause to allow children time to reflect. Then lead them in praying the Sign of the Cross.

Say: **We will sing a song in which we invite the Holy Spirit into our hearts. It is called "Come, O Holy Spirit/ Wa Wa Wa Emimimo,"** [CD 2, Track 7] **and it comes from Nigeria, a country in Africa.** Have children turn to the back of their books for the words to the song. Have children sing along while it plays.

Say: **We have invited the Holy Spirit into our hearts with this prayer. Let's allow the Holy Spirit to guide our actions every day.**

 Prayer

Thankful for the Holy Spirit

People all over the world have prayed this prayer for a very long time. Invite the Holy Spirit into your heart. Think about what you are praying as you say these words.

Prayer to the Holy Spirit

Come, Holy Spirit, fill the hearts of your faithful.
And kindle in them the fire of your love.
Send forth your Spirit and they shall be created.
And you will renew the face of the earth.
Let us pray.

Lord,
by the light of the Holy Spirit
you have taught the hearts of your faithful.
In the same Spirit
help us to relish what is right
and always rejoice in your consolation.
We ask this through Christ our Lord.
Amen.

Now take a few minutes to thank Jesus for sending the Holy Spirit to you.

66 UNIT 3 • *The Church, Our Community in the Spirit*

IF TIME ALLOWS

Come, O Holy Spirit

CD 2, Track 7 In two groups have children sing "Come, O Holy Spirit/Wa Wa Wa Emimimo." One group waves their arms during the words "Wa wa wa" to represent the wind. The second group waves streamers to represent "tongues of fire." Have children repeat the song, one group singing English verses and one group singing the verses in a Nigerian dialect, representing the languages heard at Pentecost.

FYI

Coaching Children to Pray

To prepare children to pray, say: **We are going to pray to the Holy Spirit, opening our hearts to his presence and to his great love for us.**

The Fruits of the Holy Spirit

Just as the Holy Spirit came to the disciples at Pentecost, he also comes to us. The Holy Spirit gives us the help we need to follow Jesus and to serve God and others. When the Spirit guides our actions, we can see the results of the Fruits of the Holy Spirit. The nine fruits are shown below.

Love   Patience   Kindness   Joy   Gentleness

Self-control   Generosity   Faithfulness   Peace

The Spirit in Our Actions

Read each of the Fruits of the Holy Spirit and think about its meaning. Then choose one of them. Write how it can be seen in your actions by finishing this sentence.

The Fruit of __Possible answer: self-control__ can be seen in my

actions when I __cheerfully do chores without complaining__

_____.

Reading God's Word

The Fruits of the Spirit are love, joy, peace, patience, kindness, generosity, faithfulness, gentleness, and self-control. *adapted from Galatians 5:22–23*

SESSION 11 • *Jesus Sends the Holy Spirit* **67**

IF TIME ALLOWS

Session 11 BLM

Holy Spirit in Motion Have children complete the Session 11 Blackline Master [T-309] to make a mobile of a fruit of the Holy Spirit.

Fruits of the Holy Spirit Role-Play

Arrange children into small groups and assign each a fruit of the Holy Spirit. Give them time to plan short skits illustrating actions guided by the Holy Spirit that result in their group's fruit. Have groups make presentations to the class.

---

1 Begin

Ask: **What happens when you rush through math homework?** (Possible answers: You make mistakes; you forget something.) **What happens when you are patient when you're learning a new math concept?** (Possible answer: You understand it better.) Say: **Showing patience results in better understanding.**

2 Connect

Read aloud the heading and the first paragraph. Ask: **What happens when we let the Holy Spirit guide our actions?** (We see the results of the Fruits of the Holy Spirit.) **What does it mean when we say that the Fruits of the Holy Spirit are seen in our actions?** (When we cooperate with the Holy Spirit, one of the fruits is at work.)

Ask volunteers to give examples of the Fruits, such as the fruit of generosity can be seen when clothes are donated to the church clothing drive.

Read aloud the activity The Spirit in Our Actions. Give children time to complete the sentence. Invite them to share their sentences.

Have children sing "Come, O Holy Spirit/Wa Wa Wa Emimimo" [CD 2, Track 7]. Ask them to clap with the beat. Say: **As we echo each verse, we ask the Holy Spirit to enter our hearts.** Play the song again to help children reflect on the power and love of the Holy Spirit.

3 Close

Direct children's attention to the feature at the bottom of page 67.

 Reading God's Word

Read aloud the passage as children follow along. Say: **This is from one of Paul's letters to his friends. He uses the Fruits of the Holy Spirit to explain what their communities could be like if they open themselves to the presence of the Holy Spirit.**

1 Begin

Faith Summary Read aloud this section. Ask: **What happened to the disciples at Pentecost?** (Jesus sent the Holy Spirit to his disciples.) **Who helps us be witnesses to Jesus?** (the Holy Spirit) **When the Holy Spirit guides our actions, what can we see?** (the Fruits of the Holy Spirit)

2 Connect

Word I Learned Ask: **What does witness mean?** (someone who tells others about Jesus) Have volunteers use the word in a sentence.

Ways of Being Like Jesus Read aloud this section. Have children review all of the Fruits of the Holy Spirit.

 Prayer

Ask children to sit quietly for the closing prayer. Say: **Today we learned how important the Holy Spirit was in the early Church and still is in our lives today. Let us thank Jesus for sending us the Holy Spirit.**

Pray aloud the prayer. Say: **Close your eyes and tell Jesus how the Holy Spirit helps you.** Pause for a few moments, and then have children open their eyes. Pray the Sign of the Cross together.

With My Family Ask children to read silently the three suggestions in this section. Invite children to choose one or more to complete at home.

3 Go in Peace

Collect materials and return them to the appropriate places. Encourage children to discuss the With My Family section at home. Say: **When you go home today, bring the peace of the Holy Spirit with you.**

RESPOND

Living My Faith

Faith Summary

On Pentecost Jesus sent the Holy Spirit to help his disciples continue his work. The Holy Spirit gives us strength and helps us to be witnesses to Jesus and to lead prayerful lives. The Fruits of the Holy Spirit can be seen in our actions.

Word I Learned

witness

Ways of Being Like Jesus

Jesus served the Kingdom of God by showing kindness to others. *Be kind to someone who needs a friend by eating together during lunch.*

 Prayer

Jesus, my helper, thank you for sending the Holy Spirit to support me on my journey. Help me to appreciate the presence of the Spirit in my life.

With My Family

Activity Have everyone draw a family member's name from a box. Discuss how that person shows a Fruit of the Holy Spirit.

Faith on the Go Ask one another: *Is it easy for you to be patient? Why or why not?*

Family Prayer *Dear God, help us to see the ways that the Holy Spirit guides us. Grant us patience when dealing with others. Amen.*

68 UNIT 3 • *The Church, Our Community in the Spirit*

IF TIME ALLOWS

Session Assessment Option

An assessment for this session can be found at **www.findinggod.com**.

PLAN AHEAD

Get Ready for Session 12

Consult the catechist preparation pages to prepare for Session 12 and determine any materials you will need.

The Catholic Church

3-Minute Retreat

As you prepare the session, pause for a few quiet moments. Call to mind the sense of community you feel as a member of the Catholic Church. Rest in the love of your Church family.

Matthew 16:18

And so I say to you, you are Peter, and upon this rock I will build my church, and the gates of the netherworld shall not prevail against it.

Reflection

Jesus entrusted the building of the Church to Peter, not because he was a man of superior intellect, wealth, or power, but because Peter's faith and his love of Jesus were as solid as a rock. This strong foundation of faith and love is manifested today in the Marks of the Church: one, holy, catholic, and apostolic. Today the successors of the apostles—the pope and the bishops—lead the Church. The Church finds its strength in the faith and love of Jesus.

Questions

What can I do to have a deeper faith in Jesus? How does my life show my love of Jesus?

Prayer

Pray to Jesus, using these words or your own.
Jesus, you know the depths of my being. You know that sometimes I am not a rock of faith. When I falter or weaken like sand or mud, shape me and strengthen me with your love.

Knowing and Sharing Your Faith in Session 12

Consider how Scripture and Tradition can deepen your understanding of the session content.

Scripture

Matthew 16:18–19 shows us how Jesus gives Peter authority to head the Church.

John 21:17 tells us how Jesus entrusts the care of his sheep, his followers, to Peter.

Tradition

The twelve apostles have occupied a special place in the Church because Jesus gave them a mission of leadership. Throughout its history the apostles' successors—the bishops—led the Church. A bishop is the head of a local diocese, both as a delegate of the pope and, more importantly, as a representative of Christ's. The successor of Peter, leader of the apostles, is the pope, the bishop of Rome. The pope exercises universal authority over the whole Church and is guided by the Holy Spirit. Priests assist bishops by leading parishes. Religious men and women and laypeople also exercise leadership at many levels of the Church.

Catholic Social Teaching

In this session the integrated Catholic Social Teaching themes are **Call to Family, Community, and Participation** and **Solidarity.** See page 61b for an explanation of these themes.

Window on the Catechism

The role and relationship of the apostles and bishops and Peter and the pope are explored in *CCC* 858–862 and 880–886.

General Directory for Catechesis

As catechists we participate in the apostolic mission of the Church. The role of catechists in this apostolic tradition is discussed in *GDC* 43.

One-Hour Session Planner

SESSION 12 The Catholic Church

Session Theme: *Jesus gives us leaders in the Church.*

Before This Session

▶ Bookmark your Bible to Matthew 16:18–19 and John 21:17. Place the Bible open to either of these passages in your prayer center.

▶ Display the *Finding God* poster Apostles' Creed.

▶ Read the Guide for this session, choose any additional If Time Allows activities that you might have time to complete, and gather the listed materials.

> ### Prayer in Session 12
>
> In this session children pray prayers of petition and gratitude and learn the last part of the Apostles' Creed, expressing belief in the basic teachings of the faith.

STEPS	APPROXIMATE TIME
Engage ***The Catholic Church*** PAGE 69	10 minutes
Explore ***Serving the World in God's Name*** PAGE 70 ***Our Holy Catholic Church*** PAGE 71 ***Art Print:*** *Saint Peter* ART PRINT AND PRINT BACK	30–40 minutes
Reflect ***Prayer:*** We Believe PAGE 72 ***Who Am I?*** PAGE 73	15–20 minutes
Respond ***Living My Faith*** PAGE 74	5–10 minutes

Materials

REQUIRED

▶ Bible

▶ Art Print 12: *Saint Peter* and Children's Book page 238

▶ Art supplies

▶ *Finding God* poster: Apostles' Creed

▶ CD player

▶ CD 2, Tracks 17 and 18: "Reflective Music"

▶ CD 2, Track 2: "Song of Love" (Instrumental)

IF TIME ALLOWS

▶ Computer and parish Web site (page 69)

▶ Session 12 BLM, T-310 (page 70)

▶ Parish bulletins (page 70)

▶ My Creed papers (page 72)

▶ Construction paper (page 72)

▶ Art supplies (page 72)

▶ Session 12 Assessment, www.findinggod.com (page 74)

SESSION **12**

Think about the community where you live. Then think about your church. How would you describe your church community?

The Catholic Church

Prayer

Jesus, my Savior, show me how to follow you. I want to grow closer to you.

69

IF TIME ALLOWS

Inclusion: Communication

My Church Community Children who lack communication skills may be more comfortable learning new information through computers. Provide these children access to your parish Web site. Invite children to gather around the computer and search the site. Suggest that children look for information about people who help at the parish. Point out the different ministries and events at the church.

Job Descriptions for Your Church Community

Have children work in small groups to think of things to do in your church community. Then have them write "job descriptions" for those opportunities. Examples could include someone in charge of a food drive or a gardener for the church grounds.

Go to **www.findinggod.com/sessionextenders** to learn more about the Marks of the Church. You will find articles that will give you information on these important qualities.

SESSION 12

OUTCOMES

▶ Identify Peter as Jesus' appointed leader of the Church.

▶ Identify the Marks of the Church: one, holy, catholic, and apostolic.

▶ Pray the last part of the Apostles' Creed.

▶ Define *apostolic, Marks of the Church, Mystical Body of Christ, one, pastor,* and *Vicar of Christ.*

1 Set the Stage

Play the instrumental "Song of Love" [CD 2, Track 2] as children settle in. Ask volunteers to name people who have important roles in their community, such as crossing guards, teachers, and mayors. Say: **Now we will learn about the Catholic Church and its leaders.**

2 Get Started

Have children turn to page 69 and read aloud the session title. Point to the picture. Ask: **What is this family doing?** (praying) Say: **This family and others at church gather and pray as one group. Remember, you are a member of both the community you live in and the Catholic Church, your church community.** Read aloud the text in the blue box, giving children a chance to discuss their answers.

Say: **In this session we will learn that church is not just a building. The word Church describes our community as we gather to pray and praise God.**

 Prayer

Invite children to quiet their thoughts and pray aloud the prayer with you. Say: **Remember, you can ask Jesus for help whenever you need it.** Pause and then lead children in praying *Amen.*

1 Begin

Ask: *How many of you play a team sport, such as soccer? Does the team have a coach?* Say: *The coach helps train and support the team. A coach serves the team by acting as their leader.* Read the heading to children. Say: *It takes many people to lead the Church. Now let's read about today's leaders of the Church.*

2 Connect

Read aloud the first heading and paragraph. Say: *A vicar is someone who represents another person.* Ask: *Who leads the whole Church?* (pope) *Whom does the pope represent?* (Jesus Christ) *What is another title we give him?* (Vicar of Christ) Say: *The Vicar of Christ is the person who represents Jesus Christ on earth. The pope speaks for Jesus.* Ask: *Who is the leader of the parish?* (pastor) Ask: *Who appoints the pastor to your parish?* (bishop)

Have a volunteer read aloud the activity Leading the Church. Ask: *Does anyone know the name of our pastor? our bishop? the pope?* If children do not know the names of the leaders, write them on the board. Have children work in pairs to match the names with the titles on the page. Give children a few minutes to complete the activity. When children are finished, review their answers.

3 Close

Direct children's attention to the feature at the bottom of page 70.

Reading God's Word

Read aloud the passage. Say: *Jesus is the Good Shepherd, a shepherd of people. What do the sheep symbolize?* (Possible answers: people, followers of Jesus) Ask: *Why did Jesus tell Peter to feed his sheep?* (He wanted Peter to take care of his followers.) *How did Peter answer Jesus' call?* (He led the Church.)

70 www.findinggod.com

Serving the World in God's Name

The Church is the sign that we are one with the Father, Son, and Holy Spirit. Jesus chose Peter and the other apostles to lead the Church. Today the pope, who is the **Vicar of Christ,** leads the whole Church. The bishops, the successors to the apostles, teach, guide, and lead the Church. They appoint **pastors** to lead each parish. These leaders serve the Church by helping us grow in our faith.

Leading the Church

Write the name of your parish. Then write the names of your church leaders. Ask for help if you need it.

My Parish _____

Pastor _____

Bishop _____

Pope _____

Reading God's Word

Jesus asked Peter for the third time, "Do you love me?" Peter was hurt that Jesus had asked him three times. He said to Jesus, "Lord, you know everything. You know that I love you." Jesus answered, "Feed my sheep."

adapted from John 21:17

70 UNIT 3 • The Church, Our Community in the Spirit

IF TIME ALLOWS

Session 12 BLM

A Church News Flash Have children complete the Session 12 Blackline Master [T-310] to write stories about people they admire in their Church community.

✝ *Family and Community*

Parish Bulletin

Distribute copies of your parish bulletin. Point out the names of the parish leaders and greetings the pastor may have included. Have children look for ways parish leaders are helping the Church care for others. Then have children look for ways they can become involved.

Our Holy Catholic Church

The Church can be seen on earth and felt in our hearts. This is why we call the Church the **Mystical Body of Christ.** The Church has four important qualities, or marks:

✝ The Church is **one.** We have one Lord, and we share one faith. We receive one life in the Holy Spirit.

✝ The Church is holy. The Father, Son, and Holy Spirit are holy. In the sacraments, we receive all we need to make us holy.

✝ The Church is catholic. *Catholic* means "universal." Jesus told the apostles to teach all nations. The Church reaches out to all.

✝ The Church is **apostolic.** Jesus founded the Church with the apostles. The pope and bishops continue their mission today.

The Church is one, holy, catholic, and apostolic. These are the **Marks of the Church.**

 Link to Liturgy

At Mass we pray for the Church and for our leaders, the pope and our bishop, during the Eucharistic Prayer. Listen for the names of your church leaders during this prayer.

GO TO PAGE 238

SESSION 12 • *The Catholic Church* **71**

IF TIME ALLOWS

Service: Letters to the Pastor

Have children write individual letters to their pastor, encouraging him in his ministry to their Church community. Children can offer prayers for the pastor as he works in the parish. Ask your catechetical leader if the pastor can visit your class to receive the letters.

 Solidarity

1 Begin

Have children form a circle around one child while holding a string. Say: ***Just as the children who are holding the string, the Mystical Body of Christ is the spiritual body formed by members of the Church who are bound together through the sacraments. Just as our friend stands in the center, Jesus Christ is the center and source of the life of this body.***

2 Connect

Read aloud the heading and the first paragraph. Then have volunteers read aloud the next four paragraphs.

Write *one, holy, catholic,* and *apostolic* on the board. Say: ***Name some keywords for each of the Marks.*** (Possible answers: one—one faith, one life; holy—Body of Christ, sacraments; catholic—accepts everyone, universal; apostolic—apostles, Church leaders)

Read aloud the last paragraph. Say: ***A church is a holy place where people worship, but the Catholic Church is also a spiritual body united in Christ.***

 Link to Liturgy

Obtain the Prayer of the Faithful used at a previous Mass. Make a copy for each child. Then read aloud this feature. Say: ***We pray for the Church, its leaders, and others during the Prayer of the Faithful at Mass. Let's read the Prayer of the Faithful from a recent Mass.*** Read aloud the intercessions from the Prayer of the Faithful and have children respond: ***Lord, hear our prayer.***

3 Close

Display Art Print 12: *Saint Peter.* Use the Art Print 12 instruction to teach this section. Art Print teaching instruction can also be found on page 238.

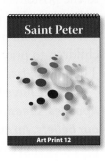

Prayer

Follow the steps to guide children through the prayer on page 72.

Children's Page

Prepare Pray the prayer in advance to become familiar with it. Display the *Finding God* Apostles' Creed poster.

Pray Remind children that they have been learning the parts of the Apostles' Creed. Read aloud the first paragraph. Point out that they have learned the parts of the Creed that express belief in God the Father and in Jesus Christ, his only Son. Explain that the section they are about to pray refers to the Holy Spirit and the truths of our faith.

Say: ***Now we're going to learn the last part of the Apostles' Creed together. Repeat each line after me.*** Read aloud each of the closing lines of the Creed and have children repeat them together.

If you wish, play the reflective music at the end of CD 2. Say: ***Let us prepare to tell God what we believe.*** Point out how the wind is blowing the wheat in the picture on page 72. Say: ***This is a reminder of how the Holy Spirit first appeared to the disciples.*** Ask children to be calm and prayerful as they fold their hands.

Say: ***Now we will pray together our words of belief. Then we will pause to reflect on our beliefs and ask Jesus for help.*** Invite children to pray the entire Creed with you. Refer them to the poster.

Read the last paragraph, pausing after each sentence. Allow time for children to pray and talk to Jesus. Then pray *Amen*.

Say: ***We have learned the entire Apostles' Creed, in which we proclaim our beliefs. An even better way to show that we believe is to live like Jesus every day.***

Prayer

We Believe

This last part of the Apostles' Creed states more of our beliefs. Think about them as you pray.

I believe in the Holy Spirit,
the holy catholic Church,
the communion of saints,
the forgiveness of sins,
the resurrection of the body,
and life everlasting. Amen.

Jesus knows what is in your heart. Be still with him for a few moments. Tell him that you believe. Ask him to strengthen your belief.

IF TIME ALLOWS

My Creed

If you have done the Creed papers as an activity, return the papers to children. Have them write the rest of the prayer. They can decorate their papers or make construction-paper covers. Say: ***Take the Creed home and learn it by heart.***

Draw While You Pray

Distribute drawing paper and crayons or colored pencils. Invite children to draw what they feel as you slowly and reverently pray aloud the Apostles' Creed a few times and play reflective music.

FYI

Coaching Children to Pray

Help children prepare for prayer by focusing on the Holy Spirit and asking for his strength and guidance.

Who Am I?

There are many helpers to guide us as we grow in faith and love as Christians. Choose a word below to answer each question.

> Holy Spirit   pope   pastor   Jesus Christ   Mary   bishop

1. I am the mother of Jesus. I love him, and I love you.

   Who am I? _____**Mary**_____

2. I came to Jesus' followers on Pentecost. I bring life to the

   Church. Who am I? _____**Holy Spirit**_____

3. I am a leader of the Church. I watch over many parishes.

   Who am I? _____**bishop**_____

4. I am the leader of a parish. I help the people in my parish

   grow closer to God. Who am I? _____**pastor**_____

5. I am the leader of the Catholic Church today. I am the

   Vicar of Christ. Who am I? _____**pope**_____

6. I give myself to my followers in the celebration of the

   sacraments. Who am I? _____**Jesus Christ**_____

Now write the name of someone who is a special helper to you in becoming a better Christian and describe how that person helps you.

_____

_____

_____

SESSION 12 • *The Catholic Church*   **73**

IF TIME ALLOWS

Give Me a Clue

Distribute paper and pencils. Have children write "What Am I?" questions, such as *I include the saints in heaven and holy people on earth. What am I?* The answer is the Communion of Saints. Invite volunteers to read their questions to the group and see if other children can answer them.

1 Begin

Play a 20-questions game with the class. Choose someone that children will recognize as your subject, such as the president or someone recently in the news, and write his or her name on a slip of paper to show the class later. After children identify the person, say: *We just played a guessing game trying to identify someone familiar. Now we will practice identifying helpers of Jesus.*

2 Connect

Read aloud the heading and the first paragraph. Say: *We're going to do the activity on this page, but first see if you can answer this question: Jesus chose me to be the first leader of the Church. Who am I?* (Peter)

When children have finished the activity, ask volunteers to read aloud the sentences with the answers so that children can check their work. Read aloud the directions at the bottom of the page. Give children a few moments to write the names of their special helpers. Have volunteers share their answers with the class.

3 Close

Take this time to play "Song of Love" [CD 2, Track 1]. Invite children to sing along. Remind them that the words are in the back of their books. Continue playing the song in the background as children work on any optional activities.

1 Begin

Faith Summary Read aloud this section. Say: ***Jesus chose Peter to lead the Church. Who leads the Church today?*** (pope) ***Who helps the pope, as the apostles helped Peter?*** (bishops and pastors)

2 Connect

Words I Learned Ask volunteers to define *apostolic*, *Mystical Body of Christ*, *one*, *pastor*, and *Vicar of Christ*. Ask children to list and explain each Mark of the Church. Have children look up each word in the Glossary.

Ways of Being Like Jesus Read aloud this section. Ask: ***What are ways to be active in your parish community?*** (support fundraisers; join the children's choir; pray for people in the parish) ***How can you spread God's love?*** (put the above suggestions into action)

✝ *Family and Community*

 Prayer

Say: ***We learned that we are all part of the Church community. Let's thank Jesus for his gift of the Church. Fold your hands and pray aloud with me.*** Pray the prayer. Say: ***Take time to thank Jesus for whatever you would like.*** Pause, then ask children to open their eyes and pray *Amen*.

With My Family Ask children to read silently the three suggestions in this section. Invite children to choose one or more to complete at home.

3 Go in Peace

Collect materials and return them to the appropriate places. Encourage children to discuss the With My Family section at home. Say: ***This week pray the Apostles' Creed often to learn it by heart. Ask someone in your family to help you.***

Living My Faith

Faith Summary

Jesus chose Peter and the apostles to be the leaders of the Church. The bishops and pastors, with the pope as their head, are today's leaders. The Church is one, holy, catholic, and apostolic.

Words I Learned
apostolic
Marks of the Church
Mystical Body of Christ
one
pastor
Vicar of Christ

Ways of Being Like Jesus
Jesus asked the disciples to spread God's love through the Church. *Take part in parish activities to spread God's love in your church community.*

 Prayer

Jesus, thank you for calling me to your Church. Support me as I follow the example of my church leaders to serve others.

With My Family

Activity As a family talk about ways you can be active in your parish community. Then choose a parish event or service project in which to participate.

Faith on the Go Ask one another: *How can we support our church leaders?*

Family Prayer *Dear God, thank you for the gift of your Church. Lead us in being a part of our parish community. Amen.*

IF TIME ALLOWS

Word Race

To review the new words in this session—*apostolic, Marks of the Church, Mystical Body of Christ, one, pastor,* and *Vicar of Christ*—play a game. As you name each word, have children race to see who can find each one in the Glossary first. The child who wins gets to read the definition.

Session Assessment Option

An assessment for this session can be found at **www.findinggod.com.**

PLAN AHEAD

Get Ready for Session 13

Consult the catechist preparation pages to prepare for Session 13 and determine any materials you will need.

The Church Prays

3-Minute Retreat

As you prepare the session, pause for a few quiet moments. Take three deep breaths and think of the comfort you receive through Jesus' presence at Mass and in your daily life.

> *Luke 7:7*
>
> *Therefore, I did not consider myself worthy to come to you; but say the word and let my servant be healed.*

Reflection

"Seeing is believing" is certainly not the credo for the Roman officer in this story. He knows that Jesus has the ability to act, regardless of time or space. He sees the power of the Word of Jesus and has faith in him. As Jesus overcame physical distance to heal the Roman officer's servant, he also reaches out to touch our lives. In the sacramental life of the Church, especially in the Eucharist, Jesus is present to help us grow in faith. Nurtured by the sacraments, our lives become one way that Jesus reaches out and is present to others.

Questions

What do I need to ask Jesus to heal today? How can I intercede on behalf of the needs of others?

Prayer

Pray to Jesus, using these words or your own.
Jesus, healer and giver of life, let your Word heal me and your sacraments strengthen me so that I can be a sign of your love in the world today.

Knowing and Sharing Your Faith in Session 13

Consider how Scripture and Tradition can deepen your understanding of the session content.

Scripture

Luke 7:1–10 tells the story of how Jesus praises the faith of the Roman officer and cures his servant.

Luke 17:20–21 tells the story of how Jesus informs the Pharisees that the Kingdom of God is already here.

Tradition

In each of the sacraments, Jesus reaches out to touch our lives. He touches us with new life in Baptism, with forgiveness in Penance, with love in Matrimony, and with nourishment in the Eucharist. The sacraments are essential ways in which the Church is built up. Baptism, Confirmation, and the Eucharist provide the Church with new members who are dedicated to the task of serving the Church and the world. Holy Orders and Matrimony fill the Church with members who are dedicated to love and service to the community. Penance and Anointing of the Sick enable the Church to grow by helping to keep its members spiritually healthy.

Catholic Social Teaching

In this session the integrated Catholic Social Teaching theme is **Life and Dignity of the Human Person.** See page 61b for an explanation of this theme.

Window on the Catechism

Specific information on the sacraments as worship is discussed in *CCC* 1123; the sacraments and Jesus, in *CCC* 947, 1088, 1097; and the sacraments and the Church, in *CCC* 798, 1118.

General Directory for Catechesis

Through the sacraments Jesus reaches out to touch our lives. The role of the sacraments in revealing God's plan is explored in *GDC* 45.

One-Hour Session Planner

SESSION 13 The Church Prays

Session Theme: *Jesus Christ is especially present in the celebration of the sacraments.*

Before This Session

▶ Provide a wrapped gift box to show during the Reflect step. Put a small gift inside for each child, such as wrapped candy, a sticker, or a prayer.

▶ Contact your church's pastor and arrange a visit for him to speak to your class about the sacraments.

▶ Bookmark your Bible to Luke 7:1–10 and Luke 17:20–21. Place the Bible open to either of these passages in your prayer center.

▶ Read the Guide for this session, choose any additional If Time Allows activities that you might have time to complete, and gather the listed materials.

STEPS	APPROXIMATE TIME
Engage *The Church Prays* PAGE 75	10 minutes
Explore *Jesus Is Present in the Sacraments* PAGE 76 *Signs of Grace* PAGE 77 *Art Print:* The Centurion Kneeling ART PRINT AND PRINT BACK	30–40 minutes
Reflect *Prayer:* Thanking Jesus for the Sacraments PAGE 78 *Gifts from God* PAGE 79	15–20 minutes
Respond *Living My Faith* PAGE 80	5–10 minutes

Materials

REQUIRED

▶ Bible

▶ Art Print 13: *The Centurion Kneeling* and Children's Book page 239

▶ Small gift-wrapped box with gifts inside

▶ Sacramentals, such as a cross, rosary, and medal

▶ CD player

▶ CD 1, Track 8: "Faith in Jesus" (9:15)

▶ Pictures of signs, such as a poison sign or railroad sign

IF TIME ALLOWS

▶ Art supplies, construction paper (page 75)

▶ Session 13 BLM, T-311 (page 76)

▶ Large cardboard boxes (page 77)

▶ Session 13 Assessment, www.findinggod.com (page 80)

Prayer in Session 13

In this session children reflect on the story of Jesus' healing of the Roman officer's servant. They pray silently, relating the Scripture story to their personal prayers. A special approach to prayer is an extended guided reflection titled "Faith in Jesus" [CD 1, Track 8]. As you prepare for the session, listen to the recorded guided reflection as a prayerful experience for yourself. When you play the recording for children, join them in reflective prayer. If you choose to lead the guided reflection yourself, listen to the recording a second time, following the script [pages T-286–T-287]. You can use the script or adapt it. An alternative approach is to use the Prayer on the children's page.

SESSION **13**

Signs of God are all around us. What signs do you see? What do they tell you about God?

The Church Prays

Prayer

Jesus, Lord, help me to be aware of your presence in the sacraments. Help me to grow in my love of God.

75

IF TIME ALLOWS

A Gift of Love

Distribute construction paper and crayons. Say: ***Jesus' gift of the sacraments is a gift of love.*** Ask children to write a thank-you note to Jesus for his gift of the sacraments they have already received. Have them fold a sheet of construction paper in half. Have children illustrate the covers and write their notes inside.

➤ Go to **www.findinggod.com/sessionextenders** to participate in a 3-minute retreat about the sacraments.

SESSION 13
OUTCOMES

▶ Describe how Jesus is present in the Mass and the sacraments.

▶ Identify sacramentals as signs that help us grow in faith.

▶ Tell the story of Jesus healing the Roman officer's servant.

▶ Define *blessing* and *sacramental*.

1 Set the Stage

Show children pictures of signs they might see, such as a railroad crossing or poison sign. Choose signs that do not have words on them. Invite children to guess the meaning of each sign. Say: ***These signs catch our attention. They give us directions and protect us.***

2 Get Started

Read aloud the session title and point to the stop signs in the picture. Ask: ***What does a stop sign tell us?*** (Possible answer: You need to stop.) Ask a volunteer to read aloud the text in the blue box. Discuss children's answers to the questions. Say: ***Like the stop sign, God's signs give direction and send important messages to us. Jesus loves us so much that he gives us special signs. In this session we will learn about those signs. We'll also learn about gifts that we receive that are signs too. What messages do signs and gifts send us?*** (Possible answer: The giver loves us and wants us to be happy.)

Prayer

Invite children to quiet their minds for prayer. Say: ***As we pray, think of how blessed we are when we receive the sacraments.*** Pray together the prayer. Say: ***Now thank Jesus for the sacraments you have received.*** Pause and pray *Amen*.

1 Begin

Ask: **When you go to Mass, who is there with you?** (Possible answers: my family, friends, the priest) **Do you think Jesus is with you at Mass?** Discuss children's responses.

2 Connect

Read aloud the heading. Say: **Jesus reaches out to us, and he works through us to help others. Let's read and find out how Jesus is always with us.**

Read aloud the first paragraph. Write the word *Mass* on the board. Say: **Help me list ways Jesus is present to us at Mass.** Record children's answers. Elicit responses, such as through the priest, the people, the Scriptures, and the Eucharist.

Have a volunteer read aloud the second paragraph. Ask: **What do the sacraments do for us?** (They help us grow in faith and live as God wants.) Have a brief discussion about the sacraments.

Ask: **Which sacraments have you celebrated?** (Baptism, Reconciliation, and the Eucharist) Ask: **How many other sacraments can you name?** (Confirmation, Anointing of the Sick, Matrimony, Holy Orders) Write all the sacraments on the board.

Have children look at the picture at the top of the page. Ask: **What is happening here?** (A child is receiving Holy Communion, the Sacrament of the Eucharist.)

Ask children to think about the day they celebrated Holy Communion for the first time. Focus the discussion on how they felt that day.

Have a volunteer read aloud the directions for the activity. Give children time to complete it.

3 Close

After children have completed writing their thoughts about their Holy Communion, have volunteers share what they wrote.

Jesus Is Present in the Sacraments

Jesus reaches out to be with us at Mass. He is present in the priest, in the people gathered, and in the Scriptures. Jesus Christ is especially present in the Eucharist.

Jesus Christ also reaches out to us through all the sacraments. They help us grow in faith and live as God wants us to. Through the Holy Spirit, Jesus Christ is present to us in the sacraments.

My First Holy Communion

Think back to when you celebrated your First Holy Communion. How does receiving Holy Communion feel during Mass now? How does this sacrament help you grow in faith? On the lines below, write your thoughts about the sacrament.

The first time I celebrated Holy Communion,

I felt _____

_____.

This sacrament helps me grow in faith by

_____

_____.

IF TIME ALLOWS

Session 13 BLM

Jesus Is Present Have children complete the Session 13 Blackline Master [T-311] to write and draw pictures about ways Jesus is present at Mass.

A Visit from the Pastor

Arrange for your pastor to visit your class. Before he arrives, ask children to think of questions they would like to ask him about the sacraments. Prompt children to include questions about sacraments they may not know much about. After the pastor's visit, ask children to share their thoughts about what they learned from the pastor.

Signs of Grace

The sacraments are outward signs of the grace we receive from God. We are immersed in water or have it poured on us as a sign of Baptism. Bread and wine are signs of the Eucharist.

The Church gives us other signs, called **sacramentals.** They are not sacraments, but they help us grow in faith. Sacramentals can be objects, such as crosses or holy water. They can also be actions or a prayer, such as the **blessing** of a person or place.

A Sacramental at Your House

Describe a sacramental that you have at home. How does it help you grow in your faith?

_____

_____

_____

_____

_____

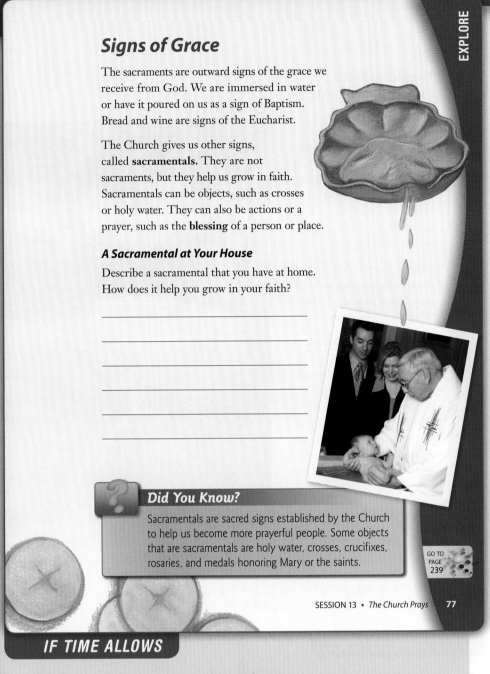

Did You Know?

Sacramentals are sacred signs established by the Church to help us become more prayerful people. Some objects that are sacramentals are holy water, crosses, crucifixes, rosaries, and medals honoring Mary or the saints.

GO TO PAGE 239

IF TIME ALLOWS

Service: Sacramentals for Others

Have children decorate collection boxes for sacramentals. Arrange with your catechetical leader to place the boxes around your parish for collection. Have children empty the boxes periodically. Send the donations to a charitable Catholic organization, to a diocese that has recently had a natural disaster, or to residents at a Catholic nursing home.

✝ *Life and Dignity*

---

1 Begin

Display examples of sacramentals, such as a rosary and a saint's medal. Ask children to name each item. Say: ***Now we will learn another word for these items and how each can deepen our faith.***

2 Connect

Read aloud the heading and the first paragraph. Ask: ***What are the sacraments outward signs of?*** (grace) ***What is grace?*** (the gift of God that fills us with God's life and makes us his friends) ***What is a sign of Baptism?*** (water) ***What are the signs of the Eucharist?*** (bread and wine)

Read aloud the next paragraph. Invite a volunteer to read aloud the definition of *sacramental* from the Glossary. Say: ***Name some sacramentals that help us grow in faith.*** (Possible answers: rosary, cross, medal)

Write *blessing* on the board. Ask: ***Both objects and actions can be sacramentals. What action is a sacramental?*** (a blessing) Say: ***A blessing is a prayer that calls upon God to care for a person, a place, a thing, or an activity. The priest gives us a blessing at the end of Mass.***

Read aloud A Sacramental at Your House and have children write their descriptions. Discuss their responses.

Did You Know?

Read aloud the information on sacramentals. Say: ***Sacramentals help prepare us to receive the grace of the sacraments.***

3 Close

Display Art Print 13: *The Centurion Kneeling.* Use the Art Print 13 instruction to teach this section. Art Print teaching instruction can also be found on page 239.

Prayer

Choose an approach and pray with the children.

APPROACH 1

Recorded Guided Reflection

 Prepare Listen in advance to the recorded guided reflection "Faith in Jesus" [CD 1, Track 8]. Decide if you will use the recording or lead the reflection yourself. If you choose to lead, listen to the recording a second time, following the script [pages T-286–T-287] and noting pauses and tone. You can then use the script or adapt it as you wish.

Pray During the session, play the recording or lead using the script, joining the children in reflective prayer. If you use the script, play reflective music softly in the background.

Children's Page

Prepare Pray the prayer on page 78 in advance to become familiar with it.

Pray Invite children to be quiet. Say: *Find a comfortable position. Relax your neck, shoulders, arms, and legs. Close your eyes, and take three deep breaths.* Pause while children do this. Say: *Now we are ready to begin.*

Read aloud the first and second paragraphs in a reverent tone, pausing after the questions.

Read aloud the last paragraph. Then say: *Now take a few moments to talk to Jesus.* Pause so that children have time to talk to Jesus. Then lead children in praying the Sign of the Cross. Say: *Jesus reaches out to others through us. Whenever we act as Jesus would, he is working through us. Let's talk about ways we can show that Jesus is working through us.* Discuss children's ideas.

Prayer

Thanking Jesus for the Sacraments

Think about the day Jesus healed the Roman officer's servant. Imagine that you are with the people following Jesus that day. You watch and listen as men approach Jesus and speak to him. What are they saying to him? What are the people around you saying?

Imagine Jesus turning toward you after he hears the officer's reply. What does he tell you? What do you say to Jesus?

Now spend a few moments with Jesus. Ask him to strengthen your faith through the sacraments. Thank him for his presence in the sacraments. Thank him for caring for you. Tell him how you will help him to care for others. Ask Jesus to help you remember he is always with you.

78 UNIT 3 • *The Church, Our Community in the Spirit*

IF TIME ALLOWS

Pray Again

If you used the recorded guided reflection, you might use this prayer page during another session.

FYI

Coaching Children to Pray

Give children sufficient time to reflect and converse with Jesus. As they become more comfortable with reflection, they may want more time to tell Jesus what's in their hearts and on their minds.

Gifts from God

God has given us many special gifts. Finish each sentence and fill in the puzzle with the missing words. Then unscramble the circled letters to find another special gift from God. Write that word in the sentence next to the puzzle.

1. Sacramentals help us grow in _____ faith _____.

2. At Mass Jesus is _____ present _____ in the priest, in the people, and in the Scriptures.

3. The _____ blessing _____ of a person or place is one type of sacramental.

4. Bread and wine are signs of the _____ Eucharist _____.

5. A _____ sacrament _____ is an outward sign of the grace we receive from God.

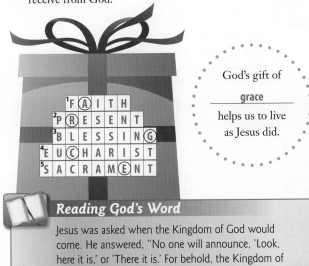

God's gift of

_____ grace _____

helps us to live as Jesus did.

 Reading God's Word

Jesus was asked when the Kingdom of God would come. He answered, "No one will announce, 'Look, here it is,' or 'There it is.' For behold, the Kingdom of God is among you." *adapted from Luke 17:20–21*

SESSION 13 • *The Church Prays*   79

IF TIME ALLOWS

Sacramental Treasure Hunt

Distribute writing paper and pencils. Tell children that they will be hunting for sacramentals. Review some examples, such as the Bible, blessings, statues, and rosary, and write them on the board. Say: **When you go home today, see how many you can find.** Tell children to write in what room they find the sacramentals. Encourage children to ask their families to help in the search.

---

❶ Begin

Show children a gift-wrapped box. Ask: **How do you feel when you give or receive a gift?** (Possible answers: excited, curious) **Why do we give gifts?** (Possible answer: for special occasions) **How do you respond when you receive a gift?** (thank the giver) Have a volunteer open the gift. Make sure the package contains something that can be shared, such as wrapped candy or stickers. Say: **Jesus loves us so much that he gives us special gifts. Now we will learn about those gifts.**

❷ Connect

Read aloud the heading. Say: **This is an activity that reminds us of God's many gifts.**

Ask a volunteer to read aloud the first paragraph. Have children complete the sentences independently and fill in the puzzle, but tell them not to fill in the last sentence because they will discuss and answer it together as a group. Walk among children as they work and answer their questions.

When children have finished, check their answers. Then ask volunteers to tell which letters are circled in the boxes. Write the letters on the board. Have children unscramble the letters to complete the last sentence. Ask a volunteer to read aloud the final sentence.

❸ Close

Direct children's attention to the feature at the bottom of page 79.

 Reading God's Word

Say: **Jesus tells us that the Kingdom of God is not just something for the future. The kingdom is now.** Ask a volunteer to read aloud this passage. Ask: **What does Jesus' answer mean to you?** (Possible answer: When we are helping people, Jesus is working through us. The Kingdom of God is among us.)

1 Begin

Faith Summary Read aloud this section. Ask: **Through the Holy Spirit, who is present in the sacraments?** (Jesus) **What are signs of grace, such as blessings or a rosary, called?** (sacramentals)

2 Connect

Words I Learned Read aloud the words. Ask: **What are some examples of special blessings?** (Possible answers: blessing of animals, homes, food baskets at Easter) Review examples of sacramentals. Have children look up the words in the Glossary.

Ways of Being Like Jesus Read aloud this section. Ask children to suggest acts of helping and kindness that they can do, such as being helpful to all children at school and helping others that have difficulty with homework.

Prayer

Ask children to quiet themselves. Say: **Today we learned about Jesus' wonderful gift of the sacraments. Let us pray a prayer of thanks to Jesus.**
    Pray together the prayer. Then say: **Take a few moments to think about being open to the grace of the Holy Spirit in your life.** Pause and then pray *Amen.*

With My Family Ask children to read silently the three suggestions in this section. Invite children to choose one or more to complete at home.

3 Go in Peace

Collect materials and return them to the appropriate places. Encourage children to discuss the With My Family section at home. Say: **Let's all go home and try to reach out to others as Jesus does to us through his gift of the sacraments.**

Living My Faith — RESPOND

Faith Summary

Jesus gives us the sacraments to help us grow in faith. Through the Holy Spirit, Jesus Christ is present in the sacraments. The Church gives us signs of grace called sacramentals.

Words I Learned
blessing
sacramental

Ways of Being Like Jesus

Jesus reached out to all people, not just those who were like him. *Reach out to someone who is different from you.*

Prayer

Dear Jesus, thank you for giving me the sacraments. Help me to be open to the grace of the Holy Spirit so that I can show my love for God and for others.

With My Family

Activity At dinner reach out to your family by talking to them about yourself and your day. Show your interest in them by listening about their day.

Faith on the Go Ask one another: *Which sacramental in your home is your favorite? Why?*

Family Prayer Dear God, thank you for blessing us with the gift of your Son, Jesus. Help us to grow in faith through his presence in the sacraments. Amen.

80   UNIT 3 • *The Church, Our Community in the Spirit*

IF TIME ALLOWS

Session Assessment Option
An assessment for this session can be found at **www.findinggod.com.**

PLAN AHEAD

Get Ready for Session 14
Consult the catechist preparation pages to prepare for Session 14 and determine any materials you will need.

Mary Is Holy

3-Minute Retreat

As you prepare the session, pause for a few quiet moments. Eliminate any distractions. Reflect on Mary as your model of a saint and what her life story means to you.

Luke 1:48–49

For he has looked upon his handmaid's lowliness;

behold, from now on will all ages call me blessed.

The Mighty One has done great things for me,

and holy is his name.

Reflection

Responding to her cousin Elizabeth's greeting, Mary praises God for the transformation in her life and for God's many blessings. As members of the Church, we honor Mary and join her in praising God. Our prayers of praise, especially in the Eucharistic celebration, draw us to a deeper unity with Jesus and all believers, living and dead. This great unity before God, the Communion of Saints, is a form of praise. The Church worldwide honors Mary in many ways, and we strive to follow her example of living in holiness and gratitude.

Question

Mary praises God for giving her the opportunity to serve him. How am I responding to God's call to serve him?

Prayer

Listen to Mary's words of praise and make them your own.

My soul proclaims the greatness of the Lord, my spirit rejoices in God my Savior. He has done great things for me, and holy is his name.

Knowing and Sharing Your Faith in Session 14

Consider how Scripture and Tradition can deepen your understanding of the session content.

Scripture

Luke 1:46–54 tells us that Mary proclaims the greatness of the Lord and his deeds among the poor and humble.

Luke 1:45 says Elizabeth calls Mary blessed because she believed what the Lord said.

Tradition

In the Apostles' Creed, we express our belief in the Communion of Saints. Mary holds a special place within the Communion of Saints because she is the greatest of the saints. For the faithful on earth, she is a role model of faithfulness to God, openness to the Spirit, and closeness to Jesus. Catholics honor Mary as Mother of Christ and Mother of the Church. We pray for her help because we believe that she will take our needs to her Son, Jesus, and through him to our Father in Heaven.

Catholic Social Teaching

In this session the integrated Catholic Social Teaching theme is **Option for the Poor and Vulnerable.** See page 61b for an explanation of this theme.

Window on the Catechism

The prayer of the Virgin Mary, the Magnificat, is discussed in *CCC* 2617–2619. The Visitation is treated in *CCC* 717. The Hail Mary is explored in *CCC* 2676–2679. The importance of the Rosary is discussed in *CCC* 971. The Communion of Saints is found *CCC* 946–959.

General Directory for Catechesis

Mary's role as a model for catechetical renewal is explored in *GDC* 291.

One-Hour Session Planner

SESSION 14 Mary Is Holy

Session Theme: *Mary is the Church's model of faith and love.*

Before This Session

▶ Bookmark your Bible to Luke 1:45 and 46–54; 2:22–35 and 41–52. Read these passages in preparation for the prayer on pages 84 and 85. Place the Bible open to any of these passages in your prayer center.

▶ Display the *Finding God* poster Rosary.

▶ Read the Guide for this session, choose any additional If Time Allows activities that you might have time to complete, and gather the listed materials.

Prayer in Session 14

In this session children review the Hail Mary and the Magnificat, Mary's song of praise. Children also begin to learn the Rosary.

STEPS	APPROXIMATE TIME
Engage ***Mary Is Holy*** PAGE 81	10 minutes
Explore ***The Church Celebrates Mary*** PAGE 82 ***We Pray the Rosary*** PAGE 83 ***Art Print:*** *Annunciation* ART PRINT AND PRINT BACK	30–40 minutes
Reflect ***Prayer:*** Events in the Lives of Jesus and Mary PAGE 84 ***Mary's Song of Praise*** PAGE 85	15–20 minutes
Respond ***Living My Faith*** PAGE 86	5–10 minutes

Materials

REQUIRED

▶ Bible

▶ Art Print 14: *Annunciation* and Children's Book page 240

▶ 6 sheets of drawing paper, each with one letter of the word *mother* written on it

▶ A rosary

▶ *Finding God* poster: Rosary

▶ CD player

▶ CD 2, Track 9: "Holy Is Your Name" (2:48)

▶ CD 2, Tracks 17 and 18: "Reflective Music"

IF TIME ALLOWS

▶ Poster board, glitter (page 81)

▶ Art supplies (pages 81, 83, 84, 85)

▶ Large cardboard boxes (page 83)

▶ Construction paper (page 84)

▶ Session 14 BLM (page T-312) (page 85)

▶ Session 14 Assessment, www.findinggod.com (page 86)

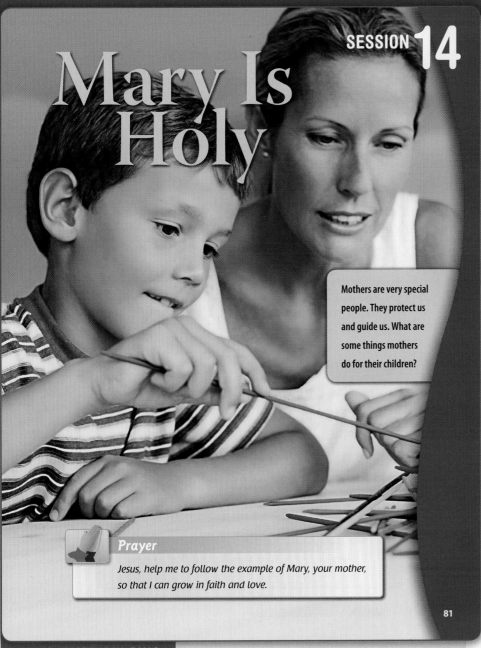

Mary Is Holy

SESSION **14**

Mothers are very special people. They protect us and guide us. What are some things mothers do for their children?

Prayer

Jesus, help me to follow the example of Mary, your mother, so that I can grow in faith and love.

81

IF TIME ALLOWS

Inclusion: Attention

Leading the Group Children with attention differences may be able to comprehend the page content more readily if you make them recorders in the mother activity in Set the Stage. In that role, they will feel like they belong in the group. They also will focus on the activity of writing words. Observe their efforts and give them frequent praise.

Celebrate Mothers

Using the activity in Set the Stage, have each group transfer the words from their paper to a large poster board. Have children decorate the poster boards with markers, glitter, and other materials, and display the posters in the room.

 Go to **www.findinggod.com/sessionextenders** to read articles on Mary and the Rosary.

SESSION 14
OUTCOMES

▸ Identify Mary as the Mother of God and the Mother of the Church.

▸ Describe the Rosary as a way of honoring Mary.

▸ Discuss how Mary is blessed by God.

▸ Discuss the prayer the Magnificat.

▸ Define *Annunciation, Communion of Saints, Rosary,* and *Visitation.*

1 Set the Stage

Greet children warmly. Write one letter from the word *mother* at the top of six sheets of drawing paper. Give a sheet to six children to be group recorders. Have the remaining children "count off" using the letters of *mother.* Have each child join the group that has his or her letter. Say: ***Think of a word or phrase that describes why mothers are special. This word or phrase should start with your letter.*** Tell children to discuss ideas with their group. The recorder should write the group's favorite answers. Then have groups share responses.

2 Get Started

Point to the picture on page 81. Ask: ***How do you think this mother and son feel?*** (Possible answers: They love each other and like to spend time together.) Read aloud the text in the blue box and discuss children's responses. Then read aloud the session title and say: ***We're going to talk about a mother we all share. Who is it?*** (Mary, Jesus' mother) Say: ***In this session we learn how Mary was blessed by God.***

Prayer

Ask children to quiet themselves. Say: ***Let's pray to Mary's Son, Jesus, who can help us follow Mary's example.*** Pray the prayer together. Then pray the Sign of the Cross.

1 Begin

Discuss with children what they know about Mary. Ask: **Where can we see images of Mary?** (Possible answers: statue in church; statue or painting at home) Say: **We will learn what Mary means to us and to the Church.**

2 Connect

Read aloud the first heading and paragraph. Ask: **Why does the Church honor Mary?** (She is the Mother of God and the Mother of the Church.) **What does Mary show us by example?** (listening to God; trusting and believing in him) Ask children what they can do to follow Mary's example. Say: **Mary is an excellent example of what it means to be a saint because she devoted her life to serving God. She loved and trusted God.** Ask: **How can we be like Mary?** (Possible answers: trust in God always, care for others, listen to God)

Read aloud the second heading and paragraph. Say: **God calls us all to be saints. When we pray together as the Church, we become one body with those who have already died. This body is called the Communion of Saints.** Ask: **What is one word to describe the Communion of Saints?** (Possible answers: togetherness, one, united) Point to the picture of people at Mass. Ask: **How does this picture show the Communion of Saints?** (Possible answers: It shows a united group.)

3 Close

Direct children's attention to the feature at the bottom of page 82.

Link to Liturgy

Read aloud this feature. Say: **In 1846 the U.S. bishops placed our country under the patronage of the Blessed Virgin Mary. We celebrate her Immaculate Conception on December 8.** Name Mary's other feast days, such as the Annunciation [March 25] and Feast of the Assumption [August 15].

The Church Celebrates Mary

Becoming the mother of Jesus was the greatest thing that could happen to Mary. She praises God for blessing her. Just as Mary praises God, the Church honors Mary. She is the Mother of God and the Mother of the Church, which means she is the mother of all of us. Mary shows us how to truly listen to God. She teaches us how to trust and believe. Mary is the best example of what it means to be a saint.

We Are All One

Each of us is also called by God to be a saint. We pray together as the Church, especially in the Eucharist. Together with those who have died, we are one body, united before God. We call this one body the **Communion of Saints.**

Link to Liturgy
There are 19 feast days honoring Mary, Mother of God, in the liturgical year.

IF TIME ALLOWS

Part of One Body

Distribute pencils and paper. Ask children to close their eyes and imagine they are gathered with others from the Communion of Saints. Ask them to open their eyes and write their thoughts or what they might say to the saints. Give them time to write and then invite volunteers to share their answers.

We Pray the Rosary

Praying the **Rosary** is one way to honor Mary. The rosary is a string of beads and a crucifix. We hold the crucifix as we pray the Sign of the Cross and the Apostles' Creed.

We use the first five beads to pray one Lord's Prayer, three Hail Marys, one Glory Be to the Father, and conclude with another Lord's Prayer. Then we pray using the five sets of ten beads, called a decade, remembering an event in the life of Jesus and Mary. We begin each decade with the Lord's Prayer, then pray ten Hail Marys, and end with a Glory Be to the Father.

When we pray the Rosary, we reflect on the lives of Jesus and Mary as the Joyful, Sorrowful, Glorious, and Luminous Mysteries. A mystery is an event in the life of Jesus, Mary, and the Church. The first set of events we remember are the Joyful Mysteries. We remember the **Annunciation**, as Mary learned she was to be the mother of Jesus. The **Visitation** tells of when Mary visits her cousin Elizabeth. These are followed by the Nativity, the Presentation of Jesus in the Temple, and Finding Jesus in the Temple.

An illustration of the Annunciation

Did You Know?

The Church named October the month of the Rosary.

GO TO PAGE 240

SESSION 14 • *Mary Is Holy*　83

IF TIME ALLOWS

Service: Be Like Mary

Explain that as Mother of the Church, Mary wants us to care for others. Collect coats, hats, and gloves for families who are homeless. Have children use art supplies to decorate collection boxes. Obtain permission from your catechetical leader before placing the boxes around the parish. Have children help you empty the boxes periodically. Donate the items to a shelter for those who are homeless.

✝ *The Poor and Vulnerable*

1 Begin

Show children a rosary and ask them to share what they know about praying the Rosary. Say: *The Rosary is a special prayer that honors Mary. We're going to learn about this prayer.*

2 Connect

Display the *Finding God* Rosary poster. Say: *As I read about the prayers we pray as we touch each part of the rosary, I will point on the poster to where each prayer is prayed.* Read aloud the heading and first paragraph. Say: *We just finished learning the last part of the Apostles' Creed, so you now know all the prayers used for the Rosary.* Remind children that the prayers appear in the back of their books. You can also refer to the Rosary on page 194 in the back of their books.

Read aloud the second paragraph, again pointing out the prayer beads.

Read aloud the last paragraph. Write *Joyful Mysteries* on the board and ask children to name the five Mysteries. List them on the board.

Did You Know?

Read aloud this section. Say: *The Rosary is such an important prayer that the Church encourages us to pray it. October 7 is the Feast of Our Lady of the Rosary.*

3 Close

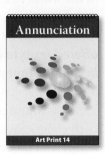

Annunciation

Art Print 14

Display Art Print 14: *Annunciation*. Use the Art Print 14 instruction to teach this section. Art Print teaching instruction can also be found on page 240.

Prayer

Follow the steps to guide children through the prayer on page 84.

Children's Page

Prepare Review Luke 2:22–35 and Luke 2:41–52 in your Bible to recall the three Joyful Mysteries not discussed in this session. Then read the prayer on page 84 in advance to become familiar with it.

Pray Invite children to sit quietly. Say: *Today we will reflect on the Joyful Mysteries of the Rosary. These are happy times in the lives of Jesus and Mary.* Read aloud the first sentence. Say: *Close your eyes to reflect on these Joyful Mysteries. Try to picture each event I describe. Fold your hands.* Pray the Hail Mary together.

You might play the instrumental "Holy Is Your Name" [CD 2, Track 10] softly in the background.

Ask a volunteer to read aloud the first event. Say: *Mary felt happy to learn she would be Jesus' mother. She is happy to love you as a mother too.*

Ask a volunteer to read aloud the second event. Say: *Mary enjoyed visiting her cousin. Mary wants to visit you the same way.*

Ask a volunteer to read aloud the third event. Say: *How happy everyone was when Jesus was born! Jesus came to the world to be your best friend.*

Ask a volunteer to read aloud the fourth event. Say: *Mary and Joseph offered Jesus to God. What's special in your life that you can offer to God?* (Answers will vary.)

Ask a volunteer to read aloud the fifth event. Say: *Mary and Joseph were happy and relieved to have their family together. How happy they are that you are part of the Christian family!*

Read aloud the last sentence and then pause to allow children to reflect silently. Pray the Sign of the Cross.

Prayer

Events in the Lives of Jesus and Mary

Let us pray together, reflecting on these special events in the lives of Jesus and Mary.

The Annunciation The angel Gabriel tells Mary she will be Jesus' mother.

The Visitation Mary visits her cousin Elizabeth.

The Nativity Mary and Joseph go to Bethlehem, where Jesus is born.

The Presentation Mary and Joseph bring Jesus to Jerusalem to be presented to God.

The Finding of Jesus in the Temple Joseph and Mary find Jesus in the Temple, talking with the teachers.

We thank God for giving us Mary, who loves us and prays for us.

IF TIME ALLOWS

Images of Mary
Provide construction paper of various colors, gold and silver paper, crayons, markers, scissors, and glue. Read aloud Bible passages on the Joyful Mysteries as children make pictures of their images of Mary.

FYI

Coaching Children to Pray

Suggest that children pray a complete Rosary at bedtime. Say: *As you pray each Hail Mary, think about one of the five Joyful Mysteries and its importance in the lives of Mary and Jesus.*

Mary's Song of Praise

Mary and Elizabeth were overjoyed. They would both be blessed with special children. Elizabeth's child would be John the Baptist. Mary's child would be Jesus, the Son of God. Mary praised God by praying these words:

> My soul praises the greatness of the Lord. My spirit finds joy in God my Savior. He has chosen and blessed me. God has done great things for me, and holy is his name! God helps the poor and feeds the hungry. He lifts up the lowly. He shows mercy to those who love him.
>
> *adapted from Luke 1:46–54*

We call this prayer the Magnificat. Like Mary, you can pray these words to thank God for all he has done for you.

I'm Thankful for . . .

Mary was thankful for all that God had given her. Make a list of people and things in your life for which you are thankful.

_____

_____

_____

_____

_____

SESSION 14 • *Mary Is Holy*   **85**

1 Begin

Invite children to share times when they heard exciting news. Then read aloud the heading. Say: *Now we'll hear in Mary's own words how Mary felt when she heard exciting news.*

2 Connect

Invite a volunteer to read aloud the first paragraph. Ask: *Why were Mary and Elizabeth so happy?* (They were going to have very special children.) *Who were these children?* (Jesus and John the Baptist)

In a voice full of praise, read Mary's words from the Magnificat. Ask: *How does Mary feel?* (honored and joyful) *What does she say about God?* (praises him for his goodness and greatness, thanks him for his generosity and his mercy) *Whom does she say God helps?* (people who are poor, hungry, and lowly) Say: *Mary seemed to be an ordinary young woman. God had a special plan for her.*

Read aloud the last two sentences. Say: *Mary prayed this prayer to praise God for the great things he had done for her.*

Say: *Mary's song of praise is put to music in a beautiful song.* Invite children to close their eyes and listen as you play the song "Holy Is Your Name" [CD 2, Track 9]. Say: *Picture in your mind Mary's visit to Elizabeth and the joy shared by the two cousins.* Have children look at the words in the back of their books so they can follow along. Once they know the song, invite them to sing as you play it again.

Read aloud the activity I'm Thankful for. . . . Give children time to reflect before they write their lists.

3 Close

Have volunteers share their answers. Once they are done sharing, reread aloud the adaptation from Luke 1:46–54.

IF TIME ALLOWS

Session 14 BLM

You Are Special Badge Have children complete the Session 14 Blackline Master [T-312] to make badges for people who care for them.

Pictures of Thankfulness

To extend the activity on this page, have children draw pictures of one or more of the people or things for which they are thankful. Encourage children to draw why they are thankful. For example, if a child is thankful for a grandparent, he or she can show the grandparent doing something to take care of the child.

1 Begin

Faith Summary Read aloud this section. Ask: **Together with those who have died, what is the body we become?** (the Communion of Saints) Say: **Mary is the best example to us of what it means to be a saint.** Ask: **What is one of the best ways to honor Mary?** (pray the Rosary)

2 Connect

Words I Learned Ask volunteers to define the vocabulary words. Then have children make a drawing that will help them remember the definition of each word. For example, children might draw Mary visiting her cousin Elizabeth for *Visitation*.

Ways of Being Like Jesus Read aloud this section. Have children review ways of following Mary's example, such as trust in God; be caring, generous, understanding, and praise God.

Prayer

Say: **Jesus and Mary are our best examples of how we should try to live. Let's reverently pray to Jesus to thank him for sharing his mother with us.** Pray together the prayer. Pause so children can talk to Jesus silently. Pray *Amen*.

With My Family Ask children to read silently the three suggestions in this section. Invite children to choose one or more to complete at home.

3 Go in Peace

Collect materials and return them to the appropriate places. Encourage children to discuss the With My Family section at home. Say: **Mary was Jesus' mother, but she is also our mother and loves us very much. Take time to praise Mary this week by praying the Rosary.**

Living My Faith

RESPOND

Faith Summary

The Church is united through the Eucharist in the Communion of Saints. We follow Mary's example of faith and love. We pray the Rosary to honor her.

Words I Learned
Annunciation
Communion of Saints
Rosary
Visitation

Ways of Being Like Jesus
Jesus loved his mother very much.
Show your love for Mary and follow her example of faith and love.

Prayer
Jesus, my guide, thank you for sharing your mother with me. Watch over me as I listen to God and trust in him as Mary did.

With My Family

Activity As a family pray the Rosary together. Talk about the mysteries and the importance of each in Jesus' life.

Faith on the Go Ask one another: *What are you most thankful for? Why?*

Family Prayer Dear God, thank you for blessing Mary as the mother of Jesus. Help us to praise and honor her. Amen.

86 UNIT 3 • The Church, Our Community in the Spirit

IF TIME ALLOWS

Session Assessment Option
An assessment for this session can be found at **www.findinggod.com**.

PLAN AHEAD

Get Ready for Session 15
Consult the catechist preparation pages to prepare for Session 15 and determine any materials you will need.

Celebrating Christmas

3-Minute Retreat

Before preparing the session, pause, be still, and be aware of the loving presence of God.

> *Micah 5:1*
>
> *But you, Bethlehem-Ephrathah,*
>
> *too small to be among the clans of Judah,*
>
> *From you shall come forth for me*
>
> *one who is to be ruler in Israel . . .*

Reflection

Bethlehem was well known in the Old Testament as the city of David. The Gospel of Matthew tells of the Magi who followed a star but needed more information. From the Jewish scholars, they learned that Bethlehem figured prominently in the expectation of a Messiah. The Magi took the Scripture to heart and journeyed to worship the Messiah. King Herod read the same Scripture and hardened his heart with envy, deceit, and murder. Let us take Scripture to heart as the Magi did so that we can worship the true Messiah.

Question

How can I read the Scriptures in ways that helps me grow in a closer relationship with God and with others?

Prayer

Pray to Jesus, using these words or your own.

Jesus, help me to take the Scriptures to heart to discover who you want to be for me and how I can be more for others.

Knowing and Sharing Your Faith in Session 15

Consider how Scripture and Tradition can deepen your understanding of the session content.

Scripture

Micah 5:1 prophesies about the importance of Bethlehem as the place where the Messiah would be born.

Tradition

Christmas, also known as the Feast of the Nativity, means "Mass of Christ." The season of Christmas begins with the first Vespers of Christmas Eve and ends with the Feast of the Baptism of the Lord, the Sunday following January 6. Christmas celebrates the birth of Jesus Christ, the Son of God. The celebration of Christmas began in the western Church in the early fourth century. It is at this time that the date for the celebration of Christmas was given as December 25. From the western Church, the practice of celebrating Christmas spread quickly. Reflecting on the meaning of Jesus' birth in the midst of winter, the Church recognizes Jesus as the true Light of the World who brings us the eternal joy of the Kingdom of Heaven.

Catholic Social Teaching

In this session the integrated Catholic Social Teaching theme is **Call to Family, Community, and Participation.** See page 61b for an explanation of this theme.

Window on the Catechism

The Christmas mystery is discussed in *CCC* 525–526.

General Directory for Catechesis

The basic Catholic understanding of the history of Salvation is found in *CCC* 108.

One-Hour Session Planner

SESSION 15 Celebrating Christmas

Session Theme: *Christmas is a time to prepare to celebrate the birth of Jesus as a Church.*

Before This Session

▶ Determine whether you will use the Unit Assessment option listed on page 90.

▶ Determine whether you will also discuss the Christmas seasonal pages in the back of the Children's Book.

▶ Bookmark your Bible to Micah 5:1. Place the open Bible in your prayer center.

▶ Obtain from your catechetical leader information about sending cards to a retirement community or to children in a local hospital.

▶ Read the Guide for this session, choose any additional If Time Allows activities that you might have time to complete, and gather the listed materials.

STEPS	APPROXIMATE TIME
Engage *Celebrating Christmas* PAGE 87	10 minutes
Explore *We Celebrate During Christmas* PAGE 88	25–35 minutes
Reflect *Mass During Christmas* PAGE 89 *Art Print: Nativity* ART PRINT AND PRINT BACK	20–25 minutes
Respond *Living My Faith* PAGE 90	5–10 minutes

Materials

REQUIRED

▶ Two different Nativity scenes or images of Nativity scenes

▶ Bible

▶ Art Print 15: *Nativity* and Children's Book page 241

IF TIME ALLOWS

▶ Voice recorder, song sheets of religious Christmas songs (page 87)

▶ Art supplies, cardstock (page 89)

▶ Session 15 BLM, T-313 (page 88)

▶ Session 15 Assessment, www.findinggod.com (page 90)

▶ Unit 3 Assessment, T-314–T-316 (page 90)

Celebrating Christmas

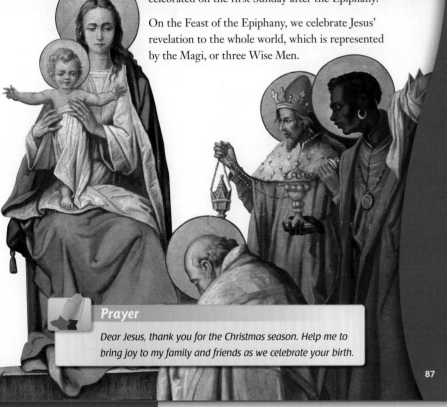

During the Christmas season, we celebrate the birth of Jesus. It is one of the most beautiful seasons in the liturgical year. This season begins with the celebration of Mass on Christmas Eve and lasts until the Feast of the Baptism of the Lord. The Baptism of the Lord is celebrated on the first Sunday after the Epiphany.

On the Feast of the Epiphany, we celebrate Jesus' revelation to the whole world, which is represented by the Magi, or three Wise Men.

Prayer

Dear Jesus, thank you for the Christmas season. Help me to bring joy to my family and friends as we celebrate your birth.

87

IF TIME ALLOWS

Inclusion: Chronic Health Conditions

Session on Audio Use this activity if you have children with chronic illnesses who are not able to meet with the group. Record children reading aloud page 87 or another page. Then record your voice, giving the child a brief summary of the group's discussion, your instruction, and any important information.

Christmas Caroling

Take children caroling to other classrooms or to a retirement home. Prepare song sheets of religious Christmas songs, such as "O Come All Ye Faithful" or "Joy to the World," for children to hold and look at as they sing together.

ENGAGE

SESSION 15
OUTCOMES

▶ Discuss how we celebrate Christmas as a Church.

▶ Explain that the Hebrew meaning for *Bethlehem,* the city of David, is house of bread.

1 Set the Stage

Play or sing a Christmas song about the birth of Jesus, such as "Silent Night." Ask: *What is this song about?* (the birth of Jesus) Say: *The Church celebrates the birth of Jesus during the Christmas season. Let's read about this special part of the liturgical year.*

2 Get Started

Read aloud the session title and the first paragraph. Ask: *When does the Christmas season begin?* (at the celebration of Mass on Christmas Eve) *When does it end?* (at the Feast of the Baptism of the Lord)

Invite a volunteer to read aloud the second paragraph. Ask: *What do we celebrate on the Epiphany?* (Jesus' revelation to the whole world) *Who are the Magi?* (the three Wise Men)

Say: *In this session we'll learn about Christmas—the time of year when we learn about Jesus' birth and how we can be more like him.*

Prayer

Call children's attention to the prayer. Say: *Take a moment to imagine the face of Jesus.* Ask a volunteer to pray aloud the prayer. Say: *Let's close our eyes and take a moment to talk to Jesus in our hearts.* Allow some time for children to finish their silent prayers. Pray *Amen* and ask children to open their eyes. Conclude with the Sign of the Cross.

1 Begin

Share how you celebrate Christmas with friends and family. Ask: **How do you celebrate Christmas with others? What are some traditions you have?** After the discussion, say: **Now we'll discuss how our parish community celebrates during Christmas.**

2 Connect

Have a volunteer read aloud the heading and the first paragraph. Discuss why it is important for the whole parish community to gather to celebrate the Eucharist on Christmas Day. Ask: **How is celebrating the Eucharist different on Christmas than on any other Sunday?** (We are celebrating Jesus and his birth on Christmas.)

Read aloud Christmas Meaning. Have children complete the activity independently or with partners.

3 Close

Direct children's attention to the feature at the bottom of page 88.

Reading God's Word

Read the adapted passage aloud as children follow along in their books. Then have children read the passage together. Ask: **How has what was foretold in Micah become fulfilled in the birth of Jesus?** (Jesus, the King, has come to be a leader of the people.)

We Celebrate During Christmas

Christmas is a time to celebrate. We celebrate the gift of Jesus, God's Son, who was born in Bethlehem. At home we can celebrate God's love at Christmas by giving gifts and cards to one another. At church we celebrate by joining our parish community for Mass. The Eucharist is our joyful celebration that Jesus is with us. We remember Jesus' life and all the ways he shows us how to love God by loving other people.

Christmas Meaning

Read the words below and think about their meaning during Christmas. Then use each word in a sentence and underline it.

Jesus	Christmas	parish
community	joy	Eucharist

_____

_____

_____

_____

Reading God's Word

But from you, Bethlehem, shall come forth for me one who is to be ruler in Israel. *adapted from Micah 5:1*

88   UNIT 3 • *The Church, Our Community in the Spirit*

IF TIME ALLOWS

Session 15 BLM

Celebrate Christmas Have children complete the Session 15 Blackline Master [T-313] to unscramble words about Christmas.

Seasonal Session: Christmas

Work with children through pages 157–160 of the Children's Book and this guide. This special session can take up to one hour to complete.

Mass During Christmas

When you go to Mass during Christmas, you will hear about Bethlehem, the city of David. The Hebrew meaning for *Bethlehem* is "house of bread." We call Jesus the Bread of Life because he came to bring bread to all who hunger.

What We Experience

When you look around your church, you may notice symbols of Christmas. The priest wears white or gold vestments, and a white altar cloth is used. White, the liturgical color of the season, reminds us of purity and joy. You may also see a Nativity scene that shows Jesus' birth in Bethlehem.

Your Nativity Scene

Draw a Nativity scene. Imagine yourself being present at the birth of Jesus. Include yourself in the scene.

Did You Know?

The word *Christmas* means "Mass of Christ."

GO TO PAGE 241

SESSION 15 • *Celebrating Christmas* **89**

IF TIME ALLOWS

Service: Pen Pals

Establish a pen pal project with senior citizens in a nursing home or with children in a local hospital. Have children make Christmas cards for their pals. As the liturgical year continues, have children make special cards during the various seasons, to maintain a relationship with their pals.

 Family and Community

---

1 Begin

Show children two different Nativity scenes. Discuss how they differ. Say: **There are many different looks to a Nativity scene, but they all have the same essential pieces: Mary, Joseph, and baby Jesus.**

2 Connect

Read aloud the heading and the first paragraph. Ask: **What is the Hebrew meaning for Bethlehem?** (house of bread) **Who is the Bread of Life?** (Jesus) **As the Bread of Life, what does Jesus come to bring to all who hunger?** (bread) Help children understand that Jesus is fulfilling a spiritual hunger.

Ask a volunteer to read aloud What We Experience. Discuss the symbols of Christmas that children might see at Mass, such as a Nativity scene, evergreens, lights, and the color white. Then invite children to complete the activity Your Nativity Scene.

Did You Know?

Read aloud the feature. Explain that the modern word *Christmas* comes from the Old English word *Christes Maesse*, meaning "Mass of Christ."

3 Close

Display Art Print 15: *Nativity.* Use the Art Print 15 instruction to teach this section. Art Print teaching instruction can also be found on page 241.

Begin

Faith Summary Ask a volunteer to read aloud this section. Ask: ***When we gather as a Church to celebrate Christmas, what else do we celebrate?*** (the Eucharist) ***Who is the Bread of Life?*** (Jesus) ***What does Jesus bring to all who hunger?*** (bread)

 Connect

Ways of Being Like Jesus Have a volunteer read aloud this section. Ask children to share their ideas. Say: ***As Jesus brings bread to all who hunger, help those in need around you.***

 Prayer

Ask children to close their eyes, fold their hands, and pray silently as you pray aloud. Allow a few seconds for silent reflection. Pray *Amen* and pray the Sign of the Cross together.

With My Family Ask children to read silently the three suggestions in this section. Invite children to choose one or more to complete at home.

 Go in Peace

Collect materials and return them to the appropriate places. Encourage children to discuss the With My Family section at home. Say: ***During Christmas this year, find ways to act more like Jesus. I can't wait to hear about them!***

Living My Faith

Faith Summary

Christmas is a time to celebrate as a Church the birth of Jesus. It is also a time that parish communities gather to celebrate the Eucharist. Jesus, the living bread, comes to bring bread to all who hunger.

Ways of Being Like Jesus

As the Bread of Life, Jesus nourishes us. *Help others who have less than you do.*

 Prayer

Dear Jesus, during the Christmas season, remind me to take time to pray for others who have less than I do.

With My Family

Activity When you go to Mass during Christmas, look around your church. Find examples of Christmas decorations and talk about what you see.

Faith on the Go Ask one another: *How can I become more involved in my church during Christmas?*

Family Prayer Invite family members to think of one friend who needs a prayer. As a family pray for these friends this Christmas season.

90 UNIT 3 • *The Church, Our Community in the Spirit*

IF TIME ALLOWS

Session Assessment Option

An assessment for this session can be found at **www.findinggod.com.**

Unit Assessment Option

If you wish, photocopy the Unit Assessment on pages T-314–T-316. Administer the assessment during the session or send it home.

PLAN AHEAD

Get Ready for Session 16

Consult the catechist preparation pages to prepare for Session 16 and determine any materials you will need.

UNIT 4

Catechist Preparation pages open each unit and session.

UNIT 4

Sacraments, Our Way of Life

The focus of this unit is on meeting Jesus in the sacraments and responding to him by living a life of service to others. In this unit children will learn the following concepts.

SESSION 16 — *Sacraments of Initiation*

We become members of the Church through the Sacraments of Initiation: Baptism, Confirmation, and the Eucharist. We belong to the People of God and receive the Holy Spirit. We begin a new life in Jesus in Baptism, receive the strength of the Holy Spirit to be witnesses to Jesus in Confirmation, and become one with Jesus through his Body and Blood in the Eucharist.

SESSION 17 — *Celebrating Reconciliation*

When we turn away from God through personal sin, Jesus calls us to forgiveness in the Sacrament of Penance and Reconciliation. God always forgives us when we are sorry. We can confess our sins to a priest and receive absolution.

SESSION 18 — *Celebrating the Eucharist*

The Mass is the most important celebration in the Church. It is the heart of our Catholic life of worship. We celebrate it every Sunday, the Lord's Day, and on Holy Days of Obligation. In the Eucharist we remember Jesus' life, Death, and Resurrection.

SESSION 19 — *Christian Living*

God gives us special talents and abilities. In this session we focus on how the Holy Spirit calls us to share these gifts. We each have a vocation or calling to a special way of life through which we serve others and the Church.

SESSION 20 — *Celebrating Lent and Holy Week*

Children learn the meaning of Lent and Holy Week, why we celebrate them, and explore how Lent and Holy Week are celebrated in our Church.

UNIT SAINT

Saint Paul the Apostle

Paul the Apostle was born in Tarsus (modern-day Turkey) and studied Jewish law. Originally he was not a follower of Jesus', and wanted to undermine the Christian Church. However, one day on his way to Damascus to arrest Christians, a bright light blinded Paul, and he heard the voice of Jesus, who had chosen him to become a follower. Paul regained his sight, was baptized, and became a missionary. Paul is an example of how our lives are changed when we meet Jesus.

Prayer in Unit 4

In this unit continue the pattern and tone for prayer that you have established with children. The opening and closing prayers invite children to reflect on a prayer that is related to the session and provide time for individual prayer. Children will reflect on the following prayers and themes throughout the prayer pages: they review their baptismal promises; pray the Act of Contrition, reflect on the image of Jesus as the bread of life; and reflect on the gifts with which the Holy Spirit has blessed them.

✝ Catholic Social Teaching in Unit 4

Following are the themes of Catholic Social Teaching integrated into this unit.

Call to Family, Community, and Participation   Participation in family and community is central to our faith and to a healthy society. As the central social institution, family must be supported and strengthened. From this foundation people participate in society, fostering a community spirit and promoting the well-being of all.

The Dignity of Work and the Rights of Workers   The Catholic Church teaches that the basic rights of workers must be respected: the right to productive work, to fair wages, to private property, to organize and join unions, and to pursue economic opportunity. Work is an important way in which we participate in God's creation.

Life and Dignity of the Human Person   The Catholic Church teaches us that all human life is sacred and that all people must be treated with dignity. We are called to ask whether our actions as a society respect or threaten the life and dignity of the human person.

Solidarity   Because God is our Father, we are all brothers and sisters with the responsibility to care for one another. Solidarity unites rich and poor, weak and strong, and helps build a society that recognizes that we live in an interdependent world.

TOGETHER *as One Parish*

Religious Education with the Parochial School

To nurture parish unity, invite each school and religious education family to write a reflection on a different Lenten-inspired Scripture passage. Collect the reflections and assemble them into a book to be distributed to all the families in the program.

📖 *Literature Opportunity*
**Going Home
by Eve Bunting**
You might wish to read aloud this story of a young boy returning home to Mexico to celebrate with his village. It shows the importance of family and the community and how strong that bond is.

✝ *Family and Community*

Sacraments of Initiation

Before preparing the session, pause for a few moments to be still. Take three deep breaths and be aware of the loving presence of God, who is with you.

> *Acts of the Apostles 8:35*
>
> *Then Philip opened his mouth and, beginning with this scripture passage, he proclaimed Jesus to him.*

Reflection

Philip had no idea why God sent him on the road from Jerusalem to Gaza, but he went because he was called to go. Philip responded to God's prompting by taking action when meeting the Ethiopian on the road. Philip taught him about the Scriptures and proclaimed the saving work of Jesus. We can see God's action in our life through the grace in the Sacraments of Initiation. God transforms, strengthens, and nourishes us. In our response to him, we are like the Ethiopian who eagerly received the gift of faith. Through the sacramental life of the Church, the gift of faith grows.

Questions

What does the grace of God I receive in the sacraments call me to do? How am I a witness to Jesus in my actions and with my words?

Prayer

Pray, using this prayer or one of your own.

> *God of action, thank you for taking the first step. Speak to my heart so that I can be a witness to your love for others.*

Knowing and Sharing Your Faith in Session 16

Consider how Scripture and Tradition can deepen your understanding of the session content.

Scripture

Acts of the Apostles 8:26–40 tells the story of Philip teaching the Ethiopian about Jesus.

Ephesians 4:4 is a statement of the Church's unity with the Spirit.

Tradition

Baptism introduces us to the Christian community as members with all the rights and responsibilities of receiving the sacraments, taking part in church activities, and being ministered to by the Church. Baptism also commits us to participating in the Christian community by helping to carry out the mission of the Church. Confirmation strengthens our connection to the community by sealing us with the Holy Spirit as we take an active role in the transformation of the world. The Sacrament of the Eucharist completes the initiation into the Christian community by bringing us together around the table of the Lord where we receive the Body and Blood of Jesus Christ.

Catholic Social Teaching

In this session the integrated Catholic Social Teaching themes are **Call to Family, Community, and Participation** and **Life and Dignity of the Human Person.** See page 91b for an explanation of these themes.

Window on the Catechism

After introducing the sacraments of initiation in *CCC* 1212, the *Catechism* treats Baptism in *CCC* 1213–1274, Confirmation in *CCC* 1285–1314, and the Eucharist in *CCC* 1322–1405.

General Directory for Catechesis

The role of catechesis in relation to initiation is explored in *GDC* 51.

One-Hour Session Planner

SESSION 16 Sacraments of Initiation

Session Theme: *Through the Sacraments of Initiation, we receive the fullness of the Spirit and become members of the Church.*

Before This Session

▶ Bookmark your Bible to Acts of the Apostles 8:26–40 and Ephesians 4:4. Place the Bible open to either passage in your prayer center.

▶ Display the *Finding God* poster The Seven Sacraments.

▶ Read the Guide for this session, choose any additional If Time Allows activities that you might have time to complete, and gather the listed materials.

> **Prayer in Session 16**
>
> In this session children review the baptismal promises as a way of recommitting themselves to God's call to be part of his family and pray prayers of petition and thanks for Jesus' continual guidance.

STEPS	APPROXIMATE TIME
Engage *Unit Saint:* Saint Paul the Apostle PAGES 91–92 *Sacraments of Initiation* PAGE 93	10 minutes
Explore *We Belong* PAGE 94 *Christian Initiation* PAGE 95 *Art Print:* The Ethiopian Baptized ART PRINT AND PRINT BACK	30–40 minutes
Reflect *Prayer:* Prayer of Our Beliefs PAGE 96 *Sacraments in My Life* PAGE 97	15–20 minutes
Respond *Living My Faith* PAGE 98	5–10 minutes

Materials

REQUIRED

▶ Bible

▶ Art Print 16: *The Ethiopian Baptized* and Children's Book page 242

▶ CD player

▶ CD 2, Track 11: "I Say 'Yes,' Lord/ Digo 'Sì,' Señor" (2:24)

▶ *Finding God* poster: The Seven Sacraments

▶ Baptismal items, such as a gown or candle

IF TIME ALLOWS

▶ Art supplies, poster board (page 93)

▶ Message Through Media: *Close Encounters with the Sacraments* VHS or DVD, media player (page 94)

▶ Large cardboard boxes (page 95)

▶ CD 2, Track 11: "I Say 'Yes,' Lord/ Digo 'Sì,' Señor" (2:24) (page 96)

▶ CD 2, Tracks 17 and 18, "Reflective Music" (page 96)

▶ Large sheet of wrapping paper, tape (page 97)

▶ Session 16 BLM, T-317 (page 97)

▶ Session 16 Assessment, www.findinggod.com (page 98)

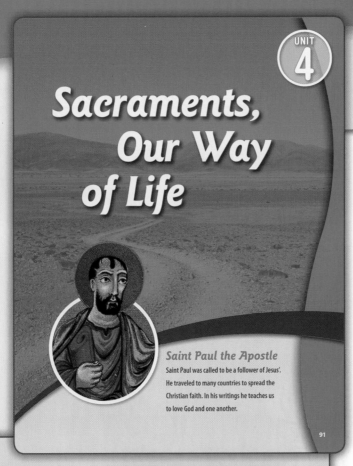

Sacraments, Our Way of Life

Saint Paul the Apostle

Saint Paul was called to be a follower of Jesus'. He traveled to many countries to spread the Christian faith. In his writings he teaches us to love God and one another.

91

Saint Paul the Apostle

Paul was born in Tarsus, in what is now the country of Turkey. He went to school in Jerusalem and studied Jewish law. Paul did not believe that the followers of Jesus were faithful to Jewish tradition. Paul wanted to destroy the Church.

Saint Paul of Tarsus announcing the Holy Gospel

Paul was there when Stephen, a follower of Jesus', was killed because he was a Christian. Paul then went to Damascus to help arrest more Christians. On the way a bright light blinded him. He heard the voice of Jesus, who had chosen him to become a follower. Paul changed his ways, regained his sight, and was baptized.

Paul made long journeys to places around the Mediterranean Sea to tell people about Jesus. He started churches in many cities. He wrote letters to the people to help them become better Christians. These letters are found in the Bible. When we read them, we learn of Paul's love for Jesus. In addition to the letters, we can learn more about Saint Paul in the Acts of the Apostles. The feast of Saint Paul is June 29.

Choose one approach to open the unit.
5-Minute Approach . . . . below
Optional Unit Opener . . . . next page

5-MINUTE APPROACH
Children's Pages

1 Begin

Before class, write the following letter on the board:

My Dear Friends,
    Today we will read about a special friend of Jesus' named Paul. He told his friends about Jesus. I think you will like learning about him.

Your friend and teacher,
[name]

When children arrive, say: *I was excited about today's session, so I wrote you this letter.* Read the letter.

2 Introduce the Saint

Read aloud the unit title and point to the picture on page 91. Read aloud the text. Ask: *What do we call someone who travels to spread the faith?* (a missionary) Say: *We will learn about the missionary Saint Paul, his travels, and letters he wrote.*

Ask children to turn to page 92. Point to the picture. Say: *This picture shows Saint Paul preaching.*

Read aloud the first two paragraphs. Ask: *How did Paul know Jesus was calling him?* (A light blinded him. He heard Jesus' voice.) Explain that Saul's name changed to Paul some time after his conversion.

Read aloud the last paragraph. Point out the map on the page. Say: *This map shows where Paul traveled. During his travels Paul started churches, preached to people, and wrote letters.* Ask: *Where can we find Paul's letters?* (in the Bible) Point out Paul's letter to the Corinthians, Galatians, Philippians, Colossians, and Romans.

This page describes a program-wide intergenerational event that is offered in a supplemental component.

OPTIONAL UNIT OPENER
Intergenerational Event

1 *Prepare*

Work with your catechetical leader to use the *Finding God Together* kit to plan an intergenerational event for Unit 4.

2 *Open the Event*

Gather families in one space. Use *Finding God Together* to open the event and discuss the main theme for Unit 4. Together, enjoy an entertaining skit.

3 *Implement the Saint Stations*

Use *Finding God Together* to help families learn more about the saints at their grade-level saint stations. Be sure all families feel welcome and are engaged in the process.

4 *Close*

Gather families in one space for a guided reflection. Use *Finding God Together* to close the event.

5 *Transition to Children's Book*

When children arrive for the faith formation session, discuss the event and review information about the unit saint. Have children open their books to page 93.

Finding **God** TOGETHER

GRADE **3**

LOYOLA PRESS.
A JESUIT MINISTRY

Unit 4

Saint Paul the Apostle
Feast Day: June 29

Image © Mary Evans Picture Library/Alamy.
978-0-8294-3213-8

Events Guide
Finding God Together: An Intergenerational Events Guide
by Mary Lynn Hendrickson and Tom McGrath

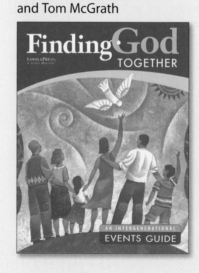

Finding **God** TOGETHER

LOYOLA PRESS,
A JESUIT MINISTRY

AN INTERGENERATIONAL
EVENTS GUIDE

FYI
Facts About Paul

Paul's conversion to Christianity occurred after the Death and Resurrection of Jesus Christ. Paul left Jerusalem around A.D. 46 and began his missionary journeys. He traveled through the eastern Mediterranean regions, preaching in synagogues and marketplaces. Paul was also well educated and tackled the broader theological issues of the new faith. Paul was executed in Rome around A.D. 65. Saint Paul and Saint Peter share a feast day on June 29.

SESSION **16**

Sacraments of Initiation

Think of a time you were welcomed to a new place. How did you feel? How did people welcome you?

Prayer

Jesus, Son of God, open my heart to the gift of faith I have received.

93

IF TIME ALLOWS

Inclusion: Hearing

A Welcoming Sign Children who have hearing impairments may find the page content more accessible if you talk directly to them. Remember to speak distinctly. If a child knows the American Sign Language sign for *welcome,* the page's most important concept, have him or her teach the sign to others. Have children practice welcoming one another to the group.

International Welcome

Ask if children know how to say *welcome* in another language. List the words on the board, along with their countries of origin. Add more ways to say *welcome* by looking them up online. Then make a colorful poster titled *Welcome to the Church.*

 Go to **www.findinggod.com/sessionextenders** to read a Knowing Your Faith article on the Sacraments of Initiation.

OUTCOMES

▶ Describe how we receive the Holy Spirit in the Sacraments of Initiation.

▶ Tell the story of Philip inviting the court official to follow Jesus.

▶ Define *People of God.*

① Set the Stage

Ask: *Imagine you are the group host or hostess and a new child is joining your group. How would you make that child feel welcome?* (Possible answers: introduce yourself, make sure there is an available desk, show him or her where the art supplies and water fountain are) Ask: *When we welcome someone, what are we telling him or her?* (that we care, accept, and are happy to have him or her with us)

② Get Started

Read aloud the session title and say: *When we become new members of a group, we usually go through an initiation. What is an initiation?* (an introduction to a group)

Have a volunteer read aloud the text in the blue box. Invite children to respond to the questions. Say: *In this session we will learn that through the Sacraments of Initiation, we are welcomed into the Church as children of God.*

Prayer

Invite children to be still. Say: *Let us pray for Jesus' help in making us faithful members of the family of God. Pray aloud the prayer with me.* After praying, say: *Now bow your head. Talk to God from your heart about your gift of faith.* Pause while children reflect. Then pray together *Amen.*

1 Begin

Read aloud the heading. Discuss any groups to which children belong. Say: **New members in an organization might receive a badge of membership. Perhaps they also say a pledge or sing a song. Now we will discuss becoming members of our Church.**

2 Connect

Read aloud the first paragraph. Write *People of God* on the board. Ask: **Who are the People of God?** (another name for the Church, family of God) **How do we begin our lives as the People of God?** (We are baptized. We become members of God's family through sanctifying grace, which is God's life within us.)

Have a volunteer read aloud the second paragraph. Point to the photos. Ask: **What is happening here?** (Children are being baptized.) Say: **After Baptism these children are members of God's family, the Church.**

✝ *Family and Community*

Play the song "I Say 'Yes,' Lord/ Digo 'Sí' Señor" [CD 2, Track 11] and have children turn to the back of their books to view the words of the song. Point out how the words in this song relate to Baptism because we say yes to God when we begin our initiation into the Church through Baptism. Say: **When we are baptized as babies, our parents and godparents say yes for us.**

3 Close

Direct children's attention to the feature at the bottom of page 94.

 Link to Liturgy

Have a volunteer read aloud this section. Say: **During the Easter Vigil, people who have prepared to become Catholics celebrate the Sacrament of Baptism. During the same liturgy, we renew our baptismal promises.**

We Belong

We are called to accept joyfully the gift of faith and to form one family in Christ as members of the Church. We become part of the Church community, the **People of God,** by faith and Baptism. Through Baptism, Original Sin is forgiven. We receive sanctifying grace, the grace that fills us with Jesus' life and helps us to be his friend. We begin a new life when we are baptized.

Baptism is a gift from God. All people, no matter what their age or background, can enter God's family through Baptism. We trust in God's mercy and, as members of God's family, we pray for those who have died without Baptism.

 Link to Liturgy

On special days the priest invites us to renew our baptismal promises at Mass. Easter is one time we do this. On Easter we think about rising with Jesus to new life. When we renew our baptismal promises, we recommit our lives to God.

94 UNIT 4 • *Sacraments, Our Way of Life*

IF TIME ALLOWS

Message Through Media: Close Encounters with the Sacraments

Have children view *Close Encounters with the Sacraments,* a 15-minute film that includes animated scenes with live action. In the film an angel appears to help an elementary-aged child with a lesson on the sacraments. Children may see themselves in the scenarios depicted. Offer topics for discussion after viewing the film.

Christian Initiation

Through the Sacraments of Initiation—Baptism, Confirmation, and the Eucharist—we receive the Holy Spirit. Each Sacrament of Initiation marks a special day in the life of a member of the Church.

Through the waters of Baptism, we begin a new life in Jesus. Our commitment to Jesus is symbolized through a candle. The white garments represent the purity of being freed from Original Sin.

At Confirmation we are anointed with holy oil. The laying on of hands symbolizes the gifts of the Holy Spirit. The Holy Spirit strengthens us and helps us to be witnesses to Jesus.

In the Eucharist the bread and wine are consecrated and become the Body and Blood of Jesus Christ. When we receive the Eucharist, we become one with him.

Together the three sacraments—Baptism, Confirmation, and the Eucharist—complete our initiation into the Church.

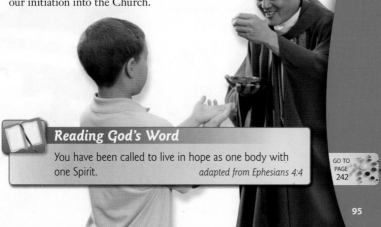

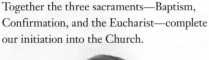 **Reading God's Word**

You have been called to live in hope as one body with one Spirit.

adapted from Ephesians 4:4

GO TO PAGE 242

95

GO TO PAGE 242

IF TIME ALLOWS

Service: Welcoming Babies

One way of welcoming babies to the world is to have children collect clothes, bottles, diapers, and other baby items for those children born to families facing challenging financial situations. Children can decorate collection boxes and check the boxes for donations periodically. Then take the items to a local shelter for distribution.

✝ *Life and Dignity*

---

① Begin

Display the *Finding God* poster The Seven Sacraments. Say: **This poster shows the sacraments in three groups. Let us look at the first group, the Sacraments of Initiation.** Ask a volunteers to read aloud the three Sacraments of Initiation from the poster. Remind children of your earlier discussion about the word *initiation*. Say: **These sacraments are the steps we take to become fully initiated into God's family, the Church.**

Display pictures of people celebrating the Sacraments of Initiation. Ask children to name the sacrament as you show them the pictures. Say: **These children are being welcomed into God's family.**

② Connect

Read aloud the heading on page 95 and invite volunteers to read aloud the section. You can refer children to pages 200–203 in the back of their books for more information on the sacraments. Ask: **What do we begin in Baptism?** (a new life in Jesus Christ) **Who strengthens us in Confirmation?** (the Holy Spirit) **What do we receive in the Eucharist?** (the Body and Blood of Jesus Christ)

 Reading God's Word

Invite children to read the passage with you. Point out Ephesians in the Bible. Remind children that it is through the Sacraments of Initiation that we become one with God and with the Church.

③ Close

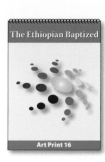

Display Art Print 16: *The Ethiopian Baptized.* Use the Art Print 16 instruction to teach this section. Art Print teaching instruction can also be found on page 242.

Prayer

Follow the steps to guide children through the prayer on page 96.

Children's Page

Prepare Pray the prayer in advance to become familiar with it.

Pray Dim the lights and invite children to be quiet. Remind children that God is with them as they reflect.

Say: **Today we learned about being welcomed into God's family. We sang special words of acceptance. What were those special words?** ("Yes, my Lord.") Say: **We say similar words when we pray the Creed together at Mass or renew our baptismal promises. We say "I do!"**

You may wish to play the reflective music at the end of CD 2 quietly in the background. Say: **Fold your hands in a prayerful position and pray silently as I pray aloud.** Read aloud the first paragraph. Say: **Respond with the words "I do" as I ask each question.** Ask the three questions reverently, pausing after each one so that children can respond.

Say: **Now close your eyes and bow your head. Listen as I read the last paragraph.** Read slowly, pausing for five seconds between sentences. When finished, take five deep breaths, then pray *Amen.* Say: **Now let us review this session and find ways to live the lessons we've learned.**

Prayer

Prayer of Our Beliefs

Leader: *We read in the letter to the Ephesians that we are called to live as one body and one Spirit. Let us answer God's invitation to be part of his family by expressing our belief in him.*

Do you believe in God, the Father almighty, creator of heaven and earth?

All: *I do!*

Leader: *Do you believe in Jesus Christ, his only Son, our Lord?*

All: *I do!*

Leader: *Do you believe in the Holy Spirit?*

All: *I do!*

Leader: *Thank God for making you part of the People of God. Ask him to keep making your faith stronger as you grow older. Thank him for making you one with him. Then spend a moment just loving him.*

96   UNIT 4 • *Sacraments, Our Way of Life*

IF TIME ALLOWS

I Say "Yes," Lord/Digo "Sí," Señor

CD 2, Track 11 Invite children to write additional verses to the song "I say 'Yes,' Lord/Digo 'Sí,' Señor." For example, encourage them to use different words for "yes," such as "I do" and "I will." Write their verses on the board. Lead the group in singing the new verses along with the instrumental track of the song [CD 2, Track 12].

FYI

Coaching Children to Pray

To prepare children to pray, remind them that as they enter the church, they make the Sign of the Cross, using holy water near the entrance. Every time we pray the Sign of the Cross, we confirm our belief in the Trinity—God the Father, God the Son, and God the Holy Spirit. Encourage children to pray this prayer slowly and prayerfully.

REFLECT

Sacraments in My Life

Each Sacrament of Initiation is celebrated using sacramentals. Think back to the day you first received the Eucharist or when you attended a Baptism or a Confirmation. Write the name of the sacrament for which each sacramental is used.

1. white garments ___**Baptism**___

2. holy oil ___**Confirmation**___

3. water ___**Baptism**___

4. bread and wine ___**Eucharist**___

5. laying on of hands ___**Confirmation**___

6. baptismal candle ___**Baptism**___

Remembering a Special Day

What do you remember about the day you participated in or witnessed a Sacrament of Initiation? In the box below, draw a picture of yourself or someone you know who received that sacrament. Include the priest who celebrated the sacrament.

SESSION 16 • *Sacraments of Initiation*   97

IF TIME ALLOWS

Session 16 BLM

New Life in Christ Have children complete the Session 16 Blackline Master [T-317], a word puzzle of important terms.

Banner for Newly Baptized Children

Ask permission from your catechetical leader to obtain the names of children recently baptized at your church. Have children make a banner for the newest members of God's family. Have children brainstorm welcoming messages. Tape a large sheet of wrapping paper to the floor and have children write their messages. Hang the banner in your church or in a greeting room.

---

1 Begin

Display items from a Baptism, such as a baptismal gown or candle. Ask: **Who has attended a Baptism?** Allow time for children to share their memories of the event. Ask: **What did the priest use to baptize the baby?** (water, to wash away Original Sin) **Let's talk about when you first received the Eucharist. What did the priest give you?** (the Body and Blood of Jesus Christ) **Who has attended a Confirmation?** Again, give children time to share their memories. **During the Confirmation you attended, did you see the priest place something on each person's head? What was it?** (holy oil)

2 Connect

Read aloud the heading and first paragraph. Make sure children understand the directions. Walk around the room and answer any questions. If necessary, refer children to page 95 for a review.

When children are finished, have a volunteer read aloud Remembering a Special Day. Allow children a few minutes to think about what they want to draw before starting. Monitor children's progress.

3 Close

When children have finished their drawings, have volunteers share their work with the class. Ask: **How did you feel about your special day? What did you see that day that you most remember?** Allow children time to share their thoughts with the group.

1 Begin

Faith Summary Read aloud this section. Ask: **What three sacraments complete our initiation into the Church?** (Baptism, Confirmation, and the Eucharist) **What do we belong to when we become members of the Church?** (the People of God)

2 Connect

Words I Learned Ask a volunteer to read aloud the definition of the term in the Glossary.

Ways of Being Like Jesus Read aloud this section. Ask: **What are some things you can do to welcome a new person to school?** (Possible answers: asking the person to join you for lunch or to play at recess, introduce him or her to your friends)

 Prayer

Say: **Today we learned about the sacraments that help us become members of God's family, the Church. Let us thank Jesus for welcoming us. Fold your hands and pray with me.**

Pray aloud the prayer. Then say: **Take a few seconds to pray silently and thank Jesus in your own words.** Close by praying *Amen.*

With My Family Ask children to read silently the three suggestions in this section. Invite children to choose one or more to complete at home.

3 Go in Peace

Collect materials and return them to the appropriate places. Encourage children to discuss the With My Family section at home. Say: **Think of how wonderful it is to be welcomed into the family of God. This week be a joyful family member!**

Living My Faith

Faith Summary

Through the Sacraments of Initiation—Baptism, Confirmation, and the Eucharist—we complete our initiation into the Church. We belong to the People of God.

Words I Learned
People of God

Ways of Being Like Jesus
Jesus welcomed everyone. *Help children who are new to your class feel welcome by talking to them and offering your help.*

 Prayer

Jesus, thank you for welcoming me to the People of God. Walk with me as I follow your example and spread your Word.

With My Family

Activity With your family, visit new neighbors and welcome them to your neighborhood.

Faith on the Go Ask one another: *When you meet a new person at school or work, do you introduce yourself? Why or why not?*

Family Prayer *Dear God, thank you for welcoming us into the Church when we were baptized. Please help us to treat all in our parish with respect. Amen.*

98 UNIT 4 • *Sacraments, Our Way of Life*

IF TIME ALLOWS

Session Assessment Option
An assessment for this session can be found at **www.findinggod.com**.

PLAN AHEAD

Get Ready for Session 17
Consult the catechist preparation pages to prepare for Session 17 and determine any materials you will need.

Celebrating Reconciliation

3-Minute Retreat

Before you begin preparing the session, pause to quiet yourself. Call to mind that you are in the presence of God. Remember that God is all-forgiving because of his great love for all people.

John 20:21

[Jesus] said to them again, "Peace be with you. As the Father has sent me, so I send you."

Reflection

The lack of peace in our world is a sure sign of the presence of sin. Sin, a separation from the loving presence of God, distances us from the ultimate source of peace. When we succumb to sin, we are not at peace with God, with others, or with ourselves. When Jesus appeared to the disciples after the Resurrection, he gave them the gift of forgiveness and peace. In the Sacrament of Penance and Reconciliation, we experience the forgiveness of sins and the healing of our relationship with ourselves, with others, and with God.

Questions

When I am not at peace, do I hear God's call to reconciliation? When and how often do I receive the Sacrament of Reconciliation?

Prayer

Pray, using this prayer or one of your own.

Merciful and forgiving God, you know me and still you love me. Give me the courage to acknowledge my sin and seek your mercy and forgiveness.

Knowing and Sharing Your Faith in Session 17

Consider how Scripture and Tradition can deepen your understanding of the session content.

Scripture

John 20:19–23 tells how Jesus gives the apostles the authority to forgive sins.

Psalm 85:9 assures peace for God's people.

Tradition

Sin can be personal, an individual's deliberate rejection of God's love. Sin can also be social when individuals join together in rejecting God's love. The source of all reconciliation is Jesus Christ, who came to reconcile the human race with God. The Church community of reconciled people is a sign to the world of God's love and forgiveness. Within the Church there are many opportunities for forgiveness and reconciliation. The Sacrament of Reconciliation is the foremost vehicle of forgiveness, but all the sacraments have the effect of forgiving sins. It is no accident that we begin the Mass with a penitential ceremony, for the first step in all our relations with God is an acknowledgment of our sinfulness and our dependence on God's mercy.

Catholic Social Teaching

In this session the integrated Catholic Social Teaching theme is **Call to Family, Community, and Participation.** See page 91b for an explanation of this theme.

Window on the Catechism

Jesus' healing power of forgiveness in the Sacrament of Penance and Reconciliation is discussed in *CCC* 1422–1470.

General Directory for Catechesis

The role of forgiveness, conversion, and the Sacrament of Reconciliation in catechesis is discussed in *GDC* 102.

One-Hour Session Planner

SESSION 17 Celebrating Reconciliation

Session Theme: *When we fail to love God and others because of sin, Jesus calls us to forgiveness through the Sacrament of Reconciliation.*

Before This Session

▶ Bookmark your Bible to Psalm 85:9 and John 20:19–23. Place the Bible open to either of these passages in your prayer center.

▶ Display the *Finding God* poster The Seven Sacraments.

▶ Read the Guide for this session, choose any additional If Time Allows activities that you might have time to complete, and gather the listed materials.

Prayer in Session 17

In this session children review the Act of Contrition, a prayer in which we tell God we are sorry for offending him. Children also pray to receive forgiveness and to thank Jesus for his special gifts.

STEPS	APPROXIMATE TIME
Engage *Celebrating Reconciliation* PAGE 99	10 minutes
Explore *Peace Be with You* PAGE 100 *The Peace of Forgiveness* PAGE 101 *Art Print: Greetings* ART PRINT AND PRINT BACK	30–40 minutes
Reflect *Prayer:* Prayer of Forgiveness PAGE 102 *Bringing Peace to Others* PAGE 103	15–20 minutes
Respond *Living My Faith* PAGE 104	5–10 minutes

Materials

REQUIRED

▶ Bible

▶ Art Print 17: *Greetings* and Children's Book page 243

▶ Adhesive bandages

▶ Art supplies

▶ *Finding God* poster: The Seven Sacraments

▶ CD player

▶ CD 2, Track 13: "Peace Walk" (2:28)

▶ CD 2, Track 14: "Peace Walk" (Instrumental)

▶ IF TIME ALLOWS

▶ Bandages, markers (page 99)

▶ Art supplies (page 101)

▶ Poster board (page 101)

▶ Session 17 BLM, T-318 (page 101)

▶ Magazines (page 102)

▶ Session 17 Assessment, www.findinggod.com (page 104)

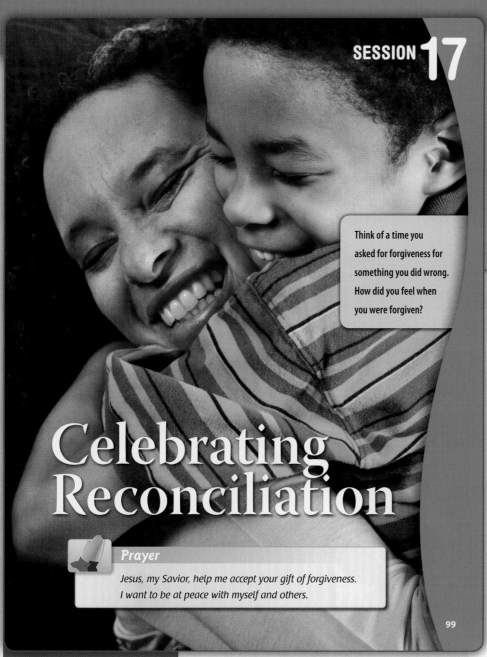

SESSION 17

Think of a time you asked for forgiveness for something you did wrong. How did you feel when you were forgiven?

Celebrating Reconciliation

Prayer

Jesus, my Savior, help me accept your gift of forgiveness. I want to be at peace with myself and others.

99

SESSION 17
OUTCOMES

▶ Explain two kinds of personal sin: mortal and venial.

▶ Pray the Act of Contrition.

▶ Discuss that we receive forgiveness from God through the Sacrament of Penance and Reconciliation.

▶ Define *personal sin*.

1 Set the Stage

Put an adhesive bandage on your hand. Greet children and ask: **When do we wear a bandage?** (when we have a wound) **What does it do?** (help the wound heal) Say: **Some hurts have nothing to do with our bodies.** Ask: **What kind of hurt is that?** (hurt feelings) **What helps it go away?** (making up after a fight, saying words of forgiveness) **How do we make up after an argument?** (Possible answers: We use forgiving words; sometimes we hug.)

2 Get Started

Read aloud the session title. Point out the picture and say: **These people are sharing reconciliation, which happens when you forgive someone and let go of bad feelings after arguing. Hugs and apologies are like forgiveness bandages.**

Call on a volunteer to read aloud the text in the blue box. Invite children to respond. Ask: **How does it make you feel when someone asks you for forgiveness?** (Possible answers: good, respected) Say: **In this session we'll read about forgiveness.**

Prayer

Say: **Let us pray to accept Jesus' gift of forgiveness. Pray aloud the prayer with me.** Then say: **Now pray silently and talk to Jesus. Think about something for which you would like forgiveness.** Pause, and pray together *Amen.*

IF TIME ALLOWS

Forgiveness Bandage

Give each child an adhesive bandage to decorate with markers. Ask children to put the strips on their arms or hands. Tell them to wear the bandages as a reminder to offer someone their forgiveness.

 Go to **www.findinggod.com/sessionextenders** for a short prayer break called the 3-Minute Retreat on reconciliation.

1 Begin

Say: **Turn to the people around you to share a sign of peace that you might use at Mass.** Give children time to exchange a sign of peace with others. Say: **We exchange this sign of peace to share with one another the peace that Jesus shares with us. Now we're going to read about Jesus sharing words of peace with his disciples.**

2 Connect

 Read aloud the heading, the first sentence, and the Scripture passage. Say: **This passage was adapted from the Gospel of John.** Show children the Gospel of John in your Bible. Ask: **How do we know that this visit to the disciples happened after Jesus died on the cross and rose from the dead?** (from the words *risen Jesus Christ* and Jesus' marks from his crucifixion) **How did the disciples feel when they saw Jesus Christ?** (joyful)

Ask a volunteer to read aloud the last paragraph. Say: **Jesus sent the Holy Spirit to the disciples.** Ask: **What two special gifts did Jesus give his disciples?** (peace and the authority to forgive sins) **When do we receive the gifts of peace and forgiveness?** (in the Sacrament of Reconciliation) Invite children to comment on the picture.

3 Close

Display the *Finding God* poster The Seven Sacraments. Point out the Sacrament of Reconciliation. Say: **Through this sacrament we receive Jesus' peace and healing.**

Refer to the bandage on your hand. Remind children how the Sacrament of Reconciliation is like a bandage for wounded feelings. Say: **The Sacrament of Reconciliation is a Sacrament of Healing because we need it to heal our broken relationships with God and with others.**

Peace Be with You

After the Resurrection, Jesus Christ visited the disciples.

> The disciples were gathered in a room. Suddenly the risen Jesus Christ came to them. He said, "Peace be with you." He showed them the marks from his Crucifixion. The disciples were filled with joy at seeing Jesus. Jesus said to them again, "Peace be with you. As the Father has sent me, so I send you."
>
> Then he breathed on them and said, "Receive the Holy Spirit. Those sins you forgive will be forgiven."
>
> *adapted from John 20:19–23*

Jesus gave the disciples two special gifts. He gave them peace to live happily together. He also gave them the authority to forgive sins. The priests who hear our confessions share these gifts. Through them, Jesus gives us peace and forgives our sins in the Sacrament of Penance and Reconciliation.

Jesus forgives our sins.

100

IF TIME ALLOWS

Reconciliation Room

Coordinate this activity with your catechetical leader in advance. Take children to visit the reconciliation room or confessional in your parish church. Say: **We can choose to talk with the priest face-to-face or from behind a screen, whichever is more comfortable for us. It is important to feel at ease when we are in the reconciliation room because we are sharing a very personal moment with our priest and with God.** Encourage children to comment and ask questions about confession. You may wish to refer children to page 211 in the back of their books to review how to celebrate the Sacrament of Reconciliation.

The Peace of Forgiveness

People have been tempted to disobey God ever since Adam and Eve. After Baptism takes away Original Sin, we can still reject God by disobeying him and being self-centered. We call this **personal sin.**

There are two kinds of personal sin. When we totally reject God, we commit a mortal sin. Sins that are less serious are venial sins. God asks us not to form a habit of committing sins, even venial sins. But when we do sin, the Holy Spirit helps us to be sorry. Then we can confess our sins in the Sacrament of Reconciliation, do penance, and be at peace with God and ourselves.

Jesus' Words of Forgiveness

Fill in the words of Jesus. Look back in this session for help.

1. _____ Peace _____ be with you.

2. As the _____ Father _____ has sent me, so I send you.

3. Receive the _____ Holy _____ _____ Spirit _____ .

4. Those sins you _____ forgive _____ will be forgiven.

Link to Liturgy

To remind us at Mass of Jesus' words, we turn to one another and offer a sign of peace.

SESSION 17 • *Celebrating Reconciliation* 101

GO TO PAGE 243

IF TIME ALLOWS

Session 17 BLM

Forgiving Footprints Have children complete the Session 17 Blackline Master [T-318] to describe situations in which they had difficulty forgiving someone.

Service: Peace "Garden"

Find a spot where children can "plant" a peace "garden." Have children draw pictures of people making peace—shaking hands or hugging—that they can hang in this garden. Children can make posters inviting others to make peace in the peace garden when a disagreement arises.

✝ *Family and Community*

---

① Begin

Say: ***When we receive God's forgiveness, we walk in peace with him and with others.*** Invite children to turn to the back of their books and follow the words as they listen to "Peace Walk" [CD 2, Track 13].

② Connect

Read aloud the heading. Remind children that Jesus forgives our sins in the Sacrament of Reconciliation. Ask a volunteer to read aloud the first paragraph. Ask: ***What sin is taken away at Baptism?*** (Original Sin) ***What kind of sin do we commit when we disobey God?*** (personal sin)

Read aloud the next paragraph. Say: ***The two kinds of personal sin are mortal sin and venial sin.*** Ask: ***When we totally reject God, what kind of sin do we commit?*** (mortal sin) ***What are less serious sins called?*** (venial sins)

Read aloud the directions for Jesus' Words of Forgiveness. Give children time to complete the activity and then check answers together.

Link to Liturgy

Read aloud this section. Ask: ***When do we exchange a sign of peace at Mass?*** (after praying the Lord's Prayer and before we receive Holy Communion) Say: ***The sign of peace we share is an expression of the unity we experience when we receive Holy Communion.*** Invite children to stand so they can extend hands and share a sign of peace.

③ Close

Display Art Print 17: *Greetings.* Use the Art Print 17 instruction to teach this section. Art Print teaching instruction can also be found on page 243.

Greetings

Art Print 17

REFLECT

Prayer

Follow the steps to guide children through the prayer on page 102.

Children's Page

Prepare Pray the prayer in advance to become familiar with it.

Pray Ask children to prepare quietly to pray. Invite them to gather at the prayer center with their books. If they completed the Session 17 Blackline Master, have them bring their footprints with them as well.

Say: ***We have talked about God's wonderful gift of forgiveness. Let us remember God is with us and be thankful for his great gift as we begin our reflection.***

Ask children to look at their paper footprints and reflect on why children made them. Say: ***When we practice forgiveness, we are being like Jesus and following in his footsteps. Know that Jesus is with us as we pray.***

You may wish to play the instrumental song "Peace Walk" [CD 2, Track 14] quietly in the background as children pray. Read aloud the first paragraph slowly and thoughtfully. Pause after each sentence, allowing children time to think of when they have hurt their relationships with God and with others.

Lead children in praying the Act of Contrition. Pray together the prayer slowly. Then say: ***Now spend a few moments with Jesus, thanking him for his gift of forgiveness.*** Pause for a few moments. Read aloud the last sentence on the page as children follow along in their books. Then pray together *Amen*. Say: ***Let us find ways to bring what we've learned into our daily lives.***

Prayer

Prayer of Forgiveness

Today let us reflect on Jesus' call to forgiveness. Think of times when you have sinned. Tell Jesus that you are sorry. Then pray the Act of Contrition.

Act of Contrition

My God,
I am sorry for my sins with all my heart.
In choosing to do wrong
and failing to do good,
I have sinned against you
whom I should love above all things.
I firmly intend, with your help,
to do penance,
to sin no more,
and to avoid whatever leads me to sin.
Our Savior Jesus Christ
suffered and died for us.
In his name, my God, have mercy.

During the rest of this week, ask Jesus to help you stay on the right path.

IF TIME ALLOWS

Celebrate Peace

Have children find pictures in a magazine of people showing forgiveness or making peace, or have children draw pictures. Have children write captions describing the scenes. Then take the pictures and captions and make a collage from them, naming it *Celebrate Peace*.

FYI

Coaching Children to Pray

To prepare children to pray, encourage them to take traditional prayers "to heart." Explain that taking prayers "to heart" not only involves learning and remembering the words of a prayer, but also listening to the meaning of each word as children pray.

Bringing Peace to Others

In the Sacrament of Reconciliation, we tell God that we are truly sorry for our sins. He forgives us, and we feel peaceful and loved. When others hurt our feelings and then tell us they are sorry, we offer them forgiveness so that they can have peace as well.

Choose Peace

For each situation below, choose what you would do to bring peace to another person.

1. You and your brother start to argue about who will hold the remote control as you watch TV. He yells at you, and then says he is sorry for yelling. You feel angry at him. You:

   a. yell back at your brother.

   b. run from the room with the remote.

   (c.) take a deep breath and say, "It's OK. I'm sorry too. We'll take turns using the remote."

2. Your best friend borrowed your favorite book and lost it. You really miss the book and wish you had never loaned it to her. She tells you that she is really sorry. You:

   a. tell her that you will never loan her anything again.

   (b.) tell her you forgive her and discuss the book together.

   c. ask her to replace the book.

3. Your mom says she will take you to a movie tonight. Then she remembers that she has already made plans. She tells you that she is sorry but will take you tomorrow instead. You:

   a. ask her to change her plans.

   b. tell her you're angry and that you don't want to go.

   (c.) tell her that you know she would take you if she could and that you're happy to go tomorrow.

SESSION 17 • *Celebrating Reconciliation*   **103**

IF TIME ALLOWS

Peace-Giving Skits

Children may enjoy acting out one or more of the scenarios in the activity on page 103. Arrange children in pairs and ask each pair to choose a situation. Give them a few minutes to plan their skits and then have each pair perform for the class. Allow some time for discussion of the decisions children made in each scene.

1 Begin

Recalling the adhesive-bandage analogy used at the beginning of this session, ask: ***How does it feel when you remove the bandage and see that your cut or scrape has healed and you are as good as new again?*** (Possible answers: excited, happy, ready to play) ***How do you feel when you and a friend apologize to each other and have accepted each others' apologies?*** (Possible answers: great, relieved, ready to play again)

2 Connect

Read aloud the heading. Have a volunteer read aloud the first paragraph. Say: ***Think about a time you were truly sorry for something you did.*** Ask: ***How do you feel when you are truly sorry and someone you have hurt forgives you?*** (Possible answers: happy, peaceful) Discuss the importance of giving other people that same sense of peace if they hurt us and are truly sorry for doing so.

Read aloud the directions for the activity Choose Peace. Make sure children understand the directions. If needed, walk around the room while children work and answer any questions.

3 Close

When children have finished the activity, ask volunteers to share their answers for each situation. If a child has made a choice that would not reconcile the two people in the situation, guide the child to see how another choice would bring peace to both people. Say: ***When you choose to forgive instead of staying angry with someone, you reconcile with that person. You both can enjoy a peaceful relationship. Remember that God wants us to forgive everyone, whether or not the person asks for our forgiveness.***

1 Begin

Faith Summary Read aloud this section. Ask: **What is a personal sin?** (a choice we make that offends God) **How does Jesus call us to forgiveness when we turn away from God?** (through the Sacrament of Reconciliation) **After we go to confession, what happens to us?** (God forgives us.)

2 Connect

Words I Learned Ask a volunteer to use the term *personal sin* in a sentence. Invite children to look up the definition in the Glossary.

Ways of Being Like Jesus Read aloud this section. Discuss situations in which children can forgive others.
　　Say: **When we forgive others, the relationships we share grow stronger.**

 Family and Community

 Prayer

Invite children to be still. Say: **We talked about forgiveness today. Let us thank Jesus for making us aware of this important gift. Pray aloud with me.**
　　After the prayer say: **Talk to Jesus silently in your own words.** Pause for a few moments and pray aloud *Amen.*

With My Family Ask children to read silently the three suggestions in this section. Invite children to choose one or more to complete at home.

 # 3 Go in Peace

Collect materials and return them to the appropriate places. Encourage children to discuss the With My Family section at home. Say: **This week live as a forgiving person. Forgive others and see how happy both you and they can be.**

Living My Faith

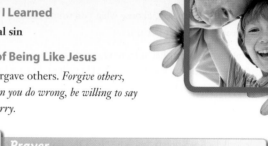

Faith Summary

Jesus gave his disciples peace and the authority to forgive sins. When we turn away from God through personal sin, Jesus calls us to forgiveness in the Sacrament of Reconciliation. We confess our sins, say we are sorry, and do penance for our sins. God always forgives us, and we feel peaceful.

Words I Learned

personal sin

Ways of Being Like Jesus

Jesus forgave others. *Forgive others, and when you do wrong, be willing to say you're sorry.*

 Prayer

Jesus, my friend, thank you for the gift of forgiveness. Help me to forgive others as you forgive me.

With My Family

Activity Family members can make "second chance" cards. When you accept an apology, offer the card to that person to show that you are ready to move on.

Faith on the Go Ask one another: *Did you forgive the last person who hurt your feelings? Why or why not?*

Family Prayer Practice the Act of Contrition with your family. Try to say it from memory.

104　UNIT 4 • *Sacraments, Our Way of Life*

IF TIME ALLOWS

Session Assessment Option

An assessment for this session can be found at **www.findinggod.com.**

PLAN AHEAD

Get Ready for Session 18

Consult the catechist preparation pages to prepare for Session 18 and determine any materials you will need.

Celebrating the Eucharist

Before you begin preparing for this session, pause to reflect on Jesus' presence in the Sacrament of the Eucharist. Remember the love that originates in Jesus' great sacrifice.

1 Corinthians 11:26

For as often as you eat this bread and drink the cup, you proclaim the death of the Lord until he comes.

Reflection

In this passage Paul reminds the Church in Corinth why people gather and celebrate. He refers to Jesus' great sacrifice as the center of the gathering and outlines how the Eucharist is to be celebrated. Even now we continue this remembrance in the celebration of the Mass. There we gather as God's family to listen, pray, and receive the fullness of Jesus in the Eucharist. At the table of the Lord, none are greater and none are lesser. We are God's children and equal in his eyes.

Question

If Paul were to write to you about how to celebrate the Mass, what would he say to you?

Prayer

Speak to Jesus, using the following prayer or one of your own.

Lord Jesus, you are the Bread of Life. Help me live in a way that shows your love for all people, despite our differences, because we are all a part of God's family.

Knowing and Sharing Your Faith in Session 18

Consider how Scripture and Tradition can deepen your understanding of the session content.

Scripture

1 Corinthians 11:23–26 tells a narrative of the Last Supper.

John 6:48 teaches us that Jesus tells the Jews that he is the Bread of Life.

Tradition

To celebrate the Eucharist, we open with a ceremony of pardoning, a way to unburden ourselves of past offenses so that we can rejoice in one another's company. Later we will share a sign of peace and reconciliation. We listen to the Bible proclaimed to us as a community. We follow this with a public proclamation of our communal faith. We then gather around the table of the Lord for our family meal. We pray the Lord's Prayer, the prayer that has identified and united Christians for centuries. We refer to the receiving of Jesus' Body and Blood as Holy Communion, a joining together of the members of the community, with God and with one another. Our celebration closes with a charge to go forth as a community and bring God's love to the world.

Catholic Social Teaching

In this session the integrated Catholic Social Teaching themes are **Call to Family, Community, and Participation** and **Solidarity.** See page 91b for an explanation of these themes.

Window on the Catechism

The ways in which the Eucharist makes us a Church community are discussed in *CCC* 1396.

General Directory for Catechesis

The importance of Christian community in catechesis and our understanding of the Eucharist are discussed in *GDC* 159.

One-Hour Session Planner

SESSION 18 Celebrating the Eucharist

Session Theme: *The celebration of the Eucharist is at the center of parish life.*

Before This Session

▶ Locate and read the Scripture passages listed on page 106.

▶ Bookmark your Bible to 1 Corinthians 11:23–26 and John 6:48. Place the Bible open to either of these passages in your prayer center.

▶ Be prepared to discuss the Holy Days of Obligation that are not listed on page 109 in the Children's Books.

▶ Display the *Finding God* poster The Seven Sacraments.

▶ Read the Guide for this session, choose any additional If Time Allows activities that you might have time to complete, and gather the listed materials.

> **Prayer in Session 18**
>
> In this session children reflect on the image of Jesus as the Bread of Life. The opening and closing prayers focus on the Eucharistic celebration at Mass.

STEPS	APPROXIMATE TIME
Engage *Celebrating the Eucharist* PAGE 105	10 minutes
Explore *Do This and Remember Me* PAGE 106 *We Imitate Jesus* PAGE 107 *Art Print: First Communion* ART PRINT AND PRINT BACK	30–40 minutes
Reflect *Prayer:* Thanking Jesus PAGE 108 *We Celebrate the Lord's Day* PAGE 109	15–20 minutes
Respond *Living My Faith* PAGE 110	5–10 minutes

Materials

REQUIRED

▶ Bible

▶ Art Print 18: *First Communion* and Children's Book page 244

▶ *Finding God* poster: The Seven Sacraments

▶ CD player

▶ CD 2, Track 2, "Song of Love" (instrumental)

IF TIME ALLOWS

▶ Session 18 BLM, T-319 (page 107)

▶ Paper plates and cups (page 105)

▶ Lined writing paper (page 106)

▶ Poster board (107)

▶ Art supplies, drawing paper (page 105, 109)

▶ Session 18 Assessment, www.findinggod.com (page 110)

SESSION **18**

Celebrating the Eucharist

We gather with our family and friends for special celebrations. How does enjoying a meal with your family make it more special?

Prayer
Jesus, my guide, help me to celebrate the Mass with love and reverence.

105

IF TIME ALLOWS

Inclusion: Cognitive

Dinner with Friends If you have children with cognitive differences, you can present the page content by having children act out a dinner. Provide directions in short, clear sentences. Use paper plates and cups as props. Bring food items, such as pretzels, fruit, or cut vegetables, and invite children to share good food and conversation. Ask children to pray before eating, pass food to one another, and talk with classmates. Praise children for showing courtesy. Repeat key points from the page content for reinforcement.

What's for Dinner?

Invite children to draw a picture of their family and friends sharing a dinner. Ask children to answer these questions in their drawings: Why are they eating together? What's for dinner? Who is there? What topics might they discuss?

Go to **www.findinggod.com/sessionextenders** for an article about celebrating the Eucharist.

▶ Describe how Jesus instituted the Eucharist at the Last Supper.

▶ Give examples of how the Mass helps us unite as one family.

▶ Discuss our obligation to attend Mass on Sundays and Holy Days of Obligation.

▶ Define *epistle* and *worship*.

1 Set the Stage

 Play the instrumental "Song of Love" [CD 2, Track 2] to calm children as they enter the room. Share a story of how your family enjoyed one another's company at a particular meal.

Invite children to talk about dinners they have enjoyed with their families. Say: **Today we'll read about a special meal that we share with our parish family. What meal is this?** (the celebration of the Eucharist)

2 Get Started

Point to the photo on page 105. Ask: **How is this dinner like your family dinners?** (Possible answers: people of various ages eating food and sharing conversation) Ask a volunteer to read aloud the session title and the text in the blue box. Invite children to respond to the question. Say: **In this session we will learn why building a strong community is so important.**

Prayer

Ask children to sit quietly. Say: **Let us pray that Jesus will help us love the times we celebrate with our parish families. Join me in praying our prayer of petition.** After the prayer say: **Pray silently as you share your thoughts with Jesus.** Pause. Then pray *Amen*.

1 Begin

Point to the picture on page 106. Ask: *What very special meal does this show?* (the Last Supper) Ask: *Where is Jesus in this picture?* (in the middle) *Who is seated with Jesus, sharing the Last Supper?* (the apostles)

2 Connect

Write *epistle* on the board and pronounce it. Read aloud the heading and first paragraph. Ask: *What is an epistle?* (a special letter written to a group of Christians) Say: *There are 21 epistles in the New Testament. Many were written by Saint Paul.*

 Say: *Follow along as I read a passage from the first letter Paul wrote to his friends who lived in the city of Corinth.* Read aloud the rest of this section. Say: *During Mass the priest prays these words during the consecration of the bread and wine. We remember Jesus' promise to be with us in the Eucharist.*

Arrange children into small groups. Give a Bible to each group. Say: *Three of the Gospel writers tell us the important story we just read about, the Last Supper.* On the board, write Matthew 26:26–29, Mark 14:22–25, and Luke 22:14–20. Point out the Gospels of Matthew, Mark, and Luke in the New Testament. Show children how to find the chapter numbers and verses. Invite volunteers to read aloud each passage. Discuss similarities and differences among the stories.

3 Close

Direct children's attention to the feature at the bottom of page 106.

 Reading God's Word

Read aloud the passage. Ask: *What does this passage mean to you?* (Jesus gives us himself in the form of bread; he is our nourishment; he gives us life.)

Do This and Remember Me

Saint Paul told many people about Jesus' life. This is what he told the Church in a special letter, or **epistle,** about the Eucharist.

On the night when Jesus was betrayed, he took bread and gave thanks. Then he broke it and said to his disciples, "This is my body that I give to you. Do this and remember me."

After supper Jesus took the cup of wine. He said, "This cup is the new agreement made in my blood. As often as you drink it, remember me."

As often as you eat this bread and drink the cup, you proclaim the death of the Lord until he comes again.

adapted from 1 Corinthians 11:23–26

Reading God's Word

I am the bread of life.   *John 6:48*

106

IF TIME ALLOWS

Thank You, Jesus

Distribute pencils and lined writing paper. Say: *When the priest prays the words of consecration, the Bread and Wine become the Body and Blood of Jesus Christ. Jesus gives himself to us in Holy Communion.* Have children write a few sentences to Jesus, thanking him and telling him what the Eucharist means to them. Examples of what they can write are a thank-you for giving himself to us or the Eucharist brings us closer to him.

EXPLORE

We Imitate Jesus

At the Last Supper, Jesus gave us a promise of his love. He called upon us to commit ourselves to God and to one another. The priest repeats Jesus' words at Mass. When we imitate Jesus in our lives, God's love is brought into the world.

At Mass Jesus Christ is present with us. He is present in the people gathered, in the priest who leads, in the Scriptures, and especially in the Eucharist, the consecrated Bread and Wine that becomes Jesus' Body and Blood.

The Mass is the central celebration of parish **worship.** It is the heart of the Church's life. It is offered for everyone, the living and the dead. An ordained priest leads us in the celebration of the Mass. We give thanks and praise to God for Jesus' life, Death, and Resurrection.

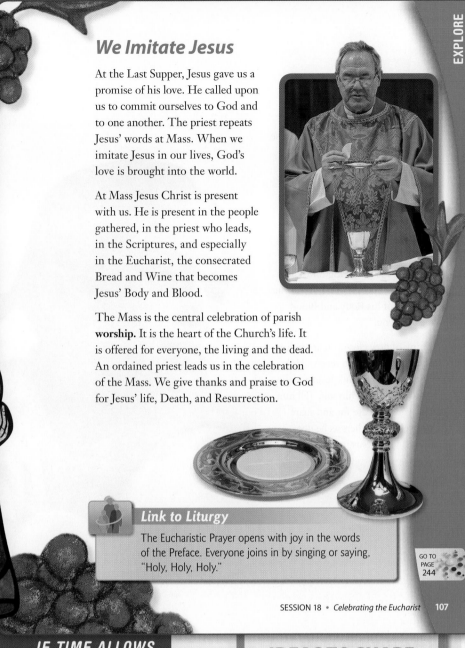

Link to Liturgy

The Eucharistic Prayer opens with joy in the words of the Preface. Everyone joins in by singing or saying, "Holy, Holy, Holy."

GO TO PAGE 244

SESSION 18 • *Celebrating the Eucharist* **107**

IF TIME ALLOWS

Session 18 BLM

Banner of the Mass Have children complete the Session 18 Blackline Master [T-319] to make a banner showing things seen at Mass.

Service: An Invitation to Mass

To enhance community in your parish, have children make posters with information about Mass times. If the parish holds a regular reception after a particular Mass, have children include that information as well. Then ask your catechetical leader where you may hang these posters.

✝ *Family and Community*

IDEAS TO SHARE

Liturgy

Write *Liturgy of the Word* and *Liturgy of the Eucharist* on the board. Explain how we hear the Word of God proclaimed from the Scriptures during the Liturgy of the Word. Point out that we receive the Body and Blood of Christ during the Liturgy of the Eucharist.

---

1 Begin

Ask: *Who were our first teachers?* (our parents) Say: *Young children often play by imitating their parents, such as playing house. Now we will learn how we can imitate Jesus.*

2 Connect

Read aloud the heading and the first paragraph. Ask: *How can we imitate Jesus?* (Possible answers: care for all people, spread the Word of God, live as Jesus lived) Say: *We commit ourselves to God and one another by loving and helping others.*

Read aloud the next paragraph. Ask: *How is Christ present with us at Mass?* (He is in the people gathered, the priest, the Scripture readings, and the Eucharist.)

Write *worship* on the board. Say: *Worship is the adoration and praise we give to God. We worship God when we take part in Mass.* Read aloud the last paragraph. Refer students to pages 204–206 for more information on the Mass.

Display the *Finding God* poster The Seven Sacraments. Review the Sacraments of Initiation. Ask: *Which sacrament did we just discuss?* (the Eucharist) Say: *We celebrate the Eucharist regularly to worship God.*

Link to Liturgy

Read aloud this section. Say: *When we sing or say these words, we are praising God.*

3 Close

Display Art Print 18: *First Communion.* Use the Art Print 18 instruction to teach this section. Art Print teaching instruction can also be found on page 244.

Prayer

Follow the steps to guide children through the prayer on page 108.

Children's Page

Prepare Pray the prayer in advance to become familiar with it.

Pray Invite children to be quiet and to clear their minds of distractions. Say: **Today we have read and talked about how Jesus gave himself to us in the Sacrament of the Eucharist. Let us spend some time reflecting on what this special gift means to us.**

Tell children that you will read aloud the reflection. Ask them to get in a comfortable position. You may wish to play the reflective music at the end of CD 2 softly in the background while you read.

Read aloud the first paragraph slowly and thoughtfully, pausing for 10 seconds at the end. Continue with the second paragraph, again pausing for 10 seconds so that children can reflect. Read aloud the last paragraph in a similar tone. Say: **Now close your eyes. I will give you a few moments to be with Jesus and tell him whatever you would like.** After a few moments, invite children to open their eyes. Say: **Let us close our prayer time by praying the Sign of the Cross.** Pray together the Sign of the Cross.

Say: **Remember that Jesus is with us every day, not just on Sunday. We can imitate Jesus in our lives by treating one another with love and kindness every day of the week.**

 Prayer

Thanking Jesus

Jesus said, "I am the bread of life." Think of how much love is in these simple words. Jesus loves us so much that he gives us himself so that we may live.

Now think of Jesus' love in giving us the Sacrament of the Eucharist. Jesus is truly present in the consecrated Bread and Wine. Thank Jesus for giving himself to you in the Eucharist. Tell him what the gifts of his Body and Blood mean to you.

Think of how close you are to him, especially when you receive Holy Communion. Thank Jesus for the wonderful gift of himself. Tell him how you will care for and share yourself with others as he does. Be still with Jesus in your heart.

108 UNIT 4 • *Sacraments, Our Way of Life*

IF TIME ALLOWS

When We Celebrate
Review People and Things I See at Mass on page 208–209 in the back of the Children's Book. Help children identify people and things that are part of the Eucharistic celebration.

FYI

Coaching Children to Pray

Remind children that, after receiving the Eucharist at Mass, they should take some quiet time to pray and to thank Jesus for the gift of himself, to welcome him into their hearts, and to take time to be with him in silence, enjoying his love for them.

We Celebrate the Lord's Day

Sunday is the day on which we remember the Resurrection. It is the Lord's Day. The Church celebrates by gathering for Mass and resting from work. We remember that we are all part of God's family. We are rich and poor, old and young. We come from all over the world, but we gather at God's eucharistic table as brothers and sisters.

Days of Celebration

As Catholics, we are called to celebrate the Eucharist on Sundays and Holy Days of Obligation. The Church asks us to receive Holy Communion as often as possible.

Holy Days Matching

Draw a line from the dates to the holy days below. Then write about how your parish celebrates these special days.

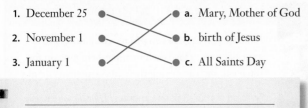

1. December 25 ●   ● a. Mary, Mother of God
2. November 1 ●   ● b. birth of Jesus
3. January 1 ●   ● c. All Saints Day

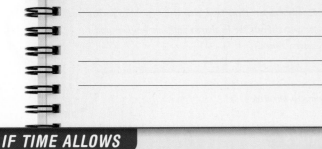

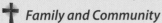

109

IF TIME ALLOWS

Sunday, Sun-Day

Distribute crayons and drawing paper. Have children fold in half a sheet of drawing paper. Ask them to label one half *Sunday* and to draw a picture of how they celebrate the Lord's Day at Mass. Have them label the other half *Sun-Day* and draw a picture of how they celebrate the Lord's Day at home with their families.

✝ *Family and Community*

---

1 **Begin**

Ask children to think about a typical Sunday at their homes. Ask: **What are some things you do on Sundays?** (Possible answers: go to Mass, play with family and friends, relax) **What is one thing that Catholics all over the world do to celebrate the Lord's Day?** (celebrate the Mass)

2 **Connect**

Read aloud the heading and invite a volunteer to read aloud the first paragraph. Say: **Catholics all over the world celebrate the Mass on the Lord's Day in a similar way. Many families make Sunday a special family day. It often begins with a celebration of Mass with their parish family.** Ask: **What is different at Catholic churches in different parts of the world?** (the language in which the Mass is spoken) **But we listen to the same readings in the Liturgy of the Word. The bread and wine become the Body and Blood of Christ in the Liturgy of the Eucharist.**

✝ *Solidarity*

Read aloud the second heading and paragraph. Say: **An obligation means a duty to do something. As Catholics, it is our special duty to attend Mass on Holy Days of Obligation, just as we do on Sundays.**

Read aloud the activity Holy Days Matching. Give children time to draw their lines and then check the answers together.

3 **Close**

Say: **In all, we celebrate six Holy Days of Obligation in our country. What are the other three?** (Assumption of Mary on August 15; Immaculate Conception on December 8; Ascension, which occurs 40 days after Easter) Have children turn to page 207 to view a list of the Holy Days of Obligation.

1 Begin

Faith Summary Read aloud this section. Ask: ***What is the most important celebration in the Church?*** (Mass) ***What do we remember at the Eucharist?*** (Jesus' life, Death, and Resurrection) ***When do we celebrate the Eucharist?*** (on the Lord's Day and Holy Days of Obligation)

2 Connect

Words I Learned Ask: ***What do you do when you go to Mass, listen to the Scriptures, and receive the Eucharist?*** (worship)

 Ask a volunteer to define *epistle*. Encourage children to locate an epistle in the Bible. Epistles appear just after the Acts of the Apostles and before the Book of Revelation.

Ways of Being Like Jesus Read aloud this section. Say: ***We can do this on every Lord's Day and Holy Day of Obligation.***

 Prayer

Invite children to be still. Say: ***Let's thank Jesus and ask him to help us be faithful members of his family.*** Pray slowly with children. End by praying the Sign of the Cross.

With My Family Ask children to read silently the three suggestions in this section. Invite children to choose one or more to complete at home.

3 Go in Peace

Collect materials and return them to the appropriate places. Encourage children to discuss the With My Family section at home. Say: ***Let's show Jesus we love him by celebrating Sunday with our parish family at Mass and by making it a "sun-day" with our families.***

Living My Faith

Faith Summary

The Mass is the most important celebration in the Church and is the central place where we worship. In the Eucharist we remember Jesus' life, Death, and Resurrection. We celebrate the Eucharist on the Lord's Day and on the Holy Days of Obligation.

Words I Learned	Ways of Being Like Jesus
epistle	Jesus shared bread and wine with his
worship	disciples. *Imitate Jesus by gathering for Mass and celebrating the Eucharist.*

 Prayer

Jesus, thank you for giving me yourself in the Eucharist. Thank you for making me one with God's family as I celebrate this sacrament.

 **With My Family**

Activity After celebrating Mass as a family, share a special meal. Have each member help prepare for the meal, such as setting the table or pouring drinks.

Faith on the Go Ask one another: *How do you prepare yourself to receive the consecrated Bread and Wine when we celebrate the Eucharist?*

Family Prayer Dear God, thank you for Mass so that we can celebrate the Eucharist with our brothers and sisters. Amen.

110 UNIT 4 • *Sacraments, Our Way of Life*

IF TIME ALLOWS

Session Assessment Option

An assessment for this session can be found at **www.findinggod.com**.

PLAN AHEAD

Get Ready for Session 19

Consult the catechist preparation pages to prepare for Session 19 and determine any materials you will need.

Christian Living

Before preparing the session, quiet your thoughts. Concentrate on your breathing and reflect on God's creation that surrounds you—in nature and in the community of people that supports you.

> *1 Corinthians 12:7*
>
> *To each individual the manifestation of the Spirit is given for some benefit.*

Reflection

Being different from your family, friends, and neighbors in appearance, personality, and talents is OK. Saint Paul points out to the believers that the Holy Spirit gives different gifts to different people. The unity of these gifts comes both in their source, who is God, and in their purpose, which is service. In the Sacraments of Holy Orders and Matrimony, the Church celebrates two vocational calls to service. We are all called to share the special talents and abilities God has given to us. Those who recognize and share their gifts with others further the mission of the Church.

Questions

What gifts has God given me for this vocational call to catechesis? What can I do to help others to appreciate their gifts and not to enter into a competitive comparison?

Prayer

Pray to the Spirit, using these words or words of your own.

> *Holy Spirit, giver of gifts, help me to use my talents to serve others and to help the children to discover your gifts to them.*

Knowing and Sharing Your Faith in Session 19

Consider how Scripture and Tradition can deepen your understanding of the session content.

Scripture

1 Corinthians 12:4–11 explains that the Spirit gives different spiritual gifts to each individual.

1 Peter 4:10 tells us that each person is a steward of the gifts God gives.

Tradition

The primary vocation for members of the Church is the call to be followers of Jesus Christ and to participate in the mission of the Church to preach the Gospel. We receive this call in the Sacraments of Baptism and Confirmation. The most common adult vocation in the Church is the call to the Sacrament of Matrimony. This is a call to live a life of committed love with a spouse and to cooperate in the creation of new life. Men are called to the Sacrament of Holy Orders and to the dedication of their lives as a deacon, priest, or bishop.

Catholic Social Teaching

In this session the integrated Catholic Social Teaching themes are **Call to Family, Community, and Participation** and **The Dignity of Work and the Rights of Workers.** See page 91b for an explanation of these themes.

Window on the Catechism

The Liturgy of the Eucharist is covered in *CCC* 1350–1355.

General Directory for Catechesis

As a catechist you have a unique opportunity to foster vocations in those you teach. This important task as it relates to catechesis is discussed in *GDC* 86.

One-Hour Session Planner

SESSION 19 Christian Living

Session Theme: *We are called by God to do special work either as a sister, brother, priest or as a married or single person.*

Before This Session

▶ Prepare a "good deeds bag" containing items a community helper would use, such as badges, tools, or articles of clothing. You might also include pictures of community helpers.

▶ Bookmark your Bible to 1 Corinthians 12:4–11 and 1 Peter 4:10. Place the Bible open to either of these passages in your prayer center.

▶ Display the *Finding God* poster The Seven Sacraments.

▶ Speak with someone from a religious order and a community helper about visiting your class.

▶ Read the Guide for this session, choose any additional If Time Allows activities that you might have time to complete, and gather the listed materials.

STEPS	APPROXIMATE TIME
Engage *Christian Living* PAGE 111	10 minutes
Explore *The Call to Share Our Gifts* PAGES 112–113 **Art Print:** *A Sunny Corner* ART PRINT AND PRINT BACK	30–40 minutes
Reflect **Prayer:** Praying About Gifts and Talents PAGE 114 ***What Will I Do?*** PAGE 115	15–20 minutes
Respond *Living My Faith* PAGE 116	5–10 minutes

Prayer in Session 19

Children pray prayers of petition and gratitude and reflect upon the talents and gifts with which the Holy Spirit has blessed them. A special approach to prayer in Session 19 is an extended guided reflection entitled "Our Gifts from God." As you prepare to share this prayer experience, listen to the recorded guided reflection [CD 1, Track 9]. When you play the recording during the session, join children in reflective prayer. If you choose to lead the guided reflection yourself, listen to the recording a second time, following the script [pages T-288–T-289]. You can use the script or adapt it. An alternative approach is to use the Prayer on the children's page.

Materials

REQUIRED

▶ Bible

▶ Art Print 19: *A Sunny Corner* and Children's Book page 245

▶ "Bag of good deeds" filled with items community helpers would use, such as a stethoscope and hammer

▶ *Finding God* poster: The Seven Sacraments

▶ CD player

▶ CD 1, Track 9: "Our Gifts from God" (10:51)

IF TIME ALLOWS

▶ Session 19 BLM, T-320 (page 113)

▶ Cardstock, art supplies (page 113)

▶ Session 19 Assessment, www.findinggod.com (page 116)

SESSION **19**

Christian Living

We each serve God in our own way. How do people serve the community in different ways?

Prayer

Jesus, my brother, guide me in the search for a way of life that can help me to serve God and others.

111

IF TIME ALLOWS

A Sharing Example

If possible, invite an adult to come to your session to tell children about how he or she shares his or her talents with others. It could be someone you know personally, a parish or community helper, or a parent of one of the children. If applicable, ask the person to bring any special tools or items used as part of the job.

 Go to **www.findinggod.com/sessionextenders** for a short prayer break, a 3-Minute Retreat, about serving your community.

OUTCOMES

▶ Describe ways we can share our gifts with others through our vocations.

▶ Discuss the Sacraments of Holy Orders and Matrimony.

▶ Explain that we all receive different gifts from the Holy Spirit.

▶ Define *Holy Orders, Matrimony,* and *vocation.*

1 Set the Stage

Ask: **What is a community?** (the area where you live) Have available a bag with items from professions in which people help others, such as a carpenter's hammer or a doctor's stethoscope. Say: **Inside my bag are items that people in our community might use to help others.** Invite a volunteer to choose one item. Let children tell who would use it or how it would be used. Repeat until all items have been discussed. Say: **Our session is about ways that people use their gifts to serve the community.**

✝ *Work and Workers*

2 Get Started

Read aloud the session title. Ask: **What does Christian living mean to you?** (Possible answer: following Jesus by helping people and doing good for others) Invite a volunteer to read aloud the text in the blue box. Discuss children's answers to the question.

 Prayer

Say: **Let us ask Jesus' help in knowing what we can do to help others. Pray the prayer with me.** Afterward, say: **Talk to Jesus about what you can do to help others.** Pause. Then together pray *Amen.* Say: **Jesus served his Father and others. We will now learn ways to be like Jesus.**

1 Begin

Ask children to name a talent that they have. Encourage children to think of subtle talents, such as being a good listener or someone who is often cheerful. Say: **Each of us has received different gifts, and we are each called to share these gifts in different ways.**

2 Connect

Invite a volunteer to read aloud the heading and the first paragraph. Ask: **With whom does the Holy Spirit want us to share our gifts?** (Church and community) **In whose name do we serve others?** (Jesus') Write *vocation* on the board. Ask: **What do we call our way of life, the way we are asked to live to share our gifts?** (our vocation)

Write *Holy Orders* on the board. Have a volunteer read aloud the second heading and paragraph. Display the *Finding God* poster The Seven Sacraments and point to the Sacrament of Holy Orders.

Read aloud the last paragraph. Ask children to tell about anyone they know who belongs to a religious order. Invite responses to the question about a sister, priest, or monk they have read about in this book, such as Saint Katharine Drexel and Saints Benedict and Scholastica.

Point to the photos on the page. Ask: **Who is this woman in the top photo?** (Blessed Teresa of Calcutta) Discuss how the people in the photos serve God and the Church. Ask: **We learned about sacramentals in Session 13. What sacramental is pictured on this page?** (a cross)

Reading God's Word

Have a volunteer read aloud the passage. Say: **Think of a gift you have received from God. Think about how you can use it to serve God and others.**

 Family and Community

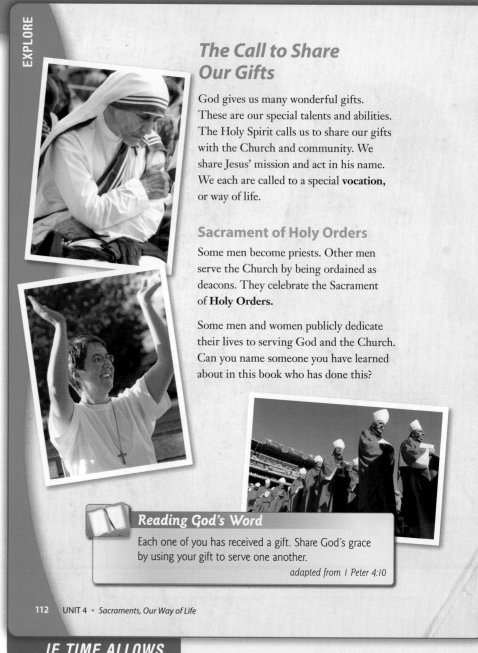

The Call to Share Our Gifts

God gives us many wonderful gifts. These are our special talents and abilities. The Holy Spirit calls us to share our gifts with the Church and community. We share Jesus' mission and act in his name. We each are called to a special **vocation,** or way of life.

Sacrament of Holy Orders

Some men become priests. Other men serve the Church by being ordained as deacons. They celebrate the Sacrament of **Holy Orders.**

Some men and women publicly dedicate their lives to serving God and the Church. Can you name someone you have learned about in this book who has done this?

Reading God's Word

Each one of you has received a gift. Share God's grace by using your gift to serve one another.

adapted from 1 Peter 4:10

112 UNIT 4 • *Sacraments, Our Way of Life*

IF TIME ALLOWS

More on Vocations

If your pastor has already spoken to your class [Session 13], ask your catechetical leader if he or she knows of a sister who could visit and talk about her vocation to the group. Before the visit have children compile a list of questions they would like to ask. After the visit encourage children to discuss their thoughts on what the sister shared.

Sacrament of Matrimony

The Holy Spirit calls some men and women to be married. They agree to live in faithful love in the Sacrament of **Matrimony.** Other people choose to remain single. Single people serve God in their lives and in the work they do in the world. No matter what our vocation in life may be, we are each called to God's service.

Your Vocation

Have you imagined what your vocation may be as an adult? Write how you could share God's love through your choice.

Meet a Saint

Saint Andrew Kim Taegon was the first Korean person called to serve God as a priest. Andrew Kim was born to a noble family and became a Christian. When he was 15 years old, he went to a seminary in southern China. He returned to Korea and began spreading God's Word as a priest. Years later he and many others were martyred for their faith. The feast of Andrew Kim Taegon and his companions is September 20.

GO TO PAGE 245

SESSION 19 • *Christian Living* 113

IF TIME ALLOWS

Session 19 BLM

Gifts from God Have children complete the Session 19 Blackline Master [T-320] to draw pictures of their gifts from God.

Service: Thank-You Cards

Have children select someone to thank for using his or her vocation to help others. Provide paper and crayons to make thank-you notes. Have children sign only their first names and then send the cards to the intended recipients.

✝ *Family and Community*

Have a volunteer read aloud the heading and first paragraph. Ask: **When men and women agree to live in faithful love, what sacrament do they receive?** (the Sacrament of Matrimony) Direct children's attention to the *Finding God* poster The Seven Sacraments. Say: **Matrimony is one of two sacraments that bless a vocation. It blesses all those who choose to marry.** Ask: **Can people who choose not to marry still serve God?** (Yes.)

Ask a volunteer to read aloud Your Vocation. Have children share what their future vocations might be and why. Ask how this relates to their gifts and how they might serve God and others. Ask children to think of symbols for their gifts, such as music notes or a firefighter's helmet. Have children draw the symbols on paper and set these aside to use during prayer.

Meet a Saint

Read the story of Saint Andrew Kim Taegon [TAY gahn]. Ask: **What does martyr mean?** (a person who accepts death rather than deny his or her faith) Ask: **What was Andrew Kim Taegon's vocation?** (priest) **What does his life show us?** (how to be strong in answering God's call)

Point to the picture. Say: **Saint Andrew is wearing native Korean clothing, but he is also wearing a red cloth. This is called a stole, a sign of priestly office worn by all priests.**

③ Close

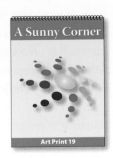
A Sunny Corner

Art Print 19

Display Art Print 19: *A Sunny Corner.* Use the Art Print 19 instruction to teach this section. Art Print teaching instruction can also be found on page 245.

Prayer

Choose an approach and pray with the children.

APPROACH 1

Recorded Guided Reflection

Prepare Listen in advance to the recorded guided reflection "Our Gifts from God" [CD 1, Track 9]. Decide if you will use the recording or lead the reflection yourself. If you choose to lead, listen to the recording again, following the script [pages T-288–T-289] and noting pauses and tone. You can then use the script or adapt it as you wish.

Pray During the session, play the recording or lead using the script, joining children in reflective prayer. If you use the script, play reflective music in the background.

APPROACH 2

Children's Page

Prepare Pray the prayer on page 114 in advance to become familiar with it.

Pray Say: **Today we have talked about the gifts the Holy Spirit has given to us. Let us reflect on how we can use our talents to serve God and others.**

Invite children to bring the symbols of their talents to the prayer center. Ask children to place the symbols next to the Bible and say "Here I am, Lord." Have children sit in a circle. Say: **Now close your eyes and take three deep breaths.** Pause. Say: **Now we are ready to begin.**

Read aloud the first paragraph pausing after each question. Then read aloud the remaining paragraphs, allowing children to spend time thinking of a vocation. Lead them in praying the Sign of the Cross. Say: **Now let us learn how we can use our talents to serve others.**

Prayer

Praying About Gifts and Talents

God has given each of us special gifts and talents. Think about your special talents. What things do you do very well? Do you use your talents at school? Do you use them to help at home?

Spend a few minutes talking with Jesus about your talents. Tell him what you think your special abilities are. Thank him for giving these gifts to you. Tell him how you will share your gifts. Ask Jesus to help you to choose a vocation that will allow you to serve others.

Be still with Jesus for a few moments. Trust that Jesus will help you use your gifts and talents to do things well and to help others.

114 UNIT 4 • *Sacraments, Our Way of Life*

IF TIME ALLOWS

Pray Again

If you used the recorded guided reflection, you might use this prayer page during another session.

FYI

Coaching Children to Pray

After the close of the prayer, offer suggestions built on the last sentence of the prayer, encouraging children to thank Jesus for the gift of their talents and for his guidance in using them to help others.

What Will I Do?

The Holy Spirit has given each of us gifts and talents that we should use to help others and to make our world better for everyone. Think about your own gifts and talents and how you can use them when you grow up. Then fill in the following sentence.

When I am older, I will help others by_____.

Sharing Gifts and Talents with Others

Complete the sentences below. Look back in this session for help.

1. God gives us gifts, which are our special _____**talents**_____ and _____**abilities**_____.

2. The _____**Holy**_____ _____**Spirit**_____ calls us to share our gifts with the Church and community.

3. We are each called to a special _____**vocation**_____, or way of life.

4. Men who become priests celebrate the Sacrament of _____**Holy**_____ _____**Orders**_____.

5. The Holy Spirit calls some men and women to be married. They agree to live in faithful love in the Sacrament of _____**Matrimony**_____.

115

1 Begin

Say: **We have talked about the different gifts that the Holy Spirit has given each of us.** Ask: **When you get older, what kinds of jobs can you do with your gifts?** (Answers will vary.) **How can you help people in your Church and community when you do that job?** (Answers will vary.) Discuss the different occupations that use a particular talent or ability that each child names.

2 Connect

Read aloud the heading. Have a volunteer read aloud the first paragraph. Give children a few minutes to think about how their talents translate into a particular occupation and then complete their sentences.

Read aloud Sharing Gifts and Talents with Others. Make sure children understand the directions. Remind children that all the answers appear in the previous pages of the session. If needed, walk around the room while children work and answer any questions. When they are finished, allow children to share their answers with the group.

3 Close

Say: **Let us ask God to guide us in using our gifts and talents to help those around us.** Allow sufficient time to let children pray, and then conclude by praying aloud the Sign of the Cross.

IF TIME ALLOWS

Guess the Job

When children have finished the activity page, allow each child a chance to read his or her completed sentence so that others can guess the chosen job. Encourage him or her to continue giving clues until others guess the job.

Begin

Faith Summary Read aloud this section and ask: **Who calls us to share our gifts?** (the Holy Spirit) **What are we called to do with these gifts?** (Use them to share God's love.)

 Connect

Words I Learned Ask: **What do Holy Orders and Matrimony have in common?** (Both are sacraments and vocations that serve God and others.) Ask volunteers to find the terms in the Glossary and read the definitions.

Ways of Being Like Jesus After reading aloud this section, ask children for specific suggestions for using their gifts to help others, such as helping a classmate with homework for a subject they know well.

> **Prayer**
>
> Say: **Today we reflected on our gifts. Let us thank Jesus for helping us use our gifts to serve others. Join me in praying aloud.**
>
> After praying ask children to spend a few moments with Jesus. Then pray the Sign of the Cross. Say: **We use our gifts every day in what we do. We can offer Jesus a prayer of thanks at any time because he is always with us, supporting and guiding us.**

With My Family Ask children to read silently the three suggestions in this section. Invite children to choose one or more to complete at home.

 Go in Peace

Collect materials and return them to the appropriate places. Encourage children to discuss the With My Family section at home. As children leave, call each by name and say: **[Name], use your special gifts to serve God and others.**

116 www.findinggod.com

RESPOND

Living My Faith

Faith Summary

God gives us special talents and abilities. The Holy Spirit calls us to share these gifts. We each are called to a way of life that will help us share God's love.

Words I Learned

Holy Orders
Matrimony
vocation

Ways of Being Like Jesus

Jesus served others. *Share your gifts and talents with someone who is struggling or could use your friendship.*

> **Prayer**
>
> *Jesus, thank you for helping me to recognize my gifts and talents. Support me as I try to use them to serve others.*

With My Family

Activity Use your gifts and talents to contribute to your family. You could use your talents to help cook, clean, or cheer up someone.

Faith on the Go Ask one another: *If you could have any talent you wanted, what would you choose? How would you use this talent to help others?*

Family Prayer Dear God, thank you for giving us special talents. Help us to use them to contribute to our family and our parish. Amen.

116 UNIT 4 • *Sacraments, Our Way of Life*

IF TIME ALLOWS

Session Assessment Option

An assessment for this session can be found at **www.findinggod.com.**

PLAN AHEAD

Get Ready for Session 20

Consult the catechist preparation pages to prepare for Session 20 and determine any materials you will need.

Celebrating Lent and Holy Week

3-Minute Retreat

Before preparing the session, pause, be still, and be aware of the loving presence of God.

Tobit 4:7

Give alms from your possessions. Do not turn your face away from any of the poor, and God's face will not be turned away from you.

Reflection

Tobit is sending his son Tobias to retrieve some money kept in a foreign land. He instructs Tobias to give alms to the poor. Later Tobit tells Tobias that giving alms not only frees one from death, but also keeps one from the "dark abode" (Tobit 4:10). It is no accident that the giving of alms is a spiritual discipline not only taught in the Old Testament, but emphasized by Jesus as well. Those who are poor are precious in God's sight, and caring for them is a sure sign of a person walking in companionship with Jesus.

Question

What opportunities do I have for practicing almsgiving during Lent and beyond?

Prayer

Pray, using this prayer or one of your own.

Jesus, help me to see all in need as precious in your sight so that I may share with an open heart.

Knowing and Sharing Your Faith in Session 20

Consider how Scripture and Tradition can deepen your understanding of the session content.

Scripture

Tobit 4:7 tells us not to turn our faces away from the poor, and God will not turn his face from us.

Matthew 25:40 teaches us that when we help those in need, we do it for Christ.

Luke 21:1–4 tells the story of the poor widow who gave all that she had to help others.

Tradition

Lent is the period of fasting preceding the celebration of Easter. It recalls Jesus' 40 day fast in the wilderness [Matthew 4:1–11]. Lent begins with Ash Wednesday and ends right before the evening Mass of Holy Thursday. During Lent the Church focuses on our need for God's forgiveness as individuals and as a community. We do so through the Lenten practice of fasting, refraining from food for a period of time to remember our dependence on God. We are also asked to consider Lent as being a period of almsgiving. To give alms is to offer our money, possessions, time, or talent to those in need. For example, we may give up one special treat a week and donate the money not spent to help those in need.

Catholic Social Teaching

In this session the integrated Catholic Social Teaching theme is **Call to Family, Community, and Participation.** See page 91b for an explanation of this theme.

Window on the Catechism

The seasons and days of penance are discussed in *CCC* 1438.

General Directory for Catechesis

The organization of catechesis around the season of Lent is discussed in *GDC* 129.

One-Hour Session Planner

SESSION 20 Celebrating Lent and Holy Week

Session Theme: *Lent and Holy Week are times to think of how we treat others.*

Before This Session

▶ Determine whether you will use the Unit Assessment option listed on page 120.

▶ Determine whether you will also discuss the Lent and Holy Week seasonal pages in the back of the Children's Book.

▶ Bookmark your Bible to Tobit 4:7. Place the open Bible in your prayer center.

▶ Read the Guide for this session, choose any addition If Time Allows activities that you might have time to complete, and gather the listed materials.

STEPS	APPROXIMATE TIME
Engage ***Celebrating Lent and Holy Week*** PAGE 117	10 minutes
Explore ***We Grow in Virtue During Lent and Holy Week*** PAGE 118	25–35 minutes
Reflect ***Mass During Lent and Holy Week*** PAGE 119 **Art Print:** *Christ on the Cross* ART PRINT AND PRINT BACK	20–25 minutes
Respond ***Living My Faith*** PAGE 120	5–10 minutes

Prayer in Session 20

Prayer during this session gives children an opportunity to ask Jesus for help in thinking of others' needs and the strength and guidance to help them. The prayer times will include time for children to talk with God in the silence of their hearts and to share with him any of their thoughts and concerns.

Materials

REQUIRED

▶ Bible

▶ Palms

▶ Art Print 20: *Christ on the Cross* and Children's Book page 246

IF TIME ALLOWS

▶ Sidewalk chalk (page 117)

▶ Voice recorder and various instruments for sound effects (page 119)

▶ Session 20 BLM, T-321 (page 118)

▶ Session 20 Assessment, www.findinggod.com (page 120)

▶ Unit 4 Assessment, T-322–T-324 (page 120)

Celebrating Lent and Holy Week

The season of Lent begins on Ash Wednesday, 40 days before Easter Sunday, and ends on the evening of Holy Thursday. During this time we prepare for the celebration of Jesus' Resurrection at Easter by praying and thinking about how to follow Jesus more closely.

The last week of Lent is Holy Week. Holy Week begins on Palm Sunday and includes Holy Thursday, Good Friday, and Holy Saturday. During this important week, we remember the suffering, Death, and Resurrection of Jesus.

Prayer

Dear Jesus, I know you will be with me during each day of Lent and Holy Week. Help me to think of others' needs and ways to help them.

IF TIME ALLOWS

Inclusion: Attention

Lenten Time Line Use this activity if you have children with attention differences. Take children outside to a large area of concrete or black-top. Have children use sidewalk chalk to work together to make a Holy Week Time Line. Encourage children to add colorful designs. Have children label the time line and sign their names near their artwork.

Make a Lent Calendar

Sometimes it is easier for children to understand the special days of Lent when they see them in a visual format. Draw a calendar on the board and have volunteers write in the following days: Ash Wednesday, Palm Sunday, Holy Thursday, Good Friday, Holy Saturday, and Easter Sunday. Then use another color to connect all 40 days.

SESSION 20
OUTCOMES

▶ Explain that Lent is a time to think of how we treat others.

▶ Discuss that Lent is a time to be aware of the needs of others and to respond with help.

▶ Define *almsgiving*.

1 Set the Stage

Display a palm. Ask: **When do we see palms in our Church?** (on Palm Sunday) Say: **Let's read more about Lent and the special days during Holy Week.**

2 Get Started

Read aloud the session title and ask a volunteer to read aloud the first paragraph. Ask: **What do we prepare for during Lent?** (the celebration of Jesus' Resurrection at Easter) **When do we celebrate Lent?** (It begins on Ash Wednesday and ends on Holy Thursday.)

Ask a volunteer to read aloud the second paragraph. Ask: **When is Holy Week?** (the last week of Lent) **What is the first day of Holy Week?** (Palm Sunday) **What do we remember during Holy Week?** (Jesus' suffering, Death, and Resurrection)

Say: **In this session we'll learn about Lent and Holy Week—a time of year when we learn how to be more like Jesus by helping others.**

Prayer

Call children's attention to the prayer. Say: **Take a moment to think about the people in your life who might need help. Is there anything you can do to help?** Ask a volunteer to pray aloud. Say: **Let's take a moment to talk to Jesus in our hearts.** Allow time for children to finish their silent prayers. Pray *Amen* and conclude by praying the Sign of the Cross.

1 Begin

Ask: **What does the expression "put yourself in someone else's shoes" mean?** (pretend you are in someone else's position, feeling and reacting how that person might to something that has happened) Say: **Lent is a time to be aware of other people's situations and how you might be able to help them.**

2 Connect

Have a volunteer read aloud the heading and the first paragraph. Discuss the difference between a person's needs and wants. Draw a two-column chart on the board with one heading labeled *Wants* and the other *Needs*. Write children's suggestions for each column and discuss them. Emphasize the importance of helping people in need of love, food, and shelter this Lent.

Read aloud the question after the first paragraph. Invite volunteers to share their answers.

 Have a volunteer read aloud the section Almsgiving. Ask: **What did Jesus mean when he said the widow put in more than the rich people?** (The widow gave all the money she had, but the rich people could have given more but didn't.)

Read aloud Earn Money for Almsgiving and invite children to complete the activity with partners. Write their answers on the board.

3 Close

Direct children's attention to the feature at the bottom of page 118.

 Reading God's Word

Read aloud the verse as children follow along in their books. Then together have children read the verse aloud. Ask: **How will you graciously give alms this Lent?** (Answers will vary.) Discuss children's responses.

We Grow In Virtue During Lent and Holy Week

Lent is a time to think about how we treat others. We look beyond our own wants and desires. Lent is a time to be aware of the needs of others and to respond with help, just as Jesus did.

What are some ways I treat others with respect?

Almsgiving

Jesus had a special love for people who were poor.

> People were putting money into a collection box. Jesus noticed a poor widow put in two coins. He said, "This poor widow put in more than the rich. She gave all the money she had, but the rich people gave from their extra supply."   *adapted from Luke 21:1–4*

During Lent we practice **almsgiving,** when we give money to people who are poor.

Earn Money for Almsgiving

Instead of asking your parents, what are three ways you could "earn" some extra money for those in need?

1. _____

2. _____

3. _____

 Reading God's Word

Graciously give alms.   *adapted from Tobit 4:7*

118   UNIT 4 • *Sacraments, Our Way of Life*

IF TIME ALLOWS

Session 20 BLM

Helping Others Have children complete the Session 20 Blackline Master [T-321] to write a prayer for a friend in need.

Seasonal Sessions: Lent and Holy Week

Work with children through pages 161–168 of the Children's Book and this guide. These special sessions can each take up to one hour to complete.

Mass During Lent and Holy Week

When we go to Mass throughout the year, we pray the General Intercessions. During these prayers we pray for the needs of the Church, the world, and the local community. On Good Friday traditional ancient intercessions are prayed. The priest invites us to pray for the Church, the pope, the leaders of the Church and government, for those preparing to celebrate Baptism, and for people who do not believe in God and Jesus. We can include our own needs with the prayers of others.

What We Experience

When you look around your church during Lent, you will notice that the church looks very simple and plain. You do not see flowers or decorations in the sanctuary because this is a season of penance. The priest wears purple vestments.

Let Us Pray to the Lord

Finish the following prayers with the needs of your community or the needs of the world.

For _____, may God _____.
Let us pray to the Lord. Lord, hear our prayer.

For _____, may God _____.
Let us pray to the Lord. Lord, hear our prayer.

Did You Know?
The number 40 occurs frequently in both the Old and New Testaments of the Bible. It is a symbolic number.

GO TO PAGE 246

IF TIME ALLOWS

Service: Audio Book

Make an audio book for a local hospital or daycare center. Have children read aloud the book and add sound effects to go along with the story. Have children practice a few songs that go with the story or the season. Record the class singing at the end.

✝ **Family and Community**

---

1 Begin

Ask: **What is a prayer of intercession?** (a prayer that asks God for help on behalf of another) Say: **Think of someone who has been on your mind lately or a group of people who you think might need your prayers. Anytime, but especially during Lent, is a good time to pray prayers of intercession.**

2 Connect

Read aloud the heading and the first paragraph. Explain that during Lent we strive to think of others, not just ourselves. Point out that one of the best ways that we can help others in need is to pray for them.

Ask a volunteer to read aloud the section What We Experience. Ask: **Do you see a lot of decorations, such as flowers, at church during Lent?** (No.) What color vestments does the priest wear? (purple)

Read aloud the directions for Let Us Pray to the Lord and invite children to complete it independently.

Did You Know?

Read aloud this feature. Tell children that many events in the Old and New Testaments contain the number 40. For example, Lent is 40 days, the great flood was 40 days, the people of Israel wandered in the wilderness for 40 years, and Christ prayed in the desert for 40 days.

3 Close

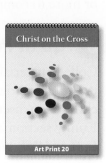

Display Art Print 20: *Christ on the Cross*. Use the Art Print 20 instruction to teach this section. Art Print teaching instruction can also be found on page 246.

1 Begin

Faith Summary Ask a volunteer to read aloud this section. Ask: **What do we prepare for during Lent?** (the celebration of Jesus' Resurrection) **How should we respond to others' needs?** (with help)

2 Connect

Word I Learned Write *almsgiving* on the board and pronounce it clearly. Ask children to suggest words or phrases that clarify the meaning of the word. Review the word in the Glossary if necessary.

Ways of Being Like Jesus Have a volunteer read aloud this section. Say: **Sometimes the best way to help people is simply to listen to what is worrying them or causing them trouble. Often just having a friend to talk to makes people feel better.**

 Prayer

Ask children to close their eyes, fold their hands, and pray silently as you pray aloud. Allow a few seconds for silent reflection. Pray *Amen* and then pray the Sign of the Cross together.

With My Family Ask children to read silently the three suggestions in this section. Invite children to choose one or more to complete at home.

3 Go in Peace

Collect materials and return them to the appropriate places. Encourage children to discuss the With My Family section at home. Say: **During Lent and Holy Week, tell me some of the ways you've found to act more like Jesus. I'd like to hear your ideas!**

RESPOND

Living My Faith

Faith Summary

During Lent we prepare for the celebration of Jesus' Resurrection. It is a time to think about how we can love others as Jesus did. We are encouraged to look beyond our own wants and desires. We strive to be aware of others' needs and respond with help.

Word I Learned

almsgiving

Ways of Being Like Jesus

Jesus treated others with kindness.
Reach out to others by being a good listener.

 Prayer

Dear Jesus, during Lent I will work hard to treat others with kindness and respect. I know you will guide me and help me to do the right thing.

With My Family

Activity Make a family alms jar. Use the jar to collect the money saved from a Lenten promise, such as giving up candy or renting DVDs. Donate the money to a charity of your family's choice.

Faith on the Go Ask one another: *What is one way that our family can help those in need this Lent?*

Family Prayer *God, help us to be aware of others' needs and think of ways we can help them. Amen.*

120 UNIT 4 • *Sacraments, Our Way of Life*

IF TIME ALLOWS

Session Assessment Option

An assessment for this session can be found at **www.findinggod.com**.

Unit Assessment Option

If you wish, photocopy the Unit Assessment on pages T-322–T-324. Administer the assessment during the session or send it home.

PLAN AHEAD

Get Ready for Session 21

Consult the catechist preparation pages to prepare for Session 21 and determine any materials you will need.

UNIT 5

Catechist Preparation pages open each unit and session.

Morality, Our Lived Faith   121

UNIT 5
Morality, Our Lived Faith

The focus of this unit is on living like Jesus. In this unit children will learn the following concepts.

SESSION 21 *Faith, Hope, and Charity*

The virtues of faith, hope, and charity help us to lead a Christian life. These Theological Virtues are gifts from God and are the foundation of the Christian life. When we practice these virtues, we grow closer to God.

SESSION 22 *Making Good Choices*

God gave us the Ten Commandments to help us follow the moral law. The commandments help us to do good and to avoid evil. With the help of the Holy Spirit, we can make good moral choices and live our lives for God and for others.

SESSION 23 *Living as God's Children*

Jesus helps us to love and respect one another. Through the grace of God, we can live in peace, harmony, and justice with our families. We share God's love by caring for others, especially those who are poor and elderly. The Holy Spirit is the source of God's help in our lives.

SESSION 24 *All Life Is Sacred*

As Catholics we are called to be aware of the needs of other people and of all creation. We treat every person as sacred and take care of God's creation. By caring for God's creation today, we help to preserve a better world for the people of the future.

SESSION 25 *Celebrating Easter*

Children learn the meaning of Easter, why we celebrate it, and explore how Easter is celebrated in our Church.

UNIT SAINT
Saint Monica

Monica, a devoted Christian, was the mother of Augustine. Monica raised her children as Christians, but Augustine was never baptized. While Augustine spent many years studying and practicing different religions, Monica persevered in her prayers for his conversion to Christianity. She finally saw him baptized when he was 33 years old. Monica is the patroness of married women and a model for Christian mothers, as well as our model of how to live like Jesus.

Prayer in Unit 5

In this unit the prayers will engage children in reflection on the following: the Theological Virtues, the Morning Offering, the gift of their own families, and other lessons they have learned this year. These prayer pages provide closure to the time your group has spent praying and growing together. The prayer service in the Review session invites children to praise and thank God with a prayer from Psalm 119:1–3. Continue the pattern and tone for prayer in the opening prayers of petition, the closing prayers of thanks, and the prayer services.

✝ Catholic Social Teaching in Unit 5

Following are the themes of Catholic Social Teaching integrated into this unit.

Call to Family, Community, and Participation Participation in family and community is central to our faith and to a healthy society. As the central social institution, family must be supported and strengthened. From this foundation people participate in society, fostering a community spirit and promoting the well-being of all.

Care for God's Creation God is the Creator of all people and all things, and he wants us to enjoy his creation. The responsibility to care for all God has made is a requirement of our faith. We are called to make moral and ethical choices that protect the ecological balance of creation both locally and worldwide.

Life and Dignity of the Human Person The Catholic Church teaches us that all human life is sacred and that all people must be treated with dignity. We are called to ask whether our actions as a society respect or threaten the life and dignity of the human person.

Option for the Poor and Vulnerable In our world many people are wealthy, while at the same time, many are poor. As Catholics we are called to pay special attention to the needs of those who are poor. We can follow Jesus' example by making a specific effort to defend and promote the dignity of those who are poor and vulnerable and meet their immediate needs.

Rights and Responsibilities The Catholic Church teaches that every person has a right to life as well as a right to those things required for human decency. As Catholics it is our responsibility to protect these fundamental human rights in order to achieve a healthy society. The only way to protect human dignity and to live in a healthy community is for each of us to accept our responsibility to protect those rights in our own interactions.

Solidarity Because God is our Father, we are all brothers and sisters with the responsibility to care for one another. Solidarity unites rich and poor, weak and strong, and helps build a society that recognizes that we live in an interdependent world.

TOGETHER *as One Parish*

Religious Education with the Parochial School

To nurture parish unity, end the year by inviting each school and religious education family to e-mail one or two photos that show their family engaged in an experience where they felt God's presence, such as experiencing a sacramental event, engaging in a service project, or participating in a special family holiday celebration. Ask them to add a caption for their photo. Compile the photos and captions into a photocopied "scrapbook" with the words *Finding God in All Things* as the title.

📖 *Literature Opportunity*
***Shota and the Star Quilt*
by Margaret Bateson-Hill**
You might wish to read aloud this story of how two young girls form a strong bond to each other and with a community. The united group works together to save their homes.

✝ *Solidarity*

Faith, Hope, and Charity

3-Minute Retreat

Pause before you prepare the session, and spend some time with God. Think of his limitless love for you. Take three deep breaths and rest in the love and comfort that God gives you.

1 Corinthians 13:13

So faith, hope, love remain, these three; but the greatest of these is love.

Reflection

Addressing the church at Corinth, Saint Paul identifies the Theological Virtues of faith, hope, and love. Faith and hope, two gifts of grace from God, are given life in our practice of charity. Charity is not only about giving to those who are poor, but also a daily practice of seeing all people as our neighbors and loving them as ourselves. Like all gifts, we need to receive the gifts of faith, hope, and charity and make them a part of our lives.

Question

How do my thoughts, words, and actions reflect the virtues of faith, hope, and charity?

Prayer

Speak to God, using this prayer or one of your own.

God, who calls me to return to you with love, cultivate in me the virtues of faith, hope, and love that I may more closely follow your Son, Jesus, and show my love for you and for those I meet.

Knowing and Sharing Your Faith in Session 21

Consider how Scripture and Tradition can deepen your understanding of the session content.

Scripture

1 Thessalonians 1:2–4 tells how Paul praises the Christian community for its faith, labors of love, and endurance.

1 Corinthians 13:13 explains that love is greater than faith or hope.

Tradition

Faith is the acceptance of God's self-revelation in Jesus Christ. It is a free acceptance and cannot be forced upon a person. Hope is the goodness of God. It involves directing oneself toward the fullness of life with God, confident that it can be attained through God's help. Charity is the love of God, our loving response to God's love. It is based on the fellowship with God that was offered to us in Jesus Christ and motivated by the Holy Spirit. Charity is expressed by our love of God and neighbor, which includes love of enemies and sinners. We call faith, hope, and charity Theological Virtues. They are gifts from God and cannot be acquired by personal effort. We can perfect the these virtues through exercise, but we can also lose them through neglect.

Catholic Social Teaching

In this session the integrated Catholic Social Teaching themes are **Life and Dignity of the Human Person; Option for the Poor and Vulnerable;** and **Solidarity.** See page 121b for an explanation of these themes.

Window on the Catechism

The Theological Virtues are discussed in *CCC* 1812–1829.

General Directory for Catechesis

The role of the Theological Virtues as integral to the invitation to follow Jesus is discussed in *GDC* 140.

One-Hour Session Planner

SESSION 21 Faith, Hope, and Charity

Session Theme: *We live like Jesus when we practice the virtues of faith, hope, and charity.*

Before This Session

▶ Bookmark your Bible to 1 Thessalonians 1:2–4 and 1 Corinthians 13:13. Place the Bible open to either passage in your prayer center.

▶ Read the Guide for this session, choose any additional If Time Allows activities that you might have time to complete, and gather the listed materials.

> **Prayer in Session 21**
>
> In this session children reflect on the Theological Virtues of faith, hope, and charity as part of a short guided reflection.

STEPS	APPROXIMATE TIME
Engage *Unit Saint:* Saint Monica PAGES 121–122 *Faith, Hope, and Charity* PAGE 123	10 minutes
Explore *Saints Who Showed Hope in God* PAGE 124 *Important Virtues* PAGE 125 *Art Print:* The Sacred Heart ART PRINT AND PRINT BACK	30–40 minutes
Reflect *Prayer:* Thanks for Virtues God Has Given PAGE 126 *She Lived Like Jesus* PAGE 127	15–20 minutes
Respond *Living My Faith* PAGE 128	5–10 minutes

Materials

REQUIRED

▶ Bible

▶ Art Print 21: *The Sacred Heart* and Children's Book page 247

▶ Construction paper hands (1 per group of 3 children)

▶ Art supplies

▶ Drawing paper

▶ CD player

▶ CD 2, Track 16: "What Does It Mean to Follow Jesus?" (Instrumental)

▶ CD 2, Track 15: "What Does It Mean to Follow Jesus?" (1:55)

IF TIME ALLOWS

▶ Poster board (pages 123, 125)

▶ Session 21 BLM, T-325 (page 124)

▶ Message Through Media: *A Memory for Tino* VHS or DVD (page 124)

▶ Shoe boxes (page 125)

▶ Art supplies, drawing paper (page 126)

▶ Computer, cardstock (page 127)

▶ Session 21 Assessment, www.findinggod.com (page 128)

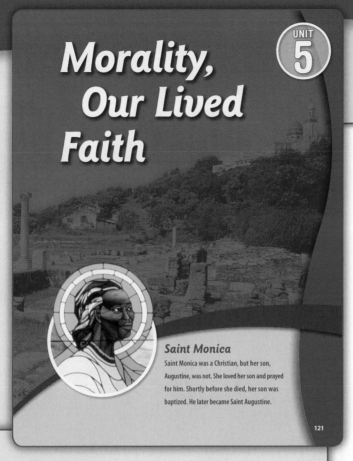

Morality, Our Lived Faith

Saint Monica

Saint Monica was a Christian, but her son, Augustine, was not. She loved her son and prayed for him. Shortly before she died, her son was baptized. He later became Saint Augustine.

121

Saint Monica

Monica was a Christian who wanted her family to share in Jesus' love. She patiently prayed for her husband, Patricius, and his mother, who were not Christians. Her prayers were answered when they were baptized. Her son, Augustine, however, did not accept Jesus.

Monica loved Augustine very much. She never stopped praying for him, even though he grew up and moved away. She continued to hope, even when he made sinful choices. Her prayers were finally answered when Augustine was baptized at the age of 33. He later became a great bishop and teacher.

Monica is the patron saint of married women. She is a model for Christian mothers. She is our model when we pray for others to know Jesus. Her feast is August 27. The next day, August 28, is the feast of her son, Augustine.

Monica and Augustine were born in Tagaste, which is now Souk Ahras, Algeria.

122   UNIT 5 • *Morality, Our Lived Faith*

Choose one approach to open the unit.
5-Minute Approach . . . . below
Optional Unit Opener . . . . next page

5-MINUTE APPROACH
Children's Pages

1 Begin

Greet children by name. Read aloud the unit title. Say: *In our fifth unit, we will learn how God and Jesus are with us with every choice we make.*

Invite children to play a game. Say: *I'll give you clues about a special person. Raise your hand when you know the person.* Use these clues: *She loves you even when you do something wrong. She prays that you will always love God.* When children guess their mothers, say: *Our mothers love us very much and want us to love Jesus. Now let's learn about a saint who was also a mother.*

2 Introduce the Saint

Ask children to turn to page 121. Read aloud the text. Ask: *Who was Saint Monica's son?* (Saint Augustine) *Why did Monica pray for him?* (She wanted him to be baptized.)

Ask children to turn to page 122. Read aloud the first paragraph. Ask: *How do we know that Saint Monica loved Jesus very much?* (She wanted her family to share in Jesus' love; prayed for her family members to be baptized.)

Invite a volunteer to read aloud the second paragraph. Ask: *What are some ways Monica showed her love for Augustine?* (never stopped praying for him, continued to hope for his conversion) Ask: *How did God answer her prayers?* (Augustine was baptized and became a great bishop and teacher.)

Invite a volunteer to read aloud the third paragraph. Say: *Some people do not know about Jesus' never-ending love for them. Like Monica, we can pray for them.*

This page describes a program-wide intergenerational event that is offered in a supplemental component.

OPTIONAL UNIT OPENER

Intergenerational Event

1 Prepare

Work with your catechetical leader to use the *Finding God Together* kit to plan an intergenerational event for Unit 5.

2 Open the Event

Gather families in one space. Use *Finding God Together* to open the event and discuss the main theme for Unit 5. Together, enjoy an entertaining skit.

3 Implement the Saint Stations

Use *Finding God Together* to help families learn more about the saints at their grade-level saint stations. Be sure families feel welcome and are engaged in the process.

4 Close

Gather families in one space for a guided reflection. Use *Finding God Together* to close the event.

5 Transition to Children's Book

When children arrive for the faith formation session, discuss the event and review information about the unit saint. Have children open their books to page 123.

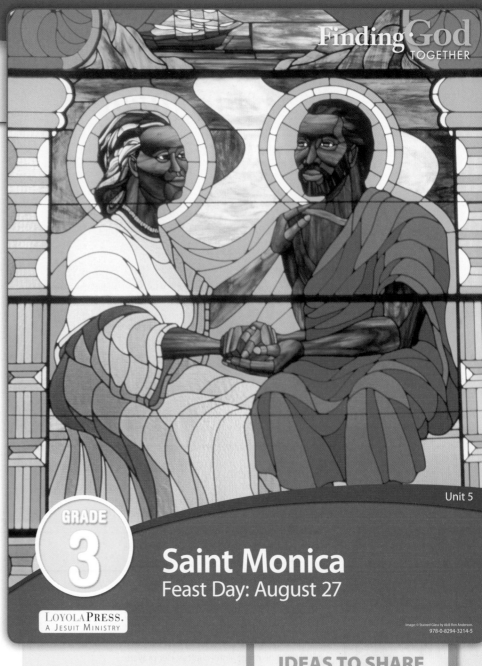

Finding God TOGETHER

GRADE 3

Unit 5

Saint Monica
Feast Day: August 27

LOYOLA PRESS.
A JESUIT MINISTRY

Image: © Stained Glass by Akili Ron Anderson.
978-0-8294-3214-5

Events Guide
Finding God Together: An Intergenerational Events Guide
by Mary Lynn Hendrickson and Tom McGrath

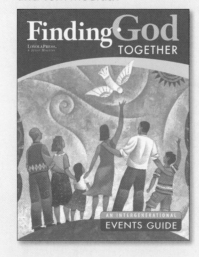

Finding God TOGETHER

AN INTERGENERATIONAL
EVENTS GUIDE

IDEAS TO SHARE

Saint Monica

Monica was born in A.D. 332. She married a pagan official, Patricius, and they had three children. She lived her life as an exemplary Christian and encouraged her children to do the same. Two of her children, Perpetua and Navigius, were baptized and entered the religious life. However, Augustine was difficult to guide toward Christian living. Monica agonized over his future and tried to convince him. Augustine was finally baptized in A.D. 387. Shortly after, Monica died in Ostia, near Rome.

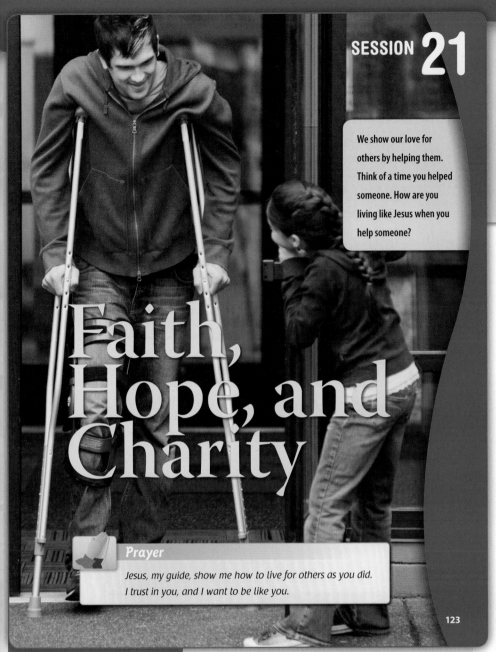

SESSION **21**

Faith, Hope, and Charity

We show our love for others by helping them. Think of a time you helped someone. How are you living like Jesus when you help someone?

 Prayer

Jesus, my guide, show me how to live for others as you did. I trust in you, and I want to be like you.

123

IF TIME ALLOWS

Catholic Charities

With the group, visit Catholic Charities' Web site at www.catholic charitiesusa.org to learn about specific programs that fight poverty and support individuals and families. Discuss the works of the Catholic Charities local and national chapters. Give children time to compare these programs to the ideas on their "hands." Write new ideas on the board and have children use the ideas to make a colorful poster encouraging others to get involved in a program to help those in need.

✝ **Solidarity**

 Go to **www.findinggod.com/sessionextenders** for a 3-Minute Retreat on the virtues of hope, faith, and love.

SESSION 21

OUTCOMES

▶ Discuss how virtues help us lead good lives.

▶ Identify Saint Jeanne Jugan as someone who served others.

▶ Define *charity, hope,* and *virtues.*

1 Set the Stage

Arrange children into groups of three and give each group a pencil and a construction-paper hand that you prepared before the session. Write *Handful of Help* on the board. Say: **We've been learning how important it is to be of service to others.** Mention a recent food or clothing drive organized by your parish. Say: **Now let's think of a "handful" of ways you can help those in your parish or community. Write these on each finger of your paper hand.** Allow time for children to work and to share ideas. Display the hands during the session. Say: **Your paper hand can be a reminder of a handful of ways to help those in need.**

✝ The Poor and Vulnerable

2 Get Started

Read aloud the session title. Then point to the picture. Ask: **How is this girl helping someone?** (The girl is holding the door for the man.) Read aloud the text in the blue box. Discuss children's answers. Say: **In this session we will learn ways to follow the guidance that Jesus provides and to use God's gifts to lead good lives.**

Prayer

Ask children to be still. Say: **Let us pray to Jesus now and ask for his help. Join me in praying aloud.** After the prayer, say: **Pray silently to Jesus for whatever you need.** Pause and then pray *Amen.*

Begin

Read aloud the heading. Say: **We have learned about many people who have trusted in God.** Ask: **How did Mary trust in God?** (accepted God's invitation to be Jesus' mother) **How did Joseph trust in God?** (took care of Mary and Jesus) Say: **We will learn more about saints and how they trusted in God.**

2 Connect

Read aloud the first paragraph. Write *hope* on the board. Ask: **What is another word for hope?** (trust)

Invite a volunteer to read aloud the second paragraph. Ask: **What did Saint Paul do to praise his Christian family and keep its faith strong?** (He wrote letters.)

 Hold up your Bible and point out 1 Thessalonians. Read aloud the adaptation of the letter that Saint Paul wrote to friends in Thessalonia. Ask: **How do you think this letter made the Thessalonians feel?** (Possible answers: happy, confident in God's love)

Read aloud the last paragraph. Ask: **What does it mean to follow "the right path"?** (Possible answers: follow God's rule, live by Jesus' example, have faith in God) Give children time to think of ways their family has helped them follow Jesus. Invite volunteers to share their thoughts.

3 Close

Direct children's attention to the feature at the bottom of page 124.

 Sacred Site

Say: **Saint Monica and Saint Augustine were good examples of the virtues of faith, hope, and charity. Monica had faith in Jesus' message. She never lost hope that her family would accept Jesus. Her son, Augustine, exhibited charity when he became Christian and gave his time and possessions to people in need.**

Saints Who Showed Hope in God

Even when her son, Augustine, was far away, Saint Monica never stopped praying for him. She had **hope**, or trust, in God. She believed that her son would one day choose to follow Jesus.

When Saint Paul was far away from members of his Christian family, he trusted in God too. He wrote letters to his friends to praise them and to keep their faith strong. Here is part of a letter Saint Paul wrote.

> We thank God always for all of you. We pray for you. We tell God about your faith, love, and hope in our Lord Jesus Christ. Know that God loves you and has chosen you to be his people.
>
> *adapted from 1 Thessalonians 1:2–4*

Like Saint Monica, Saint Paul worked hard to keep his Christian family on the right path. He praised them for their faith, hope, and love. List two ways your family has helped you follow Jesus.

_____

_____

Sacred Site

Many people visit the Church of St. Augustine in Rome. Saint Monica is buried in this church. On the walls are pictures from the lives of Augustine and Monica.

Stained glass of Saint Paul

124

IF TIME ALLOWS

Session 21 BLM

A Prayer of Hope Have children complete the Session 21 Blackline Master [T-325] to learn more about the virtue of hope in God.

Message Through Media: A Memory for Tino

This 30-minute live-action film tells the story of a young boy who becomes friends with an elderly woman who is his neighbor. Children will see how young people can be of service to others by helping and taking care of them. Children learn that sometimes the gift of time is more valuable than any store-bought gift.

faith

hope

charity

Important Virtues

God gives us gifts called **virtues** to help us live good lives. Faith, hope, and **charity** are three of the most important virtues.

Faith helps us to believe in God. We need faith to be saved and to live as God wants. Hope helps us to trust that God will always be with us. With hope we can be happy with God now and forever. We show charity when we love God above all things and love our neighbor as ourselves. Saint Paul tells us that charity, or love, is the most important virtue.

A Person of Virtue

Think of someone you know who is blessed with one of these virtues. Finish the sentence below by writing who that person is, what virtue he or she shows, and an example of how it is shown.

_____ shows the virtue of

_____

_____

_____

_____

_____ .

Reading God's Word

Faith, hope, and love each bring us closer to God; but the greatest of these is love.

adapted from 1 Corinthians 13:13

GO TO PAGE 247

SESSION 21 • *Faith, Hope, and Charity* **125**

IF TIME ALLOWS

Service: Help for Those Who Are Homeless

Have children practice the virtue of charity by filling shoe boxes with toiletries for people who are homeless. Check with your catechetical leader before calling a local agency. Have children make posters asking for shoe boxes, as well as items such as soap, socks, combs, shampoo, and toothpaste. Post the signs on collection boxes in school hallways or the church vestibule. Take the full shoe boxes to a relief agency.

✝ *Life and Dignity*

1 Begin

Write the words *God's gifts* on the board. Ask: **What are some gifts that God has given you?** List children's ideas. Say: **Now we're going to learn about three other gifts from God.**

2 Connect

Read aloud the heading and the first paragraph. Write *virtue* on the board. Ask: **What is a virtue?** (a gift that God gives us to help us lead good lives) **What are three of the most important virtues?** (faith, hope, and charity) Add these to your list on the board.

Invite a volunteer to read aloud the next paragraph. Ask: **What does it mean to have faith?** (to believe in God) **Why is faith so important?** (We need it to be saved and to live as God wants.) **What does hope help us do?** (to trust that God will always be with us) **What virtue do we practice when we show love for God and for others?** (charity) Say: **We practice charity every time we serve those in need or show compassion toward others.**

Read aloud A Person of Virtue. Give children time to do the activity. Invite children to share their sentences about the person they chose.

Reading God's Word

Ask a volunteer to read aloud the passage. Say: **Saint Paul wrote this in a letter to his friends in Corinth, a city in southern Greece. He wanted them to know how important it is for Christians to love one another.**

3 Close

The Sacred Heart

Art Print 21

Display Art Print 21: *The Sacred Heart.* Use the Art Print 21 instruction to teach this section. Art Print teaching instruction can also be found on page 247.

Prayer

Follow the steps to guide children through the prayer on page 126.

Prepare Read the prayer in advance to become familiar with it.

Pray Quiet children for prayer. Remind them that this is their special time with God and Jesus. Ask them to focus on God's presence in their lives. Say: **Today we learned about the virtues of faith, hope, and charity. These virtues can lead us to prayer. As we begin our reflection, let us think of these and other virtues that help us to live as Jesus lived.**

Direct children's attention to the prayer center. Say: **Come forward, take your "handful of help" from the wall, and bring it to the prayer center.** Give children sufficient time to do this. Children may either return to their seats or remain at the prayer center.

Play the instrumental "What Does It Mean to Follow Jesus?" [CD 2, Track 16] quietly in the background as you pray the reflection. Ask children to fold their hands and bow their heads as you read the reflection slowly and thoughtfully. They may read along or focus on the picture. Read aloud the first paragraph, pausing between sentences so that children have time to thank God for his gifts.

Continue to pray the reflection slowly, pausing after each sentence. When you have finished, count to 10 silently and give children time to talk to Jesus. Then lead them in praying the Sign of the Cross. Say: **Now let's move on to learn more ways to use our gifts from God to serve others.**

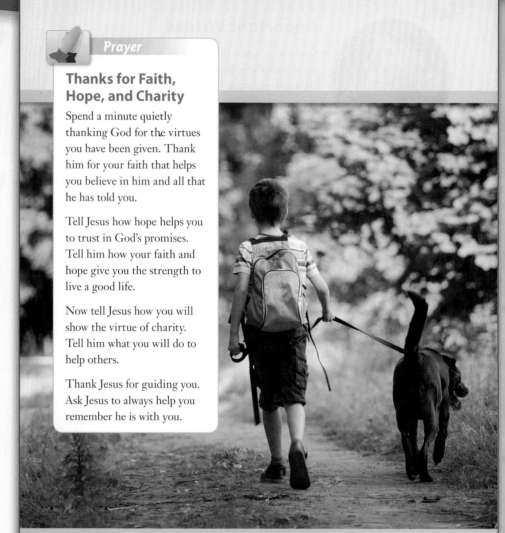

Prayer

Thanks for Faith, Hope, and Charity

Spend a minute quietly thanking God for the virtues you have been given. Thank him for your faith that helps you believe in him and all that he has told you.

Tell Jesus how hope helps you to trust in God's promises. Tell him how your faith and hope give you the strength to live a good life.

Now tell Jesus how you will show the virtue of charity. Tell him what you will do to help others.

Thank Jesus for guiding you. Ask Jesus to always help you remember he is with you.

126 UNIT 5 • *Morality, Our Lived Faith*

IF TIME ALLOWS

Working for Others

Distribute drawing paper and crayons. Ask children to imagine how many people in the world could be helped if each of us chose one thing to do to help those in need. Ask children to think about the "handful of help" they made earlier. Have children illustrate one of those ideas, preferably one they could do with their families. Invite children to share the pictures with their families.

✝ *Solidarity*

FYI

Coaching Children to Pray

To prepare children to pray, remind them that the Holy Spirit is always with us to support, guide, and strengthen us as we practice the virtues of faith, hope, and charity. Have children prepare themselves for peaceful prayer time by inhaling the strength of the Holy Spirit and exhaling any concerns and anxieties.

She Lived Like Jesus

Saint Jeanne Jugan was blessed with the virtue of charity. She was born into a poor family in France in 1792. Her father died at sea when she was a child. Her mother taught her children to live with faith and love for God.

In a local hospital, Jeanne learned how to help those who were even poorer than she was. She begged to raise money to help those who needed care. Jeanne and her friends formed a religious community to help people who were poor. Others joined and they became the Little Sisters of the Poor. This community still serves the needs of those who are poor and the elderly who cannot care for themselves.

Tapestry of Saint Jeanne Jugan displayed on the facade of St. Peter's Basilica in the Vatican

Living Like Saint Jeanne Jugan

Think how you have practiced the virtues of faith, hope, and charity in your everyday life. Complete the sentence and then draw a picture of yourself showing that virtue.

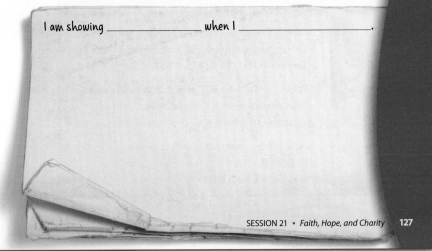

I am showing _____ when I _____.

SESSION 21 • *Faith, Hope, and Charity* **127**

IF TIME ALLOWS

Little Sisters of the Poor

Visit the Little Sisters of the Poor at their Web site. Talk to children about what you found. Say: *The Little Sisters of the Poor dedicate their lives to serving God and the Church by helping those who are poor and elderly who can't care for themselves.* Distribute paper and crayons or markers. Ask children to write thank-you notes to the Little Sisters for all that they do and to share with the Little Sisters something that they have inspired children to do. Mail the cards to the Little Sisters of the Poor.

---

❶ Begin

Say: *Raise your hands if you have given money to a charitable cause or have seen others do it.* Say: *Every time someone gives money to a charitable cause, he or she is practicing the virtue of charity.*

❷ Connect

Read aloud the heading and the first paragraph. Ask: *How did Jeanne's mother keep her children on the right path?* (She taught them to live with faith and love for God.) *What virtue did Jeanne show?* (charity)

Ask children to read silently the second paragraph and think about what happened in Jeanne's life that inspired her to help others. Ask: *What group did Jeanne and her friends form to help others?* (Little Sisters of the Poor) Say: *In Unit 4 we learned about the religious orders that women join. Do you remember some of the things sisters do?* (Possible answers: live, work, and pray together in service to God and Jesus Christ)

Point to the picture of Saint Jeanne Jugan. Say: *On October 11, 2009, Jeanne Jugan was declared a saint.*

Distribute crayons or markers. Read aloud Living Like Saint Jeanne Jugan. Make sure children understand the directions. Define the virtues listed. When children have finished, allow time for them to share their drawings. Have each child name the virtue he or she illustrated. Encourage volunteers to share the story behind their picture.

❸ Close

Invite children to listen to "What Does It Mean to Follow Jesus?" [CD 2, Track 15] Ask them to turn to the back of their books and follow the words as they listen. Ask: *How does this song help us find ways to follow Jesus?* (Children will point to examples from the lyrics.)

Begin

Faith Summary Invite a volunteer to read aloud this section. Ask: **What is a virtue?** (a gift from God) **What are three virtues that help us lead a Christian life?** (faith, hope, charity)

 Connect

Words I Learned Draw a triangle on the board. Write *virtues* inside the triangle. Say: **The triangle can be our symbol of the three most important virtues. What can we write on each side of the triangle?** (faith, hope, charity) Write *charity* at the base. Say: **Charity is the basis of the other virtues, so it will be the base of our triangle.**

Ways of Being Like Jesus Read aloud this section. Discuss ways in which children might practice charity.

 Prayer

Ask children to prepare for the closing prayer. Say: **Let us thank Jesus for his gifts. Pray aloud with me.** After praying ask children to pray the prayer silently and spend a few moments with Jesus. Pause and then pray *Amen.* Say: **Remember that Jesus is with us to help us in all things.**

With My Family Ask children to read silently the three suggestions in this section. Invite children to choose one or more to complete at home.

 Go in Peace

Collect materials and return them to the appropriate places. Encourage children to discuss the With My Family section at home. Say: **This week make your hands be like Jesus' hands. Be a "handful of help" to those in need.**

RESPOND

Living My Faith

Faith Summary

Saints Monica and Paul were examples of hope, and Saint Jeanne was an example of charity. Faith, hope, and charity are virtues. These gifts from God help us lead good lives.

Words I Learned

charity   hope   virtues

Ways of Being Like Jesus

Jesus showed charity, or love, for others. *Be friendly to a child who seems lonely. Say hello and start a conversation.*

 Prayer

Jesus, my example, thank you for sharing your life with me. Walk with me as I live my life with faith, hope, and charity.

 **With My Family**

Activity As a family, visit residents at a nearby home for those who are elderly. Play a game with them or offer to help them write letters to loved ones.

Faith on the Go Ask one another: *If you found money on your front porch with a note saying that you had to give it away, who would you give it to? Why?*

Family Prayer Dear God, thank you for the gifts of the virtues. Help me to practice the virtue of charity and think of others' needs every day. Amen.

128 UNIT 5 • *Morality, Our Lived Faith*

IF TIME ALLOWS

Session Assessment Option

An assessment for this session can be found at **www.findinggod.com**.

PLAN AHEAD

Get Ready for Session 22

Consult the catechist preparation pages to prepare for Session 22 and determine any materials you will need.

Making Good Choices

3-Minute Retreat

As you begin to prepare for the session, pause to gather your thoughts. Take three deep breaths and call to mind the guidance God gives us if we open our hearts and minds to his presence in our lives.

Matthew 4:3–4

The tempter approached and said to him, "If you are the Son of God, command that these stones become loaves of bread." He said in reply, "It is written:

'One does not live by bread alone,

but by every word that comes forth

from the mouth of God.'"

Reflection

Children often see rules as little more than a limit placed on being free to do as they please. Many adults too live under this illusion. In the same way he tempted Jesus, the devil wants us to "make our own rules." In his response Jesus sets out the truth that following the Word of God is a source of life. In the commandments, we find God's rules for life. By following these rules, we will remain connected to him and to one another. Our faithfulness is made evident by our choices, not only in what we avoid, but also in what we choose to do.

Questions

What does it mean to be free? How might I help others see faithfulness to God as a path to freedom?

Prayer

Speak to Jesus in these words or your own.

Jesus, help me to listen to every word that comes from your Father so that I may be free and faithful in life.

Knowing and Sharing Your Faith in Session 22

Consider how Scripture and Tradition can deepen your understanding of the session content.

Scripture

Matthew 4:1–11 is the account of the devil tempting Jesus three times.

Colossians 3:17 tells that all words and deeds should be done in the Lord's name and in thanksgiving to God.

Tradition

The Ten Commandments are commandments because they state the most fundamental moral obligations binding human beings to one another. The Ten Commandments make it clear that moral choices are made in terms of relationships. The challenge is to use the help we receive from the Holy Spirit in examining whether the object of what we are deciding is good, whether the action we intend is good, and whether the circumstances of the choice are good. We can never justify violating one of the Ten Commandments by saying that we had good intentions or commit an immoral act for the sake of doing something we alone think is good.

Catholic Social Teaching

In this session the integrated Catholic Social Teaching theme is **Solidarity.** See page 121b for an explanation of this theme.

Window on the Catechism

The Ten Commandments are introduced in *CCC* 2052–2074.

General Directory for Catechesis

The Ten Commandments are the framework for a healthy relationship with God and with others. This is explored in *GDC* 117.

One-Hour Session Planner

SESSION 22 Making Good Choices

Session Theme: *Jesus gives us the help we need to make good moral choices.*

Before This Session

▶ Bring treats for the Engage step. Check with your catechetical leader about children with food allergies.

▶ Bookmark your Bible to Matthew 4:1–11 and Colossians 3:17. Place the Bible open to either of these passages in your prayer center.

▶ Display the *Finding God* posters The Ten Commandments and Making Good Choices.

Prayer in Session 22

In this session children learn to pray the Morning Offering as a way of making a commitment to live that day for God.

STEPS	APPROXIMATE TIME
Engage *Making Good Choices* PAGE 129	10 minutes
Explore *How to Make a Moral Choice* PAGE 130 *The Ten Commandments Teach Us* PAGE 131 *Art Print: In the Wilderness* ART PRINT AND PRINT BACK	30–40 minutes
Reflect *Prayer:* Live Our Lives for God PAGE 132 *Following the Commandments* PAGE 133	15–20 minutes
Respond *Living My Faith* PAGE 134	5–10 minutes

Materials

REQUIRED

▶ Bible

▶ Art Print 22: *In the Wilderness* and Children's Book page 248

▶ Several healthful treats, such as grapes and carrots, enough for all children

▶ *Finding God* posters: The Ten Commandments and Making Good Choices

▶ CD player

▶ CD 2, Track 2: "Song of Love" (Instrumental)

IF TIME ALLOWS

▶ Session 22 BLM, T-326 (page 131)

▶ Cardstock (page 131)

▶ Art supplies (pages 131, 132)

▶ Drawing paper (page 132)

▶ Red construction paper (page 133)

▶ Session 22 Assessment, www.findinggod.com (page 134)

Making Good Choices

Every day we make choices. Sometimes we need help to know what is right. What difficult choice did you make this week? How did you decide what to do?

Prayer

Jesus, my helper, give me the grace to make good choices. I want to live for God and others like you did.

129

▶ Explain that God gave us the Ten Commandments to help us follow the moral law.

▶ Tell the story of Jesus overcoming temptation in the desert.

▶ Pray the Morning Offering.

▶ Define *moral law*.

1 Set the Stage

Play the instrumental "Song of Love" [CD 2, Track 2]. Bring in a variety of small healthful treats, such as fruit or cut vegetables.

Display the treats. Say: *I have enough for everyone, but they are not all the same.* Let each child choose one. Encourage children to share reasons for their choices. Then say: *We make choices every day. This choice was easy, but some are difficult. Today we will talk about many kinds of choices.*

2 Get Started

Read aloud the session title. Point to the picture. Ask: *What decision to you think this boy is making?* (which food to eat) Say: *Making decisions is like deciding which path to take.* Read aloud the text in the blue box. Pause for children to consider the questions. Ask: *Whom might you ask for advice when making a hard choice?* (Possible answers: an adult, pray to God and Jesus for guidance) Say: *In this session we will learn about how God, Jesus, and the Holy Spirit help us make good moral choices.*

Prayer

Say: *Let us pray for Jesus' help in making good choices.* After praying aloud, say: *Now talk to Jesus about whatever you would like.* Pause and then pray together *Amen.*

IF TIME ALLOWS

Inclusion: Vision

Clarifying Choices If you have children with visual impairments, display snack items in the best light possible in the room. Clearly describe each item or category and paint a word picture of each item. Provide large-print signs next to the items.

Act It Out

In groups, have children think of a conclusion to the following situations. Invite children to act out the entire scene and discuss afterward. **Scene 1:** Molly is in a store with her friends. They all buy candy, but Molly doesn't have money. Molly knows the clerk wouldn't notice her take one candy. **Scene 2:** Joe's mom asked him to take out the trash, but he's in a hurry to catch up with his friends. **Scene 3:** Amy envies Jill because she won first prize in the art show. Amy whispers to Matt about the show.

 Go to **www.findinggod.com/sessionextenders** for an article called *St. Paul on Making Moral Choices.*

Begin

Read aloud the heading. Say: **You made an easy choice at the beginning of this session.** Ask: **Did your choice involve right and wrong?** (no, just preference) Say: **Now let's read about how we can make good moral choices when we face difficult decisions about right and wrong. Remember that we always have the help of the Holy Spirit.**

 Connect

Read aloud the first paragraph. Ask: **How did Jesus overcome the devil's temptations?** (by following God's will) **Who can help us examine our choices?** (the Holy Spirit)

Ask three volunteers to read aloud the three questions and examples. Discuss how Ana's response corresponds to the question.

Say: **There may be times that we need help making a choice like Ana had to make. One thing we can do is to ask ourselves these three questions.**

Show children the *Finding God* poster Making Good Choices. Read aloud the poster, running your hand under the words as you read them. Encourage children to comment on each question. Say: **These questions will help you make the right decision when faced with a difficult moral choice. Remember that God is with you. He gives you the grace to make the right choices.**

 Close

Direct children's attention to the feature at the bottom of page 130.

 Reading God's Word

Tell children that Saint Paul reminded his friends, the Colossians, to follow Jesus. Ask a child to read aloud this section. Say: **Saint Paul tells us that our words and our actions should reflect our willingness to follow Jesus.**

How to Make a Moral Choice

The devil tempted Jesus three times. Jesus overcame these temptations by following his Father's will. Sometimes we must make hard choices too. With the help of the Holy Spirit, we can examine our choices. We can ask ourselves three questions that can help us make good choices. Read the questions below. Then read how a girl named Ana acted when she asked herself these questions. If we can answer yes to each question as Ana did, we know we have made the right choice.

Lost and Found

1. **Is the thing I'm choosing to do a good thing?**
   Ana finds a hat on the school playground. She likes the hat very much but decides to bring it to the Lost and Found.

2. **Am I choosing to do it for the right reasons?**
   Ana knows that the hat is not hers and that the owner will be looking for it.

3. **Am I choosing to do it at the right time and place?**
   Ana turns in the hat to the Lost and Found right away. Ana made a good moral choice. She feels happy because she did the right thing. The owner will be happy too because she will get her hat back.

 Reading God's Word

Whatever you do, in word or by your actions, do it in the name of Jesus, giving thanks to God the Father through him. *adapted from Colossians 3:17*

IF TIME ALLOWS

Jesus Helps

Remind children that Jesus overcame the devil's temptations by following God's will. Have children write short prayers asking Jesus to guide them and give them the courage they need to make good choices. Suggest that children keep their prayers with them often and to pray when they are faced with a difficult decision. Say: **Jesus, our Savior, help us be faithful and always follow the path to God.**

The Ten Commandments Teach Us

God our loving Father gave us the Ten Commandments. They teach us how to live for God and others. They help us follow the **moral law,** rules that help us to do good and avoid evil.

Obeying God

The first three commandments teach us to honor God. This is what they tell us:

1. I am your God; love nothing more than you love me.
2. Use God's name with respect.
3. Keep the Lord's Day holy.

Think about these commandments. What are some ways you can obey them?

Loving Our Neighbor

While the first three commandments teach us about our relationship with God, the next seven commandments teach us how to live in peace with our neighbor. This is what they tell us:

4. Honor and obey your parents.
5. Treat all human life with respect.
6. Respect married life.
7. Respect what belongs to others.
8. Tell the truth.
9. Respect your neighbors and your friends.
10. Be happy with what you have.

GO TO PAGE 248

131

1 Begin

Display the *Finding God* poster The Ten Commandments. Say: **We learned what to ask ourselves before making a decision. Now we will read the rules God gave us to help us make good choices.** Invite volunteers to read each of the commandments.

2 Connect

Read aloud the heading and the first paragraph. Write *moral law* on the board. Ask: **What is a law?** (a rule that tells us what we must or must not do) Say: **We have rules in school, at home, and from our state and country. God established a law called the moral law.** Ask: **What do the Ten Commandments teach us?** (how to live for God and others) **What does it mean to follow the moral law?** (do good and avoid evil)

Invite a volunteer to read aloud Obeying God. Then encourage children to respond to the question, offering ways such as go to Mass on Sundays and use words of respect when addressing God.

Invite a volunteer to read aloud Loving Our Neighbor. Say: **God gave us these commandments to help us love others.** Ask volunteers to read aloud each commandment.

Comment on the commandments. Ask: **Which commandment was Ana following when she turned in the hat?** (Seventh) **Which was Saint Jeanne Jugan following when she cared for all people?** (Fifth)

3 Close

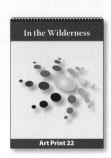

In the Wilderness

Art Print 22

Display Art Print 22: *In the Wilderness.* Use the Art Print 22 instruction to teach this section. Art Print teaching instruction can also be found on page 248.

IF TIME ALLOWS

Session 22 BLM

The Ten Commandments Have children complete the Session 22 Blackline Master [T-326], which helps them review the Ten Commandments.

Service: Follow the Commandments Campaign

Have children make mini-posters sharing the message of the Ten Commandments with other children. Distribute cardstock and markers. Have children write each poster using the language on page 131, and then decorate the poster. Display the posters with the heading *We Follow God's Laws* around the parish center or community space.

✝ *Solidarity*

Prayer

Follow the steps to guide children through the prayer on page 132.

Children's Page

Prepare Read the prayer in advance to become familiar with it.

Pray Gather children at the prayer center. Once they are quiet, say: **Today we are going to ask God to be present in our lives by praying a special prayer called the Morning Offering.**

Ask: **What does it mean to offer something to someone?** (to give it freely) Say: **When we pray the Morning Offering, we offer all our daily activities to God. We join our offerings with those of people all over the world.**

Explain the meanings of the following phrases by saying: **The "salvation of souls" means that we are praying that those who have died will be saved by the grace of God. "Reparation for sin" means that we are offering God our prayers and good actions to make up for our sins and the sins of others. "Reunion of Christians" means that we pray that one day all Christians will worship together as one.**

Play the reflective music at the end of CD 2. Read aloud the first paragraph slowly and thoughtfully. Ask children to bow their heads and fold their hands. Say: **Now listen and follow along in your books as I pray this prayer.**

Read aloud the prayer softly and slowly. Invite children to pray the Morning Offering with you. After praying read the last paragraph slowly. Pause after each sentence to give children time to reflect. When you have finished, count silently to 10 and pray *Amen.* Say: **Now let us discover ways to follow God's rule in our daily lives.**

 Prayer

Live Our Lives for God

Each day we remember to live our lives for God. Each morning we can tell God we will live for him by praying the Morning Offering. As you slowly pray this prayer, think of what you will give to God.

Morning Offering

My God, I offer you my prayers, works, joys, and sufferings of this day in union with the holy sacrifice of the Mass throughout the world.

I offer them for all the intentions of your Son's Sacred Heart, for the salvation of souls, reparation for sin, and the reunion of Christians. Amen.

Now spend a few moments with Jesus. Tell him that you want to offer everything you do to God. Ask Jesus to help you make good moral choices each day. Know that Jesus is with you.

IF TIME ALLOWS

Illustrating Your Thoughts

Invite children to respond to the Morning Offering by illustrating the works, joys, and sufferings of their day that they will offer God. Distribute paper and art supplies and play reflective music while children illustrate their feelings.

FYI

Coaching Children to Pray

To prepare children to pray, remind them that each day is a new gift from God. When we pray the Morning Offering, we remember that we are in the presence of God and we offer him everything we do. Encourage children to take this prayer to heart.

Follow the Commandments

When we follow the commandments and make good moral choices, we become more loving disciples of Jesus.

And the Correct Commandment Is . . .

Choose a word from the box to complete each sentence. Then write the number of the commandment the person in the sentence is obeying.

> God   happy   Mass   mother   respect   return   truth

1. Antonio obeyed his ____mother____ when she said it was time for bed. __4__

2. Mara goes to ____Mass____ with her family each Sunday. __3__

3. Finn told the ____truth____ when the teacher asked if he had done his homework. __8__

4. Sam likes Owen's new bike, but he doesn't want one. He is ____happy____ with his old one. __10__

5. Isabella loves God and says his name only with ____respect____. __2__

6. Jack forgot to take his skateboard home from Ben's house. Ben knew that he had to ____return____ it to Jack. __7__

7. Julia has friends who say they "worship" movie stars, but Julia worships only ____God____. __1__

SESSION 22 • *Making Good Choices* **133**

IF TIME ALLOWS

Our Hearts Are for God and One Another

Cut out a large heart from red construction paper and write *Love God* on it. Cut a smaller heart and write *Love One Another* on it. Distribute red paper and scissors. Have each child cut out two small hearts, writing his or her first name on one. On the other, ask children to write one way they show their love for God, such as following the commandments and helping others. Make a cross of hearts on the board, taping the *Love God* heart at the top and children's picture hearts in a vertical line below. Place your *Love One Another* heart in this line about a third of the way down. Tape children's name hearts in a horizontal line on either side of *Love One Another*. Tell children that the vertical line of hearts shows the love all of us have for God, while the horizontal line shows the love we have for one another.

1 Begin

Share a situation with children. Say: *Claire was nervous to take her math test. She studied very hard to prepare for the test, but she did not feel completely confident. When she picked up her pencil to begin the test, she looked up and realized that she could see Emma's test in front of her as she worked on it. Claire was tempted to cheat, but decided that she should just try her best on her test.* Ask: **What commandment did Claire follow?** (Seventh)

2 Connect

Read aloud the heading and the first paragraph. Ask: **What helps us become more loving disciples of Jesus?** (following the commandments and making good moral choices) Say: **When we face difficult choices, the commandments can help us with our decisions.**

Review each of the Ten Commandments. Use page 131 as a review, refer to the *Finding God* Ten Commandments poster, or have children turn to page 212 in the backs of their books to see a complete listing of the commandments.

Invite a volunteer to read aloud the directions for And the Correct Commandment Is . . . . Remind children to look back at page 131 if they need help remembering the numbers of the commandments. Walk among children while they work and answer their questions. Check the answers together.

3 Close

When children have finished, share the story of how God gave the commandments to Moses and the Israelites. The story appears in the Old Testament in Exodus 20:1–17 and in Deuteronomy 5:1–21.

Begin

Faith Summary Read aloud this section. Ask: ***What do the Ten Commandments teach us?*** (how to live for God and others) ***What did God give us to help us follow the moral law?*** (the Ten Commandments)

Connect

Words I Learned Ask a volunteer to use *moral law* in a sentence. Discuss decisions children might make. Decide whether the basis of each relies on preference or following moral law.

Ways of Being Like Jesus Read aloud this section. Invite children to think of a commandment that they will work at keeping this week. Ask them to write it on a sheet of paper. Say: ***Keep it where only you will see it and use it as a reminder to follow that commandment.***

Prayer

Say: ***Let us thank Jesus for teaching us how to be good people.*** Ask children to pray the prayer with you. Pause to give children time to pray and reflect on their own. Then pray together *Amen.* Say: ***When you have a hard choice to make, remember Jesus' choice to do his Father's will.***

With My Family Ask children to read silently the three suggestions in this section. Invite children to choose one or more to complete at home.

Go in Peace

Collect materials and return them to the appropriate places. Encourage children to discuss the With My Family section at home. Say: ***This week remember all the help God has given us to follow in Jesus' footsteps and to make good choices.***

Living My Faith

Faith Summary

We can make good moral choices by considering them closely. God gave us the Ten Commandments to teach us how to live for God and others. The commandments help us to follow the moral law. With the help of Jesus and the Holy Spirit, we can live our lives for God and others.

Words I Learned

moral law

Ways of Being Like Jesus

Jesus followed the Ten Commandments. *Make good moral choices by following the Ten Commandments.*

Prayer

Jesus, my brother, thank you for showing me how to be a good person. Help me to follow your example of making good moral choices.

With My Family

Activity As a family decide on a few house rules that will help your family, such as don't go to bed angry. Display them on the refrigerator.

Faith on the Go Ask one another: *Do you ever find it difficult to make a good choice? Why or why not?*

Family Prayer Practice the Morning Offering with your family. Try to learn the prayer so that you can say it by heart.

134 UNIT 5 • *Morality, Our Lived Faith*

IF TIME ALLOWS

Session Assessment Option
An assessment for this session can be found at **www.findinggod.com.**

PLAN AHEAD

Get Ready for Session 23

Consult the catechist preparation pages to prepare for Session 23 and determine any materials you will need.

Living as God's Children

3-Minute Retreat

Before preparing the session, pause and breathe deeply several times. Set aside distractions. Know that God is your Father. He loves you. He watches over you. He is present to you.

Philippians 1:9–11

And this is my prayer: that your love may increase ever more and more in knowledge and every kind of perception, to discern what is of value, so that you may be pure and blameless for the day of Christ . . .

Reflection

In this letter written while in prison, Paul expresses his great love and hopeful prayer for the growing community of faith. Families are the first community of faith. In unity with the Holy Spirit, they can be a fruitful source of love, peace, and justice. Our families teach us how to share, how to love, how to be fair, and how to serve others. We can join in the prayer of Saint Paul as we think of the families we know. In our own family, we have a wonderful opportunity to participate in the work of the Holy Spirit—to serve the Kingdom of God on earth.

Question

How can I change so that I see struggling families with eyes of love rather than of judgment?

Prayer

Speak to God, using these words or others that come to mind.

Holy Spirit, be with my family and the families in my parish so that we may grow in knowledge and every kind of perception to discern what is of value. Help us to become pure and blameless for the day for Christ.

Knowing and Sharing Your Faith in Session 23

Consider how Scripture and Tradition can deepen your understanding of the session content.

Scripture

Philippians 1:3–11 tells how Paul prays that the Christian community will increase in love and knowledge for the glory of God.

Galatians 6:2 teaches us that all are asked to bear one another's burdens.

Tradition

Our entire religious Tradition is centered on the importance of healthy relationships. In the Old Testament, we hear the divine statement that it is not good for us to be alone. God intervened in human history to form Abraham's descendants into one people. Jesus comes in fulfillment of the Scriptures as a member of a family. He teaches his followers to regard God as their Father, and he makes it clear to them that they are brothers and sisters. Jesus tried to teach his disciples how to form healthy communities.

Catholic Social Teaching

In this session the integrated Catholic Social Teaching themes are **Life and Dignity of the Human Person** and **Option for the Poor and Vulnerable.** See page 121b for an explanation of these themes.

Window on the Catechism

The "communal character of the human vocation" is discussed in *CCC* 1878–1885. The concept of love of neighbor is addressed in *CCC* 2196.

General Directory for Catechesis

The task of catechizing people into a community of faith is explored in *GDC* 220.

One-Hour Session Planner

SESSION 23 Living as God's Children

Session Theme: *Jesus helps us to love and respect one another.*

Before This Session

▶ Bookmark your Bible to Philippians 1:3–11 and Galatians 6:2. Place the Bible open to either of these passages in your prayer center.

▶ Read the Guide for this session, choose any additional If Time Allows activities that you might have time to complete, and gather the listed materials.

STEPS	APPROXIMATE TIME
Engage *Living as God's Children* PAGE 135	🕐 10 minutes
Explore *Our Call to Care* PAGE 136 *Saint Louise de Marillac Cared* PAGE 137 **Art Print:** *Saint Paul* ART PRINT AND PRINT BACK	🕐 30–40 minutes
Reflect **Prayer:** A Prayer for Family Members PAGE 138 *Peaceful Families* PAGE 139	🕐 15–20 minutes
Respond *Living My Faith* PAGE 140	🕐 5–10 minutes

Materials

REQUIRED

▶ Bible

▶ Art Print 23: *Saint Paul* and Children's Book page 249

▶ Your own family photo on an 8-inch square of paper

▶ 6-inch squares of paper and 8-inch squares of paper, 1 each per child

▶ Art supplies

▶ Poster board

▶ Glue

▶ CD player

▶ CD 2, Track 15: "What Does It Mean to Follow Jesus?" (1:55)

▶ CD 1, Track 10: "Hold Them in Your Heart" (10:43)

IF TIME ALLOWS

▶ Letter stencils, hole punch, yarn, cardstock (page 135)

▶ *The Rag Coat* by Lauren Mills (page 136)

▶ Large cardboard boxes (page 137)

▶ Session 23 BLM, T-327 (page 137)

▶ Note cards with cooperation questions (page 139)

▶ Session 23 Assessment, www.findinggod.com (page 140)

Prayer in Session 23

In this session children pray prayers of petition and gratitude for Jesus' guidance and love. Session 23 includes an extended guided reflection. As you prepare to share this prayer experience with children, first listen to the recorded guided reflection "Hold Them in Your Heart" [CD 1, Track 10]. When you play the recording during the session, join children in prayer. If you choose to lead the guided reflection yourself, listen to the recording a second time, following the script [pages T-290–T-291]. You can use the script or adapt it. An alternative approach is to use the Prayer on the children's page.

Living as God's Children

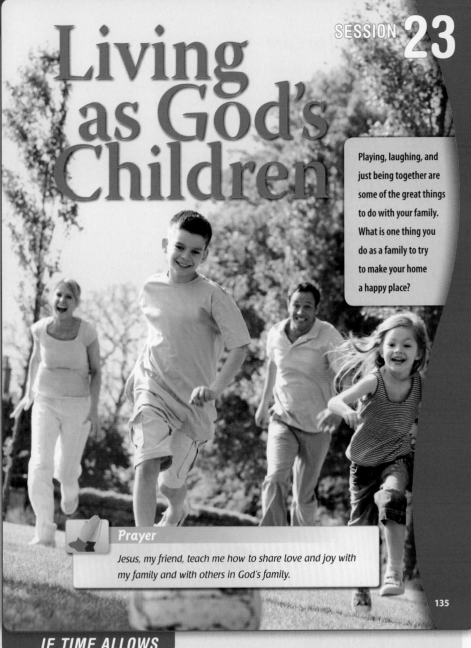

SESSION **23**

Playing, laughing, and just being together are some of the great things to do with your family. What is one thing you do as a family to try to make your home a happy place?

Prayer

Jesus, my friend, teach me how to share love and joy with my family and with others in God's family.

135

IF TIME ALLOWS

Joyful Banners

Encourage children to display their joy by making "joyful" banners. Use stencils to trace the word *joyful* in large block letters on cardstock for each child. Distribute crayons or markers and scissors to each child. On each letter, have children write one word or phrase that begins with that letter. When children cut out their letters, help them punch two holes at the top of each letter and lace the letters together with yarn to form a banner.

 Go to **www.findinggod.com/sessionextenders** for Sunday Connections about how God speaks to families through the Scripture readings.

SESSION 23
OUTCOMES

▶ Explain that the Holy Spirit helps us live in peace.

▶ Identify Saint Louise de Marillac as someone who served others.

▶ Describe how Saint Paul spread joy and love to his Church family.

▶ Define *justice*.

1 Set the Stage

Greet children and tell them a story of a happy time spent with your family. Display a family photo attached to an eight-inch square of paper. Invite children to draw a happy family time of their own. Distribute crayons and six-inch squares of paper to each child. Allow time for sharing pictures.

2 Get Started

Read aloud the session title. Point out the picture. Ask: **How can you tell this family is enjoying themselves?** (Possible answer: They are laughing.) Invite a volunteer to read aloud the text in the blue box. Allow time for sharing responses. Say: **Let's make a family "quilt" of pictures. People can make quilts by sewing together fabric from clothes or blankets. Then they look at the fabric and remember what is special about it.** Give each child an eight-inch square of paper. Have children glue their drawings in the middle and decorate the frame. Tape your picture to poster board. Have children tape their drawings around it to form the "quilt."

Prayer

Say: **Let us pray that we will always share joy with our families. Pray the prayer with me.** After praying, pray aloud *Amen.* Say: **In this session we will learn more about living as God's children.**

1 Begin

Show children a greeting card. Ask: **When do you send cards?** (Possible answers: for birthdays, when someone is sick, to congratulate) **Why do you give cards?** (to show you care)

2 Connect

Write the word *justice* on the board. Have a child read aloud the heading and the first paragraph. Ask: **With the Holy Spirit's help, how can we live in peace and harmony?** (obey and respect our parents, treat our families and others with justice) Ask: **What is another word for justice?** (fairness)

Have volunteer read aloud the second paragraph. Ask children to think about other people they could help in addition to their families, such as our parish family, friends, or classmates. Ask: **Who is the source of the help and love that we give to others?** (the Holy Spirit)

Invite children to stand up and form a circle, standing shoulder to shoulder with one another. Say: **A circle has no end. Our ability to care for others is also endless. Let us share ways we show we care for others.** Go around the circle, inviting children to share a way they show they care for family and others, such as helping someone with homework. They might say "I care when I _____."

3 Close

Read aloud the activity My Letter of Thanks. Give children time to think about what they will write. Walk around as they work and answer children's questions.

Play "What Does It Mean to Follow Jesus?" [CD 2, Track 15] Remind children that they heard this song in Session 21. Ask: **What is one thing we can do to follow Jesus? We sing about it in this song.** (care for our neighbors and families) Play the song again and invite children to sing along.

Our Call to Care

God calls us to care for one another. We start at home with our family. With the grace of the Holy Spirit, we can live together in peace and harmony. We obey and respect our parents, as Jesus did. We treat our family and others with **justice** by treating them fairly.

The Holy Spirit helps us live in peace, harmony, and justice with others. We can share the Spirit's love with one another by helping the members of our family. We can also help those who cannot help themselves.

My Letter of Thanks

We can tell our families how blessed we are to have them. Think of why you are thankful to belong to your family. Fill in this letter. Tell your family members why they are special to you.

Dear _____,

Thank you for _____

IF TIME ALLOWS

A Caring Story

Read the story *The Rag Coat* by Lauren Mills [Boston, Massachusetts: Little Brown and Company, 1991]. If you have a limited amount of time, summarize the story and share pictures from the book. When you have finished, ask children to explain the significance of the story—the need for a strong, loving community.

Inclusion: Gifted

Promoters of Peace and Justice Have children who could benefit from a more complex activity research an important figure, such as Martin Luther King Jr. or Blessed Teresa of Calcutta, who promoted peace and justice. Invite them to write a short paragraph describing how this person encouraged peace and justice and share it with the group.

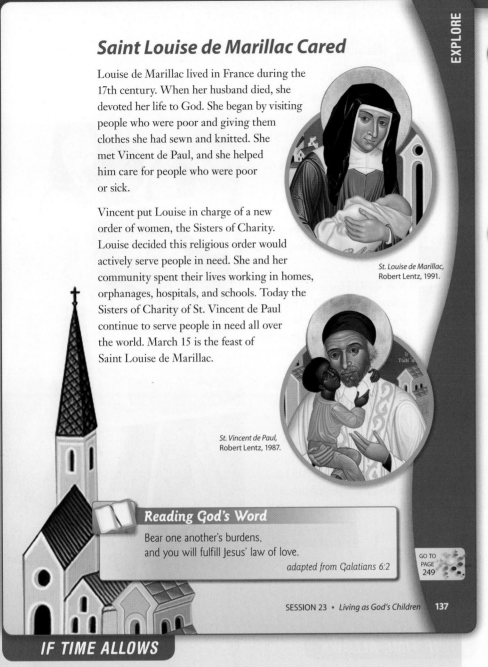

Saint Louise de Marillac Cared

Louise de Marillac lived in France during the 17th century. When her husband died, she devoted her life to God. She began by visiting people who were poor and giving them clothes she had sewn and knitted. She met Vincent de Paul, and she helped him care for people who were poor or sick.

Vincent put Louise in charge of a new order of women, the Sisters of Charity. Louise decided this religious order would actively serve people in need. She and her community spent their lives working in homes, orphanages, hospitals, and schools. Today the Sisters of Charity of St. Vincent de Paul continue to serve people in need all over the world. March 15 is the feast of Saint Louise de Marillac.

St. Louise de Marillac, Robert Lentz, 1991.

St. Vincent de Paul, Robert Lentz, 1987.

Reading God's Word

Bear one another's burdens, and you will fulfill Jesus' law of love.

adapted from Galatians 6:2

GO TO PAGE 249

SESSION 23 • *Living as God's Children* **137**

IF TIME ALLOWS

Session 23 BLM

Complete the Story Have children complete the Session 23 Blackline Master [T-327] to review what they know about Saint Louise de Marillac and Saint Vincent de Paul.

Service: Collecting Clothing

Explain that just as Saint Louise de Marillac cared for those who were poor, children can also help out those who need clothing. Obtain permission from your catechetical leader to organize a clothing drive for a local relief agency. Talk to children about collecting clothing for those who need it. Ask children to bring in clothing they have outgrown. Provide boxes for them to decorate with markers. Place the boxes in church or school entrance ways and check periodically for donations. Take the donations to the local relief agency.

✝ *Life and Dignity*

1 Begin

Read the heading and point to the two pictures. Ask: *Looking at the pictures, what kind of lives do you think that Louise de Marillac and Vincent de Paul led?* (Possible answers: religious, Louise lived as a sister, holy, cared for people in need)

2 Connect

Ask a volunteer to read aloud the first paragraph. Ask: *How did Louise devote her life to God?* (helped those who were poor, made and gave them clothes) *Whom did she meet and help?* (Saint Vincent de Paul)

Read aloud the second paragraph. Say: *"Order of women" refers to a religious group of women who follow a rule or way of life in service to God and others.* Ask: *How did the Sisters of Charity come to be?* (Vincent de Paul put Louise in charge of a new order of women.) Ask: *What do the Sisters of Charity of Saint Vincent de Paul do?* (work in orphanages, hospitals, and schools) Say: *Louise de Marillac is an example of how the smallest effort spreads God's love to many people.*

✝ *The Poor and Vulnerable*

Reading God's Word

Read aloud the passage. Ask: *What does it mean to "bear one another's burdens"?* After children offer ideas, say: *A burden is something that is difficult to carry. But problems and troubles are burdens too. When we help people with their problems, we are sharing their burdens.*

3 Close

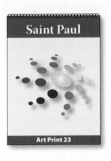

Display Art Print 23: *Saint Paul*. Use the Art Print 23 instruction to teach this section. Art Print teaching instruction can also be found on page 249.

Prayer

Choose an approach and pray with the children.

APPROACH 1

Recorded Guided Reflection

Prepare Listen in advance to the recorded guided reflection "Hold Them in Your Heart" [CD 1, Track 10]. Decide if you will use the recording or lead the reflection yourself. If you choose to lead, listen to the recording a second time, following the script [pages T-290–T-291] and noting pauses and tone. You can use the script or adapt it as you wish.

Pray During the session, play the recording or lead using the script, joining the children in reflective prayer. If you use the script, play reflective music softly in the background.

APPROACH 2

Children's Page

Prepare Read the prayer in advance to become familiar with it.

Pray Have children look at the pictures on page 138. Remind them of the quilt they made earlier. Say: **We are going to reflect on Paul's letter of love to his Church family and on how we can show love to our own families.**

Say: **Before we begin, find a comfortable position. Take three long, deep breaths.** Pause while children do this. Read aloud the first paragraph slowly, pausing for a few seconds between sentences so children can reflect on their families. Continue with the second and third paragraphs. Pause and say: **Take time to tell Jesus anything else you'd like.** Pause for personal reflection. Then lead children in praying the Sign of the Cross.

Prayer

A Prayer for Family Members

Think of Saint Paul's letter to his friends. He prays for them and holds them in his heart. Close your eyes and picture the members of your family for a moment. Think of how much you love them. Thank God for the gift of your family. Pray that you will continue to grow in love with them.

Now spend a few minutes talking with Jesus. Tell him the good things you enjoy in your family and parish. Tell Jesus how you will show your love to your family and others you meet. Tell how you will try especially to help those who cannot help themselves.

Thank Jesus for being with you. Be still and remember Jesus loves you very much. Ask Jesus to bless you and everyone in your family and in your parish.

IF TIME ALLOWS

Pray Again
If you used the recorded guided reflection, you might use this prayer page during another session.

FYI

Coaching Children to Pray

To prepare children to pray, remind them that one way we can show our love for our family members is to hold each of them in our hearts as we pray. We can look at them with Jesus' eyes of love, and we can ask Jesus to bless them.

Peaceful Families

In peaceful homes children obey and respect parents, and family members show one another how they care. Members of peaceful families help in other ways as well, such as sharing work in the family or helping one another with problems. With the grace of the Holy Spirit, we live in peace and joy with our family.

Working Together

For each situation below, write what you can do to help a member of your family.

1. Your parents have planned your little sister's birthday party for this afternoon. Many people are coming. How can you help?

   _____

   _____

2. Your grandmother, who lives with you, has misplaced her glasses. What can you do to help her?

   _____

   _____

3. You and your older brother both want to play a video game at the same time. How do you work out this problem?

   _____

   _____

4. This is your brother's first day of kindergarten, and he is afraid because he doesn't know his way around. How can you help?

   _____

   _____

SESSION 23 • *Living as God's Children*   **139**

IF TIME ALLOWS

Cooperation Station

Set up four stations in the room. At each, place a note card with a question. For example, you might ask questions from the Children's Book, such as *Why are community helpers so important?* Place children in four groups and have them assign the roles of question reader, answer recorder, and timekeeper to three of the members. Give each group paper and a pencil. Rotate groups through the stations, having them work on their answers together. Allow a few minutes at each station. Afterward, discuss answers and the value of working together.

1 Begin

Discuss the fun of riding bikes. Ask: *How many of you have bikes or share bikes with your brother or sister? Have you ever had a bike that didn't work properly?* Discuss why the bikes didn't work, such as flat tires or loose chains. Say: *When one part of a bike doesn't work, your bike doesn't work properly or at all. The parts of the entire bike need to work properly so that you can have a safe and fun time with it. That's how families work too. If everyone chips in, the family is peaceful and has fun together.*

2 Connect

Read aloud the heading and paragraph. Ask: *Have you and your family members ever worked together to do something around your home? What kind of job did you do together?* (Possible answers: rake leaves; cook dinner; make beds; fix a broken piece of furniture) Say: *When we work together with family members, we show one another that we care. By sharing the work, we help bring peace to our families.*

Read aloud the directions for the activity Working Together. Make sure children understand what they are to do. If appropriate, work through the first question with the class. Then allow time for children to think through the other problems and write their answers. When children have finished, give them an opportunity to share their answers for each question.

3 Close

Say: *Let's take a moment to reflect on our own families and how we treat one another.* Pause. *Now take a moment to thank God for your families.* Pause again for 10 seconds and pray aloud *Amen.*

1 Begin

Faith Summary Invite a volunteer to read aloud this section. Ask: **How can we share God's love?** (by caring for others) **What is a way we can show peace in our families?** (obeying and respecting our parents)

2 Connect

Word I Learned Invite children to read the Glossary definition of *justice*. Ask volunteers to use *justice* in a sentence about their families and in a sentence about their friends.

Ways of Being Like Jesus Ask a volunteer to read aloud this section. Invite children to think of more examples of specific ways they can share God's love by helping someone in need, such as reading to someone who has vision challenges.

Prayer

Quiet children and ask that they get ready to pray. Say: **Let's thank Jesus for being our example of a loving person.** Lead children in praying the Sign of the Cross. Say: **Pray the prayer with me.** After praying invite children to spend a few moments talking with Jesus in their own words. Take five deep breaths and pray *Amen.*

With My Family Ask children to read silently the three suggestions in this section. Invite children to choose one or more to complete at home.

3 Go in Peace

Collect materials and return them to the appropriate places. Encourage children to discuss the With My Family section at home. Say: **This week show your family and friends how much you love them by working and playing with them.**

Living My Faith

Faith Summary

With the help of the Holy Spirit, we can live in peace, harmony, and justice with others. We share God's love by caring for others. Saint Louise de Marillac cared for those who were poor through the Sisters of Charity. Obeying and respecting your parents is a way to show that you care about your family.

Word I Learned

justice

Ways of Being Like Jesus

We can share God's love by helping others. *Offer to do a chore, such as shoveling snow or raking leaves for someone who needs your help.*

Prayer

Jesus, help me always to be aware of those who need me so that I can serve others as you did.

With My Family

Activity As a family meet together once a week to share plans and to discuss anyone's concerns.

Faith on the Go Ask one another: *When you have differences, what is a good way to work them out?*

Family Prayer *Dear God, help our family to always be fair and respectful to one another. Amen.*

140 UNIT 5 • *Morality, Our Lived Faith*

Session Assessment Option

An assessment for this session can be found at **www.findinggod.com.**

PLAN AHEAD

Get Ready for Session 24

Consult the catechist preparation pages to prepare for Session 24 and determine any materials you will need.

All Life Is Sacred

3-Minute Retreat

As you prepare for the session, pause and take three deep breaths. Reflect on the beauty and sacredness of all creation—all life, each person. Thank God for his gift of family and friends.

> **Psalm 8:6–7**
>
> *Yet you have made them little less than a*
>
> *god,*
>
> *crowned them with glory and honor.*
>
> *You have given them rule over the works of*
>
> *your hands,*
>
> *put all things at their feet . . .*

Reflection

Some people go through their lives focusing only on their material comforts. This attitude is not in accord with that of a follower of God's. Simply consuming material resources does not enhance human dignity. According to the above psalmist, the dignity and glory of the human person is a blessing of glory and honor from God. This is linked to our responsibility to care for God's creation. Our respect for God, for one another, and for creation is shown by the choices we make. When deciding what actions to take today, we must consider how our choices affect the future.

Question

How can I use the world's resources more responsibly?

Prayer

Speak to God, using this prayer or one of your own.

> *Praise to you, Lord of all creation, you bless my*
>
> *life with an abundance of your love and give me*
>
> *what I need each day. Help me reflect your gift*
>
> *of love.*

Knowing and Sharing Your Faith in Session 24

Consider how Scripture and Tradition can deepen your understanding of the session content.

Scripture

1 John 4:7 states that everyone who loves is of God and knows God.

Psalm 8:6–10 praises God for giving humans dominion over the earth and its creatures.

Tradition

Human life has always been regarded as sacred in the Catholic Tradition. One reason is because of the value we place on human life, associating death with sin and associating life with all that is good and beautiful. Human life is the highest form of life on earth because it is directed toward eternal life. The Church defends human life against all its enemies: abortion, euthanasia, murder, and war, as well as poverty, hunger, discrimination, and homelessness. Human life is part of the web of life, and we believe that all life is sacred. There is interdependence among all life-forms, so our need to protect human life is intertwined with the care for animal and plant life.

Catholic Social Teaching

In this session the integrated Catholic Social Teaching themes are **Care for God's Creation, Rights and Responsibilities, Life and Dignity of the Human Person,** and **Option for the Poor and Vulnerable.** See page 121b for an explanation of these themes.

Window on the Catechism

Respect for human life is discussed in *CCC* 2258–2262. Respect for creation is treated in *CCC* 2415–2418.

One-Hour Session Planner

SESSION 24 All Life Is Sacred

Session Theme: *Jesus calls us to share with one another in any way we can.*

Before This Session

▶ Reread Session 1 so that you are able to compare the creation discussion with this session.

▶ Visit children's science and nature Web sites for possible activities to do with children.

▶ Bookmark your Bible to Psalm 8:6–10 and John 4:7. Place the Bible open to either of these passages in your prayer center.

▶ Display the *Finding God* poster Making Good Choices.

▶ Read the Guide for this session, choose any additional If Time Allows activities that you might have time to complete, and gather the listed materials.

Prayer in Session 24

In this session children reflect on what they have learned in past sessions about the Trinity. They thank the Father, the Son, and the Holy Spirit for their love and guidance.

STEPS	APPROXIMATE TIME
Engage *All Life Is Sacred* PAGE 141	10 minutes
Explore *A Life of Caring* PAGE 142 *Treat Others with Respect* PAGE 143 *Art Print: Light Work* ART PRINT AND PRINT BACK	30–40 minutes
Reflect *Prayer:* Thanking God for the School Year PAGE 144 *Praise for God's Creation* PAGE 145	15–20 minutes
Respond *Living My Faith* PAGE 146	5–10 minutes

Materials

REQUIRED

▶ Bible

▶ Art Print 24: *Light Work* and Children's Book page 250

▶ Pictures of various animals, insects, people, and nature scenes

▶ CD player

▶ CD 2, Tracks 17 and 18, "Reflective Music"

▶ *Finding God* poster: Making Good Choices

IF TIME ALLOWS

▶ Slips of paper, small box (page 141)

▶ Drawing paper, art supplies (pages 141, 144)

▶ Large cardboard boxes (page 143)

▶ Session 24 BLM, T-328 (page 145)

▶ Hot glue gun, glue, junk items from home (page 145)

▶ Session 24 Assessment, www.findinggod.com (page 146)

SESSION 24

We witness the beauty of God's creation when we enjoy nature. Where have you seen the beauty of nature? How would you describe it to someone who hasn't seen it?

All Life Is Sacred

Prayer

Jesus, Son of God, teach me to respect and care for God's wonderful world and all who live in it.

141

IF TIME ALLOWS

Inclusion: Physical

Picturing God's Creation Children with physical disabilities may have a difficult time navigating parts of nature, such as hiking or swimming, so invite children to brainstorm a list of aspects of nature that everyone can appreciate, such as enjoying a sunset, the scent of a flower, or the feel of snow. If children are able, have them draw what they imagined.

Describing Game

Discuss various natural settings, such as a waterfall or a desert. List them on the board. Once you have one setting for each child, write them on slips of paper and place them in a box. Have each child choose from the box and keep the setting to himself or herself. Invite children to guess the setting by playing a game of 20 questions. Explain that only yes or no questions are allowed to be asked.

 Go to **www.findinggod.com/sessionextenders** for an article about Catholic Social Teaching.

SESSION 24

OUTCOMES

▶ Identify Blessed Frederic Ozanam as someone who understood that all life is sacred.

▶ Explain that to be good Christians, we must respect all people.

▶ Describe how God calls us to live peacefully with all people.

▶ Define *Dismissal*.

① Set the Stage

Ask: **What do you remember about our study of God's creation?** (Possible answers: God created the world out of love for us; all God's creation is good; we know God through his creation.)

Say: **Imagine you are outside. Do you see animals? What do you hear? What colors surround you?** Encourage children to share what they imagined. Say: **In this session we will learn more about God's creation.**

② Get Started

Discuss the photo. Read aloud the session title. Ask a volunteer to read aloud the text in the blue box. Invite children to describe things they have seen in nature. Say: **Imagine how much God loves us to entrust his world to our care. All life is sacred, and we should help and respect others.**

✝ *God's Creation*

Prayer

Say: **Reflect on Jesus' loving presence in your lives as you pray the prayer with me.** After praying invite children to spend time talking to Jesus. Pause and close by praying *Amen*. Say: **God's presence in creation and in our lives is a blessing. Keep him in your hearts during this session.**

1 Begin

Say: **We have learned about many people who cared for others. How did Saint Louise de Marillac show her love for others?** (helped Saint Vincent de Paul work with people who were poor, helped found an order of sisters to work with people who were poor) Say: **Listen as I read about another caring person, Frederic Ozanam.**

2 Connect

Read aloud the first paragraph. Then ask: **What did Frederic Ozanam know about human life?** (It is sacred.) Invite children to look at the picture of Frederic Ozanam. Say: **Why did the artist paint a halo behind Frederic's head?** (to show that he is holy)

Read aloud the second paragraph. Ask: **Why do you think Frederic felt he should help people who are poor?** (His parents encouraged him to help others; his conscience told him to help.)

✝ **The Poor and Vulnerable**

Invite a volunteer to read aloud the third paragraph. Ask: **How did Frederic and his friends follow Jesus' example?** (gave what they had to help others, started the St. Vincent de Paul Society) Ask: **What do you know about Saint Vincent de Paul?** (He worked for those who were poor; he helped Louise de Marillac found the Sisters of Charity.)

Say: **Frederic and his friends proved that they could make a difference in the world.** Ask: **What parables have we read about small acts of love reaching many people?** (mustard seed and yeast parables)

3 Close

Direct children's attention to the feature at the bottom of page 142.

 Reading God's Word

Read aloud the adaptation. Say: **God's love lives in all of us. Praise God by sharing that love with others.**

A Life of Caring

Frederic Ozanam, Fearghal O'Farrell.

Every human life is sacred. Blessed Frederic Ozanam understood the worth of every person.

While Frederic was in college in 1832, a terrible disease broke out in Paris. Many people became sick and died. People who were poor suffered greatly. Each day Frederic would walk past the homes of these families. His parents had raised him to help others. His conscience told him he should help these people.

Six of Frederic's friends decided to help him by giving their wood supply to a widow. Soon they were helping the less fortunate people of Paris in many ways. Some people asked, "How can seven men make a difference?" But they did. They kept working, and more people joined them. They called themselves the Society of St. Vincent de Paul after the patron saint of Christian charity. In 1997 Frederic was named Blessed.

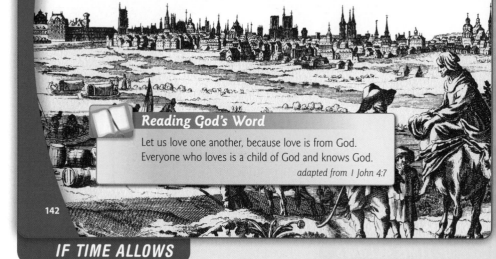

Reading God's Word

Let us love one another, because love is from God. Everyone who loves is a child of God and knows God.

adapted from 1 John 4:7

142

IF TIME ALLOWS

Going Forth

Ask children to write a paragraph about how they have learned to be aware of the needs of others and of all creation. Have children answer these questions: What are their responsibilities? How will they treat people? How will they care for the environment? When they have finished writing, allow time for children to share their thoughts with the class.

EXPLORE

Treat Others with Respect

Frederic Ozanam knew that every person is special. He knew that all people are important members of the human family. God makes each person sacred from the first moment of life. Like Frederic we are to treat others with respect, no matter where they are from or what language they speak. God wants people and countries to live peacefully with one another.

Just as Frederic helped others, we are also reminded to go and serve others. With the words of the **Dismissal** at Mass, we are sent forth to glorify the Lord by our lives. We can glorify the Lord by serving others with respect.

Make Choices That Show Respect

We can also show respect for others through the choices we make. God wants us to make choices that are good. Write the end to each sentence below, showing how you would make a good choice.

If I saw two people arguing over a game,

I would _____

_____.

If someone made fun of another's clothes,

I would _____

_____.

If a friend told me not to be friends with someone,

I would _____

_____.

GO TO
PAGE
250

SESSION 24 • *All Life Is Sacred* **143**

IF TIME ALLOWS

Service: Supplies for Pets

Talk to children about the importance of respecting the animals in God's creation. Obtain permission from your catechetical leader before having a collection for pet supplies. Have children collect food and other items for a local animal shelter. Provide supplies to make collection boxes. Have children check the boxes periodically. Arrange to take the supplies to a nearby shelter.

 God's Creation

---

① Begin

Write *respect* on the board. Ask: **What does respect mean?** (Possible answers: consideration, honor, admiration) Point to the picture and ask: **Are the children showing respect for one another?** (no, because they're whispering in front of someone) Say: **When we say we respect God's creation, we include all the people God created. Let's read how we can show respect for all people.**

② Connect

Read aloud the first paragraph. Ask: **Why are all people important?** (God makes us sacred from the first moment of life.) **Whom should we treat with respect?** (all people, regardless of their background, language, or nationality) **How does God want us to live with one another?** (peacefully) Invite children to take turns completing the sentence: **I am a peaceful person when I _____.** (Possible answers: help someone who doesn't understand my language, speak calmly to my brother when he starts to argue)

Read aloud the next paragraph. Write *Dismissal* on the board and read the definition from the Glossary.

Read aloud the activity Making Choices That Show Respect. Say: **Every choice we make affects other people. It is important that we respect others when making a choice because we are all part of God's creation and God wants us to share his love. If we do not respect one another, then we are not sharing his love.**

✝ *Rights and Responsibilities*

③ Close

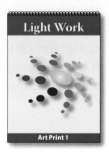

Display Art Print 24: *Light Work.* Use the Art Print 24 instruction to teach this section. Art Print teaching instruction can also be found on page 250.

Prayer

Follow the steps to guide children through the prayer on page 144.

Children's Page

Prepare Read the prayer in advance to become familiar with it.

Pray Ask children to quiet themselves. Point to the picture and ask: What do you see in this picture? (Possible answer: a child from another country standing next to a blackboard, someone happy to be in school) Ask: **What do you think this picture is trying to tell us?** (Possible answer: We are blessed to be able to go to school and learn about the world around us, God's creation.)

Invite children to be still and to listen as you read the reflection. You may choose to play the reflective music at the end of CD 2 for a prayerful atmosphere. Say: **Bow your heads and listen thoughtfully.** Read aloud the first paragraph slowly and reverently. Pause after each sentence to give children time to reflect on God and his creation.

Read aloud the second and third paragraphs in the same manner, pausing to give children time to reflect after each sentence.

Read aloud the last paragraph. Pause for 10 seconds so that children may spend time praying in their own words. Then say: **We reflected on the love and grace of God the Father, his Son, Jesus Christ, and the Holy Spirit. Let us close our prayer by remembering the Trinity.** Together pray the Sign of the Cross. Say: **Praying the Sign of the Cross reminds us of the Holy Trinity. It is a short prayer and you can say it many times throughout the day.**

Prayer

Thanking God for the School Year

Let us begin today's prayer by remembering what we have learned this year. Think of God the Father. Thank him for the wonderful world he has created for us.

Think of Jesus Christ. Thank him for teaching you about God's love and for showing you how to love God and others.

Think of the Holy Spirit. Thank him for guiding you through the year.

Sit quietly for a moment. Think about how much God loves you. He is with you always. Be still and know how special you are.

144 UNIT 5 • *Morality, Our Lived Faith*

IF TIME ALLOWS

My Prayer Space

Distribute drawing paper, crayons, and markers. Ask children to draw pictures of the various nature scenes where they like to be alone with Jesus and God to pray. Have children label their pictures with a descriptive phrase, such as *Magnificent Mountain* or *Sandy Seashore*. Suggest that they also write a brief prayer of thanks to God for his special gift. Children might model it after one of the psalms they have read this year.

FYI

Coaching Children to Pray

Encourage children to be aware of God's presence with them. Remind them that God knows them completely and loves them unconditionally. He always hears them and understands what they mean. When they pray, the bond of love between them and God is strengthened.

Praise for God's Creation

We are called to take care of all of God's creation. A bird, a river, and a friend are all part of God's creation.

> God has crowned us with glory and honor. He has asked us to care for his creation: sheep and oxen, the beasts of the field, the birds of the air, and the creatures in the sea.
>
> *adapted from Psalm 8:6–9*

Parts of Creation

Think of some parts of creation that begin with the letters below. Write the words on the lines. Use the pictures as hints or make up your own.

C R E A T I O N

C _____   T _____

R _____   I _____

E _____   O _____

A _____   N _____

SESSION 24 • *All Life Is Sacred*   **145**

1 Begin

Display pictures cut out of magazines of various animals, insects, people, and nature scenes. Be sure to have a wide variety, from whales to insects, from puddles to oceans. Scatter the pictures on the floor. Invite children to categorize the pictures any way they want. After a few minutes, discuss what the items in the categories have in common, such as bodies of water, or large animals. Then say: ***There is one thing that all these pictures have in common—they are pictures of things that God has created.***

2 Connect

Invite a volunteer to read aloud the heading and the first paragraph.

Say: ***We have said that God must love us very much to entrust the care of his world to us.*** Read aloud the passage in a tone full of praise. Say: ***When we see any of God's creatures, we are reminded that we share the responsibility of caring for them.***

Say: ***Now let's see if we can identify different plants and animals in God's creation by naming one for every letter in the word CREATION.***

Read aloud the heading and paragraph. Give children time to complete the activity. Encourage them to think of other plants and animals not pictured on the page for each letter.

✝ *God's Creation*

3 Close

Have children share their responses with the group, especially responses not associated with the illustrations in the book. Write *CREATION* on the board as many times as needed to accommodate the variety of other responses. Say: ***Look at all the living things that are part of God's creation.***

IF TIME ALLOWS

Session 24 BLM

Window to God's World Have children complete the Session 24 Blackline Master [T-328], a writing and drawing activity about finding ways to care for God's creation.

Recycled Art

Ask children to bring in items from home that they might otherwise throw away, such as cereal boxes, broken parts from a toy, and empty spools of thread. Provide glue or help them use a hot glue gun to make their own sculptures using the "garbage." Encourage children to share their garbage so that they can be creative. Host a "Junk Art" gallery after everyone has completed his or her sculpture. When children take their projects home, make sure that they know not to throw it away, but to recycle all the recyclables on their art.

① Begin

Faith Summary Read aloud this section. Ask: **What does God call us to do?** (treat every person as sacred, care for all his creation) **What to the words of the Dismissal tell us to do?** (to go forth and glorify the Lord) **What are we called to do?** (to take care of God's creation)

✝ *God's Creation*

② Connect

Word I Learned Ask a volunteer to use *Dismissal* in a sentence. Review the word in the Glossary.

Ways of Being Like Jesus Ask a volunteer to read aloud this section. Say: **How could you be like Jesus and care for someone who is sick?** (play cards together, bake a special treat, watch a movie together)

Prayer

Quiet children for the closing prayer of thanks. Say: **Let us thank Jesus for helping us know how to respect our world.** Invite children to pray the prayer with you. Ask them to pray the prayer silently a second time and to spend a few moments talking to Jesus in their own words. Count silently to 10, and then pray *Amen.*

With My Family Ask children to read silently the three activities in this section. Invite children to choose one or more to complete at home.

③ Go in Peace

Collect materials and return them to the appropriate places. Encourage children to discuss the With My Family section at home. Say: **Go in peace to respect and care for all of God's creation.**

Living My Faith

Faith Summary

As Blessed Frederic Ozanam helped others through the Society of St. Vincent de Paul, we are called to treat every person as special. God calls us to take care of all he has created. At Mass the words of the Dismissal send us forth to glorify the Lord. We are called by God to care for his creation.

Word I Learned	Ways of Being Like Jesus
Dismissal	Jesus cared for sick people. *Brighten the day of someone who is sick. Do a simple activity with them or just sit and talk.*

Prayer

Jesus, thank you for showing me how to respect people and the world. Help me always to live in peace with others.

With My Family

Activity Look into opportunities for your family to serve at a local food pantry, soup kitchen, or clothing drive. Mark your calendar to do this.

Faith on the Go Ask one another: *If someone wrote a biography about you, what is a kind act you have done that he or she could describe?*

Family Prayer Dear God, thank you for the world in which we live. Help us appreciate and care for this wonderful world. Amen.

146 UNIT 5 • *Morality, Our Lived Faith*

IF TIME ALLOWS

Words Quilt

Provide each child with a four-by-four inch square of paper. Tell them to select a vocabulary word from any of the five units, write the word on the paper, and draw a picture that represents the word's meaning. When they have finished, join the squares together to form a quilt. Use the quilt to review the vocabulary words.

Session Assessment Option

An assessment for this session can be found at **www.findinggod.com**.

PLAN AHEAD

Get Ready for Session 25

Consult the catechist preparation pages to prepare for Session 25 and determine any materials you will need.

Celebrating Easter

3-Minute Retreat

As you prepare the session, pause, be still, and be aware of the loving presence of God.

John 20:27

Then he said to Thomas, "Put your finger here and see my hands, and bring your hand and put it into my side, and do not be unbelieving, but believe."

Reflection

Thomas speaks for us at some time in our life as Christians. Times of troubles can lead us to be hesitant about our faith. Even in the Gospel of Matthew, we read that when the disciples saw Jesus some worshiped him, "but they doubted" (Matthew 28:17). As Thomas discovered, a Christian's faith is not grounded in a set of ideas but in the person of the risen Jesus. The way to live through doubt is to speak and listen to Jesus person to person. Each of us in our own way is invited to consider the wounds of Jesus and in them find his healing presence.

Question

What do I need to ask of Jesus when I speak and listen to him today?

Prayer

Speak to God, using these words or others that come to mind.

Jesus, help me to have the courage to face you, learn from you, and love you.

Knowing and Sharing Your Faith in Session 25

Consider how Scripture and Tradition can deepen your understanding of the session content.

Scripture

John 20:27 tells the story of Thomas's doubts and Jesus' invitation to believe.

Tradition

Easter Sunday begins a 50-day celebration of the Paschal Mystery, the Passion, Death, Resurrection, and Ascension of Jesus Christ. Easter Sunday follows Holy Week and is the third and final day of the Paschal Triduum, the three-day period that begins on the evening of Holy Thursday. On Holy Saturday evening we celebrate the Easter Vigil. During the Easter Vigil, a new fire is lit and the story of Salvation is told. Also that evening the Paschal Candle is lit, the baptismal waters are blessed, and new converts are received into the Church. Through his Resurrection, Christ gives us new birth in the Holy Spirit and renews the gift of life within us. We also receive the wisdom and courage to live this new life Jesus calls us to.

Catholic Social Teaching

In this session the integrated Catholic Social Teaching theme is **Family and Community.** See page 121b for an explanation of this theme.

Window on the Catechism

The mystery of Christ's Resurrection is discussed in *CCC* 639–644.

General Directory for Catechesis

The relationship between catechesis and the Easter season is discussed in *GDC* 91.

One-Hour Session Planner

SESSION 25 Celebrating Easter

Session Theme: *Easter is a time to reflect on God' merciful love.*

Before This Session

- Determine whether you will use the Unit Assessment option listed on page 150.

- Determine whether you will also discuss the Easter and Pentecost seasonal sections in the back of the Children's Book.

- Bookmark your Bible to John 20:27. Place the open Bible in your prayer center.

- Read the Guide for this session, choose any additional If Time Allows activities that you might have time to complete, and gather the listed materials.

Prayer in Session 25

During this session children have an opportunity to thank God for his merciful love and for the guidance to share this gift with others. The prayer times include time for children to talk with God in the silence of their hearts and to share with him any of their thoughts and concerns.

STEPS	APPROXIMATE TIME
Engage *Celebrating Easter* PAGE 147	10 minutes
Explore *Show Mercy During Easter* PAGE 148	25–35 minutes
Reflect *Mass During Easter* PAGE 149 *Art Print:* The Lamb of God ART PRINT AND PRINT BACK	20–25 minutes
Respond *Living My Faith* PAGE 150	5–10 minutes

Materials

REQUIRED

- Easter symbols, such as a decorated egg, lily, rabbit
- Bible
- Art Print 25: *The Lamb of God* and Children's Book page 251

IF TIME ALLOWS

- Book showing phases of the moon, book explaining the meaning behind a variety of Easter symbols (page 147)
- Drawing paper, art supplies (pages 147, 149)
- Session 25 BLM, T-329 (page 148)
- Session 25 Assessment, www.findinggod.com (page 150)
- Unit 5 Assessment, T-330–T-332 (page 150)

Celebrating Easter

During the Easter season, we celebrate the Resurrection of Jesus. We are joyful that Jesus has risen from the dead. We pray "Alleluia! Alleluia!" and sing about welcoming the risen Christ into our lives and for God's merciful love.

Easter is the most important day of the Church year. It is celebrated on the first Sunday after the first full moon of spring. During this season we also celebrate the Feast of the Ascension, the day Jesus ascended into Heaven. The Easter season begins with the celebration of the Easter Vigil on Holy Saturday and continues for the next 50 days, ending on Pentecost Sunday.

Prayer

Dear Jesus, this Easter season help me to remember the mercy that you have given us and to show mercy to others.

147

IF TIME ALLOWS

Inclusion: Specific Learning

A Full Moon Use this activity if you have children with specific learning differences. Discuss the eight phases of the moon. Display pictures and books for children to see the phases. Remind children that Easter begins on the first Sunday after the first full moon of spring. As you speak, use simple vocabulary and short sentences. Always maintain eye contact with children.

Symbols of Easter

Explain the meaning of Easter symbols. For ideas, refer to the internet and books, such as *Lilies, Rabbits, and Painted Eggs: The Story of the Easter Symbols* by Edna Barth and Ursula Arndt. Distribute art supplies and invite the children to draw some of the symbols.

▶ Discuss how Easter is a time to reflect on God's merciful love.

▶ Discuss the joy of Christ's Resurrection.

▶ Define *Lamb of God* and *mercy*.

1 Set the Stage

Display Easter symbols such as a decorated egg, lilies, or a picture of a lamb. Ask: *These symbols represent the most important day of the Church year. What day is it?* (Easter) Say: *Let's read about a special part of our Church's year—Easter.*

2 Get Started

Read aloud the session title and the first paragraph. Ask: *What do we celebrate on Easter?* (the Resurrection of Jesus)

Read aloud the second paragraph. Ask: *Is Easter on the same date each year?* (No, it is celebrated on the first Sunday after the first full moon of spring.) *When does the Easter season begin and end?* (It begins with the celebration of the Easter Vigil on Holy Saturday and ends on Pentecost Sunday). Say: *In this session we'll learn about Easter.*

Prayer

Call children's attention to the prayer. Say: *Take a moment to imagine a beautiful spring garden.* Have children close their eyes, fold their hands, and pray silently as you pray aloud. Say: *Let's take a moment to talk to Jesus in our hearts.* Allow children sufficient time to finish their silent prayers. Pray *Amen* and ask children to open their eyes. Conclude with the Sign of the Cross.

1 Begin

Say: *Think of a time someone hurt your feelings but you forgave the person.* Ask: *Did you want to forgive the person or were you still mad? How did it feel?* Invite volunteers to discuss their situations. Say: *When you forgave the person, you showed mercy to them.*

2 Connect

 Read aloud the heading. Write *mercy* on the board. Invite volunteers to read aloud the first three paragraphs. Ask: *What did Jesus do when Thomas saw and believed that Jesus had risen?* (Jesus showed them mercy.)

Read aloud the Scripture adaptation. Then read aloud from the Bible the story of Thomas, the apostle, whom we remember on the second Sunday of Easter [John 20:24–29]. Say: *The risen Jesus gives us the power to believe, even in a world of doubt and weakened faith.* Invite children to read silently the following two questions.

Have a volunteer read aloud the directions for The Mercy of Friendship. Offer an example for a prayer: *Lord, I pray that you are with my friend. She has hurt my feelings. Help me to forgive her and remember to love her as you do.* Invite children to complete the activity, but they do not need to include their friend's name in the prayer.

3 Close

Direct children's attention to the feature at the bottom of page 148.

Reading God's Word

Read aloud the verse with children. Ask: *When we have doubts about God, what can we do to strengthen our faith?* (Possible answers: pray to God, think about his gifts) Discuss children's responses.

Show Mercy During Easter

Easter is a time to reflect on God's merciful love. On the Second Sunday of Easter, we celebrate God's **mercy**—the mercy that Jesus showed to Thomas, the apostle, when he wanted a sign that Jesus had truly risen.

Thomas was not with the apostles when Jesus appeared. He wanted to see Jesus with his own eyes. The next time Jesus appeared, Thomas was present. He saw and believed. Jesus loved Thomas and showed him mercy.

We have not seen Jesus, but we are blessed by faith in him. We are called to show mercy to others and to treat others with love.

> Blessed are they who have not seen and have believed.
>
> *adapted from John 20:29*

Do I show compassion and forgiveness to others? How can I show mercy to my friends and my family?

The Mercy of Friendship

Write a prayer for a friend who needs your compassion and forgiveness.

_____

_____

_____

_____

_____

Reading God's Word

Do not doubt, but believe in me.   *adapted from John 20:27*

148   UNIT 5 • *Morality, Our Lived Faith*

Session 25 BLM

Have Mercy on Us Have children complete the Session 25 Blackline Master [T-329] to reveal that God always has mercy on us.

Seasonal Sessions: Easter and Pentecost

Work with children through pages 169–176 of the Children's Book and this guide. These special sessions can each take up to one hour to complete.

Mass During Easter

When you go to Mass during Easter, pay special attention to praying the **Lamb of God** during the Breaking of the Bread. Before receiving Holy Communion, we call on Jesus, the Lamb of God, to have mercy on us. Jesus gave up his life for the Salvation of the world.

What We Experience

When you look around your church at Easter, you may see images of the Lamb of God. This reminds us of Jesus' great sacrifice. Joyful music is played because the parish rejoices that Jesus is with us always. White is the liturgical color of the season and represents the joy of Christ's Resurrection. The priest wears white or gold vestments, the altar cloth is white, and the white lilies symbolize our new life in the risen Christ.

What Lamb of God Means to You

Choose three of the words below to write a short paragraph to describe what the Lamb of God means to you.

Lamb	sacrifice	God	Easter
mercy	Jesus	church	communion

_____

_____

_____

_____

Did You Know?

The feast of the Ascension is celebrated 40 days after Easter Sunday.

GO TO PAGE 251

IF TIME ALLOWS

Service: Spreading Easter Joy

Invite children to spread the joys of Easter to a nearby senior center or shelter. Obtain permission from your catechetical leader to decorate a social room or entrance with Easter lilies and children's drawings of Easter symbols. Distribute construction paper, crayons, markers, scissors, and glue. Invite children to draw pictures of a variety of Easter symbols, such as lambs and painted eggs.

✝ *Family and Community*

REFLECT

1 Begin

Discuss where children may have seen lambs during Easter. Ask: **Have you noticed chocolate lambs at Easter? Or little lambs made of butter at the grocery store? Does anyone eat cake that is shaped like a lamb?** Remind children that these Easter traditions symbolize Jesus, the Lamb of God.

2 Connect

Read aloud the first paragraph. Write *Lamb of God* on the board. Ask: **Who is the Lamb of God?** (Jesus) Discuss how at Easter we celebrate Jesus, the Lamb of God. Explain that as we call upon the Lamb of God to show mercy on us, the extraordinary ministers of Holy Communion are gathering around the altar. Say: **At one time lambs were sacrificed as a religious offering. We use this symbol today because of the great sacrifice Jesus made by dying on the cross for our sins.**

Ask a volunteer to read aloud What We Experience. Ask: **Why is joyful music played?** (because the parish rejoices that Jesus is with us always) **What is the liturgical color of the season?** (white)

Read aloud the directions for What Lamb of God Means to You. Invite volunteers to share their paragraphs.

Did You Know?

Read aloud the feature. Explain that the Feast of the Ascension celebrates Jesus' Ascension into Heaven 40 days after his Resurrection.

3 Close

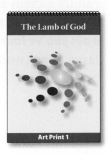

The Lamb of God

Art Print 1

Display Art Print 25: *The Lamb of God.* Use the Art Print 25 instruction to teach this section. Art Print teaching instruction can also be found on page 251.

1 Begin

Faith Summary Ask volunteers to read aloud this section. Ask: ***What do we celebrate at Easter?*** (Jesus' Resurrection and God's merciful love) ***To whom do we pray to have mercy on us?*** (Lamb of God)

2 Connect

Words I Learned Read aloud the terms. Ask children to suggest words or phrases that clarify the meaning of each term. Review each word in the Glossary if necessary.

Ways of Being Like Jesus Have a volunteer read aloud this section. Discuss situations when children have had a difficult time forgiving someone.

Prayer

Ask children to close their eyes, fold their hands, and pray silently as you pray aloud. Allow a few seconds for silent reflection. Pray *Amen* and sing an Alleluia together.

With My Family Ask children to read silently the three suggestions in this section. Invite children to choose one or more to complete at home.

3 Go in Peace

Collect materials and return them to the appropriate places. Encourage children to discuss the With My Family section at home. Say: ***During Easter this year, tell me some of the ways you've found to act more like Jesus. I can't wait to hear!***

150 www.findinggod.com

RESPOND

Living My Faith

Faith Summary

Easter is a time to celebrate Jesus' Resurrection and how Jesus showed mercy to Thomas. It is also a time to reflect on God's merciful love. We pray to the Lamb of God to have mercy on us and to show others mercy.

Words I Learned

Lamb of God
mercy

Ways of Being Like Jesus

Jesus showed mercy to others. *Forgive others, even when it is difficult.*

Prayer

Dear Jesus, thank you for your love and mercy. Help me to love others and show mercy just as you did.

With My Family

Activity Decorate your home with signs of Easter. Place a potted lily on the table and play joyful music as a reminder of our new life in Christ.

Faith on the Go Ask one another: *How does Easter make us feel? How do we share how we feel with others?*

Family Prayer Use Easter to invite family members to grow in prayer by finding "quiet time" as a family. Close your eyes and invite God into your heart.

150 UNIT 5 • *Morality, Our Lived Faith*

IF TIME ALLOWS

Session Assessment Option

An assessment for this session can be found at **www.findinggod.com**.

Unit Assessment Option

If you wish, photocopy the Unit Assessment on pages T-330–T-332. Administer the assessment during the session or send it home. Additional assessment items are available at **www.findinggod.com**.

THE YEAR IN OUR CHURCH

Catechist Preparation pages open this unit.

SEASONAL SESSIONS
The Year in Our Church

Refer to the abbreviated Scope and Sequence below for themes, Scripture, *CCC* references, and saints and holy people found in the Seasonal Sessions. These sessions can be used independently or in conjunction with Celebrating Sessions 5, 10, 15, 20, and 25.

Season	Theme	Scripture	CCC References	Saints and Holy People
Advent PAGES 153–156	In the season of Advent, we prepare to celebrate Jesus' birth.	Luke 1:26–35,38	430, 484	Mary Gabriel
Christmas PAGES 157–160	During the Christmas season, we celebrate Jesus' birth.	Luke 2:4–19 Psalm 96:1,12–13	525–526, 528	Mary Joseph Jesus
Lent PAGES 161–164	The season of Lent is a time of preparation for the Feast of Easter.	Mark 1:12–13 1 Corinthians 10:13	540	Jesus
Holy Week PAGES 165–168	During Holy Week we remember that Jesus suffered and died for our Salvation.	Luke 9:23, 23:22–26	560, 1169	Jesus Simon of Cyrene
Easter PAGES 169–172	During the Easter season, we celebrate the Resurrection and Ascension of Jesus Christ.	Luke 24:1–8 1 Corinthians 15:1–4	640–644, 647, 659–664	Jesus Mary Magdalene Peter the disciples
Pentecost PAGES 173–176	At Pentecost we celebrate the coming of the Holy Spirit to bring life to the Church.	1 Corinthians 12:4–7,12–13 John 14:16–18	731–732	Paul
All Saints Day and All Souls Day PAGES 177–180	On All Saints Day and on All Souls Day, we celebrate all members of the Church, living and dead, united in Christ.	1 John 4:11–13 1 Corinthians 12:12–13	946–948, 2177	Jesus Communion of Saints

Seasonal Sessions

Seasonal Sessions provide lessons for major feasts and seasons of the liturgical year. These sessions can be used independently or in conjunction with Celebrating Sessions 5, 10, 15, 20, and 25.

Session Steps

▶ **Engage**   a brief introduction that relates to children's life experiences

▶ **Explore**   an exploration of Scripture and Catholic Tradition

▶ **Reflect**   a Prayer Service that relates to the session theme

▶ **Respond**   a culminating activity

As a Stand-Alone Session

If your program calls for more than 25 sessions, you can offer these seven sessions separately for as many as 32 sessions. To use them independently, consider the following options:

▶ Implement a session as each season or feast is approaching.

▶ Use all If Time Allows options.

▶ Incorporate the Blackline Master.

▶ Creatively enhance the Prayer Service with local customs and traditions. You may wish to have children decorate your prayer center or sacred space for each season.

As a Supplement to a Celebrating Session

Each Seasonal Session can be used to further expand upon concepts taught in Sessions 5, 10, 15, 20, and 25. The following options integrate the Seasonal and Celebrating Sessions:

▶ In advance, review the coordinating sessions as you prepare.

▶ Based on the time you have with children, decide which elements of the Seasonal Session can be easily incorporated into instruction of the Celebrating Session. For example, you might end the Celebrating Session with the Prayer Service from the Seasonal Session, or you might have children complete the Seasonal Blackline Master after reading an Explore section in a Celebrating Session.

▶ Consider assigning a Seasonal Session as an at-home follow-up experience after you teach a Celebrating Session.

Assessment Options

▶ An assessment for each Seasonal Session can be found at **www.findinggod.com.**

▶ A unit assessment for The Year in Our Church can be found at **www.findinggod.com.**

The Year in Our Church

Liturgical Calendar
The liturgical calendar shows us the feasts and seasons of the Church year.

Advent · Christmas · Ordinary Time · Lent · Holy Week · Easter · Ordinary Time

Epiphany · Christmas · First Sunday of Advent · All Souls Day All Saints Day

Ash Wednesday · Palm Sunday · Holy Thursday · Good Friday · Holy Saturday · Easter Sunday · Ascension Pentecost

Winter · Spring · Fall · Summer

151

IF TIME ALLOWS

The Liturgical Calendar BLM

Feast and Season Booklets Distribute construction paper, crayons and markers, and The Liturgical Calendar Blackline Master [T-333]. Have children color the BLM, using the correct liturgical color for each season. Ask children to glue the calendar to a sheet of construction paper. Then invite children to make a book, using the BLM as the cover. Explain that in addition to the cover, the book should have at least seven sheets of paper, one sheet for each liturgical feast or season children will learn about this year. Tell children that as they learn about each season, they can add facts, Scripture stories, prayers, and drawings to their liturgical-calendar booklets.

The liturgical colors for the seasons are purple for Advent and Lent and Holy Week, white for Easter and Christmas, and green for Ordinary Time.

The liturgical calendar represents the celebration of the mystery of Christ, from the anticipation of his birth to the sending of the Holy Spirit. The Church marks the passage of time with a cycle of seasons and feasts that invites us, year after year, to deepen our commitment to Jesus. By inviting children into these celebrations, you help them grow in the Catholic way of life.

1 Set the Stage

Lead a brief discussion about calendars. Display calendars in different formats, such as a desk calendar and a wall calendar. Say: *These are different types of calendars. Some people like to use one or the other.* Say: *Raise your hand if you have a calendar in your home.* Ask: *Where do you keep it?* (Possible answers: on the fridge, on a desk, on a wall) Say: *Now let's discuss a different type of calendar.*

2 Get Started

Say: *The diagram on this page is a liturgical calendar. We normally keep a calendar to mark special days such as birthdays, anniversaries, and holidays. In the same way, the Church keeps a calendar to mark special times in Jesus' life, Death, and Resurrection.*

Say: *In our calendar year, we have seasons—winter, spring, and so on. The liturgical calendar has seasons too. What seasons are shown on this calendar?* (Advent, Christmas, Lent, Holy Week, Easter, Ordinary Time) Say: *The liturgical calendar also has feast days and holy days.*

Liturgical Year

At the beginning of each seasonal session, direct the children to turn to page 152 and to read the paragraph about the season they will be celebrating. You may use the following summaries to provide additional information about each season.

Advent

Advent is a season of hope and joyful anticipation. While we prepare to celebrate the birth of Jesus, we also use the season of Advent to grow in our love for Jesus. Unlike our regular year, the liturgical year begins with the first Sunday of Advent.

Christmas

At Christmas we celebrate the birth of Jesus. This celebration continues until the Sunday after the Epiphany, often the Feast of the Baptism of the Lord. During the Epiphany, we celebrate when Jesus was revealed to the world as represented by the Magi.

Lent

Lent is a season of quiet joy, for we know that the happiness of Easter will come. Throughout the 40 days of Lent, the whole Church prays, fasts, and gives alms.

Holy Week

Holy Week begins with Jesus' entrance into Jerusalem, which is Palm Sunday. The three days of Holy Thursday, Good Friday, and Holy Saturday are called the Triduum.

Easter

Because Jesus' Resurrection is the central feast of Christianity, the Church sets aside 50 days of joyful celebration. These 50 days begin with Easter and end on Pentecost.

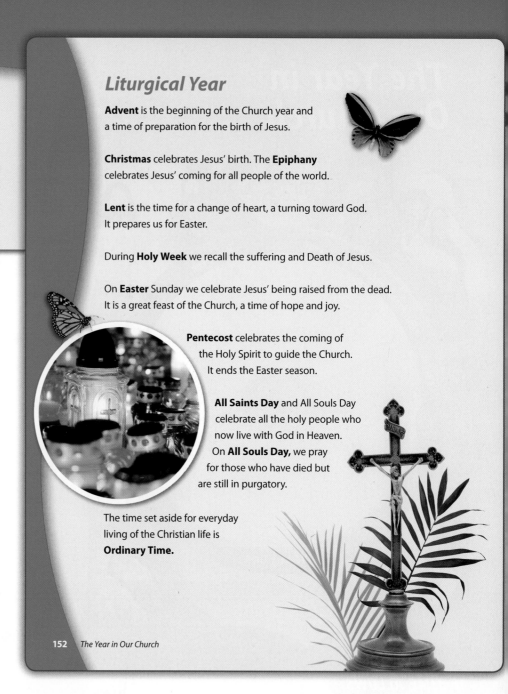

Liturgical Year

Advent is the beginning of the Church year and a time of preparation for the birth of Jesus.

Christmas celebrates Jesus' birth. The **Epiphany** celebrates Jesus' coming for all people of the world.

Lent is the time for a change of heart, a turning toward God. It prepares us for Easter.

During **Holy Week** we recall the suffering and Death of Jesus.

On **Easter** Sunday we celebrate Jesus' being raised from the dead. It is a great feast of the Church, a time of hope and joy.

Pentecost celebrates the coming of the Holy Spirit to guide the Church. It ends the Easter season.

All Saints Day and All Souls Day celebrate all the holy people who now live with God in Heaven. On **All Souls Day,** we pray for those who have died but are still in purgatory.

The time set aside for everyday living of the Christian life is **Ordinary Time.**

152   *The Year in Our Church*

Pentecost

On Pentecost we celebrate the coming of the Holy Spirit to the disciples 50 days after Jesus' Resurrection. Pentecost is our celebration of the birthday of the universal Church.

All Saints Day and All Souls Day

The Communion of Saints—those who are on earth, those who have died and are being purified, and the blessed in Heaven—is celebrated on All Saints Day, November 1, and on All Souls Day, November 2.

Ordinary Time

During Ordinary Time we reflect on our call to discipleship. The word *ordinary* refers to time as "counted" time. The Sundays of the entire year are counted or set aside as sacred time. Ordinary Time, typically 33 weeks, is celebrated following the Christmas season and then again following the Easter season.

Advent

Mary was a young woman who worked hard and prayed often. She loved God and wanted to serve him. An angel told Mary that she was to be the mother of Jesus. Because Mary said yes to God, we celebrate Jesus' birth. The Advent season is a time to prepare ourselves to celebrate Jesus' birth.

Prayer

Dear God, help me this Advent to prepare for Jesus with an open and welcoming heart.

153

MATERIALS

Get Ready for the Session

In addition to Bibles and basic writing and art supplies, you will need a shoe box, strips of paper with a good deed written on one strip, and a violet cloth or paper mat. Review any If Time Allows activities you would like to include in this session for additional materials they may require.

ADVENT

OUTCOMES

▶ Discuss the story of how Mary said yes when asked by God to be Jesus' mother.

▶ Explain how we prepare for Jesus' coming.

1 Set the Stage

Begin by asking: *Can anyone tell me what a season is?* (Possible answer: part of the year, a time of special activity) *What seasons can you name?* (Possible answers: winter, summer, football, soccer) Say: *The Church has seasons too.*

Direct children to look at the liturgical calendar on page 151. Say: *Find the Advent season on the calendar. The time before Christmas can be a busy time.* Ask: *How does your family prepare?* (Possible answers: shopping for gifts, setting up a Christmas tree) Say: *We prepare for Christmas in other ways too. In this session we will learn how to prepare our hearts to welcome Jesus during the season of Advent.*

2 Get Started

Have children look at the picture on page 153. Ask: *Who is pictured here?* (Mary) *How does Mary look in this picture?* (Possible answers: thoughtful, calm) Invite a volunteer to read aloud the session title and paragraph. Say: *When Mary said yes to God, she welcomed Jesus into her life. Like Mary, we are called to welcome Jesus.*

Prayer

Ask children to join you in prayer. Say: *Let us pray so that, like Mary, we will be willing to do what God asks of us.* Pray the prayer aloud. Then pause and give children sufficient time to pray. Lead them in praying *Amen.* Say: *Now let's read about Mary's visit from an angel.*

Begin

Invite children to discuss the excitement around the birth of a child. Ask: *Who can share a story of when you found out that you were getting a new baby brother or sister in the family? Or perhaps you found out that an aunt or a cousin or a neighbor was expecting a baby?* Say: *It is exciting to hear the news of a new baby arriving. We look forward to meeting this new person. Now we will read about when Mary was told the wonderful news that she would be the mother of the Son of God.*

2 Connect

Show children where the Scripture passage is found in the Bible. Invite a volunteer to read aloud the heading and the Bible passage. Ask: *Who brought the news from God to Mary?* (the angel Gabriel) *Luke tells us that Mary was troubled. Did you ever receive a message that troubled you?* (Possible answers: A grandparent is ill; you have to move; you didn't do well on a test.) Ask: *Why do you think Mary was troubled?* (Mary had never been visited by an angel before. She may have wondered what would be expected of her.) Ask: *What did the angel tell Mary?* (that she will have a son and his name will be Jesus) Say: *The angel's visit was a very special event in Mary's life.*

Invite a volunteer to read aloud Mary Said Yes to God. Ask: *What does it mean when we say that Mary made possible our celebration of Jesus' birth?* (Mary said yes to God so that Jesus could be born.) Say: *Once Mary said she would be the mother of Jesus, she had to get ready for his birth. We too must get ready to celebrate his birth.*

The Angel Visits Mary

God sent the angel Gabriel to a town in Galilee called Nazareth. He was sent to a young woman named Mary, who was engaged to a man named Joseph. The angel said to her, "Hail, favored one! The Lord is with you." Mary was troubled by his words, but he told her not to be afraid. He said, "You will have a son and will name him Jesus. He will be great and will be called Son of the Most High." The angel told her that the child would be holy and that people would call him the Son of God.

adapted from Luke 1:26–35

Mary Said Yes to God

Mary trusted God. She said yes when God asked her to be the mother of his Son. She made possible our celebration of Jesus' birth.

As we prepare for Jesus' birth, let us ask Mary to pray for us so that we too will welcome Jesus into our hearts.

154 *The Year in Our Church*

IF TIME ALLOWS

Advent BLM

My Advent Wreath Have children complete the Advent Blackline Master [T-334] to decorate a wreath and candles to display during the season of Advent.

Making Lists

Invite children to discuss in small groups ways they can prepare themselves during Advent, such as offer extra help at home or read books about Jesus' birth. Ask children to focus on ways to show that Jesus is welcome in their hearts and their lives, not on material preparations. Have each group choose a reporter to write their ideas. Have each group reporter read aloud one idea from the list and move on to the next group. List all ideas on the board. Invite children to choose an idea they have never done before and share it with their families to do during Advent.

Celebrating Advent with Prayer

During Advent we prepare to welcome Jesus into our hearts. We pray daily as we count the days until Christmas.

My Daily Advent Prayer

Think of some ways you would like to follow Jesus during Advent. Then use your ideas to complete these prayer starters.

Jesus, help me to _____.

Jesus, teach me to _____.

Jesus, fill me with _____.

Jesus, open my heart to _____.

Completing Your Prayer

Now use all of your completed prayer starters to compose your own Advent prayer. Imagine sharing it in an e-mail to Jesus.

From: _____
To: Jesus
Subject: My Advent Prayer

[Send]

_____
_____
_____
_____
_____

Advent **155**

I Spy During Advent

Plan a visit to your church to show children how your parish decorates for the Advent season. Have children bring a sheet of paper and pencil to jot down things they see that show the preparations. Ask them to keep their lists private. When children return to the room, see who has the most items on their list. Then invite volunteers to share one item on their list. Write the final list on the board.

Invite a volunteer to read aloud Celebrating Advent with Prayer. Say: **Mary was preparing to welcome Jesus. We are also preparing to welcome him into our hearts. Prayer is a way of letting Jesus know that he is welcome in our lives and in our hearts.**

Draw children's attention to the photo. Ask: **What is the woman lighting?** (an Advent wreath) Say: **The Advent wreath helps us count the weeks until Christmas. Each time we light a candle, we say a special prayer.**

Read aloud the directions for My Daily Advent Prayer. Allow time for children to complete the activity. Invite volunteers to share some of their prayer starters.

Read aloud the directions for Completing Your Prayer. Say: **There are lots of ways to write a prayer. Imagine sending Jesus an e-mail of what is on your mind and in your heart.**

Play reflective music at the end of CD 2 while children are composing their prayers. Allow sufficient time for all to finish and then say: **Now that you have written your prayer, let's take some time to pray it silently and reverently.**

3 Close

Show children the shoe box you brought in and the slip of paper on which you wrote a good deed you have done. Say: **As we prepare for the coming of Jesus, we will prepare for him a gift of our good deeds. It will be like the hay that made Jesus comfortable as he lay in the manger that first Christmas night.**

Read your good deed aloud and place it in the box. Distribute strips of paper to children. Direct them to write on their strips any good deeds done during the past week. Encourage children to do additional good deeds during the four weeks of Advent, record them on strips of paper, and place them in the box during upcoming sessions.

Prayer Service

On a table have the box of good deeds placed on a violet cloth or paper mat as a reminder of the season. If an Advent wreath is available, place that on the table. Have the Bible open to the Gospel of Luke 1:35–38.

Invite children to gather around the table. Ask children to look at the prayer service and find the *All* parts, which they will be reading. Select one child to serve as Reader. Explain that everyone will pray the Hail Mary together at the end before taking a few moments to pray silently.

When children have settled, begin playing the reflective music at the end of CD 2. Then proceed with the prayer service. After the final Leader part, pray the Hail Mary. Allow for a few moments of music after the prayer service so that children can reflect in silence. After a few moments, say: ***Let us return to our places and talk some more about our Advent "get-ready" time.***

1 Respond

Invite children to review the pages in the Advent session and identify two or three important things they learned about the season of Advent. Say: ***Praying helps us welcome Jesus into our hearts as we prepare during Advent for the celebration of his birth.***

2 Go in Peace

Collect materials and return them to the appropriate places. Remind children to take their Advent wreaths home and to use them during family prayer time. Say: ***Advent is a wonderful season of preparation for the great feast of Christmas. During the coming weeks, let us pray specially to Mary to help us be extra kind and helpful to others.***

Prayer Service

Leader: *During this holy season of Advent, we prepare, as Mary did, for the coming of Jesus. Let us listen to her words and ask her to pray for us.*

Reader: *A reading from the holy Gospel according to Luke.*

The angel Gabriel told Mary she would give birth to a child named Jesus, who would be the Son of God. Mary said, "I am the servant of the Lord. May it be done to me as you have said." Then the angel departed from her.

adapted from Luke 1:35,38

The Gospel of the Lord.

All: *Praise to you, Lord Jesus Christ.*

Leader: *We ask Mary to pray for us. Holy Mother of God,*

All: *Pray for us.*

Leader: *Most honored of women,*

All: *Pray for us.*

Leader: *Mary most prayerful,*

All: *Pray for us.*

Leader: *Let us close by praying the Hail Mary together.*

156　*The Year in Our Church*

IF TIME ALLOWS

Preparing for Christmas in Our Homes

Distribute paper and art supplies. Ask: ***Mary prepared her home for the infant Jesus. How do you prepare your homes for the celebration of Jesus' birth?*** Invite children to write a sentence about something they do in their homes with their families to prepare for Christmas. Then have children illustrate that activity.

FYI
Coaching Children to Pray

Encourage children to keep in mind that we can always ask Mary to pray for us, to help and support us, and to pray with us as we prepare our hearts to celebrate Jesus' birth.

Christmas

On Christmas we celebrate the birth of Jesus. The shepherds heard the angels' message and went to welcome Jesus. As we welcome Jesus, we think about what Jesus' birth means to us.

Prayer

Jesus, as I celebrate your birth, help me to share in God's life by loving others and treating them fairly.

157

MATERIALS

Get Ready for the Session

In addition to Bibles and basic writing and art supplies, you will need Christmas symbols, candy canes, and a white cloth. Review any If Time Allows activities you would like to include in this session for additional materials they may require.

CHRISTMAS

OUTCOMES

▶ Tell the story of Joseph and Mary going to Bethlehem.

▶ Discuss how the shepherds heard the angels' message and went to welcome Jesus.

▶ Discuss the meaning of Jesus' birth in our lives.

1 Set the Stage

Tell children how your family celebrates Christmas. Ask: **What does your family do to make this holiday special?** Discuss how children celebrate Christmas and ways that Jesus is recognized in their celebrations.

2 Get Started

Direct children's attention to the picture. Ask: **What do you think the children are doing?** (singing Christmas carols) Say: **We sing Christmas carols throughout the season, at school, at church, and in our neighborhood. We are joyfully welcoming Jesus at Christmas.**

Invite a volunteer to read aloud the session title and paragraph. Ask: **What do we celebrate on Christmas?** (the birth of Jesus) Say: **Although we decorate with ornaments, colored lights, and wreaths, Jesus is the real focus of Christmas. He is our great gift from God. He is the reason that we share gifts with one another. In this session we will learn about when the good news of Jesus' birth was first heard.**

 Prayer

Pause to allow children to quiet themselves. Say: **Let's pray aloud together.** Read the prayer aloud. Then say: **Speak to Jesus now in the silence of your heart, using your own words.** Allow sufficient time for private prayer. Finish by praying *Amen.*

1 Begin

Count aloud the number of children in the room. Say: **I was taking a census.** Write the word *census* on the board. Explain that a census is a count of people. Tell children that sometimes a government takes a census so that the officials know how many people live in the city or where people are moving their families.

2 Connect

Invite a volunteer to read aloud the heading and the first paragraph. Ask: **Why did Mary and Joseph go to Bethlehem?** (to be counted in the census) Say: **Because so many people had to go to Bethlehem at the same time to be counted, all the inns or hotels were filled. The only place left for Mary and Joseph to stay was in a stable for animals. They had to place Jesus in a manger, a feeding box for animals.**

Invite a volunteer to read aloud the second paragraph. Ask: **To whom were the angels delivering their message?** (shepherds) **What are the titles the angels gave to Jesus?** (Savior, Messiah, Lord) Say: **The shepherds were the first to learn of the good news of Jesus' birth.**

Invite a volunteer to read aloud the third paragraph. Ask: **Whom did the shepherds find in Bethlehem?** (Mary, Joseph, and Jesus) Say: **The shepherds told other people about what they saw and heard. Jesus wants us to do the same. He wants us to tell people that God loves them. He came to be an example of how to live.**

Read aloud the last paragraph. Review the message the angels brought. Ask: **What did the angels say to the shepherds?** (Today in the city of David a savior has been born. He is Messiah and Lord. Glory to God in the highest.) Then ask children to answer the question at the bottom of the page by writing their own messages.

Good News

Mary and Joseph went to Bethlehem to be counted in the census. While they were there, Mary gave birth to Jesus. She put him in a manger because there was no room for them in the inn.

Some shepherds were in a field nearby watching their flock. An angel came to them and told them the good news: "Today in the city of David a savior has been born. He is Messiah and Lord." Then more angels came and said, "Glory to God in the highest."

The shepherds went to Bethlehem, where they found Mary, Joseph, and Jesus. They told Mary and Joseph the angels' message. Mary remembered all these things and kept them in her heart.

adapted from Luke 2:4–19

Like Mary we can keep the message of the angels in our hearts. What does the angels' message mean to you?

_____

_____

_____

158 *The Year in Our Church*

IF TIME ALLOWS

Christmas BLM
You Were There! Have children complete the Christmas Blackline Master [T-335] to illustrate themselves in the manger on the night of Jesus' birth.

Christmas-Greetings Collage
Invite children to bring in old Christmas cards from years past or leftover ones their parents no longer need from this year. Distribute paper and art supplies so that children can cut out the covers of the cards to make a collage.

We Reflect

At Christmas we think about what Jesus' birth means to us. Jesus, the Son of God, became man to share God's life with us. We share in God's life when we love others and treat them fairly.

Symbols of Christmas

There are many symbols of Christmas. The trumpet is a sign of the angels' message to the shepherds. Christmas ornaments remind us of the beauty that Jesus brought into the world. The evergreen tree is a sign of everlasting life.

A Symbol for You

Think of a symbol for something you enjoy at Christmas. Write how it reminds you of Jesus' birth and then draw the symbol.

Invite a volunteer to read aloud We Reflect. Remind children of the importance of keeping Jesus in our celebration of the Christmas season. Ask: **How can we share in God's life for us?** (by loving others and treating them fairly)

Say: **Symbols are reminders for us. They help us remember what our celebration is all about. The color white in the Church symbolizes victory and joy. When we give presents to one another at Christmas, it reminds us of the presents the Magi gave baby Jesus. Let's read about some of the other symbols of Christmas.** Invite a volunteer to read aloud Symbols of Christmas. Ask: **Can you think of some other decorations you've seen that remind us of the Christmas message?** (Possible answers: star—guides us; crib—Jesus comes as an infant; candy cane—shepherd's crook)

3 Close

Read aloud the directions for A Symbol for You. Distribute crayons, markers, or colored pencils and give children time to draw a special symbol. Invite volunteers to share the symbol they drew and its meaning.

IF TIME ALLOWS

Presenting the Message
Arrange children into small groups. Say: **Talk with your group about what the angel's message means to all of you. Decide on a message you would like to deliver to the group about the meaning of Jesus' birth. Then choose a messenger to announce to all of us your group's message.** Encourage children to be creative. Suggest that they make trumpeting noises or act as a theatrical announcer. Make sure children understand the activity. Provide each group with the opportunity to present its message.

IDEAS TO SHARE

The Candy Cane

The shepherd's crook is representative of the shepherds who were the first to visit the newborn Jesus. The crook inspired the shape of the candy cane, which is why it has become a traditional Christmas treat.

Prayer Service

Prepare the prayer center before children arrive. Open the Bible to Psalm 96:1,12–13. If possible, decorate the table with a white cloth and Christmas symbols. If you have a recording of appropriate Christmas music, you might wish to incorporate the music into the prayer service.

In preparation for the prayer, have children look at the prayer service on page 160. Arrange them into two groups. Tell them that you will take the part of the Leader. Invite Group A to stand on one side of the prayer table and Group B on the other. Say: **Let us now gather to remember the great gift God has given us in his Son, Jesus.**

Pray the entire prayer. Pray the Glory Be to the Father together. Then say: **Now that we have praised God in prayer, let us think about other ways we can act to praise God, such as following the Ten Commandments.**

① Respond

Ask children to identify two or three new facts or ideas they learned about the Christmas season. Invite volunteers to share how they can celebrate Christmas and the good news that Jesus is born with family and friends.

② Go in Peace

Collect materials and return them to the appropriate places. When children leave, offer each child a small candy cane. Say: **Like the shepherds, recognize that Jesus' birth is good news. Spread this news to others through your words and actions!**

Prayer Service

Leader:	*During this joyful Christmas season, let us praise God.*
Group A:	Sing to the Lord a new song;
Group B:	Sing to the Lord, all the earth.
Group A:	Let all the trees of the forest rejoice before the Lord,
Group B:	Who comes to rule the world.
Group A:	He comes to rule the people
Group B:	With justice and truth.

adapted from Psalm 96:1,12–13

Leader:	*We thank God for the gift of his Son.*
All:	*Glory to God in the highest.*
Leader:	*We share the good news as the shepherds did.*
All:	*Glory to God in the highest.*
Leader:	*We share Jesus' love with the world.*
All:	*Glory to God in the highest.*
Leader:	*Let us praise God by praying the Glory Be to the Father.*

160 *The Year in Our Church*

IF TIME ALLOWS

Nativity Stories

Have children compare the Nativity stories in Matthew 1:18–23 and Luke 2:1–20. Discuss how these two writers told the story differently to emphasize different points while still highlighting the significance of Jesus' birth.

FYI

Coaching Children to Pray

Invite children to choose a time each day during the Christmas season to pause and pray "Jesus is born, rejoice!" as a reminder of the true meaning of the Christmas season.

Lent

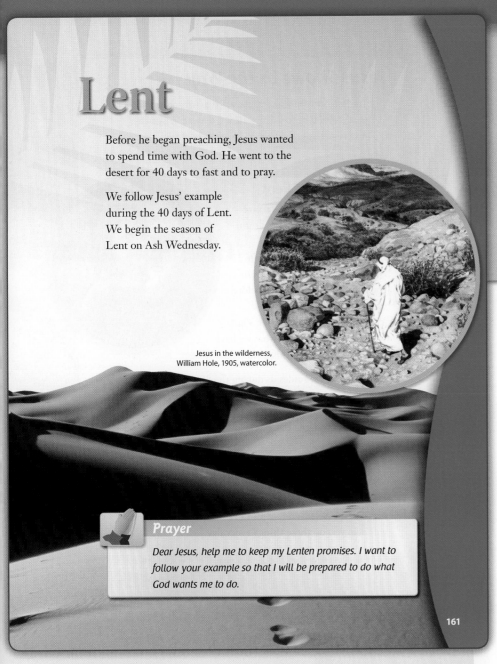

Before he began preaching, Jesus wanted to spend time with God. He went to the desert for 40 days to fast and to pray.

We follow Jesus' example during the 40 days of Lent. We begin the season of Lent on Ash Wednesday.

Jesus in the wilderness,
William Hole, 1905, watercolor.

Prayer

Dear Jesus, help me to keep my Lenten promises. I want to follow your example so that I will be prepared to do what God wants me to do.

161

MATERIALS

Get Ready for the Session

In addition to Bibles and basic writing and art supplies, you will need a bag and small slips of paper with important words from the session, *Finding God* CD 2, a purple cloth or paper mat, pictures of a desert, and ashes or sand. Review any If Time Allows activities you would like to include in this session for additional materials they may require.

LENT

OUTCOMES

▶ Discuss how Jesus was led by the Holy Spirit to the desert where he was tempted by Satan.

▶ Explain that during Lent all Christians are called to fast, pray, and share their belongings.

▶ Explain that God gives us the strength to keep our Lenten promises.

1 Set the Stage

Ask: *When you have to think about something important, where do you go?* (Possible answers: my room, outside, someplace quiet) Say: *When Jesus wanted to spend time with God, he went to a quiet place too.*

1 Get Started

Invite a volunteer to read aloud the session title and the paragraphs.

Ask: *How long is the season of Lent?* (40 days) Say: *We are called to make the 40 days of Lent holy by praying and by doing special things to honor God.* Ask: *When does Lent begin?* (on Ash Wednesday) Say: *Lent is a period of preparation for Easter. During this season we remember that Jesus died before he was raised from the dead. In this session we will learn ways that we can observe Lent.*

Prayer

Invite children to quiet themselves for prayer by breathing deeply and clearing their minds of distractions. Then say: *Let us pray together so that we will be ready to do what God wants.*

Pray aloud with children. Pause and give children sufficient time to add silently their own intentions. Then pray *Amen* together.

1 Begin

Distribute pictures of a desert. Give children time to pass them around. Ask: **How would you describe the desert?** (Possible answers: hot, lonely, sandy, without water) Invite volunteers to discuss any trips to the desert.

2 Connect

Read aloud the heading and invite a volunteer to read aloud the Scripture passage. Ask: **Why do you think Jesus went to the desert to pray?** (Possible answers: to be alone, for the quiet, because he was led by the Holy Spirit) **What happened to Jesus while he was praying?** (Satan tempted him.) Say: **We are tempted at times, but we don't always think of Jesus as being tempted. He was. Like us, he had God's help. Jesus remained faithful to God, his Father.**

Direct children to look at the picture on page 162. Ask: **What is happening?** (A girl is receiving ashes.) **On what day do we receive ashes?** (Ash Wednesday)

Read aloud the next heading and the first paragraph. Say: **We receive ashes as a sign that we are willing to make sacrifices as Jesus did. When we wear ashes on our forehead, we are witnesses to Jesus. The ashes are a way of showing others that we are beginning the season of Lent.** Ask: **From what are the ashes made?** (palms blessed on Palm Sunday the year before) **What are we asked to do during Lent?** (pray, fast, share)

Invite a volunteer to read aloud the next paragraph. Ask: **Who will guide us during this Lenten season?** (the Holy Spirit)

Read aloud Observing Lent. Ask: **What are ways we can make these 40 days special?** (pray, be kind and unselfish, be helpful)

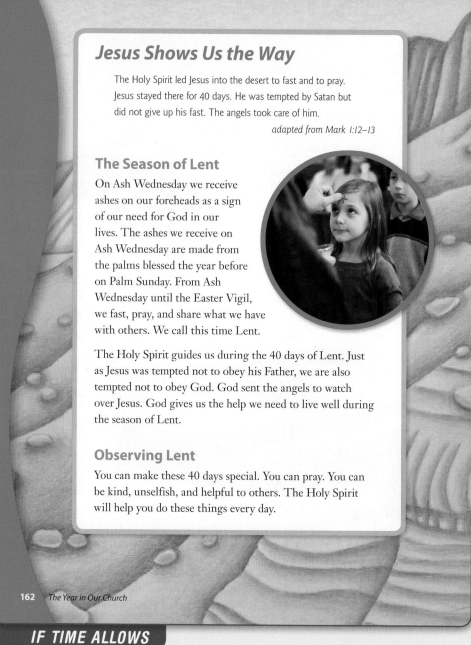

Jesus Shows Us the Way

The Holy Spirit led Jesus into the desert to fast and to pray. Jesus stayed there for 40 days. He was tempted by Satan but did not give up his fast. The angels took care of him.

adapted from Mark 1:12–13

The Season of Lent

On Ash Wednesday we receive ashes on our foreheads as a sign of our need for God in our lives. The ashes we receive on Ash Wednesday are made from the palms blessed the year before on Palm Sunday. From Ash Wednesday until the Easter Vigil, we fast, pray, and share what we have with others. We call this time Lent.

The Holy Spirit guides us during the 40 days of Lent. Just as Jesus was tempted not to obey his Father, we are also tempted not to obey God. God sent the angels to watch over Jesus. God gives us the help we need to live well during the season of Lent.

Observing Lent

You can make these 40 days special. You can pray. You can be kind, unselfish, and helpful to others. The Holy Spirit will help you do these things every day.

162 *The Year in Our Church*

IF TIME ALLOWS

Lent BLM

Lenten Calendar Have children complete the Lent Blackline Master [T-336] to record the promises they make during Lent.

Lenten Practices

Arrange children in pairs. Assign prayer to one pair, fasting to another, and sharing to a third. Continue in that manner by repeating the Lenten practices until all pairs have been assigned. Have the groups write their assigned word at the top of a sheet of paper. Say: **Under your word, list different ways you can pray, fast, or share during this season to show your love for Jesus.** Tell children that fasting doesn't necessarily mean only giving up eating certain foods, but it can also mean giving up doing certain things. Provide examples, such as for prayer—pray daily, pray for peace; for fasting—no dessert at lunch, no teasing my brother; and for sharing—letting my sister play with my puzzle, putting part of my allowance in the collection basket. Then put all the pairs for each practice together. Invite the groups to make a poster for their Lenten practice by compiling all their ideas. Display the posters in a hallway.

Lenten Promises

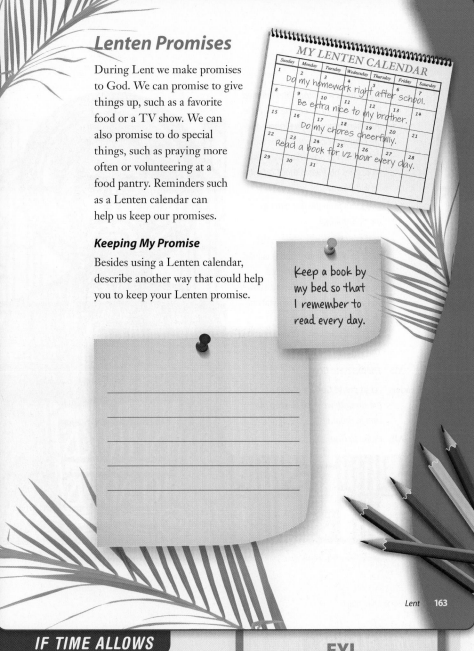

During Lent we make promises to God. We can promise to give things up, such as a favorite food or a TV show. We can also promise to do special things, such as praying more often or volunteering at a food pantry. Reminders such as a Lenten calendar can help us keep our promises.

Keeping My Promise

Besides using a Lenten calendar, describe another way that could help you to keep your Lenten promise.

Keep a book by my bed so that I remember to read every day.

Lent **163**

Invite a volunteer to read aloud Lenten Promises. Ask: *What does it mean to make a promise?* (to assure someone that you will do something) Encourage children to talk about promises they have made and the responsibility of keeping these promises, such as to take the garbage out after supper or to do homework right after school. Say: *Often it is easier to make the promise than it is to keep it, so reminders can help us keep our promises.*

③ Close

Say: *When we are tempted to break our Lenten promise, there are things we can do to help us keep our promise. Just as the Holy Spirit guided Jesus in the desert, so too will the Holy Spirit help you keep your Lenten promise. To help you keep your Lenten promise, think of a way that can remind you of your promise every day.* Read aloud the directions for Keeping My Promise. Give children time to write their ideas. Then invite volunteers to share their ideas.

IF TIME ALLOWS

Lenten Promise Beads

Invite children to make a Lenten promise bead to remind themselves of the promise they made. Distribute colorful beads and string and have children make a short beaded string, about two inches long, that they can design themselves. Encourage children to attach their beads to their backpacks or lunch boxes to serve as a gentle reminder of their Lenten promises.

FYI

Blessed Palms

Say: *Blessed palms are sacramentals that can be displayed in our homes. Before Lent begins we are asked to bring our palms from the last year to church so that they can be burned to make the ashes used on Ash Wednesday.* Encourage children to save the palms they receive on Palm Sunday so that they can be burned for use on Ash Wednesday next year.

Prayer Service

 Prepare the prayer center by placing a purple cloth or paper mat and a small bowl containing sand or ashes on a table. Have the Bible open to 1 Corinthians 10:13. Have children look at the prayer service and explain that you will read the *Leader* parts and they will be reading the *All* parts. Select a child to be the Reader.

Invite children to get up and move quietly to the prayer center. When they have gathered, pray the prayer service together.

When the prayer is finished, say: **Let us close by singing the song "Here I Am, God"** [CD 2, Track 5]. **This song reminds us that we have promised to do God's will.** Have children turn to the back of their books, where the words to the song are found. Play the song while children sing along.

1 Respond

Invite children to gather in a circle. Display your bag filled with words from the session. Use words such as *ashes, desert, temptation, Holy Spirit, Lent, prayer, fasting, sharing,* and *40 days.* Say: **We are going to review what we have learned. I have a bag here that contains words we've talked about in this session. I will ask a volunteer to draw a word from the bag and tell us something he or she learned about that word.** Have the child who talks about the word hold the bag and call on the next volunteer. Continue with the review until all the words have been discussed.

2 Go in Peace

Collect materials and return them to the appropriate places. Remind children to keep their Lenten promises. Say: **Be strong and pray always.**

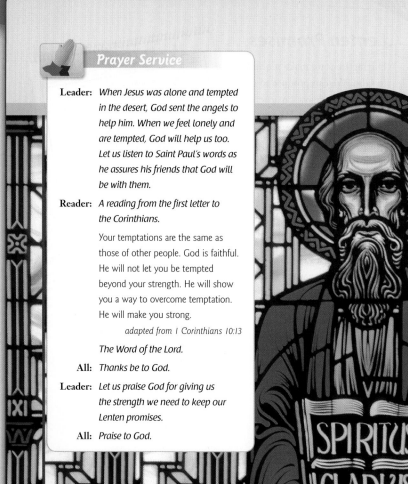

Prayer Service

Leader: *When Jesus was alone and tempted in the desert, God sent the angels to help him. When we feel lonely and are tempted, God will help us too. Let us listen to Saint Paul's words as he assures his friends that God will be with them.*

Reader: *A reading from the first letter to the Corinthians.*

Your temptations are the same as those of other people. God is faithful. He will not let you be tempted beyond your strength. He will show you a way to overcome temptation. He will make you strong.

adapted from 1 Corinthians 10:13

The Word of the Lord.

All: *Thanks be to God.*

Leader: *Let us praise God for giving us the strength we need to keep our Lenten promises.*

All: *Praise to God.*

164 *The Year in Our Church*

IF TIME ALLOWS

Exploring the Parish Bulletin

Find a recent parish bulletin containing Lenten service activities. Distribute copies to children. Brainstorm ideas of how children could help. Encourage them to choose an activity in which to participate and to invite their families to participate.

FYI

Coaching Children to Pray

Remind children how important it is to make time for silence and stillness. This helps them be aware that they are in the holy presence of God—that God is with them to make them strong when they are lonely or are tempted.

Holy Week

During Holy Week we remember that Jesus gave his life for us. The Stations of the Cross help us to remember his sacrifice for us.

Prayer

Jesus, my Savior, help me to remember your sacrifice for us. Thank you for all that you did and continue to do.

165

MATERIALS

Get Ready for the Session

In addition to Bibles and basic writing and art supplies, you will need a basket or other container and crosses made of construction paper. Review any If Time Allows activities you would like to include in this session for additional materials they may require.

OUTCOMES

- ▶ Discuss the suffering of Jesus.
- ▶ Explain how we can be like Jesus.
- ▶ Pray the Stations of the Cross.

 1 **Set the Stage**

Begin this session by discussing sacrifices. Ask: *What does sacrifice mean?* (Possible answers: giving up something, doing something that is hard) Ask: *What great sacrifice did Jesus make because he loves us?* (He suffered and died for us.)

Say: *Today we will learn about the Stations of the Cross. The Stations of the Cross tell the story of Jesus' suffering and Death.*

 2 **Get Started**

Read aloud the session title and invite a volunteer to read aloud the paragraph. Direct children to turn to pages 198–199 for a description of each station. Discuss what is happening to Jesus at the first three stations. Ask them to bookmark the pages as you will be referring to them again during the session.

 Prayer

Say: *Let us quiet our minds and think about how much we are loved by Jesus.* Pause for a few moments, then say: *Pray with me as we ask Jesus to help us follow him.*

Pray the prayer aloud with children. Give children sufficient time to pray in their own words. Then pray *Amen* together. Say: *Let us continue our journey with Jesus.*

1 Begin

Ask: **Who has been to a bus or train station? What do you do there?** (wait to get on a bus or train) Say: **A station is a stop where people can get on and off. The Stations of the Cross are stops also. They are images or pictures that we observe in order to pray and meditate on the events of Jesus' suffering and Death.**

2 Connect

✝ Read aloud the heading, the first sentence, and the following paragraph. Ask: **What did Pontius Pilate first say after he met with Jesus?** (that Jesus was innocent) **What words of Pilate give you the answer?** ("What evil has this man done? I don't think he should be put to death.") Say: **Let's read on to see what changed Pilate's mind.**

Have volunteers read aloud the next two paragraphs. Explain that to be crucified is to be put to death by nailing or tying a person to a cross. Ask: **Why did Pilate condemn Jesus to death?** (The people wanted it.) Say: **Jesus was not found guilty of any crime. Pilate didn't want the people he governed to be angry with him, so he condemned Jesus to death.**

Invite a volunteer to read aloud Being Like Simon. Remind children that Simon lived when Jesus did and so he was able to help Jesus in a way that we can't. Say: **Simon was called to help Jesus. God calls each of us at different times and in different ways. We are called in our own time to be helpers of Jesus by caring for the people Jesus loves and by helping the people around us who need help.** Ask: **What are some ways we can help others?** (comfort someone who is sad, help at home without complaining) **When we help someone, for whom do we do it?** (Jesus)

Say: **Let's turn to the pages we bookmarked.** Draw children's attention to the fourth, fifth, and sixth stations.

Trial, ceiling painting, Golgotha Chapel, Holy Sepulchre, Jerusalem.

Taking Up the Cross

After Jesus celebrated the Last Supper with the apostles, he was arrested and was brought to trial before Pontius Pilate, the Roman governor.

Pilate found him to be innocent. Pilate asked the people, "What evil has this man done? I don't think he should be put to death. I will have him whipped and released."

But the people kept shouting for Jesus to be crucified. Finally Pilate handed Jesus over to them to be put to death.

As they led Jesus away, they met a man named Simon of Cyrene. He was coming in from the country. They laid the cross on him and made him carry it behind Jesus.

adapted from Luke 23:22–26

Being Like Simon

Simon of Cyrene, a person who never met Jesus, helped him to carry the cross. We can help Jesus too. Like Simon we are called to do what is right in our lives, even if it is hard. We can comfort someone who is sad. We can help at home without complaining. Jesus said that when we do something to help someone else, we do it for him.

166　The Year in Our Church

IF TIME ALLOWS

Holy Week BLM

Stations of the Cross Have children complete the Holy Week Blackline Master [T-337] in which they make a Stations of the Cross booklet.

Our Stations of the Cross

Distribute to each child drawing paper, crayons, and a note card with a sentence naming one of the 14 stations. Have each child draw a picture of his or her station. Children may use the illustrations in the book as a guide if they wish. On the note cards, have them write short prayers to Jesus. If there are more than 14 children, some can draw while others compose the prayer. If there are fewer than 14, children who finish quickly may do more than one station. Prayers that can be used are *Jesus, lift me up when I fall from your path; Jesus, help me remember your great sacrifice;* or *Jesus, thank you for suffering for love of me.*

When all have finished, have children post their pictures around the room. Move as a group from station to station, pausing as each child names his or her station and reads the accompanying prayer.

Stations of the Cross

After Jesus' Death and Resurrection, early Christians visited Jerusalem, the city where Jesus died, to walk in his footsteps. They stopped at different places along the way to remember what happened to Jesus. They marked the places where they stopped so that others could follow. These places became the Stations of the Cross.

Like the early Christians, we can pray the Stations of the Cross to remember all that Jesus did for us. At each station we stop, pray quietly, and thank Jesus for his great sacrifice.

A Message to Jesus

Imagine you are in the crowd as Jesus carries his cross. Write what you would say to Jesus.

Jesus, _____

_____

_____

_____

_____

Holy Week **167**

The Living Stations

Invite volunteers to role-play the story of Jesus' trial and Crucifixion. Choose volunteers to play the role of narrator, Jesus, Pilate, and the crowd. You may wish to use a Stations of the Cross booklet for children as a model to follow.

IDEAS TO SHARE

Stations of the Cross

The stations are a popular Lenten and Holy Week devotion first observed in the city of Jerusalem. The practice then spread to other areas during the Middle Ages. Praying the stations involves tracing Jesus' journey from the court of Pilate to Calvary and eventually to the tomb. People walk from station to station to pray and reflect on the event portrayed in the station. There are 14 stations, but in many devotional books a 15th has been added, the Resurrection.

Ask: **What is happening to Jesus at stations four and six?** (Jesus is meeting his mother. Veronica wipes the sweat and blood from Jesus' face.) **At which station does Simon take up Jesus' cross?** (fifth)

Have children return to page 167 in their books. Ask a volunteer to read aloud the first paragraph of Stations of the Cross. Say: **After the Death and Resurrection of Jesus, many of his disciples returned to the street that Jesus walked while carrying his cross. Perhaps they also went to the hill where Jesus hung on the cross.**

Invite a volunteer to read aloud the next paragraph. Ask: **What do we do at each station?** (Stop, pray quietly, and thank Jesus.) Refer again to page 199. Say: **Let's look at stations 7 through 14 illustrated on this page. We see that Jesus fell two more times and was stripped of his clothing. What else do you see in the pictures?** (Jesus talking to some women, being nailed to the cross and dying, being taken from the cross and placed in the tomb.) Say: **We can tell as we look from picture to picture that Jesus suffered a lot even before being nailed to the cross. There can be no doubt in our minds that Jesus loves us very much.**

③ Close

Read aloud the directions for A Message to Jesus. Allow sufficient time for children to write their messages. Invite them to share their messages with the group.

Have children turn to the liturgical calendar on page 151 and find Holy Week. Ask: **On which day do we remember Jesus taking up his cross?** (Good Friday) Point out the other days of Holy Week. Say: **Palm Sunday begins Holy Week. On Holy Thursday we remember the Last Supper, and on Holy Saturday evening, we anticipate the raising of Jesus from the dead on Easter morning.**

Prayer Service

 Prepare the prayer center. Have the Bible open to Luke 9:23. Place on a table a basket or other container with the paper crosses you prepared.

Have children bring their books to the prayer center. Explain that the crosses symbolize children's willingness to help others, just as Simon helped Jesus carry his cross. Say: **After the Gospel has been read and we respond, you will be invited to take a cross to keep with you this week.** Select a child to read the Leader part and have the other children read the *All* parts. Tell them you will be the Reader.

Say: **Jesus wants us to help others. When we make the Sign of the Cross, we recall Jesus' sacrifice and tell him that we are ready to follow in his footsteps.** Begin the prayer by praying the Sign of the Cross together. After the Gospel, allow time for children to take a cross from the basket. Then continue with the prayer. Close by praying the Sign of the Cross.

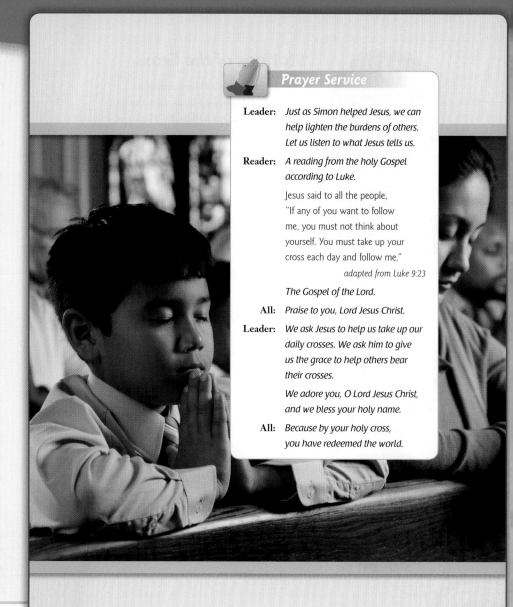

Prayer Service

Leader: Just as Simon helped Jesus, we can help lighten the burdens of others. Let us listen to what Jesus tells us.

Reader: A reading from the holy Gospel according to Luke.

Jesus said to all the people, "If any of you want to follow me, you must not think about yourself. You must take up your cross each day and follow me."
adapted from Luke 9:23

The Gospel of the Lord.

All: Praise to you, Lord Jesus Christ.

Leader: We ask Jesus to help us take up our daily crosses. We ask him to give us the grace to help others bear their crosses.

We adore you, O Lord Jesus Christ, and we bless your holy name.

All: Because by your holy cross, you have redeemed the world.

168 *The Year in Our Church*

1 Respond

Invite children to name two or three new facts they learned about Holy Week. Say: **We also learned the story behind some of the Stations of the Cross so that we could thank Jesus for his great sacrifice.**

2 Go in Peace

Collect materials and return them to the appropriate places. Encourage children to take the crosses home and put them where they will be seen. Ask children to take extra time during this special week to reflect on the Stations of the Cross. Remind them to thank Jesus for his loving sacrifice. Say: **Jesus carried his cross willingly. During Holy Week we want to follow Jesus willingly, even when it is hard.**

IF TIME ALLOWS

In His Footsteps
Distribute art supplies and drawing paper. Give children time to imagine themselves following in Jesus' footsteps by helping someone. Invite them to draw the scene and suggest that they write a short caption describing the situation.

FYI

Coaching Children to Pray

Assure children that Jesus is always present with them, even when they find it hard to follow in his footsteps. They can call on him in prayer anytime, anywhere and rely on him to strengthen their commitment and to guide them.

Easter

Jesus' friends were very sad. Their best friend had died. When they went to anoint his body one last time, they were surprised to find the tomb empty. Jesus had risen from the dead!

On Easter we remember this special day. We celebrate the Resurrection of Jesus. We share in the joy that Jesus' friends felt.

Prayer

Jesus, risen Lord, help me remember that you died and rose for me. I want to celebrate the miracle of your Resurrection by serving God and others.

169

MATERIALS

Get Ready for the Session

In addition to Bibles and basic writing and art supplies, you will need symbols for Easter and a white cloth. Review any If Time Allows activities you would like to include in this session for additional materials they may require.

EASTER

OUTCOMES

▶ Tell the story of Jesus' rising.

▶ Discuss how we are called to spread the Good News.

▶ Explain how the Church celebrates the living presence of Jesus Christ in the Eucharist.

1 Set the Stage

Begin by saying: ***Think of a time when you lost something you liked very much. Were you disappointed? Now think of a time when you found something you thought you had lost. How did you feel?*** (Possible answers: happy, surprised)

2 Get Started

Read aloud the session title. Direct children back to page 151. Say: ***Find Easter on the calendar on this page.***

Invite a volunteer to read aloud the first paragraph on page 169. Say: ***Sometimes when we find something we were sure was lost, we appreciate it more than ever. That was probably how the disciples felt when they heard that Jesus had risen.***

Invite a volunteer to read aloud the second paragraph. Ask: ***What do we celebrate on Easter?*** (the Resurrection of Jesus) Say: ***In this session we will learn about the Resurrection and the Ascension of Jesus Christ.***

Prayer

Invite children to close their eyes. Say: ***Pray in your hearts as I pray aloud.*** Pray the prayer. Allow a few moments of quiet reflection. Then invite children to open their eyes and pray *Amen* together.

1 Begin

Draw children's attention to the picture of the resurrected Jesus. Ask: **Which one is Jesus? How do you know?** (He has wounds in his hands and in his side; everyone is looking at him.) **Who do you think the other people are?** (apostles, holy people) **What do they all have in common?** (Possible answers: halos, they're all with the risen Jesus)

2 Connect

Invite a volunteer to read aloud Jesus Is Alive! Say: **The women were planning to anoint Jesus' body with spices. This is a religious custom that shows respect for people who are dead. The women did not expect the tomb to be empty.**

Point out that the tomb pictured on page 169 is similar to the one in which Jesus was placed. Say: **The women are like us in some ways. They had to be reminded of Jesus' promise that he would rise in three days. We learn many things about Jesus. Too often we forget what we learned, so it is helpful to read the Scriptures and listen to stories about Jesus' life.**

Invite a volunteer to read aloud The News Spreads. Ask: **What happened to Jesus after he rose from the dead?** (Jesus appeared to the women, Peter, and others. Jesus returned to his Father.) Ask: **What line in the paragraph is good news for us?** (We will someday be happy with Jesus in Heaven.)

Jesus Is Alive!

It was dawn on the first day of the week. Jesus' friend Mary Magdalene and several other women went to his tomb to serve him one last time. They brought spices to anoint his body. They found the tomb empty. Then two men in beautiful clothes came to them. The men said, "Why are you looking for Jesus among the dead? He is not here. He has been raised from the dead. Remember that Jesus told you he would rise on the third day." Upon hearing this, the women remembered Jesus' words. *adapted from Luke 24:1–8*

The News Spreads

After he rose, Jesus appeared to Mary Magdalene and the other women. He appeared to Peter, to the disciples, and to many more people. After some time Jesus returned to his Father, where he lives today. We will someday be happy with Jesus in Heaven.

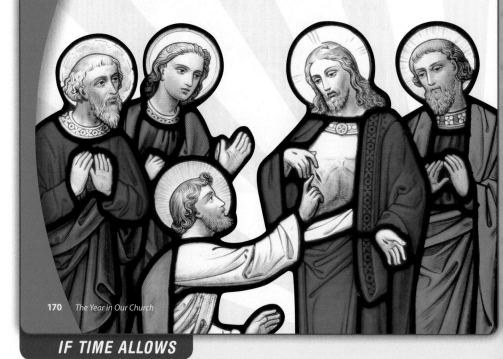

170 *The Year in Our Church*

IF TIME ALLOWS

Easter BLM

Easter Butterfly Have children complete the Easter Blackline Master [T-338] to make stick butterflies, a symbol of the Resurrection.

Resurrection Symbols

Discuss two additional symbols of new life at Easter: eggs and lilies. Invite children to illustrate a colorful garden scene, filled with lilies and butterflies. Have children hide an Easter egg in the drawing. When they are have finished, invite children to share their drawings and see if others can find the hidden egg.

The Lord's Day

On Sunday, the Lord's Day, we remember that Jesus was raised to new life. On this day we celebrate Jesus' living presence, especially in the Eucharist. Meeting Jesus in the Eucharist is important. The Church asks us to receive Jesus in Holy Communion often.

An Easter Message

After they found the tomb empty, Mary Magdalene and the other women told the disciples what they had seen and heard. We repeat their message on Easter.

Imagine you have a friend who does not understand why you celebrate Easter. In the spaces below, share the Easter message with your friend by answering his or her questions.

Friend: What happened on Easter?

You:_____

_____

Friend: Why is Easter so important?

You:_____

_____

Friend: What do you do to celebrate Easter?

You:_____

_____

Easter **171**

Messengers of the Good News

Arrange children into three groups. Distribute poster board and brightly colored markers, construction paper, and glitter. Give each group one of these words: *Jesus has risen!* Have children draw their word in large bubble letters on the poster board and decorate it. Put the finished posters side by side so that together they proclaim "Jesus has risen!" If possible, display the poster in the church entry or a public space.

Invite a volunteer to read aloud The Lord's Day. Ask: **When is the Lord's Day?** (Sunday) Say: **Sunday is the day that Jesus rose from the dead and the day that we celebrate his living presence in the Eucharist. Each time we go to Mass, we receive Jesus in the Eucharist. Celebrating the Eucharist on Sunday begins a day of celebration and relaxation for all of us.** Ask: **What are some things you do differently on Sunday to make it a special day?** Discuss ways to make every Sunday a real celebration. Ask: **What are some ways to make Sundays a real celebration?** (Possible answers: play with my family members, take a long walk, visit elderly neighbors or grandparents, go to the beach, read a book, have a picnic)

3 Close

Say: **Not everyone knows about Easter. We often meet people who wonder about our Church celebrations. Let's imagine we have a friend who does not know about the Resurrection of Jesus.** Read aloud the directions for An Easter Message. Say: **You are like the disciples and the women at the tomb. You have to spread the good news of Jesus being raised from the dead. You have to let people know that because of Jesus, we are all promised a life in Heaven after death.**

Allow time for children to think and to write. Invite volunteers to share their answers. Say: **How fortunate we are to be friends and followers of Jesus!**

Prayer Service

✝ Place a white cloth on the prayer table. Add some symbols of Easter—eggs, butterfly, flowers. Have the Bible open to 1 Corinthians 15:1–4. Select a child to be the Reader. Explain that you will read the *Leader* parts and they will read the *All* parts.

Say: **This time after Lent is a time to rejoice. During the Easter season, alleluia is said and sung over and over. It reminds us that Jesus kept his promise to rise from the dead. Because he has risen, we are saved. This is why we celebrate with happy voices and joyous hearts.**

Invite children to gather around the prayer table with their books open to page 172. If you wish, you may sing a simple alleluia with the children or say "alleluia" three times with them to begin your prayer. Pray the prayer service, ending with another joyful alleluia.

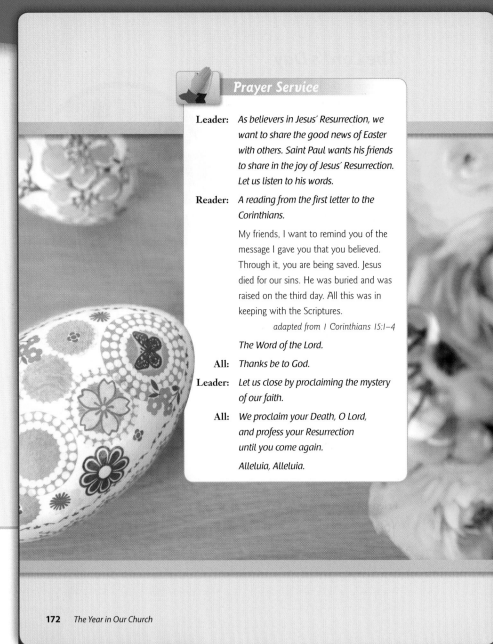

 Prayer Service

Leader: *As believers in Jesus' Resurrection, we want to share the good news of Easter with others. Saint Paul wants his friends to share in the joy of Jesus' Resurrection. Let us listen to his words.*

Reader: *A reading from the first letter to the Corinthians.*

My friends, I want to remind you of the message I gave you that you believed. Through it, you are being saved. Jesus died for our sins. He was buried and was raised on the third day. All this was in keeping with the Scriptures.

  adapted from 1 Corinthians 15:1–4

The Word of the Lord.

All: *Thanks be to God.*

Leader: *Let us close by proclaiming the mystery of our faith.*

All: *We proclaim your Death, O Lord, and profess your Resurrection until you come again.*

Alleluia, Alleluia.

172 *The Year in Our Church*

① Respond

Invite children to look back over the session and to identify two or three important things they learned about Easter. Ask: **What are some signs of a joyful Christian? What can we do to be witnesses to Jesus Christ?** (Possible answers: greet others with a smile, be more helpful, share what we have, celebrate Mass with joyful hearts, do our best at school) Say: **During Easter we share our joy. We have every reason to be happy and hopeful.**

② Go in Peace

Collect materials and return them to the appropriate places. Remind children to share their Easter activities and ideas with their families. Say: **May joy be in your hearts and in your lives. Let joy be the gift you share with others.**

IF TIME ALLOWS

Retelling the Story

Arrange children into four groups. Distribute a Bible to each group. Assign each group a different Gospel to research. Ask children to choose a reader, a recorder, and a reporter for their group. The reader reads the Gospel story to the group. Members of the group then recall details from the story as the recorder lists them. The reporter reports the findings of the group. The Resurrection accounts are found in Mark 16:1–8, John 20:1–10, Luke 24:1–12, and Matthew 28:1–10. Discuss differences and similarities among the Scripture accounts.

FYI

Coaching Children to Pray

After the close of the prayer service, encourage children to remember that the risen Jesus is with us, calling each of us to be a joyful witness of his love and to stay close to him in prayer.

Pentecost

On Pentecost we celebrate the gift of the Holy Spirit. The Church was born on this day because that is when the Holy Spirit came to the disciples. The Holy Spirit strengthens us to continue Jesus' mission. We can use God's special gifts to us, our special talents and abilities. The Holy Spirit calls us to share our gifts with the Church and community.

The word *Pentecost* comes from a Greek word that means "50." Pentecost is seven weeks, or 50 days, after Easter.

 Prayer

Dear Jesus, help me to use my special gifts. I want to live as your disciple and continue your work.

173

MATERIALS

Get Ready for the Session

In addition to Bibles and basic writing and art supplies, you will need red cloth and *Finding God* CD 2. Review any If Time Allows activities you would like to include in this session for additional materials they may require.

PENTECOST

OUTCOMES

▶ Identify Pentecost as the feast on which we remember when the Holy Spirit came to the disciples.

▶ Identify the diversity of gifts given by the Holy Spirit.

▶ Explain how the Holy Spirit guides the Church's mission.

 Set the Stage

Ask: *What do we remember on a person's birthday?* (the day he or she was born) Invite volunteers to share stories of the day they were born. Say: *On Pentecost we remember the day the Holy Spirit came to the disciples. The Church was born on that day. In this session we will be talking about a very special feast of the Church's. Pentecost celebrates the birthday of the Church.*

 Get Started

Read aloud the session title and invite volunteers to read aloud the paragraphs. Ask: *What do we celebrate during Pentecost?* (the gift of the Holy Spirit) *When was the Church born?* (on Pentecost) Say: *The liturgical color of Pentecost is red, a color of life and excitement.* Ask: *What does the Holy Spirit call us to do?* (share our gifts with the Church and community)

 Prayer

Prepare children for prayer. Say: *Pray with me in the quiet of your hearts while I pray aloud.* Pray the prayer aloud. Allow quiet time for children to add their own intentions.

1 Begin

Say: *We met Saint Paul before and know how much he liked to write letters to the people in the churches he visited. We are going to read another message that he sent to Jesus' followers in Corinth.* Remind children that Saint Paul's letters are meant for us to read too and that we can find them in the New Testament.

2 Connect

Invite volunteers to read aloud the heading, the first paragraph, and the Scripture adaptation. Say: *Saint Paul wants us to know that we are all different. We are of different races and different backgrounds. We come from different families and have different talents. Even so, we are all part of the same Church.* Ask: *When do we become one body in Jesus Christ?* (when we are baptized) *What does the Holy Spirit give each of us?* (a different way to serve)

Read aloud the last paragraph. Say: *We are going to answer the questions about our gifts from the Holy Spirit.* Play the reflective music at the end of CD 2. Have children fold sheets of paper lengthwise. On one side have them write *My Gifts.* On the other side, have them write *How I Will Use Them.* Provide an example for children to follow.

Say: *As you work remember that your gifts are given to help you be a good follower of Jesus'. Your gifts help you serve God's kingdom.* Allow enough time for children to complete the activity.

When children have finished, say: *Don't worry if you had difficulty deciding how to use your gifts. Some of the gifts you have will not be used until you are older—perhaps when you are a parent or a worker.*

One in the Spirit

Paul wanted his friends in Corinth to understand how the Holy Spirit works in each of us. He sent them this message.

> There are different gifts, but one Spirit. The same God works in all of us. The Spirit gives each of us a different way to serve. If the Holy Spirit is in you, you will say, "Jesus is Lord."
>
> We are all different. We may be Jews or Greeks, enslaved or free persons. When we were baptized in one Spirit, we all became part of the one Body of Christ. The same Spirit helps us all.
>
> *adapted from I Corinthians 12:4–7,12–13*

Saint Paul, Manolis Grigoreas, 2001.

Paul tells us that each of us has special gifts. The Holy Spirit helps us use these gifts. What are your gifts? How do you use them?

174 The Year in Our Church

IF TIME ALLOWS

Pentecost BLM

Special-Gifts Bingo Have children complete the Pentecost Blackline Master [T-339] to discover gifts their classmates possess by playing a bingo-type game.

Moved by the Spirit

Review the Prayer to the Holy Spirit. Invite children to pray along with you as you write the words of the prayer on the board. Say: *Gestures speak as well as words do. What gesture could you use to show love?* (Possible answer: hands over heart) *What if we want to say "Come"?* (Possible answer: beckoning motion) Then arrange children into groups. Tell them to think of gestures to accompany the Prayer to the Holy Spirit. When children are ready, invite each group to present its gestures along with the prayer.

Finish the Story

In this story the gifts of many people help make the church play a success. Finish the story by filling in the gifts listed below.

> kindness singing creativity
> dance joy patience

The Big Night

Backstage the third graders were warming up for the church play. Marcos cleared his throat and practiced his ____singing____. Maria put on her shoes and practiced her ____dance____ steps. Everybody was filled with ____joy____. Months of hard work were paying off. So much had gone into this play. It took the ____creativity____ of José and Brigitte to make the beautiful scenery. It took the ____kindness____ of the local store manager, who gave the cast beautiful costumes to wear. If it weren't for the ____patience____ of their director, Mr. Joyce, the third graders might never have learned their lines. Thanks to the gifts they all shared, they knew the church play would be a success.

Pentecost 175

IF TIME ALLOWS

The Work of the Spirit

Distribute Bibles. Arrange children into groups to search the Bible and discover how the Holy Spirit works in individuals and in the Church. Give each group one or two of the following passages to read and discuss: Luke 3:16, 4:14, 4:18, 12:12 and Acts of the Apostles 1:8, 6:3, 9:17, 10:44, 11:24. Have children choose a reporter to take notes on their discussion. When they have finished, ask a volunteer from each group to use the group's notes to explain what children learned from their reading.

---

❸ Close

Read aloud the directions for Finish the Story. Ask children to read aloud in unison the words in the box. Say: *Many children are involved in a church play. It takes all their talents to make the play a success. In the blanks write the words to complete the story and see what happened at this church play.*

When children have finished, invite volunteers to read aloud the story. Then lead a brief discussion. Ask: *How would the play be different if the children did not have the gifts of song or dance? What if José and Brigitte didn't have the gift of creativity? What if the store manager didn't have the gift of kindness? Or if Mr. Joyce didn't have the gift of patience? What if the children didn't have the gift of joy?* Allow time for volunteers to discuss answers to these questions. Say: *The children in the story had different talents. Yet each of these gifts from God was important to the success of their play.* Remind children that the Holy Spirit works in each of us and helps us use these gifts.

Prayer Service

✝ Have the prayer center ready with a red cloth and a Bible open to John 14:16–18 on a table. Select a child to be the Reader. Explain that you will read the *Leader* parts and they will read the *All* parts. Give the children a moment to review their responses.

🎵 Play "Come, O Holy Spirit/Wa Wa Wa Emimimo" [CD 2, Track 7]. As the song plays, have children get up with their books and move to the prayer center. When all are gathered, play the song again, inviting children to sing along. Begin the prayer service. At the end of the service, invite children to move quietly back to their places.

 Respond

Ask children to identify two or three new facts or ideas they learned about Pentecost. Say: **When we started this session, we read how the Holy Spirit strengthens us to continue Jesus' mission.** Remind children that a mission is something we are sent to do. Say: **Some of Jesus' missions were to teach us, save us, do the Father's will, and show us how to treat one another.**

 Go in Peace

Collect materials and return them to the appropriate places. Say: **Your mission is to bring God's love to all you meet in your own special way.**

Prayer Service

Leader:	*Praise be to God, who fills our lives with love and joy.*
All:	*Amen.*
Leader:	*Jesus kept his promise to send the Spirit to be with us. Let us pray that we will live according to the Spirit.*
All:	*Amen.*
Reader:	*A reading from the holy Gospel according to John.*
	I will ask the Father to send you a helper. The Holy Spirit will come to you. He will stay with you always. I will not leave you orphans. I will come to you.
	adapted from John 14:16–18
	The Gospel of the Lord.
All:	*Praise to you, Lord Jesus Christ.*
Leader:	*Jesus, thank you for being with us.*
All:	*Make us one with you and with one another. Amen.*

176 *The Year in Our Church*

IF TIME ALLOWS

Continuing Jesus' Mission
Have children define how they will continue Jesus' mission. Say: **As we move out of the Easter season, we each can carry out Jesus' mission. How can we continue Jesus' mission?** (Possible answers: speak kindly to people every day, be respectful to others, try hard in school, share with others, use personal gifts to serve God) Write a few suggestions on the board. Invite children to write on a sheet of paper how they can continue Jesus' mission and encourage them to post it in their bedrooms so that they can be reminded of it.

FYI

Coaching Children to Pray

Remind children that when we pray, we can always trust in the Holy Spirit for encouragement and support in using our talents and gifts on behalf of others.

All Saints Day and All Souls Day

We celebrate All Saints Day on November 1 by remembering those who have died and are with God in Heaven. We can ask the saints to pray to God for us today and every day. Our prayer will help us to follow the good example of their lives.

We celebrate All Souls Day on November 2 by remembering those who have died but whose souls are being prepared in Purgatory to live with God forever.

Prayer

Jesus, help me to love and serve others as you did. I want to be united with you and with others.

177

MATERIALS

Get Ready for the Session

In addition to Bibles and basic writing and art supplies, you will need a small statue of Mary, small heart stickers, and *Finding God* CD 2. Review any If Time Allows activities you would like to include in this session for additional materials they may require.

OUTCOMES

▶ Understand that All Saints Day and All Souls Day are celebrations of the Communion of Saints.

▶ Explain that in Christ we are united with the living and the dead.

▶ Discuss how the saints are examples of how we can live our lives.

1 Set the Stage

Initiate a brief discussion about Halloween. Ask: ***Does anybody know why we celebrate Halloween on October 31?*** (It is the day before All Saints Day.) Write *All Hallows Eve* on the board. Ask: ***What does hallow mean?*** (holy) Say: ***A hallowed person is a saint. We call October 31 "All Hallows Eve" because it is the eve of All Saints Day, which is November 1. This is where the name Halloween comes from.***

Say: ***In this session we will learn that the saints dedicated their lives to serving God and others, and they followed the example of Jesus. We will also pray for all those who have already died.***

2 Get Started

Read aloud the title and invite volunteers to read aloud the paragraphs. Explain that souls in Purgatory are being cleansed of sin so that they can experience fully the joy of Heaven. Say: ***The saints set an example that we can all try to follow.***

Prayer

Invite children to sit quietly and prepare themselves for prayer. Say: ***Let us now ask Jesus to help us serve God and others as the saints did.*** Pray the prayer slowly and reverently. Say: ***In your own words, pray silently to Jesus.*** Allow children sufficient time to pray, then pray *Amen*.

Begin

Invite children to share times when they have shown love to someone, such as helping a brother tie his shoe or talking to a lonely or elderly neighbor. Say: **When we serve others, God's love grows in us.**

2 Connect

Invite a volunteer to read aloud the heading and the first paragraph. Ask: **How do we become holy like the saints?** (by serving others as Jesus did) **Who gives us the grace we need to love one another?** (the Holy Spirit) **Where does Jesus want us to be kind to one another?** (at home, at school, wherever we are)

✝ Invite a volunteer to read aloud the Scripture passage. Ask: **Why must we love one another?** (because God loves us) **What happens when we love one another?** (God's love grows in us.) Say: **John says that no one has ever seen God. How can we serve God if we can't see him?** (by caring for one another) Point out to children that God is in everyone. Say: **When we care for or help someone else, we are serving God.** Ask: **Whom does God give us to help us grow in love?** (the Holy Spirit) Say: **No matter what, when we serve God, we are happy to know that we are living as God wants. As John says, God's love grows in us.**

Invite a volunteer to read aloud The Communion of Saints. Ask: **Where else have we heard the word communion?** (as a name for the Eucharist) Say: **Communion means togetherness—coming together as one. The Eucharist brings us together in Jesus Christ.** Ask: **Who is together in the Communion of Saints.** (We are together with everyone who loves God, living and dead.) Say: **The Communion of Saints doesn't just include the saints in Heaven. It includes you, me, and everyone who tries to follow the example of Jesus and the saints.**

Loving One Another

We become holy like the saints when we serve others as Jesus did. Jesus wants us to be kind to one another at school, at home, and wherever we are. Through the sacraments the Holy Spirit gives us the grace we need to love one another. In the New Testament, John tells us that God's love grows in us when we love one another.

John says, "Friends, because God loves us so much, we also must love one another. If we love one another, God remains in us, and his love grows in us. This is how we know that we remain in him and he in us. God has given us his Spirit."

adapted from 1 John 4:11–13

The Communion of Saints

We are not alone! We are united with all those who love God, both living and dead. This is called the Communion of Saints. We are to pray for one another and for those who have died.

IF TIME ALLOWS

All Saints Day and All Souls Day BLM

You're Like a Saint to Me Have children complete the All Saints Day and All Souls Day Blackline Master [T-340] in which children decorate a badge, cut it out, and give it to someone who is special to them.

Living to Serve

Make a poster board showing how we can serve others as Jesus did. Draw an outline of a church on a large poster board. Distribute magazines featuring images of people helping others. Have children cut out pictures and glue them inside the church to make a collage. As an alternative children may draw their own pictures of people serving others and glue them to the poster board. Suggest that children give the poster a title.

Saints in Heaven and on Earth

When we celebrate All Saints Day and All Souls Day, we remember all who have died and are enjoying life with God in Heaven or who are awaiting Heaven in purgatory. We remember that as followers of Jesus on earth, we are united in Jesus Christ because we are part of the Communion of Saints.

A Saint in the Making

We are living like the saints when we help others. On the lines write what you can do to follow the example of the saints. Draw a picture of yourself in the frame below.

At home I can _____ .

At church I can _____ .

At school I can _____ .

In the neighborhood I can _____ .

All Saints Day and All Souls Day **179**

My Example

Have children choose saints whose example they would like to follow. Tell children they may page through their books to choose a saint, or they may choose a saint they have learned about on their own. Have them write paragraphs explaining why they chose the saint and why they would like to be more like him or her. As an example, you may wish to tell children about your favorite saint. When children have finished, ask volunteers to read their paragraphs aloud.

Read aloud Saints in Heaven and on Earth. Ask: **What do we celebrate on All Saints Day and All Souls Day?** (those who have died and are with God in Heaven, those awaiting Heaven in Purgatory, and the followers of Jesus on earth) To explain *Purgatory*, say: **Our sins separate us from God and others. When people die, they may not have asked forgiveness for all their sins, and there may still be a separation between them and God. Before people can see God face to face in heaven, this separation must first be removed. We call this experience Purgatory. Those in Purgatory are being purified in preparation for meeting God face to face.**

3 Close

Invite a volunteer to read aloud A Saint in the Making. Say: **We can live like the saints in every part of our lives—at home, at church, at school, and in our neighborhoods. Can anyone tell me one thing he or she can do to live like a saint at home? at church? at school? in your neighborhood?** (home: clean up after dinner; church: pray for those who are sick; school: help someone understand a lesson; neighborhood: pick up litter.) Invite a volunteer to respond to each and write one example from each category on the board.

Say: **Now I want you to think of one way you would like to live like a saint in each part of your lives. Write your ideas on the lines. If you get stuck, you may get a hint from one of the examples on the board. When you're done writing, draw your picture in the frame on the page.**

♬ Play reflective music from CD 2 as you give children time to complete the activity. When they have finished, invite volunteers to tell what they wrote for one of the categories. Say: **Let's keep these ideas in mind as we try to live like saints every day.**

All Saints Day and All Souls Day **179**

Prayer Service

Have the prayer table prepared beforehand with a Bible opened to 1 Corinthians 12:12–13. Also have a statue or picture of Mary on the table. Select a volunteer to be the Reader. Point out the *All* sections that the children will be praying and you will serve as Leader. Explain that everyone will recite the Hail Mary and sing "Holy Is Your Name" at the end of the service.

Say: **As we pray we look to Mary, our greatest example of a saint. Because of this, she is sometimes called "Queen of All Saints."**

Pray the entire service. Then join the children in praying the Hail Mary. In closing, play "Holy Is Your Name" [CD 2, Track 9]. Encourage children to sing together. When finished, have children return quietly to their places.

❶ Respond

Ask children to share three new facts or ideas they learned about All Saints Day and All Souls Day. Say: **These feasts are a beautiful reminder of how we are not alone—we are part of the Communion of Saints!**

❷ Go in Peace

Collect materials and return them to the appropriate places. Remind children to share their All Saints Day and All Souls Day activities and ideas with their families. As children leave, put a small heart sticker on each child's hand. Say: **Whenever you look at your sticker, remember the example of the saints. Try to follow their example by living to serve others.**

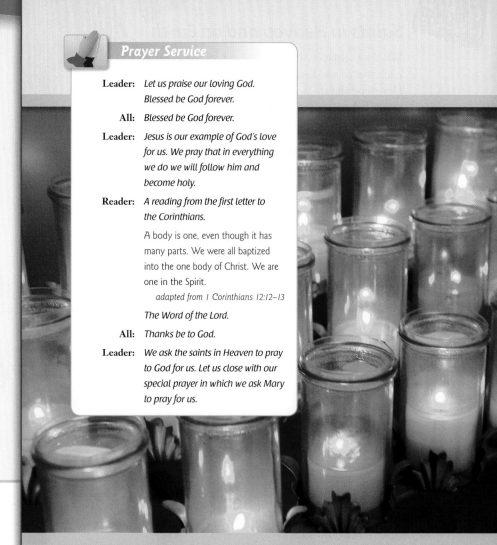

Prayer Service

Leader:	Let us praise our loving God. Blessed be God forever.
All:	Blessed be God forever.
Leader:	Jesus is our example of God's love for us. We pray that in everything we do we will follow him and become holy.
Reader:	A reading from the first letter to the Corinthians.
	A body is one, even though it has many parts. We were all baptized into the one body of Christ. We are one in the Spirit.
	adapted from 1 Corinthians 12:12–13
	The Word of the Lord.
All:	Thanks be to God.
Leader:	We ask the saints in Heaven to pray to God for us. Let us close with our special prayer in which we ask Mary to pray for us.

180 *The Year in Our Church*

IF TIME ALLOWS

Group Reports

Arrange children into four groups. Give each group one of the following questions: *How can we be like the saints? Who is in the Communion of Saints? When in our lives can we be like the saints? Whom do we remember on All Saints Day?* Give each group time to discuss their question, then have one volunteer from each group share his or her answer.

FYI

Coaching Children to Pray

Assure children that we can always ask the saints in Heaven to pray for us, especially our loved ones who have died. They are with us in a very special way in the Communion of Saints.

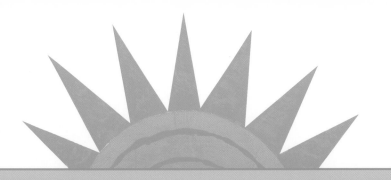

PRAYERS AND PRACTICES OF OUR FAITH

Prayers and Practices of Our Faith 181

The following resources for children are reproduced in this section for your convenience.

- **Knowing and Praying Our Faith**
- **Celebrating Our Faith**
- **Living Our Faith**
- **Songs of Our Faith**

Prayers and Practices of Our Faith

181

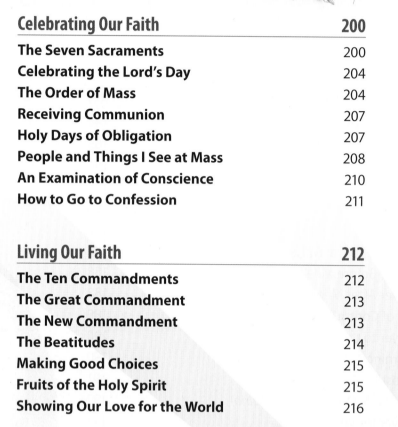

www.findinggod.com

Knowing and Praying Our Faith

The Bible and You

God speaks to us in many ways. One way is through the Bible. The Bible is the story of God's promise to care for us, especially through his Son, Jesus.

The Bible is made up of two parts. The Old Testament tells stories about the Jewish people before Jesus was born.

A beautiful part of the Old Testament is the Book of Psalms. A psalm is a prayer in the form of a poem. There are 150 psalms.

The New Testament tells stories about Jesus' life, Death, and Resurrection. In the New Testament, Jesus teaches us about the Father's love.

In the Gospels, Jesus taught, using parables. A parable is a simple story Jesus told to show us what God wants for the world. The story of the Good Samaritan is an example of a parable.

At Mass we hear stories from the Bible. We can also read the Bible on our own.

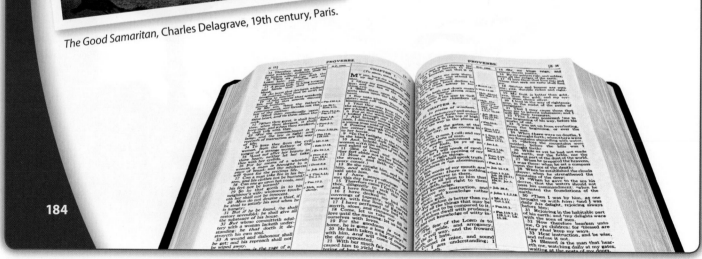

The Good Samaritan, Charles Delagrave, 19th century, Paris.

184

Prayer and How We Pray

Prayer is talking and listening to God. When we pray we raise our hearts and minds to God. We can talk to God in the special words of prayers or in our own words. We can pray aloud or quietly in our hearts.

We can pray to God often and in many different ways. We can praise God. We can thank God for what we have and ask him for what we need. We can pray for ourselves and for others.

Prayers to Take to Heart

It is good for us to know prayers by heart. To learn prayers by heart means that we not only learn, or memorize, the words but also understand and live them.

Sign of the Cross

In the name of the Father,
and of the Son,
and of the Holy Spirit.
Amen.

Lord's Prayer

Our Father, who art in heaven,
hallowed be thy name;
thy kingdom come,
thy will be done
on earth as it is in heaven.
Give us this day our daily bread,
and forgive us our trespasses,
as we forgive those who
   trespass against us;
and lead us not into
   temptation,
but deliver us from evil.
Amen.

Hail Mary

Hail Mary, full of grace,
the Lord is with you.
Blessed are you among women,
and blessed is the fruit of your womb, Jesus.
Holy Mary, Mother of God,
pray for us sinners,
now and at the hour of our death.
Amen.

Glory Be to the Father

Glory be to the Father,
and to the Son,
and to the Holy Spirit.
As it was in the beginning,
is now, and ever shall be,
world without end.
Amen.

Knowing and Praying Our Faith **187**

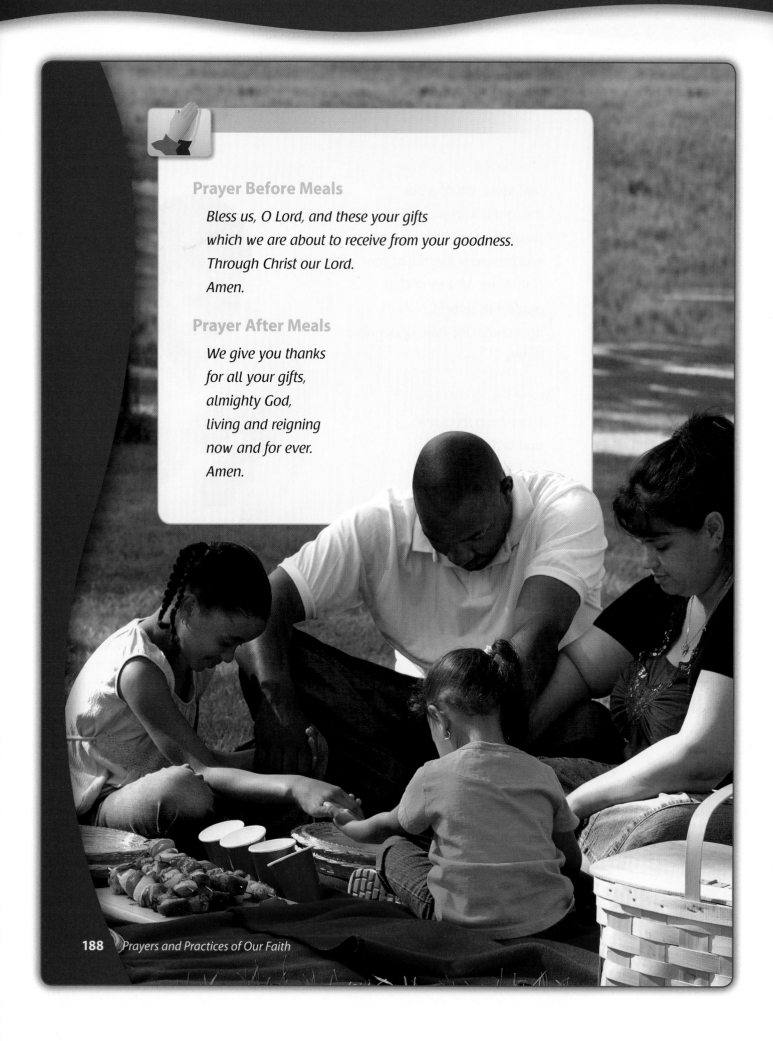

Prayer Before Meals

Bless us, O Lord, and these your gifts
which we are about to receive from your goodness.
Through Christ our Lord.
Amen.

Prayer After Meals

We give you thanks
for all your gifts,
almighty God,
living and reigning
now and for ever.
Amen.

188 *Prayers and Practices of Our Faith*

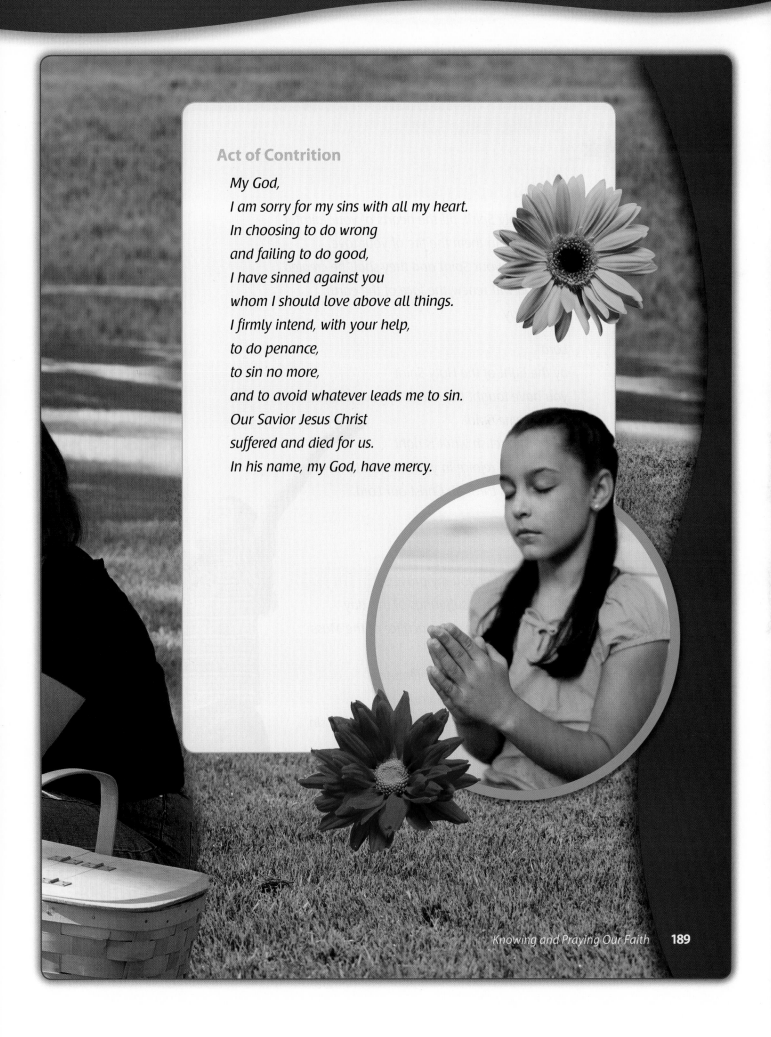

Act of Contrition

My God,
I am sorry for my sins with all my heart.
In choosing to do wrong
and failing to do good,
I have sinned against you
whom I should love above all things.
I firmly intend, with your help,
to do penance,
to sin no more,
and to avoid whatever leads me to sin.
Our Savior Jesus Christ
suffered and died for us.
In his name, my God, have mercy.

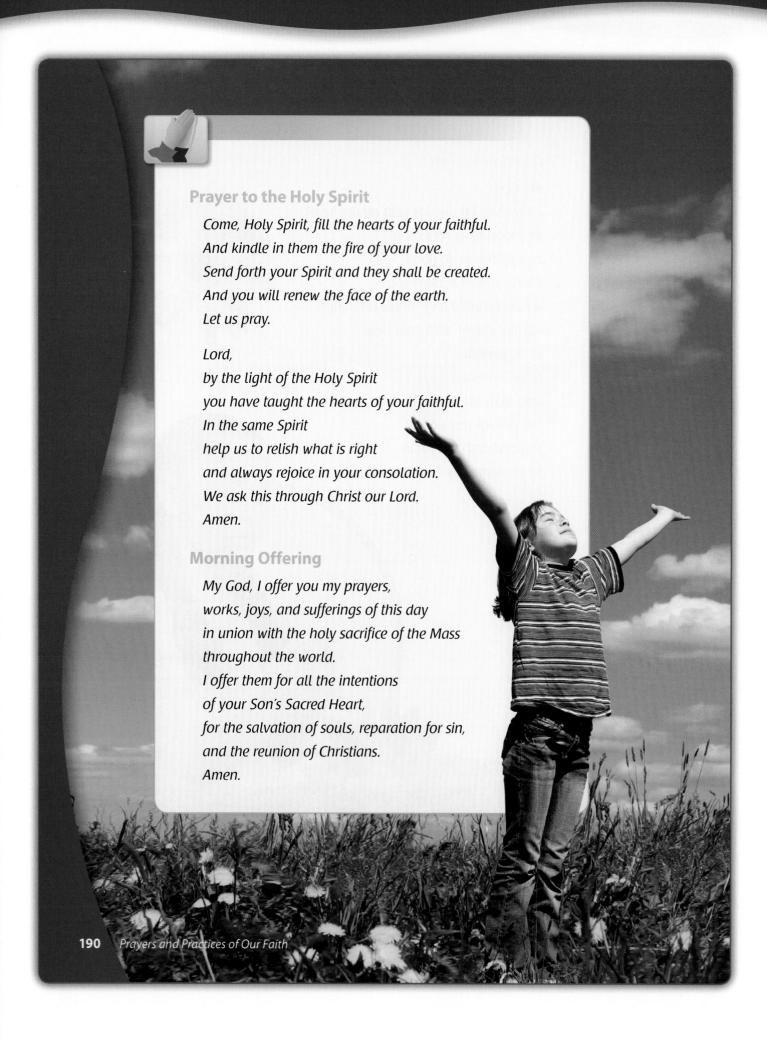

Prayer to the Holy Spirit

Come, Holy Spirit, fill the hearts of your faithful.
And kindle in them the fire of your love.
Send forth your Spirit and they shall be created.
And you will renew the face of the earth.
Let us pray.

Lord,
by the light of the Holy Spirit
you have taught the hearts of your faithful.
In the same Spirit
help us to relish what is right
and always rejoice in your consolation.
We ask this through Christ our Lord.
Amen.

Morning Offering

My God, I offer you my prayers,
works, joys, and sufferings of this day
in union with the holy sacrifice of the Mass
throughout the world.
I offer them for all the intentions
of your Son's Sacred Heart,
for the salvation of souls, reparation for sin,
and the reunion of Christians.
Amen.

Apostles' Creed

I believe in God,
the Father almighty,
Creator of heaven and earth,
and in Jesus Christ, his only Son, our Lord,
who was conceived by the Holy Spirit,
born of the Virgin Mary,
suffered under Pontius Pilate,
was crucified, died and was buried;
he descended into hell;
on the third day he rose again from the dead;
he ascended into heaven,
and is seated at the right hand of God the Father almighty;
from there he will come to judge the living and the dead.

I believe in the Holy Spirit,
the holy catholic Church,
the communion of saints,
the forgiveness of sins,
the resurrection of the body,
and life everlasting. Amen.

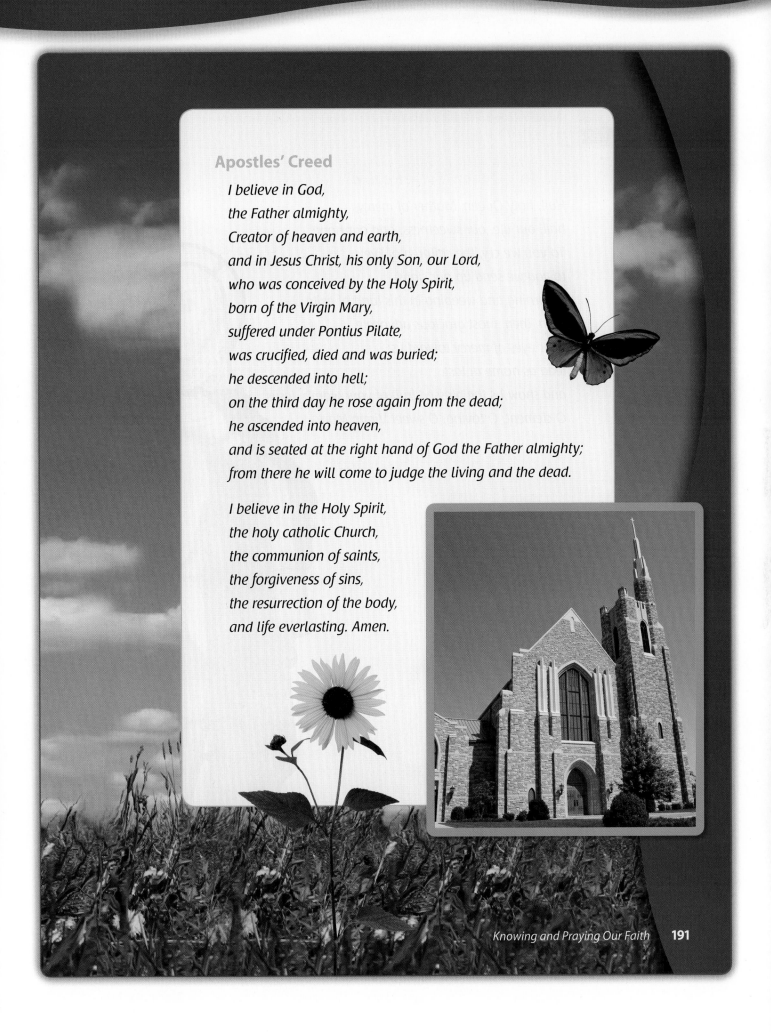

Hail, Holy Queen (*Salve Regina*)

Hail, holy Queen, Mother of mercy,
hail, our life, our sweetness, and our hope.
To you we cry, the children of Eve;
to you we send up our sighs,
mourning and weeping in this land of exile.
Turn, then, most gracious advocate,
your eyes of mercy toward us;
lead us home at last
and show us the blessed fruit of your womb, Jesus:
O clement, O loving, O sweet Virgin Mary.

Prayer for Vocations

God, thank you for loving me.
In Baptism you called me by name
to live as your child.
Help all your people to know their call in life.
For your greater glory, raise up generous leaders
to serve as priests, deacons, sisters, and brothers.
Amen.

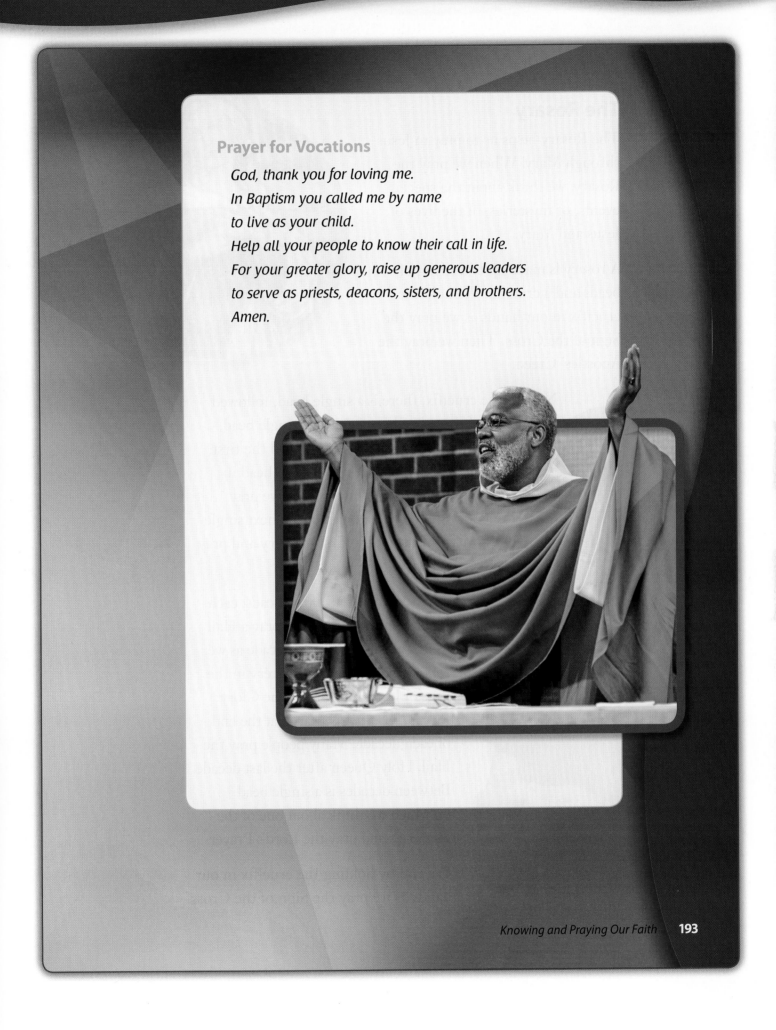

The Rosary

The Rosary helps us to pray to Jesus through Mary. When we pray the Rosary, we think about the special events, or mysteries, in the lives of Jesus and Mary.

A rosary is made up of a string of beads and a crucifix. We hold the crucifix in our hands as we pray the Sign of the Cross. Then we pray the Apostles' Creed.

Next to the crucifix, there is a single bead, followed by a set of three beads and another single bead. We pray the Lord's Prayer as we hold the first single bead and a Hail Mary at each bead in the set of three that follows. Then we pray the Glory Be to the Father. On the next single bead, we think about the first mystery and pray the Lord's Prayer.

There are five sets of ten beads; each set is called a decade. We pray a Hail Mary on each bead of a decade as we reflect on a particular mystery in the lives of Jesus and Mary. The Glory Be to the Father is prayed at the end of each decade. Many people pray the Hail, Holy Queen after the last decade. Between decades is a single bead on which we think about one of the mysteries and pray the Lord's Prayer.

We end by holding the crucifix in our hands as we pray the Sign of the Cross.

194

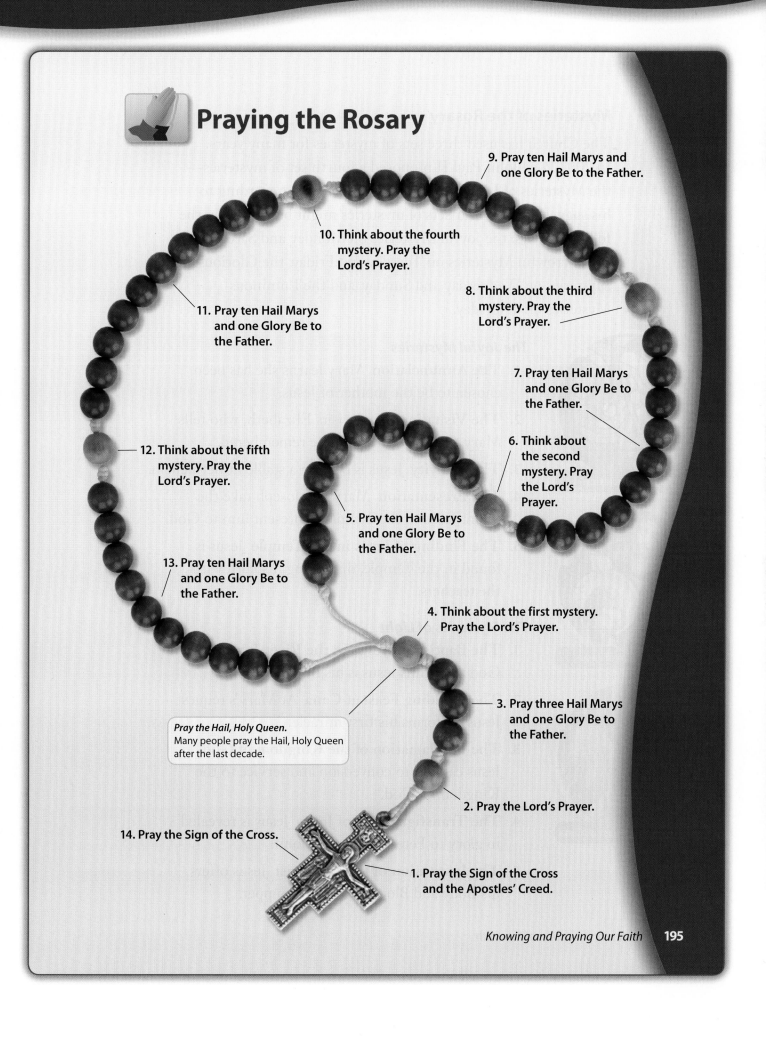

Praying the Rosary

9. Pray ten Hail Marys and one Glory Be to the Father.

10. Think about the fourth mystery. Pray the Lord's Prayer.

8. Think about the third mystery. Pray the Lord's Prayer.

11. Pray ten Hail Marys and one Glory Be to the Father.

7. Pray ten Hail Marys and one Glory Be to the Father.

12. Think about the fifth mystery. Pray the Lord's Prayer.

6. Think about the second mystery. Pray the Lord's Prayer.

5. Pray ten Hail Marys and one Glory Be to the Father.

13. Pray ten Hail Marys and one Glory Be to the Father.

4. Think about the first mystery. Pray the Lord's Prayer.

Pray the Hail, Holy Queen.
Many people pray the Hail, Holy Queen after the last decade.

3. Pray three Hail Marys and one Glory Be to the Father.

2. Pray the Lord's Prayer.

14. Pray the Sign of the Cross.

1. Pray the Sign of the Cross and the Apostles' Creed.

Knowing and Praying Our Faith **195**

Mysteries of the Rosary

The Church has used three sets of mysteries for many years. In 2002 Pope John Paul II proposed a fourth set of mysteries—the Mysteries of Light, or Luminous Mysteries. According to his suggestion, the four sets of mysteries might be prayed on the following days: the Joyful Mysteries on Monday and Saturday, the Sorrowful Mysteries on Tuesday and Friday, the Glorious Mysteries on Wednesday and Sunday, and the Luminous Mysteries on Thursday.

The Annunciation

The Baptism of Jesus

The Wedding Feast at Cana

The Joyful Mysteries

1. **The Annunciation** Mary learns she has been chosen to be the mother of Jesus.

2. **The Visitation** Mary visits Elizabeth, who tells Mary that she will always be remembered.

3. **The Nativity** Jesus is born in a stable in Bethlehem.

4. **The Presentation** Mary and Joseph take the infant Jesus to the Temple to present him to God.

5. **The Finding of Jesus in the Temple** Jesus is found in the Temple, discussing his faith with the teachers.

The Mysteries of Light

1. **The Baptism of Jesus in the River Jordan** God proclaims Jesus is his beloved Son.

2. **The Wedding Feast at Cana** At Mary's request Jesus performs his first miracle.

3. **The Proclamation of the Kingdom of God** Jesus calls all to conversion and service to the Kingdom of God.

4. **The Transfiguration of Jesus** Jesus is revealed in glory to Peter, James, and John.

5. **The Institution of the Eucharist** Jesus offers his Body and Blood at the Last Supper.

The Sorrowful Mysteries

1. **The Agony in the Garden** Jesus prays in the Garden of Gethsemane on the night before he dies.

2. **The Scourging at the Pillar** Jesus is beaten with whips.

3. **The Crowning with Thorns** Jesus is mocked and crowned with thorns.

4. **The Carrying of the Cross** Jesus carries the cross on which he will be crucified.

5. **The Crucifixion** Jesus is nailed to the cross and dies.

The Glorious Mysteries

1. **The Resurrection** God the Father raises Jesus from the dead.

2. **The Ascension** Jesus returns to his Father in Heaven.

3. **The Coming of the Holy Spirit** The Holy Spirit comes to bring new life to the disciples.

4. **The Assumption of Mary** At the end of her life on earth, Mary is taken body and soul into Heaven.

5. **The Coronation of Mary** Mary is crowned as Queen of Heaven and Earth.

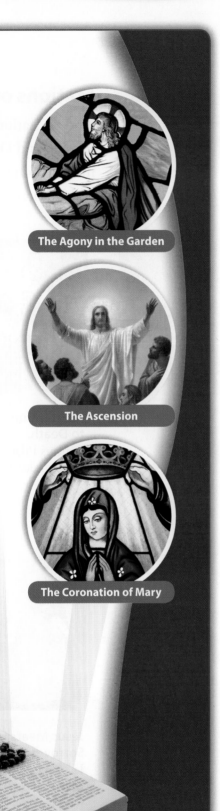

The Agony in the Garden

The Ascension

The Coronation of Mary

Stations of the Cross

The 14 Stations of the Cross represent events from Jesus' Passion and Death. At each station we use our senses and our imagination to reflect prayerfully on Jesus' suffering, Death, and Resurrection.

Jesus Is Condemned to Death.
Pontius Pilate condemns Jesus to death.

Jesus Takes Up the Cross.
Jesus willingly accepts and patiently bears the cross.

Jesus Falls the First Time.
Weakened by torments and loss of blood, Jesus falls beneath the cross.

Jesus Meets His Sorrowful Mother.
Jesus meets his mother, Mary, who is filled with grief.

Simon of Cyrene Helps Jesus Carry the Cross.
Soldiers force Simon of Cyrene to carry the cross.

Veronica Wipes the Face of Jesus.
Veronica steps through the crowd to wipe the face of Jesus.

7 Jesus Falls the Second Time.
Jesus falls beneath the weight of the cross a second time.

8 Jesus Meets the Women of Jerusalem.
Jesus tells the women not to weep for him but for themselves and for their children.

9 Jesus Falls the Third Time.
Weakened almost to the point of death, Jesus falls a third time.

10 Jesus Is Stripped of His Garments.
The soldiers strip Jesus of his garments, treating him as a common criminal.

11 Jesus Is Nailed to the Cross.
Jesus' hands and feet are nailed to the cross.

12 Jesus Dies on the Cross.
After suffering greatly on the cross, Jesus bows his head and dies.

The closing prayer—sometimes included as a 15th station—reflects on the Resurrection of Jesus.

13 Jesus Is Taken Down from the Cross.
The lifeless body of Jesus is tenderly placed in the arms of Mary, his mother.

14 Jesus Is Laid in the Tomb.
Jesus' disciples place his body in the tomb.

Celebrating Our Faith

The Seven Sacraments

The sacraments are signs of the grace we receive from God.

Sacraments show that God is part of our lives. They were given to the Church by Jesus. They help us to live the way God wants us to live. The sacraments are celebrated with us by priests.

Sacraments of Initiation

These sacraments lay the foundation for our lives as Catholics.

Baptism

Baptism is the first sacrament we receive. Through Baptism we become followers of Jesus and part of God's family, the Church. The pouring of water is the main sign of Baptism.

200

Confirmation

In this sacrament the Holy Spirit strengthens us to be witnesses to Jesus. Confirmation seals our life of faith in Jesus and helps us become better Christians.

The bishop places holy oil in the form of a cross on our foreheads. This is the main sign of Confirmation.

Eucharist

At Mass the Bread and Wine become the Body and Blood of Jesus Christ. This happens when the priest says the words of consecration that Jesus used at the Last Supper. The Eucharist is also called Holy Communion.

Sacraments of Healing

These sacraments celebrate the healing power of Jesus.

Penance and Reconciliation

We ask God to forgive our sins in the Sacrament of Penance and Reconciliation. The priest who celebrates this sacrament with us shares Jesus' gifts of peace and forgiveness.

The Holy Spirit helps us to be sorry for our sins. God always forgives us when we are sorry and do penance for our sins.

Anointing of the Sick

In this sacrament a sick person is anointed with holy oil and receives the spiritual—and sometimes even the physical—healing of Jesus.

Sacraments at the Service of Communion

These sacraments help members serve the community.

Holy Orders

Some men are called to be deacons, priests, or bishops. They receive the Sacrament of Holy Orders. Through Holy Orders the mission, or task, given by Jesus to his apostles continues in the Church.

Matrimony

Some men and women are called by the Holy Spirit to be married. They agree to live in faithful love in the Sacrament of Matrimony.

They make a solemn promise to be partners for life, both for their own good and for the good of the children they will raise.

Celebrating Our Faith   203

Celebrating the Lord's Day

Sunday is the day on which we celebrate the Resurrection of Jesus. It is the Lord's Day. We gather for Mass and rest from work. People all over the world gather at God's eucharistic table as brothers and sisters.

The Order of Mass

The Mass is the most important sacramental celebration of the Church and it always follows a set order.

Introductory Rites—preparing to celebrate the Eucharist
We prepare to celebrate the Eucharist.

Entrance Chant
We gather as a community and praise God in song.

Greeting
We pray the Sign of the Cross. The priest welcomes us.

Penitential Act
We remember our sins and ask God for mercy.

Gloria
We praise God in song.

Collect Prayer
We ask God to hear our prayers.

Liturgy of the Word—hearing God's plan of Salvation

First Reading

We listen to God's Word, usually from the Old Testament.

Responsorial Psalm

We respond to God's Word in song.

Second Reading

We listen to God's Word from the New Testament.

Gospel Acclamation

We sing "Alleluia!" During Lent we use a different acclamation to praise God for his Word.

Gospel Reading

We stand and listen to the Gospel of the Lord.

Homily

The priest or the deacon explains God's Word.

Profession of Faith

We proclaim our faith through the Creed.

Prayer of the Faithful

We pray for our needs and the needs of others.

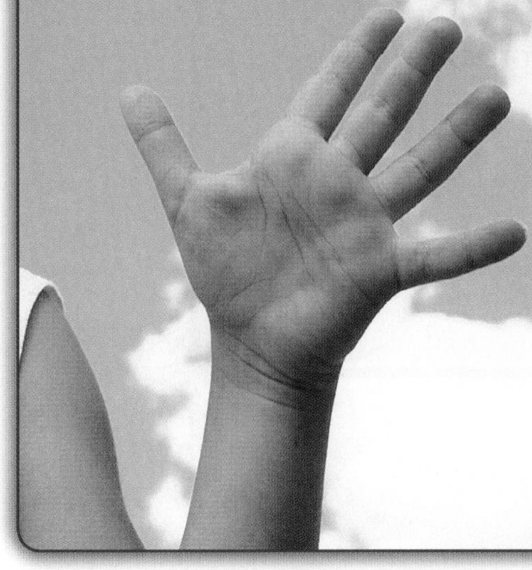

Liturgy of the Eucharist—celebrating Christ's presence in the Eucharist

Presentation and Preparation of the Gifts
We bring gifts of bread and wine to the altar.

Prayer over the Offerings
The priest prays that God will accept our sacrifice.

Eucharistic Prayer
This prayer of thanksgiving is the center and high point of the entire celebration. During this prayer the bread and wine are consecrated and truly become Jesus' Body and Blood.

- ▶ **Preface**—We give thanks and praise to God.
- ▶ **Holy, Holy, Holy**—We sing an acclamation of praise.
- ▶ **The Mystery of Faith**—We proclaim Jesus' Death and Resurrection.

Communion Rite—receiving the Body and Blood of Jesus Christ

The Lord's Prayer
We pray the Lord's Prayer.

Sign of Peace
We offer one another Christ's peace.

Lamb of God
We pray for forgiveness, mercy, and peace.

Communion
We receive the Body and Blood of Jesus Christ.

Prayer after Communion
We pray that the Eucharist will strengthen us to live as Jesus did.

Concluding Rites—going forth to glorify the Lord by our lives

Final Blessing
We receive God's blessing.

Dismissal
We go in peace to glorify the Lord by our lives.

Receiving Communion

When we go to communion, we receive the Body of Christ—in the form of bread—in our hands or on our tongues. The priest or the extraordinary minister of Holy Communion says, "The Body of Christ." We reply, "Amen."

We can also receive the Blood of Christ in the form of wine. The priest or the extraordinary minister of Holy Communion offers us the chalice and says, "The Blood of Christ." We reply, "Amen." We take the chalice in our hands and drink from it; we then hand it back to the priest or the extraordinary minister of Holy Communion.

Holy Days of Obligation

Holy Days of Obligation are the days other than Sundays on which we celebrate the great things God has done for us through Jesus and the saints. On Holy Days of Obligation, Catholics gather for Mass.

Six Holy Days of Obligation are celebrated in the United States.

January 1—Mary, Mother of God
40 days after Easter—Ascension
August 15—Assumption of the Blessed Virgin Mary
November 1—All Saints Day
December 8—Immaculate Conception
December 25—Nativity of Our Lord Jesus Christ

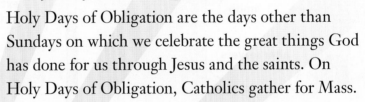

Celebrating Our Faith **207**

People and Things I See at Mass

alb

altar server

sanctuary lamp

processional cross

Paschal Candle

tabernacle

ambo

altar servers

extraordinary minister of Holy Communion

stole

chasuble

deacon

priest

lector

cantor

altar

chalice

paten

An Examination of Conscience

An examination of conscience is the act of reflecting on how we have hurt our relationships with God and with others. Questions such as the following will help us in our examination of conscience.

My Relationship with God

Do I use God's name with love and reverence?

What steps am I taking to grow closer to God and to others?

Do I actively participate at Mass on Sundays and holy days?

Do I pray?

Am I willing to turn to God often, especially when I am tempted?

My Relationships with Family, Friends, and Neighbors

Have I set a bad example by my words or actions? Do I treat others fairly? Do I spread stories that hurt other people?

Am I loving to those in my family? Am I respectful of my neighbors, my friends, and those in authority?

Do I show respect for my body and for the bodies of others?

Have I taken or damaged anything that did not belong to me? Have I cheated, copied homework, or lied?

Do I quarrel or fight with others? Do I try to hurt people who I think have hurt me?

How to Go to Confession

An examination of conscience is an important part of preparing for the Sacrament of Penance and Reconciliation. The Sacrament of Reconciliation includes the following steps:

1. The priest greets us, and we pray the Sign of the Cross. He invites us to trust in God. He may read God's Word with us.

2. We confess our sins. The priest may help and counsel us.

3. The priest gives us a penance to perform. Penance can be an act of kindness or prayers to pray, or both.

4. The priest asks us to express our sorrow, usually by praying the Act of Contrition.

5. We receive absolution. The priest says, "I absolve you from your sins in the name of the Father, and of the Son, and of the Holy Spirit." We respond, "Amen."

6. The priest dismisses us by saying, "Go in peace." We go forth to perform the act of penance he has given us.

Celebrating Our Faith **211**

Living Our Faith

The Ten Commandments

God gave us the Ten Commandments. They teach us how to live for God and for others. They help us follow the moral law to do good and avoid evil.

1. I am your God; love nothing more than me.
2. Use God's name with respect.
3. Keep the Lord's Day holy.
4. Honor and obey your parents.
5. Treat all human life with respect.
6. Respect married life.
7. Respect what belongs to others.
8. Tell the truth.
9. Respect your neighbors and your friends.
10. Be happy with what you have.

The Great Commandment

People asked Jesus, "What is the most important commandment?"

Jesus said, "First, love God. Love him with your heart, soul, and mind.

The second is like it: Love your neighbor as much as you love yourself."

adapted from Matthew 22:37–39

We call this the Great Commandment.

The New Commandment

Before his death on the cross, Jesus gave his disciples a new commandment:

"Love one another. As I have loved you, so you also should love one another."

adapted from John 13:34

Living Our Faith **213**

The Beatitudes

Jesus gave us the Beatitudes in the Sermon on the Mount.
They show us the way to true happiness.

Blessed are those who need God.
They will live in heaven one day.

Blessed are those who are sad.
They will be comforted.

Blessed are those who have little.
They will be given many things.

Blessed are those who have mercy on others.
They will be shown mercy.

Blessed are those who make peace.
They are the children of God.

adapted from Matthew 5:3–10

The Beatitudes, Jesus Mafa.

Making Good Choices

The Holy Spirit helps us to make good choices. We get help from the Ten Commandments, the grace of the sacraments, and the teachings of the Church. We also get help from the example of saints and fellow Christians. To make good choices, we ask the following questions:

1. Is the thing I'm choosing to do a good thing?
2. Am I choosing to do it for the right reasons?
3. Am I choosing to do it at the right time and place?

Fruits of the Holy Spirit

When we realize that the Holy Spirit lives within us, we live the way God wants us to. The Fruits of the Holy Spirit are signs of the Holy Spirit's action in our lives.

love	joy	peace
patience	kindness	generosity
faithfulness	gentleness	self-control

Church Tradition also includes goodness, modesty, and chastity as Fruits of the Holy Spirit.

Living Our Faith **215**

Showing Our Love for the World

Jesus taught us to care for those in need. The social teachings of the Church call for us to follow Jesus' example in each of the following areas.

Life and Dignity

God wants us to care for everyone. We are all made in his image.

Family and Community

Jesus wants us to be loving helpers in our families and communities.

Rights and Responsibilities

All people should have what they need to live good lives.

The Poor and Vulnerable

Jesus calls us to do what we can to help people in need.

Work and Workers

The work that we do gives glory to God.

Solidarity

Since God is our Father, we are called to treat everyone in the world as a brother or a sister.

God's Creation

We show our love for God's world by taking care of it.

Songs of Our Faith

Song of Love

Chorus

Thank you, Jesus, for helping me to see.
Thank you, God, for the heart you've given me.
Thank you, Spirit, for coming to me,
and for showing me how to sing your song of love.

Verse 1

I saw someone lonely by the road,
someone my age sadly all alone.
I shared my friendship, and we talked a while.
I gave my hand. Jesus gave back a smile.

(Sing Chorus)

Verse 2

I saw Jesus inside my heart,
making me God's own work of art.
If I spread my joy in life each day,
I can show my love for God's
    world in every way.

Verse 3

I saw Jesus in friends and family
by my side, sharing and supporting me.
I found my heart had room for everyone.
Thank you, Spirit, for what you have begun.

(Sing Chorus)

Lyrics by E. Strauss. Music by Neilson Hubbard.

Here I Am, God

Refrain
Here I am, God. I am coming.
My delight is to do your will!
Here I am, God. I am coming.
My delight is to do your will!

Verse 1
Pull me out of the muddy mire,
set my feet upon solid ground.
In my heart you have put new laws,
on my lips you have put new songs.

(Sing Refrain)

Verse 2
When my trouble and sins surround me,
and my eyes cannot see the way,
may your love and your kindness save me.
God, my rescuer, don't delay.

(Sing Refrain)

Verse 3
Of your love I cannot be silent;
I will shout of your wondrous plans.
You have given me ears to hear you.
Now I answer you, here I am!

(Sing Refrain)

All You Works of God

Refrain

All you works of God,
every mountain, star and tree,
bless the One who shapes your beauty,
who has caused you all to be
one great song of love and grace,
ever ancient, ever new.
Raise your voices, all you works of God!

Verse 1

Sun and moon: Bless your Maker!
Stars of heaven: Chant your praise!
Showers and dew: Raise up your joyful song!

(Sing Refrain)

Verse 2

Winds of God: Bless your Maker!

Cold and winter: Chant your praise!

Snowstorms and ice: Raise up your joyful song!

(Sing Refrain)

Verse 3

Wells and springs: Bless your Maker!

Seas and rivers: Chant your praise!

Whales in the deep: Raise up your joyful song!

(Sing Refrain)

Verse 4

Flying birds: Bless your Maker!

Beasts and cattle: Chant your praise!

Children at play: Raise up your joyful song!

(Sing Refrain)

Songs of Our Faith **221**

Come, O Holy Spirit/Wa Wa Wa Emimimo

Verse 1

Come, O Holy Spirit, come.
Come, Almighty Spirit, come.
Come, come, come.

Verse 2

Come, O Holy Spirit, come.
Come, Almighty Spirit, come.
Come, come, come.

Verse 3

Wa wa wa Emimimo.
Wa wa wa Alagbara.
Wao, wao, wao.

Verse 4

Wa wa wa Emimimo.
Wa wa wa Alagbara.
Wao, wao, wao.

"Come, O Holy Spirit/Wa Wa Wa Emimimo"
from traditional Nigerian text.
English transcription and paraphrase © 1990
I-to-Loh (World Council of Churches).

Holy Is Your Name

Refrain
And holy is your name through all generations!
Everlasting is your mercy to the people you have chosen,
and holy is your name.

Verse 1
My soul is filled with joy
as I sing to God my savior:
you have looked upon your servant,
you have visited your people,
and holy is your name.

(Sing Refrain)

Verse 2
I am lowly as a child,
but I know from this day forward
that my name will be remembered,
for all will call me blessed,
and holy is your name.

(Sing Refrain)

Verse 3
In your love you now fulfill
what you promised to your people.
I will praise you, Lord, my Savior,
everlasting is your mercy,
and holy is your name.

(Sing Refrain)

I Say "Yes," Lord / Digo "Sí," Señor

Verse 1

I say "Yes," my Lord,
in all good times, through all the bad times,
I say "Yes," my Lord,
to every word you speak.

Verse 2

Digo "Sí," Señor,
en tiempos malos, en tiempos buenos,
Digo "Sí," Señor,
a todo lo que hablas.

"I Say 'Yes,' Lord/Digo 'Sí,' Señor" by Donna Peña.
© GIA Publications, Inc.
All rights reserved. Reprinted by permission.

Peace Walk

Refrain

Come, let us walk in the way of our God,
let us walk in the way of our God.
Come, let us walk in the way of our God,
let us walk in the way of our God.

Verse 1

Pray for God's gentle peace within.
May the pilgrimage now begin.
Peace abide within our hearts.
All who love God, walk in peace.

(Sing Refrain)

Verse 2

Pray for peace in our families.
May all bitterness be released.
Peace abide within our homes.
All who love God, walk in peace.

(Sing Refrain)

Verse 3

Pray for peace and the end of war.
May the suffering be no more.
Peace abide within our world.
All who love God, walk in peace.

(Sing Refrain)

What Does It Mean to Follow Jesus?

Refrain

What does it mean to follow Jesus?
What does it mean to go his way?
What does it mean to do what he wants me to,
every day?

Verse 1

I can love my neighbor, just as Jesus said.
I can help my brother, see that he is fed.
I can show my sister kindness and care.
I can show my friends that I know how to share.

(Sing Refrain)

Verse 2

I can say I'm sorry when I've done some wrong.
I can sing his praises in both words and song.
I'll be friends with others who aren't like me.
They belong to Jesus: we all do, you see.

(Sing Refrain)

"What Does It Mean to Follow Jesus?"
by Lois Brokering.
© 1990 The Herbert F. Brokering Trust.
Used by permission.

ART PRINT
CATECHIST PAGES

The *Finding God: Exploring Faith Through Art* easel guides children to actively explore essential concepts of the Catholic faith. The beautiful and inspiring Art Prints initiate discussion, reflection, activities, and prayer for the 25 sessions.

The teaching found on the back of each Art Print is reproduced in this section for your convenience. The Answer Key for the Children's Book Art Print pages is found on the last page of this section.

FindingGod ❖ **Exploring Faith Through Art**

Paradise Garden

GRADE 3, UNIT 1, SESSION 1

Catechist Guide page 5

Faith Focus: We give glory to God for the wonders of creation.

OUTCOMES

▸ Explain that through prayer we give glory to God.

▸ Describe ways that creation reflects God's beauty and love.

About the Artist Suad Al-Attar was born in Iraq and studied art in the United States and England. In 1964, when she was 22 years old, Al-Attar was the first woman artist ever to have a solo exhibition in Iraq. Al-Attar's work is inspired by Iraqi legends and her Western education. Her work is displayed in many public and private collections, including the British Museum.

Art·i·facts *Paradise Garden* is oil on canvas. The deep blue and turquoise colors in the piece are a trademark of the artist's folklore-inspired nature scenes. Al-Attar's early work showed her affection for vivid flower- and animal-filled gardens.

For your convenience, the Children's Book page is reproduced below.

EXPLORE ART PRINT 1

Name _____ Date _____

Art Print 1 shows a lush garden filled with flowers, beautiful leaves, and birds. What beautiful gifts from God do you see around you?

God's Wonders

God created the earth and all the beauty in it.

> After God created light, God brought different kinds of plants and trees to the world. He wanted to give us delicious fruit. Later he created all kinds of animals, including wild ones, cattle, and creeping animals.
>
> *adapted from Genesis 1:3–25*

Through prayer and taking care of his creation, we can give glory to God for all his wonderful gifts.

Small Wonders

God created many wonderful things with amazing details. These details are small wonders. The dots on a ladybug, the eyelashes on a calf, and the shades of the colors on flowers are all created by God. These are all beautiful gifts that God has given us.

I Spy a Small Natural Wonder

Look around you and choose something that interests you, such as a plant or a feather. Examine it closely, noticing the details. Draw a picture of your small wonder.

www.findinggod.com   Grade 3 · Unit 1 · Session 1

CATECHIST DIRECTIONS

MATERIALS
▸ *Paradise Garden* Art Print
▸ Children's Book page 227
▸ Variety of natural objects, such as feathers and rocks
▸ Art supplies, colored pencils

TIME
🕐 10–30 minutes

1 Begin

After completing page 5 in the Children's Book, display the Art Print.

Briefly introduce and discuss the artwork, using information from About the Artist and Artifacts. Ask: **What do you see in this painting?** (plants, flowers, leaves, birds, trees) **How would you describe the plants?** (Possible answers: Some leaves are pointy while others are round; some plants have big leaves while others have small leaves.) Say: **Each of these things are created by God and can tell us something special about him. For example, the different beautiful flowers tell us that God gives us life and gives us a variety of beauty.** Ask: **What do the tall trees in the background tell us about God?** (Possible answer: remind us of his strength)

✝ **God's Creation**

Invite children to reflect on the artwork and to pray a silent prayer thanking God for all the gifts of nature, both large and small.

2 Connect

Have children turn to page 227 in their books. Read aloud the introduction and discuss the question.

📖 Invite a volunteer to read aloud God's Wonders. Ask: **How can we give glory to God for his creation?** (through prayer, taking care of his creation)

Invite a volunteer to read aloud Small Wonders. Ask: **What does the word wonders mean?** (Possible answers: something different, special) **What are other small wonders you may have noticed?** Discuss children's suggestions. Say: **All the wonderful things in nature, even the tiniest of wonders, reflect God's beauty. God must love us very much to have given us all these beautiful things.**

Take children outside to observe nature or provide a variety of natural objects, such as feathers, rocks, and pinecones. Read aloud I Spy a Small Natural Wonder. Give children time to draw their pictures. Invite children to display their drawings. Then play a game of I Spy. For example, say: **I spy something that is green and has three round leaves.** (a clover)

IF TIME ALLOWS

If time allows, complete one or more of the activities below.

Expression: Movement

Sprouts Tell children to imagine they are a tiny seed of God's love, having them curl their arms around their legs and bodies. In seed pose ask them to imagine the rain quenching their thirst as they begin to open their bodies, sprouting out of the nourishing soil toward the sun. Tell children to feel the warmth of the sun on their faces as they stretch their arms and bodies into the full, blooming expression of a flower in God's garden.

Time: 5 minutes
Materials: none

Expression: Art Studio

Your Own Garden Distribute watercolor paint and paper. Invite children to paint a garden scene of their own. Suggest that they include in their paintings both big and small wonders from God, and themselves in their garden, enjoying God's gifts. Remind children of our connection to the earth.

Time: 25 minutes
Materials: watercolor paint, paper

Expression: Using Imagination in Prayer

Praise of Wonders Invite children to close their eyes. Say: **Imagine you are walking through a field of flowers.** Ask: **What kind of flowers are they? What do you smell? What sounds do you hear?** Pause as children imagine their scene. Say: **Now take a moment to thank God for his gifts of nature.** Give children time to pray silently.

Time: 5 minutes
Materials: none

The full-scale version of this teaching instruction appears on the Art Print easel.

Finding God ❋ **Exploring Faith Through Art**

Elizabeth of Hungary

GRADE 3, UNIT 1, SESSION 2

Catechist Guide page 11

Faith Focus: We share God's love with others.

OUTCOMES

- ▸ Discuss how Saint Elizabeth devoted her life to sharing God's love for us.
- ▸ Discuss how God has given us the responsibility of caring for one another.
- ▸ Identify ways to spread God's love in our daily lives.

About the Artist   Marianne Stokes was born in 1855 in Austria. While painting at the art academy, she won a prize that allowed her to travel and study abroad. Stokes's early work focused largely on rustic scenes she saw around her. Later in her career, she focused on her spiritual life, and her paintings began to feature biblical scenes and characters.

Art·i·facts   *St. Elizabeth of Hungary Spinning Wool for the Poor* was painted in 1895. This painting was made using oil paints on canvas. Saint Elizabeth was the rich and privileged daughter of a king, but spent all her life helping those who were poor. She had a hospital built beneath her castle, so that she could aid those who were sick.

For your convenience, the Children's Book page is reproduced below.

 EXPLORE ART PRINT 2

Name _____   Date _____

Art Print 2 shows Saint Elizabeth spinning wool for people who were poor. How are you an instrument of God's love?

Sharing God's Love

Though her family was wealthy, Saint Elizabeth of Hungary lived a simple life. She devoted her life to feeding and clothing those who were poor. She started a hospital and cared for people who were sick. Elizabeth pleased God by sharing his love and by being kind to those in need.

> All love comes from God. God loves us so much that he sent his Son, Jesus, to give us life. We bring God's love to life in our world by loving one another.
>
> *adapted from 1 John 4:7–11*

Showing Your Love

In the space below, write one way that you could show your love for a friend.

_____

_____

_____

_____

_____

www.findinggod.com   Grade 3 • Unit 1 • Session 2

CATECHIST DIRECTIONS

MATERIALS
▸ *Elizabeth of Hungary* Art Print
▸ Children's Book page 228
▸ Map showing Hungary

TIME
🕐 10–30 minutes

① Begin

After completing page 11 in the Children's Book, display the Art Print.

Briefly introduce and discuss the artwork, using information from About the Artist and Artifacts. Ask: ***What are some things you notice in this painting?*** (Possible answers: the red robe, the halo, Saint Elizabeth spinning wool) Say: ***Saint Elizabeth is wearing rich-looking clothes. Her father was a king, yet she spent her time caring for people who were poor. Although the Elizabeth in the portrait appears young, she had the power and the courage to change her world because she believed she was an instrument of God's love.***

✝ *The Poor and Vulnerable*

Invite children to reflect on the artwork and to pray a silent prayer asking God to guide them in being instruments of his love.

② Connect

Have children turn to page 228 in their books. Read aloud the introduction and discuss the question.

Invite a volunteer to read aloud the first paragraph of Sharing God's Love. Ask: ***Where was Elizabeth from?*** (Hungary) Point out Hungary on a map. ***Elizabeth's family was wealthy. How did she help others?*** (started a hospital, cared for those who were sick, fed and clothed people who were poor)

📖 Invite a volunteer to read aloud the adaptation from John. Ask: ***From where does all love come?*** (God) ***How do we bring God's love to life?*** (by loving one another)

Read aloud Showing Your Love. Explain that although we know there are people in need everywhere, God wants us to begin our helping with the people already in our lives. Say: ***When we open our hearts to sharing, God will lead us to those who need us. We begin with small actions and words to spread God's love.*** Give children time to complete the activity. Invite volunteers to share their responses.

IF TIME ALLOWS

If time allows, complete one or more of the activities below.

Expression: Movement

Shine   Give children mirrors. Holding a flashlight, explain that the light from the flashlight is like God's love and that it is the source of light and love. Turn off the overhead lights and turn on the flashlight. Aim the beam at one child's mirror. Tell children to experiment with moving the light with the mirror, trying to direct the light toward another child's mirror to multiply the amount of light.

Say: ***We are like mirrors reflecting God's love. The more love we shine on others, the brighter the world can become.***

Time: 10 minutes
Materials: flashlight, mirrors

Expression: Art Studio

Portrait of a Child Helping   Distribute watercolor paint and art supplies. Ask children to consider the painting of Saint Elizabeth and to recall their helping idea from the Children's Page. Invite them to make a self-portrait featuring their ideas for sharing God's love.

Time: 20 minutes
Materials: watercolor paint, art supplies

Expression: Using Imagination in Prayer

Created to Be Together   Say: ***God does not want us to be alone. We have our families, our friends, and our Church. These communities help us feel God's love and also help us spread God's love. Now imagine a scene where you are helping someone feel God's presence by serving that person in some way.*** Give children a few moments to pray silently.

Time: 2 minutes
Materials: none

Finding God Exploring Faith Through Art

The Peace Offering

ART PRINT 3

GRADE 3, UNIT 1, SESSION 3

Catechist Guide page 17

Faith Focus: God calls us to care for others by forgiving one another.

OUTCOMES

▶ Explain that God wants us to care for one another and to live peacefully together.

▶ Discuss that God forgives us when we make mistakes and expects us to forgive others.

About the Artist Charles Haigh-Wood (1856–1927) lived in Bury, England. He was only 17 when he studied art at the Royal Academy in London. After receiving recognition for his work, he became an Academy member and traveled to Italy to study Renaissance masters, like Michelangelo and Leonardo da Vinci. When Haigh-Wood returned to England, he became famous and painted portraits in wealthy families' homes.

Art•i•facts *The Peace Offering* is a narrative piece—the picture tells a story. Haigh-Wood was famous for making paintings that inspired conversation with the stories they told. He usually painted women or families in their colorful, flowing outfits. Later in his career, he began to paint more casual, rustic scenes that recalled his childhood.

For your convenience, the Children's Book page is reproduced below.

EXPLORE ART PRINT 3

Name _____ Date _____

Art Print 3 shows two children making peace with each other. Have you ever had to say you were sorry to someone or forgive someone for hurting you?

Caring Friends

God wants us to care for others. There are many ways you can be a caring friend to those who need you. You can do this by thinking of their feelings. Listening to people can help you understand how they feel. Another way to care for people is to forgive them. God wants us to forgive others, just as he forgives us. In the Lord's Prayer, we ask God to forgive us as we forgive others. It takes love and strength to be able to forgive someone. That is why we are like Jesus when we forgive others.

What Would You Do?

Sometimes people do things that hurt us. Circle how you could show forgiveness in these situations.

1. Your little brother rode your new bike and fell. The chain on the bike came off.

   a. You tell him that he can never ride your bike again.

   b. You ask him if he is hurt and suggest you fix the bike together.

2. Your good friend went to the park with another friend and did not invite you. Later she told you she was sorry she did not include you.

   a. You tell her it is OK, and you invite both of them to play.

   b. You do not invite your friend the next time you do something special.

© LOYOLA PRESS.

www.findinggod.com   Grade 3 • Unit 1 • Session 3

CATECHIST DIRECTIONS

MATERIALS
▶ *The Peace Offering* Art Print
▶ Children's Book page 229

TIME
🕐 10–30 minutes

1 Begin

After completing page 17 in the Children's Book, display the Art Print.

Briefly introduce and discuss the artwork, using information from About the Artist and Artifacts. Ask: ***What do you see at the bottom of the painting?*** (a torn page from a book) ***What do you think happened?*** (Possible answer: The boy is offering an apple to the girl, so maybe he is apologizing for ripping the page.) ***What can you tell about the children's feelings by looking at the painting?*** (Possible answer: The boy probably feels bad, and the girl is upset.) ***Can you think of a time when you needed to apologize for something? How did it make you feel?*** Discuss children's comments.

Invite children to reflect on the artwork and to pray a silent prayer asking God for help in being open to forgiving others.

2 Connect

Have children turn to page 229 in their books. Read aloud the introduction and discuss the question.

Invite a volunteer to read aloud Caring Friends. Ask: ***How can we care for one another?*** (by thinking of others' feelings, listening to them, forgiving them) ***What do we ask for in the Lord's Prayer?*** (to forgive us as we forgive others)

Pray aloud the Lord's Prayer, calling attention to the lines that ask God to forgive us as we forgive others. Say: ***God wants us to know that we will always be loved, even when we sin. He wants us to love others even when we're angry or disappointed with them.*** Ask: ***Have you ever had an argument with someone you love? How did you feel? How did you work things out? How did you feel after you made up?*** Discuss children's comments.

Read aloud the directions for What Would You Do? Give children time to complete the activity. Discuss children's responses.

IF TIME ALLOWS

If time allows, complete one or more of the activities below.

Expression: Movement

Forgiving Others Explain that people listen to both our words and our actions. Point out that our apology is even more meaningful when we behave in a way that expresses our sorrow. One way we can do this is by exchanging a sign of peace, such as smiling, shaking hands, or hugging. Have small groups perform skits where one person makes a wrong choice, apologizes, and exchanges a sign of peace with the person who was hurt.

Time: 15 minutes
Materials: none

Expression: Art Studio

Love Means Forgiving Distribute art supplies. Give children time to reflect on a situation when they were hurt by someone and then how they felt when they made peace. Have children draw a line down the middle of a sheet of paper. On the left side, have them draw a picture showing how they felt when they were hurt. On the right side, have them draw how they felt when the problem was resolved.

Time: 20 minutes
Materials: art supplies

Expression: Using Imagination in Prayer

God's Forgiveness 🎵 Play music to set a meditative mood, such as instrumental music [*Finding God* Grade 3 CD 2, Tracks 17 and 18]. Have children put their heads down on their arms and think about any anger or sadness they may be holding in their hearts. Then have them silently ask God to take away those feelings. Say: ***Imagine feeling God's loving hands lifting away whatever heaviness you are feeling.*** Then invite children to feel their hearts being filled with God's joy.

Time: 10 minutes
Materials: CD player, instrumental music such as *Finding God* Grade 3 CD 2, Tracks 17 and 18

The full-scale version of this teaching instruction appears on the Art Print easel.

Names of Angels

GRADE 3, UNIT 1, SESSION 4

Catechist Guide page 23

Faith Focus: The names we use for Jesus reveal him to us.

OUTCOMES

▸ Review Jesus' various names and describe how they reveal him to us.

▸ Discuss the names of some of Jesus' followers.

▸ Discuss our individual names and understand their importance to God and the people who love us.

About the Artist Laura James was born in Brooklyn, New York. Her family came to the United States from Antigua, and much of her work reflects her Antiguan and African heritage. Although James was self-taught, her paintings now hang in museums all over the country, including the Metropolitan Museum of Art, the Art Institute of Chicago, and the Smithsonian.

Art·i·facts James's work is inspired by Christianity and Ethiopian folklore. Her figures are characterized by large, almond-shaped eyes and brightly colored garments. In this painting, which is an acrylic on canvas, the head is surrounded by the names of biblical angels, such as Michael and Raphael, as well as the names of angels from many countries and religious traditions.

For your convenience, the Children's Book page is reproduced below.

EXPLORE ART PRINT 4

Name _____ Date _____

Art Print 4 shows the names of different angels. What names are important to you? When you hear them, how do they make you feel?

A Name Is Special

Sometimes names can tell us about a person. We have many special names for Jesus. Each name tells us something different about him. *Jesus* means "God saves" us. Joseph knew that Jesus would also be called *Emmanuel*, which means "God is with us." The first disciples used *Christ*, which means "the anointed one."

Names of Jesus' Followers

Jesus' followers had special names too. Peter's name means "rock." That name fits him well because Peter was strong in his faith. John's name means "God is gracious." Matthew's name means "gift of God."

Our Names

Our names are special too. Some of us may be named after a saint or a family member. Do you know what your name means? Write about how your name was chosen and what it means.

_____
_____
_____
_____

Jesus
Sean
Joshua
Hannah
Katherine
Jacob
Elizabeth
Natalia
Santiago
Miguel
Andrew
Sarah
Ethan Rachel Isabella

www.findinggod.com

Grade 3 · Unit 1 · Session 4

CATECHIST DIRECTIONS

MATERIALS
▸ *Names of Angels* Art Print
▸ Children's Book page 230
▸ Baby name book

TIME
10–30 minutes

① Begin

After completing page 23 in the Children's Book, display the Art Print.

Briefly introduce and discuss the artwork, using information from About the Artist and Artifacts. Say: *Look at the angel in this painting and see if you can read the names around the angel's face.* Ask: *What names do you recognize in the painting?* (Possible answers: Mary, Michael, Raphael) Ask: *Which Mary do you think the artist is referring to?* (Possible answers: mother of Jesus, Mary Magdalene) *Who are Michael and Raphael?* (angels) Say: *An angel is a messenger from God. You may remember some Bible stories where angels bring news to God's people. What good news did the angel tell Joseph in a dream?* (that Mary would have a baby)

Invite children to reflect on the artwork and to pray a silent prayer thanking God for his special messengers.

② Connect

Have children turn to page 230 in their books. Read aloud the introduction and discuss the question.

Invite a volunteer to read aloud A Name Is Special. Ask: *What does Jesus' name mean?* (God saves.) *What does* **Emmanuel** *mean?* (God is with us.) *What does* **Christ** *mean?* (the anointed one)

Invite a volunteer to read aloud Names of Jesus' Followers. Ask: *What does Peter's name mean?* (rock) *What does John's name mean?* (God is gracious.) *What does Matthew's name mean?* (gift of God)

Read aloud Our Names. For those children who do not know the meaning of their names, provide a name book or look up their names on a baby name Web site. Give children time to find their names' meaning and write it. Invite volunteers to share the meanings with the group.

IF TIME ALLOWS

If time allows, complete one or more of the activities below.

Expression: Movement

Name Chain   Have children think of a positive quality that begins with the same letter as their first name, such as Hannah—happy, Kevin—kind, or Chloe—caring. Choose a child to stand and say his or her name and positive quality. Then invite another child to repeat what the first person said and then say his or her own name and positive quality. Have each child link arms with the children who already said their names. Continue until someone can't remember all the names and the chain is broken.

Time: 15 minutes
Materials: none

Expression: Art Studio

Angel Names   Provide children with white and blue construction paper and art supplies. Instruct them to draw a self-portrait, seeking inspiration from James's painting. Then have children mount their drawing on a sheet of blue construction paper and write their full name on the sheet. Ask them to write around their figure all the names to which they might answer, such as nicknames and names like *brother, daughter, niece,* or *friend.*

Time: 20 minutes
Materials: white and blue construction paper, art supplies

Expression: Using Imagination in Prayer

God Is with Us   Ask: *Do you remember which of Jesus' names means "God is with us"?* (Emmanuel) Say: *Now let's sit quietly with our eyes closed and think of a time that you were lonely or afraid. Then imagine that Jesus is there with you, filling you with love and courage, holding you safely in his strong hands. Silently repeat the name Emmanuel several times as you breathe in and out.* Give children a few moments to pray silently.

Time: 2 minutes
Materials: none

FindingGod **Exploring Faith Through Art**
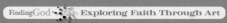

Eucharist

GRADE 3, UNIT 1, SESSION 5

Catechist Guide page 29

Faith Focus: Ordinary Time reminds us to be thankful for God's presence each day.

OUTCOMES

▸ Explain that God is present in our lives every day.

▸ Discuss how the Church community spreads God's love.

▸ Identify the ways we and our Church celebrate our relationship with God all through the year.

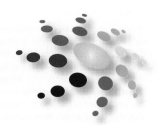

About the Artist American-born artist Julie Lonneman lives in Cincinnati, Ohio. She began her career as an art director and graphic designer. Now she works as an independent illustrator. Lonneman uses her artistic talents to explore social and spiritual themes. Her work is published regularly in books and magazines.

Art•i•facts *Eucharist* features a priest standing among members of the Church community. The picture incorporates the symbols of the celebration of the Eucharist. The Bread has become the Body of Christ. The Wine has become the Blood of Christ. The dove above the celebrant is a symbol of the presence of the Holy Spirit.

CATECHIST DIRECTIONS

MATERIALS
▸ *Eucharist* Art Print
▸ Children's Book page 231

TIME
🕐 10–30 minutes

1 Begin

After completing page 29 in the Children's Book, display the Art Print.

Briefly introduce and discuss the artwork, using information from About the Artist and Artifacts. Ask: **What are the two symbols of the Eucharist in the painting?** (the Bread and the Wine) Say: **Every Sunday during Mass, we acknowledge God's presence in our lives with the Celebration of the Eucharist. When we gather at Mass, we are surrounded by the Church community. The painting shows God's joyful Church community.**

Invite children to reflect on the artwork and to pray a silent prayer thanking God for the gifts of the Eucharist and our Church community.

2 Connect

Have children turn to page 231 in their books. Read aloud the introduction and discuss the question.

📖 Invite a volunteer to read aloud Rejoice and Be Glad. Ask: **When is God present to us?** (every day) Say: **During Ordinary Time we celebrate our Church community.** Ask: **What are some examples of what the Church provides to its members and surrounding community?** (Possible answers: support, love, prayer, friendship) **How does the Church community spread God's love?** (Possible answers: religious education classes, parish activities, parish bulletin, visiting those who are sick) Say: **We are called to live together as a community, so that we can help one another. We are instruments of God's love, and our job is to spread God's love and message.**

✝ Family and Community

Read aloud Give Thanks for Your Gifts and give children time to write. Say: **There are many wonderful occasions to celebrate, but every day is filled with the gift of God and his community, the Church. We will celebrate Ordinary Time by being aware and thankful for that gift.**

IF TIME ALLOWS

If time allows, complete one or more of the activities below.

Expression: Movement/Music

Celebration The painting shows a celebrant and church members standing in joyful celebration of the Eucharist. Say: **Let's raise our arms to rejoice and to be glad in this day that the Lord has made.** Have children stand and stretch their bodies, heads and arms, standing on tiptoe, as if reaching up to Heaven. 🎵 You may wish to accompany the movement exercise with a joyful music selection, such as "Here I Am, God" [*Finding God* Grade 3 CD 2, Track 5].

Time: 2 minutes
Materials: CD player, music such as "Here I Am, God" [*Finding God* Grade 3 CD 2, Track 5]

Expression: Art Studio

Collage of Hands Distribute art supplies. Remind children that during Ordinary Time we are called to appreciate everyday blessings, particularly the Church community. Ask children to trace one hand on a sheet of paper. Have them decorate it with symbols, words, and art representing the gifts they contribute to the community. Have them cut out the hands. Glue all the hands on a poster board to make a collage of helping hands. Label it *Our Church Community.*

Time: 20 minutes
Materials: art supplies, drawing paper, poster board

Expression: Using Imagination in Prayer

Thank You for My Church Invite children to imagine themselves working with others as one community to help a cause. Say: **When we each use our individual gifts, our gifts are greatly multiplied.** Have children prepare for prayer. Say: **God, thank you for my Church. Help me use my gifts to serve my Church family and all my community. Amen.**

Time: 10 minutes
Materials: none

For your convenience, the Children's Book page is reproduced below.

EXPLORE ART PRINT 5

Name _____ Date _____

Art Print 5 shows the presence of God in the Celebration of the Eucharist. Where do you see the presence of God in your life during Ordinary Time?

Rejoice and Be Glad

We know that God's love is present in our lives every day. We see God's gifts all around us and are thankful for our blessings. When we receive the Eucharist on the Lord's Day, we gather with other parish members together as a Church community.

> "This is the day the Lord has made:
> let us rejoice in it and be glad."
> *Psalms 118:24*

During Ordinary Time we celebrate the gift of our Church community. After Mass we show our care for our community by being more like Christ. We can help those in need in many ways. We also notice how our Church community helps us and others with the gift of caring.

Give Thanks for Your Gifts

Write a short prayer giving thanks for how your Church community helps you or someone else.

_____

_____

_____

_____

_____

www.findinggod.com   Grade 3 • Unit 1 • Session 5

The full-scale version of this teaching instruction appears on the Art Print easel.

FindingGod · Exploring Faith Through Art

Saint Benedict

GRADE 3, UNIT 2, SESSION 6

Catechist Guide page 35

Faith Focus: Saints Benedict and Scholastica spread God's love to others.

OUTCOMES

▸ Explain how Benedict's work was like a mustard seed.

▸ Discuss Benedict's rules.

▸ Define *monastery*.

About the Artist Amanda Hall is a British artist trained in graphic art and illustration. She combines crayon and watercolor paint, which she builds up, layer upon layer, to make vivid colors in her art. Her subjects include characters from myths, legends, and fairy tales. Her paintings tell stories about the history and cultures of many countries. Hall also writes children's books.

Art·i·facts The painting shows Benedict holding a raven that is believed to have saved his life. The legend says there was a priest in Italy who was jealous of Benedict's fame as a holy man, so he sent Benedict poisoned bread. The raven was Benedict's friend. It jumped up and down on the bread to warn him. Benedict understood and told the raven to dispose of the bread where no one would ever find it.

For your convenience, the Children's Book page is reproduced below.

EXPLORE ART PRINT 6

Name _____ Date _____

Art Print 6 shows Saint Benedict and his sister Saint Scholastica, both of whom served God's kingdom. How do you serve God's kingdom?

Saints Serve the Kingdom

Benedict founded a **monastery** in Monte Cassino, Italy. This monastery was a home for a group of men called monks who wanted to work and pray together. Some of Benedict's monks went on to start other monasteries. With her twin brother's guidance, Scholastica founded a convent five miles away. Benedict's work was like planting a mustard seed. The small seed of his monastery sprouted many branches.

The monks worked the land, prayed, and copied the Bible by hand. Benedict's motto was "pray and work." This motto was the beginning of several of Benedict's rules for the monastery. Benedict wrote rules for how the monks should live. Here are some of the monastery's rules:

▸ Seek Jesus' love above all else.
▸ Do not speak evil of others.
▸ Let a wise man stand at the gates of the monastery to greet visitors.
▸ A brother's clothing should be suited to the weather where he lives.

What's Your Motto?

Think of what your motto could be and write it here.

Did You Know?

The name *Benedict* means "blessed." A benediction is a blessing. The name *Scholastica* means "learned woman."

CATECHIST DIRECTIONS

MATERIALS
▸ *Saint Benedict* Art Print
▸ Children's Book page 232

TIME
10–30 minutes

① Begin

After completing page 35 in the Children's Book, display the Art Print.

Briefly introduce and discuss the artwork, using information from About the Artist and Artifacts.

Say: **Saints Scholastica and Benedict lived in Italy a long time ago. They were brother and sister as well as best friends.** Ask: **What is Scholastica holding in her hands?** (a dove) **What does a dove symbolize?** (the Holy Spirit) **What is Benedict holding in his hand?** (a raven) Say: **It has been said that the raven used to come to his window during dinner and once saved his life.** Ask: **What do you think the two buildings symbolize?** (Possible answer: the monastery and convent Benedict and Scholastica founded) Say: **Saints Benedict and Scholastica grew up to found monasteries and convents. They dedicated their lives to God.**

Invite children to reflect on the artwork and to pray a silent prayer and think how they, too, could spread God's love.

② Connect

Have children turn to page 232 in their books. Read aloud the introduction and discuss the question.

Invite a volunteer to read aloud the first paragraph of Saints Serve the Kingdom. Point out the vocabulary word *monastery*. Ask: **What is a monastery?** (a place where a group of men called monks work and pray together) Say: **Under Saint Benedict's direction, his twin sister founded a convent, and from their followers sprang many more monasteries and convents, as well as schools that spread the Catholic faith.** Ask: **Why was Saint Benedict's work like planting a mustard seed?** (Possible answer: The small seed of his monastery sprouted many branches.) **Who are other people whose relationships with God helped spread God's love?** (Possible answers: Jesus, disciples, priests, teachers, parents, or other family members)

Invite a volunteer to read aloud the remaining paragraph and Benedict's rules. Ask: **What was Benedict's motto?** (pray and work)

Read aloud the directions for What's Your Motto? and give children time to think what their personal motto might be. Invite volunteers to share.

Did You Know?

Ask a volunteer to read aloud this section. Say: **Benedictions, or blessings, are signs, or sacramentals, of God's love reaching us through the actions of the Church.** Ask: **What is a sacramental?** (an object, a prayer, or a blessing given by the Church to help us grow in our spiritual life) **What are some sacramentals?** (Possible answers: rosary, cross, picture of Mary or the saints, holy water)

IF TIME ALLOWS

If time allows, complete one or more of the activities below.

Expression: Movement

Spreading God's Love Remind children that Saint Benedict's work was like a mustard seed and that it sprouted many branches. Tell children that the actions of the Church community sprout and grow through the Church and that its members are like branches. Ask children to suggest activities that spread love, generosity, faith, or sharing. Ask volunteers to pantomime the activities as the group guesses.

Time: 15 minutes
Materials: none

Expression: Art Studio

Clay Tell children to imagine they have an animal friend, like Saint Benedict's raven, who could watch over them and warn them of danger. Distribute clay for children to sculpt their animal. Encourage children to think of a story in which their animal helps them and share it with the group when they display their sculpture.

Time: 15 minutes
Materials: clay

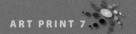

FindingGod ·:·:· Exploring Faith Through Art

Young Christian Girl

ART PRINT 7

GRADE 3, UNIT 2, SESSION 7

Catechist Guide page 41

Faith Focus: Jesus calls us to be closer to God and to show our love for others.

OUTCOMES

▸ Review that God gave us the Ten Commandments to help us live peacefully together.

▸ Discuss ways to show our love of God and our neighbor.

About the Artist Paul Gauguin was born in 1848 and lived in Paris, France. His parents were both writers. Gauguin was in the navy and also worked for a bank. It was after he saw his first exhibit of Impressionist art that he decided to become a painter. After painting in the Impressionist style, his work evolved into a new artistic style that showed concepts difficult to visualize, like beliefs, thoughts, and emotions.

Art·i·facts Artists of the Impressionist tradition painted mostly outdoor scenes, as you can see in Gauguin's subject. The girl in the painting stands with downcast eyes and folded hands. Her hands clasped together at her heart display an ancient and multicultural symbol of respect, love, and prayer.

For your convenience, the Children's Book page is reproduced below.

EXPLORE ART PRINT **7**

Name _____ Date _____

Art Print 7 shows a girl quietly praying outside. When do you make time to pray and speak with God?

Showing Our Love

Praying often is one way to become closer to God. When we show love to others, we show our love of God and our neighbor. God gave Moses the Ten Commandments to teach us how to love God and one another. Through the commandments we can become closer to God. We should also keep an open heart and always be ready to help our neighbor.

Paying Attention

Consider the following situations. Circle the letter of the action that helps you become closer to God.

1. You are playing baseball with your friends. A girl you do not know comes up to the group and asks if she can play. You should

   a. ignore her and keep playing.

   b. tell her that she can take your turn.

   c. say, "Maybe next time."

2. At school it is finally lunchtime. You notice that a boy at the next table is sitting quietly with no food. You should

   a. tease him about forgetting his lunch.

   b. tell your friends, "He must have the worst parents in the world!"

   c. offer him some of your lunch.

📖 **Reading God's Word**

For where your treasure is, there also will your heart be.

Matthew 6:21

www.findinggod.com
Grade 3 • Unit 2 • Session 7

CATECHIST DIRECTIONS

MATERIALS
▸ *Young Christian Girl* Art Print
▸ Children's Book page 233

TIME
🕐 10–30 minutes

① Begin

After completing page 41 in the Children's Book, display the Art Print.

Briefly introduce and discuss the artwork, using information from About the Artist and Artifacts. Ask: ***What is the girl in the picture doing?*** (praying) ***How do you know?*** (She has her hands together and seems like she's thinking.) ***Where did she choose to pray?*** (outside) Say: ***Following the Ten Commandments helps us stay close to God. There are also many places and times that we can feel close to God.*** Share some of your own examples. Ask: ***Where are some places or times that you've felt close to God?***

Invite children to reflect on the artwork and to pray a silent prayer, encouraging them to discuss with God anything that is on their mind.

② Connect

Have children turn to page 233 in their books. Read aloud the introduction and discuss the question.

Read aloud the first paragraph of Showing Our Love. Ask: ***What are some ways we show our love of God and our neighbor?*** (Possible answers: follow the Ten Commandments, pray often, keep an open heart, be ready to help) Say: ***When we are close to God, we show our faith by our actions.*** Encourage children to name some ways that faith is shown through actions.

Read aloud the directions for Paying Attention and invite a volunteer to read aloud each situation. Have children consider the situations and circle their answer.

📖 **Reading God's Word**

Read aloud this feature from the New Testament. Say: ***Take a moment to think of people and things you treasure most.*** Pause. Say: ***Where those things are is where your heart, or love, will also be. If you share your treasure with others, your love will spread to others as well.***

IF TIME ALLOWS

If time allows, complete one or more of the activities below.

Expression: Music

Prayer in Music 🎵 Play four song samples, one for each type of prayer: petition, such as "Here I Am, God" [*Finding God* Grade 3 CD 2, Track 5]; forgiveness, such as "Peace Walk" [*Finding God* Grade 3 CD 2, Track 13]; adoration, such as "All You Works of God" [*Finding God* Grade 3 CD 2, Track 3]; and thanks, such as "Song of Love" [*Finding God* Grade 3 CD 2, Track 1]. Have children guess which kind of song it is based on the lyrics.

Time: 15 minutes
Materials: CD player, music such as "Here I Am, God" [*Finding God* Grade 3 CD 2, Track 5]; "Peace Walk" [*Finding God* Grade 3 CD 2, Track 13]; "All You Works of God" [*Finding God* Grade 3 CD 2, Track 3]; "Song of Love" [*Finding God* Grade 3 CD 2, Track 1]

Expression: Art Studio

Good Friend Invite children to think when and where they like to pray. Distribute paper and art supplies for children to draw a scene of where it is they like best to pray.

Time: 20 minutes
Materials: drawing paper, art supplies

The full-scale version of this teaching instruction appears on the Art Print easel.

FindingGod • **Exploring Faith Through Art**

Acts of the Apostles

GRADE 3, UNIT 2, SESSION 8

Catechist Guide page 47

Faith Focus: Jesus invites us to proclaim the Kingdom of God.

OUTCOMES

▸ Discuss the mission that Jesus gave the apostles and the disciples.

▸ Examine the relationships that help us do God's work.

▸ Define *mission*.

About the Artist Raphael (Raffaello Sanzio of Urbino) was a Renaissance artist born in Italy in 1483. He was trained by his father, who was also a painter. He traveled and studied art with Leonardo da Vinci and Michelangelo. In addition to a vast number of paintings, Raphael became a skilled architect. He worked for the Vatican for 12 years and made artwork for many palaces, mansions, and churches.

Art·i·facts *The Acts of the Apostles* is a tapestry, in which colorful woven threads make an image. Many tapestries designed in the Renaissance era decorate the walls of palaces and churches. In addition to being decorative, tapestries provided insulation for big, unheated rooms, giving them some protection from drafts. This tapestry was one in a series of ten, depicting events from the Acts of the Apostles. The tapestries were commissioned by Pope Leo X to hang in the Sistine Chapel.

For your convenience, the Children's Book page is reproduced below.

EXPLORE ART PRINT 8

Name _____ Date _____

Art Print 8 shows the apostles and the disciples spreading God's Word. What is one way that you serve Jesus?

Proclaiming the Kingdom

Jesus knew he needed help spreading God's Word. He chose Peter, the other apostles, and the followers called disciples to help with his work. Jesus' apostles and disciples accepted the **mission** that Jesus gave them to proclaim God's kingdom.

Jesus depended on his friends to help him do the job God gave him. We can work together with our friends to help answer Jesus' call.

Lean on Me

Think of jobs you have at school or home. Describe a time when you depended on a friend for help.

_____
_____
_____

Describe a time when you depended on Jesus for help.

_____
_____
_____

Did You Know?

Jesus chose 12 apostles to lead the Church. The pope and bishops of the Catholic Church continue the apostles' mission today.

CATECHIST DIRECTIONS

MATERIALS
▸ *Acts of the Apostles* Art Print
▸ Children's Book page 234

TIME
10–30 minutes

① Begin

After completing page 47 in the Children's Book, display the Art Print.

Briefly introduce and discuss the artwork, using information from About the Artist and Artifacts. Ask: **What do you think is happening in this artwork?** (Possible answer: Peter and the other apostles are preaching to a group of people.) Say: **After the coming of the Holy Spirit** [Acts of the Apostles 2:1–4], **the first apostles and disciples went out to proclaim to all people that Jesus Christ had brought Salvation to all. There were a lot of people attracted by the loud noise of the wind when the Spirit descended on the apostles and disciples. Peter stood up and told the people what Jesus had done for them, and said, "Repent and be baptized, everyone of you, in the name of Jesus Christ . . ."**

Invite children to reflect on the artwork and to pray a silent prayer asking Jesus to help his followers answer his call.

② Connect

Have children turn to page 234 in their books. Read aloud the introduction and discuss the question.

Invite a volunteer to read aloud the first paragraph of Proclaiming the Kingdom. Call children's attention to the vocabulary word *mission*. Ask: **What does the word mission mean?** (a task, a project) **What does proclaim mean?** (to announce publicly) **Whom did Jesus choose to proclaim God's kingdom?** (Peter, the other apostles, and the disciples)

Read aloud the next paragraph. Say: **Even Jesus needed friends to help him with his work.** Ask: **Who helps do Jesus' work now?** (Possible answers: priests, nuns, family members, deacons) Say: **Anyone who continues Jesus' work is a disciple, and all of us can be disciples by proclaiming God's message and by doing good deeds to serve the Kingdom of God.**

Invite children to read Lean on Me silently and to write their descriptions. Encourage children to share their responses.

Did You Know?

Ask a volunteer to read aloud this section. Say: **The pope is the head of the Church. He follows in Saint Peter's footsteps.**

IF TIME ALLOWS

If time allows, complete one or more of the activities below.

Expression: Movement

Fishing with Jesus Tie a string to a broom handle and attach a magnet to the end of the string, fashioning a fishing pole. Write on note cards actions that tell how to be a good disciple, such as *tell the truth, be helpful,* or *speak kind words*. Attach a paper clip to each card. Then lay the cards on the floor and have children take turns fishing for them. Suggest that children place their card somewhere they can see it to remind them how to be a good disciple and to help Jesus carry on his work.

Time: 20 minutes
Materials: broom handle, string, magnet, note cards, paper clips

Expression: Art Studio

Jesus' Friends Distribute drawing paper and art supplies. Have children draw a picture of a present-day disciple. Explain that they may choose to draw a picture of a priest, teacher, catechist, or godparent, or they might draw themselves since they are also followers of Jesus Christ. Have them write a sentence or two explaining how the person in the picture is a disciple.

Time: 20 minutes
Materials: drawing paper, art supplies

FindingGod · **Exploring Faith Through Art**

Saint Paul the Apostle

ART PRINT 9

GRADE 3, UNIT 2, SESSION 9

Catechist Guide page 53

Faith Focus: Like Saint Paul, we can spread God's message to help others believe and be saved.

OUTCOMES

▸ Discuss Saint Paul's role in continuing Jesus' work.

▸ Explain that Jesus died to share God's message with us.

About the Artist Francesco Fracanzano was born in 1612 and lived in Italy his entire life. When he was 10 years old, Fracanzano and his brother, Cesare, worked as apprentices for Jusepe de Ribera, a respected Spanish painter. Fracanzano married Giovanna Rosa when he was 20 and continued to paint until the end of his life.

Art·i·facts This painting features Saint Paul holding the epistles that he wrote and the sword with which he was executed. The painting shows a style called *chiaroscuro*, which means a "dramatic play of light against dark." The painter Caravaggio popularized *chiaroscuro* beginning in 1584.

For your convenience, the Children's Book page is reproduced below.

EXPLORE ART PRINT 9

Name _____ Date _____

Art Print 9 shows Saint Paul with his letters that helped spread God's Word. How do you spread God's Word to others?

Remember My Message

Saint Paul wrote a letter to his friends in Corinth. He was worried that they had forgotten what he had told them about Jesus' Death and Resurrection. This is what Paul wrote, so that the people in Corinth would believe and be saved.

> Friends,
>
> Remember the Gospel I preached to you. If you believe this message, you will be saved. Jesus Christ died for our sins, as the Scriptures say. He was buried. He was raised from the dead three days later. He then appeared to Peter and the apostles.
>
> *adapted from 1 Corinthians 15:1–5*

God sent Jesus to teach his people how to follow him. Jesus died to show how much God loves us. He would do anything to help us know and love God.

What Would You Say?

Imagine you were Saint Paul. What would you want the people in Corinth to know about Jesus? Write one idea on the lines.

_____

_____

© Loyola Press.

CATECHIST DIRECTIONS

MATERIALS

▸ *Saint Paul the Apostle* Art Print

▸ Children's Book page 235

TIME

🕐 10–30 minutes

1 Begin

After completing page 53 in the Children's Book, display the Art Print.

Briefly introduce and discuss the artwork using information from About the Artist and Artifacts.
Say: ***Describe what you see in this painting.*** (Saint Paul is wearing a red robe; he is barefoot; he is holding a book and a sword.)
Say: ***Saint Paul died for doing the work of the Church, which he believed in. Many paintings of Saint Paul show him holding the sword that symbolizes his death.***

Invite children to reflect on the artwork and to pray a silent prayer asking God to guide them in spreading his message.

2 Connect

Have children turn to page 235 in their books. Read aloud the introduction and discuss the question.

Invite a volunteer to read aloud the first paragraph of Remember My Message. Locate Corinth on a world map you may have in the room. It is in Greece near Athens. Ask: ***What was Saint Paul worried about?*** (that people had forgotten what he had told them about Jesus' Death and Resurrection)
Say: ***Paul wrote this letter to his friends in Corinth because he wanted to remind them of Jesus' Death and Resurrection.***

📖 Invite a volunteer to read aloud the letter from Paul. Ask: ***What is the name of the mystery that Paul is referring to?*** (the Paschal Mystery) ***What was the most important part of Paul's message?*** (Christ died for our sins and three days later rose from the dead. If we believe this, we will be saved.)

Read aloud the paragraph below Paul's letter. Ask: ***Why did Jesus die?*** (because he loved us and wanted us to know and love God)

Invite a volunteer to read aloud the directions for What Would You Say? Give children time to complete the activity. Invite volunteers to share their ideas.

IF TIME ALLOWS

If time allows, complete one or more of the activities below.

Expression: Music

Jesus' Song of Love 🎵 Play a musical piece about Jesus' love, such as "Song of Love" [*Finding God* Grade 3 CD 2, Track 1]. Invite children to sing along. Play the piece again and encourage children to sketch how they feel about Jesus' love as they listen. Have children share their sketches after the song ends.

Time: 10 minutes
Materials: CD player, music such as "Song of Love" [*Finding God* Grade 3 CD 2, Track 1], paper, pencils

Expression: Art Studio

Maps of Paul's Travels Provide children with brown paper bags. Invite children to draw maps showing Paul's travels. Provide a map and give children time to review other maps online for reference. When children are done with their drawing, have them crumple the bag to give an "ancient" look to make the map look authentic.

Time: 20 minutes
Materials: brown paper bags, crayons, maps

Expression: Using Imagination in Prayer

Remember Jesus Is Always with Us Say: ***Saint Paul's Letter to the Corinthians was meant to remind the Church that Jesus' love would continue to be with us after his Death.*** Have children close their eyes. Say: ***Imagine yourself with Jesus. Share with him how you feel about being with him right now. Tell him that you will continue his work by helping others.*** Give children time to be alone with Jesus and then end the session by praying *Amen.*

Time: 10 minutes
Materials: none

The full-scale version of this teaching instruction appears on the Art Print easel.

FindingGod ❄ **Exploring Faith Through Art**

Prepare for Christmas

GRADE 3, UNIT 2, SESSION 10

Catechist Guide page 59

Faith Focus: Advent is a time to prepare for the celebration of Jesus' birth.

OUTCOMES

► Identify Advent as a time to prepare to celebrate Christmas.

► Discuss ways we celebrate during Advent.

About the Artist Little is known about Russian artist Sergey Vasilievich Dosekin. This may be because *Preparation for Christmas* was his only well-known painting. It is also possible that artist records during his lifetime were not kept or became lost when the Russian Revolution broke out in 1917, after Dosekin's death. We do know that art and industry experienced a surge of success during Dosekin's life. It culminated in 1896 with the All-Russia Exhibition, where Russian intellectuals displayed their work.

Art·i·facts *Preparation for Christmas* is oil on canvas. Usually an artist begins an oil painting by sketching the subject in charcoal or pencil first, then following with paint. Oil paints were used in Asia more than 1,000 years ago. Color pigments mixed with oil made a glossy, vivid finish to paint with. Oil paint became more popular from the 10th to 15th centuries as their use spread to the West. This medium has been widely used ever since.

CATECHIST DIRECTIONS

MATERIALS
► Prepare for Christmas Art Print
► Children's Book page 236
► Art supplies

TIME
🕐 10–30 minutes

① Begin

After completing page 59 in the Children's Book, display the Art Print.

Briefly introduce and discuss the artwork, using information from About the Artist and Artifacts. Ask: **What are these people doing?** (getting their house ready for Christmas) **How are they preparing?** (making decorations) **What do you see them using?** (paints, paper, glitter) Say: **We also prepare our homes for Christmas. More importantly, we prepare our hearts. The most important Advent preparation is strengthening our relationship with God.** Ask: **When you want to improve your relationship with your friends or family, what do you do?** (Possible answers: resolve misunderstandings, spend time together, talk, listen) Say: **To improve our relationship with God, those same things are important. We resolve misunderstandings through the Sacrament of Penance and Reconciliation. We spend time with God by praying and attending Mass.**

Invite children to reflect on the artwork and to pray a silent prayer asking God to help prepare their hearts for the celebration of Jesus' birth.

② Connect

Have children turn to page 236 in their books. Read aloud the introduction and discuss the question.

Read aloud Celebrating Advent. Ask: **What does Advent prepare us for?** (the anniversary of Jesus' birth, Christmas) **What is our prayer during the season of Advent?** (We pray that Jesus' love will grow in us in a more complete way.)

Invite a volunteer to read aloud Family Traditions. Give children time to reflect on their family traditions. Invite children to share their drawings. Say: **While we wait for the anniversary of Jesus' birth, we work to fill our hearts and actions with God's love.**

IF TIME ALLOWS

If time allows, complete one or more of the activities below.

Expression: Movement

Advent Game Play a version of the concentration game "I'm going on a trip." Have children sit in a circle. Say: **I'm preparing myself during Advent and I'm going to . . .** (Possible answers: celebrate the Sacrament of Reconciliation; make an Advent wreath; receive the Eucharist; pray; be kind to others; go to church; pray the Rosary) Have each child stand and say, "I'm preparing myself during Advent," repeating the preparations chosen by the students that preceded him or her, and adding a preparation of his or her own. After children say their turn, they sit down. Then invite children to pair up and act out one of the preparations mentioned. Have pairs present to the group to guess which one is being acted out.

Time: 10 minutes
Materials: none

Expression: Art Studio

Christmas Ornaments Distribute art supplies. Invite children to think about the ornaments that they place on their tree at home. Have children draw a picture of it and cut it out. Provide a large green cutout tree and invite children to tape their ornament to it.

Time: 20 minutes
Materials: art supplies, glitter, tape, green cutout tree

Expression: Using Imagination in Prayer

Prepare During Advent Ask children to imagine they are with their family preparing their home during Advent. Say: **We can say a prayer of thanks for Advent.** Pray: **Dear Jesus, help me get my house and my heart ready to receive you. I will remember that Christmas is the celebration of your birth, and I will use Advent as a time to be closer to you through prayer, Mass, and the sacraments.** Conclude by praying the Sign of the Cross together.

Time: 10 minutes
Materials: none

For your convenience, the Children's Book page is reproduced below.

EXPLORE ART PRINT **10**

Name _____ Date _____

Art Print 10 shows a family preparing for the celebration of Jesus' birth. What is something you do to prepare during Advent?

Celebrating Advent

Advent begins four weeks before Christmas. During the season we prepare to celebrate the anniversary of Jesus' birth. In the season of Advent, we thoughtfully await Christmas. We pray that Jesus' love will grow in us in a more complete way.

Family Traditions

During Advent your family might have special traditions to prepare for Christmas. For example, you may decorate a Christmas tree. Think of one family tradition that you like to celebrate during Advent. It might take place in your home, outside, in your community, or in your church. Draw your tradition in the box. Then complete the sentence below the picture.

One Advent tradition that helps my family prepare for the birth of Jesus is _____
_____.

www.findinggod.com   Grade 3 · Unit 2 · Session 10

FindingGod · Exploring Faith Through Art

The Doves III

GRADE 3, UNIT 3, SESSION 11

Catechist Guide page 65

Faith Focus: Jesus sends the Holy Spirit to be with us and to guide us.

OUTCOMES

▶ Explain that the Holy Spirit inspires and guides us to do Jesus' work.

▶ Explain that the Holy Spirit is present in our lives.

About the Artist Steve Easby was born in Derby, England, in 1958. His father was an artist, and his mother was a musician. His love of painting began at age four. He studied at St. Helen's College of Art and Design. Despite pressure to experiment with new subjects and techniques, he has committed himself to beautifully rendering his favorite subjects: gardens.

Art·i·facts Doves began to be a religious symbol in art because of the story of Noah's Ark. While Noah and the animals were on the ark, God flooded the earth. When the rains stopped, Noah sent a dove to see if the water had begun to recede. The dove returned with an olive branch, so Noah knew there was dry land. At Jesus' baptism the Holy Spirit descends in the form like that of a dove. In Catholic Tradition lilies represent Jesus' Resurrection. Both doves and lilies are used in this painting.

For your convenience, the Children's Book page is reproduced below.

EXPLORE ART PRINT 11

Name _____ Date _____

Art Print 11 shows doves, which represent the presence of the Holy Spirit. How do you feel the Holy Spirit's presence in your life?

The Holy Spirit Is with Us

Jesus sent the Holy Spirit to be with us and to guide us. The Holy Spirit helps us live prayerful lives and guides us on the journey to Heaven.

Finish the sentence to show how you can be a witness to Jesus Christ.

I can be a witness to Jesus Christ when I _____

_____

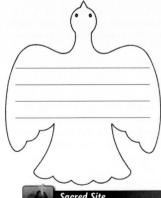

Doves

The dove has been a religious symbol in art for more than 1,000 years. Its appearance can indicate peace, hope, forgiveness, inspiration, and the presence of the Holy Spirit. On the lines in the dove, write about a time in your life when you needed the Holy Spirit.

Sacred Site

Katharine Drexel was inspired by the Holy Spirit to dedicate her life to Jesus. She gave her fortune to help others. She is remembered at the Shrine of Saint Katharine Drexel in Bensalem, Pennsylvania. It is also the motherhouse of the Sisters of the Blessed Sacrament, the order that she began.

www.findinggod.com   Grade 3 · Unit 3 · Session 11

CATECHIST DIRECTIONS

MATERIALS
▶ *The Doves III* Art Print
▶ Children's Book page 237

TIME
🕐 10–30 minutes

1 *Begin*

After completing page 65 in the Children's Book, display the Art Print.

Briefly introduce and discuss the artwork, using information from About the Artist and Artifacts. Ask: *What kind of flowers are these?* (lilies) *What objects seem similar?* (the doves and the lilies) *What is interesting to you about the work?* (Possible answer: The lilies appear to have taken flight as doves.) Explain that the artist's use of doves in his painting suggests the presence of the Holy Spirit. Say: *Sometimes we feel closest to God and the Holy Spirit when we are with God's wonderful creations in nature.*

Invite children to reflect on the artwork and to pray a silent prayer thanking God for something that has filled them with wonder, such as the ocean, a tall tree, a beautiful sunset, or a bird's nest.

2 *Connect*

Have children turn to page 237 in their books. Read aloud the introduction and discuss the question.

Ask a volunteer to read aloud The Holy Spirit Is with Us. Ask: *Why did Jesus send the Holy Spirit to us?* (to be with us and to guide us) *What does the Holy Spirit help us do?* (to live prayerful lives and to guide us on our journey to Heaven) Give children time to complete the sentence.

Read aloud Doves. Ask: *What does a dove remind us of?* (peace, hope, forgiveness, inspiration, the presence of the Holy Spirit) Then give children time to write about their experiences. Invite volunteers to share what they have written.

Sacred Site

Read aloud this feature. Say: *A shrine is a place that is set aside for people to visit because it is associated with a special person or event. A shrine can be any special place that brings us closer to God. The shrine of Saint Katharine is also the motherhouse, or main home, of the Sisters of the Blessed Sacrament.*

IF TIME ALLOWS

If time allows, complete one or more of the activities below.

Expression: Movement

I Spy the Holy Spirit Remind children that doves are often used to represent the Holy Spirit. Before going on a walking tour around the block or in the playground, hide several doves made out of white paper, on your route. Give children a few moments to see if they can find the hidden doves. Remind children that the Holy Spirit is always with us.

Time: 20 minutes
Materials: doves made out of white paper

Expression: Art Studio

Design a Shrine Explain that a shrine does not have to be a famous place like Saint Katharine's shrine. Tell children that it can be any place where we go to feel closer to God: in the woods, in our yards, in our bedrooms, or in our church. Distribute art supplies, drawing paper, and pencils, and have children draw a picture of a place where they feel close to God. Have them write a sentence describing what makes the site sacred to them.

Time: 15 minutes
Materials: drawing paper, pencils, art supplies

The full-scale version of this teaching instruction appears on the Art Print easel.

FindingGod • Exploring Faith Through Art

Saint Peter

GRADE 3, UNIT 3, SESSION 12

Catechist Guide page 71

Faith Focus: Jesus chose Peter to be the rock on which to build the Church.

OUTCOMES

▸ Explain Saint Peter's role as our Church's first pope.

▸ Discuss symbols that represent Saint Peter.

About the Artist Lucas Cranach the Elder (1472–1553) was a painter named for Kronach, the town in Germany where he was born. He moved to Vienna and painted portraits of the people he met there. Later he began an artist's workshop in Wittenburg, Germany, and enjoyed success. He had many Catholic patrons for whom he painted biblical themes.

Art•i•facts In this painting Saint Peter is holding the key to Heaven. The key symbolizes three things from Peter's relationship with Jesus: new life, authority, and the house of God. There are rocks at his feet. Keys and rocks are often used to represent Saint Peter. This painting was done using oil paint on a wooden panel.

For your convenience, the Children's Book page is reproduced below.

EXPLORE ART PRINT 12

Name _____ Date _____

Art Print 12 shows Saint Peter, the apostle whom Jesus chose to lead the Church. What qualities do you look for in a leader?

Peter and the Church

Peter became the first pope of the Catholic Church.

> Peter said he believed Jesus was the Messiah. Jesus replied, "Peter, you are the rock upon which I will build my Church. Even death will not destroy it. I will give you the keys to the Kingdom of Heaven."
>
> *adapted from Matthew 16:18–19*

Symbols of Peter

Rocks and keys are symbols of Peter. What do you think of when you see a rock? What do keys make you think of? Write your ideas on the lines. Then write about why these things are symbols of Peter.

A rock makes me think of _____

_____

_____

Keys make me think of _____

_____

_____

Rocks and keys are symbols of Peter because

_____

_____

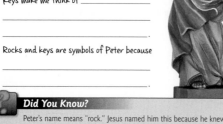

? Did You Know?

Peter's name means "rock." Jesus named him this because he knew Peter would be a strong foundation for the Church.

www.findinggod.com   Grade 3 · Unit 3 · Session 12

CATECHIST DIRECTIONS

MATERIALS
▸ *Saint Peter* Art Print
▸ Children's Book page 238

TIME
🕐 10–30 minutes

1 Begin

After completing page 71 in the Children's Book, display the Art Print.

Briefly introduce and discuss the artwork, using information from About the Artist and Artifacts. Say: **This is a painting of Saint Peter.** Ask: **What do you know about him?** (Possible answers: He was an apostle; Jesus chose him and the other apostles to lead the Church; he was the Church's first pope.) **What objects do you see in this painting?** (a key, a book, rocks) Say: **The book is the Gospels. The Gospels are the story of Jesus' life, Death, and Resurrection. It is the story upon which we build our faith. The artist placed the key and the rocks in the painting because they are often used as symbols for Saint Peter. We're going to talk about Saint Peter and these symbols today.**

Invite children to reflect on the artwork and to pray a silent prayer thanking God for people who help us grow in our faith.

2 Connect

Have children turn to page 238 in their books. Read aloud the introduction and discuss the question.

📖 Read aloud Peter and the Church. Ask: **To what object did Jesus compare Peter?** (a rock) **What will Jesus give Peter?** (keys to the Kingdom of Heaven) **Jesus told Peter he was the rock on which Jesus would build his Church and that Jesus would give Peter the keys to the Kingdom of Heaven.**

Read aloud Symbols of Peter. Give children time to complete the sentences on the page. Then ask volunteers to share their ideas about rocks and keys. Invite volunteers to share the last sentences. Say: **A rock is a symbol of strength, of something solid. A rock is very hard to break apart or destroy. Jesus wants to build the Church upon Peter's strength, and the keys represent how Jesus is giving Peter the authority over the Church and to Heaven.**

? Did You Know?

Invite a volunteer to read aloud this feature. Say: **When we look at a rock, we can think of how Jesus chose Peter to be the foundation on which to build the Church.**

IF TIME ALLOWS

If time allows, complete one or more of the activities below.

Expression: Movement

Building a Church   Provide building blocks, either large cardboard or small wooden ones, and a large square of cardboard or wood for a foundation. Invite children to build a church by each taking a turn placing one block at a time, using the foundation. Say: **This foundation is like Peter, and we can build upon this foundation. We can contribute to the Church when we are active in the Church community.**

Time: 15 minutes
Materials: building blocks, cardboard or wood

Expression: Art Studio

Key to Heaven   Show children different kinds of keys, such as standard house and car keys and more ornate keys like the one in the Art Print of Saint Peter. Give children modeling clay that hardens. Ask them to model a key. Insert a pencil while the clay is still moist so that later children can pull string through to hang the key. Tell children that when the clay is dry, they can keep the key as a symbol of their faith.

Time: 20 minutes
Materials: keys, modeling clay that hardens, pencils, string

Finding God ✦ Exploring Faith Through Art

The Centurion Kneeling ART PRINT 13

GRADE 3, UNIT 3, SESSION 13

Catechist Guide page 77

Faith Focus: Jesus Christ reaches out to all people.

OUTCOMES

▸ Explain that Jesus works through us to reach all people.

▸ Discuss that God hears our prayers and that we are worthy of his love.

About the Artist Joseph-Marie Vien the Elder (1716–1809) was born in Montpellier, France. As a boy he won an art prize that allowed him to study painting in Italy. He felt that his style was not well received there and returned to work in Paris. He taught and inspired many important painters. One of his most famous students was Jacques-Louis David.

Art·i·facts This painting tells the story of Jesus healing the soldier's servant. Jesus reaches his hand out to the soldier, but the soldier tells Jesus he is unworthy. The servant is not present in the painting because the story states that Jesus was able to cure him with his loving power from a distance.

CATECHIST DIRECTIONS

MATERIALS
▸ *The Centurion Kneeling* Art Print
▸ Children's Book page 239
▸ CD player
▸ *Finding God* Grade 3 CD 1, Track 3

TIME
🕐 10–30 minutes

1 Begin

After completing page 77 in the Children's Book, display the Art Print.

Briefly introduce and discuss the artwork, using information from About the Artist and Artifacts. Ask: **Which person in the painting is Jesus?** (the man with the blue cloak) **How can you tell?** (He has a halo.) **Where is the servant?** (He is not in the painting.) **Why is the servant not in the painting?** (He is too sick to leave his bed.) Say: **Today we will read the story of how Jesus healed the servant and learn how Jesus' mission was to serve all people.**

Invite children to reflect on the artwork and to pray a silent prayer asking the Holy Spirit to guide them in growing their faith.

2 Connect

Have children turn to page 239 in their books. Read aloud the introduction and discuss the question.

📖 Invite volunteers to read Jesus and the Roman Officer except for the last paragraph. Ask: **Did the officer know Jesus?** (No.) **Why did Jesus heal the man's servant?** (He was impressed by the man's faith, and he wanted to show that his mission was to all people.) Say: **The officer knew that he could order his soldiers to do something far away. In the same way, he believed Jesus could send his power to heal someone far away.** Ask: **How did Jesus feel when he heard this?** (amazed) **What did Jesus say then?** (I have never found such faith, even in Israel.) **When the officer's friends returned home, how did they find the servant?** (healthy)

🎧 Invite children to listen to the recorded Scripture story [*Finding God* Grade 3 CD 1, Track 3].

Read aloud the last paragraph. Give children time to write their responses. Discuss what they have written, looking for answers such as sharing, kind words, and kind actions.

Link to Liturgy

After reading aloud this feature, say: **When we invite someone special into our homes, we want everything to be just right. So, as we prepare to receive Holy Communion, we ask for God's healing grace.**

🎵 If time allows, play a prayerful song, such as "Here I Am, God" [*Finding God* Grade 3 CD 2, Track 5].

IF TIME ALLOWS

If time allows, complete one or more of the activities below.

Expression: Movement
Faith Have children dramatize the story, using the Children's page as a script. Assign the following parts: Jesus, the Roman officer, the servant, friends, and a narrator. Have children reenact the Scripture story, embellishing it by adding scenes of the officer by the bedside of his servant. Before children begin, have the class develop their roles by asking how the characters might be feeling and what they are thinking.
Time: 15 minutes
Materials: none

Expression: Art Studio
The Servant Is Healed! Distribute art supplies. Say: **The Art Print does not show the servant because Jesus is healing from a distance.** Invite children to imagine they are present when the servant realizes he is well again. Encourage them to draw what they imagine.
Time: 20 minutes
Materials: art supplies

For your convenience, the Children's Book page is reproduced below.

EXPLORE ART PRINT 13

Name _____ Date _____

Art Print 13 shows Jesus healing a servant through an officer's faith. How do you care for others?

Jesus and the Roman Officer

Before we receive Holy Communion, we pray special words. Read about when these words were first spoken.

Jesus went to the town of Capernaum. A Roman officer there had a servant who was very sick. When the officer heard about Jesus, he sent men to ask Jesus to save the servant's life. They urged Jesus, "Please do this for him. This man loves our nation, and he has helped us." Jesus went with them.

As they neared the house, the officer sent his friends to tell Jesus, "Lord, do not trouble yourself. I am not worthy to have you enter my home. Just say the word and let my servant be healed."

The officer knew that he could order his soldiers to do something far away. In the same way, he believed Jesus could send his power to heal someone far away. Jesus was amazed when he heard this. He said, "I have never found such faith, even in Israel." The officer's friends returned to find the servant healthy.

adapted from Luke 7:1–10

The officer had never met Jesus, but he had faith in Jesus. Jesus showed that his mission was to all people. On a separate sheet of paper, write how you can show you care for all people as Jesus does.

Link to Liturgy

Before we receive Holy Communion at Mass, we pray "Lord, I am not worthy that you should enter under my roof, but only say the word and my soul shall be healed."

The full-scale version of this teaching instruction appears on the Art Print easel.

FindingGod · Exploring Faith Through Art

The Annunciation

GRADE 3, UNIT 3, SESSION 14
Catechist Guide page 83

Faith Focus: Mary is blessed by God.

OUTCOMES

▶ Retell the story of Gabriel's visit to Mary.

▶ Describe how Mary felt about accepting God's blessing.

▶ Pray the Hail Mary.

▶ Explain how Mary cares for us.

About the Artist Maurice Denis was born in France in 1870. He studied art at the prominent academies in France, where he made friends with other artists who had become bored with the nature themes common to Impressionism. He joined these artists in being part of the Symbolist movement and later joined a new group called Nabis. Denis was a devout Christian and liked to paint religious subjects. The Nabis style suited these religious paintings.

Art·i·facts As an early member of the Symbolist movement, Denis made art not because he wanted to tell a story or visually describe a character, but because he wanted to make the viewer understand certain feelings. In *The Annunciation*, Mary and Gabriel's experience and emotions are more important than the details of their faces and clothing, or the specifics of the setting.

For your convenience, the Children's Book page is reproduced below.

EXPLORE ART PRINT 14

Name _____ Date _____

Art Print 14 shows Mary receiving good news from an angel about God's blessing. What gifts make you feel blessed by God?

Mary, Full of Grace

The angel Gabriel appeared to Mary and said, "Hail Mary, full of grace, the Lord is with you!" When Mary learned that God would give her a child, she knew that she had been blessed. Mary was so excited that she had to share the news with her family. She visited Elizabeth, her cousin. Elizabeth said to Mary, "Blessed are you among women, and blessed is the fruit of your womb." These words are part of the Hail Mary.

Mary as Our Mother

When God called Mary to be the mother of his Son, God also called her to be the Mother of the Church and of all God's children. We are God's children, so Mary is our mother too! We know Mary had to be special to be the mother of Jesus. She always tried to love and serve God, and she became very holy. Mary was filled with God's love.

I am blessed to have Mary as my mother because she

_____

_____

Reading God's Word

Blessed are you who believed and trusted that what the Lord told you would really happen.
adapted from Luke 1:45

www.findinggod.com   Grade 3 · Unit 3 · Session 14

CATECHIST DIRECTIONS

MATERIALS
▶ *The Annunciation* Art Print
▶ Children's Book page 240

TIME
🕐 10–30 minutes

1 Begin

After completing page 83 in the Children's Book, display the Art Print.

Briefly introduce and discuss the artwork, using information from About the Artist and Artifacts. Say: ***In this painting the angel Gabriel just announced the news that Mary is expecting the Son of God.*** Ask: ***When you look at Mary in the painting, what do you think she's feeling?*** (Possible answers: happy, surprised, blessed, honored, important) ***Does anyone have a new baby in the family or one coming soon? What did your family or another family you know do to prepare for the new family member?*** (Possible answers: buy clothes and diapers, prepare a crib, have a celebration) Say: ***These babies are gifts from God. When you were born, you were also a gift from God. We're going to read a story about a family who is preparing for the gift of a new baby.***

Invite children to reflect on the artwork and to pray a silent prayer thanking God for all the blessings he has given them.

2 Connect

Have children turn to page 240 in their books. Read aloud the introduction and discuss the question.

Invite a volunteer to real aloud Mary, Full of Grace. Ask: ***What was the name of the angel who visited Mary?*** (Gabriel) ***How did he act toward Mary?*** (He honored her by saying she was "full of grace" and reassured her by saying "the Lord is with you.") ***What did Gabriel say to her?*** (that she was going to have a baby) ***How did Mary react?*** (Possible answers: she was happy, excited; felt blessed) ***What did Elizabeth think about Mary's news?*** (Possible answers: She was in awe; She knew this made Mary special.) Then invite children to pray aloud the Hail Mary together.

Invite a volunteer to read aloud Mary as Our Mother. Ask: ***When God called Mary to be the mother of his Son, who else would she be mother to?*** (the Church and all of God's children) ***Who are God's children?*** (We are; All people are.)

Have children complete the sentence. Invite volunteers to share their responses.

📖 Reading God's Word

After reading aloud this feature, say: ***Elizabeth said these words to Mary.*** Ask: ***Why did Elizabeth say that Mary was blessed?*** (Because Mary trusted in God, he gave her his most precious gift of all—his Son, Jesus.)

IF TIME ALLOWS

If time allows, complete one or more of the activities below.

Expression: Movement
Visiting the Baby Invite children to think about what it is like to visit a mother and new baby. Ask them to imagine that they were able to visit Mary when Jesus was born. What would they say and do? Would they ask to hold the baby, help with chores, bring food, ask questions? Assign a child to be Mary and have volunteers role-play visiting her and baby Jesus, improvising a conversation with her.

Time: 15 minutes
Materials: a doll to represent baby Jesus

Expression: Art Studio
A Blessing of Ours Distribute drawing paper and watercolor paint. Say: ***We learned how the Art Print artist Maurice Denis wanted to express the experience and emotions of Mary and the angel Gabriel in this painting. Now imagine the scene of Mary sharing her wonderful news with her cousin Elizabeth. Try to express in a painting of your own the emotions of Mary and Elizabeth when Mary told her the news.***

Time: 20 minutes
Materials: watercolor paint, drawing paper

FindingGod **· Exploring Faith Through Art**

Nativity

GRADE 3, UNIT 3, SESSION 15

Catechist Guide page 89

Faith Focus: We celebrate Christmas as a Church community.

OUTCOMES

▸ Discuss how we came to celebrate the Feast of the Epiphany.

▸ Explain that Christmas is, foremost, a celebration of Jesus' life.

About the Artist Charles Walch was born 1898 in France and became interested in art when he was young. When he arrived in Paris in 1918, he studied painting at the School of Decorative Arts. He eventually became a professor of drawing. He was awarded a gold medal in 1937 at the International Exhibition and died in 1948. His joyful paintings exemplify his love of life.

Art·i·facts The word *Nativity* means "being born." A scene of Jesus' birth is called a Nativity scene, or, occasionally, the *crèche*, meaning "crib." Although Jesus' birthplace was humble and he slept in a manger, wise men traveled great distances to see the Old Testament's prophecies come to life. This Nativity painting also features an angel and the shepherd who, by legend, came along with the wise men to pay homage to Christ.

For your convenience, the Children's Book page is reproduced below.

EXPLORE ART PRINT **15**

Name _____ Date _____

Art Print 15 shows the moment when Jesus was born to us. How do you share your happiness that Jesus is with you?

Celebrating Christmas

An important feast during the Christmas season is the Feast of the Epiphany, when Jesus was revealed to the whole world. The Magi, or the Wise Men, believed that someday a star would announce the birth of the Son of God. They studied charts of the stars and waited for the special star to appear in the sky. When it finally appeared, the Wise Men packed their camels and traveled a long time to reach him. When they saw the baby Jesus, they honored him with gifts.

The Gift of Jesus

Although the celebration of Christmas comes with lights, presents, and parties, God's gift of Jesus to the world teaches us how to show our love to others. Christmas reminds us how much God loves us, and that is what we celebrate.

". . . God is love, and whoever remains in love remains in God and God in him." *1 John 4:16*

A Gift for Baby Jesus

Imagine you were traveling with the Wise Men. Draw a picture of a gift you would bring to Jesus.

Grade 3 · Unit 3 · Session 15

CATECHIST DIRECTIONS

MATERIALS
▸ *Nativity* Art Print
▸ Children's Book page 241
▸ Art supplies

TIME
10–30 minutes

1 Begin

After completing page 89 in the Children's Book, display the Art Print.

Briefly introduce and discuss the artwork, using information from About the Artist and Artifacts. Ask: **Whom can you identify in the painting?** (Jesus, Mary and Joseph; angel, shepherd, wise men) **What do you notice about Jesus?** (his halo) **What does a halo symbolize?** (Possible answers: holiness, God's light, glory) **Where is Jesus laying?** (in a manger)

Invite children to reflect on the artwork and to pray a silent prayer thanking God for his gift to us of his Son, Jesus.

2 Connect

Have children turn to page 241 in their books. Read aloud the introduction and discuss the question.

Invite a volunteer to read aloud Celebrating Christmas. Ask: **What does the Feast of the Epiphany celebrate?** (When the Wise Men visited Jesus, he was revealed to the whole world.) **How do you think the tradition of Christmas gift giving began?** (Possible answer: The Wise Men brought gifts to Jesus.)

Invite a volunteer to read aloud the first paragraph of The Gift of Jesus. Ask: **When we celebrate Christmas, of what does it remind us?** (how much God loves us)

📖 Read aloud the Scripture. Ask: **What do you think the Scripture reading means?** (Possible answer: that God and love are the same) Say: **No matter what, God always loves us. When we act like Jesus, we share God's love with others.**

Invite a volunteer to read aloud the directions for the activity A Gift for Baby Jesus. Give children time to draw their pictures. Invite children to explain the gifts they chose.

IF TIME ALLOWS

If time allows, complete one or more of the activities below.

Expression: Music

Carols Play a Christmas song, such as "O Come All Ye Faithful," which expresses the joy of Jesus' birth. Invite children to sing along. Ask them to suggest their favorite Christmas carols.

Time: 10 minutes
Materials: CD player, Christmas music

Expression: Art Studio

Our Nativity Distribute watercolor paint and paper. In groups of four, have children paint a Nativity scene on a large sheet of paper. In each group assign one child to paint a manger, another to paint Mary, someone to paint Joseph, and the fourth child to paint Jesus in a manger. Have children decide how to divide the painting of the animals, angels, shepherds, and the Wise Men. Help children make frames out of cardboard boxes and gold paint. Display the Nativity scenes to make an art gallery.

Time: 20 minutes
Materials: watercolor paint, paper, cardboard boxes, gold paint

Expression: Using Imagination in Prayer

Holy Lives Ask children to prepare themselves for quiet prayer, imagining themselves sitting near the manger, watching baby Jesus as he sleeps or interacting with him. Remind them of examples of Jesus' holiness. Say: **During this season of Jesus' birth, we will dedicate ourselves to following in Jesus' holy footsteps. Focus on one quality of his life that you can imitate in your lives. It could be his patience, generosity, love, or forgiveness.** Ask children to sit in quiet contemplation for two minutes. Pray aloud *Amen.*

Time: 3 minutes
Materials: none

The full-scale version of this teaching instruction appears on the Art Print easel.

FindingGod • Exploring Faith Through Art

The Ethiopian Baptized ART PRINT 16

GRADE 3, UNIT 4, SESSION 16
Catechist Guide page 95

Faith Focus: The disciple Philip continues Jesus' mission.

OUTCOMES
▸ Tell the story of Philip and the Ethiopian official.
▸ Explain how Baptism welcomes us into the Church.

About the Artist Lambert Sustris was born in Holland in the city of Amsterdam around 1515. As a young man of about 20, Sustris went to Rome. It is believed that he trained with famous Italian painter Titian Vecelli. Sustris never returned to Holland, instead immersing himself in Italy's vibrant art scene.

Art·i·facts Sustris was a disciple of the Mannerist movement. Mannerists painted their subjects in exaggerated settings. For instance, proportions were unrealistic. Scenes were crowded with dramatic details and dark, sweeping skies. In *The Baptism of the Ethiopian . . . by St. Philip,* the complex sky covers half the canvas. The painting shows Philip baptizing the official.

For your convenience, the Children's Book page is reproduced below.

EXPLORE ART PRINT 16

Name _____ Date _____

Art Print 16 shows Philip welcoming an official to the Church through Baptism. In what ways have you been welcomed to the Church?

Philip and the Court Official

Many disciples traveled long distances to continue Jesus' mission.

Philip was called to make one of these journeys. Philip was traveling a desert road from Jerusalem to Gaza. He met a court official from Ethiopia. The official was returning home from Jerusalem. He was in his carriage, reading the Scriptures.

The Holy Spirit told Philip to join the official. Philip ran up to him and asked, "Do you understand what you are reading?" The official said, "How can I, unless someone teaches me?" He invited Philip to sit with him and teach him.

The man was reading about someone being silent as he was led to be killed. He read about a man being denied justice. He wondered who the man was.

Philip told the official that the man he read about was Jesus. As they traveled, Philip told the official all about Jesus.

Then they came to a stream. The official said, "Look, there is water. Why can't I be baptized?" They walked to the water, and Philip baptized him. The official went joyfully on his way. Philip continued on his journey, spreading Jesus' message in each town he visited. *adapted from Acts of the Apostles 8:26–40*

Welcome to the Church
Imagine that the official is a new member of your parish. On a separate sheet of paper, write what you would say to make him feel welcome.

www.findinggod.com   Grade 3 • Unit 4 • Session 16

CATECHIST DIRECTIONS

MATERIALS
▸ *The Ethiopian Baptized* Art Print
▸ Children's Book page 242
▸ CD player
▸ *Finding God* Grade 3 CD 1, Track 4

TIME
🕐 10–30 minutes

① Begin

After completing page 95 in the Children's Book, display the Art Print.

Briefly introduce and discuss the artwork, using information from About the Artist and Artifacts. Ask: **What do you see in this painting?** (Possible answers: the sky, a town, trees, people, sheep, horse and carriage, a stream) **In the painting which person is Philip and which one is the official?** (Philip is standing over the kneeling official.) **What is Philip doing?** (baptizing the official) **Why is water used to baptize?** (Possible answer: It is a symbol of washing away Original Sin.)

Invite children to reflect on the artwork and to pray a silent prayer thanking God for being a part of the Church.

② Connect

Have children turn to page 242 in their books. Read aloud the introduction and discuss the question.

📖 Invite volunteers to read aloud the first sentence and the next three paragraphs of Philip and the Court Official. Say: **Philip was one of the 12 apostles.** Ask: **What do we call people who travel great distances to continue Jesus' mission?** (missionaries)

Have a volunteer read aloud the next two paragraphs. Ask: **Who was the person who was silent as he was lead to be killed?** (Jesus) **How was Jesus denied justice?** (Possible answer: He was an innocent man who was punished and killed.) **What did Philip do as he and the Ethiopian traveled?** (told the man all about Jesus) **When Philip and the Ethiopian came to a stream, what happened?** (Philip baptized him.) Say: **The man asked to be baptized because he understood that Jesus died for us. He wanted to become a Christian.**

🎧 Invite children to listen to the recorded Scripture story [*Finding God* Grade 3 CD 1, Track 4].

Read aloud the activity Welcome to the Church. Say: **Remember our discussion at the beginning of the session about welcoming people when you write your response.** Give children time to complete the activity and invite them to share their sentences.

IF TIME ALLOWS

If time allows, complete one or more of the activities below.

Expression: Movement
Philip and the Court Official Skit Ask small groups to work together to prepare and present a dramatization of Philip and the court official. Children may wish to use simple costumes or props in their dramatizations. Discuss the range of emotions the official had.
Time: 15 minutes
Materials: optional costumes and props

Expression: Art Studio
Paint Your Own Art Print Distribute watercolor paints and paper. Display the Art Print again. Ask children to study it closely. Then put it away. Invite them to reproduce the scene as they remember it.
Time: 20 minutes
Materials: watercolor paint, paper

Expression: Using Imagination in Prayer
Sacraments Invite children to imagine this scene happening today. Ask: **Where could a similar scene happen?** Suggest a ride on a bus, on a train, or in a car. Say: **Philip and the official might be wearing suits. The Baptism could take place in a park.** Give children time to imagine. Then invite them to pray: **God, thank you for welcoming me into your family. Help me see everyone I meet as one with you.** After a moment of silence, end with *Amen.*
Time: 2 minutes
Materials: none

FindingGod · **Exploring Faith Through Art**

Greetings

GRADE 3, UNIT 4, SESSION 17

Catechist Guide page 101

Faith Focus: When we fail to love God and others because of sin, Jesus calls us to forgiveness through the Sacrament of Reconciliation.

OUTCOMES

▶ Explain that we receive forgiveness from God through the Sacrament of Reconciliation.

▶ Describe that when we confess our sins to a priest, we receive absolution.

▶ Discuss that we share reconciliation when we forgive others.

About the Artist Jeanette Lassen began to paint on her own as a young girl. She studied formally, late in life, at Scotland's Edinburgh School of Art. Her use of bold colors and modern-day themes defined her work. She died in 2008.

Art·i·facts The bright and cheerful women of the painting greet each other by embracing each other with flowers. The painting was done using acrylic paints on canvas.

CATECHIST DIRECTIONS

MATERIALS
▶ *Greetings* Art Print
▶ Children's Book page 243
▶ Bible

TIME
🕐 10–30 minutes

1 Begin

After completing page 101 in the Children's Book, display the Art Print.

Briefly introduce and discuss the artwork, using information from About the Artist and Artifacts. Ask: *What details do you notice in the painting?* (Possible answers: bright colors, flowers, women hugging, blue skies, happy faces) *How do you think these two women feel?* (Possible answers: love, happiness, acceptance) Say: *Imagine that these two women had an argument but that they have just forgiven each other. This is how they show that they still care for each other after they've solved their differences. Jesus welcomes us always, even when we sin.*

Invite children to reflect on the artwork and to pray a silent prayer thanking God for the gift of Reconciliation.

2 Connect

Have children turn to page 243 in their books. Read aloud the introduction and discuss the question. Invite a volunteer to read aloud A Peaceful Ending. Ask: *What gives us a feeling of peace?* (when we confess our sins and receive forgiveness in the Sacrament of Reconciliation)

Have a volunteer read aloud Forgiveness. Ask: *What did you do to bring about a peaceful ending? Was it difficult?* Give children time to write about their experiences and ask volunteers to share them. Say: *Forgiving people is sometimes hard, but being a member of God's family means sometimes making hard choices. Choosing to ask for forgiveness and forgiving others brings us closer to God.*

📖 Reading God's Word

Read aloud this passage. Point out the Book of Psalms in the Old Testament of the Bible. Say: *This psalm expresses how God wants to give peace and forgiveness to his people. We receive both when we celebrate the Sacrament of Reconciliation.*

IF TIME ALLOWS

If time allows, complete one or more of the activities below.

Expression: Movement

Apologies Assign partners and ask them to write a play about forgiveness. Ask them to end each dialogue with apologies and a sign of forgiveness. Invite children to perform their play for the group.

Time: 20 minutes
Materials: none

Expression: Art Studio

Peace Signs Distribute art supplies. Brainstorm with children various peace symbols, such as a peace sign or a rainbow, or expressions of peace, such as *give peace a chance* or *smile, be happy*. List them on the board. Have children choose one symbol and expression to make a bumper sticker. Have children fold a sheet of drawing paper in half to make a long rectangle. Ask children to neatly write their message and illustrate their bumper sticker. Display the bumper stickers on a bulletin board that is made to look like the back of a car, including the bumper.

Time: 20 minutes
Materials: art supplies, drawing paper

For your convenience, the Children's Book page is reproduced below.

EXPLORE ART PRINT 17

Name _____ Date _____

Art Print 17 shows two women happy to greet each other. They accept each other. How do you show acceptance to someone who asks for forgiveness?

A Peaceful Ending

Although we try, it might be hard to get along with everyone all the time. Sometimes we do things that hurt one another or God.

When we sin, we can ask God for forgiveness in the Sacrament of Reconciliation. We confess our sins to a priest and receive absolution. Then we can be at peace with others and with God. When someone asks us for our forgiveness, we share reconciliation by forgiving that person.

Forgiveness

Write about a time you hurt someone and asked for forgiveness.

_____

_____

_____

_____

_____

📖 Reading God's Word

I will listen for the Word of God. The Lord will give peace to his people, to those who have faith and trust in him.

adapted from Psalm 85:9

The full-scale version of this teaching instruction appears on the Art Print easel.

FindingGod ▪ **Exploring Faith Through Art**

First Communion

GRADE 3, UNIT 4, SESSION 18

Catechist Guide page 107

Faith Focus: The Celebration of the Eucharist is at the center of parish life around the world.

OUTCOMES

▶ Discuss that we celebrate Mass to thank God and to ask God for his blessing.

▶ Describe how the Mass unites us as one family.

▶ Explain that when we receive Holy Communion, we feel part of one family.

About the Artist Pablo Picasso was born in Spain in 1881 and was a child prodigy. He had his first art exhibit when he was only 13 years old. He studied at the Royal Academy of San Fernando, but he found that he learned more from painting real life people and subjects. Picasso made thousands of paintings and sculptures. He is one of the most influential artists of the 20th century.

Art·i·facts Picasso began painting *First Communion* when he was 14 years old. The girl in the picture is his sister. Four years later he finished the painting and submitted it to a contest. It was considered to be his official entry into the art world to which he would dominate for 65 years.

For your convenience, the Children's Book page is reproduced below.

EXPLORE ART PRINT 18

Name _____ Date _____

Art Print 18 shows a girl receiving the Sacrament of the Eucharist. How did you feel the day you first received Holy Communion?

The Mass Makes Us One Family

No matter who we are or where we come from, participating in Mass together makes us one family. When we celebrate Mass, we gather with other members of our parish to pray together in thanksgiving and to ask God for his blessing. In some parishes Mass is celebrated in different languages. Even if we do not understand all the words, we can still know what is happening. The same Mass is celebrated all over the world.

When the time for Holy Communion comes during Mass, we process to the front of the church with other parishioners. When we receive Jesus' Body and Blood, we feel one with the Church community. No matter what language we pray in, we are all one family in Jesus Christ.

Your Special Day

On the lines below, write three special things you remember from your First Holy Communion.

_____

_____

_____

www.findinggod.com — Grade 3 · Unit 4 · Session 18

CATECHIST DIRECTIONS

MATERIALS
▶ *First Communion* Art Print
▶ Children's Book page 244

TIME
🕐 10–30 minutes

1 Begin

After completing page 107 in the Children's Book, display the Art Print.

Briefly introduce and discuss the artwork, using information from About the Artist and Artifacts. Ask: *What is the girl in the painting doing?* (Possible answers: kneeling, praying, reading her prayer book) *What is she wearing?* (a Holy Communion dress, veil, flowers on her head) Say: *On special occasions we often have special outfits we wear to show the importance of the day. Traditionally, children receiving their First Holy Communion wore white. It is still common for girls to wear white.* Ask: *Does anyone know why?* (Possible answers: White is a symbol of new life. It also represents the presence of the risen Christ living in the children.) Explain that wearing a special outfit for your First Holy Communion shows reverence and lets everyone in the parish know that you are celebrating this Sacrament of Initiation.

Invite children to reflect on the artwork and to pray a silent prayer thanking God for the gift of Holy Communion, the consecrated Bread and Wine.

2 Connect

Have children turn to page 244 in their books. Read aloud the introduction and discuss the question.

Ask a volunteer to read aloud The Mass Makes Us One Family. Ask: *Has anyone attended a Mass in a language other than English?* Encourage children to share their experiences. Say: *When we receive Holy Communion, we are one with Jesus. All Catholics are a part of one big family.*

Read aloud the directions for Your Special Day. Give children time to write about the memories they value from the celebration of their First Holy Communion. Invite volunteers to share their memories.

IF TIME ALLOWS

If time allows, complete one or more of the activities below.

Expression: Movement

Imitate Explain that when we celebrate the Eucharist, we imitate what Jesus did at the Last Supper. Point out that we learn much by imitating others' actions. Ask children to stand and perform these actions with you.

1. Make the Sign of the Cross.

2. Bless mind, lips, and heart. This is done for the Gospel.

3. Kneel.

4. Shake hands in a sign of peace.

5. Hold hands in the position to receive Holy Communion.

After each action, ask children what it is called or what purpose it serves.

Time: 20 minutes
Materials: none

Expression: Art Studio

Break Bread Have children collect pictures from magazines and newspapers of people sharing a meal at home, church, or restaurants. Have children make a collage and write words that summarize the session, such as *family, Mass, Holy Communion, sharing,* or *Jesus.*

Time: 20 minutes
Materials: construction paper, magazines, newspapers, art supplies

Expression: Using Imagination in Prayer

Being Part of the Last Supper Ask children to imagine that they were at the Last Supper with Jesus and his friends. Ask children to envision their families and friends also seated at Jesus' table, contributing to the loving closeness of the shared meal. Say: *Let's thank Jesus for his gift of the Eucharist. We thank Jesus for the loving closeness each time we are with our Church family at Mass.*

Time: 2 minutes
Materials: none

FindingGod · Exploring Faith Through Art

A Sunny Corner

ART PRINT 19

GRADE 3, UNIT 4, SESSION 19

Catechist Guide page 113

Faith Focus: The Holy Spirit gives us spiritual gifts so that we can serve God and others.

OUTCOMES

▸ Explain that we all receive gifts from the Holy Spirit.

▸ Identify our gifts and how we can use them to serve others.

▸ Discuss that our gifts are special to God.

About the Artist Charles William Bartlett was born in England in 1860 and studied chemistry and metallurgy for several years before entering the Royal Academy of Arts, London, in 1883. His travels took him to Italy, Pakistan, and Japan where he had prints produced from his paintings. He also traveled to Hawaii where his paintings and woodblock prints were well received. Bartlett quickly became an important figure in the local art world and settled in Honolulu where he died in 1940.

Art·i·facts Bartlett's favorite and most well-regarded medium was watercolors. In this watercolor, entitled *A Sunny Corner in Holland,* a boy sits working with his sister. Everyone, including children, have an opportunity and a responsibility to use their gifts for good.

For your convenience, the Children's Book page is reproduced below.

EXPLORE ART PRINT **19**

Name _____ Date _____

Art Print 19 shows a brother and sister helping prepare for their meal. How do you use your gifts to help others?

Many Gifts, One Spirit

Saint Paul wrote this letter to his friends, explaining how they can use their gifts to help others. We can learn from his letter too.

There are many different kinds of spiritual gifts. They all come from the same Holy Spirit. There are different ways to serve the same God. We each do different work, but the same God helps us. The Holy Spirit works in each of us to help us do things for the good of others.

Some of us can speak with knowledge and teach others. Some can heal sick people. The Holy Spirit decides which gifts to give us and calls us to use them.

adapted from 1 Corinthians 12:4–11

Working Together

Think of ways in which you have used your gifts to help someone in your life. Choose four people and write something you can do to serve them.

mother _____

father _____

sister/brother _____

teacher _____

neighbor _____

friend _____

Link to Liturgy

At the Dismissal of the Mass, the priest or deacon sends us forth to glorify the Lord by our lives.

www.findinggod.com
Grade 3 · Unit 4 · Session 19

CATECHIST DIRECTIONS

MATERIALS
▸ *A Sunny Corner* Art Print
▸ Children's Book page 245

TIME
🕐 10–30 minutes

1 Begin

After completing page 113 in the Children's Book, display the Art Print.

Briefly introduce and discuss the artwork, using information from About the Artist and Artifacts. Ask: ***What is the boy in the painting doing?*** (Possible answers: working, peeling fruit) ***What is the little girl doing?*** (Possible answer: helping her brother) ***What can you tell about their feelings from the picture?*** (Possible answers: They are content, happy.) Say: ***We are called upon to be helpful to our families and communities because we are all part of God's creation.***

Invite children to reflect on the artwork and to pray a silent prayer thanking God for their spiritual gifts and for the chance to help others by using those gifts.

2 Connect

Have children turn to page 245 in their books. Read aloud the introduction and discuss the question.

📖 Ask volunteers to read aloud Many Gifts, One Spirit. Ask: ***What does Saint Paul say the Holy Spirit does for us?*** (gives us different gifts; helps us use our gifts to help others) ***What are some ways we can bring joy to the work God gives us?*** (Possible answers: play music, work with friends, pray, sing, smile, be thankful) ***What kinds of gifts might you have that you can plan to use this week to serve others?*** (Possible answers: 1. I am a good artist. A picture could make someone feel loved. 2. I am a good cook. I could help make something for a new mom or someone who is sick. 3. I am organized. I can help Mom organize drawers. 4. I am good at math. I can help my brother with homework.) ***Whose work can teach others?*** (Possible answers: teacher, catechist, priest) ***Whose work can heal people who are sick?*** (Possible answers: nurses, doctors) ***Whose work can bring us relaxation or entertain us?*** (Possible answers: artists, musicians)

Read aloud Working Together. Give children time to fill in the blanks. Then ask volunteers to share their answers.

Link to Liturgy

After reading aloud this feature, ask: ***Do you recognize the Dismissal from Mass?*** Say: ***Maybe you have never noticed it before. Next time you go to Mass, and the liturgy is almost complete, pay close attention to see if you can hear it. For the rest of the day, try to remember that we can use our gifts to glorify the Lord by our lives.***

IF TIME ALLOWS

If time allows, complete one or more of the activities below.

Expression: Movement

Teamwork Have small groups make a skit that uses everyone's talents. Ask them to decide on the scene showing someone helping others and then put on the production. Point out that each person's individual gift will be needed to produce the show. Choose someone to use leadership skills to be the director; choose someone with writing skills to write the skit; choose someone with musical skills to choose sound effects and music, and so on. Encourage children to discuss the best use of their gifts.

Time: 20 minutes
Materials: none

Expression: Art Studio

We All Work Distribute art supplies. Invite children to choose one of the responses to the activity on the Children's page and illustrate it.

Time: 20 minutes
Materials: drawing paper, art supplies

The full-scale version of this teaching instruction appears on the Art Print easel.

Christ on the Cross

ART PRINT 20

GRADE 3, UNIT 4, SESSION 20

Catechist Guide page 119

Faith Focus: Lent is a time to think about how we can make our hearts ready for Easter.

OUTCOMES

- Describe how we pattern our Lenten celebration after Jesus' temptation in the desert.
- Explain how Lent is a time to prepare for Easter.
- Identify various Lenten promises to remind us of Christ's strength.

About the Artist Barthelemy d'Eyck was an active painter between 1444 and 1469. Intent on artistic achievement, he traveled to France where he worked as resident artist in the courts of kings and dukes. He managed large projects and the work of other painters, earning himself the title of "Valet of Painting." He is also believed to be the "Master of the Aix Annunciation," a triptych panel.

Art·i·facts Crucifixion was an excruciatingly painful method of execution dating back to the sixth century B.C. A Roman Emperor outlawed it as a form of punishment in A.D. 337 out of respect for Jesus' memory. The crucifix and cross have become symbols of Christianity and of our commitment to live according to Jesus' message.

For your convenience, the Children's Book page is reproduced below.

EXPLORE ART PRINT 20

Name _____ Date _____

Art Print 20 shows how Jesus sacrificed his life for us. How do you make your heart ready during Lent in remembrance of his sacrifice?

Jesus in the Desert

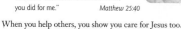

During Lent we remember how Jesus suffered and died before his Resurrection. To prepare for his sacrifice, he spent 40 days in the desert. During those 40 days, Jesus fasted and resisted temptation by the devil. By caring for those in need and resisting temptation, we can make our hearts ready for Easter. Catholics abstain from meat on Fridays. Some Christians fast during Lent by choosing a food or an activity to give up. Others choose to do something to remind them of Jesus, such as pray every morning before school.

Jesus once said this in a parable.

> And the king will say to them in reply,
> "Amen, I say to you, whatever you did
> for one of these least brothers of mine,
> you did for me." *Matthew 25:40*

When you help others, you show you care for Jesus too.

A Lenten Promise

Write an idea for a Lenten promise. Choose something that would remind you daily of Christ's strength to resist temptation and his ultimate sacrifice—his Crucifixion.

_____

_____

_____

www.findinggod.com

Grade 3 • Unit 4 • Session 20

CATECHIST DIRECTIONS

MATERIALS
- *Christ on the Cross* Art Print
- Children's Book page 246

TIME
⏱ 10–30 minutes

① Begin

After completing page 119 in the Children's Book, display the Art Print.

Briefly introduce and discuss the artwork, using information from About the Artist and Artifacts. Ask: *How does the painting make you feel?* (Possible answers: sad, angry, frustrated, horrified) *What do you think Jesus was feeling?* (Possible answers: hurt, pain, forgotten by God) Say: *The painting reminds us that Jesus was a human man who experienced real pain and sorrow in order to fulfill his promise to God and to humankind. During Lent we remember Jesus' strength and suffering as we prepare our hearts for Easter.*

Invite children to reflect on the artwork and to pray a silent prayer asking God to give them the strength to fulfill their Lenten promise.

② Connect

Have children turn to page 246 in their books. Read aloud the introduction and discuss the question.

Read aloud the first paragraph of Jesus in the Desert. Say: *During Lent we are called to honor Jesus for his sacrifice.* Ask: *What was his great sacrifice?* (Possible answers: his life; Death on the cross) *How can we honor his sacrifice?* (Possible answers: fast, practice positive new habits, care for people who need help, pray, go to church, be grateful for Jesus, think about how we treat others) *How many days did Jesus fast in the wilderness?* (40) *What does it mean to fast?* (Possible answers: to eat less, to not eat, to stop doing something) Say: *The word fast can also mean "to hold tight." You can make a Lenten promise and try to hold tight to the promise. We are called to spend 40 days paying attention to how we treat others.*

📖 Read aloud the Scripture passage and the following sentence. Ask: *What do you think Jesus is saying?* (Possible answer: When we help others, we are serving Jesus too.)

Read aloud A Lenten Promise. Ask children to spend some time thinking of a meaningful Lenten promise and to write about it. Invite them to share their ideas for honoring Jesus during Lent.

IF TIME ALLOWS

If time allows, complete one or more of the activities below.

Expression: Movement

Lenten Beanbag Toss Arrange children in a circle and provide a beanbag. Explain that when they catch the beanbag, they suggest something to do for a Lenten promise. Throw the bag 40 times, once for each day that Jesus was in the desert. Begin the game by saying a suggestion, such as "attend the Stations of the Cross," and then toss the beanbag to a child.

Time: 20 minutes
Materials: beanbag

Expression: Art Studio

Jesus in the Desert Distribute paper and watercolor paint. Ask children to paint Jesus in the desert to remind them and encourage them to keep their Lenten promise.

Time: 20 minutes
Materials: paper, watercolor paint

Expression: Using Imagination in Prayer

The Passion Ask children to think about what it must have felt like to be Jesus in the desert, knowing that to be faithful to God, he would have to suffer. Say: *Imagine how hot, hungry, thirsty, and lonely Jesus must have felt. God doesn't want anyone to suffer. Let's silently ask God to help us live our faith, even when it is difficult.* After a moment of silence, end by praying aloud *Amen.*

Time: 2 minutes
Materials: none

FindingGod • Exploring Faith Through Art

The Sacred Heart

ART PRINT 21

GRADE 3, UNIT 5, SESSION 21

Catechist Guide page 125

Faith Focus: We live like Jesus when we practice the virtues of faith, hope, and charity.

OUTCOMES

▸ Identify the symbols used for the virtues of faith, hope, and charity.

▸ Explain how virtues can be shown.

About the Artist Roy de Maistre (1894–1968) was born in Australia. He was from a wealthy family and was educated in music and art. De Maistre was known for developing a theory about the relationship between color and music. The relationship involved assigning colors to musical notes. At one time de Maistre used his theories about the relationship between color and music to devise a form of color therapy for Australian soldiers suffering from stress disorder after WWI. He was considered a leader in Modernist art in Australia.

Art·i·facts De Maistre approached paints as though the colors elicited emotional consequences. In *The Sacred Heart*, de Maistre uses bold, passionate colors. He converted to Catholicism when he was 57 years old. At that time his work became religious in nature.

For your convenience, the Children's Book page is reproduced below.

 EXPLORE ART PRINT **21**

Name _____ Date _____

Art Print 21 shows Jesus and his heart, which is the symbol for the virtue of charity. Which virtue did you show someone today?

Symbols of the Virtues

Symbols stand for something else or remind us of something. Butterflies are used as symbols of Jesus' Resurrection, doves symbolize the Holy Spirit, and water symbolizes Baptism. The cross is a symbol of our faith. It reminds us that Jesus died for our sins. An anchor is a symbol of hope. Just as an anchor holds a ship, so does hope help us hold on to Jesus. When we think of charity, or love, a heart comes to mind because the heart is a symbol of love.

Matching Virtues

Label each symbol and each sentence using *faith, hope,* or *charity.*

_____ _____ _____

1. Martha trusts that God will always guide her. _____

2. Anton shows his love by visiting a sick classmate. _____

3. Ethan believes that Jesus lived and died for us. _____

© Loyola Press.

CATECHIST DIRECTIONS

MATERIALS
▸ *The Sacred Heart* Art Print
▸ Children's Book page 247

TIME
10–30 minutes

1 Begin

After completing page 125 in the Children's Book, display the Art Print.

Briefly introduce and discuss the artwork, using information from About the Artist and Artifacts. Ask: *How do you know this is Jesus?* (by the pierced hands) Say: *Notice the cross on the heart. The sacred heart is a symbol.* Ask: *What is a symbol?* (something that stands for something else or reminds us of something) Say: *The heart in the painting is a symbol for love. The heart also symbolizes the virtue of charity.* Ask: *What are some examples of charity?* (Possible answers: goodwill to others, helping those in need, treating others with respect and dignity) Say: *Charity is how Jesus wants us to show our love for one another.*

Invite children to reflect on the artwork and to pray a silent prayer thanking God for the virtues of faith, hope, and charity. Encourage children to ask God for help in practicing these virtues often to those we meet during our day.

2 Connect

Have children turn to page 247 in their books. Read aloud the introduction and discuss the question.

Invite a volunteer to read aloud Symbols of the Virtues. Ask volunteers to name the symbols for faith, hope, and charity. Say: *Think about each virtue and how to make it present in your life. For example, you practice your faith by going to church, praying, and being thankful to God. We hope to improve the lives of all people by allowing that hope to inspire our actions. We live in charity when we love others and do what we can to help them.*

Read aloud the directions for Matching Virtues. Give children a few minutes to complete the activity, and then check the answers together.

IF TIME ALLOWS

If time allows, complete one or more of the activities below.

Expression: Movement
Virtue Charades Ask children to review the three virtues and how to incorporate them into daily life, such as praying, helping someone with chores, or hugging someone. Have children write their ideas on slips of paper and place them in a box. Ask children to select one and perform the action in front of the class. Allow the child who guesses correctly to have the next turn.
Time: 20 minutes
Materials: slips of paper, pencils, box

Expression: Art Studio
Virtue Poster Distribute drawing paper and crayons or markers. Have children draw the symbols for the virtues of faith, hope, and charity and give their posters a title. Encourage children to be creative and add details they think would enhance their poster.
Time: 15 minutes
Materials: drawing paper, markers or crayons

Expression: Using Imagination in Prayer
Faith Ask children to focus on the virtue of faith. Say: *We sometimes refer to our Catholic religion as our faith, but faith is also something personal. It is the belief that God is with us and that we will never be alone.* Have children close their eyes and imagine they are in a beautiful nature scene. Invite them to thank God for always being in their hearts, helping them to make good choices and leading them to serve others. End by praying *Amen.*
Time: 5 minutes
Materials: none

The full-scale version of this teaching instruction appears on the Art Print easel.

FindingGod ❖ **Exploring Faith Through Art**

In the Wilderness

GRADE 3, UNIT 5, SESSION 22

Catechist Guide page 131

Faith Focus: Jesus gives us the help we need to make good moral choices.

OUTCOMES

▶ Discuss the story of how Jesus was tempted in the desert by the devil.

▶ Explain that Jesus is our example for overcoming temptation.

▶ Discuss how we must often make difficult choices in life.

About the Artist Briton Riviere was born in 1840 in London, England. His art training was mainly by his father, who was an art teacher. Riviere began to exhibit his work around the age of 16 and later became a regular contributor to the Royal Academy. He made a name for himself as a portrait painter, but later in life, his main subjects were animals.

Art•i•facts Riviere painted *Christ in the Wilderness* as an experiment. He wanted to see if the story of the temptation could be told by simply casting light against dark. Light is often a symbol of good and dark a symbol of evil. Jesus' robe in the picture is the brightest color in the painting: a white that almost glows blue. Above his head is a pinpoint of white representing the evening star.

For your convenience, the Children's Book page is reproduced below.

EXPLORE
ART PRINT
22

Name _____ Date _____

Art Print 22 shows Jesus alone in the desert, praying for the strength to follow God's plan for him. What helps you make good moral choices?

Jesus Is Tempted

The Holy Spirit led Jesus into the desert. Jesus didn't eat for 40 days and 40 nights. He was very hungry. The devil came and said to him, "If you are the Son of God, turn these stones into loaves of bread." Jesus said, "The Scriptures say that people do not live only on bread, but on every word that God speaks."

Then the devil took Jesus to the top of the Temple. He said to Jesus, "If you are the Son of God, throw yourself down. The Scriptures say that God will tell the angels to protect you." Jesus answered, "The Scriptures also say you shall not put God to the test."

The devil took Jesus to a high mountain and showed him all the kingdoms of the world. The devil said, "All these I shall give you if you worship me." Jesus said, "Go away, Satan! The Scriptures say that you shall worship God alone, and you shall serve only him." Then the devil left Jesus, and angels came and cared for him.

adapted from Matthew 4:1–11

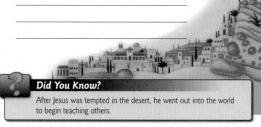

A Prayer of Petition

Write a prayer of petition, asking God for help in making good moral choices.

_____

_____

_____

Did You Know?
After Jesus was tempted in the desert, he went out into the world to begin teaching others.

www.findinggod.com   Grade 3 · Unit 5 · Session 22

© Loyola Press.

CATECHIST DIRECTIONS

MATERIALS
▶ *In the Wilderness* Art Print
▶ Children's Book page 248
▶ CD player
▶ *Finding God* Grade 3 CD 1, Track 5

TIME
🕐 10–30 minutes

1 *Begin*

After completing page 131 in the Children's Book, display the Art Print.

Briefly introduce and discuss the artwork, using information from About the Artist and Artifacts. Say: **In this painting Jesus is alone in the desert.** Ask: **What do the colors in the painting make you feel?** (Possible answers: The dark is gloomy, scary, lonely. The light is beautiful, warm, holy.) Say: **Jesus is sitting with his head down.** Ask: **What do you think Jesus is thinking about?** (Possible answer: about the important choices he has to make) **How might Jesus be feeling?** (Possible answers: tired, hungry, lonely, scared) Say: **Sometimes I have to make difficult decisions. Knowing that I am loved by God always makes me feel better. God shows me his love through my friends and family.**

Invite children to reflect on the artwork and to pray a silent prayer asking God for the strength to make good moral choices.

2 *Connect*

Have children turn to page 248 in their books. Read aloud the introduction and discuss the question.

📖 Invite three children to read aloud the paragraphs of Jesus Is Tempted. Ask: **How did Satan tempt Jesus the first time?** (He suggests to turn stones into bread so that Jesus could eat.) **What choice did Jesus make?** (He did not turn stones into bread.) **How did Satan tempt Jesus the second time?** (He told him to throw himself down so that the angels can save him.) **What choice did Jesus make?** (He did not throw himself down.) **How did Satan tempt Jesus the third time?** (He offered him kingdoms in exchange for his loyalty.) **What choice did Jesus make?** (He did not want the kingdoms.) Say: **In making these choices, Jesus never doubted his Father's love.**

🎵 Play the recording of the story [*Finding God* Grade 3 CD 1, Track 5]. Ask children to sit quietly and listen carefully to the way Jesus responds to the devil's temptations. Invite them to imagine how strong Jesus was standing up to the devil.

Read aloud A Prayer of Petition. Give children time to write their prayers.

Did You Know?

Read aloud this feature. Ask: **What did Jesus teach us?** (Possible answers: to follow God's will, to resist temptation) Say: **The Gospel of Matthew tells us that after Satan tempted him, Jesus went to Galilee to teach the people and to gather disciples. Jesus was more determined than ever to do God's will.**

IF TIME ALLOWS

If time allows, complete one or more of the activities below.

Expression: Music

Follow Jesus 🎵 Play a spiritual song that reinforces the Ten Commandments, such as "What Does It Mean to Follow Jesus?" [*Finding God* Grade 3 CD 2, Track 15]. Ask children to make notes on a separate sheet of paper of what the song suggests as ways to follow Jesus. Suggest they add some of their own ideas to share with the class.

Time: 10 minutes
Materials: CD player, music such as "What Does It Mean to Follow Jesus?" [*Finding God* Grade 3 CD 2, Track 15]

Expression: Art Studio

Temptation Distribute art supplies. Ask children to think of a time that they were tempted to make a bad choice, but instead did the right thing. Have them paint a self-portrait depicting themselves struggling to make the choice or the feeling of relief for making a good choice. Invite them to use light or dark tones like Riviere to aid in the telling of their story.

Time: 20 minutes
Materials: drawing paper, paints

FindingGod · Exploring Faith Through Art

Saint Paul

ART PRINT 23

GRADE 3, UNIT 5, SESSION 23

Catechist Guide page 137

Faith Focus: Paul was happy when he saw how his Church family grew in their faith.

OUTCOMES

▸ Describe how Paul spread joy and love to his Church family.

▸ Explain that Paul wrote letters to his friends, telling them that he loved them.

About the Artist Waclaw Taranczewski was born in 1903 in Poland. He was a famous artist and his paintings are displayed in many Polish museums. His windows are used in various locations throughout Poland. This St. Paul window is from St. Martin's Church in Poznan, Poland. Taranczewski died in 1987.

Art·i·facts Stained glass has been used to decorate churches for more than 1,000 years. Church builders believed that their beauty could raise people's souls closer to God. Glass can be tinted with metallic salts during production or color can be later painted onto clear glass and hardened in a kiln. Bright colors were used for this stained glass of Saint Paul, possibly to represent his happiness that people were growing in their faith.

For your convenience, the Children's Book page is reproduced below.

 EXPLORE ART PRINT **23**

Name _____ Date _____

Art Print 23 shows Saint Paul in bright, happy colors. Paul was happy that people were growing in their faith. How do you feel when you think of God's love?

Saint Paul's Joy

We are joyful when our family is happy and peaceful. Saint Paul was excited when he heard how some of his friends were growing in their faith. He knew that the more they grew in the love of Jesus Christ, the more they would serve others. He wrote his friends a letter telling them how much he loved them.

> I give thanks to God every time I think of you. I pray for you with joy as you help spread the Gospel. I hold you in my heart. I long to see all of you, and pray that your love and understanding will keep growing. May you continue to make good choices so that you will be pure and blameless when Jesus Christ returns.
>
> *adapted from Philippians 1:3–11*

Would you like to receive a letter like this? Which words would make you happy? _____

_____

Link to Liturgy

We hear many of Paul's writings in the Second Reading at Sunday Mass.

www.findinggod.com   Grade 3 · Unit 5 · Session 23

CATECHIST DIRECTIONS

MATERIALS
▸ *Saint Paul* Art Print
▸ Children's Book page 249
▸ Bible

TIME
🕐 10–30 minutes

1 Begin

After completing page 137 in the Children's Book, display the Art Print.

Briefly introduce and discuss the artwork, using information from About the Artist and Artifacts. Say: *You probably have seen stained glass in your church, depicting Bible stories and characters.* Ask: *What colors are used in this stained glass?* (bright ones, yellows, oranges, reds, greens, and bright blues) *What is around Saint Paul's head?* (halo) Say: *Artists have used the halo to show holiness for thousands of years. A halo symbolizes God's grace. Its circular shape is a symbol of eternity, which has no beginning and no end.*

Invite children to reflect on the artwork and to pray a silent prayer thanking God for being part of his family.

2 Connect

Have children turn to page 249 in their books. Read aloud the introduction and discuss the question.

Invite a volunteer to read aloud Saint Paul's Joy. Ask: *What did Paul know would happen as his friends grew in their faith?* (They would serve others.) *How did Paul's friends know he loved them?* (He wrote them letters.)

Say: *Paul started churches in many places. He considered his friends in the churches to be part of his family. He wanted them to be happy and to grow in their faith. He stayed close to his Church family, just as we are close to those we love.* Tell children that you are going to read aloud a letter that Paul wrote to his friends in Philippi, which is in Greece. Show them the letter in the Bible. Then read aloud Paul's Letter to the Philippians.

Read aloud the questions below the letter and give children time to respond.

Link to Liturgy

Read aloud this feature. Check the Sunday Connection on the Loyola Press Web site to find a Second Reading from Paul for an upcoming Sunday. Identify the reading from Paul and then summarize what he writes in that reading. Encourage children to listen to it on the Sunday that it will be read.

IF TIME ALLOWS

If time allows, complete one or more of the activities below.

Expression: Movement

Family Remind children that members of our church are our Church family. Tell children we can be closer to one another by expressing interest in one another. Ask children to write on a slip of paper three interesting facts about themselves. Collect the papers and redistribute to the group. Ask children to take turns standing, reading the paper, and trying to guess the person. After a few attempts, ask the person who wrote the information to stand and read the next set of facts.

Time: 20 minutes
Materials: paper, pencils

Expression: Art Studio

Stained Glass Provide children with a cross cut from construction paper. In advance cut out 2-inch pieces of its interior, allowing the paper to serve as "lead" for a stained glass window. Ask children to cut and tape colored cellophane behind the cross, making a faux stained glass picture to hang in their windows at home.

Time: 20 minutes
Materials: construction paper cross (prepared in advance of class), pencils, scissors, colored cellophane, tape

The full-scale version of this teaching instruction appears on the Art Print easel.

Light Work

ART PRINT 24

GRADE 3, UNIT 5, SESSION 24

Catechist Guide page 143

Faith Focus: Jesus calls us to share with one another in any way we can.

OUTCOMES

▸ Explain that caring for the earth and its inhabitants is our responsibility.

▸ Discuss how small acts and teamwork can make big changes.

About the Artist Louis Ward was born in 1913. Originally from England, he was a Catholic playwright and poet who fled his home because of religious persecution. He was a broadly talented artist who experimented with many mediums. He produced work in watercolor, charcoal, and oil paint. He also worked in a variety of styles. His work contains hints of Impressionism, Cubism, and American Modern. Ward died in 2004.

Art·i·facts The cheerful, sunny painting *Light Work (Strawberry Pickers)* allows us to see and feel how working with others makes our work less difficult. This painting is made with gouache on board. Gouache painting is achieved when a gum or an opaque white pigment is mixed with watercolors and is then applied to the canvas. This forms a coating and is known for the brilliant reflection of colors.

For your convenience, the Children's Book page is reproduced below.

EXPLORE ART PRINT 24

Name _____ Date _____

Art Print 24 shows people sharing God's creation and helping one another. When have you worked with others on a project or task?

Small Acts Make a Big Difference

Taking care of our planet is our job. God expects us to care for all the people, plants, and animals living on earth. This sounds like a very big job! It may feel overwhelming to consider how we could accomplish such a task. However, every big accomplishment begins with one small step. We can work together with our faith community to care for one another and all of God's creation. Working together makes the job feel smaller and more fun.

Small Steps and Teamwork

Draw a picture of yourself taking a small step toward caring for the earth or one another, or draw yourself and a few friends working together to care for God's creation. Describe the scene on the line below.

_____

_____

[blank box]

www.findinggod.com   Grade 3 · Unit 5 · Session 24

©LOYOLAPRESS.

CATECHIST DIRECTIONS

MATERIALS
▸ *Light Work* Art Print
▸ Children's Book page 250
▸ Art supplies

TIME
🕐 10–30 minutes

① *Begin*

After completing page 143 in the Children's Book, display the Art Print.

Briefly introduce and discuss the artwork, using information from About the Artist and Artifacts. Ask: *Why do you think the painting is called* **Light Work?** (Possible answer: The people in the painting are working together.) *How would you describe the overall mood of the painting?* (Possible answers: happy because bright colors are used and people are helping one another; togetherness because there are a mother and child in the picture) *Have you ever been faced with a job that seemed overwhelming? If so, what was it?* (Possible answers: cleaning a messy room, doing dishes, completing homework) *What did you do to make it easier?* (Possible answers: ask for help, work together, do a little at a time)

Invite children to reflect on the artwork and to pray a silent prayer sharing with God that they will care for his creation.

② *Connect*

Have children turn to page 250 in their books. Read aloud the introduction and discuss the question.

Invite volunteers to read aloud Small Acts Make a Big Difference. Ask: *When we have a large task in front of us, what are ways to help us accomplish it?* (begin with a small step, work with others)

Read aloud the directions for Small Steps and Teamwork. Ask: *What are some ideas for small steps?* (Possible answers: clean up the playground, be kind to your brother or sister) *What are some ideas for ways to work with others?* (Possible answers: invite a friend or a family member to volunteer for a soup kitchen; have your classroom host a bake sale to benefit a charity) Say: *Use one of these ideas or think of a new one to use for this activity.* Give children time to draw. Invite volunteers to share their drawings.

IF TIME ALLOWS

If time allows, complete one or more of the activities below.

Expression: Movement
Moving Forward Have children write an idea for helping people or the earth. Put the ideas in a box along with some negative actions prepared in advance, such as litter, fight, be grumpy, be greedy, or be impatient. Have children line up shoulder to shoulder. As you read slips aloud, tell them to take one step forward for positive actions and one step backward for negative actions. Be sure to have more positive than negative ideas.
Time: 20 minutes
Materials: positive and negative action samples, paper, pencils, box

Expression: Art Studio
Many Little Steps Distribute art supplies. Have children trace one of their feet onto a sheet of construction paper. Say: *Inside your footprint write a way in which we can take a step toward making a better world.* Have them cut out the footprint and decorate it. Collect the footprints and assemble them on a "path" drawn on butcher paper. Write a shared goal at the end of the path. Explain that our combined efforts bring us to our goal.
Time: 20 minutes
Materials: long piece of butcher paper, construction paper, markers, art supplies

Expression: Using Imagination in Prayer
God's Team Invite children to imagine being part of the strong group of people in the Art Print. Ask children to consider the power they have to make positive change. Say: *When we put our heads and hands together, we are a powerful force for good.* Ask children to close their eyes. Say: *God, help me see how my every action can make good things happen.* After a moment of silence, end by praying *Amen.*
Time: 10 minutes
Materials: none

FindingGod · Exploring Faith Through Art

The Lamb of God

ART PRINT 25

GRADE 3, UNIT 5, SESSION 25

Catechist Guide page 149

Faith Focus: Easter is a time to celebrate God's merciful love.

OUTCOMES

▶ Explain that Easter celebrates life and the joy of God's mercy.

▶ Describe how Jesus had shown many examples of caring for others.

About the Artist This art piece is an illustration for a religious manuscript. In the ninth century when it was made, religious texts were the only books. They were handwritten and illustrated by monks on vellum paper that has an opaque, waxy texture. They were rare and very valuable. The illustrators sometimes incorporated a subtle personal symbol as their form of attribution, but there was rarely, if ever, a name attributed to the work, as they considered their work to be attributed directly to God.

Art·i·facts The cross in the illustration symbolizes Jesus' triumph over sin and death. The four creatures symbolize the Gospel authors, the four Evangelists: Matthew, Mark, Luke, and John. Matthew is represented as a winged man, which symbolizes the ability to reason. Mark is represented by a lion, which symbolizes courage. Luke is represented by the ox, which is known for strength and service. John is represented by the eagle, because of John's lofty presentation of Jesus' divine nature. The lamb at the center represents Jesus.

For your convenience, the Children's Book page is reproduced below.

EXPLORE ART PRINT **25**

Name _____ Date _____

Art Print 25 shows many Christian symbols. What symbols are used in your home to celebrate the joyful time of Easter?

Celebrate Easter

Easter is the celebration of life. Jesus was born and lived to teach us how to be closer to God his Father. Jesus died so that our sins could be forgiven and our souls could be joined forever with God. God sent his Son, Jesus, to show us his mercy and love.

The Resurrection

After his death Jesus' friends came to his tomb and found it empty. His friends were afraid. Jesus appeared to Mary Magdalene and told her not to be sad. He also appeared many times to comfort and encourage the apostles. On one occasion he appeared to Peter and said, "Tend my sheep." The sheep he spoke of were his people. As disciples we are called to do the same as Peter. We celebrate Easter by committing ourselves to the service of others.

In Celebration of Easter

Jesus showed us how to treat others with compassion, respect, and mercy. In celebration of Easter, draw a picture of yourself doing one of those things.

© LOYOLA PRESS.

www.findinggod.com

Grade 3 · Unit 5 · Session 25

CATECHIST DIRECTIONS

MATERIALS
▶ *The Lamb of God* Art Print
▶ Children's Book page 251
▶ Art supplies

TIME
10–30 minutes

1 Begin

After completing page 149 in the Children's Book, display the Art Print.

Briefly introduce and discuss the artwork, using information from About the Artist and Artifacts. Ask: **What do you see in this painting?** (a cross, a lamb with a halo, a lion with wings, a winged man, a winged ox, an eagle; all are holding books) Say: **These are symbols used to give us a message. The person and animals represented in the painting all have wings, which are symbols of heavenly power. They all have books, which are the Scriptures.** Ask: **Why do you think the lamb is used as a symbol of Jesus?** (Possible answer: We call Jesus the Lamb of God. Jesus' Death on the cross was the ultimate sacrifice.)

Invite children to reflect on the artwork and to pray a silent prayer thanking God for his merciful love.

2 Connect

Have children turn to page 251 in their books. Read aloud the introduction and discuss the question.

Invite a volunteer to read aloud Celebrate Easter. Ask: **Why did God send Jesus?** (to show us his mercy and love)

Have a volunteer read aloud The Resurrection. Ask: **Why were the apostles afraid?** (Possible answers: Their leader had been crucified; they were afraid their lives were in danger; they were confused and sad, and didn't know how to proceed with Jesus' work.) **How did Jesus help Mary Magdalene?** (He appeared to her and told her not to be afraid.) **What did Jesus mean when he told Peter to tend to his sheep?** (to watch over and help his people) Ask: **How can we live as disciples?** (by committing ourselves to the service of others)

Read aloud the directions for In Celebration of Easter. Distribute art supplies and give children time to complete their drawings. Invite volunteers to discuss their drawings.

IF TIME ALLOWS

If time allows, complete one or more of the activities below.

Expression: Music

Serving Others 🎵 Play a song that reinforces Jesus' message to "tend his sheep," such as "What Does It Mean to Follow Jesus?" [*Finding God* Grade 3 CD 2, Track 15]. Ask children to listen carefully to the lyrics for the ways we can be like Jesus. After the song ask children to tell one way that they remember and list the ways on the board.

Time: 3 minutes
Materials: CD player, music such as "What Does It Mean to Follow Jesus?" [*Finding God* Grade 3 CD 2, Track 15]

Expression: Art Studio

Easter Symbols Recall the Art Print. Provide children with colored pencils and paper. Invite children to draw their own symbols for Easter. Play reflective music in the background.

Time: 20 minutes
Materials: drawing paper, colored pencils, CD player, reflective music

Expression: Using Imagination in Prayer

Mercy Give children time to reflect on God's merciful love. Say: **Imagine you went to Jesus' tomb and did not find him there. Think about how you would feel. Then Jesus appears to you with open arms. You hug him and say how happy you are to see him. He is happy to be with you and asks you to tend to his sheep by showing mercy to all. Take a few moments to think about someone to whom you can show mercy.** Pause for 10 or 15 seconds and then close the prayer time by having the group sing *Alleluia*.

Time: 10 minutes
Materials: none

Answer Key

EXPLORE ART PRINT 3

Name _____ Date _____

Art Print 3 shows two children making peace with each other. Have you ever had to say you were sorry to someone or forgive someone for hurting you?

Caring Friends

God wants us to care for others. There are many ways you can be a caring friend to those who need you. You can do this by thinking of their feelings. Listening to people can help you understand how they feel. Another way to care for people is to forgive them. God wants us to forgive others, just as he forgives us. In the Lord's Prayer, we ask God to forgive us as we forgive others. It takes love and strength to be able to forgive someone. That is why we are like Jesus when we forgive others.

What Would You Do?

Sometimes people do things that hurt us. Circle how you could show forgiveness in these situations.

1. Your little brother rode your new bike and fell. The chain on the bike came off.

   a. You tell him that he can never ride your bike again.

   (b.) You ask him if he is hurt and suggest you fix the bike together.

2. Your good friend went to the park with another friend and did not invite you. Later she told you she was sorry she did not include you.

   (a.) You tell her it is OK, and you invite both of them to play.

   b. You do not invite your friend the next time you do something special.

EXPLORE ART PRINT 7

Name _____ Date _____

Art Print 7 shows a girl quietly praying outside. When do you make time to pray and speak with God?

Showing Our Love

Praying often is one way to become closer to God. When we show love to others, we show our love of God and our neighbor. God gave Moses the Ten Commandments to teach us how to love God and one another. Through the commandments we can become closer to God. We should also keep an open heart and always be ready to help our neighbor.

Paying Attention

Consider the following situations. Circle the letter of the action that helps you become closer to God.

1. You are playing baseball with your friends. A girl you do not know comes up to the group and asks if she can play. You should

   a. ignore her and keep playing.

   (b.) tell her that she can take your turn.

   c. say, "Maybe next time."

2. At school it is finally lunchtime. You notice that a boy at the next table is sitting quietly with no food. You should

   a. tease him about forgetting his lunch.

   b. tell your friends, "He must have the worst parents in the world!"

   (c.) offer him some of your lunch.

Reading God's Word

For where your treasure is, there also will your heart be.

Matthew 6:21

EXPLORE ART PRINT 21

Name _____ Date _____

Art Print 21 shows Jesus and his heart, which is the symbol for the virtue of charity. Which virtue did you show someone today?

Symbols of the Virtues

Symbols stand for something else or remind us of something. Butterflies are used as symbols of Jesus' Resurrection, doves symbolize the Holy Spirit, and water symbolizes Baptism. The cross is a symbol of our faith. It reminds us that Jesus died for our sins. An anchor is a symbol of hope. Just as an anchor holds a ship, so does hope help us hold on to Jesus. When we think of charity, or love, a heart comes to mind because the heart is a symbol of love.

Matching Virtues

Label each symbol and each sentence using *faith*, *hope*, or *charity*.

_____ hope _____   _____ faith _____   _____ charity _____

1. Martha trusts that God will always guide her. ___ hope ___

2. Anton shows his love by visiting a sick classmate. ___ charity ___

3. Ethan believes that Jesus lived and died for us. ___ faith ___

GLOSSARY AND INDEX

The following resources for children and the acknowledgments are reproduced in this section for your convenience.

- **Children's Book Glossary**
- **Children's Book Index**
- **Children's Book Acknowledgments**

Glossary

A

Abba an informal name for *Father* in the language Jesus spoke. Jesus called God the Father "Abba." [Abba]

absolution the forgiveness God offers us in the Sacrament of Penance and Reconciliation. After we say that we are sorry for our sins, we receive God's absolution from the priest. [absolución]

Advent the four weeks before Christmas. It is a time of joyful preparation for the celebration of Jesus' birth as our Savior. [Adviento]

Alleluia a prayer of praise to God. It is usually sung as the Gospel Acclamation before the Gospel Reading at Mass except during Lent. [Aleluya]

All Saints Day November 1, the day on which the Church honors all who have died and now live with God as saints in Heaven. This group includes those who have been declared saints by the Church and many others known only to God. [Día de Todos los Santos]

All Souls Day November 2, the day on which the Church remembers all who have died as friends of God. We pray that they may rest in peace. [Día de los Fieles Difuntos]

almsgiving the practice of giving money to those in need as an act of love [limosna, dar]

altar the table in the church on which the priest celebrates Mass, during which the sacrifice of Christ on the cross is made present in the Sacrament of the Eucharist. The altar represents two aspects of the mystery of the Eucharist. First, it is where Jesus Christ offers himself for our sins. Second, it is where he gives us himself as our food for eternal life. [altar]

ambo a raised stand from which a person reads the Word of God during Mass [ambón]

Amen the final word in any prayer. *Amen* means "This is true." When we pray "Amen," it shows that we really mean what we have just said. [Amén]

angel a spiritual creature who brings a message from God [ángel]

Angelus a Catholic devotion recited three times a day—morning, noon, and evening. The devotion recalls the mystery of the Incarnation beginning with the coming of the angel to Mary, her acceptance of the invitation to be Jesus' mother, and on the Word made flesh. [Ángelus]

Annunciation the announcement to Mary by the angel Gabriel that God had chosen her to be the mother of Jesus [Anunciación]

Anointing of the Sick one of the seven sacraments. In this sacrament a sick person is anointed with holy oil and receives the strength, peace, and courage to overcome the difficulties that come with illness. [Unción de los enfermos]

apostle one of twelve chosen men who accompanied Jesus in his ministry and were witnesses to the Resurrection [apóstol]

Apostles' Creed | capital sins

Apostles' Creed a statement of Christian belief. The Apostles' Creed, developed out of a creed used during Baptism in Rome, lists simple statements of belief in God the Father, Jesus Christ the Son, and the Holy Spirit. The profession of faith used in Baptism today is based on the Apostles' Creed. [Credo de los Apóstoles]

apostolic one of the four Marks of the Church. The Church is apostolic because it hands on the teachings of the apostles through their successors, the bishops. [apostólica]

Ascension the return of Jesus to Heaven. In the Acts of the Apostles, it is written that Jesus, after his Resurrection, spent 40 days on earth, instructing his followers. He then returned to his Father in Heaven. [Ascensión]

Ash Wednesday the first day of Lent, on which we receive ashes on our foreheads. The ashes remind us to prepare for Easter by showing sorrow for the choices we make that offend God and hurt our relationships with others. [Miércoles de Ceniza]

B

Baptism one of the three Sacraments of Initiation. Baptism frees us from Original Sin and gives us new life in Jesus Christ through the Holy Spirit. [Bautismo]

Beatitudes the eight ways we can behave to live a blessed life. Jesus teaches us that if we live according to the Beatitudes, we will live a happy Christian life. [Bienaventuranzas]

Bible the history of God's promise to care for us and his call for us to be faithful to him. God asked that people be faithful first through the beliefs of the Jewish people and then through belief in the life, Death, and Resurrection of Jesus Christ. [Biblia]

bishop a man who has received the fullness of Holy Orders. He has inherited his duties from the original apostles. He cares for the Church today and is a principal teacher in the Church. [obispo]

Blessed Sacrament the Eucharist that has been consecrated by the priest at Mass. It is kept in the tabernacle to adore and to be taken to those who are sick. [Santísimo Sacramento]

blessing a prayer that calls for God's power and care upon some person, place, thing, or special activity [bendición]

Body and Blood of Christ the Bread and Wine that has been consecrated by the priest at Mass. It still looks like bread and wine, but it is actually the Body and Blood of Jesus Christ. [Cuerpo y Sangre de Cristo]

Bread of Life a title for Jesus that tells us that he is the Bread that is food for the faithful [pan de vida]

C

capital sins those sins that can lead us to more serious sin. The seven capital sins are pride, covetousness, envy, anger, gluttony, lust, and sloth. [pecados capitales]

cast lots to throw down small stones or pebbles called lots to help determine a decision needing divine guidance. Lots were cast to choose the disciple to replace Judas in Acts of the Apostles 1:23–26. Roman soldiers also cast lots to divide Jesus' clothing among them as in John 19:24. [echar a suertes]

catholic one of the four Marks of the Church. The Church is catholic because Jesus is fully present in it and because Jesus has given the Church to the whole world. [católico]

celebrant a bishop or priest who leads the people in praying the Mass. A deacon who baptizes or witnesses a marriage is also a celebrant. [celebrante]

celebrate worshiping and praising God with prayers and songs, especially in the celebration of the Eucharist [celebrar]

charity a virtue given to us by God. Charity helps us love God above all things and our neighbor as ourselves. [caridad]

chasuble the visible liturgical vestment worn by the bishop or priest at Mass. A newly ordained priest receives a chasuble as part of the ordination ritual. [casulla]

Christ a title that means "anointed with oil." It is from a Greek word that means the same thing as the Hebrew word *Messiah*, or "anointed." It is the name given to Jesus after the Resurrection. [Cristo]

Christian the name given to all those who have been anointed through the gift of the Holy Spirit in Baptism and have become followers of Jesus Christ [cristiano]

Christmas the day on which we celebrate the birth of Jesus (December 25) [Navidad]

Church the name given to all of Christ's followers throughout the world. It is also the name of the building where we gather to pray to God and the name of our community as we gather to praise God. [Iglesia]

commandment a standard, or rule, for living as God wants us to live. Jesus summarized all the commandments into two: love God and love your neighbor. [mandamiento]

Communion of Saints the union of all who have been saved in Jesus Christ, both those who are alive and those who have died [Comunión de los Santos]

community Christians who are gathered in the name of Jesus Christ to receive his grace and live according to his values [comunidad]

compassion God's fundamental attitude toward his people. This is best seen in Jesus' reaching out to care for those in need. Acting with compassion and mercy toward those in need identifies a person as belonging to God. [compasión]

confession | crosier

confession the act of telling our sins to a priest in the Sacrament of Penance and Reconciliation. The sacrament itself is sometimes referred to as confession. [confesión]

Confirmation the sacrament that completes the grace we receive in Baptism. Confirmation seals, or confirms, this grace through the seven Gifts of the Holy Spirit that we receive as part of Confirmation. This sacrament also unites us more closely in Jesus Christ. [confirmación]

conscience the inner voice that helps each of us to know the law that God has placed in our hearts. It guides us to do good and avoid evil. [conciencia]

consecration the making of a thing or person to be special to God through a prayer or blessing. At Mass the words of the priest are a consecration of the bread and wine that become the Body and Blood of Christ. People or objects set apart for God in a special way are also consecrated. For example, churches and altars are consecrated for use in liturgy. In the same way, bishops are consecrated as they receive the fullness of the Sacrament of Holy Orders. [consagración]

contrition the sorrow we feel when we know that we have sinned, followed by the decision not to sin again. Contrition is the most important part of our celebration of the Sacrament of Penance and Reconciliation. [contrición]

conversion the change of heart that directs each person away from sin and toward God [conversión]

Corporal Works of Mercy kind acts by which we help our neighbors with their everyday material needs. Corporal Works of Mercy include feeding the hungry, finding a home for the homeless, clothing the naked, visiting the sick and those in prison, giving alms to the poor, and burying the dead. [obras corporales de misericordia]

Covenant a solemn agreement between people or between people and God. God made covenants with humanity through agreements with Noah, Abraham, and Moses. These covenants offered Salvation. God's new and final covenant was established through Jesus' life, Death, Resurrection, and Ascension. [alianza]

covet the excessive desire to possess something of value belonging to another person to the point of letting envy destroy the relationship [codiciar]

creation God's act of making everything that exists outside himself. Creation is everything that exists. God said that all of reation is good. [creación]

Creator God, who made everything that is and whom we can come to know through everything he created [Creador]

creed a brief summary of what people believe. The Apostles' Creed is a summary of Christian beliefs. [credo]

crosier the staff carried by a bishop. This staff shows that the bishop cares for us in the same way that a shepherd cares for his sheep. It also reminds us that he represents Jesus, the Good Shepherd. [báculo]

D

deacon a man ordained through the Sacrament of Holy Orders to help the bishop and priests in the work of the Church [diácono]

diocese the members of the Church in a particular area, gathered under the leadership of a bishop [diócesis]

disciple a person who has accepted Jesus' message and tries to live as Jesus did [discípulo]

discipleship for Christians, the willingness to answer the call to follow Jesus. The call is received in Baptism, nourished in the Eucharist, and practiced in service to the world. [discipulado]

Dismissal the part of the Mass in which the people are sent forth by the priest or deacon to do good works and praise and bless God [despedida]

Divine Praises a series of praises beginning with "Blessed be God," traditionally prayed at the end of the worship of the Blessed Sacrament in benediction [alabanzas de desagravio]

E

Easter the celebration of the bodily raising of Jesus Christ from the dead. Easter is the most important Christian feast. [Pascua]

Emmanuel a name from the Old Testament that means "God with us." Because Jesus is always with us, we often call him by the name *Emmanuel*. [Emanuel]

envy a feeling of resentment or sadness because someone has a quality, a talent, or a possession that we want. Envy is one of the seven capital sins, and it is contrary to the Tenth Commandment. [envidia]

Epiphany the day on which we celebrate the visit of the Magi to Jesus after his birth. This is the day that Jesus was revealed as the Savior of the whole world. [Epifanía]

epistle a letter written by Saint Paul or another leader to a group of Christians in the early Church. Twenty-one of the 27 books of the New Testament are epistles. [epístola]

eternal life living happily with God in Heaven when we die in grace and friendship with him [vida eterna]

Eucharist the sacrament in which we give thanks to God for the consecrated Bread and Wine that is the Body and Blood of Jesus Christ. This sacrament brings us into union with Jesus Christ and his saving Death and Resurrection. [Eucaristía]

Evangelists the four men credited with writing the Gospels of Matthew, Mark, Luke, and John [evangelista]

examination of conscience the act of prayerfully thinking about what we have said or done that may have hurt our relationship with God or with others. An examination of conscience is an important part of preparing to celebrate the Sacrament of Penance and Reconciliation. [examen de conciencia]

Glossary **257**

faith | Heaven

F

faith a gift of God that helps us to believe in him and live as he wants us to live. We express our faith in the words of the Apostles' Creed.   [fe]

fasting limiting the amount we eat for a period of time to express sorrow for sin and to make ourselves more aware of God's action in our lives   [ayuno]

forgiveness the willingness to be kind to people who have hurt us but have then said that they are sorry. Because God always forgives us when we say that we are sorry, we forgive others in the same way.   [perdón]

fortitude the strength to do the right thing even when that is difficult. Fortitude is one of the four central human virtues, called the cardinal virtues, by which we guide our Christian life. It is also one of the Gifts of the Holy Spirit.   [fortaleza]

free will our ability to choose to do good because God has made us like him [libre albedrío]

Fruits of the Holy Spirit the ways in which we act because God is alive in us [frutos del Espíritu Santo]

G

genuflect to show respect in church by touching a knee to the ground, especially when we are before the Blessed Sacrament in the tabernacle   [genuflexión, hacer la]

gestures the movements we make, such as the Sign of the Cross or bowing, to show our reverence during prayer   [gestos]

gift of peace the peace that Jesus gives to us that flows from his relationship with his Father. This is the peace that the world cannot give, for it is the gift of Salvation that only Jesus can give.   [don de la paz]

God the Father, Son, and Holy Spirit: one God in three distinct Persons. God created us, saves us, and lives in us.   [Dios]

godparent a witness to Baptism who helps the baptized person follow the path of Christian life [padrino/madrina de Bautismo]

Gospel the good news of God's mercy and love. We experience this news in the story of Jesus' life, Death, Resurrection, and Ascension. The story is presented to us in four books in the New Testament: the Gospels of Matthew, Mark, Luke, and John.   [Evangelio]

grace the gift from God given to us without our deserving it. Sanctifying grace fills us with God's life and enables us always to be his friends. Grace also helps us to live as God wants us to live. [gracia]

Great Commandment Jesus' essential teaching that we are to love both God and our neighbor as we love ourselves [Mandamiento Mayor, el]

guardian angel the angel who has been appointed to pray for and help the person live a holy life   [ángel de la guarda]

H

Heaven the life with God that is full of happiness and never ends   [cielo]

holy one of the four Marks of the Church. It is the kind of life we live when we share in the life of God, who is all holiness. The Church is holy because of her union with Jesus Christ. [santa]

Holy Communion the consecrated Bread and Wine that we receive at Mass, which is truly the Body and Blood of Jesus Christ. It brings us into union with Jesus Christ and his saving Death and Resurrection. [Sagrada Comunión]

Holy Days of Obligation the principal feast days, other than Sundays, of the Church. On Holy Days of Obligation, we celebrate the great things that God has done for us through Jesus Christ and the saints. [días de precepto]

Holy Family the family made up of Jesus; his mother, Mary; and his foster father, Joseph [Sagrada Familia]

Holy Orders the sacrament through which the mission, or task, given by Jesus to his apostles continues in the Church. Holy Orders has three degrees: deacon, priest, and bishop. [sacramento del Orden]

Holy Spirit the third Person of the Trinity, who is sent to us as our helper, and, through Baptism and Confirmation, fills us with God's life [Espíritu Santo]

Holy Thursday the Thursday of Holy Week on which the Mass of the Lord's Supper is celebrated, commemorating the institution of the Eucharist. The season of Lent ends with the celebration of the Mass of the Lord's Supper. [Jueves Santo]

holy water the water that has been blessed and is used as a sacramental to remind us of our Baptism [agua bendita]

Holy Week the celebration of the events surrounding Jesus' establishment of the Eucharist, his suffering, Death, and Resurrection. Holy Week commemorates Jesus' triumphal entry into Jerusalem on Palm Sunday, the gift of himself in the Eucharist on Holy Thursday, his Death on Good Friday, and his Resurrection at the Easter Vigil on Holy Saturday. [Semana Santa]

Homily an explanation of God's Word. The Homily explains the Word of God that we hear in the Bible readings at church. [homilía]

honor giving God or a person the respect that they are owed. God is given this respect as our Creator and Redeemer. All people are worthy of respect as children of God. [honrar]

hope the trust that God will always be with us. We also trust that he will make us happy now and help us to live in a way that keeps us with him forever. [esperanza]

I

idolatry in the Bible, the false, pagan worship of physical images given adoration as gods. For Christians today idolatry occurs whenever someone honors and reveres something in place of God. This can mean giving honor to power, pleasure, race, ancestors, money, or the state rather than giving God the honor owed to him. [idolatría]

Jesus | Magnificat

J

Jesus the Son of God, who was born of the Virgin Mary and who died, was raised from the dead, and ascended into Heaven so that we can live with God forever. *Jesus* means "God saves." [Jesús]

Joseph the foster father of Jesus, who was engaged to Mary when the angel announced that Mary would have a child through the power of the Holy Spirit [José]

justice the strong, firm desire to give to God and others what is due them. Justice is one of the four central human virtues, called the cardinal virtues, by which we guide our Christian life. [justicia]

K

Kingdom of God God's rule over us. We experience the Kingdom of God in part now, and we will experience it fully in Heaven. The Kingdom of God was announced in the Gospel and is present in the Eucharist. [reino de Dios]

L

Lamb of God the title for Jesus that emphasizes his willingness to give up his life for the Salvation of the world. Jesus is the Lamb without blemish or sin who delivers us through his sacrificial Death. [cordero de Dios]

Last Supper the last meal Jesus ate with his disciples on the night before he died. At the Last Supper, Jesus took bread and wine, blessed them, and said that they were his Body and Blood. Every Mass is a remembrance of this last meal. [Última Cena]

Lectionary for Mass the book that contains all the Bible stories we read at Mass [Leccionario]

Lent six weeks during which we prepare to celebrate, with special prayers and action, the rising of Jesus from the dead at Easter. Jesus rose from the dead to save us. [Cuaresma]

Light of the World a name that helps us to see that Jesus is the light that leads us to the Father. Jesus lights up our minds and hearts with knowledge of God. [luz del mundo]

liturgical year the calendar that tells us when to celebrate the feasts of Jesus' birth, life, Death, Resurrection, and Ascension [año litúrgico]

liturgy the public prayer of the Church that celebrates the wonderful things God has done for us in Jesus Christ [liturgia]

Liturgy of the Eucharist a main part of the Mass in which the bread and wine are consecrated and truly become the Body and Blood of Jesus Christ. We then receive the Body and Blood of Jesus Christ in Holy Communion. [Liturgia de la Eucaristía]

Liturgy of the Word a main part of the Mass in which we listen to God's Word from the Bible and consider what it means for us today [Liturgia de la Palabra]

M

Magnificat Mary's song of praise to God for the great things he has done for her and for his plans for us through Jesus [Magníficat]

Marks of the Church | **mortal sin**

Marks of the Church the four most important characteristics of the Church. The Church is one, holy, catholic, and apostolic.   [atributos de la Iglesia]

Mary the mother of Jesus. She is called blessed and "full of grace" because God chose her to be the mother of the Son of God. [María]

Mass the most important sacramental celebration of the Church. The celebration of the Mass was established by Jesus at the Last Supper as a remembrance of his Death and Resurrection. At Mass we listen to God's Word from the Bible and receive Jesus Christ in the consecrated Bread and Wine that are his Body and Blood. [misa]

Matrimony a solemn agreement between a woman and a man to be partners for life, both for their own good and for raising children. Marriage is a sacrament when the agreement is properly made between baptized Christians. [Matrimonio]

mercy the gift to be able to respond to those in need with care and compassion. The gift of mercy is a grace given to us by Jesus Christ. [misericordia]

Messiah a title that means "anointed with oil." It is from a Hebrew word that means the same thing as the Greek word *Christ*, the name given to Jesus after the Resurrection. [Mesías]

ministry service or work done for others. Ministry is also done by bishops, priests, and deacons in the celebration of the sacraments. All those baptized are called to different kinds of ministry in the liturgy and in service to the needs of others. [ministerio]

miracle the healing of a person, or an occasion when nature is controlled that can only be recognized as God's action [milagro]

mission the work of Jesus Christ that is continued in the Church through the Holy Spirit. The mission of the Church is to proclaim Salvation through Jesus' life, Death, Resurrection, and Ascension. [misión]

monastery a place where men or women live out their solemn promises of poverty, chastity, and obedience. They live a stable, or firm, community life; they spend their days in public prayer, work, and meditation. [monasterio]

moral choice a choice to do what is right. We make moral choices because they help us grow closer to God. We make them also because we have the freedom to choose what is right and to avoid what is wrong. [opción moral]

moral law a rule for living that has been established by God and people in authority who are concerned about the good of all people. Moral laws are based on God's direction to us to do what is right and avoid what is wrong. [ley moral]

mortal sin a decision to turn away from God by doing something that we know is seriously wrong and so cuts us off from God's life [pecado mortal]

Mystical Body of Christ | one

Mystical Body of Christ the members of the Church formed into a spiritual body and bound together by the life communicated by Jesus Christ through the sacraments. Christ is the center of this body and the source of its life. In it we are all united. Each member of this body receives from Christ gifts fitting for him or her. [Cuerpo Místico de Cristo]

N

Nativity scene a picture or crèche that shows Jesus, Mary, and Joseph in the stable after the birth of Jesus as described in the Gospels of Matthew and Luke [escena de la Natividad del Señor]

neighbor according to Jesus, every person, as each person is made in God's image. We are meant to form mutually supportive relationships with our neighbors. [prójimo]

New Testament the 27 books of the second part of the Bible, which tell of the teaching, ministry, and saving events of the life of Jesus. The four Gospels present Jesus' life, Death, and Resurrection. The Acts of the Apostles tells the story of Jesus' Ascension into Heaven. It also shows how Jesus' message of Salvation spread through the growth of the Church. Various letters instruct us in how to live as followers of Jesus Christ. The Book of Revelation offers encouragement to Christians living through persecution. [Nuevo Testamento]

O

obedience the act of willingly following what God asks us to do for our Salvation. The Fourth Commandment requires children to obey their parents, and all people are required to obey civil authority when it acts for the good of all. [obediencia]

obey follow the teachings or directions given by God or by someone who has authority over us [obedecer]

oil of the sick the oil blessed by the bishop during Holy Week and used in the Sacrament of the Anointing of the Sick, which brings spiritual and, if it is God's will, physical healing [óleo de los enfermos]

Old Testament the first 46 books of the Bible, which tell of God's Covenant with the people of Israel and his plan for the Salvation of all people. The first five books are known as the Torah. The Old Testament is fulfilled in the New Testament, but God's Covenant presented in the Old Testament has permanent value and has never been revoked or set aside. [Antiguo Testamento]

one one of the four Marks of the Church. The Church is one because of its source in the one God and because of its founder, Jesus Christ. Jesus, through his Death on the cross, united all to God in one body. Within the unity of the Church, there is great diversity because of the variety of the gifts given to its members. [una]

ordained those men who have received the Sacrament of Holy Orders so that they may preside at the celebration of the Eucharist and serve as leaders and teachers of the Church [ordenado]

Ordinary Time the longest liturgical season of the Church year. It is divided into two periods—the first after the Christmas season and the second after Pentecost. The first period focuses on Jesus' childhood and public ministry. The second period focuses on Christ's reign as King of Kings. [Tiempo Ordinario]

Original Sin the result of the sin by which the first human beings disobeyed God and chose to follow their own will rather than God's will. Because of this act, all human beings lost the original blessing that God had intended, and they became subject to sin and death. In Baptism we are restored to life with God through Jesus Christ. [pecado original]

P

Palm Sunday the celebration of Jesus' triumphant entry into Jerusalem on the Sunday before Easter. It begins a week-long commemoration of the saving events of Holy Week. [Domingo de Ramos]

parable one of the stories that Jesus told to show us what the Kingdom of God is like. Parables present images, or scenes, drawn from everyday life. These images show us the radical, or serious, choice we make when we respond to the invitation to enter the Kingdom of God. [parábola]

parish a community of believers in Jesus Christ who meet regularly in a specific area to worship God under the leadership of a pastor [parroquia]

Paschal Mystery the work of Salvation accomplished by Jesus Christ through his Passion, Death, Resurrection, and Ascension. The Paschal Mystery is celebrated in the liturgy of the Church. We experience its saving effects in the sacraments. [Misterio Pascual]

pastor a priest who is responsible for the spiritual care of the members of a parish community [pastor]

peacemaker a person who teaches us to be respectful in our words and actions toward one another [paz, los que trabajar por la]

penance the turning away from sin with a desire to change our life and more closely live the way God wants us to live. We express our penance externally by praying, fasting, and helping those who are poor. This is also the name of the action that the priest asks us to take or the prayers that he asks us to pray after he absolves us in the Sacrament of Penance and Reconciliation. (*See* Sacrament of Penance and Reconciliation.) [penitencia]

Pentecost the 50th day after Jesus was raised from the dead. On this day the Holy Spirit was sent from Heaven, and the Church was born. [Pentecostés]

People of God another name for the Church. In the same way that the people of Israel were God's people through the Covenant he made with them, the Church is a priestly, prophetic, and royal people through the new and eternal covenant in Jesus Christ. [pueblo de Dios]

GLOSSARY

personal sin | psalm

personal sin a sin we choose to commit, whether serious (mortal) or less serious (venial). Although the result of Original Sin is to leave us with a tendency to sin, God's grace, especially through the sacraments, helps us to choose good over sin. [pecado personal]

petition a request of God, asking him to fulfill a need. When we share in God's saving love, we understand that every need is one that we can ask God to help us with through petition. [petición]

plague a natural calamity or disease that is seen as being inflicted by God as a remedial event to make people more conscious of their duties toward God and one another. (Numbers 14:37) In Exodus 7:14—12:30, the plagues inflicted on the Egyptians are seen as the means by which God convinced the Egyptians to free the Hebrew people from slavery. [plaga]

pope the bishop of Rome, successor of Saint Peter, and leader of the Roman Catholic Church. Because he has the authority to act in the name of Christ, the pope is called the Vicar of Christ. The pope and all of the bishops together make up the living, teaching office of the Church, the Magisterium. [Papa]

praise the expression of our response to God, not only for what he does, but simply because he is. In the Eucharist the whole Church joins with Jesus Christ in expressing praise and thanksgiving to the Father. [alabanza]

prayer the raising of our hearts and minds to God. We are able to speak to and listen to God in prayer because he teaches us how to do so. [oración]

Precepts of the Church those positive requirements that the pastoral authority of the Church has determined as necessary. These requirements describe the minimum effort we must make in prayer and the moral life. The Precepts of the Church ensure that all Catholics move beyond the minimum by growing in love of God and love of neighbor. [preceptos de la Iglesia]

pride a false image of ourselves that goes beyond what we deserve as God's creation. Pride puts us in competition with God. It is one of the seven capital sins. [soberbia]

priest a man who has accepted God's special call to serve the Church by guiding it and building it up through the celebration of the sacraments [sacerdote]

prudence the virtue that directs us toward the good. It also helps us to choose the correct means to achieve that good. Prudence is one of the cardinal virtues that guide our conscience and influence us to live according to the law of Christ. [prudencia]

psalm a prayer in the form of a poem. Psalms were written to be sung in public worship. Each psalm expresses an aspect, or feature, of the depth of human prayer. Over several centuries 150 psalms were gathered to form the Book of Psalms, used in worship in the Old Testament. [salmo]

R

reconciliation the renewal of friendship after that friendship has been broken by some action or lack of action. In the Sacrament of Penance and Reconciliation, through God's mercy and forgiveness, we are reconciled with God, the Church, and others. [reconciliación]

Redeemer Jesus Christ, whose life, Death on the cross, Resurrection from the dead, and Ascension into Heaven set us free from sin and brings us redemption [Redentor]

redemption our being set free from sin through the life, Death on the cross, Resurrection from the dead, and Ascension into Heaven of Jesus Christ [redención]

repentance our turning away from sin with a desire to change our lives and live more closely as God wants us to live. We express our penance externally by prayer, fasting, and helping those who are poor. [arrepentimiento]

Resurrection the bodily raising of Jesus Christ from the dead on the third day after his Death on the cross. The Resurrection is the crowning truth of our faith. [Resurrección]

Revelation God's communication of himself to us through the words and deeds he has used throughout history. Revelation shows us the mystery of his plan for our Salvation in his Son, Jesus Christ. [revelación]

rite one of the many forms followed in celebrating liturgy in the Church. A rite may differ according to the culture or country where it is celebrated. *Rite* also means "the special form for celebrating each sacrament." [rito]

Rosary a prayer in honor of the Blessed Virgin Mary. When we pray the Rosary, we meditate on the mysteries of Jesus Christ's life while praying the Hail Mary on five sets of ten beads and the Lord's Prayer on the beads in between. [Rosario]

S

sacrament one of seven ways through which God's life enters our lives through the work of the Holy Spirit. Jesus gave us three sacraments that bring us into the Church: Baptism, Confirmation, and the Eucharist. He gave us two sacraments that bring us healing: Penance and Reconciliation and Anointing of the Sick. He also gave us two sacraments that help members serve the community: Matrimony and Holy Orders. [sacramento]

sacramental an object, a prayer, or a blessing given by the Church to help us grow in our spiritual life [sacramental]

Sacrament of Penance and Reconciliation the sacrament in which we celebrate God's forgiveness of our sins and our reconciliation with God and the Church. Penance includes sorrow for the sins we have committed, confession of sins, absolution by the priest, and doing the penance that shows our sorrow. [sacramento de la Penitencia y de la Reconciliación]

Sacraments of Initiation | soul

Sacraments of Initiation the sacraments that are the foundation of our Christian life. We are born anew in Baptism, strengthened by Confirmation, and receive in the Eucharist the food of eternal life. [sacramentos de iniciación]

Sacrifice of the Mass the sacrifice of Jesus on the cross, which is remembered and made present in the Eucharist [Sacrificio de la Misa]

saint a holy person who has died united with God. The Church has said that this person is now with God forever in Heaven. [santo]

Salvation the gift of forgiveness of sin and the restoration of friendship with God. God alone can give us Salvation. [salvación]

Savior Jesus, the Son of God, who became man to forgive our sins and restore our friendship with God. *Jesus* means "God saves." [Salvador]

Scriptures the holy writings of Jews and Christians collected in the Old and New Testaments of the Bible [Sagrada Escritura]

seal of confession the obligation on the part of the priest not to reveal what he has heard in the Sacrament of Penance and Reconciliation under any circumstances [sigilo sacramental]

Sermon on the Mount the words of Jesus, written in Chapters 5 through 7 of the Gospel of Matthew, in which Jesus reveals how he has fulfilled God's Law given to Moses. The Sermon on the Mount begins with the eight Beatitudes and includes the Lord's Prayer. [Sermón de la montaña]

Sign of Peace the part of the Mass in which we offer a gesture of peace to one another as we prepare to receive Holy Communion [rito de la paz]

Sign of the Cross the gesture that we make that signifies our belief in God the Father, the Son, and the Holy Spirit [señal de la cruz]

sin a choice we make that offends God and hurts our relationships with others. Some sin is mortal and needs to be confessed in the Sacrament of Penance and Reconciliation. Other sin is venial, or less serious. [pecado]

sloth a carelessness of heart that leads a person to ignore his or her development as a person, especially spiritual development and a relationship with God. Sloth is one of the seven capital sins, and it is contrary to the First Commandment. [pereza]

solidarity the principle that all people exist in equal dignity as children of God. Therefore, individuals are called to commit themselves to working for the common good in sharing material and spiritual goods. [solidaridad]

Son of God the title revealed by Jesus that indicates his unique relationship to God the Father [Hijo de Dios]

soul the part of us that makes us human and an image of God. Body and soul together form one unique human nature. The soul is responsible for our consciousness and for our freedom. [alma]

Spiritual Works of Mercy | Vicar of Christ

Spiritual Works of Mercy the kind acts through which we help our neighbors meet needs that are more than material. The Spiritual Works of Mercy include instructing, advising, consoling, comforting, forgiving, and bearing wrongs with patience.
[obras esprituales de misericordia]

T

tabernacle a container in which the Blessed Sacrament is kept so that Holy Communion can be taken to those who are sick and dying [sagrario]

temperance the cardinal virtue that helps us to control our attraction to pleasure so that our natural desires are kept within proper limits. This moral virtue helps us choose to use created goods in moderation. [templanza]

Temple the Temple in Jerusalem, the most important place where the Jewish people came to pray. They believed that this was the place where they could be closest to God. Jesus often came to pray in the Temple. [Templo, judío]

temptation an attraction, from outside us or from inside us, that can lead us to not follow God's commands [tentación]

Ten Commandments the ten rules that God gave to Moses on Mount Sinai that sum up God's Law and show us what is required to love God and our neighbor
[Diez Mandamientos]

Theological Virtues those virtues given to us by God, not by human effort. They are faith, hope, and charity.
[virtudes teologales]

Torah the Hebrew word for "instruction" or "law." It is also the name of the first five books of the Old Testament: Genesis, Exodus, Leviticus, Numbers, and Deuteronomy. [Torá]

transubstantiation when the bread and wine become the Body and Blood of Jesus Christ. When the priest speaks the words of consecration, the substance of the bread and wine is changed into the substance of Christ's Body and Blood. [transubstanciación]

trespasses unlawful acts committed against the property or rights of another person, or acts that physically harm a person [ofensas]

Trinity the mystery of one God existing in three Persons: the Father, the Son, and the Holy Spirit [Trinidad]

U

universal Church the entire Church as it exists throughout the world. The people of every diocese, along with their bishops and the pope, make up the universal Church. [Iglesia universal]

V

venial sin a choice we make that weakens our relationship with God or with others. It wounds and diminishes the divine life in us. [pecado venial]

Vicar of Christ the title given to the pope who, as the successor of Saint Peter, has the authority to act in Christ's place. A vicar is someone who stands in for and acts for another. [Vicario de Cristo]

virtue | worship

virtue an attitude or a way of acting that helps us do good   [virtud]

Visitation Mary's visit to Elizabeth to share the good news that Mary is to be the mother of Jesus. Elizabeth's greeting of Mary forms part of the Hail Mary. During this visit Mary sings the Magnificat, her praise of God. [Visitación]

vocation the call each of us has in life to be the person God wants us to be. Our vocation is also the way we serve the Church and the Kingdom of God. Each of us can live out his or her vocation as a layperson, as a member of a religious community, or as a member of the clergy. [vocación]

W

witness the passing on to others, by our words and by our actions, the faith that we have been given. Every Christian has the duty to give witness to the good news about Jesus Christ that he or she has come to know.   [testimonio]

worship the adoration and honor given to God in public prayer   [culto]

Index

A

Abba, 16, 253
absolution, 211, 253
Act of Contrition, 102, 189
Acts of the Apostles, 92, 255, 262
Advent, 57–60, 152, 153–56, 236, 253.
See also Christmas
Agony in the Garden, 197
All Saints Day, 152, 177–80, 253
All Souls Day, 152, 177–80, 253
"All You Works of God" (song), 220–21
Alleluia, 253
almsgiving, 118, 253
altar, 209, 253
altar server, 208
ambo, 208, 253
Amen, 253
Andrew Kim Taegon, Saint, 113
angel, 154, 157, 158, 240, 253, 258
Angelus, 253
Annunciation, 83, 84, 196, 253
Anointing of the Sick, Sacrament of the, 202, 253, 262
apostle, 4, 49, 52, 92, 148, 253.
See also specific apostles
chosen, 46–47, 238
mission of, 234
Apostles' Creed, 4, 6, 24, 53, 54, 72, 83, 191, 194, 254
apostolic, 71, 254
Ascension, 147, 149, 197, 254
Ash Wednesday, 117, 161, 162, 254
Assumption of Mary, 197
Augustine, Saint, 121, 122, 125

B

Baptism, Sacrament of, 77, 94, 95, 101, 200, 242, 254
of Jesus in River Jordan, 196
of the Lord, 87
of Paul, 92
symbol of, 247
Beatitudes, 214, 254, 266
belonging, 94
Benedict, Saint, 31, 32, 232
Bethlehem, 88, 158
Bible, 184, 254.
See also New Testament
Gospels, 46
bishop, 71, 254
Blessed Sacrament, 254, 267
blessing, 231, 244, 254
Body and Blood of Christ, 95, 108, 201, 207, 254, 267. *See also* Eucharist, Sacrament of the
bread and wine, 95, 106, 107, 254
Bread of Life, 90, 254
Breaking of the Bread, 149

C

cantor, 209
capital sin, 254, 257.
See also sin
cardinal virtues, temperance as, 267
caring for others, 136, 137, 142, 229. *See also* charity; moral choice
Carrying of the Cross, 197
cast lots, 255
catholic, 71, 255
Catholic Church, 69–74
celebrant, 255
celebrate, 255
chalice, 209
charity, 125, 126, 247, 255
chasuble, 209, 255

Christ, 22, 28, 255.
See also Jesus
Christian, 255
Christmas, 57, 87–90, 152, 157–60, 241, 255.
See also Advent
meaning, 88
symbols of, 159
Church, the, 255
apostolic, 71
built through Holy Spirit, 65
Catholic Church, 69–74
leaders of, 70, 238
Marks of, 71
Mother of, 82
as People of God, 94
Precepts of, 264
universal, 267
Collect Prayer, 204
"Come, O Holy Spirit/Wa Wa Wa Emimimo" (song), 222
commandment, 133, 255.
See also Ten Commandments
Great Commandment, 213, 258
new commandment, 213
Communion, 17, 149.
See also Eucharist, Sacrament of the; Holy Communion
First Holy, 76
receiving, 207
Rite, 206
Communion of Saints, 82, 178, 179, 255
community, 28, 231, 255
loving, 216
compassion, 255
confession, 101, 211, 256.
See also Penance and Reconciliation, Sacrament of
seal of, 266

Confirmation, Sacrament of | *Gloria*

sacramental | yeast, parable

Acknowledgments

Excerpts from the *New American Bible with Revised New Testament and Psalms.* Copyright © 1991, 1986, 1970 Confraternity of Christian Doctrine, Inc., Washington, DC. Used with permission. All rights reserved. No part of the *New American Bible* may be reprinted without permission in writing from the copyright holder.

The English translation of the Act of Contrition from *Rite of Penance* © 1974, International Commission on English in the Liturgy Corporation (ICEL); the English translation of the *Salve, Regina* from *A Book of Prayers* © 1982, ICEL; the English translation of Prayer Before Meals and Prayer After Meals from *Book of Blessings* © 1988; the English translation of the Apostles' Creed from *The Roman Missal* © 2010, ICEL. All rights reserved.

For more information related to the English translation of the *Roman Missal, Third Edition,* see www.loyolapress.com/romanmissal.

Loyola Press has made every effort to locate the copyright holders for the cited works used in this publication and to make full acknowledgment for their use. In the case of any omissions, the publisher will be pleased to make suitable acknowledgments in future editions.

Art and Photography

When there is more than one picture on a page, positions are abbreviated as follows: (t) top, (c) center, (b) bottom, (l) left, (r) right, (bg) background, (bd) border.

Photos and illustrations not acknowledged are either owned by Loyola Press or from royalty-free sources including but not limited to Alamy, Corbis/Veer, Getty Images, Jupiterimages, PunchStock, Thinkstock, and Wikipedia Commons. Loyola Press has made every effort to locate the copyright holders for the cited works used in this publication and to make full acknowledgment for their use. In the case of any omissions, the publisher will be pleased to make suitable acknowledgments in future editions.

Frontmatter: i Rafael Lopez. **ii** Christina Balit.
iii(tl) ©iStockphoto.com/huronphoto. **iii**(tr) Christina Balit.
iii(bl) Christina Balit. **iii**(br) Hill Street Studios/Blend Images/
Getty Images. **iv**(tl) OJO Images Ltd/Alamy. **iv**(tr) ©iStockphoto.com/
gabycontrreras. **iv**(br) ©iStockphoto.com/RainforestAustralia.
iv(bl) Royalty-free image.

©iStockphoto.com: 1(t) dawnn. **6**(t) gbh007. **7**(bg) Yougen.
7(t) aloha_17. **7**(b) aloha_17. **14**(t) lisafx. **17**(b) DorianGray.
18 STEVECOLEccs. **24**(c) MariaPavlova. **25**(cl) perkmeup.
25(cr) iofoto. **26**(br) ozgurdonmaz. **31**(t) fotoVoyager. **35**(bg) mitza.
36 mandygodbehear. **37**(t) kemalbas. **38**(c) carlosalvarez.
38(b) Meggj. **40**(t) LPETTET. **42**(c) busypix. **43**(tl) SharonDay.
43(cl) MightyIsland. **43**(c) stocksnapper. **49**(bg) kentcajuan.
50(c) Royalty-free image. **50**(b) sonyae. **55**(t, cb, br) enjoynz.
55(ct) Vladimirovic. **55**(b) paulaphoto. **58**(t) huronphoto.
58(c) HelpingHandPhotos. **58–59**(b) billberryphotography. **60**(t) sjlocke.
60(c) busypix. **60**(br) redmal. **64**(tr) lumpynoodles. **65**(t) HKPNC.
66 caracterdesign. **67** lumpynoodles. **68**(t) ArtisticCaptures.
68(c) Gerville. **71**(t) KathrynSK. **71**(b) epicurean. **79** mart_m.
80(t) ManoAfrica. **85**(b) sonyae. **86**(b) THEPALMER.
88–89(b) ultra_generic **92**(bg) Bastar. **91**(b) PTB-images.
102 ImagineGolf. **102–103**(doves) ussr. **104**(t) MaszaS. **104**(bl) kirin_
photo. **107**(b) kryczka. **109**(br) MiquelMunill. **110**(bl) cglade.
115(l) Anterovium. **115**(r) ktaylorg. **116**(t) ALEAIMAGE. **118**(t) Maica.
120(t) iofoto. **120**(b) mm88. **124**(t) DNY59. **125**(t) Funwithfood.
125(c) Kativ. **130**(t) RusN. **130**(b) DarleneSanguenza. **130**(c) sextoacto.
134(b) gradyreese. **136**(l) whitemay. **136**(r) bonniej. **138** Clockwise

from upper left, (a) MentalArt. **138**(b) monkeybusinessimages.
138(c) Goldmund. **138**(d) Tsuji. **138**(e) LisaValder. **138**(f) phildate.
139 STEEX. **142**(b) horstklinker. **143**(b) monkeybusinessimages.
144 ranplett. (g) macroworld. **148**(t, bl) Faye78. **148**(bd) blue67.
150(b) nicolesy. **152** Clockwise from top, (a) cotesebastien. **152**(b) art-
4-art. **152**(d) RainforestAustralia. **152**(e) kulicki. **158** ultra_generic.
159(t) Lezh. **161**(b) rest. **163**(tl, cr, bl) RainforestAustralia.
166(b) yalayama. **169**(b) Liliboas. **173**(bg) lumpynoodles.
174(cl) duncan1890. **174**(cr) DGM007. **174**(bl) ktaylorg.
174(br) aleksandarvelasevic. **175** princessdlaf. **178–179**(t) gabycontrreras.
178(tr) shironosov. **182**(t) Tjanze. **182**(b) monkeybusinessimages.
183(b) kryczka. **184**(b) duckycards. **185**(t, c) aloha_17. **185**(bl) aloha_17.
188–189 McIninch. **190–191** gbh007. **191**(br) Stratol. **207**(b) kryczka.
210(t) juanestey. **210**(b) Kativ. **214**(bg) Yougen. **215** Maica.
216(b) sjlocke. **218**(bd) aloha_17. **218**(b) yalayama. **219**(bd) aloha_17.
219(t) STEEX. **219**(b) skynesher. **220–221**(b) antb. **224** Photo_Concepts.
226(b) nicolesy. **227**(t) 13spoon. **244** Illustrious. **249** DNY59.
250 art12321.

Thinkstock: 4(cl) Jupiterimages/Polka Dot. **30**(b) Stockbyte.
59(t) George Doyle/Valueline. **69** Jupiterimages/Polka Dot.
108(t) Jupiterimages/Creatas. **140**(b) Jupiterimages/Comstock.
146(t) Thinkstock Images/Comstock. **146**(c) Jupiterimages/Brand X
Pictures. **189**(c) George Doyle/Valueline. **197**(b) iStockphoto.

Unit 1: 1(b) From The Spiritual Journey of St. Ignatius Loyola by Dora
Nikolova Bittau. Photo by Ken Wagner @ 1998 Seattle University.
2(t) From The Spiritual Journey of St. Ignatius Loyola by Dora
Nikolova Bittau. Photo by Ken Wagner @ 1998 Seattle University.
2(b) Nik Wheeler/Corbis. **3** Blend Images/Veer. **4**(t) Royalty-free
image. **4**(cr) Royalty-free image. **4**(bl) Blend Images Photography/Veer.
4(br) Stockbyte/Getty Images. **5**(bg) David De Lossy/Photodisc/Getty
Images. **5**(t) Royalty-free image. **5**(b) Jupiterimages. **6**(b) alpha_zara/
Flickr. **8**(t) GK Hart/Vikki Hart/Photodisc/Getty images. **8**(bl) Corbis
Photography/Veer. **8**(br) Jupiterimages. **9** Onoky Photography/Veer.
10(l) Susan Tolonen. **10**(r) Hill Street Studios/Getty. **11**(t) The Crosiers/
Gene Plaisted, OSC. **11**(c) Royalty-free image. **11**(b) AgnusImages.com.
12 Corbis Photography/Veer. **13** Digital Vision. **14**(cr, b) Royalty-free
image. **14**(cl) Royalty-free image. **15** Corbis Photography/Veer. **16**(t) The
Crosiers/Gene Plaisted, OSC. **16**(b) Stockbyte/PunchStock. **17**(t) The
Crosiers/Gene Plaisted, OSC. **19**(bg) David De Lossy/Photodisc/
Getty Images. **20**(t) Photodisc. **20**(bl) Getty Images. **20**(br) Susan
Tolonen. **21** Ocean Photography/Veer. **22**(b) Photodisc/Getty.
23(t) The Crosiers/Gene Plaisted, OSC. **23**(b) Alexander Walter/Stone/
Getty. **24**(b) Royalty-free image. **25**(t) The Crosiers/Gene Plaisted,
OSC. **25**(c) Jupiterimages. **25**(c) Rubberball/Erik Isakson/Getty.
25(bl) Royalty-free image. **25**(br) Jupiterimages. **26**(t) Susan Tolonen.
26(b) Brand X Pictures/Fotosearch. **27** Phil Martin Photography.
28(t) Brand X Pictures/Fotosearch. **28**(b) Royalty-free image.
29 Stockbyte/Getty Images. **30**(t) Susan Tolonen. **30**(c) Susan Tolonen.

Unit 2: 31(b) Amanda Hall. **32** Amanda Hall. **33** Royalty-free image.
34(t, c, bl) Christina Balit. **34**(br) Jupiterimages. **35**(t) Christina Balit.
35(b) Christina Balit. **37**(b) Fred Willingham. **38**(t) Daniel Pangbourne/
Digital Vision/Getty. **39** Fancy Photography/Veer. **40–41**(b) Christina
Balit. **40**(br) Courtesy of Riverside Church, New York, NY.
41(t) Royalty-free image. **41**(b) Christina Balit. **42**(t, b) Royalty-free
image. **43**(tc) Brand X Pictures/Fotosearch. **43**(tr) Brand X Pictures/
Fotosearch. **43**(cr) Anika Salsera. **43**(b) Jupiterimages. **44**(t) Brand X
Pictures/Fotosearch. **44**(c) Exactostock/SuperStock. **44**(b) Katrina
Wittkamp/Stockbyte/Getty Images. **45** Corbis Photography/Veer.
46–47 Amanda Hall. **48** Cultura/Veer. **49** Royalty-free images.
50(t) Stockbyte/Groups: Children & Teenagers/CD disc. **51** Fancy
Photography/Veer. **52**(t) Nana Quparadze, a Georgian iconographer.
Reprinted by permission of the Holy Resurrection Orthodox Church,
Singapore (Orthodox Metrolitinate of Hong Kong & SE Asia).
52(b) Susan Tolonen. **53** Susan Tolonen. **54**(t) Corbis Photography/
Veer. **54**(b) Jupiterimages. **56**(t) The Crosiers/Gene Plaisted, OSC.
56(c) Royalty-free image. **56**(b) Jupiterimages. **57**(t) W. P. Wittman
Limited. **57**(b) Royalty-free image. **60**(bl) W. P. Wittman Limited.

Unit 3: 61(t) Royalty-free image. **61**(b) William Thomas Cain/Contributor/Getty Images News/Getty Images. **62**(t) St. Katharine Drexel, Robert Lentz, 2012, Courtesy of Trinity Stores, www.trinitystores.com, 800.699.4482. **62**(b) William Thomas Cain/Contributor/Getty Images News/Getty Images. **63** Corbis Photography/Veer. **64**(tl) Scala/Art Resource, NY. **64**(bl) Royalty-free image. **64**(br) Royalty-free image. **65**(c) Nancy R. Cohen/Digital Vision/Getty Images. **65**(b) Tom Grill/Corbis. **68**(b) Brand X Pictures/Fotosearch. **70** The Crosiers/Gene Plaisted, OSC. **72** Alloy Photography/Veer. **73** Fred Willingham. **74**(t) Susan Tolonen. **74**(c) Susan Tolonen. **74**(b) Phil Martin Photography. **75** Blend Images/Veer. **76**(t) W.P. Wittman Limited. **76**(c) Susan Tolonen. **76–77**(b) Susan Tolonen. **77**(t) Susan Tolonen. **77**(c) Phil Martin Photography. **78** Image Source Photography/Veer. **80**(c) Susan Tolonen. **80**(b) Phil Martin Photography. **81** Fancy Photography/Veer. **82**(t) Stockbyte/Getty Images. **82**(b) W.P. Wittman Limited. **83**(t) Victorian Traditions/Shutterstock.com. **83**(b) Royalty-free image. **84**(c) Stockbyte/Getty Images. **85**(t) The Crosiers/Gene Plaisted, OSC. **86**(t) AgnusImages.com. **86**(c) Phil Martin Photography. **87** W.P. Wittman Limited. **88**(t) Warling Studios. **89** Phil Martin Photography. **90**(t) The Crosiers/Gene Plaisted, OSC. **90**(b) W.P. Wittman Limited.

Unit 4: 91(b) Mary Evans Picture Library/Alamy. **92**(t) Mary Evans Picture Library/Alamy. **92**(b) David Atkinson. **93** Wolfgang Flamisch/Corbis. **94**(t) AgnusImages.com. **94**(c) W. P. Wittman Limited. **94**(b) W. P. Wittman Limited. **95**(t) The Crosiers/Gene Plaisted, OSC. **95**(b) Warling Studios. **96**(t) P T Images/Veer. **96–97**(flowers) C Squared Studios/Photodisc. **97**(t) W. P. Wittman Limited. **98**(t) Phil Martin Photography. **98**(b) Warling Studios. **99** IOFOTO/Veer. **100** Amanda Hall. **101** The Crosiers/Gene Plaisted, OSC. **103**(t) W. P. Wittman Limited. **104**(bd, br) C Squared Studios/Photodisc. **105** Laura Doss/Fancy/Alamy. **106–107**(grapes) Susan Tolonen. **106**(l) Susan Tolonen. **106**(b) The Crosiers/Gene Plaisted, OSC. **107**(t) W. P. Wittman Limited. **108**(b) Susan Tolonen. **109**(t) Susan Tolonen. **110**(t) W. P. Wittman Limited. **110**(br) Susan Tolonen. **111** Blend Images/Alamy. **112**(t) W. P. Wittman Limited. **112**(c) W. P. Wittman Limited. **112**(b) Larry Downing/Reuters/Corbis. **112**(bg) Jupiterimages. **113**(t) Moodboard Photography/Veer. **113**(c) Royalty-free image. **113**(b) Moon Hak-Jin, Korea. **114** Wealan Pollard/OJO Images Ltd./Alamy. **116**(b) Photodisc/Getty Images. **117**(l, r) The Crosiers/Gene Plaisted, OSC. **118–119**(snowflakes) Jill Arena. **118**(b) Fancy/Alamy. **119**(t) W. P. Wittman Limited. **120**(cl) Blend Images/Alamy.

Unit 5: 121(t) Roger Wood/Corbis. **121**(b) Stained Glass by Akili Ron Anderson. **122**(t) Stained Glass by Akili Ron Anderson. **122**(b) Gianna Marino. **123** Blend Images Photography/Veer. **124**(b) The Crosiers/Gene Plaisted, OSC. **125**(b) Warling Studios. **126** Dmitry Naumov/Veer. **127**(t) Maurizio Brambatti/epa/Corbis. **127**(b) Jupiterimages. **128**(t) The Crosiers/Gene Plaisted, OSC. **128**(b) Jose Luis Pelaez Inc./Corbis. **129** Randy Faris/Corbis. **131** The Crosiers/Gene Plaisted, OSC. **132** Keith Levit/Corbis. **133** Christina Balit. **134**(t) The Crosiers/Gene Plaisted, OSC. **135** Monkey Business Images/Veer. **137**(t, b) St. Louise de Marillac, Robert Lentz, 2012, Courtesy of Trinity Stores, www.trinitystores.com, 800.699.4482. **137**(c) St. Vincent de Paul, Robert Lentz, 2012, Courtesy of Trinity Stores, www.trinitystores.com, 800.699.4482. **140**(t) The Crosiers/Gene Plaisted, OSC. **141** Fancy Photography/Veer. **142**(t) Courtesy of Fearghal O'Farrell/Vincentian Family Shrine, St. Peter's Church, Phibsboro, Dublin. **143**(t) allOver photography/Alamy. **145** Royalty-free images. (h) C Squared Studios/Photodisc **146–147**(b) C Squared Studios/Photodisc **147**(t) The Crosiers/Gene Plaisted, OSC. **148**(br) Monkey Business Images/Veer. **149**(t) The Crosiers/Gene Plaisted, OSC. **149**(c) W. P. Wittman Limited. **149**(b) W. P. Wittman Limited. **150**(t) The Crosiers/Gene Plaisted, OSC.

Seasonal Sessions: 151 Susan Tolonen. **152**(c) Siede Preis/Photodisc **152**(f) Royalty-free image. **153** The Crosiers/Gene Plaisted, OSC. **154** The Crosiers/Gene Plaisted, OSC. **155** Warling Studios. **156** The Crosiers/Gene Plaisted, OSC. **157** Warling Studios. **159**(b) C Squared Studios/Photodisc **160** Hanna-Cheriyan Varghese. **161**(t) Private Collection/Look and Learn /The Bridgeman Art Library International. **162**(bg) Amanda Hall. **162**(r) Warling Studios. **163**(tr) Photodisc/Getty Images. **163**(cl) Jupiterimages. **163**(br) Jupiterimages. **164** The Crosiers/Gene Plaisted, OSC. **165**(bg) Siede Preis/Photodisc **165**(c) Galleria degli Uffizi, Florence, Italy/The Bridgeman Art Library International. **166**(t) The Crosiers/Gene Plaisted, OSC. **167** The Crosiers/Gene Plaisted, OSC. **168** Ocean Photography/Veer. **169**(t) The Crosiers/Gene

Plaisted, OSC. **169**(c) oliveromg/Shutterstock.com. **170** The Crosiers/Gene Plaisted, OSC. **171** W. P. Wittman Limited. **172** Radius Images/Corbis. **173**(cl) The Crosiers/Gene Plaisted, OSC. **173**(br) Shutterstock.com. **174**(t) Private Collection/Malva Gallery/The Bridgeman Art Library International. **176** HeQi, HeQi Arts LLC. www.heqigallery.com. **177**(l) Werner Forman/Art Resource, NY. **177**(r) Warling Studios. **178**(c) The Crosiers/Gene Plaisted, OSC. **178**(bl) C Squared Studios/Photodisc **178**(br) Charles O. Cecil/Alamy. **180** Warling Studios.

Endmatter: 181(tl) ©1996 Image Club Graphics. **181**(bl) Jupiteimages. **181**(br) Hill Street Studios/Blend Images/Getty Images. **183**(t) Warling Studios. **184**(t) Bibliotheque des Arts Decoratifs, Paris, France/The Bridgeman Art Library International. **185**(br) Warling Studios. **186**(br) The Crosiers/Gene Plaisted, OSC. **186–187**(bg) Mykola Velychko/Veer. **187**(t) Warling Studios. **187**(b) C Squared Studios/Photodisc **189**(t) C Squared Studios/Photodisc **189**(c) George Doyle/Valueline. **189**(bl) C Squared Studios/Photodisc **191**(bl) Siede Preis/Photodisc **192–193**(bg) Les Cunliffe/Veer. **192**(l) Corbis Photography/Veer. **192**(r) The Crosiers/Gene Plaisted, OSC. **193** W. P. Wittman Limited. **194**(t) The Crosiers/Gene Plaisted, OSC. **194**(b) Warling Studios. **195** Greg Kuepfer. **196** The Crosiers/Gene Plaisted, OSC. **197**(tr) The Crosiers/Gene Plaisted, OSC. **197**(cr) The Crosiers/Gene Plaisted, OSC. **197**(br) The Crosiers/Gene Plaisted, OSC. **198–199** Laura James/Private Collection/The Bridgeman Art Library International. **200**(t) Phil Martin Photography. **200–201**(b) Anni Betts. **201**(t) W. P. Wittman Limited. **201**(c) Warling Studios. **202**(t) Warling Studios. **202**(b) Susan Tolonen. **203**(tl) W. P. Wittman Limited. **203**(tr) W. P. Wittman Limited. **203**(bg) Susan Tolonen. **204**(t) Brand X Pictures/PunchStock. **204–205** Darren Kemper/Veer. **205** W. P. Wittman Limited. **208**(tr) Warling Studios. **208–209** Phyllis Pollema-Cahill. **209**(tl) W. P. Wittman Limited. **209**(tc) Warling Studios. **209**(tr) Phil Martin Photography. **211**(b) W. P. Wittman Limited. **212**(l) Corbis Photography/Veer. **213** Monkey Business Images/Veer. **214**(bl) Vie de Jésus Mafa, www.jesusmafa.com. **214**(br) RubberBall Photography/Veer. **216**(c) JGI/Tom Grill/Blend Images/Corbis. **216–217**(b) momentimages/Tetra Images/Corbis. **216–217** Jamie Grill/Tetra Images/Corbis. **217**(c) Artiga Photo/Corbis. **218**(t) ArtisticCaptures. **220**(t) The Crosiers/Gene Plaisted, OSC. **222–223** Glow Images/Getty Images. **223**(c) The Crosiers/Gene Plaisted, OSC. **225** Ocean Photography/Veer. **225**(bg) Jill Arena. **226**(t) Jose Luis Pelaez/Blend Images/Corbis. **227**(b) Jupiterimages. **231** Jupiterimages. **232** Amanda Hall. **233** Yoshi Miyake. **235** Jupiterimages. **236** Thinkstock. **237** Philomena O'Neill. **238** Courtesy of Immaculate Conception Church, Earlington, KY/photo by Ray Giardinella. **239** Amanda Hall. **240** Yoshi Miyake. **241**(b) Jupiterimages. **242** Amanda Hall. **243** Yoshi Miyake. **246** Amanda Hall. **247** photo by Greg Kuepfer. **248** Amanda Hall. **251**(t) Tony Rothberg.

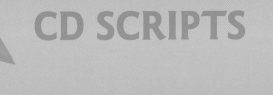

CD SCRIPTS

Faith comes alive through the dramatized Scripture stories and recorded guided reflections contained on the *Finding God* CDs. While listening to the Scripture stories, children can visualize themselves in the scene. The guided reflections encourage children to lead a more prayerful life.

The following scripts from the spoken word CDs appear in this section for your convenience.

- **Recorded Scripture Story Scripts**
- **Recorded Guided Reflection Scripts**

Based on Mark 10:17–23
UNIT 2, SESSION 7

The Rich Young Man

GRADE 3, CD 1, TRACK 1 • **TIME:** 2 min. 43 sec.

NARRATOR: One time when Jesus was on the road, a man came running up to him. The man knelt down as if Jesus were a king.

MAN: Good Teacher, what do I have to do to live forever?

JESUS: Why do you call me good? Only God is truly good. But I'll answer your question. Actually, you should know the answer for yourself. You know the commandments, don't you? Don't murder. Don't steal. Don't lie about other people. Don't cheat. Respect your parents.

MAN: Yes, I do know them. And I've kept those commandments since I was a child.

NARRATOR: Jesus took a good look at the man. He could see how much this man wanted to do the right thing, and Jesus felt deep love for him.

JESUS: All right. There's only one thing you need to do. Sell everything you have and give the money to the poor. When you do that, you will have treasure in Heaven. Then come with me. Travel with me and learn all that I have to teach you.

NARRATOR: A look of disappointment came over the man's face. He turned from Jesus and walked away. The truth is this young man was very rich, and he could not bring himself to give up all his money and all the things he owned.

Other people were traveling with Jesus—the men and women who were following him to learn about God. They watched the rich young man as he walked away from them.

PERSON: Oh my, look—he's leaving!

JESUS: It's very hard for rich people to enter into God's kingdom.

NARRATOR: The people thought a lot about what Jesus said. They wondered if they would be willing to give up the things they liked if that's what Jesus said they needed to do. As they thought about all the things they had, they realized that a person doesn't have to be rich to have trouble entering into God's kingdom. Any person who loves possessions too much will have a hard time letting go of them, even if Jesus says that that's the right thing to do.

Based on Luke 5:1–11
UNIT 2, SESSION 8

Jesus Calls Peter

GRADE 3, CD 1, TRACK 2 • TIME: 2 min. 57 sec.

NARRATOR: One day Jesus was teaching a huge crowd of people on the shore of the Sea of Galilee. The people had come to listen—they wanted so much to learn about God. But as they crowded around, they made it hard for Jesus to teach because he had no room to move.

Then Jesus saw two boats along the shore. They belonged to a fisherman who had just come in after fishing all night.

JESUS: What is your name?

PETER: Peter.

JESUS: This is your boat?

PETER: Yes sir.

NARRATOR: Jesus got into the boat, to Peter's surprise.

JESUS: Please take me out a bit from the shore. That way I can sit in the boat and teach, and the people can see and hear me better.

NARRATOR: So Peter took the boat out far enough that Jesus could get out of the crowd but still be close enough so that the people could hear him.

When Jesus finished teaching, he turned to Peter.

JESUS: Now let's go out to deeper water and catch some fish.

PETER: Ah, Teacher, we fished these waters all night long and didn't catch a thing.

NARRATOR: Jesus didn't answer. He just gave Peter a strange little smile, as if he knew a secret.

PETER: Well, all right. If you say go out, we'll go out.

NARRATOR: No sooner had they reached deeper water than hundreds of fish filled their nets. The nets were beginning to tear under the weight, so Peter signaled to his partners, James and John, to bring out another boat. They filled both boats so full of fish that it looked as if the boats might sink.

As Peter and James and John realized that they had just seen a miracle, their joy turned to awe. Peter bowed down in front of Jesus.

PETER: Lord, please go away. It's clear to me that you are a man of God, and I have many sins in my life. I shouldn't even be in your presence.

JESUS: There's no need to be afraid. You're a fisherman, aren't you? Well, from now on you'll be catching people instead of fish.

PETER: I'm not sure I understand, Lord.

JESUS: God is a fisherman too, you know. And look at all of these people; their souls are wandering in the sea, waiting to be gathered in.

NARRATOR: Peter, James, and John docked their boats and left them there. That day the men left their work as fishermen and began their journeys as followers of Jesus.

Jesus and the Roman Officer

GRADE 3, CD 1, TRACK 3 • **TIME:** 3 min. 32 sec.

NARRATOR: When Jesus was traveling around the country, teaching people about God, he entered the town called Capernaum. Many people there were interested in hearing what Jesus had to say, but one man was especially glad to know that Jesus had come to this town. The man was an officer in the Roman army.

Why would a Roman officer be interested in Jesus, the Jewish teacher? The officer was not Jewish. When the officer heard about Jesus, he called for some of the Jewish leaders to come and talk to him about Jesus, the healer.

OFFICER: Do you know where to find Jesus, the teacher from Nazareth?

LEADER 1: Yes, we were planning to go listen to him today.

OFFICER: Would you please ask the teacher's help for me? Jesus may not want to speak with me because I am not Jewish. But my servant is very sick. He is one of my best servants, and he's about to die. Please ask Jesus if he would save the life of this good man.

NARRATOR: So the Jewish leaders did as the officer requested. They found Jesus and explained the situation.

LEADER 1: Please, Teacher, this soldier's servant is close to death. He wants you to save the man's life.

LEADER 2: It's true that he is a Roman soldier, but he's not like most of the Romans. He loves the Jewish people and has always treated us with respect. Why, he even built a synagogue for us to worship in. We urge you, Jesus, to help this man.

NARRATOR: So Jesus went with the Jewish leaders to see the officer's servant. But as they got close to the house, the officer sent this message to Jesus.

OFFICER: Lord, you don't need to come any farther. I am not a good enough person for you to come inside my home—this is why I sent others to you rather than come to you myself. All you have to do is say the word, and my servant will be healed. You see, I understand what it means to have power and authority. I am under the authority of other men in the army, and many men are under my authority. I say to a soldier, "Go," and he goes. I say to another to "Do this," and he does it. A man with true power and authority can make things happen simply by speaking. So just say the word, and I know that my servant will get well.

NARRATOR: When Jesus heard this, he was amazed. He turned to the crowd that was following him.

JESUS: I have traveled and taught throughout this land, and I have never found anyone with more faith than this officer.

NARRATOR: When the messenger went back to the officer's house, they found that the servant was completely healed.

Philip and the Court Official

GRADE 3, CD 1, TRACK 4 • TIME: 3 min. 33 sec.

NARRATOR: One day the angel of the Lord spoke to Philip, a Christian living in Samaria.

ANGEL: Philip, head south on the road that goes from Jerusalem to Gaza. It is the road that goes through the desert.

NARRATOR: So Philip went where the angel told him. While he was walking on the desert road, he saw a chariot. It was brightly decorated, as if it belonged to someone important. Inside the chariot, a well-dressed man was reading. As the chariot went by Philip, he could hear the man reading aloud, and he could tell that he was reading from the Book of Isaiah.

COURT OFFICIAL: "Like a sheep he was led to the slaughter, and as a lamb before its shearer is silent, so he opened not his mouth."

NARRATOR: The Holy Spirit told Philip to go right up to that chariot. Now an ordinary person couldn't just walk up to a rich person's chariot, but Philip knew that it was all right because the Spirit was leading him. So he ran up and walked alongside the chariot, close enough that he could talk to the man who sat inside.

PHILIP: Sir, do you understand what you're reading?

NARRATOR: The man looked at Philip in surprise, but he wasn't angry at being interrupted. He seemed happy that Philip had asked this question.

COURT OFFICIAL: How can I understand unless there's someone to teach me? I'm not trained to understand the Scriptures. I take care of all the property that belongs to the Queen of Ethiopia. I understand how to manage money, but I am confused when I read from Isaiah. Please—join me and ride along for a while.

NARRATOR: Philip got into the chariot. He looked carefully at the passage that the man had been reading:

"Like a sheep he was led to the slaughter,
  and as a lamb before its shearer is silent,
    so he opened not his mouth.
  In [his] humiliation justice was denied him.
  Who will tell of his posterity?
    For his life is taken from the earth."

COURT OFFICIAL: Please, sir, I've got to know—who is this passage talking about? Is the prophet Isaiah talking about himself or someone else?

NARRATOR: Then Philip began with that Scripture and explained to the man about Jesus—about how the prophets had foretold his coming, about how he had lived and been crucified and then rose from the dead. Philip taught the court official patiently, answering his questions, and telling him how faith in Jesus could give him a new life with God.

COURT OFFICIAL: Driver—stop! Look, Philip! There's a pool of water, right here beside the road. Is there any reason you can't baptize me right here and now? I do believe what you've told me about Jesus, and I want to follow him and live a brand new life with God.

NARRATOR: So Philip baptized the court official in the pool of water. And when they came out of the water, the official went joyfully on his way. Philip followed the Spirit to the next place where the people needed to hear about Jesus. He continued to preach about Jesus as he traveled through the countryside.

Based on Matthew 4:1–11
UNIT 5, SESSION 22

Jesus Is Tempted

GRADE 3, CD 1, TRACK 5 • **TIME:** 3 min. 37 sec.

NARRATOR: Jesus was just beginning to do the work God had given him. He was about to go out and teach others about God's love. He would heal sick people and perform other miracles. But before he could begin his important work, he would have to go through a hard trial. He would have to be tempted by the devil. So the Holy Spirit led Jesus into the desert.

Jesus spent 40 days out there alone. And he didn't eat any food during that time because he wanted to concentrate on praying and listening to God.

When a person is tempted, that means that someone is trying to get him to do something he knows is wrong. The devil wanted Jesus to listen to him rather than listen to God. So, at the end of 40 days, when Jesus was really hungry, the devil came to him.

DEVIL: I can see that you're hungry. Your body needs food after so many days. If you are the Son of God, then tell these stones to become loaves of bread. Why starve to death? You have the power to do whatever you want to do.

JESUS: The Bible says that food isn't the only thing that keeps us alive. We live also because we listen to what God says and we do what God tells us is best.

NARRATOR: Well, the devil could see that he had a problem, because Jesus knew the Scriptures very well. He knew right from wrong. The devil knew what the Scriptures said too, and he decided to use the Scriptures to trick Jesus. The devil took Jesus to Jerusalem and stood him on the very top of the Temple.

DEVIL: The Scriptures say that God will send angels to protect you—they won't even let your foot get bruised on the rocks. So why don't you see if it's true? Throw yourself off this temple and see how many angels come down to catch you before you hit the ground.

JESUS: The Scriptures also say that you don't play games with God. It's wrong to test God like that.

NARRATOR: So the devil took Jesus to a very high mountain. From there, Jesus could see all the cities of the whole world.

DEVIL: If you bow down and worship me, I will give you all of this—all the world's cities and all the people in them.

NARRATOR: Jesus turned to face the devil. Oh, he was angry now.

JESUS: Get out of here! The Scriptures say that I must worship God and only God. Don't you dare ask me to bow down before you!

NARRATOR: The devil realized that his tricks weren't working. Jesus wouldn't do anything the devil wanted him to do. So the devil left Jesus. And then angels came to Jesus and took care of him.

HOW TO USE THE REFLECTION

Session 3 includes the option to use the recorded guided reflection "The Lord's Prayer" [CD 1, Track 6]. One approach for sharing the reflection with children is to listen prayerfully to the recording before the session. Then when you play the recording during the session, join children in reflective prayer.

Another option is to pray aloud, using the script of the reflection. Prepare to share the reflection by listening to the recording beforehand. During the session you may wish to use the script as is, or adapt it as you wish. When leading the reflection, play reflective music softly in the background to enhance the sense of prayerfulness.

The Lord's Prayer

GRADE 3, CD 1, TRACK 6 • TIME: 12 min.

We all like to imagine. Sometimes we imagine as we play with our friends. Sometimes we imagine stories about our toys. Today we're going to use our imaginations in a very special way.

Let's start by making ourselves as comfortable as possible. Relax. *(Pause.)* Close your eyes if you'd like. *(Pause.)* Let's all be very still. *(Pause.)* That's it. Now, breathe deeply, in and out, in and out, in and out. *(Pause.)*

Imagine that you're walking in an open field next to a forest. The weather is just how you like it. Do you feel a breeze? *(Pause.)* Is it warm or cool? *(Pause.)* As you walk, you feel happy. You're on your way to a special place. You're going to your Heart Home, that place deep inside you where you can talk with Jesus. *(Pause.)*

As you walk, you see an old woman sitting on a rock. She's smiling. You know somehow that you've seen her before, and you can tell that she's kind. "Are you looking for your Heart Home?" she asks.

"Yes," you answer.

"Here, catch!" says the old woman as she tosses you a big ball of red string. Then she says, "If you want to find your Heart Home, hold the ball of red string in front of your heart. You hold the ball of red string just as she says and repeat the words that she tells you to say, "Red string, red string, I will follow you, my red string. Red string, red string, take me to my Heart Home." *(Pause.)*

Then she tells you to toss the string out in front of you and follow it. You throw it, and the ball of red string starts to roll away into the forest. You follow it. At first the string rolls slowly by some tall trees. *(Pause.)*

The ball continues. You follow it and see a bushy-tailed fox scamper away from under a bush. Now the red string goes through an open field. There you see some deer standing still, watching you as you walk. *(Pause.)*

The ball of red string rolls past the field and up to a big hill of rocks, but it doesn't stop. It rolls a little to the right and finds a hole—a hidden pathway. You feel safe as you follow the red string along the path. *(Pause.)*

The red string leads you to a wide river. This river is too wide to cross by yourself. But the red string is there to help you. Watch it. The red string does something special to help you get across without getting wet. How does the string do this? *(Pause.)*

On the other side of the river is a forest thick with trees. You notice that the ball of red string is getting very small. You look down as you follow it. Now only the curly end of the string is left, reaching up from the ground. You look up.

You've made it to your Heart Home! You see a mailbox with your name on it. You walk around and see that it is a friendly place. What do you notice about your Heart Home? *(Pause.)*

Now you see Jesus. He's your friend, and he's here to welcome you. He smiles and calls you by name. Do you smile back? *(Pause.)* Jesus wants to talk to you and hear what you have to say. He might ask you what you've been learning about. He smiles, knowing that you've been learning about him. Tell him that you've learned about him and his Father. *(Pause.)* Maybe you wonder why he calls his Father Abba. You can ask Jesus now if you want. *(Pause.)* Does Jesus ask if you have a special name for your own father? If you do, tell Jesus the name. *(Pause.)* He tells you that God is your Father too.

What if Jesus wants to know if you've learned anything else? Maybe you have to think a minute. *(Pause.)* If you can't remember, Jesus reminds you that he taught his friends how to pray. He even gave them a special prayer. It's called the Lord's Prayer. Do you wonder why it's important to pray? Ask Jesus now. *(Pause.)*

To help you understand, Jesus might ask you how people show their love for you. What do they do? *(Pause.)* You might say, "They talk with me," "They spend time with me," or "They help me when I have a problem."

Jesus likes your answers and reminds you that God loves you too. Tell Jesus how God shows his love for you. *(Pause.)* He'll probably tell you you're right. And maybe he'll add something like, "God's always there for you, and God always knows exactly what you mean." If words are hard to find, you can just show God your mind and your heart. Do you want to think about that for a little bit? Go ahead. *(Pause.)*

You might ask Jesus how you can show your love for God the Father. You think a moment. *(Pause.)* You can pray. You can pray the Lord's Prayer. You've answered your own question.

You ask Jesus if he'll listen while you pray the Lord's Prayer. Jesus thinks it's a great idea, and so you open your heart and your mind to God and you pray:

> *Our Father, who art in heaven, hallowed be thy name; thy kingdom come; thy will be done on earth as it is in heaven. Give us this day our daily bread; and forgive us our trespasses as we forgive those who trespass against us; and lead us not into temptation, but deliver us from evil.*

When you finish, Jesus reminds you that any time you want to pray, you can find him in your Heart Home. He then leads you to the curly end of your string. If there is anything else you want to tell Jesus before you go, do it now. *(Pause.)*

You say good-bye, then tap the red string very gently with your foot. It begins to rewind. You follow it back over the river, where it helps you get across, just like before. You follow it through the rocks, through the forest, and into the field. Now you are back where you started.

You pick up the ball of red string and put it in your pocket. You pat your pocket as you remember the old woman's words: Red string, red string, I will follow you, my red string. Red string, red string, take me to my Heart Home. You smile because you know that you'll be back.

Gradually bring yourself back to this room. *(Pause.)* Open your eyes. *(Pause.)* Yawn. Stretch if you'd like, as high as you can. *(Pause.)* Look around. *(Pause.)* Our group is together again. Welcome back.

SENSITIVITIES

▶ Children's awareness of what it means to speak to God in their hearts

▶ Children's experience with reflective prayer

HINTS

When leading the guided reflection yourself,

▶ be aware of your voice quality, pacing, and the message.

▶ allow children time to reflect by pausing at appropriate times throughout the reflection.

▶ gradually decrease the volume of the background music before turning off the CD player.

REFLECTIVE RESPONSES

Help children continue the reflection by examining their own responses to either the recording or the prayerful recitation of the script. Say: ***Answer the following questions in the silence of your heart.*** Ask: ***What do you want to talk about the next time you meet Jesus in your Heart Home? What is the most important part of the Lord's Prayer for you right now?*** Encourage children to maintain a spirit of prayerfulness as they reflect on the questions.

HOW TO USE THE REFLECTION

Session 6 includes the option to use the recorded guided reflection "Kingdom of God" [CD 1, Track 7]. One approach for sharing the reflection with children is to listen prayerfully to the recording before the session. Then when you play the recording during the session, join children in reflective prayer.

Another option is to pray aloud, using the script of the reflection. Prepare to share the reflection by listening to the recording beforehand. During the session you may wish to use the script as is, or adapt it as you wish. When leading the reflection, play reflective music softly in the background to enhance the sense of prayerfulness.

Kingdom of God

GRADE 3, CD 1, TRACK 7 • **TIME:** 10 min. 32 sec.

We all like to imagine. Sometimes we imagine as we play with our friends. Sometimes we imagine stories about our toys. Today we're going to use our imaginations in a very special way.

Let's start by making ourselves as comfortable as possible. Relax. *(Pause.)* Close your eyes if you'd like. *(Pause.)* Let's all be very still. *(Pause.)* That's it. Now, breathe deeply, in and out, in and out, in and out. *(Pause.)*

In your imagination, picture a place where you'd like to be. Maybe you've been there before and would like to go back. Maybe it's some place you've read about or seen on TV. Maybe it's right at home. The important thing is that you like to be there. Be in that place in your imagination. *(Pause.)*

Someone is coming to join you. Look, it's Jesus! You are so glad to see each other. With a smile you greet him. How does he greet you? *(Pause.)* Welcome him to your favorite place. You might even want to show him around. Why don't you do it now? *(Pause.)*

Jesus probably asks how you are. How do you answer him? *(Pause.)* Share with him what's going on at home and in school. Is there something special you want to talk about with him? Tell him now if you'd like. *(Pause.)*

Jesus knows that you've learned about the parables of the mustard seed and the yeast today. You tell him what you know about these stories. *(Pause.)* Maybe you wonder why he teaches people with parables. Well, now's the time to ask him. *(Pause.)*

Jesus is likely to remind you that he speaks in parables because some things are so big, so wonderful, so precious that you can't talk about them exactly. The Kingdom of God is like that. *(Pause.)*

To remind you of the parable of the mustard seed, Jesus holds out his fist and opens it. What do you see? *(Pause.)* You're right. Jesus is holding the tiniest of seeds, a mustard seed. Touch the seed. *(Pause.)* Notice how small it is compared to your finger. What do you think will happen if you plant this seed and tend it with care? *(Pause.)* Will the seed grow? *(Pause.)* Will it take a long time? *(Pause.)* How big might it get? *(Pause.)* You remember that the mustard seed becomes a bush so large that birds can live in its branches.

Jesus is glad you remember this story. Perhaps he reminds you that this tiny mustard seed is like the Kingdom of God. A seed and a kingdom. Hmm. Jesus can see you're beginning to catch on now. And you are. You remind Jesus about the parable of the yeast. Jesus has a big smile for that one. And so he asks you what you know about it. Tell him what a little bit of yeast does. *(Pause.)* Did you tell him how powerful that little bit of yeast is, that it touches every particle of the dough to make the bread rise? *(Pause.)*

Now for the hard part. If Jesus asks you what these parables about the Kingdom of God mean to you, what will you say? Now really think about this for a moment. Will you tell him that you can be like the mustard seed, doing small things that are a big help to others? *(Pause.)* What are some of these things? Let Jesus know. *(Pause.)*

Jesus is so pleased with you that he asks you more questions. How do you make life better for other people? What do you do? How are you that little bit of yeast in your family, at school, with your friends? What do you tell him? *(Pause.)* Jesus smiles. He is so proud of you. He asks you ever so gently if you are willing to keep doing those little kindnesses, those good things, and wait patiently to grow. Are you? How do you answer him? *(Pause.)*

Why not ask Jesus to help you find ways to be a little seed, a little bit of yeast, so that his kingdom comes? You will grow into a wonderful citizen of the Kingdom of God! Spend a minute with Jesus just thinking about this. *(Pause.)*

Now, knowing that you'll be coming back to the room soon, Jesus places the tiny mustard seed in your hand. He invites you to plant it and tend it and watch it grow. You thank Jesus for the seed and for his parables. But before you leave, spend a little while telling Jesus about anything else that's on your mind. *(Pause.)*

Jesus promises to always be there to help you. With this promise in mind, you say good-bye to Jesus, knowing that you'll see him again very soon.

Now gradually bring yourself back to this room. *(Pause.)* Open your eyes. *(Pause.)* Yawn. Stretch if you'd like, as high as you can. *(Pause.)* Look around. *(Pause.)* Our group is together again. Welcome back.

SENSITIVITIES

▶ Children's awareness of what it means to speak to God in their hearts

▶ Children's experience with reflective prayer

▶ Children's experience with plants and baking

▶ Children's experience with having a special or favorite place for prayer

HINTS

When leading the guided reflection yourself,

▶ be aware of your voice quality, pacing, and the message.

▶ allow children time to reflect by pausing at appropriate times throughout the reflection.

▶ gradually decrease the volume of the background music before turning off the CD player.

REFLECTIVE RESPONSES

Help children continue the reflection by examining their own responses to either the recording or the prayerful recitation of the script. Say: *Answer the following questions in the silence of your heart.* Ask: *What are the small things you can do that are a big help to others? What are some of the little things you do that are a big help to your family?* Encourage children to maintain a spirit of prayerfulness as they reflect on the questions.

UNIT 3, SESSION 13

HOW TO USE THE REFLECTION

Session 13 includes the option to use the recorded guided reflection "Faith in Jesus" [CD 1, Track 8]. One approach for sharing the reflection with children is to listen prayerfully to the recording before the session. Then when you play the recording during the session, join children in reflective prayer.

Another option is to pray aloud, using the script of the reflection. Prepare to share the reflection by listening to the recording beforehand. During the session you may wish to use the script as is, or adapt it as you wish. When leading the reflection, play reflective music softly in the background to enhance the sense of prayerfulness.

Faith in Jesus

GRADE 3, CD 1, TRACK 8 • TIME: 9 min. 15 sec.

We all like to imagine. Sometimes we imagine as we play with our friends. Sometimes we imagine stories about our toys. Today we're going to use our imaginations in a very special way.

Let's start by making ourselves as comfortable as possible. Relax. *(Pause.)* Close your eyes if you'd like. *(Pause.)* Let's all be very still. *(Pause.)* That's it. Now, breathe deeply, in and out, in and out, in and out. *(Pause.)*

Imagine yourself walking in your neighborhood on a sunny morning. Look up to the sky. It's filled with clouds. Can you find any familiar shapes in them? That's always a fun thing to do. *(Pause.)* Who else is walking at this time of day? *(Pause.)* Notice everyone around you. Bring your whole neighborhood into your imagination. *(Pause.)*

As you walk, you feel safe and happy. Coming toward you is someone you know well. It's Jesus! He's come to be with you. You greet each other warmly. After saying hello, you and Jesus decide what you will do next. Will you continue to walk? Would you rather find a place to sit and visit? Make your decision together now. *(Pause.)*

Jesus surprises you by bringing your favorite snack. What is it? Mmm. It smells delicious. *(Pause.)* You take your time eating, knowing that Jesus is not in a hurry. He wants to talk with you.

Maybe Jesus asks what you were thinking about before he came along. Even if it was nothing, you can tell him that. It's even OK to be silent for a bit. *(Pause.)* Jesus continues the conversation by asking what you learned about today. Think for a moment and tell him. He's eager to hear what you have to say. *(Pause.)*

Jesus wants to know if you'd like to talk about how he helped the Roman officer by curing his servant. Do you wonder why Jesus would help someone he'd never ever seen or met? He's right here with you, so go ahead and ask him. *(Pause.)*

What about you? Jesus asks if you ever helped someone you'd never seen or met before? Think about it. I'll bet you have. *(Pause.)*

Maybe you and your friends made cards for someone in the parish who was sick. Or you might have collected canned foods for homeless people. Is there anything else you remember? Tell Jesus about it. *(Pause.)*

Jesus might then explain that the Roman officer was not asking for something for himself. The officer knew that Jesus had power that he himself didn't have. He believed that Jesus could cure his sick servant even without seeing him.

Jesus tells you that he was very impressed with the Roman officer. Do you think that he was impressed with the Roman officer's concern for his sick servant? Was Jesus more impressed that someone as powerful as an officer in the Roman army would ask for help? Or was he impressed with something else? What do you think? *(Pause.)*

Jesus tells you that what impressed him most of all was the Roman officer's faith. He had never seen Jesus. He had never met Jesus. He had only heard about Jesus. Yet he believed in Jesus. *(Pause.)* You can tell by the way Jesus is speaking that this is all very important. Ask him to help you see what God wants you to learn from this story. *(Pause.)*

Perhaps now you want to tell Jesus that you too believe in him. He's right here with you. Tell him. *(Pause.)* Jesus always listens. He loves you. He reminds you that you can talk with him heart to heart, anytime, anywhere.

You know we'll be going back to our room soon. *(Pause.)* Before you leave, you ask Jesus to bless you. *(Pause.)* You thank him for the gift of faith. *(Pause.)* You ask him to help you become stronger and stronger in your faith. *(Pause.)* You and Jesus spend a few moments together. There's no need to talk unless you want to. *(Pause.)*

The time has come to say good-bye to Jesus. Even though you feel that the visit was too short, you know that you'll be talking with Jesus again soon, so you leave happy. *(Pause.)*

Gradually bring yourself back to this room. *(Pause.)* Open your eyes. Yawn. *(Pause.)* Stretch if you'd like, as high as you can. *(Pause.)* Look around. *(Pause.)* Our group is together again. Welcome back.

SENSITIVITIES

▶ Children's awareness of what it means to speak to God in their hearts

▶ Children's experience with reflective prayer

HINTS

When leading the guided reflection yourself,

▶ be aware of your voice quality, pacing, and the message.

▶ allow children time to reflect by pausing at appropriate times throughout the reflection.

▶ gradually decrease the volume of the background music before turning off the CD player.

▶ adapt the neighborhood setting to children's own locale, if needed.

REFLECTIVE RESPONSES

Help children continue the reflection by examining their own responses to either the recording or the prayerful recitation of the script. Say: **Answer the following questions in the silence of your heart.** Ask: **Is there anything else you still want to say to Jesus? How can we work with Jesus to help the people we care about?** Encourage children to maintain a spirit of prayerfulness as they reflect on the questions.

HOW TO USE THE REFLECTION

Session 19 includes the option to use the recorded guided reflection "Our Gifts from God" [CD 1, Track 9]. One approach for sharing the reflection with children is to listen prayerfully to the recording before the session. Then when you play the recording during the session, join children in reflective prayer.

Another option is to pray aloud, using the script of the reflection. Prepare to share the reflection by listening to the recording beforehand. During the session you may wish to use the script as is, or adapt it as you wish. When leading the reflection, play reflective music softly in the background to enhance the sense of prayerfulness.

Our Gifts from God

GRADE 3, CD 1, TRACK 9 • TIME: 10 min. 51 sec.

We all like to imagine. Sometimes we imagine as we play with our friends. Sometimes we imagine stories about our toys. Today we're going to use our imaginations in a very special way.

Let's start by making ourselves as comfortable as possible. Relax. *(Pause.)* Close your eyes if you'd like. *(Pause.)* Let's all be very still. *(Pause.)* That's it. Now, breathe deeply, in and out, in and out, in and out. *(Pause.)*

Now imagine that you're in a place that you've visited before. It can be any place, but it's a place where you feel safe and sure and comfortable. You look around. What is it you see? *(Pause.)* You hear familiar sounds. What are they? *(Pause.)* Do you notice anything special or different about this place today? *(Pause.)* Aren't you glad you came back? You always feel so good here. *(Pause.)*

Do you hear footsteps coming toward you? You turn and see Jesus. He calls you by name and asks how you are. Answer him honestly. Do you say that you are fine or do you say something else? Jesus is waiting for your answer. *(Pause.)* Don't forget to tell him what's new with you and your family and friends. Jesus is always interested in what's going on with you. He loves to listen to you. But be sure to listen back in case there's something he wants you to know. *(Pause.)*

You look up at Jesus. Oh, you can feel the question coming. He always wants to know what it is you're learning. You tell him even before he asks. *(Pause.)* You mention that you've been talking about the special and different gifts the Holy Spirit gives each person. Jesus nods. You tell Jesus that you get gifts at Christmas and on your birthday, and that you don't mean to be impolite, but you never saw any gifts from the Holy Spirit. Well, did you? *(Pause.)*

Jesus wants you to know that when God made you, he gave you all kinds of gifts—gifts that don't come in boxes or bags. The Holy Spirit's gifts are your abilities, your power to grow and learn and do things.

To make sure you understand, Jesus might ask you to think for a moment about how you've changed since you were just one year old. What can you do now that you couldn't do back then? Name some of these things for Jesus. *(Pause.)* Did you tell Jesus that you've learned to dress and eat, and walk and talk, and read and write, and play and . . . Go on, say some more things you've learned. *(Pause.)* Jesus is always excited to hear how you've grown. He's also excited about your talents. He knows you have many. But Jesus wants to know what you think your talents are. Do you do well at music, or art, or dance? Are you good at sports? Are you a writer? Maybe you are really good in science or math. Tell Jesus about your talents. *(Pause.)*

Jesus is smiling as he listens to you. He is pleased with all you can do and have learned. But what if now he asks you to describe yourself in just one word? How will you answer him? *(Pause.)* Did you say funny? Cheerful? Kind? Silly? Helpful? I'll bet it takes more than one word to describe who you are. What are some of these other words? *(Pause.)*

Jesus is probably amused at your long list. But he won't let you off the hook. Jesus challenges you to take what you can do, take who you are, and use your gifts for others. *(Pause.)*

Maybe the thought of using your gifts makes you pause. Maybe you're not sure about what gifts to share or how you can really be helpful to others. Talk about this with Jesus. Remember that you don't always need words. Jesus knows what you're thinking. And he's very good at understanding what you mean. *(Pause.)*

We'll be returning to the room soon. As you prepare to come back, go to God in prayer. Thank the Holy Spirit for his gifts and ask him to bless you and help you use these gifts for others—just as others use their gifts for you. You are happy and sit quietly, enjoying God's love. *(Pause.)*

Now before you end your prayer, take a few more moments of silence, sharing with Jesus anything else that you've been thinking about. *(Pause.)* As you and Jesus say good-bye, he reminds you that you can speak with him anytime, anywhere. *(Pause.)*

Gradually bring yourself back to this room. *(Pause.)* Open your eyes. *(Pause.)* Yawn. *(Pause.)* Stretch if you'd like, as high as you can. *(Pause.)* Look around. *(Pause.)* Our group is together again. Welcome back.

SENSITIVITIES

▶ Children's awareness of what it means to speak to God in their hearts

▶ Children's experience with reflective prayer

HINTS

When leading the guided reflection yourself,

▶ be aware of your voice quality, pacing, and the message.

▶ allow children time to reflect by pausing at appropriate times throughout the reflection.

▶ gradually decrease the volume of the background music before turning off the CD player.

REFLECTIVE RESPONSES

Help children continue the reflection by examining their own responses to either the recording or the prayerful recitation of the script. Say: **Answer the following questions in the silence of your heart.** Ask: **Which of your talents are you most pleased with? What is one gift or talent that you most like to share with others?** Encourage children to maintain a spirit of prayerfulness as they reflect on the questions.

HOW TO USE THE REFLECTION

Session 23 includes the option to use the recorded guided reflection "Hold Them in Your Heart" [CD 1, Track 10]. One approach for sharing the reflection with children is to listen prayerfully to the recording before the session. Then when you play the recording during the session, join children in reflective prayer.

Another option is to pray aloud, using the script of the reflection. Prepare to share the reflection by listening to the recording beforehand. During the session you may wish to use the script as is, or adapt it as you wish. When leading the reflection, play reflective music softly in the background to enhance the sense of prayerfulness.

Hold Them in Your Heart

GRADE 3, CD 1, TRACK 10 • **TIME:** 10 min. 43 sec.

We all like to imagine. Sometimes we imagine as we play with our friends. Sometimes we imagine stories about our toys. Today we're going to use our imaginations in a very special way.

Let's start by making ourselves as comfortable as possible. Relax. *(Pause.)* Close your eyes if you'd like. *(Pause.)* Let's all be very still. *(Pause.)* That's it. Now, breathe deeply, in and out, in and out, in and out. *(Pause.)*

Where do you go when you really need quiet time? *(Pause.)* Do you have a special place? *(Pause.)* Do you stay in bed and pull a blanket over your head? *(Pause.)* Or do you create a private place just by closing your eyes? *(Pause.)* Wherever you go, imagine you are there now. *(Pause.)* Invite Jesus to join you. He's the one person who's always welcome, isn't he? *(Pause.)*

Jesus is with you now. He's ready to listen and talk. Jesus always likes to hear what you have to say, and so you tell him what's on your mind. *(Pause.)* Do you tell him about the ordinary things in your life: the pizza you had the other day, the movie you saw last, the friend you played with?

Or maybe some more serious things are on your mind. Do you tell him about the letter you just read, the letter of Saint Paul? You remember it's so full of love and joy. And to think that Paul wrote it from prison! Prison—not a pleasant place to be. Yet Paul stayed happy. How do you think he managed to do that? *(Pause.)* You might want to ask Jesus about it. *(Pause.)*

Did you tell Jesus about that sentence in Paul's letter, "I hold you in my heart"?* What a loving thing to say. Perhaps Jesus asks you who it is that you hold in your heart. *(Pause.)*

Did anybody ever ask you a question like that before? Maybe you could think out loud with Jesus as you try to answer. Who is it that you love? Who loves you? That's an easy way to start. Maybe you mention the people in your family first. *(Pause.)* Who else? It's up to you to name anyone you'd like. Take your time. *(Pause.)*

* Scripture citation in this reflection is Philippians 1:7.

Jesus is with you while you do this. Does he say anything to you? *(Pause.)* Now pick one or two of the people who love you very much. Your parents? Your grandparents? An aunt or uncle? Who? You know who they are. Share their names with Jesus. *(Pause.)*

How do they show you that they love you? *(Pause.)* Let Jesus know all the good things they do for you. *(Pause.)*

Now Jesus has another question for you. In his letter Saint Paul thanks God for many people. Besides the people you know and love, who do you hold in your heart? *(Pause.)* That's a much harder question, and maybe you're not sure how to answer. A good clue is to pay attention to the people you pray for. Who do you pray for at Mass, or at home, or in your heart? Can you answer that? *(Pause.)* Maybe a relative who is sick. A friend who has a hard test coming up. A family that doesn't have enough to eat. A neighbor who has no job. *(Pause.)*

Now you realize that there are many people to hold in your heart. Perhaps you wonder how you can love and care for them all. Jesus knows how. Ask him for help. *(Pause.)*

Jesus also knows how busy you might be. But nobody's too busy to glance at someone. So why not every so often during the day, give God in your heart a loving glance? *(Pause.)* Then glance down at all the people you hold in your heart. You and God can look at them for a moment and love them. You and God together, just love them. *(Pause.)*

As you get ready to return to the room, you and Jesus go to God in prayer one last time. Together you thank God for the gift of all those people who are special to you, all those people you hold in your heart. *(Pause.)* Before you end your prayer, share with Jesus anything else that's on your mind. *(Pause.)* Promise to meet him again soon. You and Jesus say good-bye now. You ask him to bless you and everyone you love. *(Pause.)*

Gradually bring yourself back to this room. *(Pause.)* Open your eyes. *(Pause.)* Yawn. *(Pause.)* Stretch if you'd like, as high as you can. *(Pause.)* Look around. *(Pause.)* Our group is together again. Welcome back.

SENSITIVITIES

▶ Children's awareness of what it means to speak to God in their hearts

▶ Children's experience with reflective prayer

▶ Diversity in family structures

▶ Children's experience with having a special or favorite place for prayer

HINTS

When leading the guided reflection yourself,

▶ be aware of your voice quality, pacing, and the message.

▶ allow children time to reflect by pausing at appropriate times throughout the reflection.

▶ gradually decrease the volume of the background music before turning off the CD player.

REFLECTIVE RESPONSES

Help children continue the reflection by examining their own responses to either the recording or the prayerful recitation of the script. Say: **Answer the following questions in the silence of your heart.** Ask: **When you thought about the people you held in your heart, was there someone there you did not expect? Who in our country, our Church, or our neighborhood can we hold in our heart-prayers?** Encourage children to maintain a spirit of prayerfulness as they reflect on the questions.

BLACKLINE MASTERS

Reproducible blackline masters appear in this section.

- **25 Session BLMs**
- **Unit Assessment BLMs**
- **Answer Key**
- **Catechist Guide Acknowledgments**

These BLMs, as well as Session Assessment BLMs, can be accessed at www.findinggod.com.

Name _____ Date _____

The Apostles' Creed

Directions: Circle the following words in the puzzle. Then write the words in the correct order to write a sentence about the Apostles' Creed.

| Apostles | Creed | faith | God | in | our |
| pray | show | the | to | we | |

```
A  P  O  S  T  L  E  S
N  R  C  H  O  E  H  W
D  A  R  O  D  A  E  E
E  Y  E  W  G  O  D  I
U  F  E  T  H  E  R  N
O  Y  D  F  A  I  T  H
O  U  R  L  I  E  V  E
```

__ __ ____ ___ ,

_____ ' _____

__ ____ ___

_____ __ ___ .

Answers: For complete answers, see page T-341.   **T-293**

Name _____ Date _____

Love Bug

The Holy Spirit helps us show God's love to others.

Directions: Make a "love bug" to remind you to show love each day.

1. Color and cut out the love bug below.
2. Glue the bug onto construction paper and cut it out.
3. Punch holes through the circles in the top of the head.
4. Poke a craft stem through each hole and twist to make antennae.
5. Decorate the bug with heart-shaped spots if you wish.
6. On the lines write some ways you can show your love for others. Then place your finished creature where it can "bug" you to show love each day.

Greg Phillips

Grade 3 • Unit 1 • Session 2

T-294

Name _____ Date _____

Praying to God Our Father

Directions: Use words from the word bank to complete the sentences.

Abba	cares	Father	Lord's	Jesus
language	wrongs	pray	revealed	taught

1. God sent _____ to show us how much God loves us.

2. Jesus _____ to us that God is our Father.

3. He _____us what God is really like.

4. A special name like Dad or Papa that Jesus used was

   _____.

5. Children call God Father in their own _____.

6. We should forgive others for the _____ they do.

7. God our Father _____ for us as his children.

8. _____ means one who loves his children.

9. Jesus taught us the _____ Prayer to bring us closer to God the Father.

10. When we _____, we raise our minds and hearts to God.

Yoshi Miyake

Answers: For complete answers, see page T-341.

Name _____ Date _____

An Angel's Visit

Directions: Complete the puzzle below, using the clues at the left to choose the correct words from the word bank.

angel	Christ	Emmanuel	Jesus
Joseph	listened	Mary	Matthew
Son of God	trust	Savior	

Across

2. New Testament writer

4. One sent by God to talk to Mary

5. The name of Mary's baby

6. Joseph placed his _____ in God.

7. Joseph _____ to the angel.

9. Jesus was to be our_____.

Down

1. Another name for "the anointed one"

2. Mother of God

3. Name meaning "God is with us"

5. Mary's husband

8. Jesus is the _____ _____ _____.

www.findinggod.com   Grade 3 • Unit 1 • Session 4

T-296   **Answers:** For complete answers, see page T-342.

Name _____ Date _____

My Parish

During Ordinary Time we give thanks for our Church community.

Directions: Draw a picture in the church below of your family attending Mass. Write the names of each family member. When you are done, write a list of community members who are special to you on another sheet of paper. Are they involved in the Mass? Do they attend church with you and your family? How many members can you name?

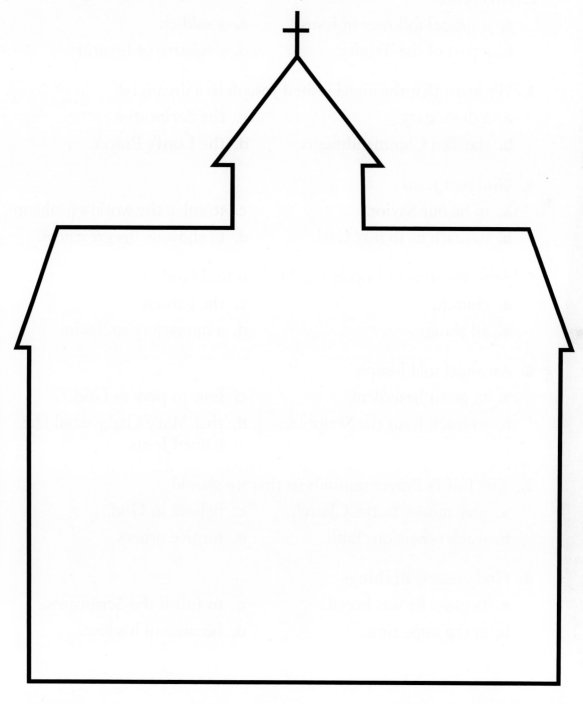

Grade 3 • Unit 1 • Session 5

Unit 1 Assessment

A. Circle the letter of the choice that best completes each sentence.

1. A creed tells people
   a. how to pray.
   b. what we believe.
   c. stories of Jesus' life.
   d. how to follow rules.

2. An apostle is
   a. a special follower of Jesus'.
   b. a part of the Trinity.
   c. a soldier.
   d. a relative of Ignatius.

3. We learn that the angel visited Joseph in a dream in
   a. a dictionary.
   b. the Ten Commandments.
   c. the Scriptures.
   d. the Lord's Prayer.

4. God sent Jesus
   a. to be our Savior.
   b. to teach us to fear God.
   c. to solve the world's problems.
   d. to show us his greatness.

5. Saint Ignatius of Loyola taught us to find God in
   a. church.
   b. all things.
   c. the garden.
   d. a monastery in Spain.

6. An angel told Joseph
   a. to go to Jerusalem.
   b. to teach Jesus the Scriptures.
   c. how to pray to God.
   d. that Mary's baby would be named Jesus.

7. The Lord's Prayer reminds us that we should
   a. give money to the Church.
   b. teach others our faith.
   c. believe in God.
   d. forgive others.

8. God created all things
   a. because he was bored.
   b. at the same time.
   c. to fulfill the Scriptures.
   d. because of his love.

Answers: **1.** b; **2.** a; **3.** c; **4.** a; **5.** b; **6.** d; **7.** d; **8.** d

Name _____ Date _____

Unit 1 Assessment

B. Circle *T* if each statement is true or *F* if it is false.

9. Joseph accepted the angel's message because he was afraid. **T** **F**

10. Ordinary Time is celebrated two times during the liturgical year. **T** **F**

11. Saint Ignatius of Loyola wrote a book called *Scripture Exercises*. **T** **F**

12. The Sign of the Cross reminds us of the Trinity. **T** **F**

13. The name *Emmanuel* means "God loves us." **T** **F**

14. Sometimes Jesus called his disciples Abba. **T** **F**

15. The Bible is the Word of God. **T** **F**

16. Our church community seeks to serve others as Jesus did. **T** **F**

17. The name *Jesus* means "God saves us." **T** **F**

18. Jesus taught us the Lord's Prayer. **T** **F**

19. The Apostles' Creed tells how to become an apostle. **T** **F**

20. The name *Christ* means "the anointed one." **T** **F**

21. We bring God's love to life in our world by loving one another. **T** **F**

22. One way to care for others is to forgive them. **T** **F**

23. The Glory Be to the Father praises the Trinity. **T** **F**

24. God the Father rarely shows sinners mercy. **T** **F**

25. The liturgical year is the Church's calendar. **T** **F**

Answers: **9.** F; **10.** T; **11.** F; **12.** T; **13.** F; **14.** F; **15.** T; **16.** T; **17.** T; **18.** T; **19.** F; **20.** T; **21.** T; **22.** T; **23.** T; **24.** F; **25.** T   **T-299**

Name ______________________ Date ____________

Unit 1 Assessment

Show What You Know

C. Write the names of the three Persons of the Trinity and tell what each one does for us.

____

____

____

____

____

____

Beliefs and Perceptions

D. Our faith tells us that we reflect God's love by the way we treat others. In what ways do you share God's love? How have others shared God's love with you?

____

____

____

____

____

____

____

____

____

 Answers: For complete answers, go to www.findinggod.com/assessments.

Name _____ Date _____

My Own Parables

We can think of our own parables to describe God's kingdom.

Directions: Write ideas for your own parables by finishing the sentences below. The first one is already completed. On the lines below the sentences, choose one parable and expand it. On the back of this sheet, draw a picture of the parable.

1. The Kingdom of God is like a garden because everything is peaceful inside.

2. The Kingdom of God is like _____ because everyone is gathered together.

3. The Kingdom of God is like a sunny day because _____

_____ .

4. The Kingdom of God is like a special gift because _____

_____ .

5. The Kingdom of God is like _____

because _____ .

_____

_____

_____

_____

top: iStockphoto.com/~art-siberia· bottom: Jan Slovak/© 1995 Zedcor, Inc./ Dover Publications

T-301

Name _____ Date _____

Singing of Love

When we sing a song, we can show what we are singing by our actions.

Directions: Sing the "Song of Love" together. Each time you reach the chorus, do the actions described below.

Thank you, Jesus, for helping me to see.
    Put your hands up to your eyes like binoculars.

Thank you, God, for the heart you've given me.
    Place your hands on your heart.

Thank you, Spirit, for coming to me,
    Reach your arms out and pull them toward you.

And for showing me how to sing . . .
    Reach your arms up and stretch them out
    like a rainbow.

Your song of love.

Name _____ Date _____

Fishing for Good Deeds

Jesus called his disciples "fishers of men."

Directions: On each fish below, write a good deed that you could do to show God's love to others. For example: *Compliment another child. Help a friend with homework. Volunteer for a chore.* Then decorate the fish and cut them out. Place the fish in a class basket. Each day someone can pull a fish from the basket to give everyone a good deed to do.

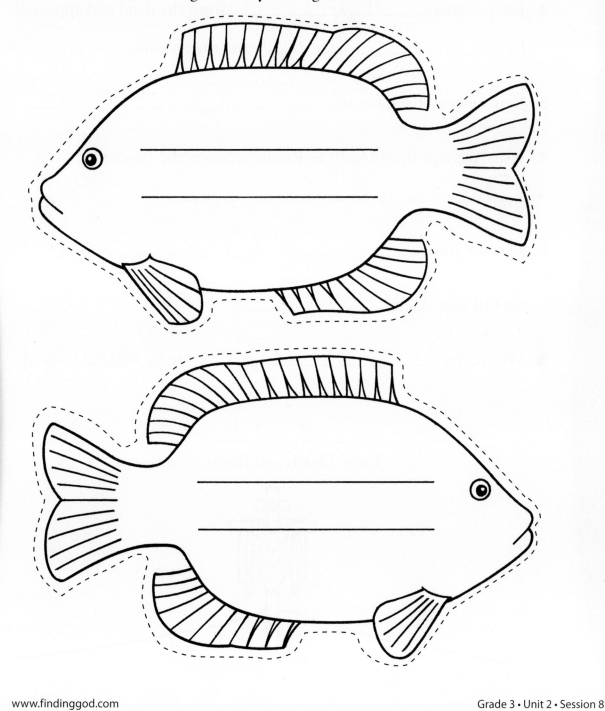

Greg Phillips

Name _____ Date _____

Paschal Mystery

Directions: Fill in the blanks with words about the Paschal Mystery. Then unscramble the letters in the circles to form a new word.

1. Jesus Christ sends the Holy ____ ◯ ____ ____ ____ ____ to share in his life.

2. Jesus Christ ____ ◯ ____ ____ from the dead and appeared to ____ ____ ____ ____ ◯ and the apostles.

3. Jesus opened the gates of ____ ____ ◯ ____ ____ ____ .

4. Jesus' passage from Death to Resurrection is the Paschal ◯ ____ ____ ____ ____ ____ ____ ____ .

5. Because Jesus ____ ____ ____ ◯ ____ ____ is God, we call him ◯ ____ ____ ____ .

6. We receive ____ ____ ____ ◯ ____ to be faithful to God.

We ____ ____ ____ ____ ____ ____ ____ ____

Jesus' Death and Resurrection.

Grade 3 • Unit 2 • Session 9

Name _____   Date _____

We Prepare for Jesus

Advent is a season to prepare our homes and our hearts to celebrate Jesus' birth.

Directions: Make a special Advent candle for your family.

1. Decorate the candle, using crayons or markers.
2. Cut out the candle following the dotted line.
3. On the back of the candle, write a prayer that you and your family can pray together this Advent.
4. Punch a hole in the top and thread string through the hole.
5. Hang your candle where you and your family can see it.

Name _____   Date _____

Unit 2 Assessment

A. Circle the letter of the choice that best completes each sentence.

1. Jesus told Peter he would soon be catching people instead of
   - **a.** butterflies.
   - **b.** mustard seeds.
   - **c.** colds.
   - **d.** fish.

2. The parable of the yeast teaches us that a little bit can
   - **a.** make a big difference.
   - **b.** make the sun rise.
   - **c.** make good bread.
   - **d.** make no difference.

3. We show love for God and others by following
   - **a.** the shortest path.
   - **b.** whatever we choose.
   - **c.** the directions for a game.
   - **d.** the Ten Commandments.

4. Jesus said that everyone who lives and believes in him will never
   - **a.** be happy.
   - **b.** die.
   - **c.** be wealthy.
   - **d.** fish.

5. The color of the altar cloth or priest's vestments during Advent is
   - **a.** blue.
   - **b.** silver.
   - **c.** purple.
   - **d.** pink.

6. The season of Advent is a time of
   - **a.** remembrance.
   - **b.** preparation.
   - **c.** celebration.
   - **d.** all of the above.

7. The story of the mustard seed is an example of
   - **a.** a psalm.
   - **b.** a parable.
   - **c.** a commandment.
   - **d.** a disciple.

8. When we mend our relationships with God and others, it is called
   - **a.** charity.
   - **b.** conversion.
   - **c.** a commandment.
   - **d.** resurrection.

Answers: **1.** d; **2.** a; **3.** d; **4.** b; **5.** c; **6.** d; **7.** b; **8.** b

©Loyola Press.

Name _____ Date _____

Unit 2 Assessment

B. Write the word that best completes each sentence.

mission	monastery	religious	Paschal	faithful
Kingdom	apostle	Gospels	grace	butterfly

9. Mary and Joseph were _____ to God's plan.

10. The parts of the Bible that tell the good news of Jesus' life are the _____.

11. Saint Scholastica and Saint Benedict each started _____ communities.

12. A community of monks lives in a _____.

13. Jesus' apostles and disciples accepted the _____ of proclaiming God's kingdom.

14. An _____ is a person who is sent forth, entrusted with a mission by Jesus.

15. The _____ of God calls us to love one another and live according to God's rule and direction.

16. Jesus' passage from Death to Resurrection is called the _____ Mystery.

17. The _____ is a symbol of Jesus' Resurrection.

18. The Holy Spirit gives us the _____ to turn back to God.

Answers: 9. faithful; **10.** Gospels; **11.** religious; **12.** monastery; **13.** mission; **14.** apostle; **15.** Kingdom; **16.** Paschal; **17.** butterfly; **18.** grace   **T-307**

Name _____ Date _____

Unit 2 Assessment

Show What You Know

C. Recall the messages of the parable of the yeast and the parable of the mustard seed. Choose one. Write what you can do in your life to reflect the message of that parable.

_____

_____

_____

_____

_____

Beliefs and Perceptions

D. We are instructed to love one another as much as we love ourselves and to love God above all else. How does God help us do this? Why is this sometimes difficult for people to do?

_____

_____

_____

_____

_____

_____

_____

_____

_____

www.findinggod.com   Grade 3 • Unit 2 Assessment • page 3 of 3

T-308   **Answers:** For complete answers, go to www.findinggod.com/assessments.

Name _____   Date _____

Holy Spirit in Motion

The Fruits of the Holy Spirit are love, joy, peace, patience, kindness, generosity, faithfulness, gentleness, and self-control.

Directions: Make a mobile using a Fruit of the Holy Spirit.

1. Write a Fruit of the Holy Spirit on the rectangle.
2. On the flames below, write three ways you've seen or experienced this fruit in your life.
3. Color and cut out the rectangle and flames.
4. Glue them to construction paper.
5. Punch out the holes.
6. Attach the flames to the bottom of the rectangle with yarn or string, as shown. Thread the yarn or string through the top hole. Hang your mobile where it can blow in the wind.

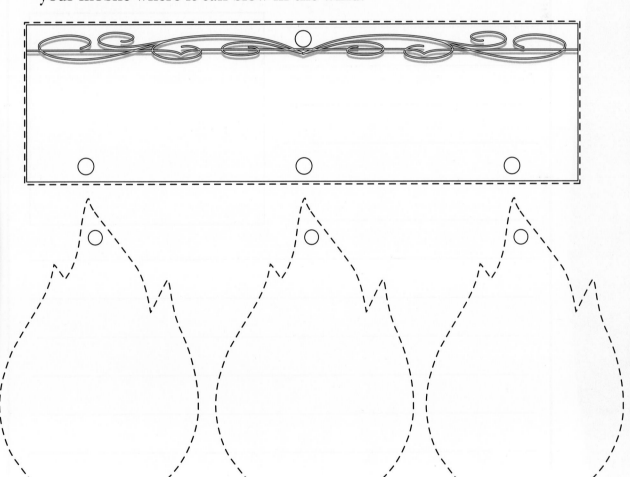

www.findinggod.com

Grade 3 • Unit 3 • Session 11

Name _____ Date _____

A Church News Flash

Directions: Think of an active member of your church community—
a family member, friend, priest, or even yourself. Write a news story
about the person you chose. Tell how the person is active in the church
community. Write a headline for the story. Then draw a picture of the
person in action.

Church News Bulletin

Volume 1, Issue 1   Serving God's Community

Name _____ Date _____

Jesus Is Present

Directions: Think of the ways Jesus is present at Mass. Recalling what you have learned, fill in the letters to finish the paragraph below. In the church scene, draw pictures of the words you have written. When you are finished, decorate the picture to make a beautiful scene.

Jesus is present in the pr ____ ____ ____ ____, in the

p ____ ____ ____ l ____ gathered, and in the

S c ____ ____ ____ ____ ____ ____ ____ ____ ____.

Jesus Christ is especially present in the consecrated

____ ____ ____ ____ d and W ____ ____ ____.

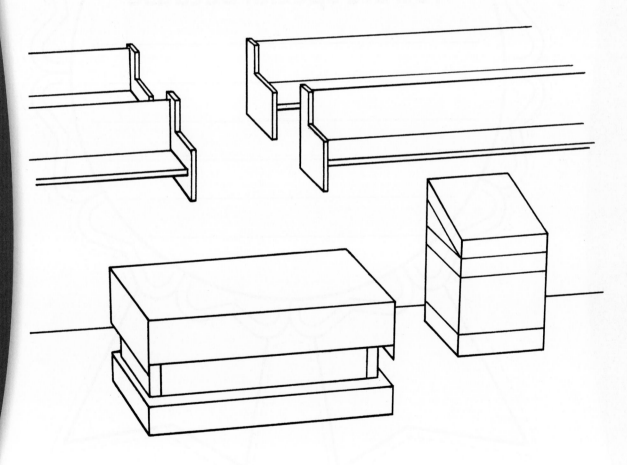

Greg Phillips

Name _____ Date _____

You Are Special Badge

Mary loved and cared for Jesus.

Directions: Think of a person in your life who loves and cares for you as Mary did for Jesus. Then write a message on the badge below, telling why you love and appreciate this special person. Decorate the badge and cut it out. Give the badge to your special person.

Dear _____,
You are special because

Greg Phillips

Name _____   Date _____

Celebrate Christmas

Directions: Unscramble the words below. Hint: the bold letter is the first letter of the word. At the bottom write three sentences, using at least one new word in each sentence. Then draw a picture on another sheet of paper about attending Christmas Mass with your family.

1. **g**rhate _____

2. **C**thasmsir _____

3. **c**ebelreta _____

4. **f**yimal _____

5. **J**sues _____

6. **c**nmoymuti _____

7. **E**rucahtsi _____

_____

_____

_____

_____

© LOYOLA PRESS.

Name _____ Date _____

Unit 3 Assessment

A. Circle the letter of the choice that best answers each question.

1. Which of these is *not* one of the Marks of the Church?
   - **a.** holy
   - **b.** prayerful
   - **c.** catholic
   - **d.** apostolic

2. The Rosary is a prayer that honors whom?
   - **a.** the saints
   - **b.** the Holy Spirit
   - **c.** Mary
   - **d.** the apostles

3. To whom did Jesus tell, "You are the rock upon which I will build my Church"?
   - **a.** Peter
   - **b.** Paul
   - **c.** the Holy Spirit
   - **d.** his disciples

4. What is another name for the pope?
   - **a.** the Apostle
   - **b.** the Body of Christ
   - **c.** the Vicar of Christ
   - **d.** Emmanuel

5. How is Jesus especially present during Mass?
   - **a.** in the Holy Spirit
   - **b.** in the psalms
   - **c.** in holy water
   - **d.** in the Eucharist

6. Which of these is *not* one of the Fruits of the Holy Spirit?
   - **a.** love
   - **b.** self-control
   - **c.** joy
   - **d.** greed

7. A cross, holy water, and a blessing are examples of what?
   - **a.** sacramentals
   - **b.** prayers
   - **c.** rosaries
   - **d.** none of these

8. On the Feast of the Epiphany, what do we celebrate?
   - **a.** Jesus' birth
   - **b.** the Mother of God
   - **c.** Jesus' revelation to the world
   - **d.** Jesus' baptism

Answers: **1.** b; **2.** c; **3.** a; **4.** c; **5.** d; **6.** d; **7.** a; **8.** c

Name _____ Date _____

Unit 3 Assessment

B. Write a word from the word box to complete each sentence.

Jesus	Bethlehem	wind	Magnificat
Fruits	witnesses	Gabriel	Church
wealth	Eucharist	prayerful	Communion

9. The _____ is Mary's song of praise to God.

10. Christmas celebrates God's gift of _____.

11. In Hebrew, _____ means "house of bread."

12. Katharine Drexel's parents taught her to use her

    _____ to help others.

13. The _____ of Saints is one body, united before God.

14. When our actions are guided by the Holy Spirit, the results

    are the _____ of the Holy Spirit.

15. We are being _____ when we tell other people
    about Jesus.

16. The power of the Holy Spirit is like the _____.

17. The _____ is called the Mystical Body
    of Christ.

18. The angel _____ appeared to Mary.

19. Bread and Wine are signs of the _____.

20. Sacramentals help us become more _____ people.

Name _____ Date _____

Unit 3 Assessment

Show What You Know

C. Imagine you are speaking with someone who has never heard of the Holy Spirit. What would you say to tell this person who the Holy Spirit is?

_____

_____

_____

_____

_____

Beliefs and Perceptions

D. We believe that the Holy Spirit gives us the strength to continue Jesus' mission in the world. How do you know that the Holy Spirit is at work within you and your family, your church, and your community?

_____

_____

_____

_____

_____

_____

_____

www.findinggod.com   Grade 3 • Unit 3 Assessment • page 3 of 3

T-316   **Answers:** For complete answers, go to www.findinggod.com/assessments.

Name _____   Date _____

New Life in Christ

Directions: Write the answer to each clue in the puzzle below. Read the word in the shaded boxes from top to bottom to find out how you can begin a new life in Christ.

1. This book contains the Word of God.

2. At first he wanted to destroy the Church, but then he became a great apostle.

3. The _____ of God are the Church community.

4. In this sacrament the Holy Spirit strengthens us to be witnesses to Jesus.

5. We receive the Body and Blood of Jesus Christ in this sacrament.

6. On Easter we think about rising with _____ to new life.

7. White garments, holy oil, and candles are _____ used when the Sacraments of Initiation are celebrated.

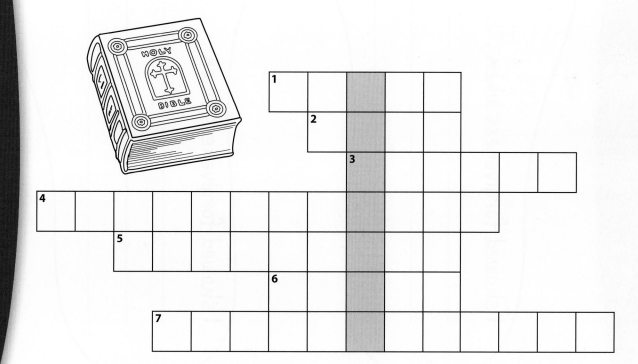

Greg Phillips

Name _____ Date _____

Forgiving Footprints

When we walk in peace with God and Jesus, our footprints are the footprints of forgiving people.

Directions: Think about times when it was hard to forgive someone who hurt your feelings. On each foot below, write about one of those times. You can ask God to help you show forgiveness if you feel this way again.

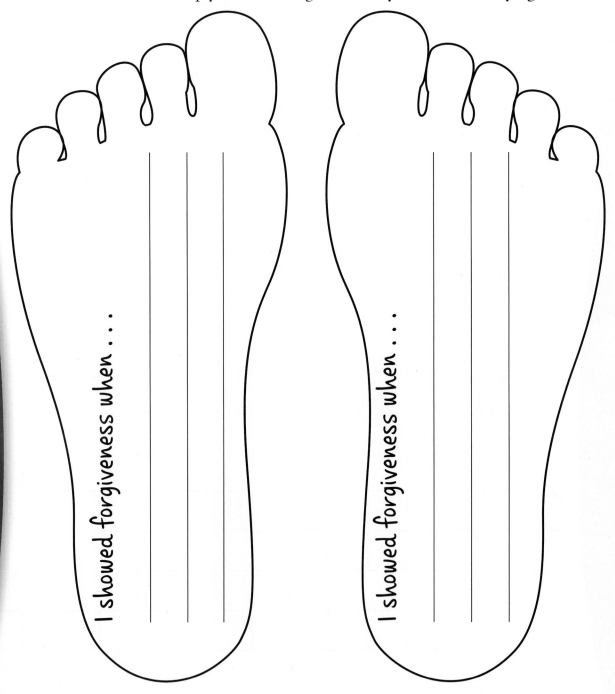

I showed forgiveness when . . .

I showed forgiveness when . . .

Name _____ Date _____

Banner of the Mass

Directions: Make a banner representing things you have seen or heard at Mass. Color the symbols of the Mass and cut them out. Glue them to poster board and decorate it. Write a special heading for your banner, such as "The Mass brings us closer to Jesus" or "Things I see at Mass."

Yoshi Miyake

Name _____   Date _____

Gifts from God

Directions: Think of the gifts God has given you. For example, are you good at painting, music, sports, or science? In each gift box, draw a picture or symbol of one of your special talents or abilities.

Helping Others

Lent is a time to help people in need.

Directions: Think about people who need your prayers this Lent, and write a prayer. Add a colorful border. On the back of this paper, make a list of friends that you will help this Lent. As you write their names, say a prayer for them.

Name _____ Date _____

Unit 4 Assessment

A. Circle the letter of the choice that best completes each sentence.

1. Original Sin is forgiven through
   a. Reconciliation.   **c.** Matrimony.
   b. Baptism.   **d.** Holy Orders.

2. We remember Jesus' words at the Last Supper in
   a. Confirmation.   **c.** the Eucharist.
   b. the Sign of Peace.   **d.** all of these.

3. The Sacraments of Initiation include
   a. Baptism.   **c.** the Eucharist.
   b. Confirmation.   **d.** all of these.

4. When we reject God by disobeying him and being self-centered, it is
   a. an obligation.   **c.** a personal sin.
   b. an epistle.   **d.** all of these.

5. When men become priests or deacons, they celebrate the Sacrament of
   a. Holy Orders.   **c.** Baptism.
   b. Matrimony.   **d.** none of these.

6. We feel one with all people when we receive
   a. a vocation.   **c.** contrition.
   b. a meal.   **d.** Holy Communion.

7. All the different kinds of spiritual gifts come from
   a. our parents.   **c.** the Holy Spirit.
   b. a priest or deacon.   **d.** an epistle.

8. During Lent we pray for the needs of
   a. the Church.   **c.** the local community.
   b. the world.   **d.** all of these.

Name _____ Date _____

Unit 4 Assessment

B. Write a word from the word box to complete each sentence.

People	worship	almsgiving	absolution	mortal
vocation	temptation	epistle	consecrated	disciples

9. After the Resurrection, Jesus Christ visited the

   _____.

10. We commit a _____ sin when we totally
    reject God.

11. Paul wrote a special letter, or _____,
    about the Eucharist.

12. The Mass is the central celebration of parish

    _____.

13. Another name for the Church is the _____
    of God.

14. Each of us is called to a special _____,
    or way of life.

15. During Lent we practice _____, giving
    money to people who are poor.

16. We make our hearts ready for Easter by resisting

    _____ and caring for those in need.

17. In the Sacrament of Reconciliation, we confess our sins

    and receive _____.

18. In the Eucharist the Bread and Wine are _____.

9. disciples; 10. mortal; 11. epistle; 12. worship; 13. People; 14. vocation; 15. almsgiving; 16. temptation; 17. absolution; 18. consecrated

T-323

Name _____ Date _____

Unit 4 Assessment

Show What You Know

C. Choose two of the sacraments you learned about in this unit. Why do people receive each of these sacraments? How does each one bring you into the People of God?

_____

_____

_____

_____

_____

Beliefs and Perceptions

D. Jesus wants us to be aware of the needs of the world, the Church, and our community. What is a need connected to each of these? What can you do to help meet each need?

_____

_____

_____

_____

_____

_____

_____

_____

_____

_____

© LOYOLAPRESS.

Name _____   Date _____

A Prayer of Hope

The passage below describes a person who trusts in God by using the symbol of a tree planted near the "water" of God's love. God promises that even though life may not always be easy, you can trust in his promises.

Directions: Read this passage from the Bible that tells about trusting God and then answer the questions.

Blessed is the man who trusts in the LORD,
   whose hope is in the LORD.
He is like a tree planted beside the waters
   that stretches out its roots to the stream:
It fears not the heat when it comes,
   its leaves stay green;
In the years of drought it shows no distress,
   but still bears fruit.

Jeremiah 17:7–8

Think about the passage and why a tree needs water. Why do you think a tree next to the stream symbolizes trust in God?

_____

_____

What is another symbol that you could use to describe a person who trusts in God? Write your own comparison in the space below.

A person who trusts in God is like a _____

_____

_____

_____

_____.

Greg Phillips

Name _____ Date _____

The Ten Commandments

Directions: Complete each commandment with a word from the word bank.

holy	neighbors	God	obey	happy
name	married	human	Respect	truth

1. I am your

   _____; love nothing more than me.

2. Use God's

   _____ with respect.

3. Keep the Lord's Day

   _____.

4. Honor and

   _____ your parents.

5. Treat all

   _____ life with respect.

6. Respect

   _____ life.

7. _____ what belongs to others.

8. Tell the

   _____.

9. Respect your

   _____ and your friends.

10. Be _____

    with what you have.

Grade 3 • Unit 5 • Session 22

T-326   **Answers:** For complete answers, see page T-344.

Name _____   Date _____

Complete the Story

Directions: Use the words in the word bank to complete the story.

Charity	clothing	community	France	Vincent
Marillac	poor	religious	together	world

Louise de _____ lived in

_____ hundreds of years ago.
She devoted her life to serving God. First,
Louise visited people who were

_____. She gave them

_____ she had made herself.

She met _____ de Paul, who
also cared for people in need.

Vincent asked Louise to start a new

_____ order of women called

the Sisters of _____. The

women in this _____ worked

_____ to serve people
in homes, orphanages, hospitals, and
schools. Today the Sisters of Charity of
Saint Vincent de Paul serve people all over

the _____.

© LOYOLA PRESS.

Answers: For complete answers, see page T-345.   **T-327**

Name _____ Date _____

Window to God's World

Every day you can look through your window into God's beautiful world.

Directions: In each pane of the window, write and illustrate one way you can care for God's creation.

We can care for the earth by

_____

_____.

We can care for the water by

_____

_____.

We can care for the air by

_____

_____.

We can care for the animals by

_____

_____.

Greg Phillips

Name _____   Date _____

Have Mercy on Us

Directions: Use the code to color the picture. Then finish the sentence below. On a separate sheet of paper, write a paragraph about a time that you showed mercy to a friend. How were you like Jesus?

1 = blue   2 = red   3 = green   4 = black   5 = white   6 = yellow   7 = brown

_____, have mercy on us.

Grade 3 • Unit 5 • Session 25

Yoshi Miyake

Name _____ Date _____

Unit 5 Assessment

A. Circle the letter of the choice that best completes each sentence.

1. Saint Monica is the patron saint of
   a. lawyers.
   b. married women.
   c. teachers.
   d. children.

2. When we have hope, we
   a. give up.
   b. put other things before God.
   c. trust in God.
   d. do all of these.

3. An important virtue is
   a. faith.
   b. hope.
   c. charity.
   d. all of these.

4. Jeanne Jugan and her friends formed a religious community called the Little Sisters of
   a. the Elderly.
   b. the Poor.
   c. the Town.
   d. the Sea.

5. When we follow the moral law, we are able to
   a. do good.
   b. avoid evil.
   c. live for God and others.
   d. do all of these.

6. When we treat our family and others with justice, we
   a. take what is ours.
   b. ignore their problems.
   c. treat them fairly.
   d. do all of these.

7. Blessed Frederic Ozanam understood the worth of
   a. every person.
   b. some churches.
   c. a good book.
   d. none of these.

8. The most important day of the Church year is
   a. the Feast of the Ascension.
   b. Holy Saturday.
   c. Easter.
   d. Pentecost.

Name _____   Date _____

Unit 5 Assessment

B. Circle the choice that best completes each sentence.

9. The cross is a symbol of our (faith   suffering).

10. Saint Monica's son, Augustine, also became a (saint   soldier).

11. God gives us gifts called (prayers   virtues) to help us live good lives.

12. Charity, or (love   praise), is the most important virtue.

13. The first three commandments teach us to (remember   honor) God.

14. The next seven commandments teach us how to live with our (enemy   neighbor).

15. The Eighth Commandment teaches us to tell the (Scriptures   truth).

16. In peaceful homes, children obey and respect (their parents   no one).

17. Every human life is (short   sacred).

18. With the words of the (Dismissal   bulletin), we are sent forth to glorify the Lord.

19. We are called to take care of (all   some) of God's creation.

20. Jesus is called the Lamb of God because he (hid   sacrificed) his life for our Salvation.

9. faith; **10.** saint; **11.** virtues; **12.** love; **13.** honor; **14.** neighbor; **15.** truth; **16.** their parents; **17.** sacred; **18.** Dismissal; **19.** all; **20.** sacrificed   **T-331**

Name _____   Date _____

Unit 5 Assessment

Show What You Know

C. How do Jesus' example and teachings help us face difficult moral choices?

_____

_____

_____

_____

_____

Beliefs and Perceptions

D. Why is love the greatest virtue we show one another? How does loving others help us be happy?

_____

_____

_____

_____

_____

_____

_____

_____

_____

T-332   **Answers:** For complete answers, go to www.findinggod.com/assessments.

Name _____ Date _____

The Liturgical Calendar

The liturgical calendar shows us the feasts and seasons of the Church year.

Directions: Color each season with the correct liturgical color.

Answers: Advent, Lent, Holy Week—purple; Easter, Christmas—white; Ordinary Time—green

T-333

Name _____ Date _____

My Advent Wreath

Directions: Make an Advent wreath for your family.

1. On the line for each week, write one way you can be faithful to God.
2. Color Candle 3 pink and the rest violet.
3. Color the wreath and flames and cut them out.
4. Glue the wreath to a sheet of construction paper. Hang it at home.
5. Glue a flame to the candle for each week of Advent.

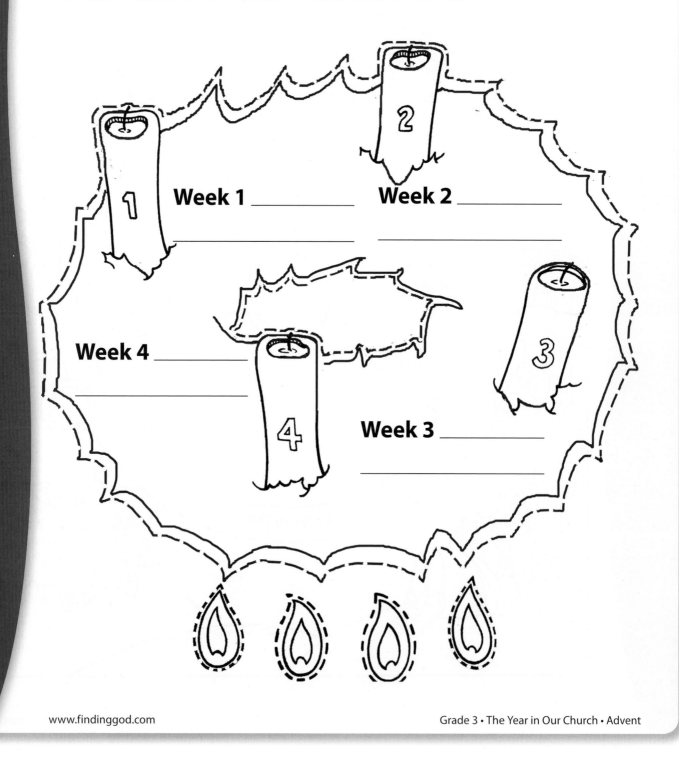

Week 1 _____

_____

Week 2 _____

_____

Week 4 _____

_____

Week 3 _____

_____

Name _____ Date _____

You Were There!

Directions: Imagine you were in the manger the night Jesus was born. Who was there? Draw yourself as a shepherd, and the people and animals who were part of the first Christmas.

Grade 3 • The Year in Our Church • Christmas

Greg Phillips

T-335

Name _____   Date _____

Lenten Calendar

Directions: On the Lenten calendar below, write one promise you will make to God for each week. Hang your calendar where it will remind you to keep your promises.

My Lenten Calendar

week 1	
week 2	
week 3	
week 4	
week 5	
week 6	

Greg Phillips

Grade 3 • The Year in Our Church • Lent

Name _____   Date _____

Stations of the Cross

Directions: Make a Stations of the Cross booklet to remind you of Jesus' sacrifice. Cut out the sentences below and glue each to a separate sheet of paper. Draw a picture of the station above each sentence. Bind the pages together with yarn and make a cover page. Use your booklet to share with someone what happened to Jesus.

1. Jesus is condemned to death.	8. Jesus meets the women of Jerusalem.
2. Jesus takes up his cross.	9. Jesus falls the third time.
3. Jesus falls the first time.	10. Jesus is stripped of his garments.
4. Jesus meets his sorrowful mother.	11. Jesus is nailed to the cross.
5. Simon of Cyrene helps Jesus carry the cross.	12. Jesus dies on the cross.
6. Veronica wipes the face of Jesus.	13. Jesus is taken down from the cross.
7. Jesus falls a second time.	14. Jesus is laid in the tomb.

Name _____ Date _____

Easter Butterfly

The butterfly is a symbol of Jesus' Resurrection.

Directions: Color and decorate the butterfly below. Cut along the dashed lines, and fold up the wings on the dotted lines. Glue your butterfly's body to a stick. Put your butterfly in a garden, a potted plant, or an Easter basket to remind others of new life through Jesus.

Name _____   Date _____

Special-Gifts Bingo

Celebrate the different gifts that the Holy Spirit has given all of us.

Directions: Sign your name under one of the special gifts on the bingo card. Then have another friend or family member choose a gift and sign his or her name below it. How fast did you fill your bingo card?

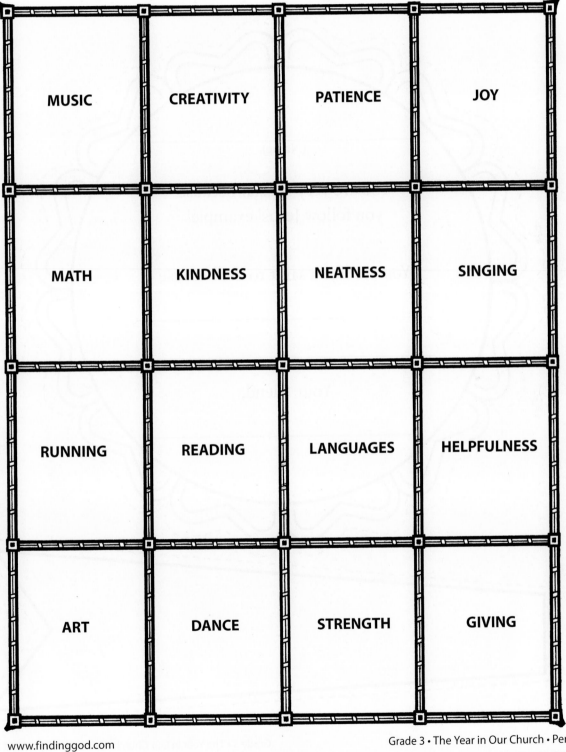

MUSIC	CREATIVITY	PATIENCE	JOY
MATH	KINDNESS	NEATNESS	SINGING
RUNNING	READING	LANGUAGES	HELPFULNESS
ART	DANCE	STRENGTH	GIVING

Greg Phillips

Name _____   Date _____

You're Like a Saint to Me

Directions: Make a badge to honor someone you know who serves God in a special way. Write the name of the person on the badge and two reasons why he or she is special to you. Color and decorate the badge and ribbon. Cut out the badge and ribbon and glue the ribbon to the bottom of the badge. Give your badge to that special person.

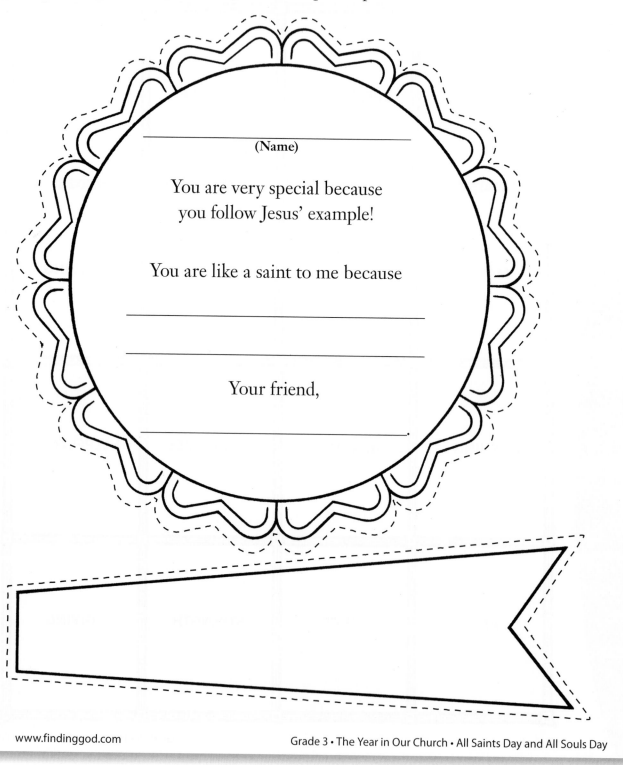

_____
(Name)

You are very special because
you follow Jesus' example!

You are like a saint to me because

_____

_____

Your friend,

_____.

Greg Phillips

Name _____ Date _____

The Apostles' Creed

Directions: Circle the following words in the puzzle. Then write the words in the correct order to write a sentence about the Apostles' Creed.

Apostles	Creed	faith	the	God	in	our
pray	show			to	we	

```
A   P   O   S   T   L   E   S
N   R   C   H   O   E   H   W
D   A   R   O   D   A   E   E
E   Y   E   W   G   O   D   I
U   F   E       T   H   E   N
O   Y   D   F   A   I   T   H
O   U   R       L   I   E   V   E
```

W e p r a y t h e

A p o s t l e s ' C r e e d

t o s h o w o u r

f a i t h i n G o d .

© Loyola Press.

SESSION 1

Name _____ Date _____

Praying to God Our Father

Directions: Use words from the word bank to complete the sentences.

Abba	cares	Father	Lord's	Jesus
language	wrongs	pray	revealed	taught

1. God sent **Jesus** to show us how much God loves us.

2. Jesus **revealed** to us that God is our Father.

3. He **taught** us what God is really like.

4. A special name like Dad or Papa that Jesus used was **Abba** .

5. Children call God Father in their own **language** .

6. We should forgive others for the **wrongs** they do.

7. God our Father **cares** for us as his children.

8. **Father** means one who loves his children.

9. Jesus taught us the **Lord's** Prayer to bring us closer to God the Father.

10. When we **pray** , we raise our minds and hearts to God.

Yoshi Miyake

© Loyola Press.

SESSION 3

T-342   www.findinggod.com

SESSION 4

Name _____   **Date** _____

An Angel's Visit

Directions: Complete the puzzle below, using the clues at the left to choose the correct words from the word bank.

angel	Christ	Emmanuel	Jesus
Joseph	listened	Mary	Matthew
Son of God	trust	Savior	

Across

2. New Testament writer
4. One sent by God to talk to Mary
5. The name of Mary's baby
6. Joseph placed his _____ in God.
7. Joseph _____ to the angel.
9. Jesus was to be our _____.

Down

1. Another name for "the anointed one"
2. Mother of God
3. Name meaning "God is with us"
5. Mary's husband
8. Jesus is the _____.

Crossword answers:
1 Down: CHRIST
2 Across: MATTHEW / 2 Down: MARY
3 Down: EMMANUEL
4 Across: ANGEL
5 Across: JESUS / 5 Down: JOSEPH
6 Across: TRUST
7 Across: LISTENED
8 Down: SON OF GOD
9 Across: SAVIOR

SESSION 9

Name _____   **Date** _____

Paschal Mystery

Directions: Fill in the blanks with words about the Paschal Mystery. Then unscramble the letters in the circles to form a new word.

1. Jesus Christ sends the Holy S (P) I R I T to share in his life.

2. Jesus Christ R (O) S E from the dead and appeared to P E T (E) (R) and the apostles.

3. Jesus opened the gates of H E (A) V E N.

4. Jesus' passage from Death to Resurrection is the Paschal (M) Y S T E R Y.

5. Because Jesus C H R (I) S T is God, we call him (L) O R D.

6. We receive G R A (C) E to be faithful to God.

We P R O C L A I M Jesus' Death and Resurrection.

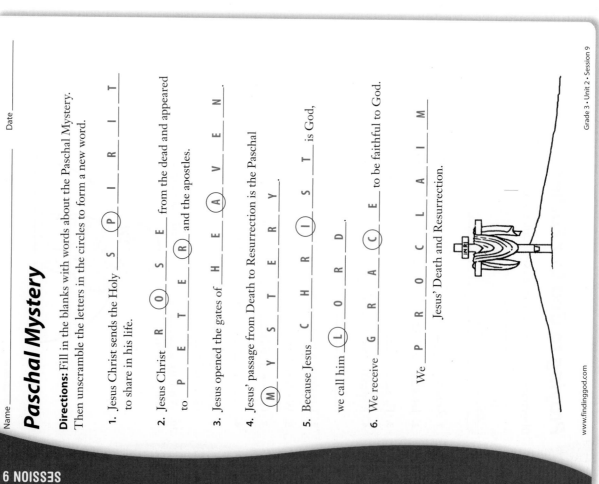

SESSION 13

Name _____ Date _____

Jesus Is Present

Directions: Think of the ways Jesus is present at Mass. Recalling what you have learned, fill in the letters to finish the paragraph below. In the church scene, draw pictures of the words you have written. When you are finished, decorate the picture to make a beautiful scene.

Jesus is present in the pr __ i __ e __ s __ t , in the

p __ e __ o __ p __ l __ e gathered, and in the

S c __ i __ p __ t __ u __ r __ e __ s .

Jesus Christ is especially present in the consecrated

B __ r __ e __ a __ d and W __ i __ n __ e .

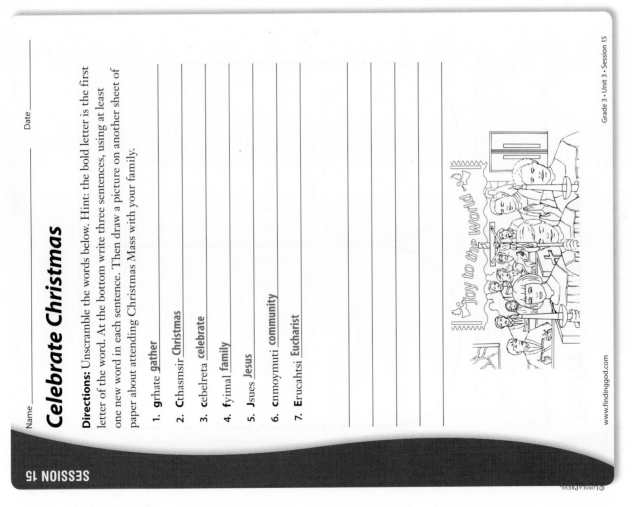

Greg Phillips

©LoyolaPress.

SESSION 15

Name _____ Date _____

Celebrate Christmas

Directions: Unscramble the words below. Hint: the bold letter is the first letter of the word. At the bottom write three sentences, using at least one new word in each sentence. Then draw a picture on another sheet of paper about attending Christmas Mass with your family.

1. grhate __gather__

2. Cthasmsir __Christmas__

3. cebelreta __celebrate__

4. fyimal __family__

5. Jsues __Jesus__

6. cnmoymuti __community__

7. Erucahtsi __Eucharist__

©LoyolaPress.

SESSION 16

Name _____ Date _____

Greg Phillips

New Life in Christ

Directions: Write the answer to each clue in the puzzle below. Read the word in the shaded boxes from top to bottom to find out how you can begin a new life in Christ.

1. This book contains the Word of God.

2. At first he wanted to destroy the Church, but then he became a great apostle.

3. The _____ of God are the Church community.

4. In this sacrament the Holy Spirit strengthens us to be witnesses to Jesus.

5. We receive the Body and Blood of Jesus Christ in this sacrament.

6. On Easter we think about rising with _____ to new life.

7. White garments, holy oil, and candles are _____ used when the Sacraments of Initiation are celebrated.

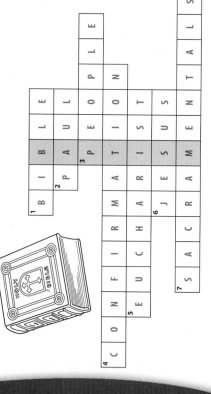

1	B	I	B	L	E						
	2	P	A	U	L						
		3	P	E	O	P	L	E			
4	C	O	N	F	I	R	M	A	T	I	O	N
	5	E	U	C	H	A	R	I	S	T	
		6	J	E	S	U	S				
7	S	A	C	R	A	M	E	N	T	A	L	S

SESSION 22

Name _____ Date _____

The Ten Commandments

Directions: Complete each commandment with a word from the word bank.

> holy   neighbors   God   obey   happy
> name   married   human   Respect   truth

1. I am your **God** ; love nothing more than me.

2. Use God's **name** with respect.

3. Keep the Lord's Day **holy** .

4. Honor and **obey** your parents.

5. Treat all **human** life with respect.

6. Respect **married** life.

7. **Respect** what belongs to others.

8. Tell the **truth** .

9. Respect your **neighbors** and your friends.

10. Be **happy** with what you have.

SESSION 23

Name _____ Date _____

Complete the Story

Directions: Use the words in the word bank to complete the story.

Charity	clothing	community	France	Vincent
Marillac	poor	religious	together	world

Louise de **Marillac** lived in

France hundreds of years ago.

She devoted her life to serving God. First,
Louise visited people who were

poor . She gave them

clothing she had made herself.

She met **Vincent** de Paul, who
also cared for people in need.

Vincent asked Louise to start a new

religious order of women called

the Sisters of **Charity** . The

women in this **community** worked

together to serve people
in homes, orphanages, hospitals, and
schools. Today the Sisters of Charity of
Saint Vincent de Paul serve people all over

the **world** .

www.findinggod.com

© Loyola Press.

SESSION 25

Name _____ Date _____

Have Mercy on Us

Directions: Use the code to color the picture. Then finish the sentence
below. On a separate sheet of paper, write a paragraph about a time that
you showed mercy to a friend. How were you like Jesus?

1 = blue 2 = red 3 = green 4 = black 5 = white 6 = yellow 7 = brown

Yoshi Miyake

Lamb of God _____, have mercy on us.

www.findinggod.com

© Loyola Press.

Answer Key   **T-345**

Excerpts from the *New American Bible with Revised New Testament and Psalms*. Copyright © 1991, 1986, 1970 Confraternity of Christian Doctrine, Inc., Washington, DC. Used with permission. All rights reserved. No part of the *New American Bible* may be reprinted without permission in writing from the copyright holder.

For more information related to the English translation of the *Roman Missal, Third Edition*, see www.loyolapress.com/romanmissal.

Loyola Press has made every effort to locate the copyright holders for the cited works used in this publication and to make full acknowledgment for their use. In the case of any omissions, the publisher will be pleased to make suitable acknowledgments in future editions.

Spoken Word and Music CDs

All CDs were produced and developed by Loyola Press in partnership with Media Creature Music, Los Angeles, California.

Executive Producer: Loyola Press
Producer: Sharal Churchill
Associate Producer: Tony Thornton
Editors: Rogers Masson, Nathanael Lew, and Kathryn Korniloff
Mixed by: Rogers Masson
Mastering: Rogers Masson
Mastered at: Moonlight Mastering
Final Mix: Sharal Churchill and Nathanael Lew, Media Creature Music

Spoken Word CDs

Scripture Stories
Narrators:
Martin Sheen and Rita Moreno

Voice-Over Actors:
Jennifer Hale: Mary, Eve, and Woman
R. Todd Torok: Grown Jesus
James Arnold Taylor: Angel, Young Jesus, Friend 1, Son, Adam, Rich Young Man, and Person 2
Nathan Carlson: Peter, Man 2, Isaiah, Joseph, Friend 2, and Angel
Abner Genece: Messenger, Shepherd 2, Elijah, and Father
Earl Boen: Andrew, Court Official, God, Isaac, and Person 2
Cam Clarke: Shepherd 1, Officer, Paralyzed Man, Disciple, Jacob, and Joseph
Jennifer Darling: Mary Magdalene, Mother, Person 1, Person 2, and Rebekah
Lloyd Sherr: Satan, Devil, Philip, Person 1, Friend 4, Jairus, James, and Leader 2
James Horan: Solomon, Person 1, Expert, Friend 3, Leader 4, Man, Man 1, and Angel

Guided Reflections
Voices: Cam Clarke and Jennifer Darling

Music CDs
Arranger: Amanda Kramer
Theme Song Arranger: Paul Gibson
Arranger/Orchestrator: Jeff Gund
Recorded at Media Creature Music and Firehouse Recording Studios
Contractor/Production Manager: Alan A. Vavrin
Music Clearance: Media Creature Music
Instrumental Music: Media Creature Music
Musicians:
Alan A. Vavrin: Drum set and Percussion
Fred Selden: Flute and Bansuri
Christina Soule: Cello
Stefanie Fife: Cello
Robert Matsuda: Violin
David W. Washburn: Trumpet
Laurence D. Greenfield: Violin
Andrew Picken: Viola
Mark Adams: French horn
Joseph Meyer: French horn
Barbara Northcutt: Oboe and English horn

Art and Photography

Photos and illustrations not acknowledged are either owned by Loyola Press or from royalty-free sources including but not limited to Alamy, Corbis/Veer, Getty Images, Jupiterimages, PunchStock, Thinkstock, and Wikipedia Commons. Loyola Press has made every effort to locate the copyright holders for the cited works used in this publication and to make full acknowledgment for their use. In the case of any omissions, the publisher will be pleased to make suitable acknowledgments in future editions.

Art Prints
Artists Rights Society (ARS) credits for art print images appear after image credits.

1 Private Collection/The Bridgeman Art Library International. **2** Private Collection/The Bridgeman Art Library International. **3** © Bury Art Gallery and Museum, Lancashire, UK/The Bridgeman Art Library International. **4** Private Collection/The Bridgeman Art Library International. **5** Julie Lonnenman. **6** Amanda Hall. **7** Sterling & Francine Clark Art Institute, Williamstown, USA/The Bridgeman Art Library International. **8** © Belvoir Castle, Leicestershire, UK/The Bridgeman Art Library International. **9** © The Bowes Museum, Barnard Castle, County Durham, UK/The Bridgeman Art Library International. **10** Regional Art Museum, Simbirsk/The Bridgeman Art Library International. **11** © Portal Painters/The Bridgeman Art Library International. **12** Musee d'Art et d'Archeologie, Moulins, France/Giraudon/The Bridgeman Art Library International. **13** Musee des Beaux-Arts, Marseille, France/Giraudon/ The Bridgeman Art Library International. **14** © DACS/Giraudon/The Bridgeman Art Library International. © 2013 Artists Rights Society (ARS), New York/ADAGP, Paris. **15** Walch, Charles (1898–1948) © ARS, NY/Nativity/Location: Musee des Beaux-Arts, Dijon, France/ Photo Credit: Scala/White Images/Art Resource, NY. © 2013 Artists Rights Society (ARS), New York/ADAGP, Paris. **16** Louvre, Paris, France/Giraudon/The Bridgeman Art Library International. **17** Private Collection/The Bridgeman Art Library International. **18** Museo Picasso, Barcelona, Spain/Giraudon/The Bridgeman Art Library International. © 2013 Estate of Pablo Picasso/Artists Rights Society (ARS), New York. **19** © Bristol City Museum and Art Gallery, UK/The Bridgeman Art Library International. **20** Louvre, Paris, France/Giraudon/ The Bridgeman Art Library International. **21** © Whitford & Hughes, London, UK/The Bridgeman Art Library International. **22** © Guildhall Art Gallery, City of London/The Bridgeman Art Library International. **23** © The Crosiers/Gene Plaisted, OSC/Waclaw Taranczewski, St. Martin's Church in Poznan, Poland. **24** Bristol Savages, Bristol, UK/ The Bridgeman Art Library International. **25** Bibliotheque Municipale, Valenciennes, France/The Bridgeman Art Library International.

Catechist Guide
When there is more than one picture on a page, positions are abbreviated as follows: (t) top, (c) center, (b) bottom.

i–ii Raphael Lopez. **OV-1–OV-3** Raphael Lopez. **OV-5**(t) ©iStockphoto .com/kryczka. **OV-5**(tc) Jupiterimages/Brand X Pictures/Thinkstock. **OV-5**(bc) Corbis/Veer. **OV-5**(b) ©iStockphoto.com/snapphoto. **OV-9** Phil Martin Photography. **OV-21**(t) ©iStockphoto.com. **OV-21**(b) Jupiter Images. **OV-22**(t) Sandra Gligorijevic/Shutterstock.com. **OV-22**(b) BananaStock/Jupiter Images. **OV-23**(t) Stockbyte. **EC-2** Greg Kuepfer. **EC-4**(t) ©iStockphoto.com/nico_blue. **EC-4**(b) Hill Street Studios/Blend Images/Getty Images. **EC-5** Steve Skjold/Alamy. **EC-6** Jupiter Images. **EC-6**(t) ©iStockphoto.com. **EC-7**(b) Mariano N. Ruiz/Jupiter Images. **2** From The Spiritual Journey of St. Ignatius Loyola by Dora Nikolova Bittau. Photo by Ken Wagner © 1998 Seattle University. **32** Amanda Hall. **62** William Thomas Cain/Contributor/ Getty Images News/Getty Images. **92** Mary Evans Picture Library/ Alamy. **122** Stained Glass by Akili Ron Anderson. **151b**(t) Chris Hill/ Shutterstock.com. **151b**(c) ©iStockphoto.com/zcw26.

Children's Book acknowledgments begin on page 275.